DOROTHY HARTLEY

FOOD IN
ENGLAND

"Your English housewife must be of chaste
thought, stout courage, patient, untyred, watch-
ful, diligent, witty and pleasant, constant in
friendship, full of good neighbourhood, wise in
discourse, but not frequent therein, sharp and
quick of speech, but not bitter or talkative,
secrete in her affairs, comfortable in her con-
sailes, and skilful in all the working knowledges
that belong to her vocation."

MARKHAM: THE INWARD AND OUTWARD VIRTUES
WHICH OUGHT TO BE IN A COMPLETE WOMAN, 1615.

LITTLE, BROWN AND COMPANY

A *Little, Brown* Book

First published in Great Britain by Macdonald 1954
Reissued in hardback by Little, Brown 1996
This paperback edition published by Little, Brown 1999

ISBN 0 316 85205 8

A CIP catalogue record for this book
is available from the British Library.

Printed and bound in Great Britain by
Clays Ltd, St Ives plc

Little, Brown and Company (UK)
Brettenham House
Lancaster Place
London WC2E 7EN

INTRODUCTION

ENGLISH cooking is old-fashioned, because we like it that way. We do enjoy foreign dishes and admire Continental cooks, but when we cook the foreign dishes, the dishes, like the foreigners, become "naturalised English".

So this book is for English cooks, and belongs to English kitchens.

The kitchens are more modern than the cooking, because we are a race of mechanics and often amenable to reason, but even our kitchens are modernised in rather an old-fashioned way—not streamlined in the transatlantic manner; and some of our best English cooking is still done in kitchens that have neither electricity nor gas, and are only just considering enclosed combustion stoves. Chaucer's alchemist used a pressure cooker, and we always used to put a flat-iron on the saucepan when we wanted anything to cook quicker; but these excellent inventions are less appreciated in old kitchens where the fire burns gently day and night—and "Something's ready for them when they come in—and dear knows when that will be!" for in the country household you cannot regulate the consumer—only the dinner. So please consider this book as an old-fashioned kitchen, not impressive, but a warm friendly place, where one can come in any time and have a chat with the cook. And here, at the very beginning, I want to thank all the kind cooks who have talked to me, and taught me, and helped me to make this book. For them I wish it was a better book; but they will know that the faults are all mine and the kindness all theirs. So I hope they will take the book as their own with all my gratitude. May I also thank the officials of the British Museum, where the history was studied and from where most of the original plates were obtained.

Now a word about the "history bits". I have already done six volumes of history, so will historians please forgive me that these bits are for cooks —not historians. Historians will see that the quotations are not those most urgent to history, and the generalities in the short condensed notes omit much of importance. Professional historians will sympathise, for they will understand the difficulty, but the general reader deserves a word of explanation.

So many well-worn quotations have been used so often, for so long, that they have become accepted as fixed facts upon their subject. But the more you study, the fewer facts become fixtures; and for every quotation giving one aspect, there are usually a dozen modifying it and capable of giving quite a different impression. Realise that for centuries the swiftest transport was by horse (or water), and the only instantaneous communication was by beacon! (and that would not convey much culinary information beyond "Victorious soldiers celebrating", so you kill the worst cow before they eat the best one; or "Not victorious—fleeing", so you take the ham out of the smoke hole and leave home).

People travelled about, but districts remained distinctive, so that there was far more regional variety, and it was harder to generalise.

Another wrong impression is that food was sharply divided for two classes: the poor, who starved on beans and black bread, and the rich, who surfeited on peacocks and cockatrice. These were two extremes. For every professional cook whose fine recipes reached the crackling parchment and fame, there were masses of working households who lived on the land and off the land, and cooked for their families because they had to and because they loved them. These poor people cooked as well as they could —probably very well indeed. The paintings of the Early Masters show that rickets and deficiency diseases were rife, but much of this work was done in cities, and our undoubtedly improved health and larger growth today is more likely to be from our knowledge of what we ought to eat than any change in the basic materials available. That these materials made a dull diet, lacking our variety of imports, can be modified by the many pungent and powerful native spices and herbs and various plants which they used and which we have now forgotten.

Another impression is of monotony—but it is we who level out the year into monotony by demanding the same food all the year round!

Mediaeval people pickled and potted and dried food to preserve it, but they did enjoy the enforced variety of the seasons! Also, the cook was only part of the communal household. It was the gardener who said in spring, "Now you eat Rounceval peas"; or, glumly, in autumn, "There's no cabbage nor 'neps." It was the shepherd who decreed when there was to be mutton; and as he ate with the other workers, it behoved him to fatten up his old crones, or his mates would find fault. In winter it was the swineherd, at last convinced that all his sows were safely in the family way, who announced, "Now you may eat the boar's head!" and the dairywoman, all flooded out from dairy to hafod, who ordered junkets, curds and whey, milk cheeses and, maybe, veal. Even the woodboy shared the general responsibility, for though all "servants at night bring in wood or a log", cooking fuel required selection, and many a joint that "would have roast" had to be boiled because the wood was damp, or the wrong sort. (Then the mediaeval cook would have a word to say to the woodboy, exactly as the cook today speaks to the coal merchant about the boiler fuel!)

So let any cook who enjoys our ancestral heritage begin at the material end and study the fuel and methods first, and remember that some cooks were old-fashioned and some used "the most modern appliances". Because they put down some unexpected result to a miracle, and you give it a scientific explanation, does not change your attitudes—you are both believing what you were taught—or trying to do so. The fact remains they were people like ourselves, doing their jobs as well as ever they could —for we English cooks (including pleasurable importations now completely naturalised) have always been our excellent selves, under all conditions in all centuries. So come now into our own English kitchen and meet friends! Here is Tusser, just back from market, at Ipswich; here a twelfth-century butler, who will mix you hyprocras; or a Yorkshire farmer, who will brew you a drink to take to bed. Captain Perry, of the North-West Passage, is poking round the stove to see how the boiler works; a couple of Elizabethan sailors are wolfing clouted cream. Haclutt is talking to the gardener; and Gervaise Markham, after a prowl round the stables, is joining Fitzherbert in the orchard. A Scottish agricultural expert brings in a sack of oatmeal; a Lancashire weaver cracks potatoes for a hot pot; a woman author brings piety and pot pie from her New England kitchen; even the mediaeval hound comes to the door for his bone. All are friendly together and make you very welcome in the kitchen they have all loved so long—the English kitchen. It is not a very tidy kitchen, because, like this book, it has been in use so long; and so many different people have worked therein, putting things into different places, so that the author does apologise to cooks—past and present—if anyone has slipped out during the blitz or turned up in the wrong recipe, for—

"So will I not be sayd
    But that to my sawe, blame may be layd,
For foule English and feble rhyme,
    Seyd oute of resun many a tyme.
Now God yield them at their ending,
    That will amende mine uncunning,
But whoso blameth and will not amend—
    He doeth not as the curteys kinde."

Also by Dorothy Hartley

WATER IN ENGLAND
THE LAND OF ENGLAND
LIFE AND WORK OF THE PEOPLE OF ENGLAND (6 vols)
MEDIAEVAL COSTUME AND LIFE
TUSSER, ELIZABETHAN FAMOUS LIFE STUDY
HERE'S ENGLAND
COUNTRYMAN'S ENGLAND
MADE IN ENGLAND
HOLIDAY IN IRELAND

CONTENTS

SOME ENGLISH KITCHENS

MY first kitchen was a stone-floored cottage in the Yorkshire dales. It had a thick rag rug on the hearth and a ceiling rack that held thin brown oatcake. When soft and newly made, the oatcake hung in loops, which later dried out stiff and brittle. The stone slab where it was baked made a little separate hearth at one side of the fireplace. The high mantelpiece had a polished gun over it, and on it two china dogs and brass ornaments. The window, almost blocked by red geraniums in flower-pots, was set deep in the thick stone wall; and most of the light came through an open door that gave onto the moor. Fresh mountain air and the smell of cooking always filled this brightly polished kitchen. I can remember a basin of mutton broth with a long-boned chop in it. A man reached up to lift down a flap of oatcake to crumble into the broth, and I remember the warm, safe feel of the big sheepdog I leant against. I remember, too, being carried high on the farmhand's shoulder, and feeling him drop down and rise up as he picked white mushrooms out of the wet grass.[1] Once a week a wagonette ran to Skipton to take people to market.

My next kitchen was in a convent of French nuns at Skipton. It had a high ceiling and a sense of space and peace. The wooden tables were

Memory of a kitchen window. The cat watches the ceaseless activity of the gingerbeer "bee" going up and down, buzzing faintly "like a bee in a bottle".

scoured white as bone, scrubbed along the grain with sharp river sand and whitening. The wide range shone like satin; the steel fender and stands were rubbed bright with emery cloth. In the wintry sunshine brass pans and silver dishcovers glittered on the cream plaster walls. To prevent clogs slipping the flags were lightly sanded, and the hearthstone was white as drifted snow. At one side of the fireplace stood an iron coffee-grinder; at the other sat a black-gowned little Sister, with white coif and blue apron, slicing vegetables, her clogs laid beside her and her white-stockinged feet on the rolled-back hearthrug.

All morning the kitchen was alive with stir and bustle, the clatter of clogs and pails, and the aroma of breakfast coffee. The range fire roared away like an imprisoned dragon behind his long bars, and the meat jack clicked and clicked as steadily as the rosary of the old Reverend Mother who slept away her last days in the warm armchair by the window. From ten o'clock to twelve the jack clicked before the fire, while on top sizzled and bubbled the pans and the big pot. Interesting noises came from scullery and pantry: the clank of the soft-water pump by the sink, the

The toast held upright between two flannel-wrapped bricks

gurgle of the new boiler, the whirr of beating eggs, the clonking thump of the heavy bread pancheons, and the scurried prayers and ejaculated responses with which the kitchen Sisters timed their cooking.

The long afternoon was still. The sunlight shone through the window, the opened range smoked gently, the clock ticked loudly, a cricket chirped. The woollen rug was spread out before the hearth and a yellow cat was asleep in the middle of it with the little "vegetable Sister" asleep at the side. At five o'clock a bell rang, and the kitchen woke up. The big kettle began to sing, the rhythmical tump-tump of the bread slicer sounded, and a yellow bowl of butter was put to warm on the fender. Sometimes the big fire front was dropped right down, and around it sat the four or five lucky girls who had drawn lottery numbers for that honour. (Other's numbers allocated prayers for the Holy Souls, weeding the grotto, or cleaning the altar candlesticks.) The toasters, armed with long wire forks, handed the brown slices back to the kitchen Sister, who at once ran them through the mangle: it was more economical to crush the crusts than to cut them off, and it allowed the butter to soak in more easily. Then the slices were arranged in a line along the hotplate, held upright between two flannel-covered bricks that looked like book-ends. Afterwards they were buttered and piled on plates on the refectory table. In each urn the tea hung in bags, with an attendant basin behind, into which the bag could be lifted after "three Hail Marys and grace" had been said, as it was bad to drink tea that "had stood". When the first missionaries brought back tea from China they reported it should stand as long as it took to say the Pater Noster slowly. [The jugs of milk were rich with cream and crystallised sugar stood in stemmed glass bowls.] When tea was over the "charge girls" carried round a bowl of soapy water and a clean tea towel. We turned round to wash our knives and spoons, dried them and replaced

Lumps of "crystallised" sugar in a moulded glass bowl

them in our silver goblets rolled up in our napkins. In true mediaeval exclusiveness we each kept our own table-ware as the mediaeval people kept their "Neps".

Nightfall in the convent kitchen was redolent of broth. The big iron pot with the screwed-on lid (called a digester) which had chuckled unmoved at the back of the stove since dinnertime, was now laid, washed and empty, on a newspaper by the hearth. "Piggy's dinner" was steaming in a bucket on the dying fire. The little "vegetable Sister" had gone to chapel. The voice of Thomas the gardener called through the backdoor, "Will you be wanting anything more tonight, Mother?" before he clumped off home leaving the watchdog under the table for the night. . . . The yellow cat and a long-legged child are drinking milk together on the hearthrug.

My largest kitchen, masculine and enterprising, was at a boys' school. Being "northern" the bread was homemade, rising each week in a huge tub set before the fire. Piles of Yorkshire teacakes came daily from the baker, and a new gas-stove supplemented the oven range. It was here I first realised the specialities of England, for my enterprising mother sent away to her Welsh home for small Welsh mutton, as she thought the large Yorkshire sheep very coarse. We had bilberries from the mountains in leaking purple crates. From the east coast came barrels of herrings and boxes of bloaters, and cream cakes in wooden shelved hampers from "Buzzards of London". Apples came from Gloucestershire, and cream, in hygienic containers that weighed a ton, from Devon. From the north came sacks of oatmeal. Oxfordshire sent crates of wonderful fruit, Moorpark apricots, and apricot hams. The beef was local: all the pressed beef and brawn moulds were learned in that kitchen and are genuine Yorkshire recipes from the dale farms. At sheep shearings huge flat baskets of beef sandwiches were carried round, each with a mustard pot tied to the handle. No one eats mutton at a sheep shearing. At cattle fairs there were rounds of beef, snowy under tufts of shaved horseradish, and big tins of Yorkshire pudding, golden crisp, with tortoiseshell markings where dripping had splashed onto them. The Craven Heifer Inn served a massive Yorkshire tea with ham, game pies, apple pies, parkin and cheese, hot teacakes, jam and honey and black treacle, and tea.

But the most wonderful memories of Yorkshire are the old-fashioned Victorian dinner parties. I remember best the desserts, the really beautiful sweet dishes of those parties. Avalanches of snowy cream deluging a sherried mixture of macaroons and candied fruits. Hedgehogs of spongecake, spiked with almonds, and swimming in custard yellow with egg yolks. There were junkets, looking virginal in silver; apricot creams moulded like Milan Cathedral; and damson cheese, crimson in a pool of port wine on a gold-washed dish, and apple cheese. There were jellies, trembling in glass, with maidenhair fern; white blancmanges garnished with scarlet geranium; apple pastry, a pleasant mixture of apples, candied peel, raisins, spice and wine, baked in a square crust, iced smooth as marble, and decorated with geometrical designs of red cherries, green angelica, and black Carlsbad plums. There was gingerbread, heraldic with gilding and cloves, and Dublin rock that always vaguely reminded me of John the Baptist. In spring, blue-veined Wensleydale cheese; in winter, Stilton, sedate in a white napkin. There were piled dishes of dessert fruit: plums, grapes, peaches and small oranges set around a spiky pineapple. And once, real strawberries growing in boxes on the table! These sweets and creams have spilled over into this book.

My next kitchen was in a country rectory in the shires between Nottingham and Leicestershire. A rambling Elizabethan house with a garden and

Victorian fruit stand

orchard, pigsties and barns; more like a small farm than a rectory. It had an apple loft with slatted shelves, and a meat larder with a pulley to lift a carcase of mutton to the ventilated roof. Strange bleached frogs swam in the underground soft-water tanks; and all the water, which was as hard as iron and corroded the kettles, had to be pumped up. The kitchen, over thirty feet long and twenty feet wide, contained a Queen Anne dresser that had twenty-four brass handles and twelve knobs to polish. There were six steps down to the larder and five up to the scullery; three steps down to the dining-room and two up from the entrance hall. Counting coal-houses and outside pumps and passages you walked about a mile per meal. We had neither gas nor electricity, and during the dark winter months there were seventeen lamps a day to be lit and trimmed, and each night a dozen flat brass candlesticks were cleaned and ranged on the oak chest at the foot of the stairs. A lovely old house with every mediaeval inconvenience. The nearest shop was five miles away, and we had no car. A butcher called once a week, a grocer once a fortnight; and the wine, coal and brewery every six months. With one maid and a weekly washerwoman it was not an easy house to run.

It was here we "did" our first pig. After the bleak north everything in the Midlands seemed warm and rich and ripe. The mutton was fat, the cakes full of eggs, and in September we made wonderful wines and jams and rich preserves. Most of the fruit and vegetable sections were learnt in this district.

Another kitchen was in a row of semi-detached houses in a small mining town near Wigan. It was barely twelve feet square, and its one window looked on a yard and directly faced an identical window opposite. In one corner a huge built-in cupboard made almost another room: the top part held stores and grocery, the middle part china, and the lower cooking pots and pans. A shallow brown earthenware sink, with a hen-bucket beneath, was fitted in the opposite corner. Over it hung the tin milk can—the milk was delivered from a churn with a brass tap—and a spring balance to weigh the meat and fish, which came to the back door in carts. Between the big cupboard and the sink was a smaller built-in cupboard. Its top served as a general work table; beneath were the shoe and blacklead boxes, the gas meter, the knife board and bath brick, and the cat's kitten basket. The treadle sewing machine was set against the far wall, and overhead was a rack for airing clothes. Being a collier's home, the wash-house was extra large and led directly into the kitchen. The miner used to leave his clogs outside and come in through the wash-house where he would swill down in the tub. His clean shirt was handed out hot from the kitchen rack; then he would come for tea at the table by the fire. Only the women and children used the upstairs bath; though one miner *did* run a slatted board from his hencoop to the bathroom window, and persuaded his favourite drake to use the bath for mating purposes. (A Wigan man can do anything with poultry.)

The cooking in this mining community was good, especially the "snapins" and the food that will keep hot without spoiling. The Wakes were always celebrated with traditional dishes, and many trotter and shell-fish recipes, as well as Lancashire Hotpot and Hindle Wakes, came from this kitchen.

Today I live on the Welsh border where the mutton is good, the beef bad, and the best fruits are the wild ones. Here there are a profusion of small fine damsons, and the blackberries hang like bunches of grapes over the Dee. Welsh cookery is based on the mountain grazing farm, the Hafod; only in the valleys do you get rich food. But now a noisy chemical works has invaded our peaceful valley. Our old big house has been divided and let, and I have lived for twenty years in a workman's cottage, with a gas-stove in one room and a log fire and pot crane in the other, and cooked—as convenient—on each. It's been a happy time, for—

"Better is the life of a poor man in a cottage . . . than delicate fare in another man's house; and better a dry morsel and quietness therewith, than a house full of sacrifices with strife" (Ecclesiasticus).

BASIC ENGLISH

The Romans first with Julius Caesar came
Including all the Nations of that name
Gauls, Greeks and Lowlands—and by computation
Auxiliaries or Slaves of every Nation—
With Hengist—Saxons, Danes with Sueno came
In search of Plunder, not in search of Fame
Scot, Pict and Irish from the Hibernian Shore
And conquering William brought the Normans o'er
... From this Amphibious ill-born mob began
That vain ill-natured thing—an English man—

The Customs, Surnames, Languages and Manners
Of all the Nations are their own Explainers
Whose relicks are so lasting and so strong
They have left a Shibboleth upon our tongue
By which, with easy search you may distinguish
Your Roman-Saxon-Danish-Norman English.

Fate jumbled them together—God knows how!
What'er they were—they're true born English now.

DEFOE.

ENVIRONMENT AND TRADITION

WE BELIEVE the first homes in England were caves such as Kent's Cavern in Devon, and Pinhole in Derbyshire. We know that England was joined to the land mass we call Europe, and the North Sea was a swamp. Uncounted aeons of ice block this time from the Neolithic Age, of which we find stone knives, pestles, and pots.

The Bronze Age made better implements, herded beasts, and grew corn; they made the long trackways, such as the Icknield Way, hogbacked paths between settlements (with stones set in line to show directions). In the Bronze Age came the Celts, from the swamp land of the south and west, and it is thought they built the marsh villages of Glastonbury. So that, as far back as we can trace, we find people of the mountain, marsh, riverside, sea coast, and forest—families whose idea of good food was ingrained by their environment. The river man trapped fish, and his wife baked it in the ash of her reed fire. The coastman collected shell fish and laid them on the hot stones of his driftwood fire to open. The mountain man ate up every inch of his hunted deer, and learnt to love the smell of bog myrtle and the peat tang of his cooking. On the saltings, where land and water meet, the small sheep ate the seaweed and took its iodine flavour (and down West today, they serve laver with mutton). On the thymey hillside the wild game were cooked with the scented herbs on which they fed; and where the early English cow herded along the waterways, beef and corn came together (and Yorkshire pudding does not seem so far off).

Mankind always liked the food he was accustomed to, and his women cooked best the food that grew around their homes; their babies were reared on it, their stomachs learnt to cope with it, and anyone who has watched primitive peoples starve rather than eat the strange famine-relief grain, understands how each type of country comes to depend upon its accustomed food. Mankind enjoys a foray, and the young try out foreign fare, but the stubborn conviction that "home-made is best" is a natural instinct. Environment diet is so marked that where a countryman is forced to move he usually takes his taste with him; so a cook can trace the invasions of foreigners by changes in the preparation of food. The basic materials cannot change, but the different recipes, the different herbs, the like or mistrust of certain local fungi or shell fish, these things are the cook's own "history book".

SAXON

The Jutes landed in Kent; and the ox plough has written Saxon history in Sussex, and still, below the south downs, they lead horses across the furrows with an ox pole.

The Saxons were wise in worts, herbs, and star lore, and studied the seasons by these. Collectors of herbs must go by the seasons, for during the winter plant-juices are stored in the roots, and later in the terminal buds, flowers or bark. They were good herbalists and used many plants we now neglect.

The Saxon law base was the Firthborth—small groups of men responsible to each other—and the Folk Moot (a village council), where vote was by clash of shield and spear. Over these collective moots was the Witan (the Wise Men's council), with the king as chairman, not a strictly hereditary king, but a man like themselves.

As the dark-haired Britons were gradually pushed into the hills of Wales and far Cornwall, the Saxons settled down over corn lands. Saxon women were fair-haired, slow and stubborn. The Saxon households gathered together under their chiefs around strong wooden-built halls, half castle, half fortified farm, and many of our basic laws, our root crops, our corn-lands, and the oxen and the moonshine in our dairies, are Saxon in tradition.

The family lived in the main hall, and there was a good meal there once a day and a feast upon occasion.

The arrangement of this Saxon main hall was curiously caricatured during the blitz by the sleepers in the Underground stations, where a rug curtained a sleeping bunk and made a separate aloof alcove, while life went on, unheeding, down the centre passageway. The units of the Saxon household also located themselves in positions between the side pillars, and went on with their working or sleeping while others were cooking or cleaning armour by the long trough fire down in the middle of the hall. There were trestle tables either side, put up for dinnertime, or laid flat on the floor as sleeping boards by night. One fixed table stood at the top end and behind this were doors leading to the private rooms of the chief (the whole shape is reproduced in the small Saxon churches—a main hall or aisle with rounded east end).

Food was of good quality: bread, stone-ground in small querns or at some mill, baked in earth ovens or under an iron pot on the hearth; mutton, roast or boiled, with the herbs on which the sheep fed; green salading; milk puddings made of barley or oats or wheat and sweetened with honey; cheese and oatcake; mead and ale. Agricultural appetites are hearty and Saxon England provided an abundance of good, varied food. They could lunch in summer on crawfish deliciously fresh from the brook, watercress, oatcake and butter, wild strawberries, and cream. In winter, a grilled pork chop with apple sauce and ale. The baby had porridge and bones to cut his teeth upon, in the most modern manner. The food was there, in England, at the hall door.

Wassail bowls and honied mead are sung by the Saxon poets, and a great many of our festal dishes are Saxon in origin.

DANES

The Danes sailed over from what we now call Denmark, Norway, Sweden and north-east Germany. They had swept around the British Isles and probably as far north as Labrador. Their towered strongholds blend with the rocks on the wild Northumberland coast, and our east-coast sailors inherit their tradition. They came in open boats, and their wool seat pads are the pegged rugs made by Northumberland wives; on their wool-padded jerkins the patterns of the quilting now done around Durham.

Danish women knew a great deal about stored butter and cheese, herb and honey drinks, and whey ferments to counteract the effects of long sea voyages. Down from the north the Danes swept like an east wind! Lindisfarne and Wearmouth were sacked, then settled; Rochester, Canterbury, East Anglia . . . further south and west they fought. One of their camps was in the stiff clay we now call Essex. They came into Wiltshire. King Alfred fought them. Some historians think wise King Alfred saw the kinship between the steady ox-strength of the Saxon and the courage of the sea-lion Dane, for, when the yellow-haired Dane settled, he was as good a farmer as the Saxon.

Land and sea hold deep peace when storms are over; men who have fought gods of earth and sea have small need to fight each other; the new god St. Dunstan had brought to England was gradually adopted and

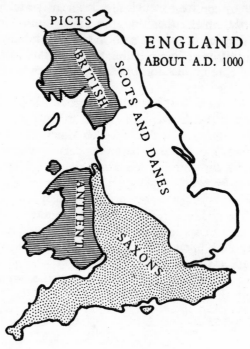

ENGLAND
ABOUT A.D. 1000

though the ground-swell of unrest rolled high, yet, after many years of bribery and bloodshed, ultimately England was at peace under the Danish King Canute.

The Dane Tower

The defence tower of the raiding Dane was less a residence than a stronghold fortress where treasure, or prisoners, could be kept safely. Many of these towers at the head of river estuaries seem to have fortified landing quays, where the returned raiders could refuge till their spoils were got away by boat. Grim and bare, and almost uniform in their simplicity, these towers stand today like sentinels on the coasts.

Some Dane towers may have been a central "keep" set in a small community of dwelling huts, but in many places the tower, thrust out upon rocks, leaves no space for the huts or even a small settlement.

The domestic arrangements within are incidental. There is a spring, or well, against siege; shelves that indicate the storage of emergency diet, and a fire in the guard-room, where men could cook themselves a hot meal. There would be "hung beef" (stuff like biltong, made of pieces of buck, pulled along the fibres, and pressed and smoke-dried), and sometimes a stone quern to grind corn for bread. A foray inland would provide stolen cattle, or a wild pig, which, sliced into thick rashers, would splutter over the firebrands. There would also be casks for drinks brewed in the tower—which argues a knowledge of dried herbs and yeasts. Men left those towers

The Dane Tower

strong and well fed, to the labour of a sea-crossing in open boats; so there was knowledge of shipping stores, and food-preservation of great skill, within those stone fortresses.

ROMAN BRITAIN

Roman Britain is an example of how a large civilised "top layer" of people can invade and rule a native population and yet leave the native fundamentally unchanged.[1] The Romans were here about three hundred years and the last generation of Romans born in England felt themselves English. Native "Roman-English" supplied the Roman markets.

[1] Africa today shows this.

The Romans worked our mines, improved our corn, our pottery and cloth; yet in a way that only a Colonial can understand, the "native" population went on living its own life separately. They met, mingled, and overlapped (and at Caerlon on Usk a Roman festival became entangled in Welsh witchcraft with curious repercussions in the twelfth century), but Rome remained aloof.

Cirencester, St. Albans, Colchester, Lincoln, Chester and York are all full of "Roman remains". Bath, the Roman spa, had a renaissance in the seventeenth century, and the "Border" believes that it was the Roman soldiers marching up Watling Street munching cherries who planted the wild cherries all along the marches!

Many foods, from cherries to snails, are reputed to have been brought by the Romans.

The influence of the Romans remained in weights and measures and figures on the kitchen clock, but there is little that the average cook can pin down to them.

TALLY

When a housekeeper today says, "Keep tally of what you spend for me", she uses something very old. Before people could read and write, tallies took many forms. The simplest was when an employer arranged with one workman to do, say, five days' work, they would split a stick and laying the halves together would cut a notch across both sticks, for each day's work. If the workman did not bring his tally to be notched, he had nothing to show he'd done that day's work. When five notches lay side by side on both sticks the tally was complete—the man was paid off. A collective tally covered sets of workers. Suppose you have ten men who must all work together for seven days clearing a field. The owner takes a strip of wood, and splits it into ten strips and gives one to each man. At sundown they come and lay the sticks together, and the owner scores a cut across the lot—each man has done a day's work.

If a man is away a day, and not there to lay his tally in line with the other nine, then his tally shows a blank for that day; it would be almost impossible to fake the score, because he would have to get both the men whose tallies lay either side of his to measure his position; and they need not be the same two people any two days. Also the "score" across was rough (notice the word); it would be almost impossible to fake that "scoring". At the end of the seven days, the tallies are checked and the score counted for each man. Tallies were strung together in bundles, like filed accounts. The labourers who could only count on their fingers used "five sets of four fingers to make a score", and there were many different "counts" for different things—eni, deni, diny, dass, catla, wena, wyna, wass was perhaps the shepherd's numbering of his sheep, while eggs or apples were counted quite differently.

NORMAN INVASION

> " So loved he the high deer,
> As he their father were,
> Eke he set by the hares
> That they might freely fare.
> His rich men mourned it
> The poor man wailed it,
> But he was so firmly wrought
> That he recked it all nought."

WILLIAM THE CONQUEROR—1066

At the time of the conquest, food was very localised; people ate the wild birds and fish in the fens, and the deer on the mountains, and the Saxons, who had become farmers, used cheese and dairy produce and such sheep and cattle as needed killing off, for winter. Because they depended on animals, they were not killed wastefully; they were hunted for the pot rather than for "sport", and because the Saxons' wealth depended upon their herds they seldom sacrificed veal or lamb. (Till as late as 1500 Tusser, an Essex farmer, warns against the use of this extravagant "froth" meat, and today the Saxon English, as a whole, dislike veal; it is the foreigners who demand it.)

William the Conqueror's strict preserving of the New Forest on the south coast may have been political. ("Who slou hert or hind he solde putte out both his eye and makyne him blind".) But it was the "hunting over farm lands", the hunting of the wild beasts that belonged to the land, and the Norman cooks' demand for the *best* farm animals (the ones the farmer wanted for breeding)—these clashes made more hatred than the war between soldiers.

As the Norman nobles brought new ideas about meat and wine, so their monks began to cultivate our mead and cider. For both Saxon and Norman, the rule was one good meal a day, served in the open hall. The same meal which we continue in "dinner" (when we bath and change and relax to music and friends). The owner and his guests sat at the end table, raised up in full view. The rest sat at long tables set either side, the "hall fire" being between these tables. The high table at the end was the first table to grow fixed legs, the others used trestles, from which the boards were lifted and laid down against the side wall, after dinner, for beds for the guards, who slept in the hall overnight.

As the Saxon churches, with their main hall, and rounded extension behind the table at the east end, reproduced the hall and its private room behind the high table, so the laying of the table cloths for dinner is reproduced in the altar cloths. To understand the laying of these cloths, you must understand "single-width" and "double-width" weaving. Holding your arms out before you, as wide apart as possible, imagine you must throw a heavy shuttle from one hand to the other—a yard is all you can manage; but if two people work, or there is a throwing arrangement of strings, you can "do" twice as wide, i.e., *double*-width. Linen was single width, and could not cover a table top and sides, and because the owner and household sat facing the hall, with their backs to the end wall, their legs would be visible under the table (and it was draughty), therefore the first cloth was hung down from the front of the table—down to the ground—the next cloth, laid at the other side, did not overhang so deeply—only to the level of the diners' knees. Another cloth was then laid along the top and down to the end at the right, and another along the top and down over the left end. The table sides being now draped, the top had a cover that came just over the edges all round—and, finally, a single "draw cloth", was laid along the "sitting-down" edge, where the eating was to be done. The narrow-width linens were always white, but soon after the Normans came we see the frontal cloth become coloured and made all of one piece, because the Normans could "do" double width.

The diners each brought their own "nef" (*see* p. 222), or set of spoons and knife and spike. These "nefs" were elaborate cases, often of great value. As soon as you were old enough to dine in hall, you were given your own nef and special drinking goblet. (Just such a "set of silver mug and spoon" as we give children today when they are christened; a symbol that they come to the Lord's Table for the first time.) There were other drinking cups, some magic ones inset with unicorn's horn, as that was considered a test for poison.

On the sideboard were kept the great flagon of washing water and a bowl, the salt cellars, and other oddments. The salt was crushed very fine and filled a handsome silver-gilt salt cellar set on the table. Smaller salt cellars graced the side tables, and as the overflow of less important people from the high table sat at the top of these side tables, the position of the salt cellars marked a social line still retained when we speak of "below the salt". The salt was crushed and served with an ivory plane rather like a modern paper knife (housekeepers will realise how very sensible this was).

The groom laying the bread takes a napkin and puts it over his shoulder and under his arm (the present-day waiter has the same gesture), fills the loose bag so formed with the bread, and goes around the board laying two flat bread "plates" to each cover, on either side of the main platter that lies before each two guests. Sometimes he will take extra napkins and "wrap up his Lord's bread in a stately way". The bishop gets a "mitre", the traveller a "shoe", the ladies a "lily tall", or the queer pulled-up shape that was so like a jousting token.

The elaborate napkin patterns old-fashioned waiters fold are still the shoe, the water lily from the ford, and the fleur-de-lis of the mediaeval dinner table!

A trumpet sounds (where we would hear the gong) and the "house party" comes in and takes its place. The lower tables draw-to on their simpler fare, and the pages bring in the food smoking hot from the kitchen, serving "roasts" on spits, straight from the fire, but boiled or stewed dishes on platters. Sauces were poured out into "saucers", conveniently placed for dipping into, and the company had napkins to wipe fingers and mouth, and might call for the page with the water and basin and towel if they got messy. The flat bread "plates" were removed between courses and the "music" echoed among the clatter of wooden bowls and talk of the side tables. A "new" dish is tried out—"My own cooks came with me from Normandy", or "Something these Saxons make rather *well*." All the interesting chatter of a dining-table goes on merrily—and in the kitchen. The hot cooks are peeping through the doors, asking the returned pages "how it ate".

Thus after the death of King Harold at Hastings a dark-headed, enterprising people of strong, warlike stock were gradually planted on to a white-haired, stubborn people, at least half of whom were only one generation settled from sea raiding, and whose flanks were constantly beset by the resentful aboriginals that they had penned up in Wales.

There was also a lively warlike mixture of peoples in the north, so that for years after the conquest the fire that burned most fiercely in England was the savage waste fire of war from the Trent to the Tweed. So fiercely did it burn, so grim was the destruction, that the "Chronicles" pass wearily across desolate tracts, despoiled manors, broken keeps, and write "Waste".

In the south the Saxon peace was shattered, and but few of the fiercest Danes and Jutes survived in the North Pennines. Today, deep loyalty and hard sense, but little southern softness, survives north of the Five Towns.

There were large communal camp fires where William's workmen squared the beams for his great stone castles. The last fierce fire in the Fens, where Hereward, last of the English, fired the reeds around his fallen stronghold. Throughout the land war and famine, fire and ash, came and went. Yet still in some unstirred corner of England some imperturbable Saxon, in his solid wooden hall, placidly ate the meat of his own herds and the bread from his corn and drank the mead brewed by his own women, and kept the Saxon tradition in England. And elsewhere in some newly acquired manor some new Norman lord held his feast cooked by his own Norman French cooks and drank his imported wine and flavoured his Saxon mutton with new and wonderful spices, and out in the Norman kitchen the Saxon slave, resentfully lugging in the firewood, learnt the new name "mutton" for his slaughtered sheep, and the yellow-haired Saxon girl, heavy with a Norman baby, smelt the new smells, and licked the gravy.

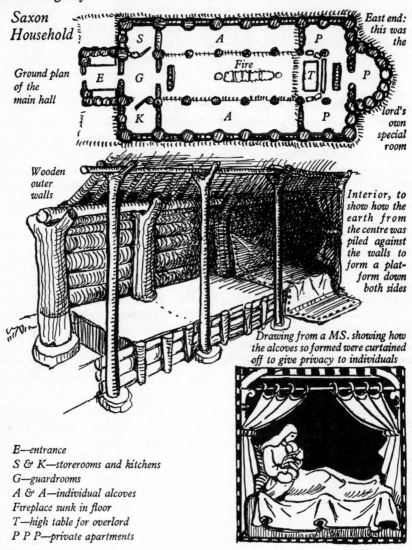

Saxon Household

Ground plan of the main hall

East end: this was the lord's own special room

Wooden outer walls

Interior, to show how the earth from the centre was piled against the walls to form a platform down both sides

Drawing from a MS. showing how the alcoves so formed were curtained off to give privacy to individuals

E—entrance
S & K—storerooms and kitchens
G—guardrooms
A & A—individual alcoves
Fireplace sunk in floor
T—high table for overlord
P P P—private apartments

FUELS AND FIREPLACES

Observe that the chimneys do smoake all about!
The cooks are providing for dinner no doubt,
O then if one calls, and no vituals appear,
O may they keep Lent all the rest of the year!
Poor Robin's Almabic.

GENERAL NOTES ON THE FOUR TYPES OF FUEL COMMON IN ENGLAND

" So they tarried and couvered them, and their horses, under the trees till the day began to appear, and such as were wet and cold, made fires to warm them, but before they made any fire, they endured much pain, for the wood was green and the ground wet . . ."

FROISSART.

FIRE IS elemental and primitive; the most miserable situation clears up when somebody gets the fire going.

We are not sensible to want an open fire, we should be hotter and cleaner with central heating, so let us face the honesty of a primitive desire.

Let hearths be of plain warm material, easy to clean, and giving the sense of being "the fire's place".

There are well-designed fireplaces that do not look too primitive for the most modern room, and will burn coal or logs; they rely on good proportion and pleasant material, and there is nothing to get out of order. A plain poker and shovel—perhaps a rough glove for shifting a log—are all you need to keep a good fire going all day. Within the regions of gas, a gas poker arranged by the fireside makes fire-lighting easy. In country places where there is no gas, keep a chest with dry sticks, and an old-fashioned pair of large bellows, as your fire equipment. In the country, too, you need a good-sized log and stick basket, and some shed outside, where large pieces of wood can be thrown to dry. An ordinary open fire should be lit, burn up, and boil a kettle within twenty minutes. Fire "night caps" can be used to keep the fire in overnight. Fire is something you must cope with daily—so treat the problem with intelligence. One should make a fire swiftly, with the happiness of one who creates a pleasant thing.

Electric fires are from tradition still built into walls, but this seems foolish, as the electric fire can stand where wood fires began, in the middle of the room. Some of the best electric fires work in connection with a fan that flutters out a live warmth most pleasantly, and though there is no need for light and heat to combine, the small reddish glow that makes the heat visible is as pleasant as it is sensible.

Either gas or electricity have advantages over the coal range, though the advantage is more in the extra intelligence usually shown in the management of the gas and electricity than the coal. A good coal range, used with sense, is thoroughly competent. Where there is "trouble with the range" it is usually the wrong type of range, or badly fitted.

   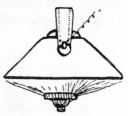

Side Heat   Base Heat

Showing the different construction needed for *side* heat from an open fire and *base only* heat from gas, oil, electricity, etc.

Side Heat
A wine mill and skillet

The new storage-heat ranges are excellent if their fuel is perfectly correct and they are treated like well-made "heat machines", but they still lack the adaptability that circumstances enforce upon farms and smaller houses. They provide perfect heat by perfect arrangement—but if the stored heat is used up and the fire has gone cold, there is no way of making a small amount of heat swiftly. In an hour's time you may have gallons of boiling water but you cannot have half a pint in ten minutes; and in a remote country house, where it is not possible to "pop on the gas or electricity", a sudden illness in the middle of the night may find the stove (correctly) closed down and cold. So the experienced country mother usually keeps the most primitive handful of dry sticks in an open grate, or an oil stove for emergency.

The worst fault of oil cookers and heaters is that they are not foolproof. An oil cooker, kept spotlessly clean, cooks excellently, but the least careless-ness makes a mess that is very hard to clean. If one person only uses the cooker, and knows it thoroughly and is entirely responsible for it, it will be all right, but a casual visitor passing through the kitchen and lighting his pipe from the flame may drop a scrap of dust on to the burner—a moth intent on suicide may get into the flame—and the "smokeless flame" has poured smuts and smoke all over the kitchen by the time the cook returns from fetching the mint from the garden patch! In old-fashioned times, when lamps and candles were used to light inns and houses, there were more people about to attend to, several people sat around one lamp, and a well-trained maid cleaned it daily. The modern oil lamp is excellently designed and will cook well, but it does need care.

A raised hearth oven from Warwickshire

Peat fires are more general than one would suppose, and could be used with far greater advantage. Many districts import coal at great expense, when they could quite well burn peat from their own lands. Cooking by peat is a craft of its own, but peat fires give out excellent heat, smell delicious, and will stay in overnight. A peat-cutter and bellows or a wheel are needed, but in country places where peat abounds, it should be more used.

WOOD

> " Let workman at night bring in wood, or a log,
>   Let none come home empty, but slut and thy dog."
>
> TUSSER, 1580.

When wood was general fuel it seemed impossible to use coal. Not until the Sussex Weald was bare came the crisis which led to coal for smelting. It takes twenty-five years to produce a thicket (that is, faggot wood), fifty to produce building timber (that is, trees), and anything from a hundred to a hundred and fifty years to produce the mixed timber for a forest.

The amount of woodland needed to keep one man warm and fed is about an acre, but increases disproportionately with increase in the community. Building of the early wooden strongholds cleared enough space for the community of that stronghold, and a continual penetration of the surrounding woods for timber and fuel pushed the virgin forest back, in proportion with the growth of the community. But with the building of stone castles the situation became acute, because they took longer to build, and required as much timber, and rather more fire wood. Few people realise the depth and weight of the timber beams required in the old stone buildings. Next time you stand within one of these ruined stone shells, count the square joist holes that mark the lines of floor and ceiling. Compute from the cellar upwards, allowing one good-sized tree to each main beam, and ten to fourteen smaller ones for the side joists. Multiply by the number of floors and then compute for the split-board flooring, seating, shutters, doors and panelling. Then add the battlement. In use, these battlements, now like squared pie-crusts to the open sky, were boarded, with an overhung gallery of timber, a top-heavy contraption probably using as much timber as two complete floors. Multiply the sum by the number of towers, then add the screen walls, and the gatehouse, and the drawbridge, and the stabling, etc. The estimate in sheer acreage of woodland is staggering! Added to this were the lodges for the masons and workmen, the lintels for huts, and all the small timber, for the wattle township which settled down around the "work".

Between these castle clearings were older townships, built almost entirely of timber. The mediaeval annual markets, which were huge temporary townships of wooden stalls, having their own special courts and laws, with regular streets and stores, covering acres, used an enormous amount of timber most wastefully. Now realise the circulatory system of domestic timber from its first usage in building to its consumption as fuel. The built-in beams lasted for centuries, but fifty years is a charitable estimate for outer buildings exposed to wind, rain, snow, bursting frost and summer suns. So, besides the dead wood and tree branches which crackle in the hall, the cook takes the rotted timber from the battlements for the kitchen; so by automatic assimilation, the clearing of wood around the castle continues all through its existence. With the later ship-building developments of Elizabethan England came another crisis in timber; and another circulatory system sets in: new timber from the forest goes down to the coast, old timber from the shipyards up from the coast. It is surprising how far inland old ships' timber will be found, shaping the twisted passages of ancient houses.

Farms used wood for their tools, so the farmer—

> " In December, he shall cut down his wood, as well to build withall as to make his fire . . . he shall also occupy himself . . . in making a thousand pretie things of wood—such as are platters, Trenchers, Spindles, Bathing tubs, Dishes, and other things requisite for household store . . . as Harrowes, Rakes, and handles for tools, he shall repair his teames, Yokes Ploughs, and all other Instruments necessarie for Cattle going to Cart or Plough, to the end that all may be in good order when they goe to labour."
>
> MARKHAM, 1500.

The country workman has always had certain rights to certain woods. He might not *cut*, but he might "take out", all the dead wood that he could get, "by hook or by crook", that is, the shepherd's crook or the agricultural labourer's weeding hook. This was a rough insurance that only official

Out of the Wood by Hook or by Crook

By hook or crook

workers (not vagrants) had access to the woods. This clearing of dead and fallen wood, that could be dragged out, was good for the timber; and where Rights of Mesyryd and Pannage (firewood and swine-feeding on the oak or beech mast, etc.) dovetailed, one imagines that the herdsman countenanced a considerable amount of oak bark-biting by his charges that he might be sure of a reasonable amount of dead and breakable small wood for next season. (As every countryman knows, there is more to wood-getting than the picking up of sticks!)

One should mention, too, that much bark (oak and willow bark in particular) was used for curing meat and tanning leather, and the waste strips of the willow, after the tan was extracted, were used for thatch and binding, and in plaster. We believe the fibres of this willow waste formed a basis for the curiously strong brown cloth specially woven for windmill sails and a few other strenuous purposes, and could be so used again today.

Outside the towns and cities, the common man's hut used little solid wood. It was built of wattle and daub, or, in some districts, chinked stone. Only the doorposts and joists were of trees and upon these, as a tally, he notched the number and heights of his family. The value of this record was recognised by laws, which permitted the preservation of the family tree, even when, as in plague, the whole hut must be destroyed.

Dressed timber was laboriously hand-sawn in pits. Rough timber was cloven—i.e., split with the grain—and this practice, which conforms to the texture of the natural material, is the chief reason for the enduring quality of some old furniture. This cleavage should be understood, for today we buy sawn wood, sliced regardless of grain and turned regardless of warp, and are surprised when it splits and breaks. Much planing by natural shape was done, especially for barns, roofs and shipbuilding, and one of the old wooden ships used as much timber as a small castle.

Any farmer's wife who enters a barn can count the number of whole trees used (root upwards) as pillars, and assess the clearance of woodland into ploughland commensurate to fill that barn with corn.

Timber fuel, owing to its grain, which makes thousands of little air channels up through it, burns fast upright with a flame, and more slowly with a hot red glow when laid flat. This is why fire-dogs in halls are high, for cheerful firelight and smokeless flame, and the roasting spits in kitchens horizontal.

When the wood fire was in the centre of the room, any baking was done under a pot (or outside the house). It was with the moving of the fire from the middle of the room to the side wall that the "oven" came to be built in.

Quite often in old cottages a hole was punched between the timbers that framed the wattle and daub, and the chimney built on outside. That is why you get stone and brick chimneys plastered against the outside walls of timber houses.

From this movement of the fireplace from middle to side developed the gorgeous open fireplaces, and all the paraphernalia of the great wood fire. The bake oven develops separately, and so does the boiler for brewing.

The Spit

The spit rested on an iron dog at either side of the hearth and was turned from the end by a cook-boy. The earliest manuscripts show that these cook-boys, to prevent themselves being roasted, usually rigged up a

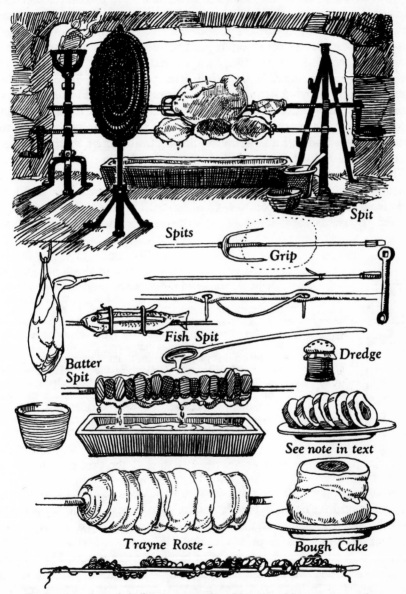

Cookery on the spit before an open fire. *Note* the old wet straw archery target used as fire screen.

fire screen (which looks suspiciously like one of the old straw archery targets—and probably was, as the target, soft and wet, would make an excellent screen), from this fire-screen (to which we are quite sure he frequently attached a small roast of his own) developed the upright toaster which stayed with us till Victorian days. The long pan set to catch the drips below the spit would be the first "dripping-pan". This drip pan is where "fried things" came from. Spits were of wrought iron, with a claw-shaped prong shrunk on to them (otherwise the spit would turn around inside the meat, instead of turning the meat). Another type of spit had holes for tying on meat. A very thin, fine spit, called a "bird spit", was small enough to string little birds. Fish or soft meat had to be tied to the spit with splints to prevent their breaking. At a banquet it was customary to carry the meat round and carve "from the spit". One mediaeval recipe threads dates and figs and apples to the spit, and then, as they roasted, they were basted with batter, till all was embedded in a thick, crisp crust. When the batter was all used up, spice or sugar was strewn over and the turning continued until the whole was firm and brown. The result was slid from the spit and sliced across and across. There is still a German cake called "Bough" cake that has a hole in the middle and is made like this.

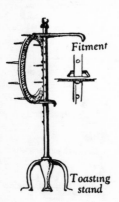

Fitment

Toasting stand

We have mentioned the circular fire-screen that served in early days to shield the blaze, and suggested (from study of many manuscript illustrations) that its common origin was an old archery target soaked in water. The straw was supported on a ring of spikes, and though we have no cast-iron evidence we think it very likely that the small roasting gadget on this page is the lineal descendant. (The design of the knotched stem is particularly clever.) It replaced the roasting jack for small flat joints. Steaks sizzled thereon to a nicety. Eight angels-on-horseback rode on it to a crisp conclusion, and rashers of bacon, herrings, and many good things, toasted on a hanging grid-iron before the cheerful red coals of the ordinary kitchen range fire.

The Cauldron

Contemporary with the spit is the iron cauldron. The man who owned an iron cauldron had a definite standing above those who cooked only in small pots or pans, for a cauldron was a "complete cooker" and hot-water system combined. The popular idea that the huge cauldron cooked nothing but large joints of meat in a swim of broth is quite wrong. Deep, strong earthenware jars were filled and sunk into the boiling water, puddings were wrapped in linen and suspended in it. An entire dinner could be cooked in one iron pot, which would simultaneously supply the bath

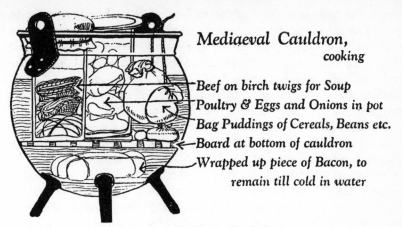

Mediaeval Cauldron,
                    cooking

Beef on birch twigs for Soup
Poultry & Eggs and Onions in pot
Bag Puddings of Cereals, Beans etc.
Board at bottom of cauldron
Wrapped up piece of Bacon, to
        remain till cold in water

Compare with illustration below

before dinner and the washing-up water after it (*see* illustration and diagram).

A wooden board, pierced with holes, is placed at the bottom of the cauldron (as is done today when wool is dyed). Below this board is a piece of bacon, covered with flour-and-water paste and wrapped round with a linen cloth to hold in the fat and juice. It will come slowly to the boil, and stay boiling throughout the dinner, and grow cold, as correct, in the water. On the board stands one jar, packed with fowls resting upon a lubricating piece of suckling pig and held down under their juice by heavy stones, or hard-boiled eggs. To the right we have sectioned a mediaeval recipe for beef tea. The earthenware pot has some birch twigs banked

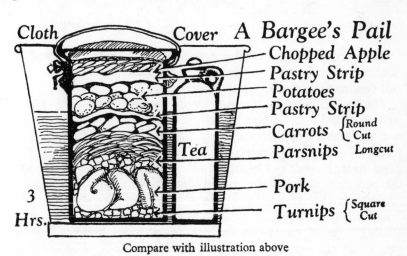

Cloth   Cover   A Bargee's Pail
                       Chopped Apple
                       Pastry Strip
                       Potatoes
                       Pastry Strip
                       Carrots { Round Cut
                   Tea Parsnips   Longcut

 3   Pork
Hrs.   Turnips { Square Cut

Compare with illustration above

across the bottom to prevent the well-scarified beef from sticking to the pan. The lid is put on, the crack sealed with paste, and the whole top tied down, air-tight, with plastered linen. It forms a perfect mediaeval pressure cooker and it presupposes the modern pressure cooker, including the possibility of going wrong and bursting; we trace several "demoniac onslaughts" in mediaeval kitchens to the mediaeval cook's desire to conserve the flavour by making everything air-tight.

Hanging loose from a string tied to the handle, are an oatmeal pudding and a bag of beans. A "great store of worts" which probably cooked conservatively, in butter, in another jar, and there is still room for the cook to put in an odd bag for his own dinner.

Now this was one mediaeval cauldron, and I hope you now understand that because there was only one cauldron on the fire there was not only one thing for dinner!

CHAUCER'S PRESSURE COOKER

> The pot to breketh! farewell al is go!
> . . . In helle, where that the feend is Lord and sire,
> Nis there more woe, no more rancour ne ire
> Tan when our pot is broke. . . .
> Every man chit . . . and halts him evil afraid—
> Some sayne, " It was too long on the fire making,"
> Some seyde, " Nay! it was on the blowing! "
> " Straw! " quoth the thridde, " Ye been lewed and nyce!
> It was not tempred as it oughte be."
> " Nay," quoth the forth, " Stent, and harken me,
> Because the fire ne was nat made of beech,
> That is the cause . . ."
>
> CHAUCER.

This mediaeval "combined operations" in cooking is still used by the unchanging workman—the open fire in the street or the bargee's dinner-pail continue a centuries-old tradition.

The "pail dinner" was drawn from life—on the Bingly Shipley cut. The jar was an old 7-lb. jam-jar, the bottle once held spirits. First the owner cup up some turnip for sweetening and laid it as a bed, then some nice pieces of pork, then a parsnip sliced into straws, then carrots, then he filled up with water and brought to the boil gently while—using some of the pork fat and flour—he made a "huff" (crust), half of which he laid lovingly on the simmering meat and vegetables—by the time this had "risen nicely", the peeled potatoes were ready to go on top—and then another layer of pastry—so the potatoes steamed between blankets of pastry. On the top, lastly, he sliced his "apple sass". (The whole pailful had been cooking all the time.) He now tied a cloth over firmly, wet the tea—"set the bucket to simmer"—and went off. The subsequent dinner, two hours later, was good. He served me some skilfully, peppering carefully, and paying due attention to the broth, which was excellent.

A.D. 1950.

THE OVEN FOR WOOD

Separate beehive-shaped ovens built alongside the kitchen range, or apart in a back-kitchen or bakehouse, formed part of the economy of the household. They were heated once a week or fortnight, and all baking, and much stewing and drying, etc., was gathered together for the "baking day". It is wrong to think of it as a great deal of trouble "just to bake bread". The brick oven did more than that; it was part of the whole arrangement of the housework. Just as washing-day—to which was apportioned all manner of cleaning as well as the laundering of clothes—meant a period of unlimited hot water, so baking-day meant a full forty-eight hours of heat that covered much more than plain bread-cooking. Starting early with pastries and pies, bread and cakes, the lowering oven heat was utilised for such divers things as feather-drying, bottling fruit,

From an old MS. about 1100—A wood-heated oven with dust slot and ash hole. Probably stone built and plastered.

preserving meats, and potting birds and fish for winter store, drying herbs and grain, and making charcoal, and, finally, drying its own firewood for the following week.

Here is an excellent contemporary description:

> " I have known a very large brick oven, heated in the middle of the day with one good-sized faggot and a log or two of cord wood, still warm enough at eight or nine o'clock at night to make delicate small cakes and macaroons and custards, and dry apples, etc.
>
> It is a great convenience and economy in many families to have a means of preparing food for several days' consumption, and heating the brick oven weekly renders them entirely independent of bakers and confectioners."

To Heat a Brick Oven (with wood)

> " Lay a quantity of shavings or light dry fuel in the centre of the oven and some small branches of faggot wood upon them; over these place as many of the larger branches as will make a tolerably large fire, and set light to it. As the wood consumes, keep adding to it, throwing in stout pieces of faggot and, lastly, two or three moderately sized logs. From one to two hours will be required to heat the brick oven thoroughly. Towards the end of the time the fire (which has been in the centre) should be spread all over the floor of the oven so that the whole floor may be heated evenly.
>
> When the fire is burnt out and the red pulsing ceases, scrape out the charcoal, letting it drop down through the slot at the

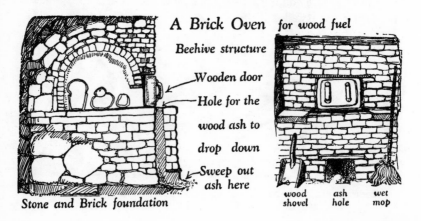

A Brick Oven *for wood fuel*

Beehive structure

Wooden door

Hole for the wood ash to drop down

Sweep out ash here

Stone and Brick foundation

wood shovel   ash hole   wet mop

oven door, and brush out the small ash with a broom of twigs. Then take a large clean mop, dip it in hot water, and mop over every part of the inside of the oven, clearing out the last of the dust, and leaving a little steam within the oven. Leave the oven closed for some little time, to even the heat, before you open it and fill it.

If the oven seems too hot, it is better to close the door, and leave the bread to cook evenly, than to try to hurry the cooling by leaving the door open, as that cools unevenly. Once the bread is packed in, do not open the oven door till two hours have elapsed, and after drawing out the bread, have the rest of your baking ready to put in, and shut the oven again instantly. And so you may go on, till your oven is quite cold. Last of all put in the kindling you will want to make the fire the following week, so that you can be sure it is ready and dry." (1800)

To Restore a Brick Oven

In case any of you have an old brick oven in your household which you would like to restore to use, first examine the casing to see that no recent new building has run timber across it or lead piping within. See that the slot in front of the oven door is clear, and drops direct to the stone or brick floor, and that the door itself fits closely. If iron, rub off the rust, and oil the hinges and clasp; if wood, put it to soak in cold water and, in any case, keep a scrap of your dough to seal up any heat-losing cracks. Sweep inside the oven wall with a small stiff brush, and if any portion of the arched roof seems loose have it repointed with fireclay. Finally scrub it out with hot water and sand, and let it dry for a day or so. Light the first fire slowly, and keep it burning for a day to dry out the surrounding masonry, rather than heat the oven. It will probably need a couple of days before the old brickwork is bone-dry. For districts where there is a plentiful supply of firewood, and a reasonably large household to cater for, a bread oven has its advantages.

In regular usage it will heat up more quickly and evenly than one long out of use.

Note: Some farmhouses have used the old oven for storing the sheep tackle or jars of harness grease, etc. This may be very difficult to burn off. Scrub the floor well with boiling water, spread with caustic soda, and leave awhile, then scrub again, and do not try lighting the first fire till you have got off as much grease as possible. The fire will soon burn out the remainder, but not until a smear of whitewash on the hot bricks stays white (and shows the grease has gone) should you attempt to cook in it.

BRUSHWOOD FUEL

"Whynnes. Indeed it is a strong weed called in the North Country Whynnes. It seldom gives place where it once footeth. . . . there is a kind of Furze . . . they grow very high and the stalks great, whereof the people make faggots and vent them in neighbour Townes, especially in Exeter . . . and this kinde of Furse groweth also upon the Sea Coast of Suffolke but the people make not that use of them . . . they suffer their sheep and cattell to crop them when they be young. Yet in that part of Suffolke they make another use . . . they plant them in hedges and the quickest of them make a strong Fence in drie and hot groundes . . . the Furse hedges which I have seen in that part of Suffolke, no cattle can peirce them.

Bayly: ' Are these [small] furze good for nothing?'

Sur: ' To brew with all and to bake and to stoppe a little gap in a hedge '."

NORDEN.

A faggot of brushwood in the wood-
man's knot

Where peat is used for the main cooking fire, bundles of the swift-burning heather furze, or faggots, may be used to heat a separate oven.

Bundles of reeds are an extreme example of fuel burning swiftly upright and slowly horizontally. It was impossible to roast in a reed district—one could heat an enclosed oven, or boil, and it is noticeable that Norfolk biffins (dried), bloaters (dried), and Norfolk dumplings (boiled) are characteristic of this fuel.

On the same principle it is possible to bake the Cornish pasty by furze, and raise the Cornish cream over the slow peat, but you can't *roast* by furze.

In every case, in this book, please note the origin of recipes, in relation to wood, peat or furze fires. Then you will realise how we have adapted our most modern smokeless fire-box, or electric cooker, to copy the old stewing, toasting, roasting and simmering of the wood and peat fuel. Our most elaborate modern stove is but a comprehensive ghost-house of accumulated experience.

PEAT

" The only fewel of the Islands is peat. Their wood is all consumed, and coal they have not yet found. Peat is dug out of the marshes, from the depth of one foot to that of six. That is accounted the best which is nearest the surface. It appears to be a mass of black earth held together by vegetable fibres. I know not whether the earth be bituminous, or whether the fibres be not the only combustible part; which, by heating the interposed earth red hot, make a burning mass. The heat is not very strong nor lasting. The ashes are yellowish, and in a large quantity. When they dig peat, they cut it into square pieces, and pile it up to dry beside the house. . . . The common method of making peat fires is by heaping it on the Hearth; but it burns well in grates, and in the best houses is so used."

DR. SAMUEL JOHNSON, *A Journey to the Western Islands of Scotland.*

Peat is still in staple use over large tracts of Britain. It varies from light-brown surface fibres (almost dried moss), to a thick dark substance (almost coal). The light, loose peat burns bright and fast. The dense smoulders and lasts longer. Peat is a gentle heat, and the clotted cream of Devon and Cornwall is a very good example of peat cooking.

Peat permeates a district. The water runs peaty, the air is acrid with the peat reek. Peat means bedding for the cattle, curing for the fish, smoking for the bacon; it is surgical dressing, it dyes wool, stains skins, flavours the tea and the whisky. It is also strongly preservative.

In some bog-lands the buried never decay. The lustrous black "bog

Turf Stack   *Peat Fuel*

Old boat tied
on against
gales
Peats built
up, hollow.

Sledge
transport

"Cornwall is a pore and very barren country, of all manner things except tin and fish. Furzes and turfs is the chief fwel."—LELAND.

Various Primitive Fire Places

Island fire place with curious Pot Hangers

A Kelpie burning fire place from West Coast

Underground Ovens

Camp Fire with Stones

Fruit

Stew

Milk Pudding

Plates

Fire Box

Flue

Long sloped Trench Fire place

Section

A convenient primitive fireplace of clay or earth, built to shelter the fire. The author found this example in a hut on the west coast, and the collection of holed stones from the beach suggested their use.

Kelpie oven from the west coast of Ireland. This is given as a good example of a drying fire.

Section through an earth oven lined with stone. When built on a slope (see above) a flue can be arranged with advantage, to create a draught. Other-

wise, the fire is simply built on the stones till they are red-hot. The fire is then swept out, the food put in (well wrapped), a stone placed over the opening, and the whole well covered in with earth and turf to conserve the heat. Note the small dust-hole below the stone on which the dish is placed. Damp leaves are often wrapped round meat to keep it moist while baking. A camp fire. The sloping stone takes the weight of the fish, which may become brittle when cooking. A piece of fat is hung above as automatic baster. If the fish should stick lay a few leaves or grass between it and the stone. A small spit arrangement in front utilises a green stick, and a shell from the beach catches the drips.
Section through a camp fireplace for stoking with wood or peat. Note the variety in heat, from the boiling pot and baking potatoes, past the hot water, to the simmering milk pudding and warm plates at the end. Crevices should be packed with damp turf.

oak" is from old trees, dug from the peat bogs. Peat is formed on water-logged land. It accumulates in the hollows of mountains, where it makes a slow-moving morass. One such mass, the Solway Moss, burst in 1771. The rain-swollen mass "boiled over" and covered five hundred acres to a depth of thirty-five feet. The heavy rainfall of the mountainous west, and the cold of the north, are conditions for forming peat, as the cold destroys the bacteria which otherwise would help in the formation of humus. In eastern England, where the rainfall is low, the peat of the Fenlands can be drained and, after scientific treatment, brought into cultivation. The absorbent quality of peat is well shown by its shrinkage under drainage, as the drains of the Fens now stand high above the sunk lands.

Peat develops its own industries. For example, in Yorkshire the light, loose peat is teased out into peat moss litter. The finer parts and the dust

Sphagnum Moss in Water

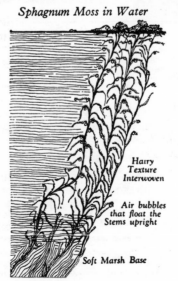

Hairy
Texture
Interwoven

Air bubbles
that float the
Stems upright

Soft Marsh Base

Sphagnum Moss. For the modern hospital.

are saturated with molasses to form the basis of cow cake. Probably some particles are not peat but the residuum of sphagnum moss, which, in its fresh state, is used for surgical dressings. Sphagnum moss is capable of soaking up an enormous quantity of water, and its iodine content makes it a natural deodorant, so it is good for children's bedding.

Usually peat is burnt on a flat hearth, though sometimes a "basket" is used.

In some places, a draught is obtained by shadrack, an underground arrangement like a small blast furnace through which the blast of a rotary fan is carried under the fire. Sometimes the ash is collected in a well below the fire, where it forms a good slow-cooking space. (Potatoes

The wheel or shadrack. A rotary fan at the side of the hearth takes the draught to an opening in the centre of the fire. The action of the blast keeps the passage clear of dust. In front of the fire is shown a peat breaker: an upright post with two shingles nailed on top form a sharp ridge across which the peat is broken into convenient sizes.

embedded in this cook perfectly.) The utensils for cooking over peat are very individual. On account of the gentle heat earthenware was used considerably; the "pot-oven" of Cornwall and the west is typical of peat cooking. The hearth-stone is made hot, swept clear, and the bread or pasty set down upon it. The iron pot covers it, and the whole is covered with the burning peat. The cool smoke from the peat had a very permeating quality, and fish and meat of all kinds were dried in the smoke fumes, acquiring the characteristic odour appreciated, and today reproduced synthetically by the chemist (*see* curing). It is the reek of the peat in whisky distilling which gives the characteristic aroma to whisky and poteen.

Peat cooking fires are seldom allowed to go out. They can be battened down and last for a very long time.

Hearthstone cooking

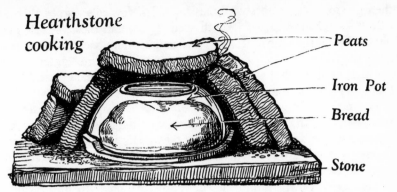

Peats

Iron Pot

Bread

Stone

An iron bake pan shown under peats. Also used under wood fires.

One can judge when the owner will return by the disposal of his peat fire. If it is a big fire, battened down under a few *wet* peats (and with other dry peats laid close) you may judge he will not be gone long, as he wants the fire to go on burning strongly and have some nice dry peats ready to put on the moment he returns. But if there is very little fire, smouldering low down under a lot of damp (not wet) peat, and the ring of waiting peats set some distance away (to dry slowly), you may know the owner will not be back for two or three days.

It is on the mountains that peat is chiefly used, and in peat districts

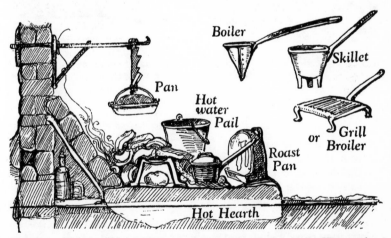

Boiler

Skillet

Pan

Hot water Pail

Roast Pan

or Grill Broiler

Hot Hearth

Diagram of a flat stone hearth and sloping stone fire-back. The cavity behind the fire-back was a good smuggler's hiding place, conveniently accessible from both sides of the wall. Section of the iron pot oven is shown. The spider, or three-legged pot for standing on the flat hearth. The pointed copper thrust pot for pushing down into the soft peat fuel (sometimes called a wine heater, as if it could be held over the coals).

"the right to cut peat goes with the land". In Norden's *Survey* (1620) we read: "The Commons . . . both yield turfe, furse, heath, and fearns (bracken) w'ch the tennaunts and inhabitauntes . . . doe take and use for fuel as they neede."

In the Welsh marches ("mearc", means land boundary) the "Right of Turbary" means the right to cut peat.

Peat cuttings are marked in Ordnance Survey maps, and so are "peat roads"—that is, the "right of way from the cuttings to the cabins". Many of these tracks and cuttings are old, past the memory of man, and the depths of some of them may be twenty or forty feet. The belief that peat "grows again" is due to the water-logged formation of most peat lands, where the high peat, slowly sliding down, causes the holes to fill up and the land apparently to rise.

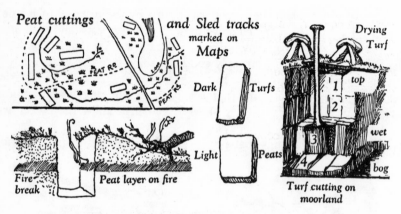

Peat cuttings and Sled tracks marked on Maps

Dark Turfs

Light Peats

Fire break   Peat layer on fire

Drying Turf

top

wet

bog

Turf cutting on moorland

"Peats" and "turfs" are not exactly the same thing, as they vary in texture and therefore in shape

COAL

" The housemaid should follow the sweep downstairs, taking care that he wipes his feet previously upon the mat and also that he does not allow the bag of soot to touch the walls as he carries it down."

The Lady, 1850.

Contrary to usual belief, coal was used from very early times in England. There were no very deep mines, but from places where the seams surfaced it was dug, very much as it is today. In other places, where the seams broke on the coastline, sea coal was gathered.

Why coal was not used on the old open hearths is understandable. The

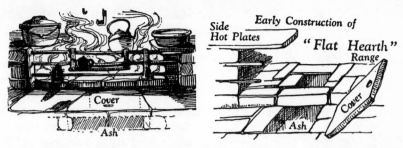

Side Hot Plates

Early Construction of

"Flat Hearth" Range

Cover

Ash

Cover

Ash

The first "ground level" ash pans. These "*ash pits*" saved the trouble of clearing out the ash dust daily—the ash accumulated for a week or more and was then collected and used for the privy. This "dry dust" was the baked earth used in the early earth closets which released a flow of dry dust on pulling the chain. Newham College used these "earth" shoots up till the 1900's.

slow kindle on the draughtless hearth designed for wood filled the rooms with smoke, and coal smoke is heavy dirt, that clings and smears, whereas wood smoke dust lies lightly, and blows off at a breath. Peat is nearer akin to coal than wood, and where peat fires are fitted with blast pipes it can usually be traced to a local tradition of smelting. Coal fires in houses were considered evil, and bad health came from sitting over "the stinking fumes".

By the time coal cooking came into fairly general usage the fireplace had moved from the middle of the room to the side wall. Chimneys had

Brick (or stone) chimney built on *outside* to an existing wattle and timber cottage. The position of the window, half blocked by the newer chimney, shows this was not part of the original cottage. A small door in the lower part of the chimney is for clearing out the soot.

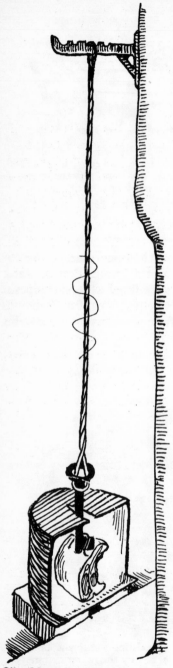

Silas Marner's "bit of roast pork
on his door key"

been built, climbing up the older houses like hollow caterpillars clinging to a leaf.

With the accepted usage of coal, hearths altered. Coal will not burn as wood does. There must be an up-draught, and space for the ashes to fall through and be cleared away, so the first basket fires stood over the old flat hearth. But though coal could be used for boiling and roasting it was impossible to use it to heat the bread oven, so the old wood bread oven stayed at the side of the hearth, and the small coal fire in the middle. The old iron cauldrons, that had lasted for centuries over wood, burned through with the new coal; also their legs were too short to stand, and they were too ponderous to balance, over the higher, raised coal. So the "built-in boiler" appears, arranged over an adjoining fireplace on the other side. Then you have (1) the bread oven, (2) the cooking fire, and (3) the boiler. And it was after this pattern of separate fireplaces that the whole "range of three fireplaces", became merged into the present "kitchen range".

With coal comes the change in roasting, from the horizontal to the perpendicular. With the narrowed coal firebox the long spits are useless, so now roasting is done upwards, with the spit swinging and turning by a dozen contraptions. By 1800 cooks wondered why they had "put up with the long horizontal spit for so long!" The simplest hanging spit was a length of cord, well twisted, that would untwist, slowly turning the meat. The difficulty was that you wanted to be able to hook and unhook the meat easily, and this is where Silas's door-key was useful.

" Silas was thinking of his supper. Supper was his favourite meal . . . whenever he had roast meat, he always chose to have it for supper. This evening, he had ingeniously knotted his string fast round his bit of pork, twisted the string according to rule over his door-key, passed it through the handle, and made it fast on the hanger. . . ."

Silas Marner.

A swift development was the roasting jack and screen. This is still in use in some country houses. Meat cooks well in this radiant heat and, contrary to general belief, there is far less waste by shrinkage, and the fat is much better preserved. Dripping, in any sort of oven, must continue to "boil" the length of time the meat takes to bake; whereas with the spit the dripping falls into a well, out of reach of the heat, and is of a clear, white quality (which makes it very understandable why the dripping of old was so valued a kitchen perquisite). The "screens" were of polished tin, and there was sometimes a little door at the back through which you could reach a ladle to scoop up the dripping and baste the meat. This dipping well had a raised-up wall, pierced with little holes that drained the dripping as it ran in, and strained out any fallen particles of meat. The jack was of polished brass, wound up with a simple key, turning clockwork that lasted about an hour. It didn't go round and round, but, like a circular pendulum, turned four times to the left, turn-turn-turn-click; then slowly back the other way, turn-turn-turn-click to the right, and so the pleasant fireside rhythm synchronised with the ticking of the grandfather clock at the far side of the kitchen, and the sizzling of the meat, the bubbling and boiling orchestration of the pots, and the purring obligato of the kitchen cat. A warm, happy prelude to dinner.

Undeniably, much good English cooking, perhaps the best of English cooking, was lost when the oven door shut on the English roast and turned it into a funereal feast of baked meats.

The Boiler Fire

In 1823 Capt. Parry's ship, engaged in Arctic winter search for the North-West Passage, is fitted with a prototype of the modern saddle boiler, to melt snow over the galley stove. The captain praises this "Simple ingenuous and effectual contrivance . . . the smoke . . . and heat issuing [up the chimney] does little or no service . . . but Messrs. Lamb and Nicholdson arrange a tank of considerable capacity: in the top a hole for inserting snow, in the lower part, a cock, for drawing off the water. . . . This apparatus was so little in the way that it could not even be seen . . . with the external atmosphere nearly at zero, it produced 65 gallons of pure water in the day—with no extra use of fuel. . . ." The good captain gives

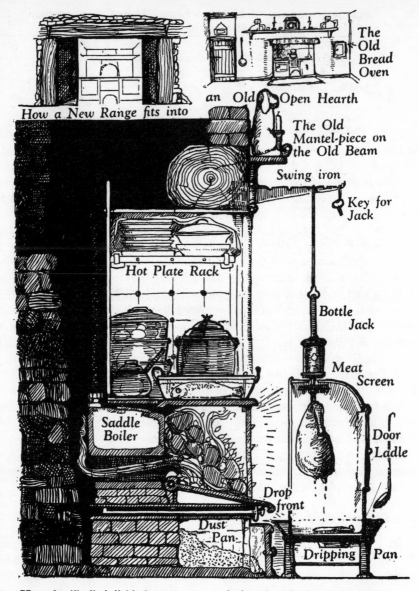

How a New Range fits into an Old Open Hearth

The Old Bread Oven

The Old Mantel-piece on the Old Beam

Swing iron

Key for Jack

Hot Plate Rack

Bottle Jack

Meat Screen

Saddle Boiler

Door Ladle

Drop front

Dust Pan

Dripping Pan

How the "built-in" kitchen range was designed to fit the already existing space of the old "open fire". In many old houses the "hollow" sound either side the fireplace (or small cupboards either side) show the ancient space is still behind there.

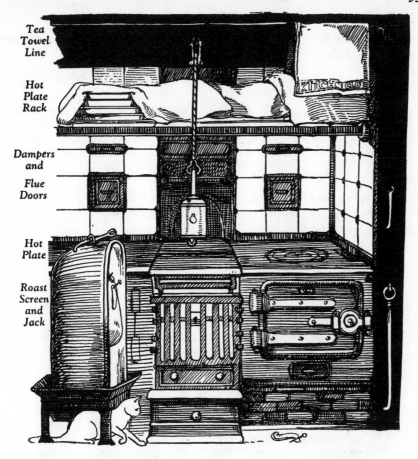

Tea Towel Line

Hot Plate Rack

Dampers and

Flue Doors

Hot Plate

Roast Screen and Jack

The front view of the range shown on page 52. Note the tiled "false back" and brick plinth to make the new range fit the old open space.

unstinted praise to its inventors, but this built-in type of boiler was not fitted to the kitchen range much before 1880.

OTHER FIRES

Beltane Fires

These do not belong to cooking: they are the cleansing fires of pagan origin still used in many districts to clear household rubbish after sickness and death, as well as to inaugurate the new spring cleaning and fresh rekindling of the hearth fire from some central source.

Bonfires

Bonfires are now festival, though for centuries used as signals to blaze news from hilltop to hilltop along the length of our island.

Hell-fires

The hell-fires of religious persecution are reflected in the country catch-word for scorched milk, which is said to have "the Bishop's foot in it".

Kilns, Furnaces, etc.

Brick kilns, smelting furnaces, clay works and all trade fires, have their own "cooking specialities" that mark the trade usage and many are mentioned in the recipes.

Moor Fires

An agricultural fire for improvement of hill pasture.

> " Whereas many inconveniences are observed to happen . . . by Moore burnings and by raising of fires in moorish grounds and mountainous countries for burning of ling heath heather furses gorse turffe fern whinnes broome and the like in the Spring time and Summer time . . . let be it therefore enacted . . . that from the last day of July next ensuing . . . it shall not be lawful for any person or persons whatsoever in the months of April May June July August September in any of them to raise kindle or begin or cause to be raised kindled or begun any fires or moor burnings in the counties of York Durham Northumberland Cumberland Westmoreland Lancaster Darby Nottingham and Liecester-shire . . . Anno VII Jacobi Regis."

Charcoal

> " He was a poor charcoal-burner, and lived in the forest."
>
> FAIRY TALE.

Charcoal-burners lived in the forests, made charcoal in "hearths" built in the clearings, and packed the black charcoal into bags when cool. The small wraiths of mist that rise so unaccountably from the woods in Hampshire and elsewhere are still called "colliers".

The chafing-dish, side heater, bain marie, and "small work" fire was for centuries more commonly a panful of hot coals raked from the main fire than the elaborate charcoal "cookers" in use across the Channel. If, with an open fireplace, you have a roasting fire, searing hot, cooking a

Early iron
"nightcap" for
keeping a fire in
overnight

Another form of the fire cover. This
was sometimes used inverted to hold
a few embers for a small side fire or
to heat a bedroom.

joint, and you want to scramble a quiet egg, it is much easier to rake a few
ashes aside to set your saucepan over than to try and cook on the main fire.

Old manuscripts show these small ash or charcoal fires (on flat stones)
being used in bedrooms to heat invalids' food, and to warm wine, but
charcoal was never a characteristic English fuel.

The "modern invention" of an iron cover placed over the fire to
keep it in overnight was used in 1500 or earlier

The Last Fire

The place where the fire burns is the glowing red heart of the household.
Our fire leaps high with our happiness, crackles and flames to our laughter,

and is stirred and coaxed to burn brightly and share special rejoicings. Fire warms us in sorrow, sleeps every night when we sleep, and rouses when we wake. Fire gives us warmth, and strength, as long as we live.

The little bright fire and singing kettle greet us when we are born; the firelight on the ceiling flickers through our childish dreams to the fire of love; and fire dies with us when we die. When the last fire dies out, there is only death and the empty room. The clink of cold cinders on the grey morning, when, on the bed, That lies, that will never be warm again, the realising that "there will be no need to make a fire" . . . That is death.

NOTES ON HEARTHSTONE, SANDING, RUSHMATTING, POLISHING FLOORS AND CHIMNEY SWEEPING

HEARTHSTONE

" Hearthstone! "
" Hearthstone! Hearthstone and Flanders brick! "

This was a street cry throughout the eighteenth century. A very "period" tract of the Industrial Revolution times gives a sad picture of the little street boy lugging heavy sacks of stones from back-door to back-door; they were pitifully cheap. Thirty years ago "hearthstones" were regular stock-in-trade of "rag-and-bone men", who came round the northern industrial towns with barrows bedecked with coloured paper "spinners", and exchanged jam-pots and bottles and rags and rabbit skins, etc., for hearthstones; the stones ranged in value from a farthing or halfpenny up to fourpence for a large one.

The regular stones were white, roughly squared to hand size (the chips and broken ones were the farthing pieces). There was a yellow stone, much liked in some districts (Glossop went all yellow for a year or so, but fashions changed), and sometimes the "stoning" would be all white, but the artist would run a yellow line round the edges. There were also composition stones, called "blue stones", but these, though softer to use, rubbed off too easily, filling the room with dust.

The stone is still mined in Surrey. It is a single six-foot seam continuous with that under Calais; the mine is believed to have been started about 1714 and has been in the same family (with interludes of French mushroom-growing and blitz sheltering) ever since. Transport was, of course, by pack pony, later by rail.

Hearthstoning obviously follows geological and cultural traits through a community. The north, with its large stone-slab building, offers fair scope, and in northern towns the stoning spreads from the hearth to window-sills and doorsteps; brick and timber building offer less stone, though I have often tracked a northern-born housewife in a southern community by her small scrap of hearthstone, being whitened with nostalgic care! Black slate is impossible to whiten, it is wax-polished or black-leaded.

Do not think of these miles of stoning as altogether useless drudgery. In kitchens and bakehouses they served a definite purpose in "taking up" the grease that would otherwise spread over the surface of the floor. In places where hot fat was spilt on the hearth, one "laid on the stone pretty thick with a little soda" and "in a few times if you put it on while the stone is hot, it will take the grease right out of the grain" (the action is like fuller's earth, used to take grease from woollen goods). Where passages and pantries had to be washed over once a week, stoning was very little extra trouble, and "showed clean finish". Wash-houses only used weekly were "set in order" after use, and when the floor was given its scrub, the gay little patterns stoned around dolly-tub and mangle were pure, spontaneous ornament, the finishing touch of the happy artist, and said in language any woman could read: "There now, that's DONE, and those tubs won't have to be moved out for another week."[1]

SANDING

" White sand and grey sand,
Who'll buy my white sand?
Who'll buy my grey sand? "

OLD ROUND.

Whereas in the south they put sawdust in public houses and butchers' shops, in the north these are sanded. This sanding was as common as rush strewing on wooden floors, but was used chiefly on stone floors. It prevented clogs slipping on the flagstones. In bar parlours sanding looked clean and fresh, and proved by its smooth surface that the floors had been properly swept.

Along passages, or over doorsteps, the sanding was sometimes done in very interesting patterns, using alternate hands and two coloured sands. Like the holystoning—and many a swain could see the white hand of his lady-love behind the pattern of her strewing, as easily as she could read his footprints in the sand!

[1] I knew one ex-mill lass who laughingly drew a " lace mat " around the household cat, which always " sat out " the last heat from the cooling boiler. She testified that the way you stoned the step reminded the pit men to take their clogs off before they stepped in!

RUSH MATS

Rush and grass strewing are now obsolete (except where certain herbs are strewn against fleas, etc.). Soft succulent leafage used to be scrubbed into floors to stain the wood before polishing; and clean grass clippings are still used to sweep over carpets. Do not think of rush strewing as being haphazard, the rushes were chosen with care. Some of the delicious scented rushes growing along the Thames once strewed the floors of Hampton Court, and many types of rush were used for different types of "wear" (just as we select carpets for their positions and usage). The low-set stretchers on the heavy oak furniture helped to hold down the rushes upon which they moved. (Single-pointed "legs" stir the rushes up into rampant tufts. Quite soon rushes were plaited into mats, very like those we use today.

These thick woven rush mats formed the truckle beds upon which women bore their babies, before being lifted up to sleep and rest upon the fine high bed. Therefore these rush mats were often reproduced under the effigies on tombs. A gentle thought, carved in stone, of another birth and longer sleep.

SWEEPING CHIMNEYS

> " The chimney all sooty, would now be made clean,
>   For fear of mischances, too oftentimes seen;
>   Old chimney and sooty, if fier once take,
>   By burning and breaking, some mischief may make."
>
>   TUSSER, 1580.

The large open chimneys of early centuries were so wide that a man went up, using one of the old scaling ladders with hooked ends designed for defence of castle walls. Later, when the elaborate tall chimneys and crooked flues of mediaeval-cum-Elizabethan homes had to be swept, boys clambered up. This continued right up till the 1900s, and an old chimney sweep in London described many houses that he had scrambled through, in his boyhood days. Some could never be swept properly now, for the manholes, where the sweepers used to stand up and use the brushes, could not be reached by any straight rod. For old chimneys sweeps can use iron balls attached to brushes and pulled down from the roof top; these balls, swinging from side to side in the flue, can be made to enter the cavities at the sides.[1]

Certain types of pine wood make a deposit of black pitch material that is inflammable, and scraping should be combined with the sweeping.

---

[1] Bomb damage displayed some of these manholes, exactly where he described.

Colliers in Lancashire always "fired their chimneys", usually on a Sunday morning when the policeman was at "parade service" (for it was illegal, but nobody minded). Quarrymen also did this, using the "shot" which they brought back from the blasting shed to make the explosion.

In some rural districts a rope was dropped down the chimney, and a holly-bush tied on to the end. It was then pulled down from below, and the soot collected and taken out.

On mountain farms, where the stone chimney-stacks were strongly built, a cow was fastened to the dangling rope, and then walked away up-hill, pulling the holly-bush up the chimney and out at the top. This was thought to make less mess.

But the general usage in the small one-storey chimneys was to "drop a hen down". These suggestions may help town people when entering old houses and cottages, as chimney-sweeping in the country is always a very "local" industry.

Note: The black stains down Malham Cove were made by little Tom, the chimney sweep, clambering down to reach the beck below, where he became a Water Baby.

CHIMNEYS, IMPROPER USE OF

> " Beware of pyssunge in draughts and permyt no common pyssyng place be about the howse and let the common house of easement be ower some water or else elongated from the howse, and beware of emptynge of pyssepottes and pyssing in chymnes so that all euvle and contagyous ayres may be expelled and clere ayre kept unputyfyed."
>
> BOORDE.

Reflector baker, which stands on the hearth and predates the roasting jack screen

MEAT

"We will cease to regard beef and mutton and pork as lifeless articles of food—but will remember that they have a close connection with the living oxen and sheep and swine. . . . If the system of flesh eating is defensible, why must the method of supply be concealed from all thought and reference? . . . Why is the slaughter-house unmentionable?"

Food Reform, 1882.

GENERAL NOTES ON SELECTION AND VARIETY

MEAT HAS ceased to have any connection with animals. Just as "wood" —so intimately known for centuries as oak, beech, ash, or apple wood, with individual qualities of their own—is now "planks", or "three-ply", etc., so meat has ceased to be anything but the "cut" or "joint". I have even heard it spoken of as a "piece" of meat—and the order for cooking it given without any reference to *what sort of animal it was*. But when you ignore selective differences you waste individual excellence; just as young, softly grown timber will serve for some purposes, and old seasoned timber be reserved for other uses, so the qualities of meat vary. In Smithfield the science of meat is taught with meticulous care, but unless the ordinary person can appreciate the result the knowledge is wasted. The cook should know the type of meat; she should know the lean mountain of mutton from the fat Southdown lamb, and treat each according to its individual excellence. The cook should understand the difference between prime beef for roasting and beef suitable only for stewing. There would be few complaints about the quality of the meat if the quality of the animal was better understood. And with the small amounts and lack of choice under present conditions this is more important than ever before. Therefore please study the matter, for if you eat meat you should face honestly the fact that it is animal, and should know the basic facts of its preparation before letting it be used for human food.

Any experienced hunter will tell you that buck killed instantaneously is best; fear and pain cause definite reactions that can be seen (and smelt) when the animal is opened. Quite definitely, trapped, hurt, or slowly killed animals are bad food. One example will serve: if you see a rabbit for sale with bloody, crushed legs, your own intelligence will tell you that it has been trapped and held in agony for hours, and should never be eaten.

Intelligent women will refuse to buy rabbit, hare, or any game that has been cut up so that the method of killing is disguised. For in meat killed in high fever, the blood stream is charged with glandular secretions and unfit for human consumption. If meat is cooked directly it is killed, and before it is allowed to become cold, it will be good (in the tropics this knowledge is indispensable). Once it has become cold, rigor mortis must be allowed to pass off completely, otherwise the meat will be unusably tough, and no amount of cooking will soften it. This fact accounts for a rather interesting mediaeval miracle.

"It happened . . . as Robert Fitz-Stephen . . . was passing through that Country an archer shot one of these birds with an arrow. Carrying it with him to his quarters, he put it in a pot to

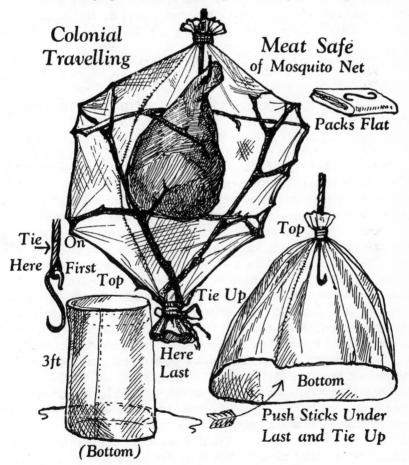

Colonial Travelling

Meat Safe of Mosquito Net

Packs Flat

Tie On Here First Top

Top

Tie Up

3ft

Here Last

(Bottom)

Top

Bottom

Push Sticks Under Last and Tie Up

For use in camp and by caravan travellers

be cooked with his meat, but after thrice supplying the fire with wood and waiting till midnight . . . he found it as raw as when he first placed it in the pot. . . . His host observing . . . exclaimed with tears ' alas that ever such a misfortune would have befallen . . . for this is one of St. Colman's birds.' The Archer soon afterwards miserably expired."

GIRALDUS CAMBRENSIS.

In cold weather some meats—e.g., mutton and venison—much improve with hanging, and may with advantage be kept a week or so before use. In this case be sure to change the position of the meat, turning it end for end at intervals to distribute the juices (unless hard frozen, when keeping, or turning, could have no effect).

Tinned and glassed meat is best chilled before turning out; then if a cloth wrung out in boiling water is wrapped around the tin for a moment, the meat will slide out with a good bright glaze. Round tins of meat should be cut open at both ends and the lower end pressed up, so as to push the round of meat out slowly. It can then be cut into thin slices very neatly.

FATS FOR BASTING, DREDGING AND FLAVOURING

MEAT FAT

That we speak of "beef dripping" and "mutton fat" is interesting, and dates from the days of the old spit roast, when the fat "dripped" off the beef; in those days mutton was less fat and more often boiled. Also, fat mutton was of more value than lean when the demand for candle-grease was great. Mutton fat was also used to grease church-bells, cart-axles, mill gear and mill wheels, and had many other uses. Dripping from beef has always been approved for cooking, and until the arrival of margarine (coinciding with the banishment of the cottager's pig), most children ate bread and dripping instead of bread and butter. Even in the opulent houses of late Victorian days, dripping cakes and dripping toast were considered excellent, whereas the mutton fat was the cook's perquisite. This is again a question of cooking, for with a roasting joint the "dripping" is there and usable at once, but with a boiled joint, the "fat" does not rise and set upon the broth till the next day. Also, the fat that dripped from a joint *before the fire* fell into a trough or basin below and remained clear. When oven baking came in, fat that had sizzled and baked in a closed oven (especially the rather uncertain early types of oven that were red-hot one side and cold the other) was unlike the clear dripping from an open roast. Note also that the big demand for fat to make candles, dips, and soap, went out about the same time as oven baking came in.

An interesting point in English medicine was the insistence on the "nature" of the animal getting in the fat (e.g., the fat from a limber hare, or active buck, was the best basis for rheumatic ointments).

We should pay more attention to this fundamentally correct idea, to the extent of cooking any meat joint with its own particular fat. This applies not only to the obvious basting fat, but throughout the recipe. The crust for mutton pies should be made with mutton dripping; for the beefsteak-and-kidney pie, with beef dripping; the pork-pie crust is always made with lard—and this use of the appropriate fat should be carried out through all forms of meat cooking.

The exception may be made for very large boiled puddings, when hard kidney suet should be used as it stands. But for a reasonable-sized mutton-and-onion pudding, the finest mutton suet is far better, and for poultry dishes the bird's own soft white poultry fat should be used whenever possible. After a boiling fowl has been left to grow cold in its broth, the sauce coating put over the bird should be made next day from the fat skimmed off this broth. The fat will have absorbed the exact flavourings of the herbs, vegetables, or spices with which the meat is now permeated, so that only by using this fat can you be sure of the sauce having exactly the same blending of flavour as the meat itself.

Exceptions are venison, a very dry game which needs supplementary fat, and the goose, whose grease is sometimes excessive.

Clarifying

Every cook knows how to clarify dripping—melting the fat with hot water and straining off into a clean cold basin. Afterwards, when cold and set, the thick dark gravy and any dark part of the dripping should be scraped off from underneath.

If you are in the country, put a handful of clean grass or hot chaff into the sieve to clear the fat. (Remember to throw it out afterwards into the hens' feed.)

Suet melts slowly; it should be shredded finely and if quite freed from skin and scraps, may be poured boiling hot direct into cold water, when it will form a dense mass that will keep good for months.

We have mentioned that suet should be used for anything that requires long cooking. Suet also has an affinity with milk foods, both being products of cereals and grass fodder. Suet will survive intense heat, so it was usable in the old bread ovens when sealing down sterilised foods. For this purpose boric acid was sometimes melted into suet, and when so prepared, was used, gently warmed, to fill and heal the painful cracks caused by the east wind chapping the teats of cows, where they grazed belly-deep in rough wet pasture in early spring.

Chopping suet is a tiresome job; it is quicker to grate it, and in very cold weather it will beat to powder under blows from the rolling-pin.

For greasing of iron girdles and bake tins, the simplest way is to tie a lump of suet into muslin; rubbed over the hot tins it will give a smooth, even film, very good against sticking.

Mutton fat should be clarified exceedingly carefully and if some vinegar is added to the clearing water it will take away any muttony taste. When mutton fat is hard, it is a good thing to warm and cream it with lemon juice before using.

If you use mutton fat for cake-making (and it makes farmhouse ginger-bread, apple cake and the homelier kinds of cake very well), beat it to a cream with the lemon juice, or a spoonful of cider, till it whips like snow.

To prepare mutton fat for a mutton piecrust, melt it over a bowl of hot water till soft, but still quite opaque; then remove it, add a good squeeze of lemon juice or vinegar (from the mint sauce), and whisk the fat quickly, in a cold place, exactly as you would whip cream, which it will shortly resemble.

Mutton fat was used in the mountain-sheep districts for the same purposes as suet or goose-grease in the valleys; being made into ointments for chapped hands, cracks from cold wind, or chilblains; to avoid chafing in babies; and to waterproof shoes. Sometimes it was melted with a tar dressing, for animals.

Mutton fat was also used as "body" for the red-raddle-earth paint used by shepherds for marking sheep, and since this old mixture was discarded and mineral-oil-bound colour introduced, the leather dressers have found deep markings coming out in the dressed skins of the sheep. Apparently the natural fat was harmless, but the commercial crude oil carried the stain by a system of osmosis up the wool into the skin.

Old mutton fat, melted and poured around boot soles in snowy weather, makes the leather waterproof; and in snow, a pair of old stockings dipped in mutton tallow and drawn on over the shoes has carried many a country child dry-foot to school.

Pork dripping, if carefully rendered down is, for most purposes, lard, but if from the basting of a seasoned and flavoured joint, it can best be used for meat-pie crusts, which it will improve very much more than the unflavoured lard.

The fat from ham can be rendered down and used for savoury dishes. Bacon fat is more definitely flavoured, and should be used as a flavouring, as well as a lubricant. Remember it will always be salt, and so where it is given in any recipe, do not add salt.

Bacon fat is especially suitable with oatmeal, so that brown bread or oat-cake are good foundations for bacon sandwiches; if mustard is not liked, put some apple sauce, or sharp pickle, to counteract the richness.

BASTING, DREDGING, AND FROTHING

Basting

Old manuscripts show scullions with long spoons continually dipping up the dripping that fell from the meat into the dripping pan below, and pouring it over the turning joint. This basting is very important, and should always be done thoroughly.[1]

Dredging

This was done between bastings. Thus you dredge with powders or spices to give flavour, or with acid juices, or chopped herbs, which the pouring fat washes down into the crevices of the roasting meat.

Finally, before you serve, you dredge with flour, or oatmeal, or breadcrumbs; let this dredging roast brown (but on no account burn) and then the final basting will give the joint that crisp brown crust that finishes it so pleasantly.

Frothing

This involved the use of steam or some flavouring liquid. The joint, when just done, is lifted from the fire and thickly dredged with flour, and boiling water trickled over it till "cooked transparent"; or the steam of a kettle is played over the floured joint for a few moments, before it is replaced in front of the fire for a final crisping of the outside.

This "frothing" is a worth-while finish to many joints. For venison, red wine is poured over; for a hare, redcurrant juice; for a rabbit, beer; and for mutton, the water in which fresh mint leaves have been boiled makes a good frothing.

FUNDAMENTAL FLAVOURINGS

It was considered very important to flavour the joint of meat *with the flavour of the food the animal ate.* Thus, for mutton from sheep bred on the mountains, the flavouring was the wild thyme whose small purple flowers made the mutton itself so spicy.

The marsh mutton (our equivalent of the pres salé of Paris) had a distinct iodine tang, from the seaweed and salt grasses of the estuary.

Therefore the laver weed, that grows there, made the hot laver sauce, a delicacy still sold at Bath spa and in Bideford and other places down west.

---

[1] There are now self-basting covered pans whose lids enclose the steam, catch the splutter of fat, and drop it again upon the meat; also some electric and gas ovens suggest that basting is unnecessary, but these are all enclosed baking methods, giving a semi-steamed soft finish, not the crisped outer crust of a roast.

c

Fat Midland mutton from the orchards had fruit sauces, such as red-currant jelly. This very old sauce is also used for game. Actually the rowan jelly is better for moorland mutton or venison.

Most sheep had their lambs down in the warm valley grazing lands where the streams ran, and mint grew in abundance. Hence mint sauce with lamb. Beef quite naturally has the milk and corn adjuncts from meadow and dairy—Yorkshire puddings, milky horse radish and corn bake.

COMMERCIAL FATS AND GELATINES

The present by-products of a leather factory are pure white fat, extracted after liming in the pits; glue and jellysquares of various kinds made from the leather trimmings; and the hair is either used for upholstery processes or in forms of fibrous plaster. Now when the pelts were dressed at home these by-products went into household use *direct*, and everybody knew about them. Today we buy in cartons and ignorance.

BEEF

Beef, Fourteenth century

> Beef is a good meate for an Englyssheman so be the beest be yonge. . . . Olde beef and cowe flesshe doth ingender mela-colye humoures. (yet)—if it be moderately powdeyd and the grose blode by salte be exhawtyd it doth make an Englyssheman stronge.
>
> Martylmas beef, which is called hanged beef, in the rofe of the smoky howse is not laudable . . . if a man have a peace hangynge by his side and another in his bely that which doth hange by his syde shall do hym more good!

DAIRY FARMING and stock rearing are quite distinct. The saying, that "the hills do feed and the valleys fill", refers both to meat and milk—that is, the mountain pastures on the whole produce more casein, making them good cheese districts. The lush valleys produce more milk, but not so much solid content.

Where a district is given over to dairy work, the beef is sometimes of very poor quality, though these districts are almost the only places where you get veal, since veal in England was mainly a by-product of the dairy herds (being the few female calves which, from some defect, were not reared for milking, or males which could not profitably be castrated and reared for beef).

Beef or "beeves" are the castrated males, bred on poor hill pasture, which gives them a strong constitution and firm bone, so that they will be

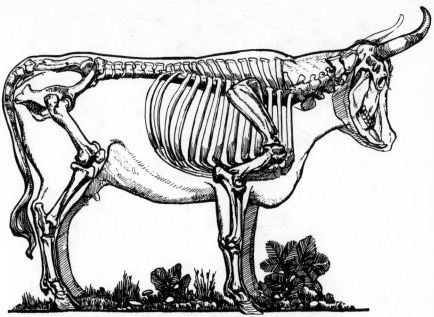

Bone diagram from a cow of the Chilworth (English) herd, renowned as one of the oldest types of cattle in the island. Note: That as a "wild" herd they do not carry great weight of meat and the leg bones are proportionately slender.

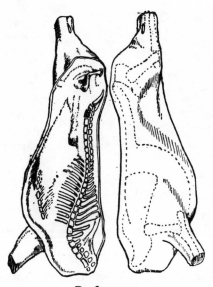

Beef carcase

THE SHORT-HORN

The short-horn is a triumph of selective breeding. This dates from the days when farmers developed their special cattle by selection *within the herd*.

HIGHLAND CATTLE

This small mountain breed have long coats suitable to wet grazing on the mountains; they are sturdy and wild (far removed from the docile "milking coo").

ABERDEEN ANGUS

These black silk-coated Scotch cattle are the prime beef of the British Isles. They are classified as dual purpose. They have been known on the east coast of Scotland for centuries. Probably they are of Viking stock.

THE HEREFORD

This is (in appearance) the " Staffordshire pottery cow " which adorns the cottage mantelpiece. She is a cheerful rich red with a white face, neck and belly. The lower legs are also white. One of the oldest English types, it is claimed by some to be the oldest pedigree cow known. A healthy strain, some herds even breed in the open in early spring. This the breeders believe to have a good effect in the high percentage of tubercular-free herds.

BELTED GALLOWAY

This prime roughland breed has a smaller carcase than the Aberdeen Angus, but its quality is unsurpassed, and for smaller joints is preferred.

THE OLD GLOUCESTER

A dairy breed, but included among two-purpose cattle, and interesting to the artist as " standard cow", being reasonably long in the leg, and having a good neck and well-carried head, with forward horns. To the students of tradition, these cows are particularly interesting, as Gloucester was the depot for the great west-country drove routes. Here the mixed herds from beyond Clun, Hereford, and the peak districts converged on the mediaeval markets. The colour, brown with blackish tone, bespeaks influences from the black Welsh cattle.

good feeders (good "doers", they call it) and put on flesh rapidly when brought down to lower, richer pastures. Bringing these young bullocks down and getting them into good condition is a separate department of farming that fits in between the jigsaw of "manure for land", and "cropping of grass for hay". Through the winter the "store" cattle may be out in the fields, or in some cases kept in hammels (big open yards) almost knee-deep in straw, which the cattle trample and turn into good manure for the fields in spring.

The notes in connection with the drawings give you some small idea of the variety of English breeds. The Scotch Angus is probably the best large beef, and the Welsh the worst small, but each can be good or bad *of its type*. So much depends on where they are grazed, and the suitability of the breed for the locality and conditions.

The method of cutting up varies. There is the Scotch cut, and the Welsh method, while the Yorkshire cut is quite different from the South and London-counties cut. Owing to present conditions, boned meat from overseas is producing another type of cutting, and one might say that there was now a "ration slice". The diagrams are basic "London-county cuts" and most deviations can be traced from them.

It is usually best to cook a joint with the bone in it, as the bone, being full of marrow fat, bastes the interior of the joint. Therefore, when boning and stuffing a joint, a plentiful supply of fat should be included in the stuffing to supply this marrow deficiency. It is better to buy a small joint from a good beast than a larger joint from a poor beast. Also, it is *very* important to cook the joint according to its qualities; the roast beef of old England is renowned, but only a small part of the beef is fit for roasting— so in cooking beef, be sure to consider your joint and cook it in the way that will bring out its best qualities.

In contrast to mutton, beef is never insipid; it may be strong, or tough, or fine, or coarse, but it is always much more definite in taste and texture than mutton, and should be cooked quite differently. It is completely wrong to use a mutton recipe for beef. On the whole, the more plain and simple the cooking of beef, the better; get the adjuncts exactly right, the cooking perfectly timed, and the basting and seasoning exact, but keep all as simple as possible.

RECIPES FOR BEEF

" On polished charger laid,
    The bulky chine, with plenteous fat inlaid
    Of golden hue, magnificently shines."

HOBBINAL.

Baron of Beef

Expert chefs roast this for great banquets. It is too large for any other usage. Beeves are also roasted whole in market squares and castle court-yards to celebrate remarkable events. In several market towns in England

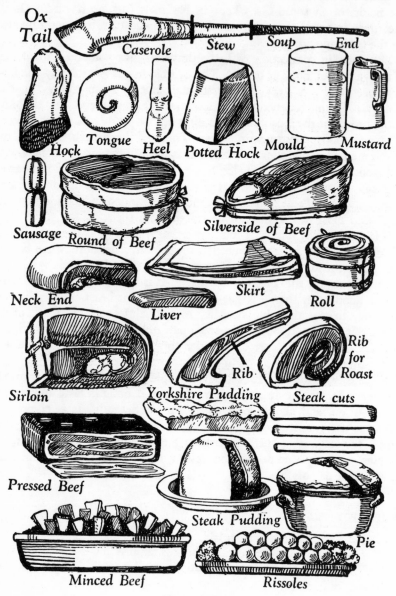

Forms of Beef

can be found the huge iron spits, and the men who have done this job. The legs are cut off at the hock, and the head and tail removed. The rounded carcase is sometimes wrapped in the fleed, or fatty inner membrane, to start the basting, and the spit is turned by one after another of the citizens. A whole beef takes about 12 hours to cook.

Sirloin (Norman-French, *sur loin*)

This is the best beef joint and should be roasted. Never have the under-cut taken out (as sometimes recommended by the too economical in order to make two joints), as this tends to make the joint dry, and loses the value of the bone marrow being cooked between both sides of the meat.

It is always best to roast a sirloin entirely and perfectly, as a well-roasted cold sirloin is almost as good as hot.

Let the sirloin be well hung; dust it lightly with dry mustard, pepper and brown flour to give a crisp crust; bed the fat end well under the lean undercut, and secure in place with string or carefully placed skewer. Roast carefully, basting frequently. If cooking in the oven, it may with advantage *start* with the fat end uppermost, till enough dripping has come to start the basting. Season, but do not salt the joint till ready to serve. The more simply this joint is roasted and served, the better.

Serve with shredded horse-radish, fresh and white as snow drift, roast potatoes, and clear hot gravy. Mustard, bread, drained green vegetables, and Yorkshire pudding, should really go with ribs, or rounds of beef, but may be served with sirloin also.

Rib of Beef

> " A good honest fellow had a spare rib, on which he intended to sup with his family after a long and hard day's work at coppice cutting. Home he came at dark, with his two little boys, each with a witch of wood that they had carried four miles, cheered with the thought of the repast that awaited them. In he went, and found his wife, the methodist parson and a whole troop of the sisterhood, engaged in prayer, and on the table lay scattered the clean polished bones of the spare rib . . ."
>
> COBBETT.

It roasts almost as well as a sirloin, but as it has no undercut, it is better to have the long ends of the bones sawn through so that the fat end can be doubled under—where the undercut comes in a sirloin.

Doing this bastes the meat on the inside and helps to make it juicy.

Baste it even more carefully than the sirloin as it dries so easily, being a thinner joint, and serve it with exceptional care with horse-radish, mustard, baked potatoes, clear gravy and fresh cooked greens.

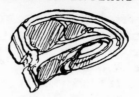

Surloin showing under-
cut and fat folded over it

Round of Beef

Boiled beef with carrots and onions is excellent, and should always be cooked with dumplings. Plain boiled potatoes should be served with boiled beef, but on no account boil the potatoes with the beef as they cloud the clear broth.

Root vegetables, which can be cooked in the broth, may be served with this dish, and celery is permissible, but green vegetables are *not* appetising with boiled meat—keep them for roast meat. A good selection of winter vegetables to serve with boiled beef includes carrots, turnips, swedes, onion, marrow, celery, beans, but not many parsnips, as they sweeten the broth too much. Swedes can be mashed and served separately. Dried peas, previously soaked and then put in a muslin bag and boiled in the beef broth, are good, and so are dried beans.

Boiled Beef with Carrots

Slightly salted beef is good for this, and a round of beef is excellent.

Take carrots, parsnips, a turnip, and a little celery, and onions, and clean and cut up and set to boil in a large pot. Tie the beef securely, and when the vegetables have come to the boil, put it into the broth, and *immediately* draw it aside from the fire, or lower the heat, so that hereafter the water only simmers. After 20 minutes or so, lift the lid and scum off any "clearing" from the top of the broth, add a *little* whole pepper, spice, close the lid again, and let it cook till the meat is tender and the vegetables soft. Serve, drained, on a hot dish, with the vegetables separately, and the broth for gravy. Dumplings are always served with boiled beef. Some people also like a white onion sauce.

Oat Pudding, for Boiled Beef

This very old form of "oat pudding" was served with boiled beef. Well grease a pudding-cloth. Take enough of the broth to moisten two cupfuls of coarse oatmeal, add a liberal dash of pepper, a little salt, and stir well. Pack *loosely* into the pudding-bag and suspend it in the pan to cook alongside the beef. The oatmeal should swell just to fill the cloth, and be served with the beef. It is *pulled* (not cut) open, and a little broth is poured over it.

(For Norfolk dumplings, *see* Bread.)
(For peas pudding, *see* Pork.)
(For other dumplings, *see* Puddings.)

Neck of Beef (oven braise)

Braising is also best for aitchbone, boned ribs, thick steak, or any thick cut without bone. Well done, a coarse joint braised is superior to roasted.

Take a thick earthenware stew-pot, thickly coat it with dripping, pepper the dripping and shred over the bottom a good bed of all manner of vegetables, carrots, turnips, parsnips, onions, swede, a few spring beans, or elderly peas. They must be shredded as fine as straw, and make a flat bed at least two inches deep. Fry the beef both sides until brown and then onto the vegetable bed lay the beef, season well, scatter with powdered herbs, and bury it two or three inches deep under more shredded vegetables, so that the stew-pot is nicely full. If the vegetables are juicy, no water at all need be added. At the most, put in about a tablespoonful, just to give it a start. Rub the inside of the pot *lid* with garlic, put it on, and see that it fits tightly.

Run a thin scrap of paste under the join of the pot lid to be sure the lid is close to the pot. Put the braise in the middle of a moderately hot oven for from 2 to 4 hours, according to the size. Don't open it till ready to serve. Then the oval brown dish should be full of succulent vegetables and meat, swimming in a rich brown gravy.

The important point is never to let it get over-heated past simmering point, and to "let it be. And not to keep worriting about, taking off the lid to poke and see how it's doing, and letting all the steam out!"

This is my aunt's recipe, and as she had to cope with tough Welsh beef and Grandad for fifty years, I have no hesitation in recommending it.

Beefsteak (several ways)

> " A wife, a steak, and a walnut tree—
> The more you beat 'em, better they be."

Grilled. The best steak should be grilled, first quickly on both sides and then more slowly till done. Sprinkle a little salt over it before serving, and pour over it the drip that has come in while cooking (not made-up

Steak

gravy). Put nothing on it, but sprigs of watercress round it. Serve with crisp potatoes.

Grilled with oysters. Open the oysters on to the top and return to the grill for a moment. In this case, do not sprinkle salt, but lightly dust with white pepper.

Grilled with mushrooms. Choose flat, dark ones, and cook under the steak while it is being turned, and finish off on top. When done, pour the drip from the grill over all, serving so that the mushroom gravy mingles with the steak gravy. Serve mashed potatoes and grilled tomatoes with this dish.

Grilled with onions. A further variation of grilled steak. First cut the onions into rings and fry them in the dripping, as they will take longer and will thus flavour the dripping ready for the steak. When brown, push aside and put the steak on. When it is done, pile the onions on top of the steak, salt lightly, and serve with Worcestershire sauce, Yorkshire relish, and chipped potatoes. Steak that might be tough may be rubbed with oil and soaked twelve hours on a plate of spiced vinegar with raw onion trimmings packed under and over it. Drain the steak, flour it thickly, and fry carefully, or, if well beaten, it may be grilled. Be sure to cook fresh onions with it; mashed potatoes go well with this dish.

Fried Steaks, unlike grilled, may be garnished with finely chopped parsley strewn over them. In all cases, be very careful to see that dripping is used for the frying, and that it is smoking hot before the steak is put into it.

Steak Pot. Fry a few onions in dripping in a shallow steak-pot.[1] When brown, put in the steak and brown that. Lift out the steak and put in some ringed carrots and fry them; a small quantity of thinly chopped swedes and fry them. Shake in a little fine oatmeal, and fry that. If winter, and it is available, a very little celery, or if it is summer, a few older peas, but do not fry either of these green vegetables. Now put back the steak, add a cupful of stock (put the peas or chopped celery which have *not* been fried on top). Rub the inside of the lid with a clove of garlic (optional) and put in a bouquet of herbs tied firmly so that it can be fished out easily. Just cover with stock, fit the lid on tightly, and set in a cool oven for two

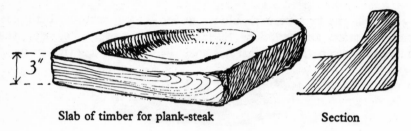

Slab of timber for plank-steak   Section

[1] Only about three to four inches deep, not a hot-pot.

hours at least. Oatmeal is better than plain flour for this dish. It should be very soft and juicy.

Plank Steak. I do not know if the Welsh for "plank" suggested this name to some Welsh-Canadian wood-cutter or if it is a relic of the older days when "treen" was in general usage. Nowadays the dish is known to all foresters.

Get a thick oak plank about a foot or eighteen inches square, and hollow the middle out a little. Rub it well with suet or dripping, making it hot before the fire and letting the fat soak in till the middle hole is full of dripping. In this lay a sprig of garlic, a bay leaf, a few rosemary leaves, or any aromatic herb available to give aroma to the cooking. See that this seasoning adjunct is well immersed in the dripping and then lay the steak over it, packing it down into the hot wood. Give any exposed part of the wood a final rub with dripping and put it in an extremely hot oven.

The steak can, with advantage, be turned once rapidly, after the first three minutes, but after that, do not take it out or open the oven door till done. The wood will char and smoke the meat while it cooks, and the hole under the meat will be filled with a delicious, aromatic gravy.

Beef Hare

Tough, or thin and ragged, steak, if too unevenly cut to grill, will make an interesting "hare". Cut the steak into strips, dust thickly with black pepper, a dash of nutmeg, and flour. Fry the strips lightly, put them into

Beef Hare

a deep hotpot, and nest on them an onion stuck with cloves, a very little celery seed, some dried mushrooms (or mushroom ketchup), a very little *shredded* parsnip (or some sweet root), cover the pot closely and either stand in boiling water, or put into a slow oven for about 2 hours. If the onion and shredded roots are sufficiently juicy it will not be necessary to add any liquid, but a spoonful of water may be added if necessary, or 2 spoonfuls of coarse red wine, with advantage.

Serve from the pot with redcurrant jelly and crisp potatoes.

Season rather highly.

Shin or Leg of Beef (Potted Hough)

The Scotch dish "potted hough", is the best use for shin of beef.

"Take a hough and bash it well with an axe. No' just break it, but have at it, till the pieces are no bigger than a wee hen's egg. Pack it into an iron pot with the brown papery skins of onions, two or three peppercorns and a blade of mace. Just cover with water, set on the lid tightly, and let it stew four hours at least.

"When the meat is away from the bone, tilt it all into a colander, strain the liquid back into the saucepan, and let it gallop while you are gathering up the meat from the broken bones. Then press the meat into a basin with straight sides, and when the meat is all in, fill up with the liquid and set aside till cold.

"It should set stiff. If it no' sets stiff, you must reduce again for it should be as stiff as glue."

Do not add vegetables, or over-season with herbs, when cooking this dish, as it is not a "made" dish, in the usual sense: it is most essentially a plain dish of solid meat. It turns out as brawn, but the texture is much more firm. The Scotch woman who gave me the recipe said, "All o' mine want no more than twa–three slices o' potted hough, and a well of baked taties, and a fresh lettuce and mustard—maybe twa–three pickles would go wi' it well—and a tankard of ale—'twill fill them fine—'tis all guid meat", and as she was the mother of four champion blacksmiths she knew what was strengthening.

Beef Cooked in Beer

" When an ox is old—with tenpennyworth of grass he shall be fit for the larder."

Walter of Henly.

I've an idea that this recipe came back from the Boer War, and was tried out by some British army cook on Transvaal oxen. If you ever have an excessively tough piece of beef, try it—I believe it would soften a frozen mammoth.

For about 8 lb. of tough beef, take 2 large onions, skin and all, and chop up. Tie the beef into a round with any fat secured underneath, between it and the bottom of the pan, and set it down upon a bunch of herbs and a pinch of pickling spice. Pour over it a large cupful of vinegar, and a small cupful of treacle, and cover with the chopped onions. Let it stand all day and then gently pour in mild beer (or dilute beer and water) till level with the top of the beef. Let it come to the "almost boil", and scum it, then put on the lid and simmer slowly for 2 or 3 hours, till the meat seems quite tender.

Lift out the beef, and serve with plain boiled potatoes, and red pickled cabbage, or hot boiled beetroot. The broth is unfortunately not much use.

Tenderising meat. Paw-paw leaves and sap, known to African cooks, make the toughest meat dissolve, through the action of the plant juices. This plant extract can now be bought in bottles, and works miracles.

Beef Spiced

The skirt or flap of beef can be used this way.

Lay it flat and cut out the ends of the bones and any gristly skin. Put these straight away to boil down for thick stock for glaze. You now have a piece of beef looking like a thick slashed blanket.

Rub it well with dry salt and leave it under a snow of salt overnight. Next day, drain, wipe and rub with powdered cloves and black pepper. ($\frac{1}{2}$ oz. of black pepper and $\frac{1}{4}$ oz. of cloves will serve two or three joints, according to the size.) Lay a few cut pickled walnuts in the bone slits, together with some pickled capsicum strips, and roll it up tightly. Tie round and round with string, like packing a parcel for the post, and set it to boil gently for 3–4 hours. Vegetable trimmings, celery-tops, etc., may be added, to flavour the tied-up beef, and for the stock afterwards.

When done, lift the beef out to drain, and set under a good heavy weight till cold. Then cut off the strings, trim and glaze. A fine glowing dish of spiced beef made like this used to deputise for the usual ham as a side dish in the West Riding.

Roll up very tightly

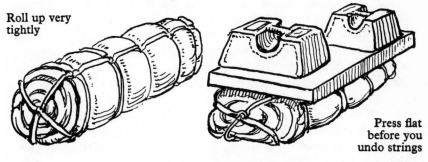

Press flat before you undo strings

Tripe

Tripe Normandy seems to have come over with the Conqueror; usually mediaevally made in autumn, we now make it when we can obtain the necessary ham trimmings.

Take honeycomb tripe (dressed) and cut into oblong pieces, chop the ham finely, and work it well into the honeycomb, spicing with black pepper; salt will not be needed. Roll up the strips, securing with a splint, put a single bay leaf at the bottom of a dish and then pack in the pieces of tripe closely, with mushrooms between and small thin strips of onion, and a sprinkle of fine herbs. Fill up the dish with thick, well-flavoured gravy made from the broken hambone and vegetable trimmings, and stew, covered, on the stove or in the oven for several hours. When almost ready, remove the cover, till the gravy has sunk just enough to leave the tops of the pieces sticking out; on these lay a fine dust of green parsley, and serve at once with dry toast and mustard.

It must be kept very closely covered while cooking, and the single bay leaf at the bottom of the dish before packing is important.

Cow-heel Brawn

Cow-heel is more strongly gelatinous than the calves' feet which are used to make jelly. It is a favourite stand-by in the cattle-market towns of the north, and jellied cow-heel used to be served at the Wakes.

Wash the cow-heel (previously cloven through by the butcher) and stew very slowly overnight, with an onion. Take out any bones and chop the meat finely. Add a large spoonful of chopped cooked bacon and white pepper and salt. Pack it into a pudding-basin, when it should set to a clear brawn. Serve cut in thin slices with mustard mixed to a thin cream with milk, and eat with bread and butter and mixed pickles.

Cow-heel, Stewed

Cow-heel can be done with brown gravy and carrots, turnips, etc., or fried, or made into a rich stew; but in the north cow-heel is considered suitable invalid diet, and so we give this simple recipe. Scald, clean, and split the heel, put it into a deep iron stew-pan with a large, mild onion, a bunch of herbs including a bay leaf, and a small spoonful of vinegar; bring to nearly boiling-point, and then draw back and let it simmer gently for 4 hours. Empty the stew-pan into a basin, wipe it, and set it back with a tablespoonful of butter in it; when melted, add a generous dust of white pepper, salt, and 2 tablespoonfuls of fine flour, cook completely, and then blend in the gravy drained from the cow-heel; leave all to cook thoroughly while you bone the heel (the bones should slide out quite easily), cut the meat up into neat pieces, slice the cooked onion and, if liked, add a little fresh, chopped parsley, put meat, onion and gravy all together inside a wall of hot mashed potatoes, and serve with mustard.

If people like tripe and onions, they are likely to enjoy cow-heel.

Heart: Mock Goose Method

Heard in Wigan Market:

> *Collier*, admiring pendant heart, windpipe, and lungs outside a butcher's shop: " I say, guv'nor, how much for your watch and chain?"

In the beef-eating north poor folk sometimes cooked bullock's heart instead of a goose for Christmas. A few days before wanted, wash the heart well, and set it to simmer overnight with a good dash of vinegar in the water and a few peppercorns. If necessary, let it simmer two or three nights, till it is really tender, leaving it to grow cold in the broth, and on Christmas Eve skim off the fat from the broth, take up the heart, and stuff it with forcemeat made of breadcrumbs, the fat from the stock, a heavy seasoning of sage and onions chopped (the onions should have been cooked whole in the broth). Pepper and salt. Moisten the forcemeat with broth, or egg, and stuff the heart and sew it up. Flour thickly, tie some rashers of bacon across the "breast", and roast, basting as if you were cooking a goose. Adorn the mock goose with a ring of sausages and some roast potatoes, and serve with apple sauce. In texture and flavour it much resembles goose.

Tongue and Ox-Cheek Brawn

At a boys' school in the West Riding we made a special beef-brawn. My mother got the recipe from one of the large farms "up the Dales", and it was probably "as old as the hills".

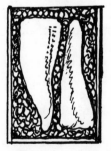

Section showing how the two tongues are embedded in the round of the brawn

Two ox-tongues and two ox-cheeks were first lightly salted, and two cow-heels split and cleaned. A large iron pan was placed on the fire, into which were put trimmings from vegetables, including onion skins, celery tops, chopped parsnips, etc. Then the ox-cheeks and tongues were rinsed from the salt and packed in, with a few peppercorns and a large stick of *cinnamon* and the cow-heels. The whole was covered with water and brought slowly to the boil and simmered all day long. Salt was not added, as the meat was already salted.

The liquid was then strained off *through muslin* and put into a pan to boil down rapidly. The tongues were skinned, and trimmed, and the meat taken from the cheeks and the cow-heels.

The tongues were then placed top-to-tail and side by side in the tall brawn tin and the other meat packed around them. The liquid, well reduced by boiling, was then poured in, filling the tin to the top, and the brawn was set aside to cool.

The double-tongued brawn would take at least 24 hours to stiffen in a cold stone larder (there were no refrigerators in those days). It was then turned out upright on to a dish on the sideboard, and the hungry boys used to "level it off" vigorously across and across. It was always popular with the menfolk, and we usually had one "in cut" for breakfast all summer. Beside this dish always stood the tall white jug of the traditional mustard sauce, not plain mustard, but a creamy, thick sauce—which has been served with brawn since the fourteenth century (*see* Mustard Sauce).

Potted Beef

Properly made potted meat used to be served as a "dish" for breakfast or lunch.

If, instead of framing the tops as pictures (for which they were never designed), the old decorated potted-meat jars were hunted up and put to their proper use, they would cheer the modern breakfast table very pleasantly.

This recipe is a very old one, re-written about 1750, when some of the best pots were designed by Staffordshire potteries. *To pot beef:* 2 lb. beef, rather lean, about ½ lb. good dripping, pepper, salt, and powdered mace. Put the beef into a stone jar with the dripping, cover it very closely, and let it bake slowly, or else set it in a pan of boiling water for about 4 hours.

Take the meat out and, whilst hot, pound it with a pestle and mortar (or a rolling-pin in an iron pot), moistening with the gravy from the jar and adding the black pepper, powdered mace and salt as you work. It should start dry, but gradually take up all the grease and juice from the pot while being pounded. When quite smooth and soft, put it into the jar which has been rubbed with a clove of garlic or onion.

Pour a little well-clarified butter or very white dripping over the top and leave it overnight to stiffen before serving. Some lay a bay leaf at the bottom of the jar before filling it up.

Uses for potted beef. Excellent with hot buttered toast and coffee for breakfast.

Or with crusty crescents and chutney and a glass of beer for lunch.

Or with mustard-and-cress and wholemeal bread and butter, or with watercress and bread and butter, for high tea.

And grand for packed lunches (with an apple or tomatoes in the other pocket).

Note. On no account let the meat bake hard or boil. As it is close-

covered it will not lose weight by cooking slowly for several hours at some
time when the range is hot.

Ox-head

Get this prepared by the butcher, who will send it to you split in two
(*see* notes on Pig's Head). Lay it in strong salty water overnight and rinse
under a briskly running tap till thoroughly clear.

The tongue should be salted separately.

Put the head into a pan with water to cover, a few peppercorns, salt,
a bunch of herbs, and vegetable trimmings. Simmer till the bones and meat
all fall to pieces, then drain into a basin. Take out every scrap of bone and
gristle and chop the meat finely, sprinkling with powdered herbs and pepper.

Press into a mould set with a weight on top, and turn out when cold.
Garnish with parsley and serve with pickles and roast potatoes. The broth,
strained and boiled with oatmeal, onions, or a strongly flavoured vegetable
such as celery, makes a meaty soup.

Note. Be sure you put the remnants, bones, vegetables, etc., out for the
fowls to pick clean. There is enough miscellaneous picking on an ox-head
to keep an industrious hen busy for hours.

Ox-pith

The pith of an ox is often mentioned in old books—it is the marrow
of the spinal cord. A small portion may be seen across the end bone of
ribs of beef (as the spine cord of a sheep makes that small portion of marrow
across the head of a mutton chop). This pith is the finest pure marrow fat,
and in the days of home slaughtering was carefully collected and used for
"marrow puddings" and "toasts" as very delicate fat (*see* Marrow Bones.)

Ox-palates

Old recipes using ox-head or calf's head for broth often removed the
tongue and palates and cheeks to use for separate dishes. The palate is
tougher meat than the soft tongue, but of the same type. Cooked longer
than the tongue, it can be used to supplement its bulk, in tongue and
brawn or jellied meat dishes.

Here is an eighteenth-century recipe:

> " Have ten or twelve Ox palates—boil them till tendre, and peel
> them and cut into squares then slay and draw two or three
> chickens, and cut them between every joint and season with nutmeg
> salt and shred thyme—fry them with butter, then put in rich gravy
> with the ox palates and let stew together. Thicken some more
> gravy with the yolks of three or four eggs, beaten in a glass of
> white wine, and a piece of butter, and 3 or 4 spoonsful of cream.
> Dish it up garnished with pickled grapes."

Ox-tail

As animals store reserve fat in their tails, a winter ox-tail is an unexpectedly meaty joint. If a small family, use the largest joints to make a braised dish the first day, and the smallest end joints the second day for soups.

Ox-tail Pot

Take the larger joints, pepper them well, and roll around in a basinful of flour till well coated all over. Fry till brown.

While frying, cut up an onion, a carrot, a turnip (or a small slice of swede, or a smaller slice of parsnip, i.e., some sweet root), and a small stick of celery if available, and a bunch of herbs. Roll these cut vegetables in the flour, but do not pepper *them* heavily as you want to keep their *individual* flavour. When the ox-tail is brown, take it out and fry the vegetables. When they are brown, take them out and fry the flour, and when that is brown, froth it up with stock or water to make a rich gravy.

While the gravy is cooking pack the pieces of ox-tail and vegetables into a fireproof casserole, pour the gravy over, and bake close-covered, till the vegetables are tender and the meat loose on the bone.

Note. This dish is very rich, so some people prefer to make it overnight so that the fat which rises to the top can be taken off when it cools. In this case, only re-heat it the following day. On no account cook it twice.

Ox-tail Soup

The *ends* of ox-tails should be used for this.

To a good tail end allow about $\frac{1}{4}$ lb. of bacon bones, the outer leaves and sticks of a head of celery, carrots, a turnip, an onion and a bunch of herbs.

Flour and brown the jointed ox-tail, and put the pieces into a pan. Put two or three cloves into the onion and add it, with chopped-up vegetables and bacon bones. Put in also a few peppercorns and cook all slowly, in just enough dripping to prevent them burning, for a good twenty minutes. Then add rather less than a quart of water and let it simmer till the vegetables are tender and the pieces of bone can be taken out clean.

This soup is characteristically rich. If too rich, it must be left to get cold overnight, when it can be skimmed, but if a rich winter soup is wanted it can be served direct, thickened in the usual way.

Just before serving, a glass of port wine or burgundy is a great improvement.

Beef Dripping

Beef dripping, well creamed with a spoonful of thin mustard, is better than butter for beef sandwiches.

Beef dripping creamed with a generous spoonful of Worcestershire sauce, or Yorkshire relish, makes an equally good spread for potted beef.

Do not forget the horse-radish when making beef sandwiches.

Beef sausages should be fried in beef dripping, and served with mustard.

Hot dripping toast, for tea on a winter's evening, should be well salted and peppered.

For all beefsteak pies, or beef-filled pastries, use beef dripping to make the pastry. It can be clarified till white and firm as suet.

Beef Dumplings

"My housekeeper will have these in her new fashion, although I tell her that when I was a young man, we used to keep strictly to my father's rule, 'No broth no ball; no ball no beef', and always began dinner with broth and white suet dumplings boiled in the broth with the beef, and then the meat itself. If we had not supped our broth we had no ball, which we liked a deal better, and the beef came last of all, only to those who had done justice to the broth and the ball. Now folks begin with sweet things and turn their dinners topsy-turvy."

Cranford.

Dough dumplings. Where bread is made at home, a portion of the dough is always taken for dumplings, and cooked with the boiled beef. Dumplings for boiled beef are as much a matter of course as Yorkshire pudding for roast beef.

Light dumplings. The proportions are three tablespoonfuls of flour to two eggs, and only just enough milk to make a stiff batter. Put the flour into a basin with a pinch of salt, make a small well in the middle, into which break the egg-yolks, keeping the whites separate. Stir the yolks into the flour, add the milk, beat the batter well until it is of the consistency of whipped cream, beat the whites until they are very stiff, and fold them into the batter. Drop spoonfuls of the batter into the boiling broth and simmer till well risen and cooked.

These bread (yeast) or batter (egg) dumplings are best with meat as they can be cooked *with it*, but suet dumplings need *boiling*.

Beef-melt

The melt is attached to the inner side of the ribs and is sometimes sold separately by country butchers. It makes a coarse, kidney-flavoured gravy, and is mentioned in eighteenth- and nineteenth-century workhouse recipes as an addition to meat puddings and suet dumplings. If you can't get enough kidney for the gravy of a large beefsteak-and-kidney pudding, the melt can be used for those who like the kidney flavour.

When I spoke of beef-melt to an old Devon woman who used to cook for men in a sailors' home, she told me that they made a meaty gravy with an ox-melt and a shallot that was very popular with the old toothless men—"but we'm didn't use no separate fat; no, we'm boiled bacon and peas and beans one day, and after the bacon was ate, we used rind we cut off, and some of the broth, to make the melt gravy, and gave it with dumplings for the next day."

Meat gravy for a Vegetable Pie

This, a good ploughboy dinner gravy, can also be used with suet rolls. Cut up an ox-melt or a piece of kidney into pieces the size of sugar lumps, and as much of bacon rind, or ham or bacon trimmings and chopped shallots; fry all together slowly in an iron pot till brown (about fifteen minutes). Add enough fine oatmeal to dry up completely, and continue cooking till all is brown—but unburnt; add slowly as much boiling water as will make a good thick gravy, and continue cooking slowly about one hour. Strain, season well, and add chopped parsley and a small spoonful of made mustard before serving.

Beef Sausage

Yorkshire and Lancashire specialise in beef sausages, the proportions being: suet one; lean beef two; bread a half; spice and black pepper to taste (not much spice, but rather heavy with the black pepper); sausage skins.

These sausages are rather thinner and longer than pork sausages, of a dark-red colour, and are usually fried in dripping till very crisp, and served with mashed potatoes and Yorkshire pudding. We suggest horse-radish sauce as an alternative. They also make a very good toad-in-the-hole with a Yorkshire-pudding mixture.

Aberdeen Sausage

The mixture is two parts minced beef, one part very fat bacon, one part fine oatmeal or spice, and pepper and salt to flavour. The whole is boiled in a tight, well-greased cloth, in good beef stock, left to get cold, then unrolled. (It will have absorbed enough liquid to swell the oatmeal, and have made a firm smooth sausage.) It is then brushed over with light brown glaze, or crumbed, and served sliced.

During the war we had so many tins of nondescript "luncheon meat", served in flat pink disks, which might have been beef, pork or anything, that the "cut sausage meat slice" became unpopular; but a good, well-made, meat sausage, freshly sliced, is wholesome and appetising.

The Aberdeen sausage is about a foot long and 4 or 5 inches in diameter.

Beefsteak-and-Kidney Pudding

Cut beefsteak and kidney into rather small pieces, according to the size of the pudding, and shake the pieces well in a bowl containing flour and pepper till all the pieces are well coated. Then use the peppered flour, with some salt, and the suet from the kidney chopped very finely, to make a light suet crust.

A Bag Pudding

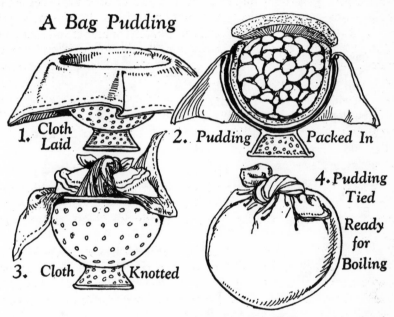

1. Cloth Laid
2. Pudding Packed In
3. Cloth Knotted
4. Pudding Tied Ready for Boiling

Boiled puddings were made in cloths and hung in boiling water or broth (*see* Cauldron Cookery, page 36).

Grease the basin with dripping, line it with the crust, put in the seasoned meat and some very finely chopped onion. Fill up the basin with stock or water to near the top, put on the pastry lid, seeing that the edges are well brought together to keep in the steam. Cover the whole pudding with a floured cloth and simmer 3–4 hours. On account of the long boiling the crust should be made rather damp. The diagram on this page shows how to mould this type of pudding without a basin if necessary.

Mushrooms—the dark ones—are excellent additions. Cut up raw and pack in with the beef, but, as you want their gravy to escape and flavour the dish, do *not* flour the mushrooms.

Beefsteak-and-Kidney Pie

This is made on similar lines as the pudding, but has a light short crust on top. This is the basic beefsteak-and-kidney pie. At your discretion may be added mushrooms, fresh or dried (if dried, soak beforehand and chop up rather small). The black-gilled mushrooms are nicest, and make the gravy very rich. Some young, small carrots, peas and morells make useful additions. Oysters are sometimes added, not too successfully, however, as the prolonged cooking is apt to make them hard; cockles are better, but don't overdo it, and in this case pepper well, but go carefully with the salt.

Beef Tea

" Take a grete glasse [pot] and do thi beef therein, and do onyone mynced and whole cloves and maces and pouder of pepur, and a lay splinters in the bottom [of the pot] that the flesh hit not and stop it well, that no eyrie goo oute, and seethe hit with an esy fyre—[or] sethe it ina pot with water in a cawdron, but top it well that no eyre goo oute."

A. BOORDE, 1500.

This old recipe cannot be improved upon.

The "grete glasse" was a pot standing inside a cauldron of boiling water, and the "splinters"—which are to lift the beef up in the pot, so that it does not lie sodden in the gravy—were, according to a contemporary cook, best made of birch, as they do not boil soft but remain springy. (From experience I know birch twigs give a slight, pleasant aroma.)

In modern usage, for the "grete glasse" take a 7-lb. jam-jar, and lay the twigs at the bottom, and lay the beef (cut and scored across the grain) over the twigs, with a little shredded onion and the clove and mace and pepper; stopper up the jar closely and set it to boil in a deep pan of water. After some hours, lift out the beef, and the jar will be full of rich, well-flavoured beef tea.

Note. Beef *extract*, which is far less pleasant, is made from raw beef at doctor's orders.

Skink: an inferior beef tea

" Skink is beef boiled down to a thick broth."

SILVOCEAS, 1800.

Cut 1 lb. of beef into dice—put $\frac{1}{2}$ oz. of butter into a deep pan and cook the beef cubes in it till brown. Add 2 pints of boiling water, 1 teaspoonful of salt and a pinch of sugar, 1 clove and $\frac{1}{4}$ of an onion cut in two parts.

Simmer slowly for 30 minutes and serve with a little pepper and toasted bread.

Mince

For grown-ups, "mince" is usually made into rissoles or shepherd's pie, but children sometimes like it plain.

To serve this, cook it very gently in a little good gravy, and when done, cover it all over with triangular snippets of very thin dry toast, prodded in edgeways. This is important, as it gives something to chew. Served inside a ring of potatoes and vegetables, it is a simple nursery dinner.

A sprinkling with raw finely chopped parsley adds to its value as food, and makes it look much more appetising.

Rissoles

Boorde in the fifteenth century gives it as *Risshe shewes*, but the spelling varies: "And then make stuff as thou doest for resshewes." A piece of batter falling off the spit into the dripping pan certainly makes the sound of the word—and they are usually reshows of meat.

Cut cold meat finely or put through a mincer; if it is roast beef, put through also a scrap of horse-radish; if the rissoles are of cold boiled meat some of the vegetables cooked with it may be chopped together also. Season rather highly and flavour with fresh green herbs; parsley and chives are good.

Shape the meat into small balls, binding with beaten egg, and roll in egg and crumbs, and fry briskly. Cold potatoes, mashed and seasoned and made into balls to match, go well with rissoles, and all rissoles should be served with some good tart fruit sauce, or well-flavoured gravy.

When making mutton rissoles, a small bunch of red currants embedded inside makes a juicy centre (*see* Mutton).

Be sure the gravy or sauce is good.

Suet Cough-cure

A farmhouse cure for a winter cough. Take 1 pint of hot milk, and set to boil on the fire. Stir in, when just boiling, 1 tablespoonful of *pounded* (chopped and then pounded fine-as-dust) suet, and whisk thoroughly while on the fire, till it froths. Serve in a glass wrapped in a hot napkin, with a pinch of salt. Emollient, laxative, and guaranteed to loosen a tight chest cough. For children a spoonful of honey was substituted for the salt.

Suet for Milk Puddings

A spoonful of finest oatmeal mixed with a spoonful of *pounded* (not merely chopped but pounded fine) suet stirred into a slowly baked milk pudding will make it exceedingly rich and creamy.

Suet Dumplings

12 oz. of flour; 6 oz. of thinly shredded suet; and about 4 oz. of fine white breadcrumbs; white pepper; salt.

Mix to a paste with a little broth or cold water; form into dumplings and drop into absolutely boiling broth and keep them bubbling about until light and puffy. They are usually cooked with the beef, but as you do not want the beef to boil, it is better to first cook the dumplings by themselves in broth taken from the meat after it has become well flavoured. Once the dumplings are risen and firm they can be put back with the simmering beef to continue cooking.

BEEF MARROW BONES

> " These cokes how they stampe and streyne and grinde
> And turnen substaunce into accident
> Out of the harde bones knokke they
> The mary (for they caste nought a wey
> That may go through the golet softe and swote)
> Of spicerye, of leef, and bark, and roote,
> Shall been his sauce y-maked by delyte
> To make him yet a newer appetyte."

Marrow

Marrow is the most light and digestible fat, and should be given to children and invalids who require building up. The only people I have found who appreciate the value of marrow bones are some children's nurses (specially trained in dietetics), and Army cooks, who can count on getting a couple of pounds of "butter" out of the canteen marrow bones.

Mediaeval people loved marrow, and used it chiefly for sweet dishes. A favourite recipe was whole barley, oats or wheat steeped in milk with honey and chopped marrow (and raisins or currants). Our modern rice pudding is obviously a copy of this, with foreign materials.

To make it the old way with modern English materials, take 2 cupfuls of pearl barley and simmer in milk gently until swollen. Press 2 table-spoonfuls of finely chopped marrow at the bottom of the dish (just as if you were buttering it for a milk pudding), put the barley on top, sprinkle with sugar or a spoonful of honey or treacle, add a little more of the finely chopped marrow on top, and bake slowly.

A *few* currants or raisins may be put in but it is very good plain.

In Georgian days marrow bones were served baked; with a small crust on top of the cut end to prevent evaporation. They were wrapped in a napkin and sent to table with pepper, salt, and wafer-dry toast. They were eaten from the bone with the long silver or Sheffield-plate marrow-

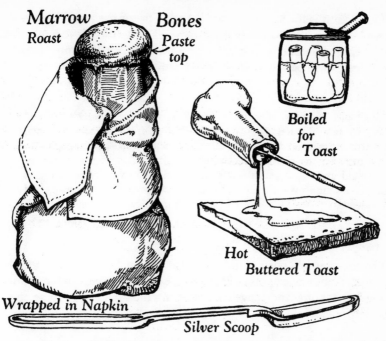

Marrow *Roast* **Bones** *Paste top*

Boiled for Toast

Hot Buttered Toast

Wrapped in Napkin

Silver Scoop

Marrow bones should be sealed with a huff paste before roasting. The long silver spoons are usually of Georgian silver.

spoons, which are a feature of Georgian silver. They are still served thus at the Mitre, Oxford, and a few knowledgeable eating houses.

In Victorian England this bone fare was served for men, being considered "unladylike", but Queen Victoria ate marrow toast for tea every day. For this the bones, previously baked or steamed, are disgorged on to freshly made hot toast, sprinkled with pepper and salt, and sent to table piping hot. A fine strewing of parsley improves the appearance of this delicious tea-time dish (which was certainly not correct diet for her plump Majesty).

Marrow Butter

This is excellent for thin nervous children.

Melt the marrow out of the bones very gently (the best way is to break the bones with a meat chopper, and pile them into a deep dish in a cool oven). When all the marrow is melted out, strain it off into a warm dish and add a scrap of sugar and a well-rubbed-in clove of saffron. When the marrow is almost cool, it may be whisked with a beater like whipped cream, which will make it very light, but if left to set stiff in a cool place, can be used on bread in exactly the same way as butter.

The saffron is for colour, colour is such a factor for young children that because it *looks* like butter, it is far more likely to be enjoyed.

Its best food value for children who need it, is with brown bread and watercress, or good home-made meat sandwiches.

Ox-gall

> " 3 lb. of yellow soap, sliced into a jar with one bullock's gall and one pint of water. Set it in the brick oven after the bread is drawn (or simmer on the stove) till all is melted, cool, and shape into balls for the cleaning of carpets and rugs. A spoonful of household ammonia, and a few drops of oil of cloves, beaten in as it cools, improves the colour-reviving properties of the soap, and leaves a refreshing smell in the room, which discourages moth."
>
> Housekeeper's book, 1700.

Ox-rein for Clockmakers and Drovers

The long testicle cord of the bull was valued by drovers as a lash. It was hung from a hook with a heavy weight at the end to stretch it out. Its strong gut texture and length was also used as pulleys in some sorts of grandfather clocks.

Ox-hides

The hair from the ox-hides was pickled off in the lime vats, before making leather, and this "neat's hair" was the basis of the fibrous plaster of which walls and ceilings were built. The hair preserved thus in old plaster walls is interesting, as showing whether the local type of cattle has continued, or changed. This hair was also used for upholstery.

The trimmings and cuttings of the hide from the leather-works now make jelly squares, and the scraped-off fat—bleached white by the lime process—makes commercial suets.

BEEF TRACKLEMENTS

Horse-radish

Horse-radish was a notable stomachic and antiscorbutic. We have always found it grown in large quantities around mediaeval landing-stages and inns, where the extracted juice of the root probably formed a hot cordial for cold and seasick man and beast. The expressed juice still forms an embrocation. Its usage with hefty joints of beef is easily understood. We think it likely that the expressed juice, eaten something like mustard, may have taken the place of the snowy, fluffy piles of white root now served with the hot roast (*see* Vegetables).

Mustard

> " English mustard was first made at Durham about 1730, and the recipe was kept a secret for many years by an old woman named Clements, of Durham.
>
> She ground the seeds like wheat and made a little fortune by going from town to town on a packhorse. She even secured the patronage of George I."
>
> *Mustard Secret Kept.*

Mediaeval mustard seems to have been more like a creamy white sauce than the present yellow gum. We have made it to serve with brawn, then, following mediaeval directions, poured it like thick cream over the thin slices as they lay in the dish. Up to William Shakespeare's day, Master-mustard-seed was gathered and used by English people with their roast beef, and I believe a certain firm of mustard-makers are still enjoined to give anyone who needs it a small quantity of the expressed mustard oil, so valuable was it considered as a cure for rheumatism.

Parsnip

Roast beef and parsnips, boiled beef and carrots, these go together. The parsnip is interesting. It was one of our earliest English dairy plants, being used, both root and leaf, to enrich the milk and sweeten the cheese. (This is the reasonable connection we find for roasting it with beef.) The roast potato, at first a sweet potato, followed the roast parsnip (*see* notes in Vegetables).

Mixed Vegetables

Boiled beef and carrots are good, for when carrots and beef are old, they take about the same time to cook together very gently. The turnip or swede also supplies the sweet element. In many country places, after the boiled beef has been eaten hot with the vegetables in the broth the first day, the carrots, turnips, parsnips, etc., are all chopped up together, heated with a little broth, and served as the hot vegetable with the cold meat the following day.

Pickles

Cold roast beef is so excellent it should be served plain. Good pickles and fresh salad should always be served with cold meat.

Yorkshire Pudding

It is said that this can only be made correctly in Yorkshire or Lancashire. Probably the brisk, bright coal fires of the Black Country and the way they

All sorts of Beef Vegetables

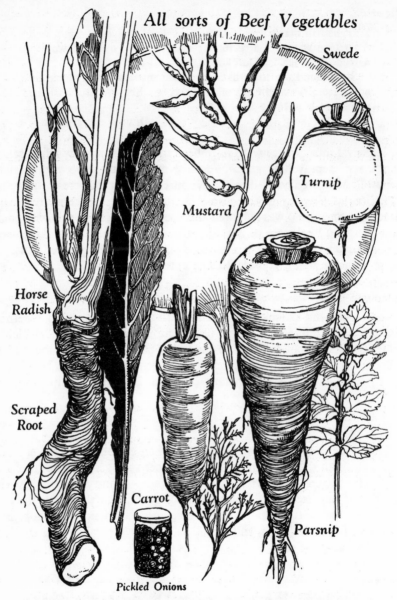

Beef tracklements. Some vegetables that are traditional with beef

hang their roasting meat over the pudding below, have something to do with it.

The recipe is eggs, whipped to snow, with almost as much flour as they will take up well beaten in. The batter is then thinned down with a little salted water till as thick as good cream. Whip the whites of the eggs to snow before whipping in the yolks. Make this batter early, when you first put down the beef to cook. When the beef is nearly done (at the moment when you give it a final basting), lift the joint up a little, or, if you are baking it in a tin, raise it higher on the grid above the dripping in the pan. Give the standing batter a good beating up and pour it quickly into the boiling dripping in the tin. It should "frou-frou" as it goes into the hot fat like an omelette. Let the beef drip on to it as it finishes cooking. Yorkshire pudding should be puffy and crisp and brown, and ready to serve at the same moment as the beef. Slice it into 'crisp squares at once.

Cab-shelter Sauce

This dark-brown spicy sauce used to fill the stoppered bottles on the scrubbed tables of the shelters, where the cabbies had their meals in the "growler" and hansom cab period. Most "cab cribs" made their own version, but this was "foundation" sauce:

1 pint pot full of chopped shallots, 1 clove of garlic (London East), 1 teaspoonful of salt, 1 teaspoonful of black pepper, 1 tablespoonful of sugar, and mushroom catsup, or other spice to the host's opinion. Add enough cold water to cover the ingredients, and boil thoroughly together till the shallots are pulp. Sieve, pressing well, cover with 1 pint of good sharp vinegar, boil up, and bottle. Shake the bottle and pour over steak, chops, or London eggs.

Rajah's Sauce

Outside Reading is a deep well through the chalk, sunk at great expense by an Indian rajah for his English friends. This sauce comes from that district, but we cannot guarantee the connection. It *must* be cooked in an earthenware pot, and is very fiery. Strain the juice of six lemons with their thinly cut and sliced yellow rind. Add 1 small teaspoonful of salt, and 1 dram of cayenne pepper; boil up once, simmer for 5 minutes, and strain into a small dry bottle and cork tightly. Sprinkle sparely over cold meat.

Spice Sauce (sauce for fish or flesh)

" Take a quart of sharp cider, and take jamaica pepper [long peppers], sliced ginger, some mace, a few cloves, some lemon peel, horse-radish root sliced, some sweet herbs, 6 schaloys [shallots], 8 anchovies, 3 spoonfulls of shred red peppers, bang all and put into a bag in the cider, and keep it warm and shake it often. A spoonful cold or mixed in sauce for fish or flesh."

Indian Soy

This dates from the East India Company days. Soy is the fungoid product of the soy bean (*see* Fungi).

Worcester Sauce
Yorkshire Relish

Both these sauces are of ancient ancestry and were served in Inns and Post Houses.

Nun's Sauce (a Convent recipe)

This very old form of relish was made by nuns in a Yorkshire convent more than eighty years ago. Most of the large farms in the north made their own relish to eat with their beef.

¾ oz. of cayenne pepper, 2 tablespoonfuls of soy, 3 cloves of garlic, 1 tablespoonful of anchovies (these came in barrels, and the scraping of the barrel was used), a few cloves, 3 or 4 shallots, 1 large spoonful of sugar, and 1 quart of vinegar. Pound all dry things with the dry sugar, chop and add the onions, etc., put into a leadless glazed demijohn with the vinegar, and cork lightly. This jar was then left at the foot of the kitchen stairs for a month, and everyone passing up and down to chapel (twice daily) had to give it a shake. At the end of the month it was strained off through muslin into the tall glass bottles in the old-fashioned cruet stands.

> " Old fish and young flesh wolde I have ful fain,
>   Better is, quoth he, a pyke than a pickerel
>   And bet than old beef, is the tendre veal."
>
> CHAUCER.

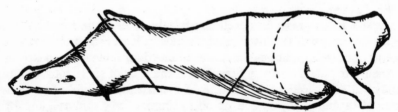

Cutting for veal (as also for goat) varies considerably. Veal is valued for its white meat and gelatinous bones; goat has the same long bones in proportion to the meat, but the meat is dark and the bones thin and hard.

VEAL

VEAL IN ENGLAND

> " Who eateth his veal, pig, and lamb, being froth,
>   Shall twice in the week go to bed without broth."
>
> TUSSER, fifteenth century.

VEAL HAS never been popular in England. From an economic view, veal was wasteful meat, while there was plenty of rough grazing to rear young beef. Besides being "froth" and disapproved of, veal was usually suspect, for one did not slaughter a calf unless there was something wrong with it. Separate dairy herds (such as were kept on the Continent) were not part of general English usage. The conquering Normans demanded veal—and the Saxons resented the spoiling of their cattle; also, the vile method of bleeding the calf while still alive, as practised on the Continent, was commented upon during the French wars; and its resemblance to the kosher methods fostered the dislike through the Middle Ages. All these combined causes made a definite English resentment against veal. It continues strongly today in rural England. "Blancmange" of the old cookery books is really white meat dressed in milk. Dishes like calves-foot jelly became "sweet-meats", because they were made of white meat. In early times veal seems to have been used only in its youngest gelatinous forms. With the specialising of dairywork in the eighteenth century (and prevalent French fashions) veal recipes are found more often—but veal is not a typical English meat.

RECIPES FOR VEAL

Barley Cream of Veal (seventeenth century)

This is a "special soup for invalids".

1 lb. of lean veal, shredded small, a handful of pearl barley, seasoning, and 1½ pints of cold water. Bring all to the boil slowly in a jar inside a pan of boiling water, and stew very gently till all is soft. Rub both barley and veal through a sieve, returning the liquid, which should be as thick as a good cream, to the pot. Warm up again, adding a spoonful of cream, and serve, delicately seasoned, with snippets of dry toast.

Liver

Calf's liver is very tender. It should be brushed with oil or melted fat and grilled or fried with a few curls of bacon. Fried onions are good with liver—be sure to do them first so that their flavour permeates the liver.

If the calf's liver is inclined to be tough, a good way is to stuff it. Get the butcher to cut a deep pocket, and set the liver to soak for an hour in a soup-plate or baking-pan full of spiced vinegar. Meanwhile, make a stuffing with sage and onions, seasoning it rather highly with herbs, pepper and salt. Fill the pocket with the stuffing and secure the opening with a small skewer. Fry it in hot dripping in a baking pan for 1 minute, first on one side and then on the other. Then pour off the dripping, lower the heat, put a tassel of bacon-rinds lattice-wise across the top of the liver to keep it basted, and cook in a very slow oven till tender. It may take an hour or more, according to size. 10 minutes before serving, remove the bacon scraps and let the dish brown appetisingly. A few slices of bacon browned on top, a glass of red wine or a spoonful of Worcestershire sauce, and another of apple or damson jelly poured round in the juice, transform a tough piece of liver into a very succulent dish. Do not omit the red wine, or some tart fruit element; red-currant juice, or crab-apple, will serve quite well.

Make the stuffing as damp as possible, as it is the steam, engendered *inside* the steak, imprisoned by the frying fat outside, which penetrates the liver and makes it tender.

Muggety Pie

The umbilical cord of the calf was washed, soaked in salt water, and cut into short lengths which were then split open end to end twice, and cut, so making small oblong pieces. These were then boiled, till soft, with onions and seasoning, chopped again and made into a pie, using the gelatinous stock and some milk to make the filling gravy. The whole white pie was then covered with crust and baked.

I have not made this myself; the description was given to me by an old farm-hand in Gloucestershire, who assured me "all jelly soft it was", and "it was the jelly gravy was the best part—some did put in taters and a turnip and sech, but 'twas best plain, and good cold".

It's interesting how the dairy districts and the valleys seem to like these gelatinous dishes, such as cow-heel and potted hough, and the Highland districts, on the whole, like the cereal thickening.

Tripe

Tripe and onions are a classic.

There are several different sorts of tripe: the honeycomb, the sponge, and the black. The honeycomb and sponge, being white, are generally used for this dish, the darker tripe being better served with a brown gravy or cut into squares, egg-and-breadcrumbed, and fried.

Let the onions be simmered till tender with the tripe before using the liquor with an equal quantity of milk to make a white sauce, which should be thickened with flour and butter. Afterwards let the sauce boil well, separately, to cook the starch thoroughly; and it should cool a little before the pieces of tripe and the cooked onion are put back into it. A dash of mace or a bay leaf may be added to the sauce, but onion should strongly predominate.

Veal Loaf (nineteenth century)

This was popular for Victorian picnics in the summer. Lightly grease a plain pottery mould and decorate it with slices of hard-boiled egg, strips of thin pink ham, and sprigs of parsley. Cut the veal into small squares about the size of a lump of sugar, add the choppings from the ham, white pepper and salt, and pack it into the mould, being careful not to disturb the decorations.

Fill up the mould with good strong veal stock (that can be relied upon to jelly when cold) and bake all gently for 1 hour. Let the mould get cold, turn out, and garnish with parsley, peas, and young spring carrots. Serve with brown bread and butter, and watercress or dandelion salad with a "bite" to it. Lettuce is rather too insipid for this delicate mould.

Veal Fritters

This recipe from a cook's book of Richard I, 1390, is a very useful one for using up small pieces of cooked veal. The scraps scraped off a bone that has been used for soup are enough to make a small dish of these fritters.

"Nym vell and seeth it well and hak it smal and grynd bred, peper, safron [seasoning to taste] and do thereto and frye yt—presse it wel upon a Bord and dresse it forthe."

In modern usage: Take scraps of cooked veal (and ham if possible) and mince up with an equal quantity of fine white breadcrumbs. Season carefully with white pepper and salt (unless a little ham is used when it will supply the salt). In place of the "safron" modern taste prefers a suspicion of lemon rind or finely ground lemon thyme. Bind the mixture with a little of the veal broth and shape into cutlets—flattening them between two boards. Dip into batter, fry till crisp, serving hot with slices of lemon.

Veal Pie

"Raise a high pye, then cut out a fillet of veal into three or four fillets, season with spice, mynced sage and sweet herbs, lay fillets in the pye with slices of bacon at the bottom and betwixt each piece lay on butter. Close the Pye-bake." This cannot be improved upon for simplicity and flavour, but if you do not wish to "raise a high pye", use a very deep pie-dish, and cook (cóvered) a while before putting on a rich, seasoned short-crust.

> "When an eating house keeper sets down afore his customers and deliberately eats one of his own Weal pies, no man can refuse confidence."
>
> SIMMONS, 1858.

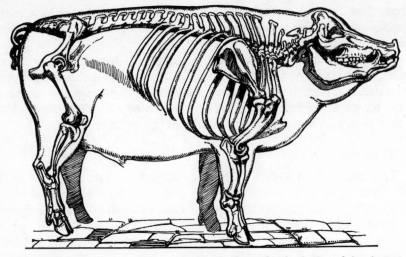

Bone structure of a pig. Contrast with the long slender bones of the sheep.
Note the pigs short leg bones and heavy jaw. The young porkling must have
bone-forming feeds and exercise to make this strong frame *before* he puts on
weight. The wild boar had a long hairy swishing tail and pricked-up ears.

PORK

" Look at Pork. There's a subject!
If you want a subject, look at Pork!"

DICKENS, *Great Expectations.*

GENERAL NOTES ON "PORKERS" VERSUS "BACON PIGS"

" Good October and a good blast,
To blow Hog acorn and mast."

TUSSER.

PIGS TO be eaten as pork are different from those destined to be bacon
and hams. The type of animal is different, and the feeding is altered to suit
the purpose for which the pig is required. Bacon and ham pigs used to be
wanted large, and in country places, 40- or 50-lb. hams, and sides of
bacon to match, glistening with salt, sparkled aloft between the top of the
grandfather clock and the dresser; but for pig-keepers in a small way,
pigs are usually killed when just "full grown" and used partly as fresh
pork and partly for salting.

The greatest dietetic change came in England when the law was passed forbidding the keeping of pigs near the house. Previously every cottager kept a pig, and the pig ruled the diet all the year round. In autumn pigs were killed, not all at once, but a few at a time, so that in any village there was a constant relay of fresh meat from September onwards, beginning with black puddings and the soft entrail meats, to the pork joints, and going on all through the windfall apple season.

Thus every worker, tired after harvest, had a good steady feed, and put on weight, before the cold weather set in. In this healthy "laying on of fat" and resistance to cold, sage and onions (both dietetically commendable), added to the effect, as did the important apple sauce.

Later, the boar's duty done for the last time, the Christmas dinner of boar's head and fruity mince-pies saw the last of the boar pig.

His pig-sty was left open to the scouring snow and cleansing frost of winter, and only the breeding sow survived to farrow in the early spring.

From Christmas onwards the lard, saltings, pies, boiled pork and ham and bacon "filled in". The accepted country worker's diet was toasted bacon for breakfast, with fried potatoes from the night before, the children getting bread dipped in the dripping. The bread was usually home-made with a fair mixture of oatmeal or bran. Oatmeal porridge, milk, swedes or turnips, and apple sauce, were all obtainable free.

Lard was the basis for the hot, solid puddings and pies of winter. Bread spread with bacon fat and cheese supplemented the small winter butter. Frequently the country family kept a goat, and a few hens which provided eggs for the eggs-and-bacon, for custards, or for scrambling with scallions. Rabbits were often cooked with the bacon, and rabbit-and-pork brawn was made. In cold weather, brawns kept well, and provided cut meat to be eaten with potatoes and pickles and winter greens from the garden.

Frequently the cottage kept a bee skep which provided honey for the curing of the bacon, besides very wholesome mead to drink.

And so till springtime, when they again cleaned out the pig-sty, mended the roof and put in the next young porker.

It was a much healthier diet than our present tinned fish, white bread, margarine, mineral waters and Swiss rolls. The removal of the "cottager's pig" was an urban legislation forced upon rural populations. It was certainly unsuitable to keep a pig in crowded urban districts, and rightly abolished there. It was open to abuse in the country if the pigs were not kept clean, but it was to the interest of the entire family to keep their pig clean and healthy, and they usually did so.

It is wrong to deny the useful pig, the basis of the farm workers' diet, to rural workers. Every encouragement should be given, by cutting costs of pig-wire fencing and supplementary feeding stuffs, to those willing to grow their own meat and fat rations.

BERKSHIRE

A characteristic "stocky" English breed, descendant of the mediaeval pig, who fattened in the beech and oak woods in time for Christmas and winter salting. He requires no special foods, fattening best on ordinary diet to a nice lean ham, for which reason he is best at large—given freedom, he develops a bristly independent nature and fends for himself on a naturally selected diet. Rooting and foraging in the wooded uplands of Berkshire, his colour blends well with the rich clear browns of the beech woods. Characteristically, this pig does well in the Australian and New Zealand bush country. His carcase is especially good for small, firm pork joints, and he cuts up with very little waste. Altogether, a free, roving, active pig, maturing to a live weight of 120 lb. in twenty-one weeks.

GLOUCESTER OLD SPOTS

This is an individualist pig, appreciated in his own fruitful valleys for centuries, before being spotted in show pens. The "Gloucester Old Spots Pig-Breeding Society", was founded in 1914 upon his (or rather her) estimable maternal qualities. They were bred to produce two litters a year, to do well on grazing and vegetable refuse during the working months, and have the acumen to fatten rapidly during the short orchard harvest, where they save their bacon on the fallen fruit (which would produce belly grouting in other breeds).

A decorative pig, his spots should be few, and of a pleasurable diversity, the low belly particularly full and thick to afford streaky bacon, a high and twisted tail, the general appearance of the sows redoubtable, large and roomy.

Her motley accords pleasantly with the dappled shadow dance of the Gloucester apple orchards. In that sheltered valley-land, she lies out all the year round littering easily and prolifically in open sheds. The small spotted piglets, scuttling and squalling beneath the apple-blossom, are delectable pork in time for the young spring beans. We expect the last dish of sucking pig will be served in Gloucestershire.

WELSH

As all animals in the Principality, he is comparatively small. Little but good. He has been kept by every Welsh miner, quarryman, and farmer, for centuries. Foraging free round the hillside in youth, he develops activity and sagacity. He is a "good doer" for his small self, and later, in the small stone sties, he fattens quickly on household waste, in nice time for the Christmas pork and winter bacon.

He was, and still is, the cottager's pig to perfection, and propinquity induces a very friendly disposition. His demeanour and his forward-carried ears give this pig a notably docile aspect.

His compact body plumps out a smooth, unwrinkled, skin, his bright eyes and nimble toes give him a very alert look. He is well-bristled against the mountain cold and his small bush tail curls cheerfully.

In 1929 this old-fashioned, peaceable, capable, thrifty, neat little porker popped up suddenly in a London dairy show and astonished everybody by trotting off with two challenge cups (Cwym Ucha!).

Note. The mild Welsh leek and wild sage of his mountain environment are his natural accompaniments into another sphere (*see* Pork Tracklements).

LARGE WHITE YORKSHIRE

This pig's blonde aspect and fine upstanding build are seen most handsomely on the green grass by the banks of the dales. He is named " white ", but against the chalk-white limestone he shines clean pink, with brighter gold hairs. His firm bone stands up well to his heavy weight. The pink and white York hams (originally smoked with oak sawdust from York Cathedral) are long-shaped rather than square, and show his tall, well-built legs. There is a tough knuckle for the stewpot, and a fine trotter for the Wakes. We believe, from length of bone, that this pig was capable of walking long distances from hill farms to market without undue fatigue or loss of weight. A characteristically handsome Yorkshire breed, with a firm, free action.

To quote from " His Majesty's Live Stock Returns ": " No breed has done more to raise the world standard of pigs, and year after year overseas breeders return for breeding stock."

TAMWORTH

The Tamworth is probably our finest English strain. When all country families, from the landowner to the cottager, raised their own pigs, the Tamworths were notable as giving a long side of bacon, and large hams of fine quality. The integrity of this stock was preserved, and its stamina improved, by select breeding. Early Tamworths migrated to Canada, founded a parallel strain in the New World, and then sent back worthy descendants full of vigour, which, again allied to the strong ancestral stock, have bred a truly noble and vigorous pig. The shape is particularly handsome, holding securely the erect proportion and carriage of the wild boar, the colour, a warm golden sand, glinting almost to brass when the sun shines upon the strong lustrous bristles. The head is notably fine, and a Tamworth's boar's-head a fine dish. They are long-lived and hardy, and Tamworth boars of good strain are highly recommended for crossing, to improve the flesh and refine the shape of shorter, fat-producing types. A classic example of a finely domesticated pig and an interesting American alliance.

ESSEX

This is an indigenous pig, descended from the small half-wild swine who were herded in the afforested and reeded Essex of the Middle Ages. His ancestors snorted about, digging roots and scouring tree-barks, champing in the reeds and relishing fish waste—in short, thriving upon anything they could find along the muddy Essex coastline.

He is a singularly good-looking pig: his finely marked black and white, long silky bristles, and well-set-up frame are very pleasing against the dark, tarred barns and bleached white stubble of his native lands. These pigs are an extremely hardy breed, stubborn (as everyone in Essex), and like all good Essex males, they continue to hold closely to the ways of their forebears. The healthy sows are reliable mothers, and, though only averaging eight pigs a litter (as against the prolific breeds' twelve or sixteen) they continue to live and breed and rear steadily for ten or eleven years. Their excellence is commended in the pork and bacon trade of Smithfield Market, where their sterling qualities are deservedly appreciated.

CUTTING-UP OF THE PIG

Practically nothing is wasted in a good pig. The head might be cooked whole as a "boar's head" dish, but more likely the cheeks were made into "Bath chaps". The gristly ears, head, bone and tail are at once put down to make the strong jelly stock.

The soft meat—that is, the pig's fry, kidneys and liver—were eaten at once. If the first consideration was bacon, the fore-legs were cut with the sides for bacon, and the hind legs only for ham. In this case the bones of the shoulder, cut from inside the pieces, made a separate joint. The "spring piece" (as we called the lower part of the side) was sometimes boned, and made bony pie, or rich savoury stew with the last of the broad beans. Sometimes one side of the pig was cured as bacon, and the other side used as loin of pork, when the pork side was laid out, boned, spread with forcemeat, and rolled up into a large roasting joint.

All the meat joints were eaten with large quantities of apple sauce and plain boiled potatoes. When a piece was boiled, dumplings were cooked in the broth (*see* Oats).

All trimmings of the meat were chopped into a basin which had been rubbed with onion. The meat was then scattered with chopped sage and black pepper ready for pork pie. The flead was set in an iron pot on the stove for lard.

The trotters and tripe were usually cooked with onions and white sauce, and the extracted bones from the trotters were added to the head and trimmings already simmering, to be made into brawns. Black puddings had been made by the butcher with barley, oats or rice. When no more lard could be squeezed from the scraps in the iron pot, they were "fried to a finish", and the crisp brown pieces called "scratchings" were sprinkled with freshly chopped parsley and a dash of vinegar. They were served hot with baked potatoes, or later, pressed into a pan and allowed to get cold; these scratchings were cut into thin, marbled slices to be served with cold meat and pickles.

It is not only the amount of meat you get off a pig, but the extraordinary variety of the dishes and the great length of time it goes on supplying the main dish for a hungry family. A pig killed in November would still provide fresh meat and brawn and pie till Christmas, and ham, bacon, and lardie cakes for an entire year.

JOINTS OF PORK

Roast Pig

"One item of entertainment was a roast pig, its brown and glossy back making a very conspicuous object at one side of the board. ' I thought I'd surprise you all ', remarked the satisfied hostess; for she knew the pig was done to a turn, ' and anything you don't expect tastes twice as good; I knew Ma liked pig better'n anything; and I think myself it's the top sheaf. . . . Uncle Tim, do you just give Mrs. Barclay some of the best of that pig . . . and the stuffin' . . . and the gravy, and plenty of the crackle; Mother, it's done just as you used to do it.' "

Nobody, a novel, 1882.

Sucking Pig

Sucking pig should be killed under a month old, and used the day after killing. It is obtainable on farms where it is not economic to raise a full litter. The butcher will "scald and scrape", if you have a cauldron of boiling water ready for him (as it should be done before paunching). After paunching, it's more troublesome—the legs should be tied, and boiling water poured over the hairs to loosen them, for if you dip the open carcase into boiling water it may lose shape and be more difficult to cook. Rub against the lie of the hairs with a coarse cloth till all are out, then wrap in a cold wet cloth and leave the pig in a cool larder till you cook it.

To cook: Rub over inside with lard, and pepper lightly; make a stuffing of sage and onions, and pack tightly; sew or skewer the opening, and truss back the legs either side (remove the lower bone ends and secure them to the sides). Put some lard into your baking pan, and tie some flead (or fat) onto the pig's back. Roast as hot as possible for a few minutes, then reduce heat, and continue, basting frequently till cooked (about 2 hours). Remove the fat, and let the pig brown crisply, dredging with flour, and basting over it, till the crackling is brittle and crisp. The pig is usually jointed before serving, being split down the back, and across head and haunch. Apple sauce, bread sauce, and good brown gravy should be served, with some sharp pickle, as the dish is very rich.

Loin of Pork

This is best roasted. Score the crackling very thoroughly and rub it well with lard before putting it in the oven. Roast pork should be thoroughly well done. It is better to overcook than undercook it, but be very careful not to let it dry up.

Forcemeat balls are good made with sage and onions and pepper and

Score the crackling and baste while roasting, but never let the skin touch the boiling fat in the dripping tin, or it will fry, and become "as tough as leather". It will become "Cuir Boullie", that is "boiled leather armour plate" (which was specially manufactured in olden days to withstand battle axes!); so keep your crackling well raised above the fat in the pan.

put in under the meat half an hour before it is cooked. Turn them once or twice when you baste the meat and see that they are very crisp.

All meat should be raised on a grid in the baking-pan, otherwise the bottom part fries continually in the dripping. (This is the reason that the crackling is sometimes so hard it is inedible. Properly roasted crackling

Loin of pork

should be brittle and crisp; but if you immerse the skin in fat, and fry it, it becomes like shoe leather.) Plain boiled potatoes, apple sauce, beans or well-drained cabbage are all good with roast pork.

Loin of pork may also be boned, and stuffed. The bones taken from a rolled loin of pork make good broth, and with a pease pudding makes a hot dinner for a cold winter's day.

Pork Chops

Plain pork chops should be cooked as plain pork chops. Trim them, removing any superfluous fat. Brush the lean over with a little lard, dredge the fat lightly with flour, and grill quickly at a clear fire, cooking them very thoroughly.

They should be a crisp brown outside and white inside.

Serve with hot apple sauce, brown gravy and boiled potatoes.

Shoulder of Pork (inside cut)

For a complete shoulder, you can roast as you would roast any joint of pork, but more usually the inner part of the shoulder and blade bone make a separate joint, taken from behind the bacon piece.

This inner joint is without any outer skin. Find a deep baking-tin or casserole that will fit the joint, and in it fry some onions till tender but not too brown. Take them out, flour and pepper the joint, sprinkling it well with fine sage. Put it in the pan, pile onions round it, cover and bake very thoroughly.

When nearly done, remove the cover, drain off the fat and give it another few minutes to brown before serving. As all pork joints, this is very rich, so should be sent to table with plenty of apple sauce and plain boiled potatoes. The gravy should be made very clear of fat. As this inner joint has no crackling, it is sometimes breadcrumbed before browning.

Leg of Pork

This joint especially is better roasted before the fire. If baked in the oven, take it out after a few minutes, and wrap the thin end round with a thick cabbage leaf[1] or something to slow up its cooking, otherwise it will be dried away to nothing before the thick end of the leg is thoroughly

Vegetables to eat with Pork

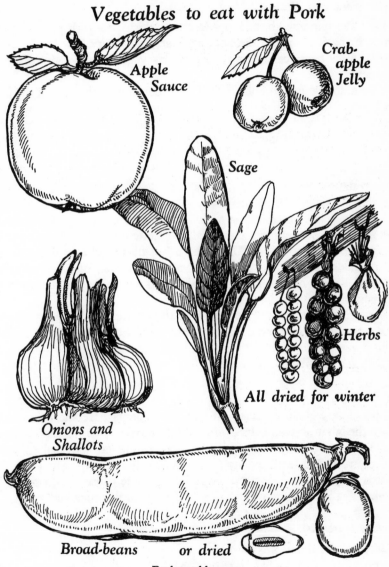

Apple Sauce

Crab-apple Jelly

Sage

Herbs

All dried for winter

Onions and Shallots

Broad-beans   or dried

Pork tracklements

[1] If the leaf is put on the raw meat it will make it sodden.

cooked through. For this reason we recommend boning a leg of pork and stuffing with sage and onion stuffing. It is easier to cook evenly.

The gravy for roast pork should be made with extra care. Pour off every scrap of the fat before thickening the residue in the pan and frothing up into gravy. Onion and apple sauces are both served with roast pork leg.

Boiled Pork and Pease Pudding

Take the joint, wash, and put it into a thick pan with plenty of cold water. Bring it slowly to the boil, add carrots, turnips, parsnips, swedes, onions, a cabbage, celery tops, in fact any vegetables you have, except potatoes.

Take a double handful of old peas, or according to the size of the joint, put them in a muslin bag with a sprig of mint, allowing plenty of room for them to swell, and suspend the bag inside the pan with the pork. Add to the water a few peppercorns, a large spoonful of sugar or treacle, and a cup of cider. Put on the lid and let all simmer very gently indeed for several hours.

At your discretion, if the joint is very large, put the meat on before you add the vegetables. When ready to serve, drain, and arrange the pork and the vegetables together on a dish. Lift out the pease pudding (and if well made the peas should have swollen together so that it comes out like a large green cannon ball). Unroll on a hot dish, *pull* it in two with two forks (do not cut). Put a knob of bacon fat, a dash of black pepper, a spoonful of hot broth on to each half, and serve it with the pork and vegetables.

Note. You don't need potatoes with this pease pudding, but slices of brown bread can be served. Thick white onion sauce is sometimes made to pour over this dish, but it is an effeminate trimming. The broth is really a much more suitable lubricant.

Pig Haggis

This is very good, especially if you like tripe. (In Ireland this was the gift to the labourer who helped with killing the pig.) The stomach is turned inside out, scrubbed clean, soaked overnight in strongly salted water, and then stuffed with potato, sage-and-onion stuffing, sewn up, and roasted in the oven, being well basted during the process with bacon fat. It takes 2–3 hours to roast and is served with apple sauce and gravy.

Yrchins (Urchins)

Very colourful and mediaeval.

"Take Piggis mawys [belly] skalde hem wel and take groundyn porke and spicerye and put hit in the mawe and fill and not too fulle then sewe hem with fayre thread [roast him] and take almonds and cut into shreds and frye them and take a litel pricke and prick the yrchin and puttee in the holes the almonds every hole half and each for other and lay to the fyre and when they be rosted dore them sum with white flour and sum grene and sum blake with blode and serve forth."

These are small haggises, filled with spiced minced pork, roasted, and then stuck over with split almonds and browned to a finish. "Sum" were to be made gold (dore) with a batter (of egg and flour). "Sum grene" (chopped parsley) and some black (like black puddings). With the white almond spikes they look like brightly coloured spiked "sea urchins".

Sweetbreads

The pig's sweetbreads usually form part of the mixed dish known as pig's fry.

There are three different breads: the heart, throat, and pancreas. Being white meat they are considered suitable for invalids. First blanch them, by soaking in salted water for an hour, then put into fresh cold salted water and bring to the boil as slowly as possible. Drain, clear of any skin or gristle, and slice fairly thickly. They should now be as white as a piece of bread. They can be egg-and-crumbed and fried, or served in a number of ways, but for invalids this is perhaps the best.

Sweetbreads in White Gravy

Put a small, thin slice of ham or mild bacon into an earthenware pot and fry gently, together with a little celery chopped very finely, and a bouquet of herbs. Season, drain off all the flavoured fat, and use it to make a small quantity of fine white sauce. Now put the sliced sweetbreads into the pot on top of the scraps of celery and ghost of the ham, season the sauce delicately and pour over; cover and cook gently till the breads are very tender. Serve in the pot, with slices of dry toast.

Black Pudding

> " Small otemeale mixed with blood, and the liver of either sheep, calf or swine, maketh that pudden . . . whose goodness it is in vaine to boast because there is hardly to be found a man that doth not affect them."
>
> *English Housewife's Booke*, 1600.

Probably the earliest pudding made and traditionally interesting. Every illuminated manuscript shows the winter pig-killing and the making of black puddings. Nowadays the butcher usually makes them, except on farms, or country houses, where the pig is killed on the presmises.

In the south and west the puddings are usually cooked in earthenware

Black puddings

Made of pig's blood and cereal filling,
usually brushed over with blood before baking, which makes them black.
These are shown being made in all
the winter "slaughter scenes" in
early manuscripts.

pans (in Bideford Market I have counted eight or nine different types of
this pudding), but in the Midlands, east and north, they are made in thick
skins and frequently polished a handsome jet black, set off with marbling
of glistening white suet. A "set piece" at a Wigan market stall regularly
attracted much attention. The design was finely heraldic:

> "Treen scrubbed, five bladders full of white lard, displayed in
> a chevron argent, set about with a frieze of black puddings,
> sable with cabouches of parsley vert, mantled with sausages rouge
> or. In the midst a boar's head all proper on a trencher of the
> field."

The supporters were savoury ducks, the whole achievement coming
straight from the Middle Ages. The pork butcher himself was a great
upholder of tradition, never killing except when the moon was on the
wane. (In his spare time he bred racing pigeons.)

Brawn

       "Set forth mustard and brawne."

               RUSSELL, *Boke of Nurture* (1460).

Brawn was made of any trimmings from cutting up the meat, and that
part of the head which was not used to make "Bath chaps". It was not
prepared at once. The gristle and bones were set aside to simmer while
the head and larger pieces of meat were put straight into brine. Sometimes the pigs' feet were put into the simmering pot.

When ready to prepare, the head was taken from the brine, rinsed,
and put with the feet, ears, tail, tongue, bones and gristle trimmings into

the same large iron pot, and set to simmer. A bunch of herbs—chiefly sage and marjoram—and the yellow skins of the onions, were tied tightly and slung inside the pot together with a few peppercorns and the bits out of the nutmeg box that were too small for grating—in fact, use these occasions to "turn out" the spice box, as brawns should be seasoned strongly, otherwise they "eat monotonous". Sage predominated, and we usually put in some fresh bay leaves (fresh, because the tree grew outside the kitchen window).

When the bones were quite loose and could be lifted out easily, the pan was emptied into a large basin, and rinsed out. The stock was then strained back into it through a couple of thicknesses of muslin. This stock was then set on the fire to "gallop down", till reduced, while the pieces of meat were lifted from the bones and chopped up, seasoned nicely, the tongue skinned and sliced, and the whole neatly arranged in the brawn tin. It was a slow, tiresome job, and by the time it was done the stock had usually boiled away to just enough to fill the brawn tin to the brim.

The tin was then carried into the coldest place in the larder and left to set for at least 24 hours. When wanted for use, boiling water was poured very quickly over the outside of the tin and instantly! a tall, glistening, marbled brawn slid out to quiver resiliently on its bed of parsley.

The men were very fond of a slice of brawn with baked potatoes and pickles for lunch. Mustard sauce was *always* served with brawn—cold, in a large jug (*see* p. 93).

Pork Dumplings (excellent and unusual)

I think this old recipe is a sailor's. It has a very "galley" aroma, and the Dutch herring boats fought around the eastern coasts where the recipe came from.

A pastry crust for boiling (made with raw bacon fat) is stuffed with finely chopped pork, sliced onion rings and an apple grated or chopped, three to four sage leaves, and a spoonful of golden syrup or honey. Fill in any cracks with water, seal up closely, and boil well.

Soaked salt pork and well-soaked beans or peas will also do for this pudding. When the dumpling is opened it should be full of rich, savoury juice from the chopped onions and fat pork.

This is a good recipe for using one thick slice of too salt bacon. Or one pork chop with plenty of onion and apple will make a fair-sized pudding.

Flead

Flead is the inner membrane of the pig's inside, a fine thin skin full of particles of pure lard. This was beaten into the flour to make a form of light lardy cake. It is curious that in a Lincolnshire cook-book of the late eighteenth century a "proper paste for tarts" is made by beating butter and sugar into the flour in exactly the same way.

The recipe takes equal quantities of flour, sugar and butter, and is made rather like shortcake, as it is mixed entirely dry and pressed into shape.

Flead pastry. Clear the flead from the membrane, and use the same proportion as you would lard (but it makes a much shorter crust). Cut the flead into the flour and salt it lightly, and make up into a firm paste with a very little cold water. Then lay it flat upon a firm board, or smooth stone, and bang it hard, with the rolling pin—folding and turning till the pieces of hard flead are finely incorporated with the flour. Roll out then, and use as pie crust.

Flead cakes were made in the same way, but sugar and spice were added instead of salt, and after beating, the pastry was cut into square cakes, and "crusted" with white of egg and crushed sugar before backing.

The secret was to "bang and whang" the brittle bits of flead till they powdered down into the flour. It was a splendid way of working off a bad temper.

Scotch Slim Cakes

There are so many versions of the thin girdle cake that this is uncommon only in its simplicity. Take ½ lb. of flour, 3 oz. of fine pork dripping, 2 eggs, salt; and enough warm milk to mix into a dough. Roll out, cut into rounds the size of a saucer, and bake them on the girdle, turning once. Spread with bacon fat and pepper and salt *while on the pan*, and serve on the instant while hot.

Pork Tarts made with Scratchings

The scraps left over after the last of the lard is rendered from the membrane may be served up in various ways: cold, pressed into a mould and turned out (a white marble and gold slab) and sliced; or hot, strewn with parsley and grilled tomatoes, etc. Sometimes these pieces were made up in pastry like a sort of post-flead cake, and sometimes as a curious kind of open spicy cake of which I do not know the name, but as it was very good I give instructions how to make it.

Grease an oven plate and cover with a thin short crust. Chop the scratchings very thinly and cover the paste with them about a quarter-inch deep. Pat it smooth and cover with a layer of coarse brown sugar, pat that smooth, and cover the sugar with grated nutmeg or cinnamon. Chopped apples and a layer of raisins are then added, and a spoonful of ale or home-made wine is poured over the top, just enough to moisten the sugar.

The tart is then cooked in a rather hot oven and the sugar, fat, fruit, and spice melted down into a mound of gummy sweetness (the colour of an autumn beech leaf) inside its crisply baked crust.

Showing the "egg" whites of his eyes, round a black pickled-walnut pupil and red beetroot rim. Celery sticks form his tusks, and piped lard his decorations

Boar's Head

" Hey! Hey! Hey! Hey!
Hey! Hey! Hey! Hey!
The Boar's head in hand I bring,
With garlands gay in carrying,
I praye you all with me to sing
Hey! Hey! Hey! Hey!
Hey! Hey! Hey! Hey!
Lords and Knights and Squires,
Parsons, priests and vicars,
The Boar's head is the first mess!
Hey! Hey! Hey! Hey!
The Boar's head is armed gay! "

OLD SONG.

"Ye Olde boar's head" may be bought, handsomely prepared, at provision stores in the Christmas season. When made of a wild boar it is always justifiably expensive, but the homely version was peasant fare down the centuries, and if your men like cold boiled bacon, rather highly spiced, and you think it worth the trouble, a pig's head makes a very imposing side dish at very small cost.

A very simple boar's head dish. Get the head split and prepared at the butcher's. It should be in two halves except for the joining skin at the top. Eyes, ears, snout and all the bone at the back should be removed and the brains wrapped separately. When it reaches you, lay it down quite flat and soak it in running water for an hour, rubbing it with salt and leaving it overnight in a large tub of strong salt water. Next day, drain, wipe dry, and rub it well with salt and saltpetre (in the proportion of 1 drm. of saltpetre to 1 oz. of salt), pickling spice, and black pepper, then lay it in a kit, or large earthenware basin, which it will soon fill with brine. Keep rubbing on the salt daily, turning and rubbing thoroughly for a week (you may have to use more salt according to the size).

At the end of a week or ten days take it up, drain, and you now have a piece of salt pork which could be plain boiled or baked; but if it is for Christmas fare, put the head to boil very gently with vegetable trimmings, a large bunch of sage, onion-skins, marjoram, bay leaves and peppercorns. Let it simmer *till the bones are loose*, allow it to cool in the broth, then lift it from the pan, and pull out the bones carefully. Skin the tongue, replace it, and truss the hot meat into a good conical shape. Dust with a little pepper and a suspicion of powdered mace as you work. Tie it very firmly into shape and leave it overnight under a weight.

To make the glaze. Meanwhile, ears, bones, gristle, etc., should have been boiled with plenty of flavouring herbs and spice till very stiff. Add a tablespoonful of brown vinegar and a couple of crushed egg-shells (these give it a bright clearness). Strain into a jar, and by the time the pig's head is cold the glaze should be solidified to a stiff brown jelly.

When the head is cold, brush the liquid glazing over it several times till smoothly coated. The last coating should be *poured over* and left to set.

Serve "hym" on a convenient carving board, laid on a clean, flat fir bough. Give hym split almond tusks, and whatever your artistic eye suggests of trimmings of golden cut lemon peel, cut vegetable stars, bright green parsley, or wrinkled black shiny prunes for eyes, and finish with a wreath of holly; stand alongside a bowl of mustard sauce (*see* p. 126). It carves best lengthwise, is a very savoury form of cold spiced bacon, and looks very handsome on the sideboard at Christmas.

If, in damp weather, the glaze becomes cloudy, it may be wiped with a pastry brush dipped in hot water.

BORES HEAD CAROL

" The Bores hed in handis I brynge
With garlondis gay and byrdis syngynge
I pray you all helpe me to synge
Que estis in convinio

The bores hed I understand
Yo cheffe serwyes in all this londe
Where so ever it may be fonde
Servitur eum sincfio

The bores hed I dare well say
Anon after the XIIth day
He taketh his leve and goth away
Exiunt tune di patria."

BALLIOL MS.

Twelfth-night Pie (a happy ending to Christmas left-overs)

After Christmas the remains of the boar's head (rather fat) and the clearings of the Xmas ham (rather lean) were used to make a special "raised pie". Any sausages left over were added, and any cold bacon or brawn. All the meat was chopped together, with a generous spoonful of chopped herbs and some black pepper; the whole mixed with the remains of the gravy, seasoned and packed into a raised pie crust.

The space on top of the pie was filled with finely chopped fresh apples, and the whole baked and served hot with roast jacket potatoes.

Pigs' Ears

To make a ragout of pigs' ears (about 1680).

Stew them in water with a glass of wine or plenty of vinegar to "cut" the gristle substance. When this is soft, cut it up into small square pieces, and roll in seasoned flour and fry in bacon fat with an "escholot or two". Make a good brown gravy, adding mustard, nutmeg, some lemon slices, and two anchovies and "make it perty thick"; put over the pigs' ears, and garnish with red barbaries.

Pigs' ears, as turtle soup. The larger pigs' ears were the basis of a "mock-turtle soup" much liked in the Midlands for "tenants' dinner parties" and "farmers' rent dinners". Sometimes the pigs' trotters were added to thicken the stock, but it could be made of "earmeat" alone. Stew the ears in 2 quarts of water, with one large clove-stuck onion, and a faggot of herbs—including marjoram, basil and thyme (*excluding* sage and salt)—and a dash of vinegar, and leave on stewing all night till the fire dies down. Next day, skim off the fat, and take out the ears (they should be soft jelly) and skin and cut into strips. Strain the stock and boil it down (getting it as clear as you can), season it with white peppers, mace, lemon juice, and a glassful of sherry just before adding the sliced and hot ear-strips and sending it to table in a hot tureen. It is a clear strong gelatinous soup, with almost transparent meat strips, and a great flavour of real turtle soup.

Note. It cannot be made without the marjoram and basil.

Pig's Tail

The old wild boar had a straight swishy tail, the modern pig's tail is a gristly twist. It should be chopped up and cooked with the gristly parts of ears and snout to make the stiff jellied stock with which pork pies and brawn are set. If by any unlikely chance you get a leg of pork with the tail on it, cut the tail off and make stock, as it's mostly gristle.

A pig's tail is mostly gristle. Put it into stock.

Pigs' Pettitoes

These are not pigs' trotters, but a special dish.

The feet, heart, liver, and some of the lights of a pig, a small piece of lard, and a little flour to thicken, a slice of lemon, salt, 1 egg, 2 spoonfuls of milk and a little grated nutmeg. Boil the heart, liver and lights and the feet together for 15 minutes, then take up the meat and mince very fine. Let the feet go on stewing till tender. Then take them up and split them lengthways. Thicken some of the liquor in which they have been boiled, using flour and lard to prepare a thick sauce, put in the minced meat, with a slice of lemon and salt. Cook a few minutes. Beat the yolk of the egg with the spoonfuls of milk and a little grated nutmeg into a pan, and the pettitoes into it, and shake over the fire till the egg is set and they are coated (but do not let the mixture become too hot). Lay snippets of toasted bread all around a dish, pile the hot meat and gravy in the middle of the dish and the half feet on top.

Pork Rissoles and Pommes Dorés

"Golden apples" are a very old mediaeval dish. They are a little troublesome to make, but were popular, being light and crisp and crunchy, very much the texture of an excellently fried fritter.

The old Norman-French recipe is:

"Take fylettys of raw porke and grynde hem wyl, do salt, pouder pepir thereto, than take the white of Eyroun [eggs—plural] and make them so harde [beat stiffly] and throw therto [wrap the pork mince into the egg foam, and bind it into balls] and make round as a appul. Make fyre withoute smoke, than take akmond milk and flour and do hem together and take sugure and putte hem [the rounds of pork-egg] in [this] batture; and make them on a spit, and dore him with the yolks of the eyroun, and some, do with sum grene thing, percely [chopped small and dusted over the batter]. And sum men boyle him in brothe or they be spetid, and dore with the yolks of eyroun mengyed with jus of haselle leuys."

Do not shudder at the sugar put into pork recipes—today the modern American enjoys well-spiced and sweetened "pork loaf" in tins, and we taught America how to sugar-cure hams.

I give the same recipe in two forms because I do not want you to have the impression that each old recipe is an isolated historical instance: there were more cooks than scribes able to write down the recipes, but the recipe books that do exist prove that the same types of dishes were cooked in different households and different districts—using local materials. There was diversity of old; householders travelling took their cooks with them, so that any tour of the Justices, any marching of an army from one castle to another, or any visiting of relatives and friends from one district to another, took the exchange of *ideas* into the kitchens, but the *materials* must be obtained on the spot. The methods were probably discussed, boasted, and cried down, while the visitors were there, and tried out after they'd gone! So that you often get the same recipe from several sources. Compare these two from two different manuscripts: they differ in the same way two different cookery books would do today.

"Lean pork and hen's flesh pounded with spice and bound with egg [the whole egg used this time, no attempt to keep the interior of the pomme white by using the white of egg only]. Shaped into round balls the size of small apples." The size is important, as experience shows it the right size to have the meat cooked by the time the outside batter is crisp; after that—"loke you have a panne sething over the fire and do theron the pelettys, and late hem not sette to swythe [cook gently and don't break] whan cold and set spit on a hasselle rod [green, so it would not burn] and leave an inch between them and roast before the fire, and caste battur on hem, and make one batture green with perceley, and the other leave yellow."

Result: *Pommes doré*—white meat balls, of spiced pork, crusted with yellow batter—and *Pommes garnez*—yellowish meat balls, crusted with alternately green and yellow batter covers—six of one and half a dozen of the other. And two thirteenth-century cooks each firmly convinced of the superiority of his own recipe.

A modern version—not using the spit:

Cold pork, minced and formed into rissoles with added herb seasoning and spice, bound with egg and coated with rather a stiff coating batter, fry in deep fat till golden and crisp. To make the green "pommes", roll half of them on to fresh "percely", chopped fine as mist, and leave the others yellow. They are extremely rich! and should be served very crisp and dry.

Pork and Apple Pie

When making our pork pies near Melton Mowbray, some of the pie meat was made into a "dish pie" to be eaten that day. The recipe is also good for any small quantity of pork or fat bacon (such as the knob end of a "Bath chap", or hock), or it can be made with the spare meat from a pork bone.

Take a deep dish, lay a layer of pork, chopped very small, at the bottom, cover with a layer of apples cut rather roughly, and a dust of sugar. Shred a small onion finely over this, and a dust of pepper, cover with another thin layer of pork, and continue these layers till the dish is full, letting the top layer be pork. Press it down *firmly*, and then fill up with a *very little* stock, barely enough to moisten it. Cover with a thick potato crust, and bake slowly, browning nicely. Some add a leaf of sage minced over the pork layers, but don't put in too much. A simple dish for a busy day's dinner, as it does not need any accompaniments.

A Leicestershire version of this pie. Line a deep cake tin with the pork pie crust, keeping a round for the lid. Fill with alternate layers of apple and pork, sprinkling the apple with sugar and the pork with pepper, and putting a few sage leaves and fine minced onion here and there. The whole is then moistened with a little mild ale, the lid put on, and baked according to size, 1 or 2 hours. At the small farms around Market Harborough and Charnwood Forest, they make this pie very well.

Pork and Apple Stuffing

This is particularly good if the meat or poultry is inclined to be dry.

Four large peeled and cored apples, four onions, and about as much fat bacon; chop all these roughly, and add six sage leaves, a sprig of lemon thyme, or lemon balm, or lemon peel, chopped *very* finely.

Mix all these together with a tablespoonful of cider, or stock, and beat in enough dry, floury, mashed potato to make a smooth stuffing. Season it well and pack it in *very* tightly (because both apple and onion, and fat, will melt down and make juice while cooking).

If the joint or bird is very small it may be wise to part-cook the apples, onions, etc., before use—but as a rule they will be cooked by the time the meat is done.

Pork Pies

Pig Pye.
"Flea Pyg and cut him in pieces, season with pepper and salt, and nutmeg, and large mace, and lay in your coffin[1] good store of raisins and currans, and fill with sweet butter and close it and serve hot or cold."

FOURTEENTH CENTURY.

We lived many years within a few miles of Melton Mowbray, the home of pork pies, and so give the Melton recipe.

We used some herbs—about one sage leaf per pie, and a small sprig of marjoram, and we also put a faggot of herbs into the stock. Every farmhouse, hunting lodge, and inn, in the shires, used to have its own special pork-pie recipe, but I think one general thing which made the Melton Mowbray pie slightly different from other excellent pies was the *anchovy sauce*. A very small amount was used, but it made the Melton Mowbray pies pink inside, whereas in most other districts the meat content of the pies is brownish, or grey.

The ingredients and method follow on page 122.

[1] "Coffin" or "coffer"—mediaeval pie-crust "raised" exactly like ours today.

PASTRY SHAPES IN ENGLAND

The Cornish Pasty, has a join down the top, as being less likely to spill gravy
when baked in the old Cornish hearth ovens.

The Lancashire Foot, further south called a Turnover, was baked on a flat
over shelf, and fitted into the inner pocket or tin.

The Raised Pie was made of hot pastry and moulded, or raised, round
wooden moulds. This is the oldest form of pastry case, and was known as a
coffyn, or coffer, *i.e.*, a little box or enclosure it lent itself to elaborate
traditional decorations, on both top and sides.

The Checky Pig is very curious. It is mentioned by many old writers, and I
found it still made in Leicestershire. Two thin strips are laid across the
central round and folded in to form the "two-ears and long tail". Its likeness
to a "cheese peg", a cross-handled awl-shaped tool, suggests its name, for the
ears and long tail are most unlike any pig (though most lovable design).

The Dumpling has two structural forms—the single round, tucked together
underneath, and the Victorian two circles, with a central join.

The Crowthie has thin flat undercrust and puffy thicker top crust. The *Maid
of Honour* and *Gable Tart* are traditional shapes as also the *Banbury* and
Clifton and *Coventry* foldings; and the twisted *Horn*, and *Triangular* (jam)
Puff. The covered china dish is a *Pie*, and the same boiled in a round basin a
Pudding. N.B. This distinction irrespective of fillings.

The traditional "sheaf of corn" in pastry.
Roll a thin strip and shred each side
finely, nicking or criss-crossing the "head-
of-corn" side, and cutting a few more wide
strips to form leaves and a 'tie for the sheaf.
Roll up the sheaf, spreading out the stalk
ends to make it stand firmly, and binding
the centre and bending down the drooping
leaves (which also helps steady the sheaf).

For the crust: 1 stone of flour, 4 lb. of lard, 4 pints of slightly salted water.

For the filling: 9 lb. chopped pork (good weight), 3 oz. of salt, ½ oz. of white pepper, 1 dessertspoonful of essence of anchovy. We personally added one sage leaf and marjoram per pie.

For the jelly: stock made of the tail, ears, trotter bones, and trimmings of the pig, a truss of herbs, chiefly sage and marjoram, and the *cores* of all the apples used for sauce since the pig was killed (for the subtle almond flavouring of the pips and the slightly acid value).

The salted flour for the crust is put into a large warm panchon before the fire and a well made in the middle. The iron pot containing the lard and water boils above it, and one person, tilting it forward, pours the boiling lard and water steadily into the well in the flour below, while the maker stirs round and round with a wooden spoon. It is better to have too much water than to run short before the flour is all stirred in, but with judgment and reasonably new flour, the flour should take up about that much water and lard.

The pouring and the stirring should be done very steadily till the lard and water and the flour in the bowl are used up simultaneously. You will understand that this is a serious proceeding.

The panchon now holds a hot mass of alabaster paste and this should be "worked" as soon as the fists can bear the heat, pummelling it up and down, and kneading and pounding it for about half an hour. Now leave it to prove for an hour, turning the panchon now and again before the fire so that it keeps evenly warm.

Pies can be raised by hand, without the use of a wooden mould

Now to raise the pies. Take a wooden pie-mould in your left hand and, standing it into a round of paste, press and coax the paste up round the mould. Keep the pastry warm so that it is pliant, and get it as even as possible. When up to the top of the mould roll it sideways, as this will smooth the outside and loosen the pastry. Lift out the mould and press in the pork meat, packing it down tightly. Trim the top edge of the pastry with scissors and have another round of paste cut out ready for the top. Lay this on, damping and nipping the edges together. Make a neat round hole in the middle of the lid, which is decorated with cut leaves or scrolls or lattice, as your fancy is inclined. Pie art has moved with the times, and the most modern pies have now an austerity of outline. Nevertheless, an acorn or a rosette is suitable, and four oak leaves or a beech-nut in paste show a nice feeling for the pig's previous environment.

When the last of the pig is suitably enshrined in its paste, send it to the bakehouse or oven. It should take about 4 hours. If you favour a polished pie, brush it over with egg beaten in milk and return to the oven for 10 minutes to glaze.

Immediately the pies are cooked, have the well-flavoured stock piping hot, and pour it into the pies through the hole at the top till they are quite full. This should be done at once, whilst the pies are hot. Leave them to cool down in the warm kitchen overnight. By next day they should be a very firm and juicy set of pork pies.

The art is to get the crust crisp and firm, but not hard, and the jelly surrounding the meat very clear, firm and well flavoured.

It is a great pity more raised pies are not made. They are not so difficult as they sound, they keep well, and are substantial and wholesome.

Special hinged pie-cases can be bought which are clasped round outside the pie when put in the oven, and lifted off to brown the pastry just before taking out.

Around Nottingham they used to make a raised pie with green gooseberries and a sweetened crust, afterwards filling it with melted apple jelly. The white, green and pink were very pretty and, served with whipped cream, a raised gooseberry pie took a lot of beating.

Veal and ham was another filling for raised pie, and another version of the pork pie was made in a long bread tin with whole hard-boiled eggs and pickled walnuts inset down the length of it. This "long pie" cut up very economically.

Mutton pies were made, but were smaller, had onion flavouring, and on the market stalls were garnished with sprigs of mint to prevent their being mistaken for the pork pies, which always wore sage sprigs.

Pork Fat and Potato Stuffing

Slice and cook one large onion in a lump of lard the same size. Let the onion cook till soft but not browned. Shred in five or six leaves of sage, pepper and salt. Have ready a bowl of mashed potatoes and stir the potato into the well-flavoured fat. Keep on stirring in potato till the fat will moisten no more. Do not overload the fat as this stuffing is used to fill poultry, rabbit, or meat which requires lubricating and larding. The principle is, that in baking, the potato renders up the extra lard into whatever it stuffs, and so forms an inside basting.

Savoury Ducks (sometimes called *"faggots"*)

These are really a rich forcemeat ball made with pieces of pork offal. They are especially popular in the north of England.

Take the pig's liver, lights, and fat, onions, and an equal weight of breadcrumbs soaked in milk (or soaked oatmeal or barley or wheat instead of crumbs, according to the district in which the savoury ducks are made), and a seasoning of herbs, including basil and marjoram in the south, or sage and bog myrtle in the north—in fact, any herbs according to district. Add also salt, pepper, nutmeg or mace.

Mince the pork, liver and onions together and mix well with the soaked breadcrumbs, herbs and seasoning. Press the mixture into a baking-tin and cover with the flead, i.e., the fine membrane marbled with fat, from the inside of the pig. Cook slowly in the oven. The fat in the pork and the skin should be sufficient to bind the mixture.

When nearly done, mark it into squares. When pork and liver seem thoroughly well cooked and the top is crisp, take it out and leave it to grow cold in the pan. When cold, break the "ducks" apart. They should have the consistency, and somewhat the appearance, of small, square penny loaves. They can be served cold with salad, or re-heated with a good brown gravy and apple sauce. Home-made, they are very savoury, economical and appetising, and very sensible usage for caterers and canteens, as they can use up waste breadcrumbs, and, served with a helping of greens and gravy, have a really good food value.

Sausages

> " I always think sausages ain't sausages if they ain't stuffed. Aunt Anne won't have the plague of it; but I say, if a thing's worth doing at all, it's worth doing the best way; and there's no comparison in my mind."
>
> SUSAN WARNER, *Nobody*, 1832.

Probably "Aunt Anne's" sausages were not put into skins but plain rolled into egg-and-crumb coverings.

Mace around
the nutmeg

To make pork sausages for a private family (this is a recipe of about 1800). "To every pound of lean pork $1\frac{1}{4}$ lb. of fat, pepper and salt, nutmeg, a handful of pennyroyal and marjoram shred small. Put all into the guts, twist into lengths, dry a little before you fry them."

Basil is used for some sausages—as Sam Weller said, "It's all in the flavouring!"

"To be Continued"

PORK TRACKLEMENTS

" Though plenty of acorns, the porkling to fat,
Not taken in season, may perish by that;
If rattling or swelling, get once to the throat,
Thou losest thy porkling, a crown to a groat."

TUSSER.

Enterprising hens like to follow a loose pig—a lucrative partnership that comes to a succulent end in eggs and bacon on the breakfast table. The ranging pig rooting in the woods or digging up the pasture always had a following of hens, to whom, dietetically, he was a godsend. A less subtle circumstance accounts for roast pork and apple sauce. Pigs will always eat windfalls when they can get them, and probably in mediaeval days when the pomace[1] of small crabs, from the making of verjuice, was thrown out of the mediaeval kitchen, it was cooked with the perquisite piece of pork by the scullion.

The mediaeval "onion" was often wild garlic. Even the genuine old onion was more leek-like than the rounded Spanish onion (which did not come into cultivation till later). Pigs could certainly eat the wild garlic and the wild sage, thus following the sensible mediaeval culinary procedure of "serving what flavoured the animal, when we ate him".

Pork and beans are seasonal. Piers Plowman speaks of a few beans left over to last him till the spring, and it was the dried and salted pork, that was cooked with the dried beans, that formed the winter diet for centuries. Remember the pork would be less heavily salted and more honey used, so the beans would be much sweeter. (*See* Preserving and Drying.) At Christmas pork went with dried beans, so young spring pork has always been eaten with young broad beans. They go excellently well together.

[1] See cider—the dry sour apple mash left in the press after the juice is extracted, often mixed with straw. POMACE is the older spelling but PUMICE is modern usage in trade to-day.

Apple Sauce

This is best baked while the roast pork is baked.

Cut and quarter the peeled apples: put into a deep earthenware dish, just cover with water, add a knob of butter and a small spoonful of sugar, cover closely and cook alongside the meat at the last 15 minutes or so. Beat down with a wooden spoon and serve in the dish it was cooked in; it makes a better sauce than when the apples are boiled separately.

Mustard Sauce

Since before A.D. 1200 "brawne" was always served with mustard. Mediaeval mustard was a creamy white sauce which was flooded over the slices of "brawne" as they lay in the "dyshe".

We always made this "mustard sauce for brawn" in the north, and it was a direct mediaeval survival.

To make it, melt some lard in a pan and blend with as much fine flour and dry mustard (half and half) as it will soak up. Let it cook very well before gradually adding milk till the whole has the consistency of thick cream. Let it boil well and serve cold.

The dry mustard and flour should be mixed together first, and the proportions of half and half, as above, should at first be tried, then if you want the sauce more keen add more mustard.

Another method is to mix the mustard with real cream, but this is too rich and expensive, and the cream sauce will not keep fresh for more than one serving.

VENISON

> " But old Sir Thomas thought daintier cheer
> A pasty made of the good red deer."
>
> BARHAM, " *Witches* " *Frolic.*

GENERAL NOTES ON VENISON

BUCK IS in season from the end of June; doe venison in the winter only. All venison varies. Park-fed may be lamb-like or tough. Some wild deer are very fine meat, some coarse and dry. The best is stalker's venison, clean shot buck, fat and well-conditioned. Venison should be hung as long as possible. The old-fashioned meat larder had a pulley that swung the game right up to hang between the ventilators in the roof, which were gauzed against flies.

In mediaeval days meat was hung by the smoke-hole in the roof. It was far enough away from the open fire to be fairly cool, and the blue

Venison

haze which hung around the smoke-hole was the only fly-proof spot. Firewood of resinous firs was definitely used as fly preventative.

Venison should be well cleaned out round the rump and tail, and the old custom of peppering the meat and covering with cool, green leaves has much to commend it. Whether the prejudice against venison in some districts has any traditional significance we leave to anthropologists to determine. In some localities deer meat is approved, in others despised— almost feared.

In war time I have seen a queue of native country people in an agricultural town go without their Sunday dinner rather than buy the excellent venison in the butcher's shop, though unrationed, uncontrolled, attractively displayed and cheap. Whereat the Purveyors of Meat in the more expensive shops took over the stock, put up the price fifty per cent, and sold out to the knowledgeable town evacuees by lunch-time; the old country women said: *Woolton or not, they were not going to eat wild animals! They would go home and get their husbands to catch them a rabbit!*

Near London and some university cities, where evacuated intellectuals and week-enders have leavened the community, venison is now served in pubs, and around ancestral parks its use is disseminated through the tenants on the estate. But in my long, inquisitive life, I have never managed to locate the political, agricultural, or occupational mapping of districts allergic to shrimps or venison.

Venison is a very dry meat. There is practically no fat on some joints, so if you have saved the rind off a ham or bacon piece, wrap it round the venison and cook it so wrapped. The salt rind will redden the venison, but that is no harm and the flavour will be excellent. Otherwise, you can lard it, or tie on a lump of mutton fat, or well wrap it in buttered paper—in fact, roast it exactly as you would lean mountain mutton and serve it with red-currant jelly, rowan jelly or red-gooseberry jelly, fine gravy and chipped potatoes. French beans and braised lettuce are good vegetables, and the bread should be oatcake or brown bread.

Wrap up in the fat rind taken off the
ham before rasping, and cook with cider

On no account make a thick brown gravy to serve with venison. It should be made with any juice that comes from the meat and a glass of red wine (or failing that, the melted jelly) and should be clear, bright gravy.

Venison takes rather longer to cook than most meat, and must on no account be hurried or it will be tough. Try it with a skewer. When it goes into the thickest part easily the meat is done.

The haunch is the best joint. The neck is usually treated as chops, the shoulder as haunch. If reasonably tender, steaks are cut from the top of the leg. Shoulder or leg may be braised or, if several steaks have been cut off the thick end, the thin end may be treated like potted hough.

Haunch of Venison

" To my mind a fine well cooked haunch of venison—such as is served during the season every Tuesday and Thursday at the Albion Hotel opposite Drury Lane Theatre is the finest dinner obtainable."

A Man about Town (1850).

If it arrives by rail, take it out of the hutch, in which it will probably be packed with heath or fern, wipe with a cloth wrung out in cold water and hang up in a cold draught till dry, then pepper it thoroughly all over with black pepper and let it hang as long as possible. Just before cooking, wipe again and rub over with butter or sweet oil before covering thickly with a layer of clarified fat. On to this fat press clean vine leaves, or grease-proof paper, and then wrap the whole joint inside a covering of huff paste, sealing it carefully. Roast it for 3–4 hours according to the size; half an hour before it's done, remove the huff paste and leaves and dredge lightly with flour, return to the oven and baste it continuously till lightly browned. A glass of red wine poured over while basting is good and the gravy should be the drip from the meat, with the addition of this wine, or a little red-currant juice.

If huff paste is considered wasteful, several layers of heat-proof paper can be used—the whole rind off a ham was old-fashioned usage; the point to remember is the dryness of venison and the need for keeping the flavour in the meat by basting it well.

Venison Steaks (cut from the leg)

Rub the steaks over with oil, melted mutton fat or lard, and grill very swiftly on both sides, then more slowly, till well done. If the steaks can be done in a Dutch oven before the fire, as in camps, they can be basted while toasting, and this much improves the meat. Any good, clear fat can be used for the basting, and a glass of red wine.

When done, put a pat of butter in the centre of each steak, dust with pepper and salt, and serve quickly. For grilled venison steaks, put mush-rooms under in the dripping and serve with crisp potatoes, french beans, red-currant jelly and a fine sauce of the dripping and red wine. This is excellent fare. On no account smother this or any other grill with thick brown gravy and soft potatoes. Let the grill be dry and crisp and the small juicy gravy clear and spicy.

Venison Cutlets and "End-bones"

These are cut from the small loin and the long end of the bone is removed. Grill as for steak.

They may be served packed into a crisp hot pastry case, garnished with watercress, crisp potatoes and red-wine gravy. A small pat of butter, well peppered, should be put on each cutlet immediately before serving. The end bones of the loin, cut off from the cutlets, may be cooked as a joint. Remove the bones, spice and roll tightly, and braise. This is really a by-product of veal cutlets and very good for sandwiches, as the lean and fat become well mixed.

Venison Braised

Tough venison should be braised, and it is better to bone it first as this allows it to become more tender. Lay the boned joint as flat as possible and beat it well with a wooden rolling-pin, up and down, end for end, and then sideways (do not pound it with the end of the pin, dinting it, but use the length of the pin flat, like a flail). Pour over it some lees of red wine or a little vinegar, and oil the opposite side.

Venison pies look very jolly with red
jelly and a sprig of sweet gale

Venison Pastry

Put the bones and trimmings of venison to boil for stock with the papery outer skin of a shallot, a small piece of nutmeg *or* a clove. Cut some of the lean meat into pieces, dredging them with pepper, salt and a trace of spice. Fry the pieces of meat very lightly and put them into the stock made from the bones, when it has cooled down a little. (Do not put them into the boiling stock, or they will be as hard as nuts.)

Let the venison barely simmer in the stock till tender and use as filling for the crisp pies, which fill up with a little of the stock to which has been added a spoonful of red-currant jelly after baking. These little venison pies are very good to take out with a flask for a pocket lunch, or, if a larger pie, it can be made as a raised pie (*see* Pork Pie). Bake, and fill up through a hole in the crust, as in pork pie, only in this case use strong stock with a glass of red wine in it. Be sure the stock will set stiff so that the pie will cut handsomely.

The small round pies (about the size of little mutton pies) look very attractive with their white crust, rich brown meat filling and bright scarlet jelly. A dozen or so, each with a tiny sprig of bog myrtle, on a brown wooden platter, served with watercress and a flagon, look very jolly about lunch-time.

Venison and Game Pie

Miss Florence White gives this as a speciality for Ashdown Forest, but it is also made of any game in the northern and eastern counties. It is a dish popular with " game-keepers ".

Thoroughly grease a deep pie-dish with bacon fat. Flour a thin fillet of beef or venison and lay it at the bottom. Joint a bird, or a brace, flour and pepper well and pack down with plenty of diced bacon and small mushrooms, if available. Set it in the oven to cook, dry, while you make a light suet crust. Season the crust lightly and roll it out to fit the pie-dish. By now the floured meat in the dish should have browned slightly and the bacon be crisp. Fill up the dish with stock and the lees of any red wine. Put on the lid and bake till the crust is well risen.

Suet is advised for the crust as the pie needs long baking, but any light crust will serve and, if the steak, bird, etc., is cut in small pieces and well fried in the dish first, they should be tender by the time the crust is done.

In any large pie it is better to cook the meat a little before putting on the crust, but put on the crust as soon as you can to keep in the flavour.

This type of "game pie" gave cause for the pie-crust ware of the potteries, as the meat was cooked in the dish and the pie crust of pastry held in the aroma, thus leading to the casserole direct.

Umbles of the Deer

"He did give us the meanest dinner of beef shoulders and umbles of venison." PEPYS.

The word "umbles" has been given many meanings in different dictionaries, and the original cookery books and hunting books, from which the dictionaries derive, are equally confusing. I believe that umbles were the stones, sweetbreads, and what (in a modern pig) we should call the "best parts of the 'fry' ", and as much a delicacy as the "lamb stones" of the old sheep-farming days. Later the word seems to be used for a much coarser selection of "fry", including liver and lights—and in 1725 we get a reference to "the umbles or dowsets" in a contemptuous term. Yet curiously, dowsets is also the name of a white soft hasty pudding. Speaking as a cook, and an historian, I believe that the choicer parts of the usual "fry" might be considered umbles. And note that they would be used *fresh*—the hunter's first dish—and *served at once*. (Which accounts for the number of times the returned hero is regaled with this dish upon a sudden and dramatic arrival.)

The chief recommendation for this unprepossessing dish is that there was only one of it!

By an interesting analogy, I found the buck hunters of the veldt always ate the perishable (and unportable) head of their buck, roasted neck down in the camp-fire overnight, with somewhat the same forced enthusiasm.

Buck Biltong

"The hardened flesh of mountain deer."—SIR WALTER SCOTT.

Vidame of Chartres, reporting on Scottish customs (Edward VI) says that they ate deer's flesh, raw, but compressed between two batons of wood till hard and dry.

It is probable that the making of biltong came to the Cape through Scotch settlers rather than Dutch seamen. The pulled flesh (not cut but pulled by the length of the fibre) is piled up to drain—and sometimes compressed under weights till the lymph has run out, before spicing and drying.

The early form of cider or wine press (English, thirteenth century) would be used by any countryman, and may have been the batons referred to.

Cider Venison

I think it was in the Forest of Dean—or was it the Wye Valley?—where I had venison which had lain overnight in the dripping trough of the cider barrel.

Take the soaked venison, wipe it, pepper it, flour it and fry it till brown, then lay it in the braising pot with a few peppercorns, a dusting of allspice, wine (or dash of cider or vinegar), one or two bay leaves and barely enough water or stock to moisten. Cover closely, packing the peats around and over the pot, or set your casserole in the oven and let the joint cook as slowly as possible, keeping the lid well closed down.

If the joint is small, you can braise it with vegetables; in this case you will need no water or stock at all, but butter or lard the bottom of the dish very well and press the vegetables very carefully over the joint. Dot with butter or marrow, put in the lid tightly, and the meat will cook in the vegetable juice. Serve in the dish, which should, when cooked, have plenty of rich, savoury gravy under and around the meat. Flat, dark mushrooms laid all over the top of the braise make this a capital dish.

Serve fresh, green vegetables, crisp potatoes, watercress and fruit jellies with venison and mountain mutton. Onions, celery, etc., are better kept for beef and fat mutton.

QUICK GRILLS OF VENISON OR MUTTON

Grilled Mutton Chop or Venison Chop

> " . . . It's very true
> He ain't been brought up common
> Like the likes of me and you,
>
> .   .   .   .   .
>
> So they took him into hospital,
> And gave him mutton chops,
> And chocolate and arrowroot
> And bones and malt and hops."
>   *Bab Ballads.*

Bat flat, pepper it lightly, rub the grid bars with mutton fat, give it 10 minutes—2 minutes first side, turn, and then 2 minutes the other side (to seal it); finish cooking, put on a hot plate, with a pat of butter on it, salt, and any juice from the grid. Serve immediately, with plain potatoes.

Grilled Small Steak

Rub with dry mustard, bat flat, rub the grill bars with suet, give 10–20 minutes according to size and thickness. Turn after the first 2 minutes each side; lay a chopped onion on the top side while cooking. Serve on to a hot plate, salt, put a pat of butter on top; or don't salt, but put an oyster on top; or put butter on top and a small tuft of horse-radish. Serve with plain potatoes—or bread—and Worcestershire sauce.

Skewer cookery (all that is left of the "spit")

Venison Slice Grilled

Rub thickly with lard, wrap in a vine leaf and grill comparatively slowly. After the fat is absorbed, remove the vine leaf for the last moment to brown meat. Put on to hot plate, serve with a spoonful of red-currant jelly and put a pat of butter on top.

Hunter's Grill (sometimes miscalled Umbles)

Small pieces of fresh deer meat threaded on to skewers between rounds of mushroom, bacon fat, onion—and grilled over the red embers of the camp fire. In the illustration the grill is threaded on to the metal tent pegs; the original method would be to use green sticks.

Cold Meat

Cut thick slices of cold meat (underdone), rub well with dripping, pepper (no salt); grill very quickly till crisp and brown. Serve with tomato sauce, potatoes, and fresh salad.

DEER HORNS

Hartshorn

Hartshorn ("hart's horn", the antlers of the deer) was the chief source of ammonia, which in old books is spoken of as "spirits of hartshorn" or "Salarmonica".

But the bone itself was also a staple gelatine, cheaper than calves' feet. It is a great pity that we do not still use this simple, useful by-product.

Much of the modern commercial gelatine is now made from trimmings from the leather-makers (the coarser leathers, and hoofs and gristle go to the glue manufacturers). This is dissolved—by chemical action and material processing—and cleared and flavoured, and the resultant jellies are quite wholesome and very convenient. It should be possible to supply the plain shredded hartshorn equally simply and much more cheaply. It used to be available at any chemist's for twopence or so for a large bagful—enough to make many jellies.

Ivory turnings, and ivory dust, were also used, and are mentioned in some cookery books.

Hartshorn Flummery (old Scottish recipe, 1700)

"Put a pound of hartshorn shavings into 3 quarts of spring water; boil it very gently till consumed to 1 quart, then strain through a fine sieve into a basin and let it stand till cold. Then just melt it over the fire and put into it ½ pint of white wine, 1 pint of thick cream and 4 spoonfuls of orange-flour water. Scald your cream and let it be cold before you mix it. Put in refined sugar to your taste, then beat it all one way for an hour and a half at least—for if you are not careful in thus beating it will never mix or look to please you. Let the cups you pour it into be dipped in clear water. When you send to table you must turn it out and stick over the top with blanched almonds cut in slips. Eat it with cream or wine, whichever you like best."

VENISON TRACKLEMENTS

Red-currant jelly with the juice of a lemon squeezed into it. (1730).
Red-currant jelly melted in port wine. (1880).
Red-currant jelly. (1900).
The flavour of venison is improved if the meat be packed for transport with sweet gale (the shrub that grows on the mountains). This plant is in full flavour and scent between February and May, the season for venison.

Barley and oat puddings were cooked with venison.

The rowan berries make a red smoky-flavoured jelly that goes well with venison.

The mountain herbs, thyme and wild sage and gale, are better seasoning than garden herbs.

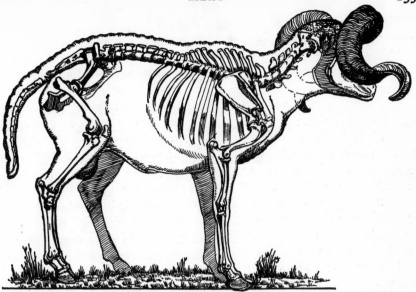

Bone structure of a mountain ram. Note the weight of the fighting ram's head,
the light active legs and long tail.

MUTTON

Of the sheep is cast away nothing,
His horns for notches[1]—to ashes goeth his bones,
To Lordes great profit goeth his entire dung,[2]
His tallow also serveth plastres,[3] more than one,
For harp strings his ropes serve everyone,
Of whose head boiled whole and all
There cometh a jelly, and ointment full Royal.
For ache of bones and also for bruises
It is remedy that doeth ease quickly
Causing mens stark points to recure,
It doeth sinews again restore to life.
Black sheeps wool, with fresh oil of olive,[4]
The men at armes, with charms, they prove it good
And at straight need, they can well staunch blood.

THIRTEENTH-CENTURY VERSE

[1] In the old breeds of English sheep the ewes also had horns; these short rough-ridged horns formed perfect ends for the bows, where the bowstring was fastened on; when the bow was bent and the loop of the bowstring slid down, it hooked into the bone notches.

[2] Sheep were folded each night on the lord's fields to fertilise them. Shepherds are instructed to look for bare places, and to set there a scratching post to encourage the sheep to congregate in that spot.

[3] The lanoline from around the udders of sheep (still in use).

[4] The same clean oily (yolk) wool will matt across a wound, and cause the blood to congeal. A spider's web is still used in the same way in any carpenter's shop.

GENERAL NOTES ON MUTTON

> " Sante Julyane, in til his tyme was ne glotonne
> Na wont was moch to ete motone."
>
> *Legends of the Saints* (1375).

Do not treat all types of mutton in the same way, and always differentiate between lamb and mutton by quality, not size. Of old, lamb was a small, young sheep; it was definitely immature meat—or "froth".

But the present "lamb" is castrated mutton, and may, at two years old, be larger than the ewe. It is still technically called "lamb", but in all respects is very dull mutton. The real old mutton was usually four years old (as ewes were killed off after breeding), and that mutton was lean and well flavoured, and quite different from the fat castrated ram lambs.

Nowadays the hirsels upon the mountains keep the natural grouping and it is sometimes possible to buy the genuine lamb and elderly mutton, but the bringing down of the castrated rams to the lower pastures and finishing them off for meat is much more general, and the ewes are bred from for so long that they seldom reach the butcher.

Even under this rearrangement the mountain breeds never put on fat like the Lowland mutton, and the spicy thyme and herb fodder of the hills makes them much the best mutton obtainable. All recipes for cooking mountain mutton, therefore, should be studied to bring out the special qualities of a rather lean and very well-flavoured meat.

Another very popular type of mutton is the Southdown, which, unless spoilt by too-long root feeding in enclosures, is also a well-flavoured mutton, but with much more fat than the mountain breeds.

The really large Midland breeds are not well flavoured, and should be cooked quite differently from either of the previous types, using fruitier and sharper condiments.

The less common type of salt-grazed or marsh mutton is flavoured by the salt grass and weed of its sea-coast pastures, and requires pungent condiments, such as samphire or laver, to make the distinctly iodine flavour pleasant. The principle is that as the sheep grazes on the iodine-and-salt weeds, its meat becomes *slightly* flavoured with them. Therefore if as condiment you use some of the weed direct, and full strength, it will cover, and blend with the slighter flavour in the meat.

I have arranged the recipes into groups suitable for the different types. Please look up and use the type of recipe for your own special type of mutton—*and do not cook all types of mutton in the same way.*

Note. It has been impossible to do so in some cases. The mountain sheep keep their tails, the downs sheep have theirs cut off. You can't make lambtail pies from long-tailed sheep!

LEICESTERSHIRE

Nowadays this is the standard English mutton; the routine of fattening on hay or sugar-beet tops is probably the cause of the disparaging " only mutton ". This is unjust to the Leicestershire sheep, who, upon grassland, supply large plump joints of succulent meat, needing only the tart barberry or bright red-currant jelly to bring out admirable qualities. (At Smithfield, in 1915, the weight of three Leicestershires was 8 cwt. 1 qr.)

We have drawn these really excellent large sheep between the mountain Blackfaced and the hardy Cheviot, as Cheviots are usually sent south and crossed, producing the Border Leicestershire, which fattens rapidly as prime lamb for the wholesale meat trade.

It is to be regretted that the modern trend of mass-production has invaded the meat market. The average urban consumer now buys " mutton ", and, as the general source of supply nearly always depends upon cross-breeding, the " general usage " of urban English mutton becomes rather dull.

It is unfortunate that so few people nowadays appreciate the individual excellence of the different breeds.

ROMNEY MARSH

Romney Marsh sheep are huge, and big-boned and sturdy, up to 10 or 12 lb. weight for a leg. To see a small leg of Welsh mutton beside a huge Kentish joint, you would never credit it was the same kind of animal. The lambs are sent upland for store, and come down to be finished off on the rich marsh grass, which puts them into good weight for the butcher. The meat is good quality, though a little coarse in texture. The name " Marsh " is misleading, as they are fine reclaimed pasture " walks " of phenomenally quick growth and rich " bite ", but it serves to describe a type of mutton well developed for a special market.

SOUTHDOWN

Southdown lamb is the best lamb in England. The spicy fine turf-grazing on the chalk, fine fattening and careful breeding, have made Southdown herds' reputation with connoisseurs, but again, the modern mass-production method, which brings flocks of Southdown lambs off the downs, to fold them on sugar-beet tops, and turnips, is changing the flavour and quality till it might be Leicester or Oxfordshire, a dull, rather mediocre, mutton. If you ever can get really good Southdown off the downs you will have had one of the best dishes in England. A nice leg of Southdown lamb is plump, fat and well flavoured and should be served with mint sauce, green peas, and new potatoes—but it must be real Southdown, not root-fed mutton.

BLACKFACED—LARGE MOUNTAIN TYPE

An agile mountain breed, whose wool was valuable when long, straight staple, with the springy hair in it, was used for the hard-wearing worsted stockings. This wool was almost as damp-resisting as goat's hair, and when the fleece "counted", the Blackfaced was valuable. Some Blackfaced herds have worked the same sheep-walks for centuries and by knowledge, transmitted through the herd leaders, can find their ways about, and pick up a living on barren moors, where other herds would starve. On this account one may never sell a complete hirsil of Blackfaced but must leave some wise old ewes, and a knowledgeable ram or two, on the mountain to teach the new sheep. Their wild, free, natural life makes them very intelligent and clever. It is almost impossible to fence in Blackfaced; they can clear a six-foot stone wall with a running jump, and will ford or climb any dyke. Their hooves are a weak point for foot-rot on damp grazing.

The rams are so quick and strong, that the north sheepdogs are trained to overthrow them by a sideways thrust and tug, before they can round up the ram's following herd; this trick disqualified many north dogs for the Southern trials where it disqualifies a dog to touch a sheep.

CHEVIOT

This favourite sheep is spreading rapidly, taking over many of the moors originally walked by Blackfaced. In shape, the joints are very like the Leicestershire, and when brought into condition on the lower pastures, the meat is similar, though not so fat, and better flavoured—that is, if well fed. But like all free rangers, it loses badly in quality on too much artificial food. There is nothing to choose in badness between a moorland sheep fatted to weight on dry hay, and roots, and a Southdown fatted to weight on sugar-beet. The individual goodness of either type depends upon its own special grazing.

SMALL WELSH

Now the small Welsh mutton is acceptedly the best. The herds are free-ranging, and on most of the hills there is an abundance of wild thyme, the spicy herb which gives the Welsh mutton its characteristic flavour. The joints are very small, so that a hindquarter is cut quite as usually as a leg. A small leg of Welsh mutton may be only 3 or 4 lb. in weight. In the Lowlands and on the border they are frequently crossed with the Shropshire to obtain larger lamb. This is useful, but it is a pity the modern demand for lamb has practically put an end to the market for really good Welsh mutton, because old Welsh ewes are now kept to breed from year after year, till they are long past the stage when they could fatten up to finish as " good " Welsh mutton. This universal change in the breeding system has little to recommend it, and many in the Principality regret the really good, old-fashioned, well-hung, four-year-old Welsh saddle of mutton.

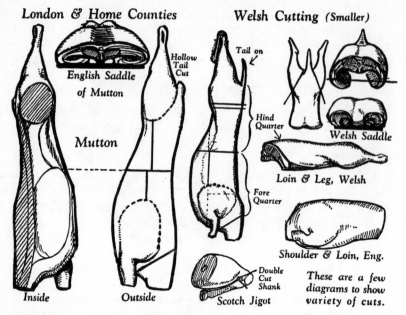

London & Home Counties   *Welsh Cutting (Smaller)*

English Saddle
of Mutton

Hollow
Tail
Cut

Tail on

Mutton

Hind
Quarter

Welsh Saddle

Fore
Quarter

Loin & Leg, Welsh

Shoulder & Loin, Eng.

Double
Cut
Shank

These are a few
diagrams to show
variety of cuts.

Inside   Outside   Scotch Jigot

The cutting up of mutton varies with the type of sheep and the locality of sale

SPECIAL COOKING FOR MOUNTAIN MUTTON[1]

Saddle

Saddle of mutton from the Welsh hills, or Scotland, is a joint for an epicure. Let it be well hung, dust the entire joint with pepper and dry flour and strew it with powdered herbs. The herbs may be thyme, parsley, mint, marjoram, etc., though the wild thyme should be definitely predominant. A suspicion of wild garlic is a great improvement, but only a slight aroma— a head of the dried flowers, rubbed into the mixed herbs, is quite enough. A slight dust of mace is also permissible (as for mushrooms).

Mountain meat being characteristically dry, the hill people often "butter" the joint over with mutton dripping, dust with flour, and roast for a few minutes in a hot oven, then again baste and again dredge with flour, thus forming a thick crust over the meat to keep in the juice. Set the joint before a brisk fire or into a hot oven till sealed, then reduce the heat, but cook as quickly as you can to prevent waste. Realise that the joint, being smaller than usual, will cook more quickly, but it must be basted well and often.

When the joint is just done, give it a very brisk finish to crisp the

[1] The post-war trouble over "ewe-mutton" showed that people had forgotten its qualities; they tried to cook it like fat lamb and so made it uneatable.

outside, and serve on a hot dish. The gravy should be strained carefully, and if the herbs have been well chosen, it should be found to be well seasoned. It is a mistake to serve quantities of thick brown gravy with roast mountain mutton; the thin brown gravy from the roast should be enough. Serve rowan jelly, mint sauce, plain boiled potatoes, and a light green vegetable, such as string beans. Onion sauce may be served in winter, but see that it is not too strong. The delicacy of mountain mutton is in its aroma and flavour, which should not be spoilt by coarser flavours.

Leg and Loin

These two joints were sometimes cut and served as one, not very successfully, as the thin loin is apt to be done before the thicker leg portion. If they must be toasted as one, make a good forcemeat stuffing and fit under the loin section. For serving, *see* notes above on saddle.

Roast Leg of Mutton

" For dinner we had salmon and leg of mutton; the salmon from the Dee, the leg from the neighbouring Berwyn. . . . As for the leg of mutton it is truly wonderful; nothing so good had I ever tasted in the shape of a leg of mutton. The leg of mutton of Wales beats the leg of mutton of any other country, and I had never tasted a Welsh leg of mutton before. Certainly I shall never forget the first Welsh leg of mutton which I tasted, rich but delicate, replete with juices derived from the aromatic herbs of the noble Berwyn, cooked to a turn, and weighing just four pounds."

GEORGE BORROW, *Wild Wales*.

The best little joint there is and this is how it would have been cooked for Borrow. The shank should be removed, broken up, and boiled separately, to obtain stock for gravy, as there should be very little drip from the small joint. Pepper first, then "butter" with mutton fat and flour thickly. If you get the leg that has the tail attached, and it is late summer and the tail is fat, bend it round across the meat and secure with twine, and arrange the joint upwards, or hang it from the hook from the thick end first, *long enough for the fat from the tail to give the meat a basting.* Then reverse, and hang from the shank in the usual way. As the leg of mutton is very small be sure to "butter" it thickly before roasting. See that the outer skin is crisp and the gravy well made. Accompaniments as for the larger joints. Do *not* overcook small Welsh joints.

Loin Chops

In the loin of mountain mutton the chops are so small and the meat at the long end of the bones so thin, that it is better to saw them across, half-way down, then the small, loose end of the bone can be slipped out and the flap, which will contain any fat there may be, should be wrapped round over the inner side of the loin (see diagram, p. 144). This will give you a joint of small, rounded cutlets in a row, much more compact, and it will be found to cook more juicily. The other alternative is to fill in the end side of the loin with forcemeat stuffing made with herbs, bread-crumbs and any suet which can be obtained from the kidney, which should be left in position under the chops.

Shoulder of Mutton

See instructions for roasting and serving saddle and haunch. As this joint is particularly thin and extra care must be taken that it is not dried up.

Cold Roast Lamb and Mint Sauce

The joints of mountain mutton are so small that there is usually little to eat cold, but the mountain saying "The nearer the bone, the sweeter the meat" holds good, and it is a great pity not to eat these good cold meats plain. Well-made mint sauce may be served with them, also rowan or jelly. Crab-apple jelly, green-tomato chutney, or any of the more lightly flavoured pickles, but not the strongly flavoured ones; salad, green vegetables, and plain boiled or buttered potatoes. On no account serve hot, sticky vegetables with cold mountain mutton; they should be light and crisp.

If the small joint has unfortunately been carved so badly that it is unappetising, the following way will preserve excellency of the meat (but do not cut it from the bone until just before it is wanted). Take a small dish, and cover closely with a very fine green film of chopped young spring onions and shredded lettuce, or in summer with finely chopped mint, lettuce, and a sprinkling of tarragon vinegar. On this bed lay your slices of mutton cut from the bone. Dust the whole lightly with pepper and salt, and send to table as quickly and as cold as possible.

Spiced Mutton (old sheep)

> " If you wish mutton tendere it must be hung as long as it will keep; then a good eight-tooth [i.e. four-year old] mutton is as good eating as venison."
>
> *Enquire Within*, 1858.

Here is a very old way of cooking mutton, either shoulder, loin or leg, or, preferably, saddle. The mutton should be four years old and well hung. Bone the joint (unless the saddle), rub it well with black pepper, powdered thyme, mace and fine meal (no salt). Work the herbs and spices well down into the bone cavities. Wrap the whole joint round in a strip of flead, or the entire rind that has been removed from a ham after cooking.

Or, if neither are obtainable, cover thickly with mutton dripping, and wrap in several layers of cabbage leaves. Roast rather slowly, basting with cider (or crushed crab-apple juice) removing the wrapping in time to brown and crisp to a finish. Serve, as venison, with red rowan jelly, burgundy, or some dry red wine in the clear gravy, and a salad of watercress.

The correct cutting and packing of a stew

Neck of Mutton

The neck portions are best made into lobscouse.[1] Chop the joint neatly and, bending it, rub pepper and powdered thyme into the slits, and cover all with a dusting of seasoned flour. Put a lump of fat at the bottom of an iron saucepan and fry the meat in this till lightly browned. Meanwhile, cut up carrots, turnips, a little swede or parsnip, some onions, or if you are using leeks they will be found to make a very delicate dish and should be sliced across and across. Add a sprinkling of barley. (On no account put in either onions or leeks *uncut*; or they will stew to a soft, stringly lump, instead of permeating evenly.) Add these to the meat and then cover the whole with a layer of sliced potatoes followed by a layer of whole potatoes. (The idea of the cut layer is that they will simmer down in the cooking to a creamy mass and thicken the gravy.) Add a good sprinkling of mountain herbs and fill up just to the level of the *whole potatoes*. (*Note*. The whole potatoes should not cook in the broth, but in the steam above the water level.) Put on the lid closely, and simmer very gently *without stirring*, till the top potatoes are cooked through (by which time the smaller vegetables, lower and nearer the heat, will be done, and the meat just leaving the bone). This dish is best served direct from the pot. If it is taken out, lift the potatoes and arrange them round the dish, and put the meat and vegetables in the centre.

Grilled Mutton Chops

" The supper was an excellent one too . . . the tea service was extremely plain . . . but the bread and the mutton chops, and the butter, and even the tea, were such as Mrs. Powell's china was never privileged to bear."

Susan Warner's description of a Welsh farmhouse, about 1850.

[1] Lob=sheep; couse=broth.

The Welsh sheep would provide mutton chops about three or four inches long—very small indeed, but "excellently" juicy, tender and well flavoured. They would be grilled over a quick fire, and served on a dish, each chop having a lump of butter melting upon it when served, with pepper and salt. Plain bread and butter, and perhaps rowan jelly, would be the only condiments.

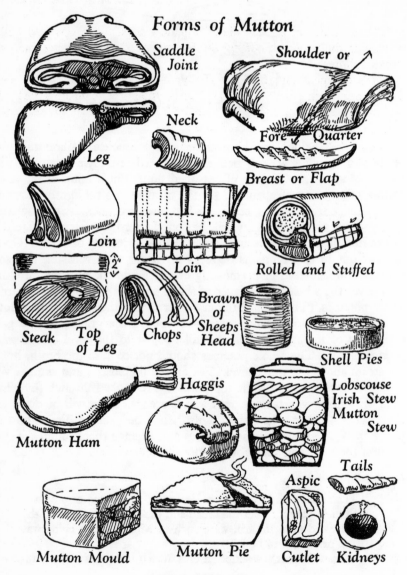

Forms of Mutton

Saddle Joint

Shoulder or Fore Quarter

Neck

Leg

Breast or Flap

Loin

Loin

Rolled and Stuffed

Steak

Top of Leg

Chops

Brawn of Sheeps Head

Shell Pies

Mutton Ham

Haggis

Lobscouse Irish Stew Mutton Stew

Tails

Mutton Mould

Mutton Pie

Aspic

Cutlet

Kidneys

Forms of Mutton

Lamb Cutlets and Green Peas

" Never you mind about the piece of needlework, the tambouring and the maps of the world made by her needle. Get to see her at work upon a mutton chop, or a bit of bread and cheese, and if she deal quickly with them, you have a pretty security for that activity, without which a wife is a burden instead of being a help."

COBBETT, *Advice to Young Men.*

The diagram on p. 144 shows you how to shape chops into cutlets, removing the bone and curling the fat tail round and securing them with small splinters.

Shell the peas and boil the shucks[1] vigorously, drain off the liquid, and use it with a little milk and butter and flour to make a fine white sauce. Put this in a shallow casserole. There should be just enough to cover the chops, which are then laid in it. Cook gently until the chops are tender. Cook the peas (with mint and sugar), drain, put over the dish, and serve.

Lamb Chops

Lamb chops are excellent grilled over a clear fire. Season with pepper and salt just before they are done, and serve on a base of mashed potatoes, or with new potatoes and peas, and butter on each chop.

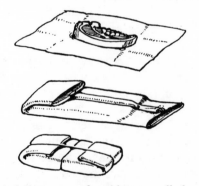

A delicate way of cooking a small chop

Steamed Cutlet for an Invalid

Trim the fat closely and season the chop lightly—if possible add a few young green peas. Take a piece of strong buttered paper and wrap the chop closely—as shown. Steam 10–20 minutes according to size and serve *in its paper*, which should be full of juice.

[1] Shucks or pods.

Lamb's Tail Pie

Mountain and Wiltshire lambs keep their tails; but this recipe comes from the Cotswold district. Instruct the shepherd to keep the docked tails warm, packing them into a sack, and let him bring them straight to the kitchen. Scald, removing the wool, joint the tails, and stew with whatever root vegetable is used locally for feeding the sheep, parsnips or swedes, etc. Add a sprinkling of barley and just enough water to cover. When tender, pack into a deep pie-dish with a chopped-up hard-boiled egg and green peas. Cover with a short curst and bake quickly.

In regard to the cooking of sheep's tails, it is interesting that the fat-tailed sheep were used at the Cape of Good Hope as early as 1700. The fat is so soft that, once melted, it does not readily harden again, and is used like hog's lard, as a contemporary writer says:

"May not the shepherd conclude he had made a valuable acquisition since he had not only a sheep that gave him as much wool, milk and flesh as the rest of his flock, but had a tail which in addition gave him a comfortable meal, and what is more valuable, plenty of grease for his toilet."

Sheep's Head (Lowland Scotch)

> " Oh Lord, when hunger pinches sore
> Do thou stand us in stead
> And send us from thy bounteous store
> A tup or wether head.
> Amen."

A BURNS GRACE FROM THE GLOBE TAVERN, DUMFRIES.

An excellent dish, but one that takes time. Let the butcher prepare the head, splitting it in two and removing the eyes and offal and brain. Wash in running water till it runs clear, then put into a thick stewpan with 2 whole onions, 2 chopped carrots, the top part of a stick of celery, a couple of cloves, a bay leaf and a faggot of herbs, 3 or 4 peppercorns, salt and about 3 quarts of water (or less—the head must be completely covered). Set over heat, and as soon as it boils, skim carefully (this is important). When it stops "throwing up" scum, draw the pan aside and let all simmer for about 2 hours, or till the bones are loose and lift out easily. Tilt the whole boiling out into a collander, or sieve, rinse out the pan, and pour back the liquid, adding a handful of whole barley and a fresh supply of nicely cut and prepared root vegetables—carrots, turnips, celery, parsnips, etc.—in great variety (but not potatoes, as they cloud the broth). While these boil in the broth, carefully pick over the meaty pieces from the head, pepper them lightly and scatter with some very finely minced parsley (not much of this). Re-warm the pieces of meat with the freshly cooked vegetables and serve the meat and broth in deep bowls, with the vegetables, and bread or potatoes handed separately. Dumplings are added if liked, but they should be small and very light.

It is the cooking of the bones and trimmings of the vegetables in the first broth, and the addition of the fine vegetables and meat to the same strained broth, that gives the double richness to this dish. The old trimming vegetables will, after the long boiling with the bones, be uneatable pulp, but all their suave juices will be in the stock, ready to welcome the new supply of fine vegetables that will now cook quickly and lightly, and be pleasantly firm to eat with the meat. A properly prepared dish of "sheep's head meat" is a very delicate and very nutritive dish. *Note.* The onions are put in "whole", as the outer skins make the broth a rich golden colour.

Sheep's Head (mould). (*See* diagram, p. 144).

If the above dish is wanted cold, add sheep's trotters, as the extra glutinous bone will make a very stiff jelly. Proceed as above, then arrange the cooked vegetables around a basin, place the pieces of meat and barley in the middle, boil down the stock till thick and pour in gently to fill the basin to the brim. Set it aside till next day, when it should turn out firmly. The very thin skin of white fat should not be removed before turning out, and a little should be served with the jelly slices.

Young dandelion leaves, endive, or watercress are the best salad with this gently flavoured mutton mould, and oatbread and salt butter are good accompaniments.

Mutton Pudding

" But Mutton! thou most nourishing of Meat!
Whose single joint may constitute a treat,
When made a Pudding you excel the rest
As much as that of other food is best."
                                                    KING.

Mutton pudding is as important in the hill districts as beefsteak pudding in the valleys. Required: one sheep's kidney, embedded in its fat, and about 2 lb. of mutton. Make a crust of flour and the hard mutton suet. Season this crust spicily and mix it rather damp.

Chop all the lean mutton, with the kidney, sprinkle well with parsley, juicy chopped onion, flour, black pepper and a little salt. Pack into the crust and fill up with mutton stock made from the bones. Boil for 2 hours.

In summer, season the mutton pudding with wild thyme flowers (pale, pinky mauve) from the hillside. In autumn, pack with rowan berries or the last of the red currants. In winter, pickled damsons are spicy, and after Christmas a scattering of capers is usual.

The main thing with a mutton pudding is to see there is plenty of juice.

Haggis

> "The groaning trencher there ye fill!
> Your hurdies like a distant hill,
> Your pin wad help to mend a mill
> In time of need.
> While thro' your pores the dews distil
> Like amber bead."

BURNS, *Ode to Haggis.*

Nowadays haggis are issued sewn up, but years ago in the kitchens of the Cape Wrath Lighthouse I ate a haggis made by "herself" and it had three wooden skewer pins down its belly, making it look like a debauched black beetle. But it was "warm reeking rich", and the fat within had distilled "like amber beads". It was very savoury.

I watched it being prepared. The paunch and pluck were boiled whole in a big iron pan; with the windpipe hanging over the edge to drain off impurities. I give two recipes to show how this dish remains fundamentally unchanged through the centuries.

Old recipe (dated about 1300). "Take the Roppis [pluck] with the tallow [white fat] and parboyle them and hack them small with pepir and safron, salt and brede [oat bread] and yolks of eyroun and swete mylke.

Haggis. Pluck boiling, with wind pipe hung out.

Do all togederys into the wombe of the sheepe and sethe hym and serve forth."

The modern version. A sheep's paunch and pluck (it is the honeycomb tripe stomach of the sheep), some of the porous lung, liver and heart, and sometimes the kidneys. Take the suet from around the kidney and chop it finely. Add about a pint of medium oatmeal, a good amount of chopped onion, a tablespoonful of salt, a strong dash of black pepper, half a nutmeg, a handful of currants, raisins or any available fruit element (small wild damsons or garden currants). Mix and pack into the paunch.

The secret of making a good haggis is to allow for the swelling-up meal to fill the elastic stomach tightly, without bursting. It may be necessary to prick the haggis a little when the boiling is beginning, to let out the air. It is easier to sew it up, though the correct fashion is to wrap the stomach over, using wooden skewers.

Nothing is served with haggis, except bagpipes and whiskey.

Afronchemoyle (a form of haggis; a Norman-French marrow bone)

This form of haggis appears in 1390, in *The Form of Cury* (cookery) by one of the royal cooks of Richard II. In effect, it is a delicate rich dish of tripe and eggs.

"Nym Eyren with al the wyte and myse bred and scheps talwe get as dyses grynd peper and safron and caste thereto and do hit in the schepys wombe seth it wel and dress it forth."

The modern version. Take eggs, white and yolk together, and mix with white bread crumbs and finely diced sheep's fat (the soft interior fat rather than mutton suet); season with "peper and safron" (this would make it golden in colour) and stuff a sheep's tripe with the mixture, sewing it up securely. Steam or boil the "haggis", and drain it before serving. The swelling bread would form a firm forcemeat, and the wrinkled tripe outside and white fat-flecked yellow centre would much resemble a sawn-across marrow bone.

Mutton Sausages

In mountain countries mutton interchanges with pork on many hill farms, and mutton hams (*see* Preserving) and mutton sausages are a matter of course.

The proportions are 1 lb. lean mutton to ½ lb. mutton suet and bread-crumbs, in equal proportions. If possible, add a little cold boiled bacon or ham. Press into sausage skins and cook exactly like pork sausages.

They are good fried in mutton fat in the oven, with mint sauce and mashed potatoes. On some farms they put in a little crushed onion juice, in that case the sausages must be eaten at once.

Braxy Mutton

This has always been known from hard times in the bleak Highlands. The term not only covered sheep which had died, but those which were killed after an accident.

"Si une berlyz murge sudeynement il mettent la chas en ewe aulant de dure com et entre mydi e noune. Et pus le pendent sus e kant le ewe escule le fount saler e pus ben secher."

("If a sheep die suddenly you must put it in water during the hours between mydi and noune (roughly all day), and then after you have drained the water away you can salt it (dry salt?) and you can then eat it.")

Note. We do not recommend this.

Mutton—Marking with Raddle

The red earth gathered from the screes of Helvellyn (and sometimes other red pigment earths) are mixed with melted mutton fat to make the red paint or raddle with which sheep are marked.[1]

I tracked an interesting development of this.

Some commercial firms pushed an oil-bound, lead-basis red paint upon hill shepherds, to use in place of the old mutton fat and earth raddle. As a result the chamois leather and skiver workers were worried by curious *stains* which appeared in the sides of their sheepskins—invisible till the skins had been far processed towards leather, when it showed up as a stain *within* the texture of the skin. The explanation was that the bought "paint" had worked up the wool and, unlike the reabsorbed mutton fat and sedimentary colour, the paint stain had penetrated the skin and left a deposit therein.

FAT STOCK MUTTON

" O the mountain is the sweeter,
  But the valley is the fatter;
  And so we deem it meeter
  To carry off the latter."
                    BORDER RAIDING SONG.

The fat Shropshire, or succulent Leicester, mutton should be cooked in exactly the opposite way to the small dry mountain mutton. Whereas in

---

[1] A dry powder is sometimes dusted on the chest of the tup, so that the shepherd can see which ewes will bear his lambs the following Spring, but as this blue does not have to withstand a long season's weathering, it is seldom grease bound.

the mountain mutton the job was to get enough fat to cook it with, with the fatter mutton, the job is to keep it from being too greasy.

SPECIAL COOKING FOR FAT STOCK MUTTON

Roast Saddle of Mutton

This is even cut differently from the mountain mutton, which has a tail (this, being tucked under, serves to baste the meat). The larger mutton has no tail, and is a square-shaped, rather than oblong joint. Do not attempt to encase the fat mutton in any way, though a light dusting of pepper and flour will do no harm, and will crisp the outer fat. The joint should be cooked quickly till the juices are sealed, and then very slowly till done thoroughly. The loss of fat from a fat joint is less, proportionately, though it should be kept well basted. If cooked in the oven it should rest on a grid; otherwise the bottom part of the joint will lie in the fat and fry instead of roasting. These larger fat joints can be lifted out and kept hot *before* the fire (not covered in any way, or they will lose their crispness) while the gravy is made.

In making fat mutton gravy, see that the fat is poured off absolutely clear. See also that the thickening be thoroughly well browned. Nothing is so unappetising as a greasy, pale sauce. A little chopped onion and parsley should be added to flavour the gravy, and, after it is strained out into the tureen, a spoonful of red-currant jelly and a dash of pepper are a great improvement. If lamb, mint sauce may be served. If mutton, make a good onion sauce, or a caper sauce (*see* recipes). There will be enough fat to cook your roast potatoes. Root vegetables, chopped or mashed, and kale, cauliflower or spring cabbage are all good with this type of mutton.

Haunch and Leg of Mutton

The same observations apply to cooking these joints. The leg of mutton, especially, may be rather fat. Do not remove any fat before cooking, as it bastes the meat, but see that the mutton is very carefully drained before serving. Especially for a leg of mutton, a final dusting of seasoned flour and a dredging of herbs is good, to render the outer casing of fat crisp and crusty. The shank need not be removed from this type of mutton, but it is rather wasteful to leave it on as it quickly dries out.

Boiled Leg of Mutton with Caper Sauce

" A select company of the Bath footmen presents their compliments to Mr. Weller . . . a friendly soiree consisting of a boiled leg of mutton, with caper sauce, turnips and potatoes."

Pickwick Papers.

If not too fat, or inclined to be tough, this type of mutton may be boiled instead of roasted. Put mint, thyme and other herbs with the onions and a good dash of pepper and salt into the water, and let them boil till the liquid is well flavoured, before putting in the meat. See that the meat is completely covered and then withdraw the pan and let it only simmer thereafter. A few minutes after putting in the meat, skim, and again at intervals, the last time just before serving, as you want to lift the meat out very clean and white-looking. If it is a large joint, it is better to boil the skins of the onion and trimmings of vegetables to flavour the mutton, but cook the vegetables you are going to eat separately, for, if they are young, they will not need such long cooking as the mutton itself. In this case, add a double handful of barley or some soaked beans and peas. Dish up your boiled mutton with a good hot caper sauce and serve the boiled vegetables and barley chopped up together in a hot bowl. If potatoes are served with this dish they should be plain boiled. The meat should be juicy and tender from long simmering; the vegetables and barley tender and well mixed; the potatoes and broth should be handed separately. Like this, plain boiled mutton can be a very appetising dish.

Cold Mutton

To serve this dish cold, return the joint to the pot to let it grow cold in the broth (so that it will remain juicy instead of drying out on the larder shelf). Then before serving, lift it from the broth, wipe dry and mask appetisingly with the caper sauce, decorating it with whole capers and slices from the boiled carrot, etc. Serve with hot jacket potatoes and fresh vegetables.

Breast of Mutton (three different ways)

Dust well with flour and pepper, and fry lightly. Butter a shallow casserole, lay a bay leaf at the bottom of it, and put in the square of meat.

Then fry some finely chopped onions and shake these over the mutton. Add a large cupful of peas—the ones that are already a little old will do very well—or small vegetables. Cover with stock, just to the level of the onions (so that the vegetables cook in the steam). Put on the lid tightly and cook slowly until the meat is tender.

Alternatively, lay the meat flat, cut out the bones, and score it deeply across half a dozen times, pepper well and salt lightly. Make a good force-meat stuffing, using chopped parsley, thyme, and, if possible, lemon peel; otherwise lemon balm or lemon thyme, and a little mint. Let the forcemeat be rather damp, and press it well into the holes left by the bones. Roll up and tie it round and bake, putting it into a square bread tin. It will take about 2 hours to cook. Serve hot, with gravy and roast potatoes. Alternatively, leave it in the tin till cold, cut it out (when it should be a neat brown loaf) and serve sliced, with red-currant or rowan jelly and salad.

Sheep's Trotters with Oatmeal

Sheep's trotters are the ceremonial part of the Bolton Wanderers football team dinners. Only the heavy types of mountain sheep, such as the Pennine Range sheep, can make this dish well. (I don't think a sparrow could make a meal off a Welsh trotter, but in the larger breeds of sheep, the trotters are almost as meaty as a pig's.)

Sheep's Trotters

Get the butcher to cleave four trotters carefully. Stew gently in salted water till the bones can be removed. Mix a little fine oatmeal, with the water, to a paste, pour over it the boiling stock from the trotters (it should thicken instantly), pepper well, replace the trotters and cook gently for about ten minutes.

Alternatively, some people cook this dish with flour and milk, making a white sauce, and onions may be added. It is best served poured out over a slice of hot buttered toast.

Battered Trotters

Clean the trotters and set them to stew slowly (in Lancashire they put them upon the back of the hob all day), together with onion trimmings, carrot and celery scrapings, a peppercorn or two, and a spoonful of salt. When you return from work at evening time, take out the trotters and bone them, dip them in good thick batter and fry them. While doing this the liquor drained off from the stewing is being boiled down to be thickened and served as gravy with the battered trotters, the whole making a substantial "tea relish".

Note. The batter being made beforehand rather stiff is left to stand all day in the pantry while the stewpot stands on the hob—and a few spoonfuls of the trotter gravy are used to thin it down to the right consistency just before use, thus ensuring that the batter is flavoured correctly to go with the trotters. If this simple dish was prepared *before* you went to work at 6 a.m., it wouldn't "take a minute to put into batter and fry it up" when you get back from work at 6 p.m.—and "trotters was cheap and t'trimmings cost nout".

When you find some people making some dishes over and over again, and specially well, you can nearly always see *why*.

Shanks Jelly

> " Roste or sodden wholesome is mutton
> And of the bones be made a broth full restorative
> And a gelly right royalle."
>
> TWELFTH-CENTURY DISCOURSE ON SHEEP.

Soak twelve shanks of mutton, brush and scour them clean, lay in a saucepan, with three blades of mace, an onion, a few black peppercorns, a bunch of savoury herbs and a slice of very brown toast, cover with 3 quarts of cold water and bring to the boil, skim, cover, and set to simmer "for as many hours as sheep" (i.e., as long as possible). Strain into a basin, remove grease when cold, and use as basis for mutton broth, or in the preparation of mutton brawns.

The cleaned shank-bones of the sheep were scraped, sawn with a slant across, and whittled into apple scoops for removing the cores of apples. A dozen or more scoops were not too many, for everyone lent a hand at the autumn apple-paring and drying.

Broth

> " Though never so much a good huswife doth care,
>   that such as do labour, have husbandly fare;
>   Yet feed them and cram them, till purse do lack chink,
>   no spoon-meat, no bellyfull, labourers think."
>
> TUSSER.

The liquor of all meat is "broth" in history, but because beef was more often roasted and mutton boiled, broth is usually "mutton broth", and beef broth is called beef "tea" (*see* Teas) or soup.

The seething of the mutton in the cauldron was not likely to be a lonely affair in a mediaeval kitchen; the various puddings and nets full of food hung in the common pot must have made a diverse mess that varied daily. Broth, therefore, is made automatically by all the boiling recipes given for mutton; the sheep-head, the boiled leg of mutton, etc., all make broth.

When broth was specially needed, and could not be worked into the rest of the household economy, the scrag end of the neck and shank bones were bought, broken up and put into the pan with a sliced onion and some vegetables cut up, a bunch of herbs, salt (or bacon rind), and the whole covered with cold water (none of the brown frying suggested for soups or stews) and simmered slowly till the bones were clean and the vegetables soft; it was then strained into a basin. Next day the fat was skimmed away, the clear broth poured off to heat up with a handful of barley, and pieces of meat and vegetables. The broth was again simmered till the barley was tender and served hot in bowls with pepper and salt and oatcake.

Mutton broth, as made in 1893 by my own old nurse.

Probably most of the kings of England were reared upon this same mutton broth, which is a democratic excuse for describing this process in detail.

The fire was an open one, coal and wood mixed; the range had an oven at one side, but still kept a pot crane over the open fire in the middle. Nurse took a thick iron pot and rubbed the bottom inside well with the fat tail of a mutton chop (the point being that she did not want it to burn). She then fetched a scraggy, bloody end of a sheep's neck and, laying it on the *stone* (not pottery) sink, she chopped it up with an axe and put the pieces in the pot, together with a bunch of bacon rind plaited together. This pot she now hung upon the hook high over the fire, and fetched some vegetables from the outhouse. Onions (shallots) were skinned and cut in two and added, and some washed turnip, sliced. Then a small bundle was made up of wiry thyme, a sprig of green mint, a twig of marjoram and the brown-paper peels from the onions; this was tied tightly with twine, and secured to the handle of the pot, hanging the bunch inside. Then the kettle that hung alongside the pot was tilted up and some water poured in (warm to prevent the cracking of the hot iron pot), and the whole filled up with cold water. When it boiled, she skimmed the dark scum off very carefully, and replaced the lid till dinner-time. A scoopful was poured into a basin and a brittle yard of West Riding oatcake was lifted down from the rack overhead; a spoon and plate were set at the wooden table by the window and dinner was served.

Curiously, it was *not* greasy; I expect the meat was so lean and the slight fat from the bacon rinds so thin, that the short preliminary cooking used it up. There was a velvety sheen on the surface and the yellow onion skins had given the broth a golden colour. Next day, after it had gone cold, it was skimmed and barley added, but this was definitely another dish, having barley and bits of meat and vegetables in it and needing a soup plate to eat it in. This first day's boiling was plain "broth".

China Chilo

This dates from the East India Company's time, and was a clear white and green dish much fancied by the ladies of that period, and also thought to be good for the blood after the sea voyage back from the East. It was one of the dishes you made a little boastfully—to show you had overseas connections and to point out the new lacquered tea-caddy, the Cashmere shawl and the gossamer-fine Indian muslin *he* had sent to you last season. This recipe dates from the days when Warren Hastings was a young hero.

1 lb. of mutton, raw and minced finely, 2 or 3 lettuces shred small, 1 pint of green peas, salt, white pepper, 2 oz. of butter, a very few spring onions chopped up (leafy ends and all). Cook all together in a pan over the fire,

tossing lightly with a silver fork. Add 3 or 4 spoonfuls of water and set on a high trivett (that is, lift it high away from the fire); cover closely that it may stew as softly as possible for 2 hours. One or two sliced cucumbers may be added towards the last, and a few small button mushrooms. It should be sent to table, piled high on a platter of white boiled rice, "with a light white wine".

It makes a pleasant summer evening meal—with a flavour of white muslin and spinets.

The large Pennine sheep have long chop bones. The straight tall pot fits them upright and cooks well in the side ovens.

Mutton Hotpot (from Lancashire)

Make a big brown earthenware hotpot with a fitted lid "right hot". Put a bay leaf in a spoonful of dripping at the bottom.

Get some mutton chops and flour and pepper them, then fry till brown both sides. Take them out and pack them into the pot standing on their heads, tails up. If the chops held a kidney, put that in too.

Chop up an onion for each chop, and fry that, and pack it amongst the chops. Take some carrots and chop them and flour them and brown them, and pack them over the onions; then cut some potatoes into thick slices and put them on over the top, overlapping like slates on a roof. Pepper and salt as you go and if you get a dozen oysters you can put these under the potatoes (don't fry them first).

Now take the fat that you have fried all in, thicken it with flour till brown, pour in boiling water from the kettle, and stir till the gravy is well cooked. Season it with pepper and salt and a good sprinkling of sugar (this is important). Some people put in a drop of Yorkshire relish or a suspicion of anchovy sauce.

Pour in the gravy till it comes up to the level of the potatoes, put on the lid and bake with a good fire for 2 hours. Ten minutes before dinner take off the lid, rake up the fire and get the potatoes properly brown on top. It's champion!

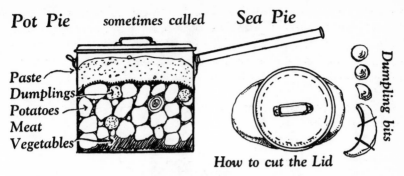

Pot Pie *sometimes called* Sea Pie

Paste
Dumplings
Potatoes
Meat
Vegetables

Dumpling bits

How to cut the Lid

The lid is a good guide to cut the pastry cover. The small trimmings are placed in the broth like dumplings.

Mutton Pot Pie

"Before the fire stood a pretty good-sized kettle, and a very appetising smell came from it to Ellen's nose . . . her ride had made her hungry. It was not without pleasure that she saw her kind hostess arm herself with a deep plate and tin dipper, and carefully taking off the pot-cover so that no drops might fall on the hearth, proceeded to ladle out a goodly supply of what Ellen knew was that excellent country dish called pot-pie. Excellent it is, when well made, and that was Miss Janet's. The pieces of crust were white and light like new bread; the very tit-bits of the meat she culled out for Ellen; and the soup gravy poured over all would have met Miss Fortune's wishes, from its just degree of richness and exact seasoning. Smoking hot, it was placed before Ellen on a little stand by her easy-chair, with some nice bread and butter; and presently Miss Janet poured her out a cup of tea, ' for,' she said, ' Leander never could take his dinner without it '."

ELIZABETH WETHERELL, *The Wide Wide World.*

For this useful dish you require a strong iron saucepan, or a thick, straight-sided aluminium pot.

Fry small pieces of bacon or ham in the pot and then fry in it chopped and seasoned cubes of meat that have been well rolled in seasoned flour. Add chopped and seasoned root vegetables of all sorts, several onion slices, some beans or peas. Roll these vegetables also in the seasoned flour, and fry lightly for several minutes with the lid on the pot, shaking it at intervals. Now cover with water or good stock, and set it on the stove to come to the simmer gradually while you make a crust.

A plain good suet crust is best (it is a tip to make it slightly drier than usual). Roll it out once and cut out a thick round exactly the size of the cooking pot.

A raised mutton pie has red-currant jelly on top

(*Note*. If you stamp it out by the lid of the pan you will find it will fit exactly.)

Any small trimmings left may be rolled into little dumplings and dropped into the stew, which should, by now, be simmering well.

See there is plenty of broth in the pot, well seasoned and flavoured. Lay the round pie-crust gently on top so that it rests on the stew. Replace the lid and don't lift it again for at least an hour. The crust should have risen well, nearly to the top of the pan, and should be light and puffy and permeated with the savour of the stew.

You will probably find it necessary to cut out a slice before you can lift the crust whole. In fact, it is better to serve direct from the pot to the plate as Ellen had it.

Mutton Spicy Pie

A very old English recipe and a very good winter dish.

Make a short crust, using mutton dripping, and season with salt and pepper. Cut the cold mutton into rather small bits, but do not mince. Let there be half fat and half lean, season well, and add an equal quantity of coarsely chopped apples (hard windfalls are best for this). Pack the mutton and apples in alternate layers, sprinkling each layer of apples with a little sugar and a good grating of nutmeg. A few currants or chopped prunes are a great improvement and should be tucked amongst the mutton pieces.

Cover the top layer with finely grated mutton suet, then put on the crust and bake quickly. Do not add any water, as the apples should cook down to a spicy apple sauce over the meat.

Mutton-melt

This bloody piece of meat is legally "entrail" or offal, but it is usually left attached to the inner side of the loin of mutton, especially by country butchers. It is of somewhat the consistency and flavour of kidney and makes a dark meaty gravy. In farmhouse cookery and cottage economy melt is often used separately to make the meaty gravy served with herb puddings. In this Victorian family recipe, it is mentioned as:

> " A good cheap gravy suitable to pour over suet dumplings and also suitable to cover chopped potatoes and cabbage for the mid-day nursery dinner." (1840)

Cut a large melt into thin slices and brown in bacon fat in an iron sauce-pan, then sprinkle in enough flour or fine oatmeal to dry up *all* the fat completely, and continue to stir and cook till all is well browned but not at all burnt (about 15 minutes). Now slowly pour on about two pints of boiling water, stirring well all the time; add a slice of raw ham cut up small, or the knuckle-bone of a bacon hough, or the trimmings off a ham-bone; an onion sliced and cut up—yellow skin and all—a bunch of herbs; and seasoning. Boil all well up, and set to simmer till wanted.

"Strain carefully into a hot jug, test the seasoning and salt and pepper it nicely, and you will have a good thick brown gravy for meat puddings or children's spoon meat."

Mutton Hams

To dry a leg of mutton like a ham:
> " Cut it like a Ham and take 2 oz. salt-petre and rub the Mutton all over and let it lie a day and make a Pickle of Bay Salt and spring water and put the Mutton in and let it lie 8 days and take and hang it in a chimney for 3 weeks, and then boil it till it is tender.
> The proper time to do it is in cold weather."
>
> EIGHTEENTH-CENTURY RECIPE.

These were cured like pork. They were pressed flat to "Westphalia" shape and boiled with a truss of hay (*see also* Curing and Salting).

Lanoline

A natural lubricant and salve for use in the lambing season, or for any hurt, was made by shepherds from the fat near the sheep's udders. Sometimes it was melted with flower of sulphur or broom buds. Lanoline and mutton fat were used as ointments on hill farms just as hog's lard or goose-grease were used on valley farms. On account of the extreme hardness of well-clarified mutton fat, when used as a basis for ointment it was usually warmed before being applied. For shepherd's or milkmaid's chapped or badly cracked "winter" hands the sovereign cure was to warm the fat, when the hands were dipped in bodily, and the grease worked well in. The hands were then held under the cold tap and gently wiped. This treatment made it possible for the worker to carry on with his job without his hands being too sticky, and the ointment did not melt off easily during the day.

Collier's Roast (Colliers originally meant charcoal burners)

Colliers, working night shifts, and "being able to see in the dark" were noted as poachers, so when a small family had a whole sheep to dispose of—tactfully—and they did not dare make hams of the legs, they salted them in brine, and then, (having eaten the rest of the animal) fished the legs out of the barrel, washed them very well in running water, and roasted the lightly salted meat.

Another report says this was the charcoal burner's way of baking the mutton, under the hearths in the woods, where, unless the hearth was disturbed (spoiling the charcoal), the carcase could not be discovered for several days. It is of use if you have a joint of mutton that must be kept some time. Salt it in brine (*see* Mutton Hams), and afterwards wash and treat it like the salt-grazing mutton. The meat will be reddish (the broth too salt to use). Par-boil and finish off in a quick oven, serve with plain potatoes and laver sauce.

Cottage pie has a potato cover

Vicarage Mutton (two versions)

       1. " Hot on Sunday,
          Cold on Monday,
          Hashed on Tuesday,
          Minced on Wednesday,
          Curried Thursday,
          Broth on Friday,
          Cottage pie Saturday."

2. A complete joint *is* sometimes the best solution for a small family—and this way does supply more variety than most others.

1st Joint: Cut a deep steak at least two inches thick from the broad end, and braise. Serve with plain boiled potatoes and tomato sauce.

2nd Joint: Remove the shankbone and knuckle end, crush the bone and set to stew for broth, with onion and barley, and use the knuckle, well sliced, to make a small lobscauce.

3rd Joint: Take the main piece left, remove the bone (for gravy), stuff the centre with good forcemeat, and baste and roast. Serve this roast joint with red-currant jelly and roast potatoes.

4th Joint: Broth, followed by the cold joint, served with salad, jacket potatoes and mint sauce.

Cold mutton need not be unappetising. It is a pity to spoil good joints by re-cooking, and better to serve them plain cold, with pickles and salad, keeping less interesting joints for made dishes. The pickles for mutton should always have a fruit element, or be green: pickled damsons, pickled ash keys, spiced cauliflower, french-beans, etc., or small white pickled onions. Mint sauce and caper sauce may also be served with the cold meat.

MUTTON TRACKLEMENTS AND CONDIMENT

Rosemary

Rosemary is an old-fashioned herb good with fat lamb or mutton. It is especially useful in winter, when we get imported fat lamb—but no fresh mint.

It is more aromatic than flavoursome, so should be used like bay leaf—for the savour only; not to be eaten. Therefore, lay a bunch in the gravy, or under the joint, do not mince it up in the stuffing or sauce. To try it, lay a long wisp of rosemary along the inside of a loin of lamb when stuffing; roast or bake as usual. If you leave a little piece of the *stalk end* of the rosemary sticking out, you will find the sprig slides out quite easily, for the smooth leaves, you will notice, all lie closely folded upwards. It is worth trying this very pleasant herb with any fat roast or baked mutton, be sure to pack it against the fat, or, if using in the baste, see it is *in* the butter or dripping, because it is the aroma of the essential *oil* which you want released, and not the flavour of the leaf.[1]

For the proper method of making mint sauce to serve with lamb, *see* Vegetables.

Since the earliest times red-currant jelly has been served with mutton,

[1] There is the same dual flavour in an orange. The orange essential *oil* aroma is in the yellow rind; the flavour in the juice. So you rub off the rind as well as the juice to get the aroma as well as the flavour.

Tracklements for Mutton

The mountain mutton. The fat valley breeds. The South Down and the marsh-
or sea-grazed mutton all take different flavours.

and for most of the valley breeds of mutton it is still the best. Gloucestershire, Oxfordshire, Leicestershire, Shropshire, and all such breeds take
red-currant jelly. To the east—Leicester and Norfolk and the uplands—
an excellent jelly can be made from the barberry. It is slightly more acid
and tart than the red currant, and seems to suit the meat better. The jelly
for Welsh and mountain mutton should be the rowan or mountain ash.

(The very delicately flavoured mountain mutton is lost under the stronger tart red currant.) The subtle, slightly smoky flavour of the rowan suits its own climate and locality very much better. Rowan jelly is more golden than red-currant but is equally clear. The berries are ripe from October onwards, as soon as they hang down.

With the rather dull winter mutton of the garden lands, hot onion sauce is very comforting. The salt-marsh mutton, or saltings mutton, should be served with hot laver sauce. This is gathered on the sea-coast between tides (*see* Laver). It is sold ready-prepared in many places: Mother Yeo's shop in Bideford, in shops in Exeter, markets in Devon, Cornwall and South Wales. Samphire grows on the cliffs (though why Shakespeare referred to gathering samphire as a "dread calling" only a Warwickshire man knows). It grows on the golf-course at Westward Ho! It is pungent, strongly aromatic, and brings out the flavour of the saltings perfectly.

Caper sauce is served with any of the sturdier types of garden mutton. In default of the imported caper, pickled nasturtium seeds are good. There is also a very good batter, and a grain "under-pudding" for fat mutton. Both should be cooked under the drip in the same way that Yorkshire pudding is cooked under the drip from beef (*see* recipes). Some joints of mutton may very well be stuffed with forcemeat. Be sure that seasoning for this forcemeat is made of the same herbs that are used when cooking the meat.

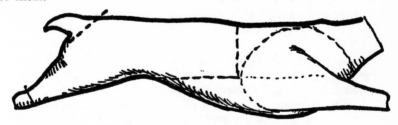

Venison cuts (the usage varies locally)

GOAT

GENERAL NOTES ON GOAT

" Younge Kyddes flesshe is praysed above all other flesshe—although it be somewhat dry.

Old Kydde is *not* praysed."

" Likewise our predecessors had the flesh in such loathed detestation as they would not deine to touch it . . . notwithstanding if necessity doe force us to feed upon it, as many pore peasants dwelling in villages doe (hauving good store of goats, and which are the store of their powdering tubs) (i.e. salted for winter) . . . they boyle it in a pot not couvered, and in great quantitie of water, with good store of spices."

G. MARKHAM, *Adaptation to English Usage*, 1600 (?)

GOAT MEAT varies very much—good pasture-fed kid is like mountain mutton, old wild goat is more like bad venison.

So select your recipes according to the goat.

For paddock goat, of best quality, any of the recipes for mountain mutton apply. The bones being longer, the shank of the leg-bone should be sawn through higher up than for mutton, to get a better-shaped joint, or it may be more convenient to roast the top portion and keep the shank end for stewing.

Goat grazed on the salt pastures near the coast, had better be treated as the pres salet mutton, with laver sauce and samphire pickle.

Very old tough goat is better cooked by venison recipes.

Goats do well on rough pasture, give excellent milk and are reasonably good meat also. Their cheese is less well liked, being usually rather strong.

Kid

Kid should be cooked by any of the mountain mutton recipes, as most of these were originally used for cooking goat. If the kid is very young, treat as lamb, if full grown, as yearling mutton.

Goat meat also makes a good curry (*see* Goat, Spiced).

Goat, Young

"I ordered Friday to take a yearling goat, betwixt a kid and a goat, out of my particular flock to be killed, when I cut off the hinder quarter and, chopping it into small pieces, I set Friday to work to boiling and stewing and may have a very good dish, I assure you, of flesh and broth, having put some barley and rice also into the broth."

Robinson Crusoe.

Goat chops can be treated like mutton chops (*see* general notes as to type). The only difference is that the longer bone should be removed, as it only sticks out and dries up; break it off close to the head-bone and cut it away, leaving the tail of fat. Fold this up two or three times and fit it into the inner side of the chop, securing it with a small skewer. Then cook as a mutton chop of the same type.

Goat, Old

Cut up as mutton, but if using the loin, saw through the bones twice, and fold under; if the leg or shoulder, saw through the bone in several

places and insert wedges of onion or shallot, bay leaf and lump salt[1] into
the gashes, to hold them well open. Then put the joint into water and
bring slowly to the boil. Pour off this water and, while the meat is hot
and damp, season again, adding a dust of powdered cloves, or a little
curry powder, if intending to curry the meat later. Fill up again, adding
a cupful of cider or vinegar and a few peppercorns, and simmer to rags.
(In camp it is left on the fire, the pan half-buried in hot ash.)

Take up when done, remove the bones, and shred the meat; meanwhile boiling barley or rice in the broth. When ready to serve, pile the
drained barley or rice on the dish, arrange the meat in a well on the top
of the mound, cover the whole with fried onions and sweet pickle, pouring
some of the broth over all just before serving.

Goat, Spiced

This seems to have been an early English attempt to copy an Arabian
dish; and probably is a "hearsay" from the last Crusade period. I have
rendered its old recipe into modern usage.

Simmer the meat then take a quart of broth. Put the broth into a pot
with a bunch of herbs, in which marjoram, scented herbs, rosemary and
thyme predominate. Add also some greens, such as spinach or endive.
When it boils, add a lump of dripping or fat shredded finely and then
spices, powdered mace, cloves, cinnamon and a few pieces of ginger root.
(The spice added after the grease is there to absorb the aroma; the herbs
are placed in the liquid broth.) In a bag in the same pot boil currants
and prunes, raisins and dates; add a spoonful of cider or vinegar. When
all has boiled well and the fruit is well swollen and fat, put in the meat
again and let it stew a while. Now take out the meat and cut it into
pieces on a dish, and put the hot fruit on top; take a little of the flavoured
broth, add sugar and cider and boil till syrupy, then strain over the hot
meat and fruit in the dish, garnish with slices of orange and almonds and
so "serve it forth".

Note. The cider should be dry and sharp; grape juice from sour grapes
is better and probably nearer to the original idea.

This recipe is good for almost any form of old tough meat—so coarse
and tough that it would be uneatable by any other method.

Goat Broth

" My food was now regulated thus:
I ate a bunch of raisins for my breakfast; a piece of the goat's
flesh broiled for my dinner."

Robinson Crusoe.

[1] To draw out the blood and strong flavour.

Brewis

> " He caused some biscuit and cakes to be dipped into the pot
> and softened with the liquor of the meat which they called brewis
> and gave everyone some to stay their stomache."
>
> *Robinson Crusoe.*

This "brewis" is a Welsh dish called also "tea kettle broth".

Goat Hams

> " They had smoked and dried goat hams and bacon; with bara
> aych [oat bread] and buttermilk or whey to drink."
>
> *Tour in Wales,* 1798.

Goat hams were eaten in Welsh hill farms (*see* recipes for Mutton and
Venison).

They were probably made for economy (to use unwanted he-goats as
store meat), for lack of fat would make goat ham a dry bite! However,
they are on record as late as the 1800s.

Goats' Milk (*see* Milk)

> " When sea voyages are so stormy as to kill geese, ducks, fowls
> and almost pigs, the goats are well and lively—when a dog of no
> kind can keep the deck a minute a goat will skip and leap about
> on it as bold as brass."
>
> COBBETT.

For centuries goats' milk was more used than cows' milk by the common
people and a milking nannie was commonly taken on sailing ships.

ODD ANIMALS

SUNDAY MORNING—1399.

" Forasmuch as divers artificers, labourers, servants and grooms
keep greyhounds and other dogs and on the holydays *when good
Christian people be at Church hearing divine service,* they go hunting
in parks, warrens, and connigries of lords and others to the very
great destruction of the same. . . . No artificer, labourer or
layman which hath not lands or tenemented to the value of 40/- a
year, nor any priest or clerk, if he be not advanced to the value of
£10 per annum, shall have or keep from henceforth any grey-
hound, hound or other dog to hunt, nor shall use fryets, nets,

harepipes nor cords nor other engine to take or destroy deer, hares nor conies nor other gentlemans game upon pain of one years imprisonment."

GAME LAW (Richard II).

GENERAL NOTES ON LEVERETS AND HARES

" Yet can I neither sol fa, ne synge, ne seyntes lyves rede
But I can fynde in a felde, or in a fourlonge an hare."

The Vision of Piers Plowman, 1362.

MEDIAEVAL PEOPLE thought the hare was good sport but indifferent meat. There are different types of hare, and more difference between a tender young leveret and his elderly grandfather, than between two quite different makes of animal. One is white meat, almost like chicken, and the other a strong, rich-flavoured meat; so study your hare before you decide upon the appropriate recipe. Cooked right, hares are good; cooked wrongly, very bad. You can tell young leverets by the size, and the softness of pad and claw and ear. Also their teeth are small and sharp. They should be skinned, paunched, and dressed at once, unlike an old hare, which should be hung.

Roast Leverets

To roast a leveret whole, follow the recipe for roast rabbit. Hares are really better (and much easier to serve) if jointed first; and, as the joints vary so much in thickness, it is better to cook the thick meaty ones rather differently from the thin, bony joints. Really young leverets are better grilled.

Grilled Leverets

Joint neatly, putting the head and ribs to boil down for gravy. Pepper and flour the meaty joints, and fry quickly and lightly in a little butter. Put them, spread flat, on the grid, in a bake pan, dredge with *lemon* thyme, baste well, and cook 20–30 minutes, basting frequently with butter and hot milk, which you scoop out from the pan under the grid. Do not let them lie in the pan or they will just stew in the liquid. They should be raised above it an inch or so, then they will bake brown nicely, and at the same time the steam from the hot buttery milk below will prevent them drying up. Just before they are done, put some tiny rolls of bacon to toast on the grid alongside the hare pieces. Pour off the basting liquid and use it to make bread sauce. Have everything ready for making this sauce beforehand, as you must let it cook a clear 5 minutes while the joints are having their final crisping.

Pile the nicely browned pieces of hare on to a mound of crisp potato wafers, arranging the curls of bacon on the top, with a border of fresh watercress twigs.

Serve with the bone gravy and bread sauce handed separately. Young green salad or small early carrots are good service with grilled leverets.

HARE

GENERAL NOTES ON HARES

" A hare doth no harme nor displeasure to man . . . yet he maketh gentlemen good pastyme; and better it is for the houndes and dogges to eat the hare after they have killed it, than man should eat thereof, for the Byble sayeth the hare is an unclene beaste and doth engendre meloncoly humours."

A. BOORDE.

A meaty, old hare should be hung a week, and should not be paunched or skinned until required for use. Dressing a bloody, old hare is a gruesome job. If you can, let a butcher do it. It is not usually possible to use the liver, and few people nowadays appreciate the head, though it makes good gravy.

Hares can be cooked whole, stuffed, trussed, and sewn up like any other roast. Sometimes the shoulder—that is, the forepart and meaty back, is stuffed with forcemeat and roasted as a small separate joint. Basted with red-currant jelly and butter, it is very good, and with the forcemeat stuffing, a good sauce, and some black mushrooms, makes a capital dish.

This leaves the large back legs to serve another dinner, and the head and trimmings make a rich soup for yet a third dinner, so that a hare is very economical for a small family.

Roasted Hare and Mushrooms

Unless cooking it whole, joint it, wipe, but on no account wash, the joints, and strew them with black pepper, fine oatmeal, and a suspicion of ground cloves as you do so.

Put the head and top part of the neck to simmer for gravy, with the trimmings from the mushrooms, a clove, and a bunch of herbs, chiefly thyme and marjoram.

Fry the joints briskly till brown, pile onto a grid over the bake-pan, cover with scraps of butter, and roast gently, basting frequently with the melted butter from the dripping-pan, under the meat. The hare should take about 40 minutes, so about 20 minutes before it is done, lift the grid, put the flat black mushrooms to cook in the bake-pan, underneath the drip. Hare and mushrooms should be done at the same time.

To dish up, drain the liquid from the bake-pan and use it with the stock from the head and a thickening of fine oatmeal to make a rich brown gravy. Season rather highly, using black pepper only (you put the cloves to cook with the head), salt at the last minute, cover a hot dish with a straw of chipped potatoes. Lay the pieces of hare on these, with tufts of fried parsley. Strew a pinch of finely powdered herbs, thyme and marjoram, over each piece of meat, and send it to table with the gravy separately, bread sauce, and red-currant jelly. Large Spanish onions, braised in the oven—they take the same time as the hare—are an ideal vegetable with this rather strongly flavoured dish.

Roasted Old Hare with Beer

Unless cooking it whole, joint it, wipe, but on no account wash, the joints, and strew them with black pepper, fine oatmeal, and a suspicion of ground cloves as you do so. Fry the joints briskly till brown, and then pile into a bake-pan, cover with scraps of butter, and roast gently, basting frequently with beer. When quite tender (and the more slowly cooked the better), lift up the pieces, drain, flour and baste them with a little bacon fat and let them brown while you complete the thin bone gravy.

To dish up, lay the now browned pieces of hare on a hot dish between tufts of fried parsley and send to table with the gravy and red-currant jelly. Brown bread and butter is better than vegetables with this dish on account of the malt flavour of the beer.

Forcemeat Stuffing for Hare

A good spicy forcemeat for hare is made thus:

2 cupfuls of brown breadcrumbs, $\frac{1}{2}$ cupful of fine suet, $\frac{1}{4}$ cupful of fine onion, $\frac{1}{4}$ cupful of mixed fresh herbs—parsley, thyme, lemon balm, marjoram, etc.—a good dust of nutmeg, a small spoonful of anchovy sauce, and black pepper and salt. Mix thoroughly, moisten with a glassful of red wine and a little extra cider or stock in which the hare trimmings have been cooked. Do not bind this forcemeat with egg or milk. This

would only curdle with the wine and spoil the spicy crumbiness of the stuffing, which should cut rather on the dry side.

Note. The suet is required for a large or old hare, that takes at least 1 hour to cook. For a small joint use bacon fat, and remember to use less salt.

Jugged Hare

An old 7 lb. jam or pickle jar makes a good "jug" pot. Buckley Potterie used to make special tall fire-proof stewpots that were even better, as they had lids.

For this rich, dark "jug" you cook, also, all the head, neck, ribs, and all the blood and liver. Pepper the joints and flour them with fine oatmeal, and fry them lightly and put them into a deep earthenware "jug". Then add a shallot, stuck with half a dozen cloves, a glass of red wine, claret or port, a tart apple cut into six, a lemon cut into six, a dozen peppercorns, a dozen black mushrooms, and a good big bunch of herbs—thyme, bay, parsley and marjoram—tied by a string to the handle of the pot and hanging down in the jug. Sprinkle freely with fine oatmeal and black pepper as you pack the jug, and then fill up with good beef stock. Cover the mouth of the jug with a bladder to keep in the savour, and set it to cook in a deep saucepan of boiling water. (It *can* be cooked in the oven, but the saucepan of boiling water is much better.)

While cooking, make good forcemeat balls, using breadcrumbs, lemon thyme, seasoning, etc., coat with egg and breadcrumbs before frying.

When the jug is done, take off the bladder top, give it a good stir round, and pile the forcemeat balls on top. Fold a white napkin around the jug (to keep it hot and to look nice), and send to the table with red-currant jelly and string beans. Racks of dry toast are served with this dish and red wine only.

Potted Hare

> "What a breakfast! Pot of hare; ditto of trout; pot of prepared shrimps; dish of plain shrimps; tin of sardines, beautiful beef-steak; eggs, muffin; large loaf, and butter, not forgetting capital tea. There's a breakfast for you!"
>
> GEORGE BORROW, *Wild Wales.*

This is given direct from a 1780 cook-book, and is just what Borrow would find at his White Hart Inn.

"Take 3 lb. of flesh of hare, to 1 lb. of pork or bacon fat and beat them together in a mortar till you cannot distinguish each from other. Season with pepper, salt and a large nutmeg, a handful of sweet herbs (sweet marjoram, thyme, parsley, all shred fine, double quantity of parsley).

Beat all together till very well mingled, then put into a pot, laying it lower at the middle than the sides,[1] and paste it up [i.e. cover it with an airtight crust]. Two hours will bake it. When it comes out of the oven, have clarified butter ready, remove the crust, and fill the pot an inch above the meat, while it is hot. When 'tis cold, paper it up, so keep it; which you may do three or four months, before 'tis cut. The fat of pork is much better than the fat of bacon."

This is a particularly good recipe, when there is much over-fat mild cured bacon on the market, and large old tough hares are obtainable cheaply from Scottish moors. The proportion of fat to lean may be increased with advantage, and firm, well-clarified fat can well take the place of the clarified butter. The pot should be brown earthenware, and set in a ring of watercress.

LEVERET

An Old Lincolnshire Recipe

Here is a recipe from the *Lincolnshire Family Jewel*, a cook-book of 1808.

"Catch a hare of middling size, it will take near 3 pints of milk and ½ lb. of butter, you must put the milk and butter into the dripping pan and baste the hare well with it till it is all soaked up and the hare is cooked enough . . . I count this a good way to roast a hare."

Roast Hare

All good cook-books tell you to truss the hare with the head and ears erect, as if lying in the dish, but the gruesome effect does not suit modern ideas, and most cooks now remove head and lower part of leg and use them for gravy.

"Wipe the hare dry with a clean cloth and fill belly with stuffing, sew

---

[1] As a large thick pot would tend to cook solid at the sides while the middle was still soggy soft, the result would be to get a more level surface when cooked through—one does the same with soft dough cakes that are required level for icing.

up, and truss with legs well drawn into body and secured with skewers right through, so that the whole makes a thick round and cooks evenly. Pour a little melted dripping over it, put in a hot oven, and then reduce the heat. Baste it well with milk and dripping alternately till the pan under the hare be full, and then spoon that up and over it (the hare should be on a grid over the pan). Just before it is done, sprinkle with flour, and baste again to make a fine crisp crust over the meat. Dish on a hot dish, remove the skewers, and serve with the gravy in a tureen, and red-currant jelly." (1908).

The hare takes at least 2 hours roasting and the more it is basted all the time the better it will be.

Hare Pasties

Eaten with crisp oatmeal bannocks, these make a very successful luncheon dish. A rather rough red wine is a pleasant accompaniment in a luncheon basket, but out on the hills the white wine of a waterfall is sufficient to wash it down. The pastry should be well salted, rolled thin, and the lightly cooked hare boned, and cut up, and well peppered; a few slices of tart apple can be added, to make the filling more moist.

Hare's Foot.

The "hare's foot" was used for centuries as a toilet brush for powder and rouge—and continues in favour in the theatre today. To prepare, wash the pad thoroughly in soft soapy water and stand the bone end into a jar of strong disinfectant, dry out, cover the bone end with the finger of a glove (for handle) and you have a neat efficient powder brush.

The same was sometimes used to brush glaze over pastry, but a bunch of feathers had a lighter touch.

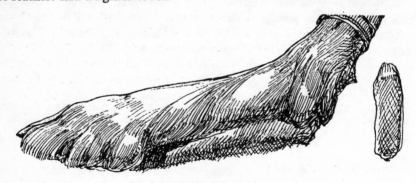

Hare's footpad

RABBIT

GENERAL NOTES ON RABBIT

" Rabettes flesh is best of all wylde beestes, for it is temperate and doth nourissh and is syngulerly prazed of Physiche."

A. BOORDE.

Wild v. Tame Rabbit

Rabbits vary a lot. A young rabbit, clean shot in the fields, is white like chicken and should be treated as such, roasted and served with bread sauce, green peas and new potatoes. Specially bred and fed rabbits, kept in hutches for meat, are delicate and easily digested meat, and should also be cooked like chicken.

Fat old country rabbits make good pies and stews. Thin, scavenger rabbits, trapped, broken-legged, and killed in fever and slow misery, should not be eaten at all. They are definitely unhealthy food.

Young Rabbits

Skin, clean and trim into joints. Put the head and ribs (that are fidgety eating) to simmer for gravy. Wash the white joints in water and a dash of vinegar, flour them lightly whilst still damp, dust with white pepper, brush over with melted butter, dripping or bacon fat, and grill, turning the pieces twice and cooking them with frequent basting till they are brown and crisp. The meat will be as white as roast chicken breast. Serve the grilled joints on a pile of green peas and new potatoes, and hand bread sauce separately. The drip from the grill, with a knob of butter, should be sufficient gravy. The stock made from the head and bones will be brown, and can better be used in rabbit pie made from older rabbits.

Young Rabbit in White Sauce

Prepare as for grilled rabbit, putting the bony parts, head and dark meat aside to stew for stock. Simmer the white meaty joints—with a bunch of herbs, a bay leaf, pepper and salt—in milk and water till tender. Then

make a good, thick, white sauce with this milk, butter and flour, cooking
the sauce very thoroughly, and put the kept-hot rabbit joints on to a hot
dish, pouring the white sauce over them.

A very slight dusting of fine parsley looks nice, but only garnish with
it, as you cooked with a bay leaf and want to preserve that faint aroma
and the delicacy of the rabbit.

Serve this dish with new young beans and young potatoes.

Middle-aged Rabbit (in a bake-pan)

Middle-aged rabbits, corn-fed or domestic, are good cooked "Dorset
fashion"—i.e., oven-fried.

Skin, joint (putting head and ribs to stock as usual), and brush each
meaty piece with lard, white-peppering the lard as you work. Flour well
with fine oatmeal. Put some bacon fat in a flat earthenware baking-pan
and scatter it with chopped onion, and over this some fine breadcrumbs.
Pack the rabbit joints on to this flooring and cover each piece with a slice
of fat bacon. Set to bake in a hot oven whilst you make a nice forcemeat
of breadcrumbs, chopped parsley, lemon thyme, and finely minced bacon
fat. Season with a dust of nutmeg, pepper and salt, and bind with egg
or milk. Form it into balls about the size of a bantam's egg, coating them
in breadcrumbs.

Open the oven door. By now the bacon will have run considerably, and
the pan be sizzling hot with fat. Take the forcemeat balls and pack into
the spaces between the joints, and if you have any little button mushrooms,
pack them down too. Do not take the hot pan out of the oven while doing
this. The point is to put the forcemeat balls into the boiling hot fat. After
3 minutes, open the door again and turn them, joints and all, and give
them another 3 minutes. Then drain off all the superfluous fat thoroughly
and put the bake-pan on to a cooler shelf and let it cook more slowly
until the forcemeat balls crack open, the rabbit meat is white and tender,
and the scraps of bacon have slid off into little crisp rolls here and there.
Lift out the dish, sprinkle it with cider, and send it to table just as it is,
serving straight from the dish.

Note. The oatmeal and well-fried onion and crumbs should have made
a sort of crumbly crust underneath each piece of rabbit, so that each joint
with its congruent forcemeat ball and bacon roll cuts out on a little brown
raft.

For meat baked in the oven the instructions are usually to raise it above
the fat on to a grid. But not in this case, as the rabbit joints are actually fried
a little before baking; therefore it is necessary to drain the fat very
thoroughly after the first quick frying process is finished.

Elderly Rabbit (in pie)

An elderly rabbit is best in a pie. Joint it, putting head and ribs to boil down for gravy. Rub the meaty joints with lard, then pepper and dust with fine oatmeal. Put a slice of bacon over a bay leaf at the bottom of a deep pie-dish; lightly fry the joints and pack down on to it, scattering chopped parsley and onion on top, small chopped carrots, parsnip thinnings, mushrooms if you have any, and some elderly peas—a few capers are good; lacking mushrooms, a spot of mushroom ketchup will not come amiss, or if you can, pack the old rabbit with a little finely chopped ham, or bacon, a blade of mace, nipped up fine. A spoonful of cider, or a chopped apple, should be added, and season well, making it good and spicy. Whatever the filling, let the top layer be thickly sliced potato, capped with chopped parsley and butter.

Rabbit pie

Fill up the pie-dish with gravy from head and ribs and put on a thick white pie crust. Start the pie in a hot oven to raise the crust, and then let it cook slowly until the meat is tender. Make sure that there is plenty of gravy in the dish, and when done it will be found to be good either hot or cold. It is better to start the pie cooking before putting on the lid, as an old rabbit is a slow job.

An Old Tough "Rabbit Pot"

This should be pot-stewed using the pie mixture, but after browning each piece, pack them *into the pot* with the bacon, bay leaf, onion, and a cupful of cider. Fill up like a hotpot, and, if you like, you can put a suet crust on top. Cover and let it simmer a very long time.

Do not omit oatmeal and potatoes, because they help to thicken the gravy; or the cider, as that makes it tender.

"To Smoar an hole old Cony" (1670)

This recipe begins "Take and put him in a jufkin [or jug] head down-ward and tayle upwards", and uses the recipe already given, but adds a large tablespoonful of vinegar or the acid "pulp from the cider press if the old Cony is a tough one".

Rabbit Mumbled

To mumble rabbits—a nineteenth-century recipe, which we recom-mend for tough ones, or those shot on the mountains.

"Clean skin and fill the bellies with parsley and onions whole, and stew them till the meat falls from the bones (which pick out). Chop up the meat, onions, and parsley and meanwhile thicken the gravy in the pot, with flour and butter, and season with pepper, spice and cider, return the chopped meat and onions into this thick sauce to reheat—and serve on snippets of fried toast." We add button mushrooms or old garden peas to this "mumble". Lacking cider, use sour apples, or a small spoonful of vinegar while stewing.

Rabbit Brawn

This is a summer dish made in harvest-time from the young rabbits shot in the cornfields.

Take your rabbits; skin; remove the heads and dark back meat; clean; and cut up. Put the heads and dark meat aside, and put the white meat to

Colander

stew down with the remains of a ham or bacon bone (there is usually ham or bacon "in cut" during harvest), some parsley, pepper and a little milk. Let this simmer slowly till pink ham scraps and white rabbit meat are all loose from their bones. Pour through a colander, immediately putting back the broth to go on boiling. Lift out all the bones and pack the meat into a rinsed mould, putting the pink ham and white rabbit disposedly, and alternately. Rapidly boil down the broth to a strong white stock. If the weather is hot, add a sheet of gelatine to make sure of a firm set. Fill up the mould and leave to stand.

Turn out onto a dish garnished with watercress, cold peas, and tiny carrot thinnings, and serve with a white potato salad. It is a very cool dish for a hot summer's day, and yet solid enough to work on.

Serve with bread and butter, and a cup of white coffee, and you will have a complete light luncheon.

Rabbit Cup

Equal parts of rabbit white meat, lightly cooked, and mashed potatoes, seasoned lightly, and pressed into a buttered and breadcrumbed cup. Bake till firm and lightly browned, and turn out onto a sprinkle of finely chopped parsley. A very simple dish for a small child, or light diet for an invalid.

A variant is made of chopped rabbit meat and breadcrumbs, soaked in the rabbit broth. Old farmhouses used deep tin pattypans for "cups".

A cockatrice should be decorative

COCKATRICE

As this "antient conceit" uses up elderly fowl or rabbit well, and makes a decorative dish that delights children (for parties), it is given in modern equivalents. It is some trouble, but with a refrigerator the first part can be prepared beforehand.

The original is capon and sucking pig, but a boiling fowl and good domestic rabbit will serve. The meat of both must be of the same colour, and take the same amount of cooking time.

Dress the boiling fowl whole, but dress the rabbit by removing head and front legs completely and setting the hind-legs out flat. Now truss the ribs of the rabbit well into the rib cage of the fowl, slitting the fowl's vent and skewering the fowl legs back over the body of the rabbit. Tie into shape and simmer gently, with seasoning and herbs, till quite tender; leave it to grow cold in the stock. Next day, lift out, remove string, and drain; stuff with forcemeat, and roast till dry and brown and the forcemeat cooked. Again leave to cool. When ready to serve, glaze the whole with bright dark glaze, picking out the shape with powdered egg yolk. As it is a "show dish" it should be made specially decorative, with cut beet, egg white, etc.

Set it high on a nest of green parsley, add a small carved head, with scarlet leather, or gilded cock's comb at the cock end; set the two wings either side the body, and display the four legs (with gilded claws) out behind. A gold egg between the paws, or gilded skewers, or anything decorative, may be added, and a "collar" of cut parchment or of plaited straws should be put around the neck of the wooden head. The "joint" should be arranged upon a wooden board, both for appearance and for ease in carving.

For the forcemeat: A usual mixture, but add a good lining of chopped fat ham before the forcemeat is pressed in (this helps to baste the cockatrice while roasting); spice the filling rather highly, as it is to be eaten cold.

For the glaze: the usual aspic glaze may be used, but for children a quick substitute may be made by dissolving a jelly foundation with 2 tablespoonfuls of best vinegar and meat extract. It need not be clear, if it sets with a fine bright glaze. Brush on rather thickly, till well coated, and pour the final glaze over last, quite liquid, to get a good finish.

Children of all ages and many centuries seem amused by this weird creature with a bird's head and wings, and four legs, yet, like the elaborately decorated boar's-head, it is fundamentally a very plain dish.

HEDGEHOG

The gypsies encase them in clay and bake them in their open fire. When cooked, the case is broken off, bringing with it the prickles and skin; it is like very tender chicken. But hedgehogs are completely harmless, and do an enormous amount of good in the fields and gardens by devouring snails and slugs. They become very tame, especially in dry weather, when they are glad of water. They are very fond of bread and milk, which trait has caused them to be accused of stealing it from cows—a complete fallacy. They also eat fallen fruit in the orchard, and are credited with rolling in it in order to carry it off on their backs. Thousands of these harmless little Furze-pigs are run over by motorists on the roadways at night; they do not bolt when frightened, but roll up, lie still, and are crushed to death. *No one should harm a hedgehog.*

Dark
Shell
Edible

Common
Snail

SNAILS

Helix Pomatia is a large-shelled snail with shadowy marks on the shell.
Helix Nemoralis, the wood snail, is smaller and has darker "tabby"
markings.

Helix Aspersa, the large garden snail, is nearly as large as *Pomatia*.

The extremely large garden snails found in parts of England are said
to be the descendants of the edible snails of the Romans. The edible ones
are eaten in Soho and Swindon and a few other places. In some parts the
small "dew slugs" were considered good for nourishing backward children.
They were gathered and dissolved in salt broth, or dissolved in salt first
and added to the child's broth. The tough-shelled garden snails used to be
calcined for lime diet. There is a substantial account in the *London Gazette*
of 23rd March 1739, of five thousand pounds' reward being paid to one
Joanna Stephens on her medicine having been tried and approved, this
medicine being chiefly calcined snail and egg-shells powdered and made
into pills with soap and honey.

Edible Snails

The large edible snail, supposed relic of the Roman days, was probably
imported and fattened up in England, but the largest ones in England
today are as big and as fat as the French snails, so anyone who enjoys
Esargotis l'epicurienne can prepare them by this old English recipe.

Collect the snails into a covered tub, or onto some grass plot, and
fatten them for a week, on bolted lettuce, onion, and soft oatmeal porridge.
Fruit peels, savoury herbs and fresh water should be provided daily, and
the snail pasture should be shaded from the direct sun (and, of course,
from thrushes). The washed snails are then thrown singly into fast boiling
salted water and simmered for twenty minutes, and allowed to get cold
in the broth. The shells are then emptied and the meat left in the broth
while the shells are dried and polished with a scrap of fat (if you wish to
make the shells really ornate they can be dabbed with gold-leaf). Arrange
the shells in a line along a split cane, and set them to keep warm. In a
mortar pound a small shallot, parsley, pepper, a scrap of salt ham or
bacon, and a pinch of spice. When smooth, rub a gallipot with a clove
of garlic, and put the seasoning into it with enough butter to melt into
a smooth warm sauce. Put the snails, drained from the broth, into this

strongly flavoured sauce and cook another 10 minutes till hot through. Half fill the shells with the sauce, and put the snails into them; fill up with the rest of the sauce, and sprinkle over the top some finely powdered herbs. Take any of the flavoured butter that is left and heat up with a little of the cooking broth, and send to table separately.

Lacking the silver prongs of Soho (epitomes of the two-pronged mediaeval fork), use clean splinters of reed or fine skewers.

SNAKES

Adder

> " The fat of an adder *is said* to be the antidote to its sting."
> COBBETT, 1822.

Note it "is *said*"—the sign of unbelief. Up to the fourteenth century faith was complete; if the cure did not work, the fault must lie in your application of it. From the fourteenth century to the seventeenth grows a new mistrust. Such a thing is "supposed to cure". With the nineteenth century comes the tentative "is *said*" and by the twentieth these things are "superstitions".

"Fysshe of the Mountayn"

> " Take a mountain serpent, that hath a black back and white belly, and cut off his tail even hard to the place where he sendeth forth his excrements, and take away his head to the depth of four fingers."
> TOPESELL.

The flesh was then skinned, and cooked with wine or vinegar in the water, and spiced (rather like a small eel). Curiously, a Dutch farmer in the Transvaal expressed horror because the African native cooked and ate a serpent in this way—using lime juice instead of vinegar.

POULTRY AND GAME

" Being by conjecture 500 Leagues from any land the ffowles which naturally lodge and breed at land did com so infinitly to Our Shipp so far off at sea . . . they fell upon all partes of the Shipp to rest themselves, takeing (us) as it seemed for Mooveing Rocks, without any feare of harm . . . suffered themselves to be taken . . . with hands without motion or remooveing away . . . as if they had been commanded of God to yeild themselves to be meat for us."

SIR FRANCIS DRAKE.

GENERAL NOTES ON POULTRY

" Your Hen must be perfectly bred as your Cooke . . . her head would be smal, her eye very cheerfull and her Crowne armed with a double Cofpel or Crownet; her body would be large, for so shee will cover her Broode the better, and the feathers on her brest would be long and downie, for that is most comfort to the Chickens . . . if she have no spurres it is better for her Broode and no impeachment to her Valure. Lastly looke that she be a painfulle layer, awilling Sitter; and above all things loving and kinde to her Broode. If your Hen chance to crow, which is an evill and unnantural infirmity in her, you shall forthwith pull her wings and give her wheat scorched and mixt with powder of Chaulke and keepe her . . . from the companie of all other Pulline."

MARKHAM.

PEOPLE who do not keep hens may not know why poultry is cheap at some seasons and dear at others. Chicks are generally hatched in spring, but some, in incubators, before Christmas. These autumn-hatched hens begin to lay in spring, when eggs are scarce and valuable, but, as only one cock is required (or none, if breeding is not done), the young male birds are sold off. Hence a "spring chicken" is nearly always a cock. Therefore if you see a cockerel sold in spring, you can buy it, knowing that it *is* a chicken, and sure to be young and tender.

But sometimes in country markets you do get a young hen because the eggs may not breed true and a smallholder, recognising offspring from a hen known to have been troublesome, will count her off to fatten with the cocks. So, if you are given the reason why that hen bird has been killed, take her, because of the two, hens are better than cocks.

Now we come to summer fowls. The farmer's wife says: "These pullets [young hen birds] have not begun to lay yet. If they don't start by next market day I shall put paid to them!" and that is why in summer roasting birds will mostly be hens, for the young cocks will be gone.

After that, all poultry is very scarce and expensive until autumn, when the hens, having laid their natural clutches, go broody. When a hen leaves off laying, you decide whether she is worth keeping to lay again at Christmas (to "lay about Christmas" is the ultimate virtue for which the hen is born!). Or she may become "a boiling fowl or would roast". That is why, after July, nearly all "fine fat birds" are mostly broody hens.

In summer, as soon as the new young cockerels are old enough, the old cocks go. But an old cock is *not* a roasting bird! The honest market woman commends his weight, and labels him "Nice Boiling Fowl". If he is fat, buy him. He will have a lot of meat on him, and is the bird you want for Cockaleekie.

Now I do hope this small lecture on how to choose poultry is more use than telling you to waggle the breast-bone or look at its claws (which have probably been cut off).

> " Of all tame fowls a capon is moste bests for it is nutytyne and soone dyggestyd—A Henne in wynter is good and so is a chyken in somer especyallye cockrellys and polettes . . . (the which be untroden—i.e. virgin chicken.)
>   The fleshs of a cocke is harde of dygestyon but the broth or gely made of a cocke is restoratyve."
>
>   **FOURTEENTH-CENTURY COOKERY BOOK.**

Capons[1]

Capons are made by castrating the cock bird, usually at 6 weeks old. The bird then tends to grow large and put on weight; a note on farm management says that the custom was abandoned in Scotland earlier than in England, where the London market was kept well supplied up to the end of the 1800s. Fatted poultry from Norfolk were sometimes sold under the name "capon" at this date.

---

[1] Capons are now obtainable; and injection, and chemical, and special-content diets, are now in experiment to control growth.

Cramming Poultry

" If the farmer's wife have a dozen birds to cram, there she sits, with a leathern apron before her, with a bowl of warm milk, or some greasy water, taking a turkey out of the coop, onto her lap, forcing its mouth open, with her left hand, putting in the balls with the right, and stroking with her fingers the outside of the neck to make them descend."

Amicus Curiae, 1847.

The whole principle of cramming is abhorrent and unnatural, yet it is difficult to draw the line between these old forcible methods and the modern over-feeding induced by spicing the food to bring on thirst, or over-eating. To study the diet that will produce the most fat birds in the least time is legitimate only so *long as their health does not suffer*.

PRINCIPLES OF STUFFING

Before cooking poultry, the principles of stuffing should be understood. Birds, being hollow, dry out while roasting, therefore stuffing should be designed as an internal basting, to give off a savoury steam which will permeate the meat, and fat, to be absorbed by suction through the fibres inside, as the heat is roasting the meat outside. When this principle is realised, the cook will understand why it is reasonable to brush over the inside of poultry with oil or butter, or put lard, beef steak, fat pork, etc., inside a bird. For large fowls that are slow to cook, the stuffing must be mixed with suet or a slow-cooking fat, and as it will be some time before this fat is released for absorption, the bird should also be greased inside, as well as stuffed, to start the internal basting, till the suet is cooked sufficiently to carry on the work. It would be silly to stuff a small bird that only takes 20 minutes to cook with a suet stuffing that takes 40 minutes before it is edible, or for a heavy bird, that takes nearly 8 hours to cook, to be stuffed with a butter or lard stuffing, as by the time the bird is edible there would be no butter or lard left. I hope I have made this side of the question quite clear.

Now, "to stuff or not to stuff"! That is the next question. Nearly always it is safe to oil or lard the bird inside, but whether or not to add to the flavour by stuffing is a distinct problem. Fat absorbs flavour, therefore the stuffing itself takes the flavour of the bird in which it is cooked, and in return imparts its flavour to the bird. So if you have a strong-flavoured bird, as a rule use strongly flavoured stuffing, or leave it empty, substituting only some fat or a piece of juicy meat for lubrication. For example, goose is well flavoured and can stand up to a pretty strong sage and onion stuffing, but for duck, which is more delicately flavoured, the onions and

Our Main Poultry

Feather Bed

Turkey

Goose (House)

Arrows

Cock (Capon cote)

Hen (Pen)

Duck (Pond)

Pillow

Pigeon (Columbarium or Loft)

Guinea Fowl

In a cold dark mediaeval night, groping for a fowl to cook for supper, you were instructed to "take the one roosting next to the cock"—she was sure to be the fattest. Punctual-crowing cocks were genuinely useful on winter mornings. Giraldus Cambrensis notes with disapproval that cocks "crow at a different time in Ireland".

sage should both be parboiled first. The goose, taking 80 minutes to cook, can have its own goose grease; the duck, taking less than 40 minutes to cook, requires a little butter or lard.

Wild duck, teal, grouse, etc., being birds with a strong, distinct flavour of their own, are best left unstuffed, but need some fat or juicy meat inside to prevent drying.

Herbs should be mixed with the fat ingredient, as fat absorbs their flavour, before being mixed with the dry crumbs. Pepper, salt, spice, etc., being dry, mix better with the bread crumbs. Lemon peel, lemon thyme, etc., should be used sparingly, and when ham and bacon are used, it is worth the trouble of pounding them with the fat before adding the crumbs.

Here is a delicate stuffing for a small roast chicken: 1 teaspoonful of parsley chopped fine, 1 teaspoonful of lemon thyme, ¼ teaspoonful of onion, a dust of mace, 1 tablespoonful of cold cooked ham. Pound all with 4 oz. of bird fat, white pepper, and about 6 oz. of breadcrumbs. Mix all with a well-beaten egg or, failing that, milk. Lard or butter the bird inside, and mix the stuffing fairly moist. A good test is that you *can* just lift the stuffing into the bird with a fork, but a spoon is easier.

RECIPES FOR COOKING FOWLS

Roast Spring Chicken

Pluck, draw and truss, putting the liver and gizzard inside the bird (it is silly to cook these under the wing, as they dry up). Wipe the inside very carefully, and butter it well before stuffing with a very delicately flavoured forcemeat of crumbs, lemon, thyme, and parsley, nicely seasoned, and bind with an egg or milk. (The rind of quarter of a lemon, two good sprigs of parsley, and one small sprig of thyme, are plenty for one bird.)

Roast the chicken, basting constantly. Brown it delicately, and serve with tiny rolls of grilled bacon, bread sauce, small pork sausages, young potatoes and peas.

Roast Fowl (older than chicken)

Hang for a day or two and then rub the skin with lemon juice. Wipe the inside with a cloth dipped in cider or mild vinegar, and coat inside with lard or butter before stuffing with a well-flavoured forcemeat of breadcrumbs, parsley, lemon thyme, marjoram, etc., the same as for spring chicken, only more so. Serve with peas, beans, or braised lettuce, and gravy.

Roast the fowl very gently and baste it well.

Boiling Fowl

A fowl of uncertain age is better boiled.

Truss as if roasting, but instead of stuffing, put the liver and gizzard inside with two large onions stuck with a clove. Flour the bird thoroughly and put into a pan full of boiling water, immediately draw from the fire, and never again allow to come above simmering point.

After the bird has been in a few minutes, skim the pan very carefully, and after it has cooked a little, shred in a really good mixture of nicely prepared vegetables, carrot, turnip, one stick of celery (don't overdo this, as it is very strong flavouring), and a good bunch of herbs.

Simmer till, when you lift the drumstick, the joint gives way easily.

If the bird is to be eaten hot, lift out, drain and serve on a hot dish with the vegetables around it. Remove the trussing string and skewers, and sprinkle just enough finely chopped parsley over it to look appetising, or

The indispensable oval boiler of the country woman. It boils joints, hams, fowls, salt meats—takes bones and vegetable trimmings for soup—fits bottles for preserving and bottling fruit—boils and dyes cloth and makes hen, pig or horse mashes.

coat with thick sauce (for boiled fowl has a pallid look). Serve with hot onion or parsley sauce made with the broth, plain boiled potatoes, and the mixed vegetables which have been cooked in the broth.

It will be very tender and juicy. The best gravy is its own clear broth.

If it is to be eaten cold (and a cold boiled fowl is less dry than a cold roast one), *leave it to grow cold in the broth.* Then drain and pour a very thick lemon sauce over it. A little green parsley also sprinkled on the bosom makes it decidedly better looking; so do cut vegetable shapes laid on it.

Garnish around with watercress and the red carrots in alternate piles.

Cold boiled fowl can be a very decorative dish, as well as a very succulent one.

Note. The reason people do not like boiled fowl is that it is usually watery when served. This is a pity, for a well-boiled fowl should be juicy and succulent. The secret is to drain it very carefully. When lifted from the pot, let it hang upright in a warm place for several minutes. It is quite a good trick to hang it from the hook in the roasting jack or warm oven. When it has ceased to drip and is steaming, put it on to a slice of hot toast. Then you may mask it with sauce, decorate it with vegetables, and serve it upon a triumphantly dry, hot dish.

Old Fowl for Pot-Roast

The secret of this dish is to cook slowly, *closed*, so that the juices soak through and through—thoroughly.

Joint the bird, pepper and salt each joint nicely. (Put the back to boil down, with the giblets, for gravy.) Lay slices of bacon at the bottom of the baking-pot and pack the joints down on to it, in layers, between cut carrots, turnips, parsnip, peas, beans and tiny whole potatoes; in fact, use any small root or pulse vegetable that is in season. The vegetables must be cut up quite small and the pan packed quite closely. A very slight sprinkling of herbs and a few mushrooms are a great improvement.

When the dish is well packed, fill it up with good stock made from the bones. Rub the inside of the lid with a clove of garlic and put on closely, sealing all round with a rim of paste. Then let it bake very s-l-o-w-l-y.

A Very Tough Old Fowl Exploded

How to make a really tough fowl tender.

For this, get the largest bird you can find. *It does not matter how tough it is.* Draw it and truss it. Put a couple of onions inside and set it to simmer very slowly overnight, letting it grow cold in the water as the fire dies down towards morning. There should be a skin of fat on the broth. Take this up and set it aside, but leave the fowl to soak in the broth.

Two or three hours before dinner next day, bring the pot again slowly up to boiling point. Meanwhile, have your oven ready as hot as possible, fiery hot—and a baking pan well greased with the fat from the fowl. The minute the water begins to boil, lift out the fowl, dredge it thickly with pepper and flour, and instantly shove it into the hot oven. Close tightly and leave it 10–20 minutes, according to size.

When taken out, the breast and skin should be brown, and crisp as if roasted, but the fowl still damp and juicy, inside. Scientifically done, it will almost fall to pieces when carved, as the steam from the boiling broth, superheated in the hotter oven, explodes, and, quite literally, blows the whole contraption to pieces.

Note. The peppered-flour dredging *must* be done quickly, and the bird *must* be boiling hot, when thrust into the oven.

Bread sauce and condiments as for a roast fowl should be served with this dish.

Cockaleekie

" Now just such a mess of delicious hot pottage
Was smoking away when they entered the cottage
And causing a truly delicious perfume
Through the whole of an ugly old ill-fashioned room.
   Poor Blogg when seeing the reeky
Repast placed before him, scarce able to speak, he
In ecstasy muttered, ' By Jove, Cockaleeky'! "

BARHAM.

The Scotch have kept this fine old soup unchanged through the centuries. (I don't like to think of what would happen to any foreigner who tried to tamper with Cockaleekie.)

It is not generally known that an old cock bird gets far more tough than any hen.[1] The oldest cock is the best for Cockaleekie.

Pluck, draw, *but do not truss*, the cock, and lay him at the bottom of a well-greased iron pot. Pack around him leeks, cut as shown, add pepper, salt, and a double handful of barley. Cover with about five quarts

How to cut leeks or bottleneck onions slantingly to make rings of larger size

of water and let it simmer and simmer and simmer—and then simmer, till the bird is rag and the leeks are pulp, and the broth is lovely.

If cooked over peats, put on overnight, bringing the peats up, over and under the pan, and it will be ready for supper-time next day. The fat may be skimmed off, but with a really skinny old reprobate of a cock there should not be much fat.

To serve, take out the skeleton and skin, shake the meat back into the pan and ladle meat, barley, and leek into each bowl of soup. Don't spoil this superb old dish by doing things to it. It has withstood the test of centuries.

Chicken Broth (fourteenth century)

" *Hennys in Bruette*
Take the henneys and skald them and open them and wasshe them clean and smite them in gobbets and sethe with fresh pork and take pepyr ginger and bread ground fine and temper it up with some brothe or a little ale and colour it with safren and sethe it togeder and serve forth."

[1] A really old patriarchal bird is put head first, feathers, legs and all, into a hogshead to make cock ale.

This fourteenth-century recipe for chicken broth reads fantastically to the average cook, yet it is not so far removed from modern usage when studied closely.

We followed it with a tough old boiling "henn" and the excessive fat cut from a piece of very fat salt bacon. (A mediaeval lean hen had probably no fat at all—hence the pork fat was needed.) One old boiling fowl was cleaned and cut into pieces (again, with perfect accuracy, she was so tough we had literally to "smite her in pieces", using a chopper). The pork was also cut into small dice, pepper was added (the bacon fat supplied the salt), and the pinch of ginger (which does practically nothing but intensify the strength of the pepper, and was probably added in mediaeval recipes because they used the same whole peppers over and over again, till they must have become weak). The bread used was plain, dry, crushed oatcake (the mediaeval cook would certainly have mentioned specially if "fine" or "Manchete" bread). The whole was well simmered over a wood fire, with a generous pinch of saffron; we left it on simmering overnight. Next day, we removed the cold caked fat, ladled the clear golden-coloured broth out into a basin, "sorted" the mass of bones and meat and added the loose tender pieces of the latter to the broth. There was a little oatmeal sediment, but most of the meal had jellied (like long-cooked porridge) and thickened the broth. The meat was also a fine gold colour, and the whole extremely good chicken broth. There was a slight aroma of saffron (perhaps I put in too much?), but it tasted of well-cooked chicken, which is what chicken broth should taste of, and it was "all henn" and very satisfying and good; whereas modern chicken broth, made of the scraps after the chicken has been eaten, tastes mostly of bone and onion.

It was not wasteful, as we ate ALL *the fowl, completely;* no skin and scraps were lost on the plates, the skin had gone into the broth, and the bones that were left were empty, white, and clean.

Having eaten the pieces of meat in the broth the first day, the following day we reheated the remainder of the broth, full of finely chopped vegetables, and again got a satisfying meal. The only modern difference we could see was the colour; the modern cook would have used "browning" in place of the "goldening" saffron of the mediaeval cook.

Hindle Wakes ("Hen de la Wake" or "Hen of the Wake")[1]

This very old English recipe has come down through many centuries unchanged. The white meat, with its black filling and yellow and green garnish, must look as handsome and gaudy as it did on any mediaeval table. The older recipes use the blood of the fowl to mix with the stuffing. (The blood of a pig, making black pudding, is also extremely old.) All the recipes vary, but the essential filling of dark fruit and spice remain the same.

[1] We believe the Flemish spinners settled at Bolton le Moor responsible for this recipe.

This modern version was collected from a Lancashire family, near Wigan, about 1900. An old boiling fowl was brought in from the allotment the week before the Wakes, plucked and drawn, and hung up in a cold larder, and the stuffing prepared in a big "crock". Half a loaf of dry bread was crumbed and mixed with twice that amount of soaked (but not cooked) stoned prunes (the stones were cracked and the kernels added). This was seasoned with pepper and mixed herbs, and made moist with a cupful of vinegar. A handful of coarsely chopped suet was stirred into the black prune mixture, and the fowl was *firmly* stuffed from end to end, trussed into shape, and set to boil gently overnight in water to which another cupful of vinegar and a large spoonful of brown sugar had been added. It simmered all night on the hot stove, and was left to grow cold in the broth. Wake night it was lifted out, drained, and coated with a thick lemon sauce (the grating of the yellow peel dusted over the top). Set and cold, it was a "stand to" dish on the high-tea table. Halved prunes and quarters of lemon were patterned over the handsome dish. Each family has its own special recipe, but the basis is old hen and fruit filling. Excellent.

"Nek podyngs"—neck puddings

Necks

The long necks of poultry, now made into giblet soup, used to be stuffed and roasted as a small, separate dish. It is only worth the trouble for very meaty necks, when this old recipe may be tried out.

"Take percely and the liver and herte and perboyle. Then choppe hen smal and put raw yolkye of eggs therto and take mace and cloves and littl pepir salt and bred [crumbs] and lay them along the crop and prycke hym and roste hym."

The modernised version is as follows. Part cook the liver and heart (if not served with the rest of the bird) with some parsley—and then chop all together and season rather highly with pepper, salt and powdered cloves, and use with breadcrumbs to make a forcemeat. Bind it with egg and fill the neck of the bird, bind tightly, and roast quickly; cut it into small slices before serving and garnish with fried parsley. It is better to chop the bone side of the neck before roasting as then the swelling forcemeat forces the long sausage-shaped "joint" into sections more easily divided afterwards.

Cutlets of Chicken or Cold Fowl

The fat of the bird is its natural lubricant for basting or stuffing. For basting, tie a piece of fat over the breast, and also put a piece within the bird. The fat of a boiling fowl (not being so used), may be rendered down and used in pastry for the chicken pies, or to form the basis for chicken cutlets.

Chicken Cutlets

Take 4 tablespoonfuls of fat (the clarified fat skimmed from the top of the stock in which the fowl was cooked). Melt it to boiling point in a smooth deep saucepan, shake in flour—it is impossible to give exact measure, as flour varies so much, but keep on stirring in the flour, and stirring and cooking and sprinkling it in, a little at a time, till the fat will "take up" no more, and the mass in the saucepan begins to crumble. Cook for 5 minutes more—*at least*—and then gradually add double the quantity of chicken broth, stirring and beating all the time, so that the mixture leaves the sides of the pan clean, and the whole has a cooked transparent look. (The secret of all sauce making is in cooking thoroughly.) Now add a little good milk (till it is just fluid, not so sloppy as sauce, nor so thick as blancmange), season carefully, and add about four table-spoonfuls of chopped chicken, one of ham or cooked bacon, and, if liked, a small quantity of chopped parsley or a chopped hard-boiled egg. Stir all well together, turn out on to a plate, and leave till cold. When cold, divide into pieces the size of an egg, mould into round shapes, dip in egg and breadcrumbs, and fry in smoking fat till brown and crisp. Serve with fresh green salad and bread and butter, or potatoes and peas, or chips. The cutlets should be firm and crisp outside, but the inside should be soft and creamy.

This recipe may be used for many different sorts of cutlets, but it is especially useful in finishing off small scraps of cold fowl and cold bacon.

Giblets

These can be made into a pie, but most people prefer them simmered down into a good broth. Take the head, neck, legs and all bones and trimmings of the bird, and break them up with the *outer* skins of onions,[1] the outer stalks and trimmings of celery, a few herbs, and any suitable rough vegetables. (It is better to use these outer coarser parts of the vegetables, as they have more flavour, and as they won't be eaten, their stringy texture does not matter.) Lay a few bacon rinds at the bottom of the pan, pack the bones and vegetables down on to them, together with a few pepper-corns and a very little salt, put on the lid of the pan, and let all "sweat"

[1] These outer skins give a rich golden colour to the broth.

together for 10 minutes or so, without burning or frying. Then add just enough water to cover, put on the lid again tight, and set the pan where it will simmer slowly for several hours (in the hot ashes overnight is good). In the morning, skim off the fat, strain off the broth through a fine sieve or muslin, and reheat with barley, rice or peas, seasoning delicately. Serve hot with fried dice of bread.

Rennet Gallino (Spanish "rooster")

Rennet Gallino is a very fine rennet made from the rough skin covering the gizzard of fowls.

A nice "table bird". The liver is displayed to show health and age. It should be removed for cooking.

DUCK

Duck and Green Peas

Traditional in the spring. A chicken and green peas, ready for Easter Sunday, prove to an appreciative family that you are nice and forward with the work. Duck and green peas take their place for Whitsuntide.

If a young duckling, the sage-and-onion stuffing should be very delicately made. 4 *small* onions and 4 sage leaves for 4–6 oz. of breadcrumbs, salt and pepper, melted butter, also a small quantity of milk to moisten, or bind the stuffing with an egg, if possible.

Boil the onions, changing the water twice, and slip the sage leaves into the last water as you take the onions out. Chop onions and sage leaves finely, mix with a good big knob of butter and a drop of milk (or use a beaten egg), and dry off with as much fresh white breadcrumbs as it will take up lightly.

Put a breast-plate of fat over the duck's front, and some inside, and roast it very moderately, basting well. Small pork sausages may be served with the duck, or, in some districts, a piece of hot boiled bacon is cut at the same time. Apple sauce, green peas, and new potatoes are the correct accompaniments.

RUNNER DUCKS

Smaller than Aylesbury Ducklings, but excellent eating.

Prepare them in the same way as duck, but they will take less time to cook.

"The End"

GOOSE

" No quoth the goose . . .
  Nor how could Arrows, profit and alight,
  To meet our enemies and grive their visage,
  And from their Armies, save us from Damage ?
  Flight of My Feathers! despite Sheep I tro'
  Us shall defend, against our mortal foe."

DISPUTE BETWEEN GOOSE, SHEEP AND HORSE, DATE ABOUT 1300.

The long bow, pride of the English army, was dependent upon its "feathering" of goose quills, and its "notches" (end-pieces, where the cords were attached) of sheep horn. Flight of the English arrows was said to resemble a snow storm. The English goose has always been a festive bird (turkeys were much later). Traditionally the goose is stuffed with sage-and-onion stuffing.

Roast Goose

A large slab of his own grease should be tied over his breast and allowed to melt enough to grease all his skin before roasting starts. The skin of the goose is the most delicate part and the lump of grease should be removed and the breast nicely browned before serving. Apple sauce, bread sauce, plain boiled potatoes and greens are the right English usage with roast goose.

Cold roast goose is quite as good as hot and should be accompanied by a fresh watercress salad.

The drumsticks of the goose should be reserved and devilled next day.

Harvest or Michaelmas Goose

> " For all this good feasting yet art thou not loose
> Till thou give the Ploughman in harvest his goose.
> Though goose go in stubble, yet pause not for that,
> Let goose have a goose be shee leane be shee fat."

TUSSER.

The Michaelmas goose was fattened up on the stubble and gleanings left by the reapers. Young rabbits were fat from stolen corn at the same time, and, synchronising, there were also the first windfall apples for the apple sauce and the new corn for the "fermety puddings" and the "scallion onions" that must be eaten quickly. It is not accident, but design, that arranges such things as goose-and-rabbit pudding, sage-and-onion stuffings, apple sauce and dumplings.

Goose Roast with Rabbit

In a large family with many children, a farm labourer's wife told me that they used to pack the legs of a couple of rabbits into the goose, among the sage-and-onion stuffing, with slices of fat bacon. The rather dry rabbit meat absorbed the flavour of goose and stuffing, and smaller children got these "inside pieces" for their serving, as it was not so rich, and left more goose for the hungry men.

Another scheme was to roast joints of the rabbit under the goose, putting them in, when the goose was half done, and letting the rabbit be basted by the dripping goose grease. This is very good indeed, and interesting to know the idea has come down in use from the fifteenth century.

Goose Pie with Rabbit

Here is an old recipe for "Goos in a Hogepotte".

"Take a goos and make him clean and hack her into gobbets. And put in a pot and water thereto and seethe togederys. Then take pepir and hewed bread and grinde it with ginger and galingale and comyn and

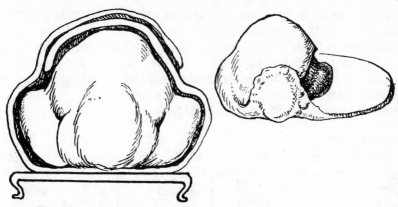

Wrapping up a bird in a huff crust before roasting (or boiling)

temper with ale and put it therto, and mynce onions and fry them and do thereto and a portion of wyne.

"Break the bones of your goose then parboil hym and season hym with salt and a little clove and you may tak a rabbet or two in it, because your Stubble geese are very fat and your Rabbets dry, so you need no Lard neither. Bake it in a paste."

An excellent compromise. We recommend that you parboil the goose together with the rabbits, then take both up and carve into neat joints, or even bone completely, and season. Break the taken-out bones and boil till reduced to a good strong stock, and use this to moisten the meat when packed into the suet crust, or into the piedish covered by a short crust.

This is a useful recipe for using up a cold goose with rabbits. The white joints only of the rabbits should be used, and they will be quite as good as the goose.

Goose (or Chicken) Pudding

This is an old English dish, and survives in Sussex and perhaps else-where. It is an elderly goose close-wrapped in paste and boiled in a cloth. Onions packed inside the goose permeate and flavour the whole. The rich fat from the bird is caught by the pastry which *would be served with the goose.*

Before potatoes, puddings of this type were more common, the solid crust forming the basis for the meat.

Chicken pudding is made in the same way. A modern recipe suggests jointing the chicken and packing it into a deep basin with a little chopped bacon or ham, green peas, very small young carrots, pepper and salt, and covering with a light suet crust. Steam as you would any boiled pudding. A fine white mushroom sauce is good with this.

Goose Grease

The fat of most fowls is soft in texture, yellow or white (stearin and elain, in varied proportion), and it all melts easily. Goose fat being the softest (liquid at 111° F.) is always called goose grease; Turkey fat is more like chicken (melting point 113° F.); while Duck fat melts at 126° F. From these figures you realise why duck, roasted, needs a quick strong heat "to start it", compared with goose or turkey.

Goose grease is always treasured by country people as very useful. Well beaten to a cream, with vinegar, lemon juice, finely chopped onion, and chopped parsley, it is used as a filling for sandwiches. It is more appetising than it sounds, having the creamy white consistency of thick mayonnaise. Where the more sturdy Teuton element has remained in Britain, it is eaten on bread, seasoned only with salt and pepper.

In most farmhouses some goose grease is kept in the medicine chest and used in many ways. The old-fashioned hot poultice, so useful in relieving an old person's bronchitis, or easing the "tight chest" of a child, is temporarily out of hospital fashion. Poultices do entail trouble and care, both in application and in easing them away, and substituting warm flannel to guard against chill—but they serve a useful purpose, especially in the country, and many a doctor, long delayed by snow or distance, has arrived to find pneumonia averted, a warmed and soothed child placidly asleep. For any fomentation, goose grease, being water-proof, is rubbed on to the skin beforehand, to prevent the moist heat unduly soaking the skin, and a little is often added to the linseed for the same reason.

Goose grease and fine lard are the only creams permitted in the dairy, both for the dairymaids' hands and the churn fitments. It is also used, in east winds or snow, to anoint the udders of cows to prevent chapping. It was used by mothers with babies for the same reason, and later when children had colds in the head, noses and lips were rubbed with goose grease, before going out into the cold.

Goose grease is also used to soften stored leather, old straps, harness, shoes, etc., or suitcases and bags were smeared with goose grease (or neat's-foot oil) and left to stand in a warm room overnight, before being rubbed soft with dubbin or washed with saddle soap.

Goose grease, melted, beaten full of yellow broom and gorse flowers, and strained, made a yellow ointment much approved for skin trouble of man and beast. A green version, made with watercress juice was more liked by the sailors and fisherfolk (*see* Cress). Both ointments probably had real value, combined with the treatment of washing and fomentation. Goose grease, melted with horse-radish juice, mustard, and turpentine, and shaken till white and creamy, made embrocation for stiffness and rheumatism. Another form was emulsified with yolk of egg, or Irish moss solutions.

Warm goose grease gently smeared into the sheep-dog's ears, and between his pads, helped him through long days out in wet snow.

Finally goose grease was good in the stable for cracked hoofs, and was also much used by proud poultry-keepers, waggoners, and shepherds, to polish the beaks, legs, hoofs, or trotters of any animals going on show. It improved the texture of the translucent horn, and showed up its natural colour.

Goose Quills and Feathers

" There were three fat ducks that once I knew—
Fat ducks and pretty ones they were too.
But he with the feather curled on his back—
O he was the fattest one! Quack, quack, quack! "

OLD SONG.

These curled feathers are sold for making paint-brushes and fishing tackle. Flight quills for pens. This is now a commercial matter between poulterers and manufacturers.

The country people themselves use the goose quills to make teats for bottle-fed lambs, and for fishing floats. In old-fashioned country houses no housemaid's box was complete without a couple of goose pinions, those strong firm plumes which were so excellent for dusting ledges. A stiff, trimmed goose pinion is also kept by the lady's-maid for taking the dust from velvet.

Quills were also used as valves and indicators for brewers and in ferment bottles. By the rise and fall of the liquid in the quill could be seen the condition within the bottle.

All painters and artists use the quills of birds to hold their brushes of beaver, camel, or sable hair. The sizes of brushes attest to this. One brush for lettering work and miniatures is made from the single small tuft of sensitive feathers that curl upon a drake's back.

We quote instructions for making a goose-quill pen from an eighteenth-century *Young Man's Companion*.

"Take the first or second quill of a goose wing, and scrape it, and hold it in your left hand, with the feather end from you. Beginning even with the back, cut a small piece off sloping, then make a slit, enter the knife in the midst of the first cut, and slit the quill up so far as you desire it. When the slit is done, cut away a piece from the other side, and fashion the nib by cutting off both sides equally. Place the nib on the nail of your left thumb, draw the edge [end?] into it half through, then turn it and turn the edge down, and cut it off. Let your ink be thin, and your paper be white and well gummed. Rub your paper lightly with gumrack, beaten fine and tied up in a linen cloth—which makes the paper bear the ink better and the pen run more smoothly."

TURKEY

" Turkeys heresays hops and beer
All came to England in one year."

Being a north-country woman, I have no enthusiasm for turkey.[1] Some people like veal stuffing, some chestnut stuffing, and some recommend that veal stuffing be put one end and chestnut stuffing the other, which seems sensible.

Turkey Roast

To roast, butter the bird well and hang it, legs up, before a clear fire. Baste it very well. Half an hour before it is done, remove the butter paper, rub the breast well with butter, and let it brown nicely. Serve with bread sauce and baked sausages.

Cranberry sauce is served with the turkey, also chestnut sauce made by rubbing chestnuts through a sieve, and adding a spoonful of white sugar and a glass of sherry.

Veal Stuffing

Take ½ lb. of very fine breadcrumbs, 5 tablespoonfuls of finely chopped suet, 1 tablespoonful of chopped parsley, 1 teaspoonful of powdered thyme, 1 teaspoonful of lemon rind chopped up very fine, and pepper and salt. Mix these some time before wanted, and before using the bird bind together with a beaten egg.

Chestnut Stuffing

Take four to five dozen chestnuts, cut a small slit in the skin and fry the nuts till the peel comes off easily. Then boil them in a little gravy till quite done. Mash lightly into half their quantity of breadcrumbs, add salt and pepper, and an egg of butter, and stuff the turkey.

[1] Northern farmers have chicken for Easter, duck and green peas for Whitsun, and a fine meaty goose for Christmas. Most northern farmers say that turkey is only like a big fowl. The best turkeys come from Norfolk.

GAME

" But yet men; rage not beyond thy need,
Deem it not glory to swell in tyranny,
Thou art of blood; joy not to see things bleed,
Thou fearest death; think; they are loath to die—
A plaint of guiltless heart doth pierce the sky."

SIR PHILIP SIDNEY.

Blackcock

A rather dry bird. It should be hung as long as possible, then drawn, wiped, trussed as a fowl, and a piece of fat placed inside it before roasting. Baste it sparingly; it will take about half an hour if large. Just before serving, crisp a slice of oaten bread in the basting fat, squeeze lemon juice over it, and place the bird on it to serve. Gravy may be served with this game, and a rich well-flavoured bread sauce.

Grilled Blackcock

Split flat, spatchcock fashion.

Rub both sides with butter and grill quickly, turning and basting frequently.

Serve with potato straws, and the dripping from the birds seasoned with a squeeze of lemon juice or a suspicion of cider, in a hot tureen.

Capercailzie

Roast like chicken, covering the breast, but as it is rather a dry bird, a piece of well-pounded juicy steak and a knob of butter inside is a great improvement.

Serve with fried breadcrumbs and watercress salad.

Try brown toast, or oatcake, as an accompaniment.

Grouse

Roast Grouse. Roast like chicken, putting on a breast-protector of fat bacon, and if possible wrapping around in vine leaves. Brush inside and out with oil or melted butter before cooking. Place a slice of lightly browned toast under the birds, while the cooking is done, to catch the dripping, and serve the birds on these slices, with seasoned gravy made from the bones of the neck and a glass of red wine.

Bread sauce, piles of fried crumbs, watercress, and wafer potatoes are the correct accompaniments.

Sportsman's grouse. Very well hung: for a fortnight is best. Stuff with butter and rowan berries, or better still with the little wild raspberries of the mountainside. The juicy fruit melts almost away during cooking, but the melted, spicy, buttery juice is all the gravy required.

Grouse pie with hare.

> " Grouse pie with hare in the middle is fare
> Which duly concocted with science and care
> Doctor Kitchener says is beyond all compare
> And a tenderer leveret Robin had never eat."
>
> *Ingoldsby Legends.*

(1893 recipe.) Cut thin slices of venison, sprinkle with black pepper and lay in a deep dish. Joint two pigeons, and a brace of grouse, and pack around the sides; take the best parts of a hare, two mutton kidneys, a teacupful of chopped mushrooms, 2 hard-boiled eggs quartered, and fill the spaces with diced bacon. A few forcemeat balls may be added near the top. Make a good gravy with the bones of the hare, the trimmings of the birds and meat, and a glass of port wine; fill the piedish and cover closely before baking. Just before it is done, cover with a rich short pastry. Serve hot or cold.

Guinea Fowl

In season February to June. Keep it as long as possible and treat like roast fowl. If stuffed, put some finely chopped bacon in the forcemeat, and butter the bird well as it is inclined to be dry.

Partridge

Can be grilled or roasted like blackcock.
Gypsies stuff them with mushrooms.

Autumn Partridge Pot. A Norfolk dish; for old tough birds.

Pluck and dress, discarding the rib-bones and necks, but keeping the backs. Put necks and rib bones to stew for gravy, while you prepare the "pot".

Roll each joint in seasoned fine oatmeal (*not* flour). Put a slice of fat ham or bacon at the bottom of the dish, and pack the joints down on to this, filling spaces with peeled fresh mushrooms, sliced onion, and a few small tomatoes. Add a clove for each bird, and a bay leaf in the middle of the pot. A light strewing of powdered herbs (chiefly thyme), and pepper and salt (unless the bacon is very salt). Now strain into the bone gravy a glassful of sharp red wine (the sediment from the bottles of burgundy or port were treasured for this dish). See the joints are completely covered (the pot lid should be fitted on with a rim of huff paste to get a close fit). Bring very slowly to boiling point, remove at once and let it stew on the cool stove overnight.

It is usually eaten cold for breakfast with brown bread and butter or hot dry toast.

Peacocks

" Peacock is euyll fleashe to disiest, for it can not be rosted or soden ynough."

1480.

"At a feeste Roiall Pecokkes shall be dight on this Manere. Take and flee off the skynne with the fedurs tayle and the nekke and the hed thereon, then take the skyn with all the fedurs and lay hit on a table abrode and straue thereon grounden comyn. Then take the pecokke and roste hym and endore hym with rawe yolkes of egges and when he is rosted take hym off and let hym coole awhile and take and sowe hym in his skyn and gilde his combe and so serue hym forth with the last cours."

Pheasant

There is as much difference between pheasant well hung and cooked as game, and the same bird cooked fresh, as there is between two different breeds of birds. One is game, the other practically brown chicken.

Pheasant fresh. If fresh, it is mild, and should be treated exactly like chicken. It may be stuffed with a very light closely minced forcemeat, or, better, a stuffing containing fat sugar-cured pork. It is rather a dry bird, and the fat and the steam from the stuffing keep it juicy. To be served cold, brown appetisingly (removing the fat from the breast), and as soon as you take it from the oven, wrap it closely in a cloth wrung out in cold water, or cider. Wrap it very carefully, putting another cloth outside again, and slip it into a haybox or wrap in a rug. As the bird is well greased from roasting, the damp will not penetrate, but it will keep the steam in and the bird will be more tender when cut.

Pheasant well hung. Take a well-hung game pheasant, pluck very carefully (as the skin will be soft), and flour with oatmeal. Add a piece of well-pounded juicy steak inside the bird, previously brushing the bird inside and out with melted butter to keep it succulent while cooking.

Serve with bread sauce, fried crumbs and red gooseberry jelly.

Note. The pheasant (a foreign bird) is good stuffed with raisins and apples, or, after well buttering within, with a small bunch of red grapes.

Pheasant poached. Pheasant is fairly common in England in summer, when the cock invades the cottage gardens to sneak the peas. You catch him quietly, with a paper bag and raisins.

Smear the paper cone inside with treacle or gum, put a few raisins at the bottom, and prop the bag up amongst the peas. When he sticks his head in he cannot see where to go, so he stands still till you fetch him.

Pigeon

> " A pigeon tower frame of stone,
> A fishpond dark and deep to see
> To cast nets in when need there be
> Which never yet was known to lack
> A plenteous store of perch and jack."
>
>   *Iola Goch.*

Woodpigeons, plump on stolen corn, are like tiny brown poultry. They are meaty little birds, and should be cleaned and plucked very close, and finished off with a stiff brush dipped in oil or lard. A thick chest-protector of fat bacon or ham should be tied over their breasts, and they may be stuffed, grilled or roasted exactly like very small chickens, and served with gravy and bread sauce.

The livers, pounded with any left-over pigeon, mace, and pepper and salt, make a good potted meat.

Pigeon Pie (with dumpling crust; very substantial)

Pigeons that are old and tough had better be cooked in a pie. Take 4—6 pigeons, dress and joint the birds, and at once put the neck and backs to simmer for gravy with 4 cloves, salt and pepper.

Take a piedish, grease it well, and lay at the bottom either a bay leaf, a scrap of garlic, or a little shredded shallot (one or the other, not all three). Cover these with a thin slice of raw beef, notched into squares, and put the pigeon pieces over, seasoning well. Pack in half a dozen small mush-

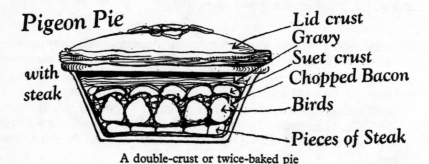

A double-crust or twice-baked pie

rooms and, over all, the scraps from a ham-bone, or bacon trimmings diced small. Fill up with half of the spiced gravy, and cover with a very thin suet crust that should lie flat down on the meat inside the piedish. Cover the dish with a lid and bake the pie for about an hour. This inside crust keeps in the aroma, and by the end of an hour should be thoroughly cooked and light as bread.

Take out the pie, cut this dumpling crust into squares, and pack it down amongst the pigeon meat, which should be now really tender. Fill up the dish with the rest of the hot gravy, put a light shortcrust paste over the piedish in the usual way and return to the oven to bake for another 20—30 minutes till the crust is done crisp and brown.

To serve, cut a slice out of the top crust, lift out a square of the dumpling paste, arrange a pigeon, the piece of beef it cooked upon, some mushrooms, and ham or bacon scraps, upon this square of paste (like fellow travellers on a raft); pour gravy round, and top it off with the slice of pie crust. The suet crust will have absorbed all the flavours and be very savoury. This "Inside paste" or "Huff pastry" is an old fashioned idea, and takes the place of potatoes or bread to eat with the meat. It was this double crust that gave the idea to the potters. Sometimes the inside suet crust is not broken but just submerged under more gravy, hard-boiled eggs quartered, more mushrooms or fruit, or some filling that does not take so long to cook as the main dish.

Woodpigeon as Ortolan

> " What tooth or stomach is strong enough to feed
> Upon a goose my grandma kept to breed?
> Why must old pigeons; and they stale; be dressed,
> When there are so many squab ones in the nest? "
>
> KING.

In the corn-growing counties woodpigeons are too plentiful, especially in the autumn in harvest-time—and it is at that time you are thinning the coldhouse vines for grapes, so prepare a few pigeons this way. Pluck, dress, and trim very clean (ortolans are not drawn, but pigeons must be), wipe inside and out, and put to soak in a deep plateful of cooking oil— olive oil is best, but unsalted lard, melted, or any very liquid cooking fat will serve. Meanwhile boil enough pearl barley to stuff the birds, with a scrape of fine garlic and a bunch of sweet herbs, such as marjoram, basil, lemon balm, tarragon, etc. (all freshly picked); we must leave the exact selection and blending to your good taste and garden—choose the lemon-scented and aromatic ones, and use as fresh as possible. Drain the now well-flavoured barley, season it, and toss in a little butter; drain the pigeons, put a bay leaf and a drop of onion juice inside each bird, stuff tightly with the barley; wrap each in a vine leaf, grease well (don't put a slice of bacon on their breasts for this dish, but butter or lard should be rubbed over the vine leaf), and roast, or braise gently until tender.

Remove the vine leaves 5 minutes before the birds are done, to brown them nicely, and fill the dish with the small, rather sour thinnings of the English grapes, piling them round the birds, and giving the fruit just time to burst and the juice to run and mingle with the gravy. Serve on slices of toast garnished with vine leaves and fresh grapes, and serve a sauce made from the grape juice and butter, strained, to accompany the dish.

Note. If the grapes are very tart (unripe) it is permitted to put a little sugar or a spoonful of honey among them while cooking, but don't overdo this.

Plover

Pluck and truss. It is incorrect to draw the bird.

Tie fat on the breast and roast for 20 minutes, basting well, remove the fat just before it is done, and dredge with flour to brown nicely. Put slices of toast under the grid to catch the drip and serve on this toast, garnished with cress and with lemon juice in melted butter.

Some people prefer to draw the bird. In this case wipe well with butter inside and out and put a hot roast apple and a pat of butter inside just before roasting. This keeps it nice and moist, and the acid is good. Crab-apple juice in melted butter is also good for serving with the birds.

In Norfolk, where these birds are plentiful, plovers are made into a pie.

Plover's eggs. Should be boiled for 15—20 minutes, cooled in cold water, and rubbed over with just a scrap of oil to polish them.

They are served as laid, in a rosette, points to the middle, in a nest of moss.

Ptarmigan

Roast like grouse. Serve on toast that has been cooked beneath the grid, and with bread sauce very well cloved.

Quails

These never seem really English. They should be wrapped in vine leaves and roasted like any other small bird.

Leave the vine leaves on, and lay them on a fresh vine leaf when you serve them.

Snipe, Ortolan, Plover and Woodcock

Experts decree that these birds should be plucked, trussed, and roasted undrawn. It is also correct to leave on the heads, turning the long beak of the snipe sideways, to act as a skewer.

They are roasted with fat bacon and ham, and are served on squares of toast with wine sauce.

Teal

Brush over, inside and out, with butter or unsalted lard, and roast within half an hour, basting frequently with the juice and turning once.

Serve garnished with watercress, slices of lemon, and a tart vinegar sauce.

Widgeon

Roast and serve with orange juice.

Rooks

A rook pie is not worth making unless some large rookery has to be thinned, when it is a pity to waste the bag of young birds brought in by the countrymen. Rooks mate in November, and live paired till the spring, when they nest together. Notice the pattern of paired birds in the winter flights and subsequent "sets" of two adults and five to eight young birds grouped in the summer flights. Rookeries are well-organised communities.

A pie

Young Rook Pie. These young rooks "cleared" in spring are the size of a small pigeon, but the breast and top part of the thighs are the only parts which are edible. The back and skin meat is bitter and black. Therefore the birds must be skinned, and divided completely before cooking. The pieces of breast meat are only the size and something the shape of a large cockle-shell.

Put these pieces to simmer in a dish of milk and water. Meanwhile butter a shallow dish, lay at the bottom a slice of juicy meat, preferably thin steak, or a slice from a round of beef. Pepper and salt it and lay down the rook breasts, bone side down and round side up (looking like a cobbled pavement). Cut thin strips of bacon, weave them into a lattice over the birds, cover with crust, bake briskly and serve with mustard.

Wild Duck

Should be lightly roasted. It has a pleasant salt tang, but if from the low seaflats may taste as bad as any oily seagull.

Wipe inside and out and butter well all over. Roast in a hot oven for 20 minutes, basting every 5 minutes, the last time dredging with flour, and peppering lightly in order to brown crisply. Serve with hot burst oranges.

The first time I came across this English recipe was in the Transvaal. While the ducks were roasting, small mandarin oranges were laid, like a golden floor, over the bottom of the pan 10 minutes before cooking was finished. They were then swollen, bursting, and soft. Just before serving the pips were scooped out with a small spoon, and a lump of butter and sugar put into each orange. Watercress and burst oranges make so bright a garnishing that wild roasted duck is one of the most pleasant dishes. Fine wafer potatoes are the only vegetable needed, though string beans are permissible, and a crisp salad commendable.

Small Birds

Larks, sparrows, and small blackbirds.

These should not be taken for food as it upsets the balance of the countryside, and the lack of the birds causes plagues of insects amongst the crops. To be sure, blackbirds and thrushes steal fruit, but before that fruit is ripe they have reared two or three families on small insects.

Roast Swan

Prepare as a turkey if young. If old the same treatment as an antique fowl.

Brush over inside and out with clarified dripping, and dust, also inside and out, with powdered mace, mixed herbs, and a little allspice. Stuff, using plenty of chopped fat pork in the stuffing, and sew up tightly.

Make a crust of flour and water and a scrap of dripping, roll it evenly, and encase the bird in it, damping the paste and wrapping a double thickness over the breast.

Roast in a moderately hot oven 2 or 3 hours, according to size. Try with a skewer, and if this pierces it easily, it is tender. When done, crack off the crust. You will find it cracks off easily in large pieces if the bird is previously green greased and thickly dusted with the herbs, as these form a steamy, aromatic casing over the inside surface of the bird.

Dredge with flour and pepper, baste very well, and return to the oven or to the spit to roast quickly for about 20 minutes. The condiments are the same as those for goose.

The Barnacle Goose. From a MS. of 1100.

Puffins and Barnacles

" There are likewise many birds called barnacles which nature produces in a wonderful manner . . . they resemble marsh geese, but are smaller. Being at first gummy excrescences from pine-beames floating on the waters, and then enclosed in shells to secure their free growth they hang by their beaks, like seaweeds attached to the timber. Being in the process of time well covered with feathers they either fall into the water or take their flight in the free air, their nourishment and growth being supplied while they are bred in this very unaccountable manner from the juices of the wood in the seawater. I have often seen with my own eyes more than a thousand minute embryos of birds of this species on the seashore. No eggs are laid by these birds. . . . In no corner of the world are they seen either to pair or build nests. Hence, in some parts of Ireland bishops and men of religion make no scruple of eating these birds on fasting days, as not being flesh because they are not borne of flesh. But these men are curiously drawn into error."

Giraldus Cambrensis.

Puffin Island, off the coast of Anglesey, and Penmon's beautiful Columbaria, share testimony to the monks' good appetites, because though the pigeons and poultry were *meat*, the puffin, being a seabird (and distinctly fishy in flavour), *could* be eaten on fish days.

Possibly puffins were the original of the mediaeval barnacle goose—that mediaeval marvel, which was a shell-fish fastened to a tree by the water for half its life, and then, opening, dropped its embryo into the water where it developed into a bird.

The mediaeval historian was probably misled by seeing some ducks—which nest in trees—getting their young ones down to the water. That, and the clusters of huge river mussel shells clinging to submerged tree trunks in tidal estuaries, very likely gave rise to the legend.

EGGS

EGGS (Historically)

"Hens' eggs are the best eggs, and the best be those that be new."

FOURTEENTH-CENTURY COOK-BOOK

At least eight different sorts of eggs have been eaten in England. Domestic hens were general, and breeds localised. A very short-legged hen called a "Creepie" laid small eggs, Ducks eggs varied in fashion, Goose eggs, plovers eggs, seagulls eggs of several sorts were gathered, and guinea fowl eggs came later. For religious purposes fish eggs (cod's roe, or the "wombe of a luce") counted as eggs, not fish. Eggs of swan and other wild birds may have been taken, specially in the fen districts, but, as we read of peacock eggs being set under a hen as early as the eleventh century, they were probably too precious to eat. Turkey eggs (from the sixteenth century), were carefully kept for sittings under an experienced "Broody". Curiously, eggs were not often boiled before the sixteenth century; they baked well in the soft ash of the wood fire (you can't do this with coal ash—the embers are too fierce).

Eggs were seldom eaten more than one or two at a time. The generally accepted opinion was that "one egg is gentility, two sufficient and more excess", and a note says "all eggs hard roasted be grosse meat".

Eggs were often poached, and, knowing the exquisite etiquette of the early Middle Ages, I wondered how they ate a poached egg with their fingers when sharing a platter with a partner at the table. (The modern taking of partners into the dining-room is a reminder of the days when you shared one plate together when you reached the table.)

At the end of the thirteenth century one learns that "a fried egg does not need instruction, but dig not at it with your thumb turned down—move it about with the point of your knife". But the softly poached egg remained a problem—till I learnt that "one egg must NEVER be served between guests" (you get one each), and "after stripping off the white with the fingers, you may mop up the yolk with a piece of bread". In the fifteenth and sixteenth centuries eggs were plentiful, but it is not till the flush of farming in the eighteenth century that one reads the lavish "Poach an ample sufficiency of eggs and lay on buttered toast on a flat dish and cover with a cream of butter and new milk". After the "enclosures", the loss of common lands, and change-over in harvesting methods reduced poultry-keeping as a farm by-product. The old name "Michelmas goose" was a direct result of the birds being set to glean the cleared cornlands, and the hen-wife, or goose-girl, moved the flocks out to the fields or the commons, or along the seashore, as part of the routine of egg production. (Bee-keepers still move their bees to the changing flower localities in this way.) Till the twelfth century the "doing of things" in county houses (from cheese-making to slaughtering,) made the old-fashioned household life far better for the keeping of hens—even during my mother's childhood, in the 1870's, eggs were still 25 for a shilling, and plentiful at that!

But the present-day hen has to rely almost entirely on expensive "poultry food" and the most diligent hen could toil for miles after a combined harvester without getting a peck.

A fair conclusion, bringing this short sequence to the twentieth-century war time and ration period, is a cartoon showing one of England's stately homes, with the impoverished owner sitting forlornly at one end of his baronial dining table, while the housekeeper bends respectfully to enquire, "How will you take your egg this month, my lord?"

Now to date (1953) there are modern methods of importing foreign eggs and classifying and collecting the home-grown, but the new-laid eggs from hens kept under natural conditions on grass cannot be imported. The intensive egg-forcing in horrible wire batteries may produce more eggs, but they are not of perfect quality and flavour (and, knowing the conditions of production, one cannot like them).

Birds are very adaptable, and I have seen road-making parties in the High Bush setting hens under the trees behind their tents; so I wonder if our new afforested lands upon the mountainsides could not be combined with hen farms. The birds would keep down the insect pests and pick up a natural diet to supplement the one evening feed that would bring them into the laying-pens. It might be worth trying to combine these two rural industries, and it would give the foresters' isolated womenfolk their own interest. The wind in the trees is their music; but the cluck of an industrious hen and new-laid eggs for breakfast should add to the amenities. They might start with guinea-fowl, who fly up into the trees to roost and so avoid foxes. Mediaeval people kept hens loose in the woods, so it might be worth retrying.

Wild-birds' Eggs

"Arnshead, a promontory, consists of high cliffs which shelter pigeon-gulls, razorbills, ravens, guilemots, coramants and herons and many other birds; the eggs of these, and the Peregrine falcon, are sought after as delicious food and considered a great

treat to the Epicurean. The price paid is sufficient inducement
for the poor to follow the adventurous trade of eggtaking."

GUIDE, 1700.

Seagulls' eggs are still a seasonal industry in some districts, but nothing
like the old days, when they were collected from the rock face and lowered
in baskets to the boats waiting below.

The Bass Rock was for years considered valuable for the sollan geese
there; some eggs were taken, but more often the young geese were sold
for eating, and the feathers and down were also valued in the days when
all who could slept on feather-beds. In *Catriona* R. L. Stevenson mentions that the minister's stipend of N. Berwick was paid partly out of the
Bass products. The seabird eggs sold around the coast were sometimes
fishy in taste (like the penguin eggs sold at the Cape), but were usually
eaten after so many herrings, so that the flavour passed unnoticed. I had
gulls' eggs in Durness, served on hot buttered toast spread with bloater
paste. They were very good.

Breakfast Eggs[1]

The breakfast egg was a Victorian institution (only a century old);
whatever else there was for breakfast—kidneys, chops, bacon, or ked-
geree, with tea or coffee, marmalade or honey—there was always a
meek little cluster of boiled eggs, set modestly apart upon a chased silver
stand, with their spoons beside them (like St. Ursula's virgins on shipboard).

Really nice homely families kept their little flotilla of breakfast eggs

The china hen, covering a shallow hot-water dish, which
kept the family eggs coddled nicely, on the breakfast table

[1] In one of her detective stories Dorothy Sayers skilfully indicates disorganisation in
a ducal household by giving them bloaters for breakfast on Sunday morning instead of
sausages, and for years it was customary to say of the unknown breakfaster, "If he don't
eat fish he can always take an egg."

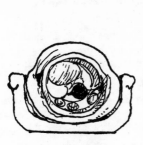

| Boned and stuffed fowl in earthenware bakepan (section) | Boned and filled fowl, set in a pastry case, with pastry head and frilled paper tail, a copy of the "china hen" | Pastry head baked round a pie prop |

coddled in hot water under a china hen. Many of these hens were beautifully modelled. Our hen is of pure-white china with dull-gold beak, her crimson topknot is studded with white raised dots, in toadstool pattern, her tail smoothly plumed, and her basket-nest most carefully moulded and touched with gold. She has a pure but friendly eye. There were handsome black hens (like plump matrons in black alpaca). Black hens usually had gold-lustre spots and white wattles. There were naturalistic brown hens on yellow baskets, and rather coarse red-and-white Staffordshire hens on green tub bases.

The bases in all cases held the eggs in hot water, which kept them from going hard and drying up. (*See* Boiled Eggs.)

An interesting point about the china hens was their artistic influence. Just as the potters had been constrained to copy the cook's pie-crust design in making "pie-crust ware", so the Victorian cook copied the potter's design, and when making a boned fowl galantine used to model the pastry-case on the china hen off the breakfast table, adding a pastry-head (baked on a pie lift) and a cutlet frill-tail and putting a plaited wreath

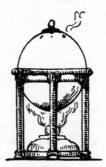

A silver spirit lamp and eggboiler
for the breakfast table or sideboard

of dough around the top of the pastry crust. This dish was almost a direct revival of the mediaeval open "coffyn".

Smaller, larger, or less-punctual households had table egg-boilers and "did" their own eggs for themselves as they came down. These silver boilers shared "spirit lamps" with the coffee-pot and the long polished "sluggard" that held the toast, hot milk, bacon, etc.

"Breakfast trays" and "single gents" had egg-cosies—not today's church-bazaar fancies, but solid thick woollen coats. Cooks today crack the boiled egg on top "to let the steam out", but the old-fashioned idea was to keep the steam in—as a new-laid egg should be steamy and milky within.

According to superstition, empty egg-shells should always be broken up—lest witches make boats thereof. After pulverising, the shells were put, with pounded oyster shells, into the hens' food pail. Raw egg-shells are used to settle coffee-grounds and clear aspic jelly.

My grandfather's thick efficient egg cosy knitted in scarlet wool, with a pom-pom atop. Like a nightcap.

An egg timer (three minutes and a half)

Boiled Eggs

Boiled eggs take $3\frac{1}{2}$ minutes if put into boiling water, but new-laid eggs should not be boiled, as the white hardens before the yolk is properly set. This accounts for the egg which "seems done" when cautiously tried, but discloses an unexpected raw jelly round the centre. The completely cooked but not hard egg is coddled, by being put into boiling water and then the pan drawn aside so that the egg lies in "just-not-boiling" water for 5 to 6 minutes. Eggs cooked in this way can be kept in hot water for some time without becoming hard, and it preserves the natural moisture in the new-laid egg.

Poached Eggs

Poached eggs are cooked directly in boiling water and served on hot buttered toast (pepper-and-salt the toast also). Eggs cooked *over* boiling water in little patty-pans are steamed eggs.

A poached egg on spinach is classic, but set upon a wheel of small carrot "thinnings" is less well known.

A buck rabbit is a poached egg on a welsh-rabbit's bed of toasted cheese, between two fried tomatoes.

Some affirm that this is a Buckinghamshire rabbit. Two eggs poached in well-seasoned meat extract or vegetable bouillon make a quick light meal. They can be drained and set upon hot buttered toast, with the bouillon served separately, or the bouillon may be poured over freshly made dry toast and the eggs laid on top (serve with extra-dry toast separately). (This is rather a good dish for people not able to take butter.)

Fried Eggs

Fried eggs should be broken into boiling fat in a shallow pan; and though they may be basted, or the white wrapped over the yolk (using a long hot iron spoon), the eggs must not be left in the pan after the fat has ceased boiling or they will lose their crisp brown frilled edge and become limp and greasy.

Scrambled, Buttered, or Rumbled Eggs

There are two main schools: one (which I believe to be correct) breaks in the eggs direct, so that particles of clear white and clear yellow remain in the creamy mass. The other school beats the eggs together first, maintaining it gives a smoother texture. Melt butter in a saucepan, pepper-and-salt it (about the size of a walnut of butter for each egg is average, though some farms put about as much butter as egg). When the butter is hot but not boiling break (or pour) in the eggs and stir round and round over a gentle heat till soft and creamy. It must not boil or burn, and the instant it creams scoop it out on to hot buttered toast and serve at once.

If the toast is spread with anchovy or bloater paste it is good, but in this case go easy with the salt in the egg mixture.

Omelet

A good omelet requires skill and thought. Allow two eggs for one person, three for two people, five or six for four people, and eight for six people. Never make larger sizes unless you have exceptional equipment, or the outside film (which should be as fine as gold-beater's skin) becomes tough before the interior is set. Also serving too large an omelet without crushing the texture is difficult—even for four people it is better to cook two pans simultaneously, otherwise folding over spills the suave juice.

An omelet is a friendly dish—the friends must be seated and have wine or coffee served to them, so that they await cheerfully. Never cook the omelet till you have seen the recipient seated, with his napkin tucked down, ready to begin. No omelet should take longer than 5 minutes, and $3\frac{1}{2}$ minutes is usually enough.

Method for a Savoury Omelet for Two Persons

Set the filling to cook gently in butter. (Chopped mushrooms, shreds of chicken and ham, or freshly chopped herbs are plain savoury fillings; crisp bacon dice and fine onions are good in winter, green peas or asparagus tips in summer.) The filling should be slight, but very well flavoured and juicy.

In this case we make an October filling:

Dice two dark mushrooms, cut four inches of fine bacon diced, a sprinkle of fresh herbs, and pepper (no salt—the bacon will supply that). Fry slowly and thoroughly in a little butter in a rather deep frying-pan that should be kept for omelets only. While these are cooking, break three eggs, putting the whites into one basin and the yolks into another. Take one half egg-shell of water to each egg, measuring into the shells as you break them (this measures accurately according to the size of the eggs). Put the water with the yolks, and add salt and pepper, but add nothing but a dust of pepper to the whites. Beat the whites till light snow, but not so long that it becomes cream (i.e. till the whites have expanded their fullest froth and there is no trace of clear white below when left to stand a minute). Now, without wiping the whisk, beat the yolks, and water, and they should also raise a fine froth. Now drain the cooked filling from the omelet-pan and set both to keep hot—see the butter is again smoking hot—tilt the yolks into the whites, blend lightly together and instantly pour the whole golden foam into the pan. It should make a delicious "frou-frou" sound as it greets the hot butter, and the top of the foam should quiver delicately. Do not touch it at this stage—let it set for an instant, then slip it under the grill to seal the top, or hold a red-hot pan (or salamander) over it, the principle being to enclose the juices of the egg within a silken skin, so that the heated froth expands upwards and outwards. Some people like the egg centre to be still slightly runny; if so, take it off sooner. If you want a firm set, cook slightly longer—see it is loose round the rim (it should have become free of the pan almost at once) —and slide out on to a hot dish, putting in the filling and folding over in one swift movement. Serve instantly.

A sweet omelet may be flavoured with rum or sherry and have fruit or jam filling. Honey and cinnamon, with a sprinkling of hot cider on the folded top, is uncommon. The filling should suit the occasion, and the flavouring of the egg mixture should suit the filling.

Wild Omelets

To travellers: the best omelets on earth are made over the white ash of the camp-fire. Brown the tops with a red-hot charcoal of timber, held almost two inches above the omelet's surface as it rises in the pan.

Egg-and-Apple Soufflé

The ordinary type of soufflé is often made—but this older apple-and-egg dish seems very like the Anglo-Norman coffer pastries.

Butter the *outside* of a cake-tin (or baking jar) and cover with thin short crust. Bake it standing upside-down, and when cool slip out the tin. Brush over the inside with melted butter. Have ready some baked apple pulp that has been sweetened with castor sugar and into which you have incorporated some finely sliced lemon peel (candied). Half fill the pastry-case with this light pulp, and then cover it with an almost equal quantity of stiffly whipped white of egg that has been lightly sweetened and strewn with fine lemon-peel. Return to the oven long enough to set this white meringue. It can be eaten hot, but is usually a cold sweet, and may be very prettily decorated with angelica and lemon-peel. The yolks of the eggs are made into "glass custards" and served with the cold sweet, and should have a little orange-flower water added. The use of orange-flower water, rose water, and elderflour, etc., used to be very general for egg-and-cream sweets—they are very delicate and pleasant. They should be used sparingly, as they are more for aroma than flavour.

Caramel Custard

Proportions can vary to taste. This is of average richness.

Take a deep round cake tin, and in it dissolve two heaped teaspoons of sugar in two egg-shells of boiling water. Boil this syrup carefully till it turns a golden brown and is a mass of froth. To test: set the tin on to a plateful of cold water, and if sufficiently cooked the bubbling sugar will flatten out into a smooth base of hard amber toffee. If it does not set hard, boil a little longer, but on no account let it burn.

Caramel pudding

Meanwhile, beat two eggs into a pint of milk, sweeten and flavour with ratafia. Pour this custard upon the firm toffee base and bake in the slowest possible oven till just set. Turn out when cold. The caramel juice that flows down and around is the only sauce needed for this pudding.

A spot of ratafia added to the boiled sugar just before setting improves the flavour of the caramel juice.

Custard for a Hedgehog

This is not a furze-pig, but a sponge cake baked in a hedgehog mould and soaked in noyau or cherry or almond brandy. The hog is then turned out on to a dish and covered with split almond spikes (set in rows backwards). Two currants make his eyes, which are almost submerged under the pool of custard that flows round his base.

Relic of the days when hedgehogs were supposed to suck from cows' teats as they lay sleeping on the grass. A thirteenth-century story of the witch who was supposed to send a leather bag "to suck the kyne in the pasture" was probably based on seeing some innocent hedgehogs scuttling back from where they had been eating the grass slugs that clustered round the cow-droppings in the farm fields. They would look, in the dusk, like little brown leather bags, and hedgehogs are very fond of milk. (In dry weather, the surest way to make friends with a hedgehog family is to put out milk for the mother who is suckling her kits.)

To "make a hedgehog" use the sponge-cake recipe—and this custard:

One pint of milk, the yolks of four eggs and whites beaten separately, sugar to taste, and either two laurel leaves infused in the milk (they give an almond flavour) or noyau. Boil the milk (with flavouring and sugar), and when just off the boil pour over the beaten egg yolks, stir in the beaten whites, and return to a gentle heat (a double saucepan or water bath is best) and stir gently till thick. Add the noyau and pour round the hoggie.

English Noyau of Beech Leaves

In a close-covered jar steep as many beech leaves as the jar may hold and be covered by gin. Steep for six days, and strain off the gin (repeat if not sufficiently strongly flavoured). To every pint of gin add 1 lb. of sugar dissolved in about ½ pint of boiling water, and a dash of brandy. Mix, and bottle when cold. A few bitter almonds in their brown skins may be added, and some makers use more brandy. It varies locally, and seems to be a Buckinghamshire speciality. One old lady said they made it of beech *nuts* in her young days.

"Caudele eyren myt amydon" (Custard with Cornflour and Eggs)

This is an interesting Norman introduction to the use of cornflour in thickening custards. (The very ancestor of all the modern makes of "custard powder".)

> "Nym eyren and sweney well togedere. chauf ale and do therto.
> Lye it with *amydon*. Do therto a porcion of suger and a perty of
> hony and a perti of safron. boillehit and gif it forth.

"*Amydon*—to make. Nym whete at midsomer—salt yt and do it
in a faire vessel. Do water therto that the whete be heled. Let it
stande 11 days and 11 nights and every day whesh well thy whete
and at the end of IX days bray hit wel in a morter and drie hit in
ye sonne. Do it in a faire vessel and couvere hit forth [with]."

The Old English Sponge Cake

This was made entirely of eggs, sugar and fine flour. It was the basis
of many "made up" sweet dishes (such as "hedgehog") and was frequently baked in specially designed tin moulds. When served as a cake
a crust was given to the sponge by greasing and then dusting the inside
of the mould with a thick coating of sugar and flour. A tall architectural
mould, crusted this way, turned out a cake that looked like a miniature
cathedral carved in ivory.

The method of making a "light sponge" varies with each expert—some
beat the egg mixture over hot water, some beat whites and yolks separately, but the resultant cake is a feathery-light texture of sugared egg.

Later the Victorians added butter, which gives the sponge mixture a
different texture, halfway to a Madeira sponge (which is compounded
completely differently). This more solid type baked better in flat tins
and resulted in the "Victoria sandwich", which was spread with jam
and dusted with sugar. Nowadays nearly all sponge mixtures are baked
flat and miscalled after their fillings as "cream sponge", "sandwich cake",
"chocolate sponge", etc.; and the Victorian sandwich sponge is gradually
becoming a "layre cake" (which is again completely different in method
and texture).

We give one simple old-fashioned sponge cake of eggs. Take three
fresh eggs and beat lightly in a deep basin—add one large cup of sugar
that has been softened with two large tablespoons of boiling water. Beat
the eggs and dissolving warm sugar vigorously for 30 minutes. By this
time it should be a firm froth. Now fold in, very lightly, a large cup of
fine fresh self-raising flour. Put the mixture into the previously crusted
baking-tin and cook in a hot oven for 10–15 minutes. When the top
feels firm to the touch it is done. Allow a few minutes for it to shrink
away from the sides of the tin before tilting it out on a wire tray on the
kitchen table. Do not carry the cake into a cold room till it is quite cold
and the crust crisp. Some makers add the hot water direct to the egg-
and-sugar mixture, and some (if the eggs are not quite fresh) use a little
more water, but this is an excellent average proportion.

Sponge Fingers

The long savoy biscuits are a form of crisp sponge, and were served
with egg nogs and light sweet wines, such as Madeira cake was served

with Madeira wine. In some country districts they were nicknamed "funeral fingers", being laid out with the sherry to greet visiting mourners. My aunt told me that in Wales in the 'seventies it was correct to give little faggots of these biscuits, neatly tied up with black tape and tissue paper, to children to eat on the long cold drive to the funeral.

Their more cheerful use nowadays is to serve as a crisp barrier around standing creams and jellies.

Egg and Lemon Jelly (using Sponge Biscuits)

Coat the inside of a straight-sided mould with a little melted jelly and line it with savoy biscuits, neatly fitted together. Leave a small pool of the jelly at the bottom of the mould and decorate this as you like. (White split almond daisies around yellow lemon-peel centres are pretty; or cut angelica leaves simple, and the flavour blends well.) Now dissolve two lemon jelly squares with 8 tablespoons of hot water, and stir in the juice of four good lemons. Whip the whites of four eggs to snow, and gradually whip in the cooling jelly mixture and a few spoonfuls of castor sugar.

Egg and lemon jelly. Section: clear
jelly, cloudy foam

Keep the whole as light and fluffy as possible, and when on the point of setting pour gently into the lined mould to set.

Note. Any biscuit ends that stand out above the surface of the jelly must be cut off level—otherwise the mould will not stand steady when turned out. It is very brittle and should not be turned out long before serving.

It is impossible to give absolutely exact proportions, as lemons vary so much in quality; but water and lemon juice together should make up rather less than the given quantities advised for the jelly squares used.

The yolks of the eggs can be used for custards.

Egg Nog

"'Here take this,' pouncing upon a glass of egg nog; 'I made more than half of it myself. Ain't it good?' 'Yes, very. What is it?' 'Oh, plenty of good things'."

Wide Wide World.

Again, a recipe probably pre-Elizabethan and varied by continual use in two continents. As "Nancy" was there one day and only "made half", we judge Aunt Fortune's Nog was this type.

Take the yolks of two eggs and a tablespoon of sugar and beat to foam with a glass of brandy. Boil a pint of milk and pour over the egg mixture, stirring at low heat till a custard forms. Add shred almonds, and nutmeg, and a very little finely cut candied lemon-peel. Allow to cool. Next day (this is where Nancy came in) beat the whites of the eggs with castor sugar and brandy (only a flavouring), mix with an almost equal quantity of stiffly whipped and flavoured cream, and pile upon the custard just before serving.

Curried Eggs

The word curry has changed meaning. A "form of curry" is an old cook-book—"Pety Cury" names a little cook-shop passage. Curry, as we use the word today, names an admixture of spices that did not reach England till after the East India Company officers began to return home on leave.

A dozen cook-books of that period give "Lord Clive's special curry"— and all are different! Real curry cannot be made excellently well in an ordinary English kitchen, because the native cook-boys grind the spices freshly, pounding them to dust on certain polished stones, and adding spice, oils and blended peppers with loving skill. Most of the spice oils are so fugitive that the aroma is lost unless used fresh.

This should be understood and the curry flour or paste we purchase should be closely stoppered and used fresh. To follow a precedent, we will call this single English version: Lord Clive's curried eggs:

Boil half a dozen of the *smallest* eggs you can find for 20 minutes and drop into cold water and shell. (Indian eggs are small and the flavour should penetrate well.) Slice four medium-sized onions into rings and shake them dry in a floured cloth. Fry in butter to golden brown and pepper lightly. Wash two cups of rice and boil swiftly in ample salted water till soft but unbroken. Drain and toss dry before the fire.

Take a spoonful of your curry paste (according to its directions) and mix with a little strong vegetable stock or some of the rice water. Melt a little butter, thicken with rice flour (ordinary flour will do), cook thoroughly, and use the curry powder and stock mixture to form the sauce. Put in the eggs, cover closely and cook for a good 30 minutes. A few raisins and almonds may be added if liked.

To serve, lift out the eggs and slice in two *across*. Arrange the pointed halves together in the centre of the dish, with the rounded ends clustered round them. Surround the dish with a wall of the rice—topped with the onions, and pour the curry sauce over the eggs so that it makes a deep pool between the white rice wall and around the almost submerged island of eggs. You can garnish with cut lemon, mango slices, or tamarind, etc., but if it is a plain English curry thin slices of tart fried apples serve well.

Mayonnaise

It has been said that the French doctor of the Queen of Scots invented this mixture of eggs, oil and cream to allay sea-sickness—"mer en aise." Bad sailors cannot believe this and consider "mer malaise" more probable! I do not think the early sauces of oil and verjuice that were "caste upon" mediaeval dishes were mayonnaise as we know it today, but the mixture of oil allied with vinegar is very ancient and egg yolk is a natural soap to form the emulsion.

Most cooks have their own methods. This is a very simple one.

Two yolks of eggs, add salt, pepper and a little dry mustard. At least one large tablespoon of tarragon vinegar to 1 pint of salad oil. Use a rotary whisk and beat the eggs and seasoning with a little oil to "start the cream". Now very gradually add the vinegar and oil in alternate drops, beating all the time, and continue till a thick cream is formed.

It may be thinned down with more vinegar, but do this very carefully. In hot weather it is best to work in a cold room, or chill the basin over ice.

Wrexham Pudding

A hot rich pudding using eggs.

This is taken direct from a cookery book of 1890 and is one of the few hot winter puddings that uses many eggs.

It was probably one of the Wynstey Hotel puddings, when that post-house was famous for its catering. This is more likely, because a pudding of the same style is still served on the old Pen y Pass route to Holyhead (*see* Snowdon Pudding) that connected with the Wynstey.

½ lb. of breadcrumbs (brown if possible), 1 lb. of suet (finely pounded), 2 oz. of sago (also pounded), 5 oz. of moist sugar, 7 oz. of orange marmalade, six eggs, one wineglass of brandy, butter and raisins.

Butter a basin thickly and press on to it raisins to "make a device". Mix the pounded suet, breadcrumbs, pounded sago, sugar and marmalade together, add the well-beaten eggs and the brandy. Another egg may be needed if six do not sufficiently soak the breadcrumbs and the sago. The brandy should be put in last, and the pudding immediately put into the buttered basin, covered and steamed for a good long hour. It was served with a choice of either marmalade or brandy sauce made with egg-custard foundation. The sago was comparatively new at this date, considered "very sustaining" and giving the pudding an interesting texture.

"Crypspey"

An early form of crispy noodles made with eggs.

> "Take whyte of eyroun and mylke and floure and a lytel berme
> and bete to gederys so that it be renning and not too styf. Caste
> sugre thereto and salt, than take a chafer full of fresshe grece
> boyling and put thy hand in the lature and lat hym renne down
> thy fyngerys, into the chafere. Whan it is runne togedere on the
> chafere and is y now nym a skymer and take it up and let all the
> grece renne out and put it on a fayre dyssche and cast theron sugre
> and serve forth [with]."

Eggs and Apple Savoury or "Marigold Eggs"

This is Worcestershire and Oxfordshire, and probably very old.

Line a shallow dish with thin short crust, butter the bottom, and cover it with thinly sliced apples, and set it to bake until the apples are just cooked. Make a custard mixture of eggs beaten in milk, season strongly with pepper, salt and thyme, a very little chopped sage, and a lot of marigold petals (the common yellow marigold). Pour this savoury custard over the cooked apples and return it to the oven to bake till set. I was told it was served with roast pork, like Yorkshire pudding is served with roast beef (the sage and apple indicate this), but the marigold is more usually a cheese condiment.

Fruteure or Fritters

> "Take yolkes of eyreune, drawe them through a straynour, caste
> thereto fair floure, barme and ale, and stere togedre till hit be
> thicke. Take pared appelles, cut them like oblies [like sacra-
> mental wafers, in oval slices] lay them in the batur. Then
> put them into a frying pan and fry them in faire grece or butter
> till thei ben browne & yellowe. Then put them in disshes and
> strawe sugar on them y nough, and surve forthe."

This is almost exactly farmhouse apple fritters: egg yolks and flour, stirred together with enough ale to make a thick batter, apples pared and cut into round slices and flipped into the batter and fried in butter till "thei ben browne & yellowe"; even the strewing of sugar is completely modern.

Scotch Eggs

These are hard-boiled eggs encased in sausage meat, egged and crumbed and fried brown. They are usually eaten cold, sliced across, but can be served hot with gravy.

Lemon-and-Egg Curd

Lemon-and-egg curd is traditional, and varies with each family. Four eggs, four lemons, to about 1 lb. of sugar and ½ lb. of butter.

Grate the lemon zest on to the sugar and squeeze the juice on to it, add the butter and melt together in a water bath till they can be beaten to blending. Now add the beaten eggs and stir over a very gentle heat till the mixture is thick and creamy. Pour into pots and cover at once.

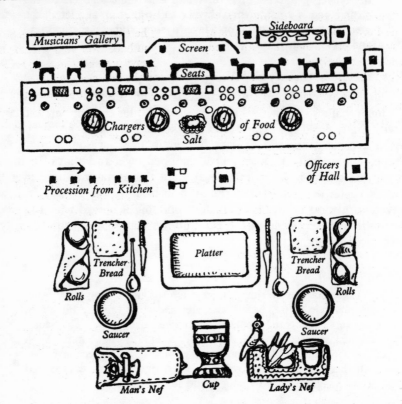

This diagram plan of a high table might be of any date towards the end of the fifteenth century. Earlier, the board would be narrower, and there would be few saucers, and perhaps no platters. The chargers might be of wood or silvergilt, and later they might be of pewter. The small squares behind each chair show the position of the personal pages, who would come round and carve *before* the table as required, or fetch wine or wash-hand water. The larger squares either side of the sideboard and at the end of the tables are hall officers.

The entrance across the front of the table of a "course" led by a steward and two trumpeters is shown, also the great saltcellar. With the help of the key cover the smaller details can be placed. The nefs and drinking cups along the front of the board would not be there after a service of tableware was usual, and people no longer carried their own nefs.

MEDIAEVAL FEAST AND FAMINE

DINING OUT AT THE CASTLE

" When thou come to a lordis gate
The Porter thou shalle fynde thereate
Take [give] him, thou shalt, thy wepyn
And aske hym leve in to go
When thou come the halle dor to
Do off thy hode, thy gloves also
In myddys the halle upon the flore
Whille marshall or ussher come fro the dore
And bydde thee sitte, or to the Lord the lede
Lay thy trenchour thee before
And sitt up ryght for any sore!

When you come,
The footman opens the door,
you hand over your stick or bag.
Leave your hood and gloves, etc.,
in the hall cloakroom.
You then go into the main hall
and the servant will take you to
your host, if you're expected, or
show you where to sit and wait.

Pare they brede and kerve in two
The over crust the nether fro
Spare brede or wyne, drynke or ale
To [till] thy meese of kochyn [kitchen] be
    set in sale
Lest men sayne thou art nongur lyten
Or ellis a gloten that all men wyten

At table, sit before your plate, cut
your plate bread into two platters.
But on no account start eating
or drinking till dinner is served.

Byt not thy brede and lay it down
That is no curteyse to use in Town
But breke as muche as thou wylle ete
The remelant [remains] to the pore thou
    shalle lete.
Let never thy cheke be made too grete
With morselle of brede that thou shalle ete
If any man speke that time to thee
And thou schalle answare? hit will not be!
But waloande and abyde thou most
(That is a shame for alle the host)
Thou shalle not laughe ne speke ne synge
While thy mouth be fulle of mete or drynke
Ne suppe not with grete soundynge
Nother potage [soup] ne other thynge
Ne blow not on thy dyshe ne mete
Nether for colde—neither for hete
Let not thy spoone stand in the dysche
Whether thou be served with fleshe or fishe

Don't bite your bread (we never
do so today from this tradition)
as these bread plates are later
handed down to the lower tables
—or the poor.
Don't bite off more than you
can chew.
Don't talk with your mouth full.

Eat quietly, without noise.

Don't blow to cool food.

Do not leave your spoon in the
dish (or cup).

Also eschewe, withouten stryfe
To foule the borde clothe with thy knyfe   Do not wipe knives on the cloth.

With mete ne bere thy knyfe to mouthe   Don't eat with your knife,—
Whether thou be set, be strong and couthe
Clense not thy tethe at mete sittande
With knyfe be stre, styke, ne wande
While thou holdes mete in mouth be war   nor drink with your mouth full.
To drynke—that is anhonest [unhonest or
    ugly] char
Drye thy mouthe aye wele and fynde [fine]   Wipe your mouth on your napkin
When thou shalle drynke (either ale or wyne)   before and after drinking.

Ne calle thou *NOT* a dysche agayne   Do not call for dishes that have
That is take from the borde in playne   been taken away.

If thy own dogge thou scrape and clawe   Don't let your pet dog be a pest.
That is holden an vyse among men who know.

If that thy nose thou clense (as may befalle)
Loke thy hand thou clense, as wythe alle   Wipe your nose privately.
Prively [privately] with skyrt do hit away
Or ellis thurge thy tipet that is so gay

Lene not on elbowe at thy mete   Do not lean your elbows on the
Dip not thy thombe [or fingers] thy drink into   table nor put fingers into your
Ne backward sittand . . . and ever eschewe   drink.
To flye [dispute] at borde that may be rewe
Nor telle thou never at borde no tale   Nor tell any tale to make anyone
To harm or shame thy fellowe in hall."   uncomfortable.

This simple courtesy remains. We substitute hat and stick for the helmet and spear but the rest is our own usage today. On arrival we hand over our impedimenta and packages at the gate and ask to see our host and hostess. If we have the right to enter, we are led from the gatehouse to the main "halle dor" where we remove outdoor things. Here, we are probably offered a wash and brush up.

Now the marshal of the hall, that is, the head servant, comes to show you where to sit and wait by the fire, or, if you are to go direct to the family, he will "to the Lord the lede". Greetings over, you will probably be given a drink and a short rest and be introduced to others—the equivalent of our cocktail before dinner. On the blast of the trumpets (our gong sounding) you find your seat at table and wait, politely still, until all the company are seated and the meal begins. Notice that you may cut your trencher bread, thus preparing your plates for dinner—these "trenchours", and your own knife and spoon, you might lay ready for use; but it was then, as now, unmannerly to begin to crumble bread or drink before dinner begins.

"Byt not thy brede and lay it down" is also usage today. It is because in these early centuries their first bread, which became soaked with the gravy and sauces, was, after the first course, collected and distributed among the lesser people at the lower tables. Therefore, to *bite* that bread would have been a grave discourtesy to those having it after you. Not to ask for dishes once removed (or to demand things not served), is plain politeness in any century. Not to leave a spoon standing in cup or dish, not to put elbows on the table, nor to tell any story that could make anyone at the table uncomfortable; these are the courtesies when "dinning out at the Castle".

AN ELABORATE FEAST

" A Franklen may make a feste Improberabille
  Brawne with Mustard is concordable
  Bakon served with peson
  Beef or moton stewed seruysable
  Boyled Chykon or Capon agreable
  Convenyent for the season.
  Rosted goose or Pygge fulle profitable
  Capon Bakemetes or Custade Costable
  When eggis and crayme be season
  The stuffe for household is behovable
  Mortroves or Musselle are delectable
  For the second course by reson
  Yhan weel Lambe kyd or cony
  Chykon or pygeon rosted tenderly
  Bakemeats or dowcettes with alle
  Then following frytours and leche lovely
  Such seruyse in sesoun is fulle semely
  To serue within both cambur and Halle
  Then appuls and peris with spices delicately
  Aftur the terme of the yere fulle deynteethy
  With bred and chese to calle
  Spised cakes and wafurs worthily
  With bragot and nethe, theese men may meryly
  Plese welle both gret and smalle."

                                            BOORDE.

LE PREMIER COURS
BRAWN EN PEUERARDE   Brawn with sharp sauce.
                            A pudding to eat with the main dish, which was

VIAUND RYAL	Head of a boar, armed with tusks and decorated
TESTE DE SELERE ENARMEZ	elaborately,
GRAUNDE CHARE	With hot spiced gravy. These three made one complete service.
SYNGALLYS	Cygnets (young swans), rather dry and meaty birds.
CAPOUN DE HAUT DE GRACE	Capon in the highest state of fatness and richness.
FESAUNTE	Pheasants.
HERON	Heron. (The neck always worried cooks; see note about it.)
CUSTARDE LUMBARDE	This was a baked custard in pastry case, with dried fruits.
STORIEOUN GRAUNT LUCES	Sturgeon, with a sauce of pike.
A SOLTTE. . . .	An elaborate centrepiece of sugar and paste edible in part.

Cours 2

VENYSON en FURMETY	Venison cooked in a stew of corn—a spiced and gamey mixture.
GELY	Red-currant jelly(?).
PORCELLE FARCE ENFORCE	Sucking pig, stuffed with forcemeat.
POKOKKYE	Peacocks, garnished with their feathers, and very handsome.
CRANYS	Cranes (see note on herons).
VENYSON ROSTE	Roast venison.
CONYN	Rabbit. Probably white meat only in this case.
BYTTERE	Bitterns.
PULLE ENDORE	Chickens cooked with saffron and made golden with egg yolks.
GRAUNT TARTEZ	A tart vinegar sauce, to serve with the rich
BRAUN FREYEZ	Fried brawn.
LECHE LUMBARDE	A bread and dried-fruit dish.
A SOLTELLE	Another elaborate amusement, that could be taken to pieces and eaten—anyhow in part—afterwards.

Cours 3

BLAUNDESORYE	Was a basis of white curd and white meat, mixed with almonds, and set in a dish.
QUYNCYS IN COMFYTE	Quince pie.
EGRETEZ	Uncertain what bird this is, but probably an egret.
CURLEWYS	Used again in the last war, they were on sale in Chester and elsewhere.
PERTYCHE	Perch.
PYIONYS	Pigeons(?).

QUALES	Quails.
SNYPES	Snipes.
SMALL BYRDYS	Larks and other small birds, probably in a pie.
RABETTYS	Rabbit, as distinct from cony? I think all the animal was cooked.
EYROUN ANGELE	Eggs in jelly. (Plover's eggs in aspic?)
FRYTOURS	Frittures, fritters.
DOUCETTES	Sweetmeats—rather like marzipans and fancy cakes.
PETYPERNEUX	Little lost eggs. Were fancy pastry, golden egg yolks and mincemeat.

A SOLTETTE

The sets of dishes making up a course, were all available together, but each course was completely removed before the next came in. For example, the first main course was boar's head, with a sort of Yorkshire pudding and gravy. As alternative, if you did not want this main hot dish, you could have cold brawn and sauce, or the ladies, perhaps, preferred the poultry course of capon or swan. The roast pheasant and herons were side dishes to balance the fish dish (which would have to come in every course, in those religious days). The "Custarde Lumbarde" is a sweet dish, and would be there in case anyone wanted it (as a modern hostess might say anxiously to a guest, "There *is* a milk pudding, if you like?"). Everybody did not eat everything! If you consider the guests, each choosing *one* thing from each course, you only have a four-course dinner, though more elaborately arranged than we consider possible.

This was a dinner party of exceptional grandeur.

Ordinarily, meals would vary with the season; in summer, fresh meat, poultry, fruit, pies, puddings and creams; in one district wine, another mead, another cider—not usually all together. The single meal in hall was a really good solid feed; and though the fine food and spices were kept for the household at the top table, we believe the main dish—the roast beef, the boiled mutton or whatever it was—was shared pretty well throughout the hall (last come worst served). But the sending down of a serving from the top table to the lower was more than a form of patronage. It was a mediaeval form of supervision. The head of the household thus saw that the servants' dinner was well cooked, and the servants saw that the head *saw them well served*. If it sizzled and smelt good, the head probably directed his page to cut him a slice; and it is very reassuring to any servant to feel that, except for the flavourings and spices, "we have what they have themselves". It was this sense of unity in hall that was so valuable. If some hunter (down by the salt) had been out with his master hawking, one of the birds, on a plate of trencher bread, would come down from the high table; or, if it was a trusted retainer, the gift might be reversed, with laughter! But when it was a new over-lord, and conquered retainers, this unity was lost; and in the later centuries comes the sad division, when the lower tables feel cut off because: "Now have the rich a rule to eat by themselves in a separate chamber because of the poor in the hall" (*The Vision of Piers Plowman*). Even then, for special occasions all met together in the old fashion.

"SPECIAL FEAST FOR A BRIDE"

A coming-of-age, or a wedding in the family, is still a matter of importance to the tenants on any estate in the country, so here is how

" ffor to make a feste for a bryde

The ffirst cours: brawne, with the borys hed, lying in
a felde, hegge about with a scriptur, saying on this
wyse:
    ' Welcombe you bretheren godely in this hall!
      Joy be unto you all . . . '
ffurmete with veneson, swanne, pigge
ffesaunte, with a grete custarde, with a sotlete,
A lambe stondyng in scriptour, sayng on this wyse;
    ' I metely unto you, sovrayne, am sente
      to dwell with you, and ever be presente.'
The ij cours: Veneson in broth, viaunde Ryalle,
veneson rosted, crane, cony, a bake mete,
leche damaske, with a sotelte, An anteloppe
standyng on a sele that saith with scriptour;
    ' beith all gladd and mery that sitteth at this messe
      and prayeth for the kyng. . . . '

The iij cours: Creme of Almondys, losynge in syruppe
betoure, partrich, plover, snyte, pouder veal,
leche veal, wellis in sotelte, Roches in sotelte, Playce
in sotelte; a bake mete with a sotelte, an angell with a
scriptour, ' thanke all, god, of this feste '.

      ' A Sotlety '
The iiij cours: Payne puff chese freynes, brede hote, with a
cake and a wif laying in childe-bed with a scriptour
saing in this wyse:
    ' I am comyng toward your bryde '
    ' If ye disste onys loke to me ward, I wene ye nedys muste.' "

A SOLTETEE

"SOLTETEES BE MADE OF SUGAR AND WAX" and a soltey had as many forms as spellings, and delighted the mediaeval kitchen staff.

Historians differ in their exact definition, but from pictures and recipes, they seem to have been prototypes of the elaborate stage "cakes" of today that open to disclose "a fair maiden with congratulations" or the "fish" dragged in at some arts ball that cuts open to spill gifts and balloons. For smaller affairs the soltety might be an elaborate erection of real pastry and sugar, which, after it had been duly admired, could be broken up and eaten.

The solteety was more an excuse for admiration and laughter than an eatable part of the meal. The parade of the dish all across the dining-hall was part of the fun, and, as it was carved at a sideboard, the gay elaborate trimmings could be stripped off before the pages carried the portions around. Some soltys were set on the table, some carried around, and some carved out of sight and served in "portions", but no feast was complete without its soltytte.

THE LIVERY CUPBOARD

THE OPENWORK livery cupboards (sometimes called mistakenly game cupboards) of the period from the eleventh to the sixteenth century, are the prototypes of the modern snack bar. The great dinner-in-hall was the more or less punctual cessation of the day's employments for lord and labourer alike. It was attended by all as a matter of course. It was the one time of day when your absence would be noted. Therefore, if absent, your steward or page would annex a portion of the food for you, collect a flask of wine, some bread, cheese and meat, and cache it away for you " in the livery cupboard ". In this cupboard were also kept salt, verjuice (vinegar type), bread, cold meat, or small game that could be grilled quickly over the open fire in the hall. The servant in charge of the hall saw that the cupboard was replenished with suitable light foods, and that clean cloths and napkins were stowed in his sideboard. Anyone returning unexpectedly, and needing a meal to keep them going till dinner-time, could be fed from the livery cupboard. Cold ham, meat pies, bread and cheese and pickles, and something to drink, would be livery cupboard snacks.

Do not confuse the livery cupboard with the sideboard, which was set at the side of the high table. At dinner time the sideboard was laid with a white cloth, and on it stood the gold and silver salvers, and the ewer and bowl for hand-washing at dinner-time. The livery cupboard had pierced openwork carving, for air inlets, and shelves and hooks to hold stored food. With the sixteenth century, smaller cupboards of this type appear in bedrooms, and it becomes the pleasant custom to keep hyprocras and cakes there.

If you wished for a little private dalliance, or had an undignified chill, you instructed the groom of the bedchamber to see your bedroom cupboard was suitably arranged.

Already, a century earlier, Boorde had frowned upon this custom, and said that firm housekeepers should forbid it! All this laughing and chattering, and snack meals and spiced wine served in bedrooms, becomes wasteful and expensive for a man who does much entertaining.

MEDICAL EPISODE

There is a good story quoted in one of Dr. Coulton's reprints, of a passing doctor-priest being stopped by a ploughman whose wife complained of a devil ("possession"). The doctor turns aside to the house, examines the patient, and diagnoses "self neglect", "starvation" and "general feebleness". He tells the husband to see that his wife eats properly "good meat and good drink", and at night before retiring she is "to drink a quart of hot ale, hot as she can sup it", "with a nut of butter in it", and go straight to bed. The ale (home-brewed) would be soporific, the butter mildly aperient and the cure pleasant. . . . What could be more sensible? The date is 1300. It's impossible to generalise, but one does notice that, the simpler the household, as a rule the simpler the medical usage. It is in later and more complicated communities that we get the fantastically complicated medicines; and the more wealthy the patient, the more likely he is to die of his expensive treatment!

THE FAMINE YEARS

(*"hoc anno cira pestilentium"*)

> " I have no penny polettes for the bigge
> Nor goose nor grys but 2 green cheese
> A few croddes and creyme and a cake of oates
> And bread for y barnes, of benes and of pease
> I heve no salt bacon nor cokery by Cryst !
> But I have polett plontes—perseley and scalones,
> Chiboles and chirvylles and chives sam node
> And a coo and a calf and a cart mare
> To draw a field y donge—the while drought lasteth
> And by this we must abide till lamasse tyme
> By which time I hope to have harvest in y croft
> Then may I dight y dinner as me liketh! "

The Vision of Piers Plowman.

THE WILD game was becoming scarce or "strictly preserved", and the people on the land lived very close to their small fields, and lacked reserve stores. The Crusade period was ended, but the crusades had taken many of the able-bodied men away from the land to travel overseas. The returned Crusaders had brought new spices and new ideas of cooking, but, like returned adventurers, had lost touch with work at home and the English seasons.

To realise how desperate was the famine you must know the seasons as the starving peasants knew them—close and vital knowledge. Autumn meant the end of all the green food from woods and commons, the last wild fruit was finished, and the corn had been gathered (they cut it high by hand, with reaping-hooks, and the cattle browsed on the straw). The geese and hens had eaten the fallen grain and been eaten in turn, the pigs had eaten the fallen acorns and beech mast, and now the pigs were killed off for winter, one by one. Winter came, and there were salt and dried meats, and some parsnips. After a good harvest these lasted well enough, but as the winter dragged out, the last of the fresh meat went; only the few beasts necessary for breeding in the spring remained. . . . When necessity compelled the poor to eat those beasts, famine came since there was *no possibility of fetching supplies from elsewhere*. Other districts might have missed the storms or rain, but they were too far away to fetch food from; nor could the hungry move over to join another community, for the others had only enough food for themselves. Some movement about the land had been possible, but now the shortage of labour ties men to their own ground, and summer sees them still there and still hungry. Autumn brings no extra food. Lacking plough beasts, no fields are tilled. So comes the terrible time when berries are gathered for food and wild roots of pig-nut and acorn are ground to make a miserable ash cake. Fish from the rivers, wild birds killed with sling stones, snakes, shellfish, braxy mutton—anything is food that will fill the belly. Then illness, and the desperate eating of the very last beast they kept for breeding! After that, no hope ahead, no future animals, no grain for seed— all gone, and a wild escape from one part of the country to another only stopped by law, and death. Within the period of the Black Death it is believed that one in every five died, either of the plague, or weakness and starvation.

TRADE, MAGIC AND RELIGIOUS COOKING

TRADE COOKING

" All these trust in their hands, and everyone is wise in his
work."

ECCLESIASTICUS.

"TRADE" SPECIALITIES

I F YOU ever find some "special" type of cooking in a district where there
is no "foreign influence" or other cause to account for it, study the local
trades. It was young Watt, watching his mother's kettle-lid dancing up
and down, who made steam work for mankind; and to assess the genius
of the eighteenth-century engineers realise that the first Manchester to
Liverpool canal was built before steam power was developed. Roads and
aqueducts, all over industrial districts, show the structural thought—and
that is engineering at its best—and many stone aqueducts and tunnels are
as beautiful in their simplicity as any ornate mediaeval cathedral. These
great feats moved a mass of specialised workers about the country, often
keeping them in residence in the same district for several years together
(like cathedral and castle-builders of earlier centuries).

These clusters of workmen, coming from one part of the land to
another, carried their own special cooking methods with them, and in
turn learnt local ideas and materials. Anyone who has to keep a large
party of workpeople happy in a strange district knows how a consign-
ment of "food from home" will cheer the whole party; and when you
study the large undertakings *of any century*, it is pleasant to find sudden
consignments of unexpected food being brought, at great expense, from
some remote place—to vanish, apparently, into thin air.

Sometimes it is a cargo of salt herrings by waggon, or a curious sudden
bill for "sum pygges" (that makes one think there had been complaints
about the local bacon).

The same thing had happened when William the Conqueror took his
castle-builders to work in Saxon land; when the Flemings came to settle
in South Wales (twelfth century); when the lace workers came to the east
Midlands; and the same will always happen where *sets of workers* who
serve one trade work the same hours and eat the same food.

Thus clay and pottery workers cook in their own kilns—encasing raw
meat, fish, game, etc., in clay to bake it. The rich carefully preserved

aroma of the "enclosed cooking" made them invent pottery jars with close-fitting lids and pottery "cases" to save the expense of the huff paste.

Painters and workers, using certain chemicals, developed a compensating taste for salt and acid flavourings, and their natural cooking used these abundantly. Field workers in Scotland were given free barley water, slightly acid, and well-salted oat porridge to replace their "sweating" in the dry harvest fields.

Leather workers became so impregnated with the tannin from the oak and willow bark used in dressing the hides, that their bodies did not decay after death, but shrivelled and dried up like old leather sacks.

Lime workers were issued with extra butter, grease or cream to save their skins and eyelids, and (so I have heard) developed a compensating taste for vinegar and milk.

Iron workers, by reason of the furnace heat, learnt much about light beers and strengthening ales and liquors.

All the various trades cooked and flavoured according to their special requirements. The engineer was ever a good cook under all circumstances, and what he learnt on his trade furnaces he later incorporated into the iron cooking ranges he invented.

The modern Thermos flask and "works canteens" have put an end to much of the unofficial cooking that went on around the old factory-heating stoves. I worked for five years in a shipwright's factory heated by great coke stoves. The stoves were ridged and spaced into hollows, like a big black honeycomb, and from 6 a.m. to 6 p.m. these heated hollows would be packed full of things cooking, "tins" boiling, tea mashing, chops, potatoes, or even bread and pie, baking! Some of the men would come "on" direct from their allotment gardens, and big round onions baking used to scent the night shifts. (Often an apprentice boy got his "kit" for being good at cooking.)

Quarry men, working on a "face" a long distance from home, often became expert cooks, their "bakstone" supplementing the iron gridiron over the fire in their blast shelter. Slate will not stand heat, and some stones "fly" dangerously, but some mountain men used to keep goats, or even a cow, up near their jobs. The queerest "churn" I ever encountered was where some Arenig men took their spare milk down in a can slung below the rattling trucks; it was good buttermilk, and butter for tea by the time it reached the valley.

Foresters cooked at a wood fire, and the "plank steak" is direct from their specialised craft cooking. They also used the slow "buried iron oven bake" that the peat burners used on their open hearths. Lancashire mill hands, working long shifts, developed many special dishes that could be left to cook all day, and "finished in a few minutes" on their return home. That the size and shapes of the pots and pans depended upon their owner's job is understandable, but you will also find long-boned Yorkshire sheep required a different-shaped stewpot from its neat-boned southern lamb! The "shepherd's lambstones", and "lambtail pies" are farming examples of "the job and the food". The sprouts of the buried swede turnip, and the cut tendrils of the hop, are agricultural local foods, and cod's liver[1] and clams were discoveries of the fisherman. Such remote connection as the sawdust from York Minster flavouring York hams shows how interesting trade and craftsman's cooking can become!

MAGIC COOKING

" O where are your bloodhounds Rendel my son
    O where are your bloodhounds my sweet pretty one?
    They swelled and they died—Ah make my bed soon
    I am sick at my heart, and fain would lie down."

Until the Reformation, no one ate meat on a Friday, and on some fast days, only preparations of vegetables or grain. If any modern woman feels exasperated by her household being "allergic" to certain foods, let her remember that her predecessor had to cater both materially and spiritually. For example, this simple matter of Friday's fish; did it count throughout the whole of Lent or not? and what about eggs? (Assuredly, "eggs hard rosted be grosse metes; and evil of digestion".) But what about fish eggs? Would the priest consider the "wombe of a luce" as fish or egg? Then there was a creature called a barnacle goose, that was born a shell fish, on tree stumps over tide water; when these shell fish were ripe, they opened and small birds dropped out into the water. Were these mediaeval mixtures? birds or fish? spiritually cooking? Puffins were oily, but their dwellings underground in burrows made them legally meat, not birds. Even vegetables were not without difficulty, as Varro had said "a bishop should not eat beans" and "cabbages out of season" were most unhealthy. Stars, and the position of the moon, required consideration. As a general rule things were best killed or gathered with the wane of the moon, but things on the increase, with the increase of the moon. This is not superstition, as animals kept awake by bright moonlight usually wake up and feed extra, so are likely to weigh heavier than those killed after dark nights, and roots are most full of substance just before they burst into growth in spring. Thus the top part of a parsnip, just at the base of the leaves, contains most sugar.

The calendar was also governed by saints' days; and certain peas or

---

[1] Codliver oil, discovery of Cape Cod fishermen, as scurvy antidote and means of keeping warm in arctic seas.

beans were, by experience, planted "before St. Edmund's Day", or after Lamas.

Poison tests were a matter of course in court circles, and most nobles arranged for all food to be officially tested before they ate it. Lord Rendel's symptoms suggest Amantia mussari, or some form of fungi poison, but aconite, deadly nightshade, or even hemp seed, can make you very ill. Foxglove was a queer, uncertain herb. Arum maculatium (Jack-in-pulpit) has a root that burns like fire if bitten. Lettuce juice, dried and made into white cakes, was used to induce insensibility and sleep, as were poppy heads. Yew is so poisonous to cattle that it was planted around the graves in the churchyard to keep them untrodden (and also to supply bow wood).

One of the best tests for poison was unicorn's horn; the unicorn was so fierce that no man could catch one, but a pure virgin could go forth and put her girdle around the wild beast and lead him whither she would. The mediaeval people, taking these allegories of passionate love materially, noted that a pure unicorn stooping to drink, dipped his horn in the water first, and so avoided poison; therefore cups made of unicorn horn were considered completely safe poison testers. The enormously long "unicorn's horns" cherished in some cathedrals till today are narwhal horns, and were possibly used for testing deep wells. By 1400 spurious unicorn horn was being sold by dishonest eastern traders (so you are warned to test your horn by poisoning a pigeon before purchase). These beliefs are no more absurd than our own faiths of today. We do not know what is inside half the pills we swallow; we are *told* they will act, and we believe our doctors; the mediaeval people believed their doctors and felt the same confidence.

Sir Francis Drake, the most level-headed navigator of the world, wrote of unicorns.

> " The Floridians have pieces of unicorn's hornes which they weare about their necks whereof the Frenchmen obtained many pieces. Of those unicorns they have many, for that they doe affirme it to be a beast with one horne which coming to the river to drinke, putteth the same into the water before he drinketh."

Giraldus Cambensis, in the twelfth century, thought Apuleius really was turned into an ass, and cured by eating roseleaves. The mediaeval ingredients mentioned in *Hamlet* were completely trusted, and even the phantasy of Bottom's head was a lively possibility to an Elizabethan audience. (There was a recipe for making the ointment for doing this trick —you began by cutting off the ass's head while it was still alive, and cooked it for three days. . . .)

It was difficult for a cook to distinguish between religion and magic in its effect upon food. For example, St. Colman was patron of certain sea birds; an archer shot one, and boiled it for hours, but it remained tough as a stone! This was attributed to the influence of the saint, and the unfortunate archer miserably expired (*see* Meat Section).

St. Werburg ordered the wild geese from her corn, and they obediently left, but her cook, having meanly caught one of the religious captives, made a goose pie, so the wild birds refused to leave, and St. Werburg had to do a miracle and let the bird out. These were not "stories" but firm beliefs in mediaeval days. The tremendous power of magic in the Holy Wafer of the Mass was extended to almost anything that was consecrated to the church. One instance was connected with mutton fat. The church candles being of mutton tallow, that valuable fat was perquisite to the church, and blest for church use. The refuse from the candle making was used to oil the church bells, and soon rubbed into a thick black grease. Some poor mother, needing grease to rub her child's chest, risked committing·sacrilege and sneaked a dab of the grease (which had not only become blackened by the strength of the metal bell, but had a blessing over it, so would be doubly efficacious).

After the Reformation, some New World sailors, grinding trade axes for the Indians, may have used the same lubricant, for the Indians, confusing the arrowproof steel breastplate with the black grease the soldiers rubbed upon it (for camouflage, and to preserve it from rust) began to buy the axle grease as a strengthening ointment for themselves! These things "stick like burrs", for in a Leicestershire village I was asked to hold the ladder while an old woman climbed up for "church-bell grease", for her grandson's chest! Thus the apotheosis of mutton fat, when rendered down with religious magic!

RELIGIOUS COOKING

" When I went into the Refectory, I found a Hall fit for a King, with broad scoured tables, and wide benches, and windows of glass; and a Friar, feeding alone from a livery cupboard, O a great fat churl, his belly as big as a barrel, and his white face blown up like a lard bladder. His cheeks lagged and waggled either side his chins, where the top chin lolled on the soft chins below as big as a goose egg."

The Vision of Piers Plowman.

Few of the early and strict religious houses ever ate meat. Bread and water diet was not "a slice of bread and glass of water" but all the range of cooked and raw cereal foods, a broth of boiled barley with all manner of root vegetables, and leeks.

A solid oatmeal dumpling filled with fruit (like a boiled apple pudding); greens, cooked enclosed in jars with a lump of butter; two poached eggs on "spinnage" followed by oatcake and cheese, or a bread-and-butter pudding with honey and black currants, would all be allowable, and for invalids, jelly, and barley water, and a coarse, invigorating red wine. Where fish and game were permitted they had great variety, and the monastic dairy work was excellent. It is to the Cistercians that we owe our variety of sheep, and ewes were always milked, as well as goats.

The large religious houses had fish ponds in which they kept and bred fish. The lords of the manors had the river, and many were the fights over fishing rights in the mill streams. A "kettle of fish" was originally a "kiddle *for* fish"—a large fish trap set in the river, and strictly illegal. If one was found, the entire community was under suspicion, and punishments were widespread, involving innocent and guilty alike. It was a very serious "kiddle of fish"! Parts of the coast were marked off as fishing reserves. Salted herrings were sent incredible distances by pack horse, and later by cart. Dried stock fish was cooked in milk.

Towards the end, before the Reformation, the monasteries were renowned for their excellent cooking of sumptuous fare.

A "side-line" of their catering establishments were the praiseworthy small "cells", or resthouses, that seem to have been built near every river port, landing stage, or ford. These hostels had an open shed below, where horses were sheltered, a cookhouse with a permanent warden, and an upstairs dining-room dormitory, with a wash place and clean rush bedding. The great plantations of horse-radish and cumphrey that run wild around these ruins show that broken bones, and internal chills, and saddle galls, and stiffened legs, were well arranged for, and when the rough sea sounds in the estuary, and blue woodsmoke hangs in the chilly dusk, there shines a warm glow within those old hostels that may be the setting sun through the broken window frame, or the benediction of the many seasick, weary travellers who sojourned there.

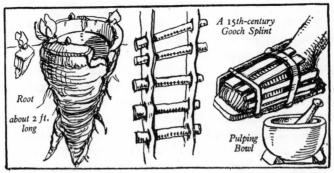

Cumphrey: *symphytum officialie*; boneset; knitt bone, etc.

FISH

GENERAL NOTES ON FISH OF ALL KINDS

ENGLAND IS an island entirely surrounded by fish. Unfortunately the very diversity of the fish has been the cause of waste, because the ordinary housewife regards all as "fish", without regard to type.

The fried-fish shop has much to answer for in this, the batter-covered catfish is sold as "fish" and, except for the fish that goes with "chips", the working man knows only "herrings" and "cod steaks" (and fries both!). I've seen turbot, mullet, and many good fish left unsold in country markets with the indignant query: "Haven't you got any *proper* fish?" So please forgive a rather elementary lecture on "types of fish".

We know that the vegetable or herb that the beast feeds upon is the best condiment to it when cooked, so do not disguise the natural good flavour of fish, but develop it, by using appropriate adjuncts.

Fresh-water fishes from the mountain streams require only the most delicate aroma of herbs and fresh butter to develop their natural flavour. Thus, thyme for mountain grayling, watercress for brook trout. So important is this for fresh-water fish, that expert anglers will often collect the appropriate herbs *from the very pool* where they catch the fish.

For salt-water fish, redolent of the sea, use more hearty flavours. Laver, samphire and shell fish (such as shrimp or cockle sauce), and green garden herbs of strong taste, are often good condiments, but usually unsuitable with dried, smoked, or oily fish, for which dried oatmeal, baked barley, etc., are better, as they absorb the already too-strong flavour of the oil.

Some fish, such as pike, are dry, and the skin so tough and smooth that basting butter does not get inside. For such fish, rubbing the inside over with lard and stuffing with a rich flavoured stuffing (incorporating chopped bacon or fat ham), greatly improves the fish. For some dry fish we recommend half slicing (as if for steaks) and inserting a buttered bay leaf or slice of thin bacon between the slices.

Unless fisherman's pride dictates that the fish be cooked whole, or if the head is large and full of flavour as in mullet, it is often sensible to remove the head and tail altogether and use them, with the fins, to make fish stock for the gravy.

Always cook fish flat; the trick of bending them round, and fastening the tail through the eye or mouth is a silly affectation. The twist leaves the inside compressed and raw, and the outside is stretched and overcooked.

SALT-WATER FISH

" Here followeth of the natures of the fisshes of the sea which be ryght profitable to be understane."

L. ANDREWS.

COD

Cod's Head and Shoulders

Cod's head is usually cut with the shoulders, because the shape of this thick fish makes the head end difficult to cut into round steaks on account of the lower fins being set rather far back under the gills. Custom varies, and in some parts they cut quite high up and sell the top-end steaks with thick, long flaps.

London does not now count as a fishing port, but most deep-sea ports still serve "cod's head and shoulder" because fishermen say "cod's head is the best part of the fish", the thick tongue and cheeks being particularly rich and nutritious and the deep cut at the nape of the neck is very firm and fine fish; a helping from both parts should be served together. The main problem for the modern cook is to prepare this dish so that it shall not be unsightly. We recommend this method.

Slit open underneath and clean the head well, scour with dry salt and rinse under running water (but do not leave it soaking in water). Have a fish-kettle ready with just enough boiling salted water to cover the head, which should be lowered into it, slit side up. At once move the pan from the heat and simmer gently till the bones are loose. Lift the fish and, working from the open underside, remove the bones gently, beginning with the lower jaw, the long bones, and all the grey gills. The skull-bones, eyes and back can then be lifted out and the space filled with cooked cod's roe. Press the whole into shape, season well with pepper and salt (and, if you like, chopped parsley and finely scraped onion), and slide it on to a hot dish, turning it over as you do so. The thick skin may now be lifted off the top of the head and shoulders and you have a seemly "joint" of excellent-quality fish. To complete, dredge with fine fresh breadcrumbs and roast before the fire 10 minutes, basting well with good dripping. Use the fish water to make a brown, well-flavoured sauce and, when the fish is browned, dried, and smoking hot, dish it up on a garnishing of parsley and lemon. Serve the sauce in a tureen and hand brown bread and butter, or plain boiled potatoes. A large cod's head and shoulders makes a substantial dish for three or four people.

Salt Cod and Parsnips

This is a very old English dish; most of the mediaeval fish dishes add sugar as condiment, and the common parsnip would be the sweetening agent for the poorer people. The "salt cod" of the middle ages was probably exactly the same as today. The dish is still made in Catholic rural communities, and both salt cod and frosted parsnips are at their best during early Lent.

Wash the dried fish and soak in running water for several hours (in Ireland I have seen it pegged down in a running brook). Put it into a kettle with plenty of cold water and bring very slowly to almost boiling point; throw off the water, add warm water and heat again. If the piece is thick, this may be done two or three times, as it draws out the salt, but be careful never to let it actually boil, or the fish will break. Let the last filling be half milk and half water, and add the parsnips cut in long strips, replacing the fish last (on the fish-tray or in a cloth), simmer gently for half an hour, or longer, till quite soft. Lift out the fish and set to drain before the fire. Meanwhile, strain off the parsnips and mash till creamy with a lump of butter and pepper (salt will not be needed). When parsnips are mashed and fish dried, serve them together. The symphony of white fish and creamed parsnip is completed by yellow egg sauce, made with the golden yolks of eggs beaten into the sauce *after* it has been well made and boiled. Give the yolks a minute to cook in the hot (not boiling) sauce and serve in a hot tureen as the only accompaniment to this dish. It is really very good.

Buttermilk is the best drink with this, as the salt destroys either tea or coffee, and malt drinks are even worse. Mutton fat, clarified, can be substituted for the butter.

Creamed Fish

A simple dish. Take about 1 lb. of fish—cod or hake. Put it, bones and all, into a small enamel pan with herbs and peppercorns, and just enough salted water to cover, and cook it till the fish leaves the bones. Pick the bones out and put the fish aside. Strain and boil up the water in which the fish was cooked and use it, with an equal quantity of milk, a lump of butter, and flour, to make a thick sauce. Boil this sauce thoroughly and incorporate a little finely chopped ham trimmings, or a rasher of bacon cut small. Add a little chopped parsley (or taragon leaves) and pepper well (but go easy with the salt if you use ham). Take the sauce off the fire, flake the fish into it. Put a layer of mashed potatoes into a buttered piedish, pressing them well up the sides to form a wall; pour in the fish cream, brown on top, and serve.

This is really an excellent fish dish, simple to make and very useful when fish is scarce, but it must be made very carefully. Good cooking is not elaboration—it is good simplicity.

HADDOCK

A thick, meaty fish of excellent quality. It is usually gutted at the fish-monger's and should hang up by the gills in a cool draught in the larder. The liver should be cooked at once with a little onion and herbs.

Baked Haddock

Scale and clean and rub the fish well, inside and out, with salt, wiping it off and trimming the fish neatly. To make the stuffing, chop the cooked liver finely, add 4 or 5 spoonfuls of fine breadcrumbs, salt, pepper, mixed herbs, and a little clarified dripping or butter, melted just sufficiently to bind the mixture. Pack the stuffing into the fish and tie it up. Take a deep bake-pan, grease it, strew the bottom thickly with *finely* chopped onions and crumbs. Cover the top of the fish with small dabs of dripping (to make it brown nicely), pour into the dish just enough fish stock (made from the trimmings) to damp the onions, and bake all in the oven about 40 minutes (according to the size of the fish). Serve the dish just as it is—the onions, the stock and the dripping should have melted together into a rich brown gravy (you should have a look at the fish while baking and, if necessary, add a little more stock to ensure this).

Haddock, Steamed

Haddock can also be steamed and served with parsley sauce. Personally, I think anchovy sauce swamps the delicate flavour of most fish, but this is a matter of taste—and it also depends upon the quality of the fish.

There is a pleasant salt tang to fresh-caught fish, which passes off if they are stored on ice too long. They will still be good, but flavourless; in this case anchovy may be useful, but if firm and fresh, steamed fish should be served as simply as possible and reserve the savoury flavours for the roasting process, which blends them better.

"Haddoke in Cynee"

Very spicy—local name "Douch" (?)

"Shal be yopaed and ywasshe clene, and ysode and yrosted on a gridel, [with] grounde peper, saffron, bread and ale." While the "Haddoke" is grilling: "mynce oynouns and fry hem, and do therto salt and ale and boil it and do thyn haddock in plates and the curiey above and gif forth."

The ale puzzled me, till a west-country friend showed me a dish called "douch". She substituted flour and potatoes for the bread, otherwise it is the same. Grill a fresh haddock, peppering well (no salt, as it is salt enough), fry the onions in fat till crisp and brown, and pile them on the (now turned-over) haddock. To the onion-flavoured fat in the fry-pan, add a measure of flour (this would be the bread), and after cooking make into a gravy with a measure of ale or cider. Put the haddock on the plate, pile on the onions, and pour the spiced gravy around.

Findon (or Finnan) Haddock

" Chuse skilfully salt-fish, not burnt at the stone, but such as be good, or else let it alone : Get home that is bought, and go stack it up dry, with pease-straw between it, the safter to lie."

TUSSER.

Catfish v. Haddock

There is a skeleton in the cupboard here. The *genuine* haddock has a stiff, firm backbone and, when split open to become a "haddie", that bone protests his noble ancestry in a strong curve, like a wave, all down one side.

The skin of a haddock is silver-grey and fine, and the rounding to the pointed tail shows the shape of the original fish. Both skeleton and skin prove that a fine fresh haddock has been gutted, split, cured and smoked

to make your fine "finny haddie". To get such a fish, pay a good price for it; it is worth it. But nowadays a lot of catfish are landed on the quays; they used to be thrown away or used for bait (as they are a poor-quality fish, of little flavour and worse texture) but such is commercial duplicity that I have watched catfish being beheaded, skinned and packed into barrels and sold as "dressing fish", and a lot of "boneless haddie" is nothing more than this catfish, dipped in pickle and yellow colouring dye. It *is* edible and, thanks to the pickle, quite palatable, *but it's not haddock—* it should not fetch the price of haddock. The *real* haddock is far superior in flavour and value.

"Buttered Haddie"

Take a large real "haddie"; lay it, skin side down, on a well-buttered bake-pan, pour over just enough boiling water and milk (half-and-half) to barely cover the fish, cover the bake-pan closely, and set in a hot oven for 20–30 minutes, according to size. Do not uncover the dish, as you want to keep in the aroma.

To serve, slide the fish on to a hot plate, pour the white "gravy" over it, put a pat of butter on top, dust it with white pepper, and send to table quickly with brown bread and butter—or hot mashed potatoes. Real haddie is a very savoury dish.

"Haddyanegg"

A "special" supper in some industrial districts is "haddyanegg", that is, a "haddie" steamed in butter and milk, with an egg poached on top of it. The egg is cooked in the rich salty gravy from the fish and the "plateful" served with brown bread and butter, and a cup of tea. It is a favourite "high tea" before evening technical institute classes.

Catfish Haddock

To cook the "boneless" yellow substitute—lay it in a dish—pour boiling water over it, slowly, till the long wiry bones can be picked out.

Then butter a piedish, put a layer of the fish, a dust of pepper, a pat of butter (in bits) and a layer of mashed potatoes, and add fish and potatoes in layers till the piedish is full—rough up the top potato layer—and bake in the oven for a good half-hour.

HERRINGS

> " Fresh herring plenty, Michell brings,
> With fatted crones,[1] and such old things."
>
> TUSSER.

[1] Fattened crones were old ewes, too old for breeding, fattened up for mutton

Fresh herrings straight from the water are firm, bright fish. There are many ways of cooking herring. They are very rich in oil and, therefore, can be fried without any fat in the pan.

This recipe was taught to me in 1920, crossing to Stornaway. (There was blue sky and flying cloud overhead, and the spray flung over the deck as the ship's cook showed me this method.)

Take an iron pan and put in a pinch of salt for each fish, and gut and trim the fish, taking off the fins and head; wipe them *bone dry* with a cloth dipped in fine oatmeal and put them in the pan on to the *hot* salt, and keep shaking the pan so that they do not stick. Cook till they are done one side, and then turn over with a knife and do the other side; when cooked through, and crisp outside, slide out of the pan on to a hot plate, put a lump of butter and a dash of pepper inside each, and eat with a slab of buttered oatcake.

Grilled Herrings

Fresh herrings are best plain grilled. Gut them, cut off heads and tails and fins, and split open down the backbone, drawing it out together with as many of the fine bones as possible. Wipe the fish, pepper and salt it, and dip it in fine oatmeal, pressing this on well, inside and out. Dot with a very little bacon-fat, and grill, first one side and then the other, for a good 10 minutes (as you want the oil in the herrings to be drawn out and permeate the oatmeal covering, which should be crisp and bright brown). Serve instantly on a hot plate, with the drips from the grill and a pat of butter on each. The correct condiment with herrings is mustard sauce. Serve with brown bread and butter and freshly made tea.

Bloaters

Bloaters are a speciality of Yarmouth. They are herrings salted and preserved in their natural form.

"The common English mode of 1840: Take fresh Yarmouth bloaters, cut off the heads and tails, and open the herrings down the back; grill over a red fire on a gridiron. Rub over with a lump of cold butter, sprinkle with black pepper and serve plain, smoking hot, with thick bread."

Red Herrings

Red herrings are a form of super-salted bloater, very popular on the western seaboard, specially Ireland. They produce a terrible thirst—all artists seem to like them: I cannot account for this. Rudyard Kipling makes his "Hal o' the Draft" cook salt herrings in the cathedral, but he provides the only corroborative authority that I can produce for this notable dietetic discovery.

Note. At Hogmanay, if the Glasgow friend wishes you well, he slips a red herring down his sleeve into the palm of your hand as he grasps it.

MACKEREL

" When Mackrell ceaseth from the seas,
    John Baptist brings grass-beef and pease."

                                                    TUSSER.

This is the most beautiful fish. When the shoals come in to the bay, mackerel is suddenly very plentiful and cheap; at other times there may be none for weeks. Its delicacy makes it one of the most difficult fish for transport and it spoils so rapidly that there were special laws permitting it to be sold on Sundays, even in Scotland.

Mackerel, so fresh that the light shines from it like a rainbow, should be treated exactly like trout, and grilled and served as swiftly. For this the smaller fish are best. The very large mackerel, full of roe, are better split and stuffed with a good herb seasoning (as they have less flavour). Therefore small mackerel, grill as trout; large mackerel, bake with stuffing.

Note. On no account boil or stew mackerel, as it loses all flavour and tastes like a wet pin-cushion.

Large Mackerel

Take 4 oz. of fine breadcrumbs, 2 oz. of fine dripping or lard (just melted), 1 teaspoonful of powdered herbs, 1 small onion scraped finely, salt, pepper, and a spot of anchovy sauce. Beat together, binding with an egg, dry the fish, put a strip of bay leaf inside each, fill up with the stuffing, dust with seasoned flour, and dot over well with dripping or butter before baking in a medium oven for about 30–40 minutes (according to the size of the fish). In this case (i.e., a *very large* and therefore rather less-flavoured fish) it is permitted to serve with a full-flavoured sauce—anchovy or parsley.

Note. Any soft roe may be mixed in with the stuffing, but the hard roe is better baked under the fish.

PILCHARDS

These are also called Cornish "fair maids"—a corruption of "formade", from the Spanish word "fumade" or smoked.

Pilchards were important to the industries of the west country, and this eighteenth-century description of bulking pilchards for oil probably described a far older process, and some of the reputed prehistoric hut circles around the coast may have been only these curious sunk pits.

" The fish were now laid out on the raised slabs that ran round the court. First a layre of salt was spread, then a layre of pilchards and so on, layres of pilchards and salt alternating till a vast mound was raised. Here they remained a month or more. Below the slabs were gutters which convayed the brine and oil which oozed out of the mass, into a large pit in the centre of the court. From three to four hundred-weight of salt was used for each hogshead. After remaining in bulk for a sufficient time, the pilchards were cleaned from the salt and closely packed in hogsheads, each hogshead containing about 2400 fish, and weighing 476 pounds. The pressure to which they are subjected forces the oil out through the joints of the cask.

No portion is lost. The oil and blood is sold to the curriers, the skimmings of the water in which the fish are washed before packing is purchased by the soapboilers, and the broken and refuse fish are sold for manure. The oil, when purified, formed an important part of the profit."

MICHAEL PENGUYNE, Kingston S.P.C.A.

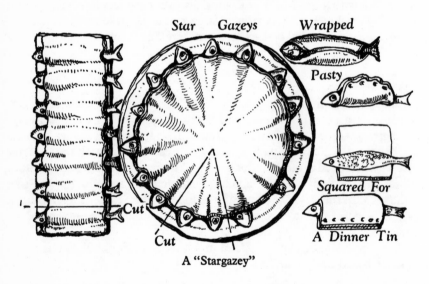

Star   Gazeys   Wrapped

Pasty

Squared For

A Dinner Tin

Cut

Cut

A "Stargazey"

Stargazey pies. These are properly made of pilchards, and are a good example of structural design. The pastry cover probably derives from the clay-workers' kiln (*see* Huff Paste). When eatable pastry was used, it was wasteful to cover the uneatable fish-head—yet, if the fish-head was cut off, the rich oil in it was lost. Therefore, it was better to cook the fish whole, so that this oil could drain back into the meat (as marrow out of the bones internally bastes a roasting joint). So the cooks covered the body of the fish—but left the head sticking out.

Now note the structural design of an economic idea! It becomes possible to construct a communal pasty, and divide it into slices with great exactitude. For family use, the circular pie-plate. For market stalls and meetings, the fish can be laid side by side along the first strip of pastry and covered over with the second, quickly pressed down between individual slices and sold—by the yard.

Common Stargazey

Slit and gut the fish, removing small fins and wiping off the scales; season well, putting a spoonful of finely chopped onion and green herbs into the belly (this improves the flavour and keeps the fish moist while baking). The pastry should be a plain short-crust, and the underside crust rolled out rather more thinly than the top cover. The tops may be brushed over with a little saffroned milk—or beaten egg, to give them a golden colour.

The stuffings vary; a spoonful of mustard, pummace from the cider press, or pickled samphire, if the flavour is liked, or plain crumb-and-herb stuffing, but keep it moist to act as gravy.

A Victorian "Rich Stargazey"

Scale, gut, and bone pilchards or herrings, laying them flat; open, season lavishly with pepper, spice and chopped herbs—roll up and pack down into a dish thickly coated with butter and equal quantities of finely chopped onion and breadcrumbs. Place slips of fat bacon among the fish and fill up the dish with well-seasoned egg-custard—cover closely. Bake long and slowly, so that the whey from the custard, the juice from the onions, and the gravy from the fish commingle with the bacon fat and seasoning, and permeate the whole.

Just before it is done, remove the cover and place over it a short-crust pastry.

In Victorian cookery, the herring heads gazed upwards, clustered through a hole in the centre, with parsley in their mouths, while the tails of the fish decorated the outer rim.

CONGER

Conger eel is more like a fish than an eel—thick and fleshy and gelatinous. It has always been very popular with old Cornish miners. The middle cut was usually roasted whole; the ends made into pies.

In the Cornish Women's Institute recipes they cook the conger eel in milk and butter, but in that case the old recipes add sugar and currants and make a different type of dish.

Roasted Conger (middle cut)

Take the whole middle cut (twelve to eighteen inches, and "thick as a drumnie"), clean it and dry it, rub the inside well with cut onion, and wipe over with a little dry mustard. Stuff it with a good, well-flavoured forcemeat and sew it up strongly. Cut an apple in two and use each half to plug the ends, before tying it up with tape like a packet.

Roast it thoroughly, basting with dripping and cider. The cider is

The apple used to plug the ends should be well pressed into the roll,
as it is thrust outwards in the heat of baking (as shown).

specially needed to soften the gelatinous texture. The dish splutters badly, and was obviously better cooked on the flat hearth under an iron pan oven. If using a top oven put paper, or a tin, over it while spluttering, but do not enclose the fish, or it will be steamed not roasted. Remove the tapes before serving very hot. Pickled red cabbage is good with this dish, or samphire pickle, if you like it.

SKATE

The "ray" fishes do not have roes like most fish, their young are born alive, so it is important to eat them *only* when in season. It is one of the best fish when good, and quite the worst when bad. The wide wing-like fins are tiresome to eat on account of the bones, so it is sensible to serve separately. The fish will steam well, or, cut into steaks, it fries very well.

Skate and Tomatoes

Cut the skate into slices two or three inches long and the *width* of the fish (it is understood you have removed the side "wings"). Let the slices lie on a plateful of diluted lemon juice, vinegar or dry cider (some mild acid) for an hour or so, turning them. Drain dry, dip in beaten egg and crumbs, and fry golden brown, turning carefully with a slice. Have another pan full of even-sized tomatoes frying side by side, and serve the hot skate slices with a sizzling red tomato on each, and a garnish of green fried parsley round the sides.

Skate "Wings"

These should be simmered flat in well-salted water with a dash of vinegar (as this "cuts" the gelatinous bone). When they seem done (probably 15 minutes), lift out gently and, holding flat, with a cloth wrung out in cold water, you'll find you will be able to draw out all the bones sideways, like a row of pins.

The slices may then be served under a thin glazing of melted butter.

RAY

" St. Austyn he took his way
  Goddes word for to say,
  Besides Rouchester, in the land
  Of South East Britain, a folk he found
  That to Gods word gave no heed,
  No; nor grace had they in deed,
  For there—whereas he stood to preach
  Their salvation them to teach
  Behind him, to his clothes they hung
  Ray's tailes ! on a string! "

                                E. E. T. S.

The ray differs from the skate and has rather wider flaps and longer devil tail. But it may be cooked in the same way. The curiously long flakes of this fish make it very appropriate for cold mayonnaise salads.

SOLE

This is the best flat fish, so it should be cooked carefully and served simply. A small sole is very delicate, steamed between two plates; put a pat of butter under and over it, add a little salt and a spoonful of liquor (for which the head and fins have been boiled down). Pepper it before serving and use the broth which runs in cooking as gravy. Serve rolled brown bread and butter or fine dry toast with it.

A fine thick sole is usually expensive, but if very large it may also be flavourless, in which case you are justified in cooking it more elaborately.

Clean and trim off the fins along the sides, but leave on the head. Cut a slit from head to tail on the dark side and across from behind the head on both sides. Slide a pliant knife along the bones each side (as if you were going to fillet it) and snap the bone in two above the tail; then turning back the flaps and levering up by the head, it is possible to lift out the entire "harp" still attached to the head. Fill the pocket slit so left with green

Removing the bones

butter, season delicately, and press the fish "shut" again, coat it with beaten egg and a little fine flour and bake a delicate golden brown; serve it with wafer potatoes, grilled tomatoes, a sprig of watercress, and thin rolled brown bread and butter.

Green butter is made thus: pour boiling water slowly over a handful of parsley till it is limp and vivid green; then squeeze dry and chop it fine as green mist, crush a small onion to pulp and squeeze the juice of that on to the parsley and the juice of half a lemon, add pepper and salt and beat it into as much warm (*not* melted) butter as will hold it.

PLAICE

They can be treated like sole, but are a much cheaper fish and more often larger.

Trim, gut and clean—wipe dry, with some salt on the cloth. Put a generous pat of butter, lard, or clarified bacon-fat into a bake-pan and put in it a shallot, chopped up, and some lemon thyme and parsley, chopped fine. Let them cook till the butter is well flavoured (do not *fry* them, just cook gently), take them out and then raise the heat till the butter *does* boil and dip the fish into it for a moment, both sides. Lay a bay leaf under the fish, put the herbs on top, cover with greased paper, and bake gently till done—serve in the bake-pan.

A small glass of white wine stirred in just before serving makes the liquid in the bake-pan the best sauce for the fish.

Baked Plaice and Shrimps

This is a thoroughly Victorian recipe from a "refined periodical" of the period.

"Put a pat of butter into a shallow earthenware dish, large enough to hold all the fillets of plaice laid flat. Heat the butter and slip the floured and seasoned fillets into it. Cover closely with buttered paper and bake until tender. Meanwhile put a handful of picked shelled shrimps into another deep pot with a scrape of butter, and enough milk to cover, and set it into the oven alongside the plaice. (Time shrimps and plaice to be perfectly cooked at exactly the same time.) Take up the dish of fillets and spread half of them with the shrimps; cover with the other fillets and pour the hot milk and butter sauce from both dishes, over the pink and white fish sandwiches on a hot dish. Garnish the top of each slice with a few of the best shrimps and serve with thin white bread and butter."

DABS

Very small plaice and sole are sometimes sold as "dabs". They are only a few inches long, and should, rightly, have been returned to the sea, but this is not always possible. Dabs are best "buttered".

Clean and trim the dabs, removing head and tail and cutting off the fins with scissors. Rub a flat baking-pan with butter, using a cut garlic; dip the dabs in seasoned flour and arrange them flat all over the pan—overlapping the thin tail ends with the thick head ends (like tiles on a roof); *grate* some cold butter over all (so that it falls like fine snow), and put under the grill, till the fish is done and just beginning to crisp at the edges—5–10 minutes.

Note. We repeat that this "dab fish" is a massacre of innocents, but if they must be used, this is the best way.

THORNBACKS (name varies locally)

These fish are coarse and should be cooked in the same way as herring. Skerries (above Dublin) was famous for thornbacks. They were used also to supply the crude oil for lighting.[1]

The oil-burning light from thornbacks is not to be confused with the phosphorous glow of old fish, or rotten wood, which was used for primitive path lighting (as mentioned by the Board of Northern Lights and Hans Andersen).

GURNARD

As the round head of this fish is so large, it is usually cooked on the fish, but if you cut it off, when you trim the fins and tail, use the pieces to make liquor for the pan. Gurnard roasts best and, though it is not good to mix meat and fish, in this case, a slice of fat *mild-cured* bacon over it helps to keep this thick fish basted during the long cooking.

Clean, wipe dry, and dress the fish; rub the inside over with a cut onion, pepper it, brush a little butter, lard or bacon-fat over the inside of it; and stuff it with a nice mildly flavoured forcemeat (a tablespoonful of finely chopped fat bacon—pepper, salt, a pinch of herbs, and a fine slice of lemon rind minced small; bind with an egg). Roast, basting very thoroughly all the time—it may take an hour if large and thick—do not make sauce with this roast fish, but strain off and thicken the liquor in the pan; a glassful of white wine improves it.

[1] The fish themselves were stuffed full of linen waste, and pressed till the "wick" was saturated, and actually burnt as "candles", being lit at the "top end". Two or three tied together in an iron holder made a torch.

TURBOT

This is one of the best large flat fish. Rounder than the sole, it has tiny knobs of bone within its thick skin. It is far too good and well-flavoured a fish to spoil by over-dressing. Clean out carefully, but do not remove the fleshy fins. Rub it with salt and a cut lemon till clear, and, if liked, a small wedge of cut lemon may be left inside the fish. It is one of the few fishes really best steamed. Lay it on the drainer in the turbot kettle over well-salted water. When it seems loose on the bones, lift, drain, and serve with a cream sauce. It is one of the fishes where oyster or shrimp sauces are good, otherwise a plain egg or parsley sauce is suitable, but on no account overdo the flavour of the sauce, so that it swamps the flavour of the fish, for which reason plain white bread and butter, rolled, is the best accompaniment.

RED MULLET

These should be cooked whole without cleaning. Season lightly and butter thickly, before wrapping each one up in a piece of oiled paper, tie securely and bake for about half an hour, turning the packets around once, but being careful not to tilt up or spill any juice.

They are served direct on to the plates, the sauce being the butter and gravy that pours out of the packet when undone, though a little white wine may be added.

LING GOLDEN

> " Ling perhaps looks for great extolling being counted beefe
> of the sea, and standing every fish day [as a cold supporter] at
> my Lord Maior's table; yet it is nothing but long cod. When it is
> salted it is called Ling . . . the longer it lyeth . . . the better it is;
> waxing in the end as yellow as a gold noble."
>
> *Babees Book.*

The same ambiguity holds today, and dried cod is sometimes called "ling". I am told that the small ling sometimes caught off the Yorkshire coast are called "drizzles". It is a solid fish and should be served as a complete meal, and the mediaeval idea of ling "yellow as gold" cannot be improved upon. This is the modern version of the old recipe.

Slice the fish one inch thick, rub it well with onion and salt, then dust it with fine pepper, coat thickly with fine oatmeal, and fry it golden brown. Take it out, and arrange it in a shallow fireproof dish. Then take onion chopped fine, and parsnip chopped very fine, and fry them also till golden brown; pack these over and around the fish, and fill in the cracks with chopped herbs. *Season well,* fill up the dish with well-flavoured stock

(made from the fish and vegetable trimmings boiled down with a single
clove of saffron). Cover and bake at least 40 minutes in a very slow, steady
oven.

Serve in the dish in which it is cooked. It should be yellow as gold and
very tender and savoury.

Note. It is important to use fine oatmeal in order to make the gravy
thick and rich. The parsnip gives the important sweet element, and the
saffron (use *very* little) its particular aroma and fine gold tint.

If saffron is missing, a "gold" stew may be had by packing the gold
outer skins of the onions over the fish while cooking (removing before
serving). The yellow outer skins will colour the fish, but the flavour of
the saffron will be missed.

Blanket Ling

Ling, or stockfish, is only salted—not smoked (as a rule). The island
people do it under most difficult weather conditions, when it would seem
impossible to dry anything. They put the fish, on ladder-like racks, in
the wind, till very much the consistency of a well-scoured white board.
You often see stockfish for sale in towns. The north-country people soak it
in *running water*, then stew it in buttermilk, and afterwards rub it with a
dry cloth, while hot, till it fluffs up into a blanket-like consistency, very
light and white. But the more general usage is to stew slowly on the
peats with milk and butter and thicken the gravy with eggs before serving.
Catholic Ireland and parts of Scotland make this dish to perfection.

"Stockfysshe" with Walnuts

> " Take currylles of walnuys and clouys of garleek and piper
> bred and salt and cast in a morter and grynd it smal and tempre
> it with some of the broth that the fysshe was sode in, and serue
> forth."
>
> **FOURTEENTH CENTURY**

From experiment I believe the "kernels of walnuts" to have been
pickled, as the dark-brown spicy gravy on the white fish is just the "design"
a fourteenth-century cook would delight in. Had the walnuts been shelled,
assuredly saffron or saunders or some other colouring would have been
"caste" in; there are no pale pastel shades in Gothic cookery!

Here is the modern version:

Soak a dried "stockfysshe" and bring slowly to the boil twice, throwing
away the water, and the last time filling up with fresh water and letting it
simmer, flat out, in a shallow pan. Shred onions and strew them over the
fish, and let it go on cooking, covered up, till both onions and fish are
tender.

Meanwhile make a sauce with butter, flour and pepper, chopped pickled walnuts, and add the onions from the fish, temper it with some of the fish broth and boil up. Drain the fish and replace in the dish with the brown sauce over it, garnish with a few halved walnuts and tufts of watercress. The sauce should be distinctly sharp, so add a little of the vinegar from the walnuts, if not sharp enough. If we were in the habit of "grinding" raw materials together, probably we should "grind" the raw onions with the walnuts and pepper all at once, and the resultant gravy would be stronger flavoured.

WHITEBAIT at Greenwich (A.D. 1890)

(This recipe is for July to the end of August only.)

In the "nineties" and earlier it was a gay and pleasant summer outing to take your lady-friend down the river to luncheon at Greenwich, where, in an inn overlooking the river, the whitebait were cooked fresh from the nets. This was from "The Inn overlooking the River" at Greenwich.

"The fish should be lifted straight in the net, rinsed in seawater and thrown directly on to dry, thickly floured cloths—the cloths must be lightly tossed and shaken between the outstretched hands—and the cloth then released and the fish dropped lightly down on to sieves to shake out the surplus flour. These sieves are then plunged straight into boiling fat, and almost instantly lifted out, the fish being cooked crisp." Correctly cooked, whitebait should be silver tinted with gold and "piled high on a hot silver dish without any napkin" (this dates the period) and sent instantly to table with cut lemon and slices of thin brown bread and butter "on wide plates".

To the cook who has to get the whitebait from the fishmonger, we suggest that they should be rinsed in strongly salted water, in lieu of seawater, and carry on the old recipe from there. The rinsing, in salted water, directly before flouring and drying and frying, is what is required to make the flour coating even and close and to get the crisp finish. If the small fish are unevenly damped, the flour sticks unevenly and they cook unevenly. Method: Wet, flour, dry, fry, serve.

Water Souchy (Greenwich recipe)

While waiting for the whitebait to be cooked, this soup was often served. It was made from the small odd fish that were taken out of the whitebait nets.

Throw the well-rinsed fish into rather more water than sufficient to cover them, adding $\frac{1}{2}$ oz. of salt to the quart, a dozen peppercorns and a large bunch of fresh parsley, *with its roots*, all chopped up. Simmer 1 hour and strain through muslin. Throw in any small neat white pieces of the cooked fish and a sprinkling of freshly chopped green parsley. Add the juice of half a lemon, or rather more, to taste, and add a thin slice of the lemon to each serving of soup. This clear green fish broth was accompanied with fine hot toasted brown bread, and was excellent while chatting to your friends, watching the river traffic, and awaiting the whitebait.

FISH POT (and fish by the yard)

This old country dish was made of any damaged or broken fish that was no use for market or the odd fishes left over in packing sheds. Such fish was by custom given away at the quayside. Some old "fishwomen" would sell it on barrows in the streets. Often they did not sell by weight, but "by measure", having a small wooden board about a foot long by six inches wide and laying the strangely assorted fish out along the board—in a ragged row—long and short, thin and fat, side by side. "A shilling a boardful, missus! Hall frush fussh!"

This "mixed fish" was put into a brown earthenware hot-pot that had been well greased with plenty of dripping, a chopped onion added, the whole close-covered and baked. The bones were then removed, also skins and tails, etc., and the hot fish and onion flaked up with an equal quantity of hot mashed potato, well seasoned, and returned to the oven, without the lid, to brown (like a hot-pot). Eaten with thick slabs of bread and dripping and cups of scalding hot tea, about six o'clock, it went down very comfortably on a cold night.

The points to remember are that the "pot" lid should fit closely (so that the fish steams in its own juice), that there should be ample well-clarified dripping, and the onions large, mild and juicy, to make plenty of rich fish gravy. Serve it straight from the oven in its own pot.

FISH ROE (fourteenth-century recipe)

"Take the womb of a luce [pike] and seethe it, and Kut [shred] tendre chese, and grynd them 'in frere' [together, 'in brotherhood'] with peper and sugre. And take flour and egyroune [plural of egg] and do togeder— [i.e. make a batter coating] and loke the eyroune [the roe] been hote and lay over the paste and serve."

In modern version: take cod's roe and stew it, shred a *little* soft cheese and mix all together with pepper, salt, and a little sugar (it improves many fish dishes very much), and make a batter of flour and eggs and water, and coat the fish-cakes and fry or bake them and serve. "Loke the eyroune *been* hote" means that it must not be cooked *again* after the cheese is added ("eyroune" being plural for egg, and *been* is past tense).

DOLPHIN

> " The dolphin and the bonetta being fresh are most wholesome nourishment, and fitt for Kings; but being salted and dryed are most dangerous and contagioue to breed leprosye."
>
> DRAKE'S VOYAGES, 1628.

Interesting, as the dried and salted fish of East Africa and India is suspect today by research workers on leprosy. Also, the extra salt in the diet on shipboard, in the tropics, would force up any other skin trouble that might stimulate leprosy.

FRESH-WATER FISH

> " Fysshe, the which is in ryvers and brokes, be more holsome than they which be in ponds and mootes, or other standing water, for they doeth labour and doth skower themselves. Fysshe and els that do feede in the fen or morysshe ground doth saver of the moude."
>
> BOORDE.

Clear Stream versus Muddy Pond

Muddy-bottom fish has to be specially cooked or it will taste muddy. The skill was taught to me by an old fisherman of the Fens, where I first cooked bream. In detail he showed why all muddy-bottom fish have special overlapping and fringe scales—these keep the mud clear from the fish's skin while the fish is full, and swims against the stream; but once the fish is limp, and the scales are disturbed, the mud gets under them, and touches the absorbent skin of the fish. Therefore pond fish must never be washed, or even moved, more than can be avoided. Take the fish by the head, and smooth it down lightly towards the tail in clay or paste, and bake it quite flat without turning. For this reason you must roast it, raised up on a grid, or a handful of twigs, anything that will allow the underside of the fish to cook dryly. When done, this crust can be broken off, skin and all, and the fish will be clean-tasting and of very fine quality.

SALMON

> " I tell you, captain, if you look in the maps of the world, I'll warrant you shall find comparisons between Macedon and Monmouth. . . . That the situations look you is both alike. . . . There is a river in Macedon, and there is also, moreover, a river at Monmouth—it is called Wye at Monmouth . . . 'tis as alike as my fingers to my fingers . . . and there is salmons in both."
>
> SHAKESPEARE, Henry V.

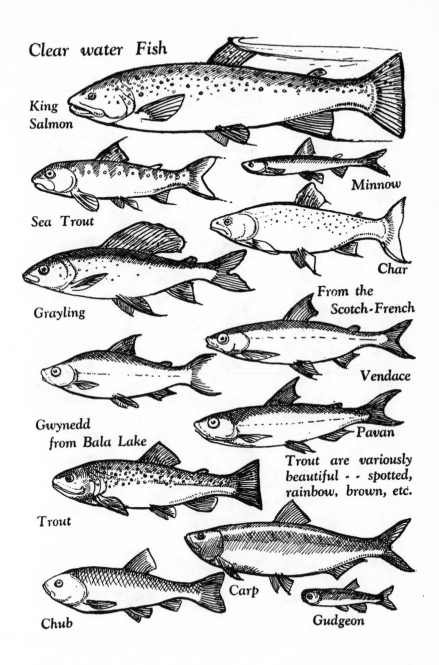

Clear water Fish

King
Salmon

Sea Trout

Minnow

Char

Grayling

From the
Scotch-French

Vendace

Gwynedd
from Bala Lake

Pavan

Trout are variously
beautiful - - spotted,
rainbow, brown, etc.

Trout

Chub

Carp

Gudgeon

The Muddy Water Fish

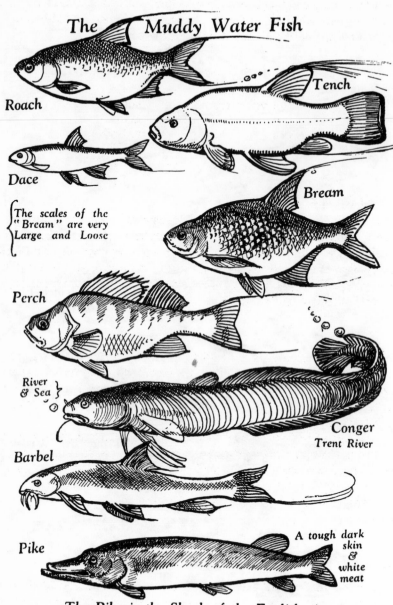

Roach

Tench

Dace

The scales of the
"Bream" are very
Large and Loose

Bream

Perch

River
& Sea

Conger
Trent River

Barbel

Pike

A tough dark
skin
&
white
meat

The Pike is the Shark of the English river

Salmon should never be taken out of season, as it is a fish which changes character completely between fresh-water and sea periods. Fishermen recognise half a dozen different periods of salmon, according to their movements in the river, and their breeding seasons.

" Salmon—Nomenclature[1]

1 year's growth	—	smelts
2 years' growth	—	sprods
3 ,, ,,	—	morts
4 ,, ,,	—	forktails
5 ,, ,,	—	half fish
6 ,, ,,	—	salmon."

EVANS, 1798.

Salmon Steamed

Salmon is best cooked very simply. To steam: wrap the whole fish, or portion of the fish, in greased paper and lay it over fast-boiling water till cooked. Slide it out gently on to a hot dish and serve with its own broth. A small bouquet of herbs may be laid under it, to give aroma, but do not over-season. Cook gently and serve plainly. If any sauce is needed, it is usually fennel (*see* under Sauces).

Roast Salmon

An old way to roast salmon. Season the round, or length, of the salmon with nutmeg, and salt, stick with a few cloves, and within put some buttered bay leaves and a little spray of rosemary. Roast and baste it with butter and add to the gravy, for sauce, a very little vinegar, butter, and slices of orange.

For a piece of salmon needed for mayonnaise next day, season it, wrap in buttered paper, and enclose in a covered pot, so that it is completely sealed. Bake, and leave it unopened till wanted next day, when it will be found in a pool of rich gravy and the meat very delicate and juicy.

All fish to be eaten cold is good cooked thus, as it retains the juice and flavour.

TROUT

Everyone in England eats trout whenever they can. Land proprietors preserve special trout streams at great cost. Hotels and club-houses advertise "fishing rights" in trout streams, and charge accordingly.Week-enders from industrial towns follow trout streams for miles. Country

[1] These names vary according to the river.

rectories, mountain farms and lakeside inns produce trout for breakfast. Half the fly-rods of expensive fishing tackle purchased by country visitors are "for trout". Small boys lie on their tummies and tickle trout. (In my granddad's time all quarrymen and miners used to go down to the streams and lift out enough fish for Sunday morning's breakfast. Nowadays they buy sausages.) Trout vary as much as the water they swim in. Trout from shallow streams tend to have shorter pelvic fins. They look as if they have been rubbed off on the stones. Very green trout probably come from deeper rivers where green trees shadow green weed below. Limestone streams have very silver trout. Scotch trout, Welsh trout, Irish trout all differ. Rainbow trout originally imported from the North American lakes are bred in the Ceiriog Valley in North Wales. *All* are slightly different in colour and shape, but all trout have spots and all are good eating.

Trout and Leek

A single folded leek leaf holds a trout very neatly for grilling.

GRAYLING

I believe the grayling the most beautiful fish in the world. Where Kilsey Craig stands up like a rampart below Hatton Gill there is a stone bridge over clear water, running over pebbles white as mushroom tops, spotted with water snails black as ebony. The fine turf either side of the Wharf is grey-green. In the swift places of the water the grayling rests, a fish of silver and pearl, fanning the stream gently with graceful fronds of bronze silk. He looks as if he rested still, and let the stream ripple through his soft fins, but he is keeping his place with effortless grace. Sometimes he lets go and drifts down stream, swift as the shadow of a flying bird; and then a flicker of pearl light, and he is back at rest again. At evening time when the stream is dark, he shines like white pewter in the moonlight. I hate to give you the recipe for cooking him.

He is flavoured of thyme—as are all things living on those thyme-scented moorlands—so when you have caught him, pack him in your creel with a bunch of the wild thyme that grows in scented purple and grey close to the stream, and cook some of it with him. He is far superior to trout.

BARBEL

This fish is easily distinguished by its beard, i.e., barbe. It is rather attractively coloured yellowish-brown with reddish and greenish lines, according to the locality. We often find this fish in Nottingham market. It was caught in the Trent on Sundays by men with baskets and Thermos flasks, sitting on camp-stools on the grass, all, along the flat green agricultural Trent Valley. It is a better-looking fish when washed and wiped, but like all mud browsers is best covered with clay or paste and baked, the skin and crust being broken off before serving.

CARP

" The Carp is the queen of rivers; a stately, a good and a very subtil fish. . . . The physicians make the galls and stones in the heads of Carps to be very medicinable. But it is not to be doubted but that in Italy they make great profit of the spawn of the Carp, by selling it to the Jews, who make it into red caviare; the Jews not being by their law admitted to eat of caviare made of the Sturgeon, that being a fish that wants scales . . . by them reputed to be unclean."

IZAAK WALTON.

The date of their arrival from China is controversial. According to the early English records—the *Book of St. Albans*, 1496—the carp was a "dayntous fysshe but fewe in Englande". Izaak Walton puts their arrival in the sixteenth century. Fish experts in Germany had long developed the carp as a domestic fish. It was one of the last unfortunates to be sold piecemeal from tanks, and was literally "cooked alive" as late as 1850, though even earlier cookery books rebel against "crimped carp" as being inhuman. They have always been a cultivated fish and were almost certainly bred in the monastery fish ponds, but whether the old pet carp in the ornamental pools of cathedral cloisters are descendants of "holy orders", or not, is disputatious. Mirror carp and gold carp are variants of the common carp.

CHUB

"The Chub, though he eat well, thus dressed yet as he is usually dressed, he does not. He is objected against, not only for being full of small forked bones, dispersed through all his body but that he eats waterish . . . nevertheless, he may be so dressed as to make him very good meat . . . First scale him, and then wash him clean, and then take out his guts; and to that end make the holes as little, and near to his gills, as you may conveniently, and especially make clean his throat from the grass and weeds that are usually in it; for if that be not very clean, it will make him taste very sour. Having done so, put some sweet herbs into his belly; and then tie him with two or three splinters to a spit, and roast him, basted often with vinegar, or rather verjuice and butter, with good store of salt mixed with it. Being thus dressed, you will find him a much better dish of meat than you, or most folk, even than anglers themselves do imagine."

IZAAK WALTON.

A chubby little fish in shallow streams or mill dams and waterwheel races. He is disappointing to cook, as his plumpness is all held out on splints inside.

Izaak Walton gives the recipe for cooking him, but most fishermen throw him back. To avoid disappointing some young fishermen, the fish can be made into broth, and the following "young fisherman's soup" (from a book of 1869) was probably the solution of this difficulty:

1 lb. of fish, different kinds (small and bony), 1 tomato, 2 carrots, 2 onions, a bunch of sweet herbs, 1 cupful of vinegar, 1 spoonful of soy, and some celery if available. Chop all coarsely and boil rapidly for a few minutes, then simmer 1 hour. Strain through a tammy.

Fish Mould with Salad

Follow the soup recipe, but add one small handful of isinglass to the mixed vegetables. Simmer for 1 hour, stirring at intervals, strain off through tammy and let it set over night. It should set to a stiff, clear jelly. Melt until just liquid and pour into moulds. Fill up with any small cooked vegetables, such as green peas, carrots, and a little chopped parsley, and when cold and set, turn out and garnish with sprigs of watercress and serve with mashed potatoes.

It is really very good, and the young fishermen seem to think it more solid worth for their catch than "just soup".

Minnows

The tiddlers caught by small boys should be put back. The minnow proper is two or three inches long, a blunt-nosed, sturdy, clean little fish, rather like a trout, and should be cooked like whitebait or sprats according to size. Mediaeval people used minnows as garnishes to larger fish.

Izaak Walton gives a "minnow tansie":

"And in the spring they make of them excellent Minnow-tansies; for being washed well in salt, and their heads and tails cut off, and their guts taken out, and not washed after, they prove excellent for that use; that is, being fried with yolk of eggs, the flowers of cowslips and of primroses, and a little tansy; thus used they make a dainty dish of meat."

CRAYFISH

> " A crewes—dyght him thus—departe hym a sonder, and slyte
> the belly and take out y fysshe, pare away the reed skynne and
> mynce it thynne—put vynegre in the dysshe and set on ye table
> without hete."
>
> 1400.

The monks were very fond of crayfish, and it is said it was they who
introduced them to many of our streams. The finest I ever saw were
out of the Eleanor Beck, near Bolton Abbey. They resemble small lobsters,
and are cooked and eaten in the same way.

English Crayfish

Kill the fish instantly by a thrust through the spine behind the head,
through the carapace. Plunge into absolutely boiling salted water till
bright red and cooked (10–15 minutes). Put into clean cold water to cool.
Shell as you would small lobsters, and serve on a flat tray of watercresses.

PIKE

> " First, open your Pike at the gills, and if need be, cut also a little
> slit towards the belly. Out of these, take his guts; and keep his
> liver, which you are to shred very small, with thyme, sweet
> marjoram, and a little winter-savoury; put to these some pickled
> oysters, and some anchovies, two or three; both these last whole,
> for the anchovies will melt, and the oysters should not; to these,
> you must add also a pound of sweet butter, which you are to
> mix with the herbs that are shred, and let them all be well salted.
> If the Pike be more than a yard long, then you may put into these
> herbs more than a pound, or if he be less, then less butter will
> suffice: These, being thus mixt, with a blade or two of mace, must
> be put into the Pike's belly; and then his belly so sewed up as to
> keep all the butter in his belly if it is possible; if not, then as
> much of it as you possibly can. But take not off the scales. Then you
> are to thrust the spit through his mouth, out at his tail. And then
> take four or five or six split sticks, or very thin laths, and a con-
> venient quantity of tape or filleting; these laths are to be tied
> round about the Pike's body, from his head to his tail, and the
> tape tied somewhat thick, to prevent his breaking or falling
> off from the spit. Let him be roasted very leisurely, and often
> basted with claret wine and anchovies, and butter, mixt together;
> and also with what moisture falls from him into the pan. When
> you have roasted him sufficiently, you are to hold under him,
> when you unwind or cut the tape that ties him, such a dish as
> you propose to eat him out of; and let him fall into it with the
> sauce that is roasted in his belly; and by this means the Pike

will be kept unbroken and complete. Then, to the sauce which was within, and also that sauce in the pan, you are to add a fit quantity of the best butter, and to squeeze the juice of three or four oranges. Lastly, you may either put it into the Pike, with the oysters, two cloves of garlick, and take it whole out, when the Pike is cut off the spit; or, to give the sauce a haut gout, let the dish into which you let the Pike fall be rubbed with it: The using or not using of this garlick is left to your discretion.

This dish of meat is too good for any but anglers, or very honest men; and I trust you will prove both, and therefore I have trusted you with this secret."

IZAAK WALTON.

ELVERS *in the Rhynes of Somerset*

The discovery of the breeding-place of the eels, in shallow warm water across the Atlantic Ocean, cleared up the long mystery of the elvers which pour up the western rivers in spring. From March onwards, the stream of fish begins, and lasts perhaps a week or more. It happens in most of the western rivers, but very especially in Somerset. This land used to be half under water, and the shallow entrances and waterways made it a perfect ground for the eels. Now the land has been drained, but whether from instinct, or some turn of the sweeping tide, the elvers continue to pour up the Bristol Channel and turn south down the Rhynes. The Somerset people are divided into "farmers" and "marsh folk". (The latter live on the reclaimed lands and at present run a large willow industry.) These marsh people, who live in the lands around Wells Cathedral, all know elvers.

The elver shoal itself looks like a mass of jelly swimming in the water; it consists of millions of elvers, and can best be described as transparent spaghetti. The fish are caught by dipping them out of the rhynes in scoops made of cloth, or buckets and pans, as any net would let the fish through. They are washed in running water and then cooked at once. As soon as the transparent mass touches the hot pan or fat, it turns opaque (exactly as white of egg becomes opaque and visible). It is stirred and turned till it is all evenly cooked, and eaten with salt and pepper and bread and butter. It is best hot, cooked loosely, like whitebait (though never so crisp), but the marsh folk also make "elver cake", which is the same mass of fish, seasoned with chopped herbs (a suspicion of onion and butter or bacon-fat added), and the whole turned into a dish, and pressed down till set and cold. This elver cake then turns out and can be cut in slices. There is no bone in the fish, it is all pure soft fish, and becomes firm and almost textureless after cooking. It is especially good for children. (The marsh folk point out the fatness of young ducklings, which are hatched out in time for the elver feed.) It is certainly good food and could be the basis of a seasonal canned-food industry. There is no fear of the fishing of these elvers destroying the future eels, if the main shoal, which sweeps up the channel, is left untouched, as the rhynes will be drained, and therefore all the elvers trampled and destroyed, when the willows are cut a month later.

There is a witchcraft story, vouched for down west, that one old marsh mother having moved up-country to Swindon, her dutiful grandson, a driver on the railway, stopped and left a bucket of elvers at her cottage. The old woman rejoiced loudly in broad Somerset speech, and set the bucket of elvers on to cook, causing an outcry of "Witchcraft!" For she was "seen to take a pail of clear water and set it upon the fire, murmuring incantations, and behold! half an hour later *she was enjoying a hot fish dinner*", and her black cat said it was fish too! (The elvers are invisible in clean water.)

Elvers have always been eaten in parts of the west, and were one of the seasonal dainties for which Bath was famous. It is still possible to obtain a dishful at some of the oldest and best hotels in the district.

Cat-fish

EELS

" It is agreed by most men, that the Eel is a most dainty fish. How to make this Eel a most excellent dish of meat. First, wash him in water and salt; then pull off his skin below his vent or navel, and not much further; having done that, take out his guts as clean as you can, but wash him not; then give him three or four scotches with a knife; and then put into his belly and those scotches, sweet herbs, an anchovy, and a little nutmeg grated or cut very small; and your herbs and anchovies must also be cut very small; and mixed with good butter and salt; having done this, then pull his skin over him, all but his head, which you are to cut off, to the end you may tie his skin about that part where his head grew, and it must be so tied as to keep all his moisture within his skin; and having done this, tie him with tape or pack-thread to a spit, and roast him leisurely; and baste him with water and salt till his skin breaks, and then butter; and having roasted him enough, let what was put into his belly, and what he drips, be his sauce.

When I go to dress an Eel thus, I wish he were as long and as big as that which was caught in Peterborough river, in the year 1667; which was a yard and three quarters long."

IZAAK WALTON.

Eel Pie (fifteenth century)

"Grease a pye dish and rub it well with garlic. Break off pieces of the ele, and roll them in poudered mace, pepir and salt and, if you would have it golden, a little safron rubbed up in a spoonful of water, pack very closely, and press down in the cranies mashed apple." (*Note.* I expect the pomace from the cider-press suggested this.) When the dish is packed, pour on vinegar to the brim, cover closely, and let it bake while you make the crust—take out, fit on the crust, and complete baking.

Verjuice, the mediaeval extract of crab apples, was a very sharp acid sauce, likely to have been replaced by the modern vinegar or cider. The pie could be eaten hot or cold, as it sets into a stiff jelly.

Jellied Eel

> " Elis and lampurnes rosted where that ever ye go
> Cast vinegre and powder thereon furst get the
> bonus them fro."
>
> > BOORDE.

From this and other evidence we believe that small eels, etc., were treated as soused herrings, to "gette the bonus them fro" thus:

Lay one or two bay leaves at the bottom of a shallow earthenware dish, and cut the eels into lengths rather less than the height of the dish sides; arrange the pieces upright, packing them loosely together with small bunches of thyme, parsley and roughly chopped onion. Add a few peppercorns, and fill up with vinegar to the brim of the dish. Cover, and bake slowly for 2 or 3 hours, according to the size and thickness of the pieces. Remove the herbs (leave the onion), and when cold, next day, most of the bones will have dissolved. Turn out, and serve on a bed of crisp salad, with brown bread and butter, and mustard and sliced lemon.

> " Lord! Let me catch a fish
> So large that even I,
> In telling of it afterwards,
> Shall have no need to lie."

LAMPREY

This curious fish, with the historic tradition of a king's death, is very uncommon nowadays. I can find no direct evidence, but it seems possible that when tidal waters were more regulated (for working mills, etc.) and fishing rights vigorously upheld by weirs and fish dams, some type of breeding may have been carried out with estuary fish, such as was certainly done with inland fisheries.

I have never cooked lampreys myself, so give two old recipes, one fifteenth century:

"Take lamprons and scalde hem with hay and make faire paste and couch two or three lemprons thereon, with poudered giner salt and pepir, and let bake, and samon in fair brode peces and bake in the same maner."

Though of late date, this nineteenth-century recipe from Bath seems nearest to the mediaeval dish that killed the king.

Soak in salt water and bleed them well, and wash in hot water and scour with hay to get rid of the slime. Cut in pieces and fry in butter, till almost done, then add a little white wine and season with spice and sweet herbs, add a bay leaf and any blood you have saved to the gravy in the pan, shake the pan and leave close-covered till all is soft. Dish up, straining the gravy over the slices.

TENCH

> " Un Techne and steue hym in a potte with wyne and when he is y now—pipe out the bonys and stampe hem in a morter, then take him uppe and put him in the brothe that he was sothe in and caste thereto mace, cloves, pepir, and cimmon and caste him in a dyshe. Put vinegre pouder ginere ciman ynow."
>
> FIFTEENTH-CENTURY MS.

SHELLFISH

OYSTERS

> " And Somers sighed in sorrow as
> he settled in the South
> For the thought of Peter's oysters brought
> the water to his mouth.
> He longed to lay him down upon the
> shelly bed and stuff,
> He had often eaten oysters but
> had never had enough."
>
> *Bab Ballads.*

Oysters should be served in the rounded shell, with cut lemon and brown bread and butter.

Oyster Patties

These are made of the lightest puff pastry or flaky pastry, very small and light; the cases are baked and then opened and the oyster, in a spoonful of melted butter sauce, dropped into the cavity, closed, and put back into the oven for one minute to heat through. On no account must the oyster overcook or it becomes leathery.

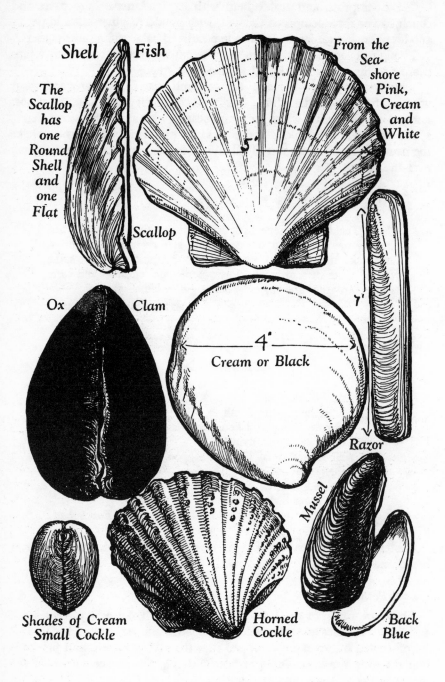

Shell Fish

The Scallop has one Round Shell and one Flat

Scallop

From the Sea-shore Pink, Cream and White

5˚

7'

Ox Clam

Cream or Black

4˚

Razor

Shades of Cream Small Cockle

Horned Cockle

Mussel

Back Blue

Oyster Cutlets

These are very good made from the tinned or bottled oyster. Make a firm foundation sauce of butter, flour, milk, some of the liquor from the fish, and seasoning of pepper; let it cook thoroughly well, then take from the fire, and beat in the fish and the remaining liquor. The mixture should be reasonably stiff; pour out on to a plate, and leave till cold. Next day, cut into small pieces, shape a little, into rounds, egg and bread-crumb thoroughly, and fry lightly; serve hot.

Oyster Sauce

This is made with a melted butter foundation and the liquor from the shells, and the fish itself stirred in after it has cooled slightly, though the sauce should be kept hot some minutes to be sure the fish is cooked and hot.

Roast Oysters

"(Fleda) had spread a glowing bed of coals on the hearth, and there lay four or five of the big bivalves, snapping and spluttering . . . in a most comfortable manner . . . she was shielding her face, and making efforts to persuade a large oyster shell to stand, so, upon the coals, so as to keep in the juice. . . . How long it is since we had a roast Oyster! How pleasant they smell!"

Queechy, 1870.

LOBSTERS

The finest are caught in "pots" on rocky bottom, out at sea. They should not be taken near towns with sewers. A freshly caught lobster is dark blue green (they turn scarlet after boiling). Both crabs and lobsters are sold by weight as much as size; if light, they should be thrown back into the sea. Cooks should insist on lobsters being killed instantly when caught. Keeping lobsters in huge, floating tanks in the sea is permissible, but the claw-tied, mutilated, living creature, with sensitive feelers torn, eyes crushed in, and cracked grinding carapace, nailed up in crates, and jolted miles by railroad to be shown, alive and quivering, on the fishmonger's slab, is a disgrace to civilisation. This senseless torture of animals must cease, before clean, wholesome food is safe for human beings to eat.

To serve lobster.

A large lobster takes about 40 minutes to boil, in a large pan completely covered. Afterwards wrap in a wet cloth till cold. Take off the huge front claws and small legs and remove the head, keeping the meat of the back part only. Cut the whole body in half, lengthways, and take away the stomach and long dark intestine-line (all the rest is white meat).

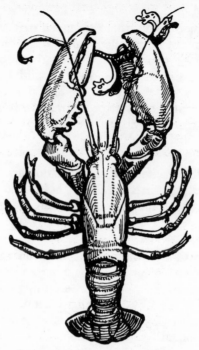

The Lobster should have good claws

Crack the small legs and claws, and pick out the meat, mix it with any saved from the back part of the head, and trimmings of the tail, and shred this up, with seasoning (or pound with the coral butter), pile it up in a piece of the shell—lay the two tail pieces either side and the claws top and bottom—garnish with the coral and cress, and serve with oil, vinegar, and brown bread and butter.

Lobster picks, and nut-crackers for the claws, should be provided.

A lobster salad can be very elaborate. Shred enough crisp lettuce to almost fill a deep bowl, rub the bowl well with cut onion, and have ready a spoonful of sugar, a spoonful of salt, a small spoonful of white pepper, oil, vinegar, some small, very new potatoes, green peas and sliced hard-boiled eggs. Shred the lobster meat, keeping pieces of the claws whole and prepare the coral as butter. To serve, shake the lettuce into the bowl in a spiral way, seasoning as you go, and following the green spiral with the white lobster spiral. Finish by pouring the mayonnaise into the centre, and adding the coral butter, alternately with the whole pieces of the claws, and the sliced egg on top of the cream centre. See the vinegar is very fine, and use very little. This dish is sometimes fussed about so much that you lose the lobster—it's better served plainly.

For the Victorian picnic we recommend packing the lobster meat into a mould, and filling the interstices with clear aspic jelly; carry this and the green salad separately, with a bottle of dressing cream, "to combine in the appropriate chosen spot".

Coral Butter

The red coral in the female lobster is usually pounded (use the mortar) with an equal amount of butter and lobster meat, a spicing of cayenne, mace, the smallest suspicion of clove, and made into lobster butter. Used to decorate a mould of lobster or a mayonnaise salad.

CRAB

> " A crabbe broke hym asonder into a dysshe make ye shelle clene and put in the stuff agayne tempre with vynegre and pouder [salt and spices] then cover it with bread [crumbs] and send it to the kytchen to hete [bake it] and broke the grete clawes and laye them in a disshe."
>
> BOORDE.

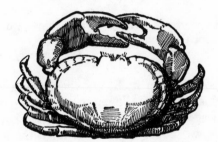

The Crab should be heavy

Much said about lobsters applies to crabs. They should be very heavy for their size, and not less than eight inches across. The smaller ones are not worth eating and should be thrown back into the sea. Crabs that have just shed their old shells and got their new ones are never taken by experienced fishers; they are light weight and the hollow sound of the empty shell, not yet refilled, can be heard at once.

Crab-pot men stun them with a mallet, before dropping them into boiling water to cook. They take 30 to 40 minutes, according to size.

Dressed Crab

Remove the big claws and legs whole, crack and pick the meat out of the small claws, and put it in a basin. Now take away the front fringe part, and cut around the crab on the white side, so as to take away the whole of the white under-shell (there is a natural crack between the shells easy to follow). Remove the head and the green intestinal part, and then scoop all the brown crab meat into a basin.

The "dressing" of the crab meat is a matter of taste—do not deluge it with mayonnaise, most men prefer it plain seasoned. If you have never dressed a crab before, try this simple dressing the first time and afterwards adapt it to suit your own taste.

For one sizeable crab, take 1 heaped tablespoonful of fresh bread-crumbs, 1 small saltspoonful of salt, and 1 large saltspoonful of black pepper, 1 large dessertspoonful of oil, and 1 small dessertspoonful of vinegar mixed with a little made mustard. Put all in the basin with the brown crab meat, and leg scraps, mix lightly, and pile back into the deep-red back shell; a teaspoonful of finely chopped parsley dusted over the top improves the dish. The big claws should be laid on either side—and picks provided. Brown bread and butter go with this dish, which most working men like very much for their late teas. Crab is a much more flavoursome fish than lobster, and should never be iced.

MUSSELS

> " A farthings worth of mussels or a farthings worth of cockles were a feast for them on a Friday."
>
> *The Vision of Piers Plowman.*

No mussel is poisonous in itself, but they vary a lot in quality. The smaller mussels clustering and clinging to the stanchions of the pier and encrusting the sewage pipes at watering-places are not edible, because of the dirty water from which they are taken, but it is the water that is impure, not the mussel.

Mussels from clean water are wholesome food; far cheaper than oysters, easy to prepare and very fine in flavour. Therefore the Ministry of Agriculture and Fisheries has realised their value and has special centres where good wholesome mussels are prepared for food. They are sold with a guarantee, and well worth the extra price.

You should know about your food, so without going into technicalities, here is the process. The mussel is a little pumping machine which passes through itself at least 10 gallons of water a day. The mussels, good meaty ones, are brought by the fishermen from the sea and put into tanks where they are thoroughly washed till clear of sand and weed. The tanks are repeatedly refilled with sterilised water and the mussels allowed to pump themselves clean till the water is absolutely pure. They are given a last refill of sterilised clean water, and, as it drains off, they close tight, sweet and clean. No better closing or more tightly sterilised container than their own shells could be invented, so to keep them closed in transit, the shells are sprayed with a clean preparation of limewater and the hermetically sealed mussels are despatched to the consumer in sterilised bags, stamped with the Government seal. Get your mussels with this seal and be sure of good, well-prepared food.

To open the mussels, rinse the shells and put them, still sealed tight, into just enough boiling water to cover. Leave them to cook till open and use at once.

Shellfish baked in their shells

> "As to the smoak we saw, it might have been travellers who were rosting of oysters and shell fish on the shore."
>
> *Slave Traders' Log at Sligo*, 1600

This roasting in the shell was laying them on heated stones by a bonfire on the shore, as the kelp women do. Butter is put into the shells as they open.

"Muscules in Shelle (steamed)

> " Take a pike faire muscles, and cast hem in a potte and caste hem to myced onyons and a good quantiti of peper and wyne and a lite vynegre; and assone as thei begynneth to gape take hem from ye fire and serve hit forth with the same broth in a dissh al hote."   E.E.T.S.

Mussel Pie

Empty the fish from the shells into a buttered pan and sprinkle them with a tablespoonful of white wine. Scatter very finely chopped parsley over and two small onions chopped finely; pepper and salt, and just cover flat with fine white breadcrumbs. Dot over with butter and fill up just to the level of the crumbs with some of the liquor from the mussels. (The crumbs should be thoroughly damp, but not covered with the liquor.) Bake 20 minutes in a very moderate oven, and serve hot. The dish should be crisp and brown on top, the underneath fish swimming in a luscious buttery liquor. Serve with dry toast and black pepper. Bottled mussels make this dish very well.

"Muscules in Broth" (1400?)

> " Take Muscules and sith [seethe] them, and pike them, oute of the shell, and drawe the broth through a streynour into a faire vessell and sette hit on the fire. Then take faire brede and stepe hit with the broth and draw hit through a streynour and caste into a potte with the sewe: and menge onyons, wyn and powder-pepper, and let boyle and cast thereto the Musculis and powder ginger and saffron and salte and then serve ye hit forthe."
>
>   E.E.T.S.

Boiled Mussels

Shell three dozen mussels. Simmer a pint of milk with a chopped onion, a clove, and a bunch of herbs, or the clove may be omitted and a blade of mace substituted. Melt an egg of butter or lard and bind it with a tablespoonful of flour until well cooked and translucent. Add the flavoured milk gradually and stir until your sauce is well thickened. Cook it very well, to get it creamy. Let it get off the boil, then put in the mussels and let them stand and cook in it (but do not let them boil), for about 10 minutes, while you make some slices of hot buttered toast. Sprinkle the toast with cayenne, pour the mixture over, and use instantly with tiny slices of lemon made hot.

Note. The mixture should be of the consistency of a scrambled egg.

A Few Mussels

If there are only a few mussels, use them to fill bread rolls, crisp from the oven; pull out the centre crumbs and replace by the mixture as above. Rub the rolls over with hot butter and serve with sprigs of watercress.

COCKLES

Cockle-gathering has altered a lot. There was a time when cockles were much in favour, especially to garnish other fish dishes; "with hot cockle sauce" appears in the recipes for old-fashioned banquets. In country places near the sea they were served in all manner of ways, and considered a delicacy. Since transport made it possible to send heavy shell-fish inland quickly and fairly cheaply, it is the markets in the black countries that have the biggest demand. Lancashire favoured the mussel "on hot toast with pepper and pikelets at tea-time"; on the north-east coast they gathered very large-sized cockles. The huge "king cockle" was also found and eaten, especially among the islands, and razor shell, and a shellfish locally known as a "clam". This I found being dug as a side-line by the cockle-getters near Cley in Norfolk. But the man who spoke about these "clam fish" said they "ate them themselves as few folk nowadays remembered how good they were". They are very like oysters, but more solid. Scallops are one of the few English shellfish that seem to be increasing in popularity and the price is mounting accordingly.

On the east coast the smaller black cockle is raked from the black sand, and further south in Essex, at Leigh-on-Sea, are the famous cockle-sheds where the cockle-boats fetch in the cockles from the Goodwin Sands and the fish are mechanically scalded open, tossed out, preserved in brine or sold on small china saucers, or in limp muslin bags to be carried away. These are a very small cockle. One year, off Anglesey, we got some of the

Digging for bait and collecting clams

fine large white cockles; at Exmouth they were digging the medium darkish cockle.

Cockling is a peaceful sort of job. You take a basket (small) and a sack (large) and, according to whether the sand is soft, or full of sharp shells and rocks, you wear your oldest shoes or go barefoot. The end of a worn-out garden rake with short blunted teeth is about as good as anything to "scrat" with. Some professionals have a half-moon-shaped rake, others use an old knife. Having found your cockle-beds, you set to work—and scratch them. Experience only can tell you where the cockles lie close together; if you "scrat" and they're *there*, you've found the place. If you haven't, you "scrat" somewhere else. Sometimes you can notice the two little cockle marks in the sand shining against the sunlight.

About two inches down, pick up the cockles, drop them in the basket. A genuine tight alive cockle you can't possibly open with your fingers; that's a test. When the little basket is full of cockles, you wade into the water and wash off the sand and mud, lifting the basket up and down in the water, then you put the clean cockles into your sack, take your little basket and go at it again. Don't throw the cockles into the basket, you may crack the shells. Choose a clean sea-shore, free from drain outlets, and see that the cockles pass the test above. You can always consult a local professional, for I never met a cockle expert yet who feared amateur competition!

Francatellis' Cockle Soup

Wash and scald about four dozen cockles; as they open pick out and empty into a bowl. Put 4 oz. of butter into a stew-pan and, as it melts, mix in 4 oz. of flour, moisten with $1\frac{1}{2}$ pints of milk. Season with a little pepper, nutmeg, and a teaspoonful of anchovy. Stir over the fire for quarter-of-an-hour's gentle boiling. Remove from the fire and, if possible, add a generous spoonful of thick cream. Pour over the cockles in the hot tureen.

Cockle Pie

Butter a deep piedish and pepper lightly. Take the cockles, scald, and as they open, drop them into a little milk. When all the cockles are open, strain off the liquor and use it, with a spoonful of anchovy and a generous lump of butter and flour to make a thick sauce. Add a dust of nutmeg. Shake brown breadcrumbs into the piedish, cover with tiny dabs of butter, and spread with a layer of cockles; pour over a layer of sauce, then a layer of crumbs, more butter, more cockles, and more sauce, so that the dish is full. Let the last layer be of sauce. Cover with a thin crust of mashed potatoes and bake for half an hour. Serve hot with a squeeze of lemon juice.

Fried Cockles

At the seaside I have had fried cockles. The bacon was lifted from the pan and the cockles, previously rolled dry in flour and pepper, were fried crisply in the fat. They should be very brown and crisp.

SCALLOPS

These beautiful shellfish are sold open in fish shops; this is a pity, as they lose their fresh salty taste once opened. Those purchased in the shops are ready prepared. If you get them from the sea, you must scrub the shells, give them a shrewd knock, or set to open in shallow boiling water, rounded side down; when open, cut off the flat top shell and take away any black part, leaving only the white and orange fish. Season the fish with

Whelks, Periwinkles and Limpets

pepper and salt, and a sprinkle of lemon juice, cover with fresh white breadcrumbs, and dot with butter; cook in a very moderate oven. They will take about 40 minutes, perhaps longer if large—so it is well to cover with butter paper for the first part of the cooking.

WHELKS

The whelk-stall serves this delicacy plain steamed (this takes about 1 hour), and turned out on to little saucers to be swallowed oyster-like, or covered with sauce and pepper (from bottles clustered on the stall). There used to be special orders in the Potteries for whelk saucers—they are about three inches across, and piles were sold at the average price of a penny each.

Another name was "coop s'aucers", because "you use them to set your cup on and save t'cloth whilst you drink out of the saucer".

Whelk Fritters

If you have whelks, but lack both saucers and courage, try them as fritters. Put the whelks for some time in clean cold salted water, then plunge into boiling water and leave for 1 hour to cool. Remove shells and hard cover bits, drain the fish, roll in seasoned flour, dip in batter, and fry crisp. Serve garnished with pickled red cabbage and watercress, and white bread and butter. They can also be treated like cockles.

"Welkes Boyled"

"Take welks and cast hem in colde water and lat boyle but a littul, and caste hem into a vessell and pyke hem oute of the shell and picke away the horn of hem, and wasshe hem, and rubbe him well in cold water and salt two or three waters and serve hem colde and caste upon hem leves of perceley wet in vinegar."

The recipe is unchanged. Wash the whelks and drop into boiling water, but immediately draw aside, as they must not actually boil or they harden. Unshell, removing the little hard coverpiece, rinse clear of any particles of sand and serve with parsley sauce, or cold, with mayonnaise sauce and garnished with parsley.

If the whelks are bought from a fishmonger they will be ready washed, but if direct from the shore they should be kept in cleaned changed water till free of all sand (*see* Mussel).

WINKLES

" I merely quote wot the nobleman said to the fractious penny-winkle ven he wouldn't come out of his shell by means of a pin."
Pickwick Papers.

Periwinkles were popular in 1850—sixpence a bushel for gathering in Oban, then shipped to Glasgow, Liverpool and London, where they were sold for threepence a pint. Welks were gathered from Mull.

The historical succulent lore of the winkle is purely traditional. Nowhere is it confirmed in writing.

You will not find winkles mentioned in cook-books, even the gentle Victorian books "preserve an elegant reticence". As they say, "anyone will *tell you* how to prepare winkles", but "you will not find it written down".

Gathering Periwinkles. The close season begins in April.

Therefore, for centuries, the tradition of the winkle must have been handed down, as you might say, from father to son—or a wife might, so to speak, "marry into winkles". If they were just a few unexpected edible shellfish, you could understand this, but *thousands of tons of winkles are consumed yearly—millions of winkles are eaten daily*, and yet, to put it crudely, would you think of eating a winkle if somebody else did not put you up to it? Also, their spasmodic distribution is intriguing. London eats tons; so does Blackpool; Chester eats but few. At some country places the winkle statistics may be high, and yet in an adjacent hamlet the winkle will be practically unknown.

I learnt "winkles" from a night watchman. He used to sit by his big red coke fire-bucket, a bit of folded blanket over his knees, his mug of hot tea, and a little enamel bowl full of winkles. And he would turn up the little tab-end at the bottom of his waistcoat, pull out a long pin, and take a winkle. . . . And then he would chuck the empty shell neatly over his shoulder into the canal with a tiny "plop". He did it quite slowly, and he always paused (I can see him now, red in the firelight, head aslant, his huge hand still half-open—curved like a hoary brown shell). He always paused just that second till he heard the tiny plop, before he bent and picked up the next winkle. His old woman had put him "a reet proper breakfast", and he had a basket with a bottle in it. But, as he said, "Winkles, they *do* pass the time along very pleasantly".

Winkle-eaters have a punctuated outlook on life. Winkles are one of the queerly unexpected things, like pigeons and *Old Moore's Almanacks*, that country people take to towns with them.

Pickled Winkles

This recipe is direct from the pen of the countrywoman who sent it to me c/o the old *Daily Sketch* in 1934.

"One quart winkles, boild. Put in coald water.

"Take a long pin. Pull it out of shell. Have a large glass jar, fill with brown vinegar. Put each winkle in (with scab off). Put very thin paper to cover jar. Prick the paper with small owls [holes?]."

A PURKINS COOK.

CLAMS

There is some difficulty in locating the local names for these, as in some districts "all that's not cockles nor mussels we call clams". In other districts I have had fine scallops offered to me as clams. Near Hunstanton I was told by one fisherman that "a very knowledgeable chef in one of the hotels, he counted them as bettern oysters" and "useter keepn them for his own supper". But as the oxhorn cockle, the scallop, or the largest horned cockles, may all be sold to you as "clams" I advise you to take local advice as to cooking.

LIMPETS

Limpets are gathered and eaten in the Isle of Man. They must be picked with the fall of the tide, when they can be lifted off as they slide over the rocks. Scrap them from the shell and cook by any mussel recipe.

OTHER SHELLFISH

Cardium edul, the common white cockle, is the one usually eaten. In certain localities of black sand and mud this cockle is locally known as the "black" cockle, and has darker markings, like stains, over the shell.

Cardium rusticum is larger, and both that and the *Cardium aculeatum* have rough raised brown and reddish ridges on their shells.

Myatruncata is also eaten, but is apt to be sandy.

Solen siliguia, the razor-shell (much prized in Japan), is gathered in Anglesey and elsewhere by the old families, though they are shy of introducing them to strangers. They are best boiled out of their shells, and are often served vinegar-pickled.

Isocadia, the big black Oxhorn cockle, is very meaty (the shells look as if made of dark rough horn, ridged slightly, and very thick and strong). Boil for 10 minutes, till shells open, fry the fish in egg and breadcrumbs with a sauce made from the liquor.

The *Purpura lapillus* used to be gathered in Connemara and used for dye for the scarlet petticoats of the womenfolk.

Melica coerulea, being abundant in the Hebrides, was used by fisherfolk to make nets. They found them durable.

SHRIMPS

" The traveller dines on potted meats,
    On potted meats and princely wine
    Not wisely but too well he dines,
    And breathing forth a pious wish
    He fills his belly full of fish."

ROBERT LOUIS STEVENSON.

Shrimp Teas " Down South "

Shrimp Teas " Up North "

There was a little house that said "Shrimp Teas". We went through a little wicket gate down a flagged yard (for it was in the grey north). There was a holly-bush growing over a stone wall and a wooden bench went along the wall. There were three strong round wooden tables and against the three tables leant twelve strong square wooden chairs. On the tables were white cloths. You went to the door and told Betsy "We've come". Then you sat down and "drew in".

Betsy brought out a pot of tea, with a woollen tea-cosy on it, sugar and cream, a cup and saucer each, two big plates of thin bread and butter—brown and white—a big green plate of watercress, and a big pink plate of shrimps. And that was all, except an armoured salt cellar and a robin. Then you "reached too".

Presently Betsy Tatterstall came out again, with a big white apron over her black gown, took the teapot in to replenish it, and see if you wanted any more bread and butter (you always did). And you ate, and talked, in desultory fashion (there is something very conversational about a shrimp tea), and the robin hopped about on the table.

Presently you wiped up and sat back, and Betsy carried a bowl of pink-bewhiskered debris to the hens, and you bought some fresh eggs, and a jar of potted shrimps to take away with you. . . .

Betsy sold that paste in white jars, with whole shrimps embedded in it, and smooth white melted butter on top. It *was* the best in the district, and that, mark you, in a district that was notable for fish paste.

There was always a white jar of potted fish or potted meat on the table for the big Yorkshire high teas. Sometimes, if it was a new jar, they would thoughtfully cut thirty degrees out, and lay neatly across the top, just to encourage you to begin.

A white china pot of pink Shrimp Paste. "Betty's Best".

Shrimp Paste

This was Betsy Tatterstall's shrimp paste.

Weigh the shrimps, and take an equal quantity of fine flaked white fish. Shell the shrimps, and put heads and shells to boil in enough water to cover. Drain, remove the shells and heads, and now cook the flaked fish in this shrimp water till soft. Let cool, and pound to a smooth paste with a careful seasoning of powdered mace, cayenne and one single spot of anchovy sauce. Now measure, and add an almost equal quantity of butter. When smooth, stir in all the whole shrimps, make all piping hot, press into pots, and flood with melted butter on the top.

The effect was a solid potful of shrimps, cemented together with a soft, delicately seasoned pink butter. It was a great delicacy, and always served in fine white china.

Shrimps in Mediaeval Manner

" Shrympes welle pyked the scales away he cast
Round about a sawcer ley he them in haste
the vinegre in the same sawcer that your lord, he attast
Then with the said fische he may fede hym and of them
    make no wast."   BOORDE.

Shrimp Sauce

Shell 1 pint of shrimps, putting shells and scraps into an enamel pan, just cover with water, or if you are making a sauce to accompany boiled fish use that water. Meanwhile toss the whole shrimps into a tablespoon-ful of butter, and put them into a hot sauceboat. Cook a small tablespoon-ful of flour in the same butter, adding gradually the strained liquor from the shells, and, if required, add a very little extra milk. Beat and boil the sauce well, then pour over the hot shrimps, stir and serve.

PRAWNS

Prawns are usually caught in nets or pots. Lately, off the coast of America, they seem to have discovered an inexhaustible supply of prawns and some special boats are being equipped for the "new industry". Prawns always fetch a good price. They look like huge shrimps, but are different. Scientifically speaking, "the prawn is a long-tailed decapod marine crustacean, *Palaemon serratus*. In the Palaemonidae family, the first two pairs of legs are chelate, and in crangonidae, shrimps, the first legs are subchelate, and the carpus of the second pair not subdivided."

Prawns are usually served in salads or in aspic.

SAUCES FOR FISH

" What do you think of our fish? I never ate it before but I want the Harvey or Reading sauce.

Pray let me entreat you to use none other sauce than the water in which it was boiled. I assure you that this is the true epicurian way of eating fresh salmon and for trout use only a little vinegar and mustard."

SALMONIA DAVY, 1828.

The net is pushed along from the wooden shaft end, held at hip level. The sacking tied below this cross bar pads the hand grip. The mesh for shrimp and prawn is the finest made, and so heavy in the water, and the pushing slow.

Watercress Sauce

This is excellent with most freshwater fish. Follow the directions for parsley sauce exactly, only be cautious with the pepper, as the cress itself is hot.

Taragon Sauce

This may be made the same way, but use very little. It is rather strongly flavoured.

Fennel Sauce

Fennel leaves are best boiled soft and rubbed through a sieve. Use the water with the fish stock to make the sauce.

Parsley Sauce (strong flavour)

Take a large handful of parsley for 1 pint of sauce. Strip the fine leaves, chop the coarse stalks roughly, and put them to simmer in a ½ pint of water, or if the sauce is to go with fish, to a ½ pint of fish stock. Meanwhile chop the leaves very finely (they are most easily chopped after dipping them for one moment in boiling water). Melt a tablespoonful of fine bacon-fat in your saucepan, and blend with a tablespoonful of flour. Cook thoroughly, seasoning with pepper; salt will scarcely be needed, the bacon-fat supplies that. Strain in the liquid from the boiled stalks, and when thoroughly cooked, take off the fire and put in the parsley. Put a spoonful of cream into a hot sauceboat, pour on the sauce, and serve quickly.

No Sauce

We have mentioned wild thyme for grayling; a little may be cooked within it, but no sauce should be served with this fish, nor with trout. Put a pat of butter to melt on them, and send to table with crisp salads.

Fish traps of this type were legally used in "runs" of fish, or to stop some mill race in private waters; but when they were set up at random, in open rivers, they could ruin the fishing of an entire district in one season

SEAWEEDS

"Ah! call us not Weeds, but Flowers of the Sea,
For lovely and gay and bright tinted are we
Our Blush is as bright as the Rose of thy Bowers.
So call us not Weeds, but the Ocean's gay Flowers.

Not nursed like the plants of a Summer Parterre
Where winds are but Sigh of an Evening Air,
Our exquisite fragile and delicate Forms
Are reared by the Ocean, and rocked by the Storms!"

FROM A VICTORIAN SEAWEED PICTURE.

GENERAL NOTES ON SEAWEEDS

IT IS not often realised that there is a season of growth among sea plants as among land plants. They shoot as buds, and grow lavishly through the summer, and wither and die in winter. They are "cropped" at various times (according to their content and use). At one time seaweed was lavishly used as manure—and is still the best dressing available for seakale, asparagus and other special vegetables. Most of the edible seaweeds have very high content of mineral salts, and for some glandular and deficiency complaints are a valuable form of diet. The iodine flavour is sometimes disliked at first (but few people care for olives or oysters, instantly!) so give the seaweeds a fair trial before you condemn them, as they offer very delicious meals, and in some cases have genuine medicinal value.

LAVER

"Deos wyrt pe man sium odrum naman
Laber nemnep bya cenned oh woetum stowun."

ANGLO-SAXON CHRONICLE.

Which means "That wort named Sion, or by another name 'laver', is kenned on wet stones."

So, as it grew by sucking upon stones in the water, our Anglo-Saxon forefathers used it as a cure for the stone in the bladder—"eaten sodden, or raw, it draweth out the calculi". (There is a plausibility among medical men.)

Laver

Purple laver (*Porphyra laciniata*) and green laver (*Ulva Latissima*) are common around the west coast of Great Britain and Ireland. It is a smooth, fine seaweed, which clings to the rocks like wet, brown silk. Laver is one of our oldest salads. The gatherer plucks it from the rocks, gives it a preliminary rinse in a clear sea pool, and finally washes it and boils it for hours, and packs it into a crock.

The home-tied wives of fishermen had the gathering of laver for their own special industry; and they supplemented their small earnings by preparing and selling it.

In fashionable Bath of the eighteenth century where everybody specialised in diet, " Fine potted laver" was a street cry; but I'd judge its genuine dietetic properties by old sailors, for their hard life on slow voyages in small ships taught them its value, and our mediaeval English sailors were, for their times, singularly free from skin and blood illnesses.

To country people laver belongs to the sail-grazing mutton as characteristically as thyme and mint belong to our mountain jigots.

Laver Sauce

" A capital dinner! you don't get moor mutton, with hot laver
sauce every day! "

COLLINS, 1875

Wash the weed in running water, stirring repeatedly till clear of any trace of sand. Then boil down to a stiff green mush (this is best done in a double saucepan as it sticks easily). In this state it will keep several days. When wanted, put two cupfuls to a lump of butter the size of a walnut, and the juice of half a lemon or Seville orange, *not* a sweet orange— beat it well with a silver fork, and send to table in a hot water dish.

Another method is to melt the butter, thicken with flour, add milk gradually, and heat till the sauce is well cooked and liquid as cream, and then beat in the laver—but real devotees prefer their laver neat and strong.

Laver has a queer "iodine" taste—few people really like it the first time, but once you've caught the taste, you want more. It is very invigorating and clears the palate and is supposed to have a marvellous, health-giving content.

IRISH MOSS (*Chrondrus Crispus*) *or Dorset Moss*

Though now thought of as an Irish speciality, was called "Dorset weed", and near Cerne Abbas I found it hung up in bags in cottages, where they used it medicinally. In Yorkshire it was made into blancmanges.

The chemist knows it as "Iberian moss". It is vegetable gelatine, and can be used instead of gelatine or isinglass. As it has iodine and other valuable salts it is rightly considered better than ordinary jelly for invalids. It is specially valuable for some gland troubles. Children with adenoids or sore throats were dosed with it hot at bedtime.

It is gathered in April or May (realise that there is a season for plants in the sea as well as on the land), and when gathered it is light brown; or sometimes you can gather it, already bleached, on the shore. Wash it well in running brook water, and spread it out to dry on the grass. If the wind blows you must pack it down under a fish-net so that it does not get blown away. Keep pouring buckets of fresh water over it, or if it rains, that is very good. When bleached a creamy white, trim off rough places, stalks, etc. (you can see to do this better when it is white than when it is brown). Give it a final wash, dry thoroughly, until it is really crisp, and then store it in bags hung up in a dry place.

Note. Properly prepared, it will keep indefinitely, but if you have not got the salt out, like all salt things, it will pick up the damp.

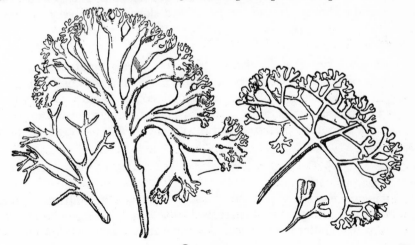

Carrageen

Carrageen or Irish Moss Blancmange, Plain

Rinse the moss till uncurled and plaint (about 1 minute). Take one cup of moss to three cups of milk, add sugar to taste, and flavouring. Simmer the moss in the milk, stir occasionally till it is nearly all melted away, strain to get rid of any undissolved pieces, and pour into a rinsed mould and turn out when cold.

Irish Moss Ginger Jelly

It makes a very good ginger mould, and in this case simmer the ginger roots in water with the weed, adding sugar and the rind of a lemon. Strain into a wet mould and turn out.

Irish Moss Blancmange, Thicker

Three cupfuls of milk, one cupful of the soaked moss, simmer together till the moss has almost gone, then press all through a coarse sieve. Sweeten, flavour, and put to set. Turn out when cold and stiff. This is more like a cornflour mould.

Irish Moss Custard

1 cupful of soaked moss, 2 cupfuls of milk; simmer, strain, and beat in, while hot, one yolk of egg beaten in a $\frac{1}{2}$ cupful of cold milk. When still hot enough to cook it, but not boiling, whip stiff the white of the egg and fold that in also. Sweeten to taste and flavour as you would any custard.

Irish Moss (for a child's chest cold)

A glass of hot milk with a teaspoonful of soaked moss dissolved in it, a spoonful of honey. It must be swallowed slowly, and is very soothing.

Emulsions

Irish moss was the chemists' vehicle for making emulsions, such as cod-liver-oil emulsion. It blends well with the oil and adds useful mineral salts to the medicine. Unfortunately, commercial chemists took to preparing emulsion with gum tragacanth, which gave the more snowy-white effect that the public preferred, but the profession still considers the moss a superior vehicle.

Other Uses for Irish Moss

This same moss is much used in many manufactures: it prepares paper, surfaces, coloured printings, marbles, endpapers, prints leather and silver surfaces, fills plaster pores, makes wallpaper dressings, is used in printing fabrics, and fixes false teeth.

SLOKE (*Porphyra palmata*)

This sea spinach, much akin to laver of the south and west, is brown when gathered from the rocks, but turns into a blackish green pulp on cooking. You can often buy it ready-prepared in seaside villages in Wales, and as it is rather tedious to prepare it is worth enquiring after it.

If you gather it yourself, wash it well, preferably in a running stream, shake dry and pack down into an iron saucepan over a slow fire and let it cook almost indefinitely. When it is quite soft (like over-cooked dark spinach), add butter, pepper and salt, and a squeeze of orange or lemon juice or a spot of vinegar. Beat it well and serve, smoking hot, as an adjunct to roast marsh mutton.

Sloke can also be eaten cold as a salad with cold mutton. In some districts it is served hot with hot boiled bacon, which makes me sure it was a special diet item in the Middle Ages.

Sloke Cakes

Prepare the sloke with butter, cream, and pepper and salt, and while hot beat into it as much hot medium oatmeal as it will take up. Form it into small flat cakes, roll them in oatmeal and fry them when you are cooking the breakfast bacon.

DULCE (*Rhodomenia palmata*)

This red seaweed is only eaten in a few places today, usually on the west coast. I think its use must be very old, and dates probably from Eskimo and Icelandic settlements, probably supplying a deficiency in diet for seafaring people. It is interesting that I found it most popular

Dulce.

in places near the sites of old whaling stations, whereas some other weeds and sea vegetable products are more easily traced to monastic influences. I have heard that it has been prepared and smoked like dagga,[1] as it burns with a curious arid smoke. *Sarcophyllis edulis* Dillick is gathered and used in west Ireland and Scotland. It is used medicinally on the western seaboard, and in Scotland as a vermifuge.

Dulce, Stewed

For such a frail material it takes astonishingly long to cook. If put on about 2 p.m., it is soft and edible at 7 p.m. Add butter, salt and pepper and eat it hot, with potatoes.

SAMPHIRE

> " One who gathers samphire—dreadful calling."
>
> SHAKESPEARE, *King Lear.*

This line has always puzzled me, for Shakespeare is sound on food, and would know samphire was served with marsh mutton. Samphire grows on rough shingle; there is a lot on the pebble ridge at Bideford. You can smell it before you find it. Among all the delicate subtle scents of the country, samphire holds unique place. People who dislike it say it smells of sulphur, but others sniff it ecstatically, and seem to make themselves slightly drunk on the aroma. Then, surprisingly, someone who dislikes it the first time will try again, and find they like it extremely well! It's the most complete puzzle—I have never yet met anyone who was neutral to it. There is something "magic" about samphire.

You can sometimes buy it in country markets, but the liking for it is so uncontrolled that you find some families—miles away from the sea—getting it sent to them, as a delicacy, while the rest of the community look on in bewilderment. Try it; for if you like it you will have added a very pungent, enjoyable, and health-giving item to your diet.

Samphire Hash (a recipe of about 1650)

"A handful of pickled cucumbers, some capers, and samphire. Chop all with a little vinegar and strong broth, add a lemon cut small, pepper and nutmeg. Let boyle. Thicken with butter and yolk of egg and a pinch of sugar. Dish your meat upon snippets, pour on your samphire sauce and garnish with samphire and barberries."

This is a curious "curry type" of sauce. We poured it over some tough beef which (by reason of the vinegar) it made more tender. The garnish looked beautiful: blue-green samphire and red barberries.

---

[1] Dagga, used in many parts of Africa: a narcotic, but having somewhat the effect of hashish. Burnt in a hole in the earth and smoked through a reed.

Samphire Boiled

Those who like samphire enjoy it plain steamed, like asparagus, and served with melted butter.

Glasswort

It is sometimes eaten as samphire. It grows upon salt marshes, and is so pregnant with soda and salts that it was used in the manufacture of old English glassware. It has a very interesting history, but this is a cookbook. So suffice to say: prepare like samphire, and if someone likes these curious flavours very much, probably they are supplying some deficiency in their diet, and should be indulged.

One of the difficulties in locating the owner of an illicit "kiddle" was that everybody made their own baskets and creels, and a creel was shaped *very* like a kiddle. In this example the creel is for heavy peat carrying, and the central stick is left to form a spike that will touch the ground and take the weight, when the owner straightens up to rest.

FUNGI

" A large and complex group of thallophytes of low organisa-
tion, the moulds, mildews, rust, smuts, mushrooms, toadstools,
puff balls, and the allies of such."

Webster.

THE COMMON field mushroom (*Psalliota campestria*) is dainty pink and
white when young, the gills turning brown, then almost black, as it grows
old. You will find them in pastures usually where cattle graze. They may
be anything from four to twenty-four inches across, the average size
being about six to eight inches. The small unopened ones are known
as button mushrooms; these are best for pickling, or making white sauce
dishes, and are very delicate cooked in milk. The rounder, pink-gilled
ones can be cooked many ways. When fully opened, flat, and just brown
underneath, they are suitable for grilling; when darker underneath but
still dry, they are good for drying and flavouring; and when they have
gone quite black, they are really only good for ketchup.

Length of stem varies, and you can easily find the soft torn ring which
sealed the button mushroom still fastened to the stem, and when you pull
them up, the end of the stem is rounded, but not much thickened. There
may be a few white fibres or hairs, but the stem goes into the ground quite
cleanly and straight.

Cultivated mushrooms, grown from spawn, in boxes, are usually
brownish and dry in texture. They are a good useful mushroom for cooking and flavouring, but lack the delicacy of the field ones, and the aroma
of wind and rain and the tang of autumn that comes into the kitchen with
a basket of field mushrooms.

The horse mushroom (*Psalliota arvensis*) is a clumsy version of the
field mushroom. The top is thicker and the stem lumpy, and the colour
of the gills less pink. The smell is that of the field mushroom. The buttons
can be treated in the same way as button *campestris*; the cup-shaped
ones with their thick tops are solid enough to bake, holding a tomato, well
spiced, or an egg, or chopped ham. If they open flat they can be grilled,
but are not so good for grilling as *campestris*. In fact, very thick horse
mushrooms are really better with the tops cut down, or chopped up and
put in a pie.

Both these mushrooms peel easily. Both vary according to their locality
from snow-white to a faint pinkish or creamy colour, but if a horse

The "Common" Mushroom (*Agaricus Campestris*)

The "Horse" Mushroom — *Psalliota Arvensis*

B.1. B.2.

The Common "Puff Ball" (*Lycoperdon Perlatum*)

C.1. C.2.

The "Fairy Ring" (*Champigone Marasmius Oreades*)

D.

E.

These should be cut from their tough thin stalks and dried for winter use

The Bluet or Bluetail

The "common" refers to the field or "common grazing" (Campestris) where these pink and white mushrooms grow to perfection.
The Bluetail will not dry, and must be used fresh.

mushroom stains yellow, when cut or bruised (not a faint tinge, but a definite bright yellow as if dabbed with mustard or yolk of egg) discard it as it may be *Psalliota xanthoderma* which, though not deadly, has been known to cause illness. It is the solitary dead white fungus that should be regarded with suspicion. It is the Death Cap (*Amanita phalloides*) which is most dangerous. Luckily it is unmistakable by sensible adults, for though it has a superficial resemblance to *Psalliota xanthoderma* and *arvensis*, if you saw them together the difference would at once be apparent. To begin with *Amanita phalloides* gills never turn pinkish or dark brown (like *campestris*) but remain a cold clammy white. Its frilly ring round the stem is different, hanging down smooth and limp from the top. Its top is tinged olive green or yellow instead of the creamy colour of *arvensis*. And most definite of all, if you dig down to the base of the stem with your fingers, you will find it has come up out of a glutinous case; called a volva. (Sometimes bits of this case membrane are found sticking to the top.) This volva is a sure sign of the Death Cap. That is why it is so important to look at fungi when growing. Children especially should be taught to examine fungi right down to the roots when gathering. If you can find the utterly unmistakable tall stinkhorn fungi in some wood, the volva of that is so large that it can easily be seen, and the smaller volva of the Death Cap easily recognised afterwards.

Button Mushrooms in a White Stew (a memory of childhood on a farm)

A pint of small mushrooms, peeled, are thrown at once into slightly salted water. When all are done a pint of new milk is put into a double saucepan, and the drained mushrooms added with a good dab of butter and the least possible dash of pepper and mace, and the whole is left to simmer for nearly an hour (this slow cooking *under* boiling-point is the value of the dish).

Serve in a bowl with a spoon and a good stiff rusk. For grown-ups, the same dish is made, but the milk thickened to a white sauce.

Flat Mushrooms Turned Brown

These are best grilled, and well basted with butter while cooking. If cooked with bacon, grill them smooth side up first, then put them gill

Strips of bacon rind used to baste flat grilled mushrooms

side up, under the grill, with strips of bacon, which drips on to them. Done this way, they grill both sides, simultaneously with the bacon. Dust with pepper and salt.

Mushroom Sandwiches

Country people make delicious sandwiches of brown bread and butter and finely sliced up mushrooms (raw), the mushrooms being sprinkled with lemon juice. Similarly, thin slices laid on beef in sandwiches are much enjoyed by most folk in the fields. They keep the sandwiches nice and moist.

Thick mushrooms placed over tomatoes, with basting fat above

Horse Mushrooms with Tomatoes

The large rounded horse mushrooms bake well, and, being less delicately flavoured, combine well with other materials. As tomatoes are ripe at mushroom time, any thinned out, cracked, or irregular-shaped fruit combine well with the varied shape of the mushrooms. To prepare, pepper and lightly salt the mushrooms inside, and add a small dab of bacon fat. Invert and press in a neatly fitting tomato, previously skinned. Turn down upon an oven dish and impale a small strip of bacon upon the top. Bake all in a fairly hot oven till mushrooms are tender and the tomatoes have made a rich juice sauce.

For the thickest, clumsiest-shaped horse mushrooms, cut a slice off the thick white top, so that they stand evenly, pepper, salt, and press in the tomato as before, but pack the filled mushrooms upright, like cups, tightly wedged into a deep bake-pan. Put small strips of bacon fat across the tops and a little broth into the pan and stew slowly till the mushrooms can be pierced with a fork and seem cooked through.

Stewed Horse "Buttons" with Red Fruit

The rounded "button-shaped" horse mushrooms may be quite large. These are best stewed in milk, with a suspicion of *mace* (nutmeg is too strong); when soft, drain, pack the rounded mushrooms into a deep dish and use the milk to make a thick coating sauce (using as much butter as

Tomatoes inside mushroom cups

possible). Pour over the hot mushrooms and garnish the white dishful with sprigs of barberries, made hot, to bursting point, in the oven, or a spoonful each of butter and red-currant jelly, that will melt in combined yellow and red sauce. The slight garnish of tart fruit brings out the smooth aromatic delicacy of the mushroom sauce.

Dried Mushrooms for Winter

Fairy-ring mushrooms (*Marasmius oreades*) are best for drying.

Also known as "champions" (champignon?), they are not always true to their habit of growing in rings, especially where lea has been broken. But the delicate "fairy-ring mushroom" is unmistakable. They are seldom more than two inches across, and carried comparatively high on slender stems.

Threaded on string and hung up to dry

The gills are very deep and regular, one long, one short, like the minute marks around a clock. The top is buff, and the gills are very much paler. The slender stems are stringy and tough, so cut them off. *Marasmius oreades* have a strong mushroom flavour, and are the dried mushroom of the French and Italian shops in London. We recommend drying these for winter use; using a darning needle, thread them on a string and hang them across the ceiling or in a hot airing cupboard till crisp.

These dried mushrooms are excellent in beefsteak pies and puddings, or a rabbit pie; or cut into strips with scissors, they make appetising dark stripes along a galantine or in soup. Another method of drying these small mushrooms is to thread on fine splinters of wood, which are put in rows grid-wise across the oven shelf ledges overnight for several nights.

Mushrooms dried on sticks laid across the bars of a cool oven

If you have no continuous oven, but use an electric fire, or have a hot radiator, burning continuously, spike the mushrooms on to a nice twiggy bough, wedge the bough in a flower-pot before the fire and keep turning it round and round; it looks curiously decorative like the ghost of a willow-pattern tree.

Mushroom Ketchup

When mushrooms are "in a glut", make mushroom ketchup. Put all peel, stalks, broken mushrooms, and the spicy rich black old ones (too ripe to cook otherwise), into an earthenware jar, strewing them with salt. Cover the jar and set it at the back of the stove to keep warm. You can keep adding to it whilst the mushrooms last, salting each layer lightly and pressing well down.

When the jar is full, and the dark liquid flowing, set it in the oven and give it a good, steady boiling. Strain through muslin, pressing well, and for each quart of liquid add an ounce of black pepper and three to four blades of mace *or* a quarter of a nutmeg broken to bits.

Give it a good boil-up, and strain into hot, well-scalded bottles, which cork immediately. If put into sterilised bottles, it will keep indefinitely, but the delicate aroma of mushrooms is naturally fugitive, and a bottle once opened should be used quickly.

THE PUFF-BALLS (LYCOPERDON)

While finding *campestris* and *arvensis* you will probably find plenty of puff-balls. You may find also the enormous puff-balls *Lycoperdon giganteum*. The little puff-balls vary from one to two inches or more across, but the giant puff-ball may be as big as a football. They are both exactly the same texture (solid white, like smooth, white cream-cheese), and the outer covering is fine as white kid. Once you have lifted them, only a few white strands will show where they were fastened to the ground. When they get old, the inside turns yellowish, greeny brown, and finally turns to powdery dust, the "white kid" skin bursts, and the empty cases, full of dry dust, lie about all winter.

Mushrooms dried before an open fire

Puff balls, to my mind, are the most delicious fungi. The little round ones should be gently stewed in milk, till you can pierce them easily with a skewer. Then pour off the milk, and use it to make a white sauce with butter and a dust of mace, some pepper and salt. Return the puff-balls to warm through and serve hot, with brown bread and butter. The Giant Puff-Balls (*Lycoperdon giganteum*) are exactly like sweetbread, both in texture and flavour. Slice and fry them, and serve with a squeeze of lemon juice. The giant puff-ball is a feast in itself, and I remember a huge one found by a shepherd of the wolds near Loughborough. It was about twenty-four inches in diameter. We cut it in slices, egg-and-breadcrumbed them, and fried them; and one giant puff-ball served six people.

Smallest Puff-Balls

Very small puff-balls, walnut size, are best dipped in batter and fried like rissoles. Drain and serve as a pebble beach around a pool of green spinach.

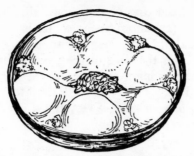

A snow-white dish garnished with burst scarlet
barberries and bright green cress or parsley

Medium-sized Puff-Balls

Take one dozen puff-balls, about the size of hens' eggs, wipe them
carefully, and see that all are firm and white. Roll them in flour, white
pepper, and salt, and drop them into a deep earthenware pan with barely
enough milk to cover them. Add a small bay leaf and a scrap of onion,
and simmer gently till soft. Lift them out carefully onto a hot dish. Thicken
the milk in which they were cooked with butter and cornflour, season
delicately, and cook thoroughly. Pour back over the puffs, and garnish
the white dish with tiny bunches of scarlet barberries and sprays of green
parsley. In a round brown dish, the smooth white puffs in their own
creamy sauce, white against the translucent scarlet berries and the vivid
green parsley, look good and taste delicious.

Giant Puff-ball Egg-and-Crumbed

The giant puff-balls are too large to cook well whole, but their fine
texture cuts clean and crumbly like close white bread. Use a breadknife,
and slice into rounds half an inch thick. Dip the slices into well-beaten
egg and milk, and then into fine dry breadcrumbs. Press the crumbs
on firmly, and let the slice stand an hour or two to make the coating
firm, then fry the slice in hot bacon-fat, turning once. Lift with a slice,
drain on kitchen paper, pepper and salt, and serve piping hot, sprinkling
with cider or vinegar.

THE PARASOL MUSHROOMS, *Open and Shut*

The parasol is another unmistakable mushroom. It grows from late
August onwards in fields—sometimes where long-establised lea is broken
—on stubble or ploughed earth. The mechanism of the parasol is exact;
it rises closed, held to the stalk by a white loose ring which slides up
the stem as the parasol opens; and finally tears loose, as the top spreads

wide open, the now freed ring of membrane slipping loosely down the stem. The raised boss (or umbo) in the centre is well marked, the stem long and slender, and the top rough with tufts of up-curling membrane, which also fringes the edge of the parasol top. The light setting of the head is another distinguished feature, the gills being clear of the stem, so that the head rocks lightly on the stem if touched. Pick when just opened flat; remove the stem and, if very thick, cut a little off the umbo to make it cook more evenly.

Cooking the Parasol, Open

Put it between two buttered saucers or soup plates (according to size) and steam over a pan, season lightly and eat with bread and butter. Do not overcook this mushroom, as its flavour is very delicate, and the texture as light as a good omelet. If late, the top skin may be tough; if so, cut it off and shred the parasol across, from side to side, into strips about an eighth of an inch thick, and toss in butter till cooked; pile on to hot buttered toast and serve quickly.

Stuffed Parasol, Shut

Find half a dozen parasol mushrooms in the cup stage. (The long fibrous stem must be discarded as tough.) See they are perfectly clean, and fill them with a fine sage and onion forcemeat. Turn them upside down on to a flat baking dish, secure a small square of fat bacon to the top with a skewer, and bake upwards of 30 minutes, the bacon-fat. Some partly boiled potatoes may be roasted at the same time, and the parasol mushrooms, served with these and apple sauce, they make a very "meaty" dish.

Pieces of fat bacon used to baste baked mushrooms

CHANTARELLE (Cantharellus cibarius)

One of the prettiest of fungi. You find them, suddenly, in the autumn woods, sometimes clustered so close that they look like a torn golden shawl dropped down amongst the dead leaves and sticks. They are all the same clear, egg-yolk yellow, the stem coming up straight, and springing and spreading stiff as a tiny fountain spurting gold. The top surface is damp and glossy yellow; the underside crinkly matt yellow; and they smell faintly of apricots.

Being more solid than they look, they are best sliced across and across, before stewing gently in milk and butter. When quite soft (they may take nearly an hour), lift the slices and drain onto a hot dish, thicken the milk to a cream with butter and flour and pour over the waiting slices. They are so delicate that only a trace of white pepper and salt is needed for the dish, though some think it improved by a dust of white sugar and mace.

COMMON MOREL (Morchella rotunda)

" Q. What are morels?
  A. A kind of fungus found in woods and used for thickening and flavouring sauces and soups. They are preserved by being strung on a pack thread and dried."

Mangal's Questions, 1850.

A truffle, not a mushroom. I believe they used to teach dogs to nose for them. I have found them in the Hampshire woods. They resemble knobs of deep brown honeycomb on hollow, short white stems. They are a spring fungus and grow well on chalk soil. They are so thin, brittle and hollow that there seems to be nothing to them, but they are well flavoured and are sold abroad as a grocery for flavouring stews and pies. When dried and the stems cut off, they shrink so much they look like wrinkled thimbles. If you find one morel, hunt round thoroughly for more, as they are rare in England, but sometimes come up in quantities in some locality, and they are a very great delicacy.

EDIBLE BOLETUS (Boletus edulis)

This is found rather late in autumn and is common in beechwood districts. It is so exactly like a glossy penny bun, that any other description seems superfluous. Even the texture is bun-like, for underneath, instead of gills, it has a golden porous texture (really myriads of small spore tubes).

The stem bulges towards the base and is finely covered with a tracing that looks as if someone had been scribbling on it. In woods, it is so like the golden brown beech leaf that it is easily missed, but a sweep of boletus, looking as if someone had tipped a basketful of penny buns out onto the emerald autumn grass, is a joyous sight.

I believe the Italian-English in Soho cook them in oil, and that some people recommend cutting out the spongy underneath part, but if clean, and there are no insects, just cut off the stem, shake pepper and salt over the porous surface, flatten the top of the dome a little so that they lie level, pour over melted butter, and bake in a shallow bake-dish till tender. They have then to be turned over and, just before serving, they should be given a good final basting.

BLUE TAILS, BLUETS, BLUITS

These have always remained popular where the French people settled. Bluits in Nottingham used to fetch a higher price than mushrooms and are sold in Northampton and many Midland markets. They are the shape of a mushroom, but a pleasant smooth fawn brown, with lighter gills underneath. The bluit (in contrast to the white opaque mushroom) is translucent, with a delicate blue stem. There is no ring or volva, nor any surface peel—the texture is exquisitely smooth and even throughout and, though moist, never sticky. Bluits come rather late in September, and on account of their moist substance they do not fry well, nor dry, and should be eaten stewed.

Bluits, when cooked, have exactly the substance and aroma of the very best reed tripe. Therefore, to those who like tripe, we strongly recommend the following.

Bluits Stewed as Tripe

As bluits vary in size, I usually measure quantities by amount of chopped-up stems (as this is a simple automatic adaptation for both number and size).

Take the bluits, cut off and chop up the stems, and allowing one stem to measure about a tablespoonful when chopped, measure an equal number of tablespoonfuls of chopped onions, and of milk, and enough water to just cover the bluits as they lie flat in a shallow dish. Pack the chopped stems and the chopped onions into the bluits, together with a small sage leaf (also chopped finely) and a knob of bacon fat. Cook slowly

Served in a ring of mashed potato

for half an hour or more, until the onions and bluits can easily be pierced with a silver fork. Draw off the liquid, and thickening with flour and butter, boil it thoroughly well, and season lightly. When this sauce is thoroughly cooked, pour it back over the bluits and onions and let the whole stew, close-covered, for another quarter of an hour. Serve the hot stew within a well of mashed potatoes.

The likeness to a very delicate dish of tripe and onions is curious, both in texture and flavour, but bluits are very digestible and lighter even than tripe. If liked, apple sauce and snippets of dry toast may be served with the dish, which you will find excellent.

OTHER FUNGI

Horn of Plenty (Graterellus cornucopoides)

The handbook of the Ministry of Agriculture states that these fungi are comparatively common and used to be sold at Covent Garden, but (by some chance) I have only twice found them, and never once in a condition to cook.

My father recognised it as a fungus he had had in Norway, baked with butter, but in this chapter I am only quoting the fungus I have actually cooked and eaten myself.

Pepper Milk (Lactarius piperatus)

This rather rare fungus is for the expert. It cannot possibly be mistaken, for it is hotter and more peppery than the fiercest chillies. It is not poisonous, and is eaten a good deal in Russia, usually salted. It is pure white and large and gracefully undulating, and when broken spills out a copious white juice. In age it is sometimes attacked by a mustard yellow parasite fungus. I have tried small slices in curry, and think it would be a valuable pickle adjunct for making chutneys. It shows how useful an international cooks' bureau would be, as we have not so many pungent indigenous plants to miss using this one.

Funnel Organe (Clitocybe maxima)

This is a little like the chanterelle, but the colour is less clear, bright and constant, and the gills are more like mushroom gills, though deeply cut in the middle and petering out at both ends to where they touch stem and margin. The gills are much paler in colour than the top. It lacks the frilly, graceful effect of the chanterelle. It loses its funnel shape as it grows older, being more like a deep golden-brown basin, with a slightly raised bottom. It may be as much as a foot across.

It has a pleasant texture, but is better with bacon, tomatoes, or something more interesting than its wholesome but rather solid self.

The Ink Horn Fungus

Quill Pen

Ink Pots

Scribe's Sheeps Horn

When old, they turn black inside and drip sepia-black "ink"
and resemble a mediaeval ink horn and quill

Inkytops or *Inkorns* (ink-horns?)

These tall, brownish hedgeside fungi, with dark gills and long, whitish stems, are exact replicas of mediaeval inkhorns, with a quill pen stuck into the ink. When the fungus has become soft and full of dripping black juice, the resemblance is perfect. They usually come in clusters. When young enough to eat, the inside gills are white. They go through brownish pink shades till when old they turn quite black and damp, almost liquid.

They are edible but have little flavour.

Soy

Soy is a fungoid growth on the soya bean. Soy appears after the seventeenth century, first as a condiment, and next as a flavouring in the kitchen. Like anything that showed an overseas connection with the new East India ventures, soy became "a fashion" and permeated everything. It was a convenient gift to bring home. Sailors abroad having learnt to like it, glass bottles of all types were filled with the rich dark juice.

Cultivated Mushrooms

The forced mushrooms bought in shops are rather dry and lack the full flavour of those gathered in fields, but they are excellent for serving under game or with roast rabbit. Having little natural juice, they are best "buttered".

Peel, cut stems level (include the extra stem pieces), sprinkle with salt, and for every pint of mushrooms melt about 2 oz. of butter in a thick pan with a blade of mace and cayenne pepper. When melted (not boiling), add the mushrooms, and simmer and cook in the very hot butter till soft and browned. The butter will be well flavoured also, and they are far better served thus than by any of the "liquid" methods used for the juicy wild mushroom.

ELIZABETHAN HOUSEHOLDS

" Swepynge of howses and chambres ought not to be done as long as any honest man is within the precynts of the house, for the dust doth putryfy the ayre making it dence."

BOORDE.

BY this time the great hall dinner is old-fashioned. It continues in use in farmsteads, where master and men eat in relays at the great farmhouse table in the kitchen (as they do in good farms today). It was still part of farm life, but as Piers Plowman cried a century before: "Now have the Rich a rule to eat by themselves—in a room with a chimney"; and these small intimate family meals form a distinctive new series of pictures in all the manuscript books from the fourteenth century onwards. Very cosy, small tables set close to a fire, with the wife setting the dishes or spinning, while the servant "carries in"—and the cat sits by! Notice that compared with the Norman and Saxon dinners cooking has become much more simple. The Tudors' taste was for "basic English" fare! and the Norman pork is called *Pigge!*

SIMPLICITY AND RICHES (A Court Dinner, 1575).

First Course

Pottage of stewed Broth	The soup eaten before the meat.
Boyled Meat	Cooked in it.
Chickens and baken	Chickens and bacon.
Powdered Biefe	Salt beef (probably spiced).
Pies and coffers	A century before called " tarts " and " coppyns ".
Pigge	Sucking Pig?
Rosted Beefe	
Rosted Veale	
Custarde	Probably baked and savoury, like Yorkshire pudding.

Second Course

Rosted Lamb	
Rosted Connies	Rabbits specially fed for table.
Chickens	
Pea Hennes	
Baken Venyson Tarte	Fish and meat " tarts ", were probably " open shape ".

SIMPLICITY AND POVERTY

This description of a croft in the Orkneys is by Captain Frobisher in 1577.

"Their houses are very simply builded of Pibble Stone, without any chimneys, the fire being made in the midst thereof. The good man, wife and children, and other of the familly, eate and sleepe on the one side of the house, and the cattell on the other. They are destitute of wood, their fire is turffes, and cowshards. They have corn, bigge and otes, with which they pay rent (to the King of the island). They take great quantitye of fish, which they dry in the wind and sunne. They dresse their meat without salt. . . . They have egges . . . and fowle . . . their bread is eaten in cakes, their drink is ewe's milk, and in some parts ale. . . ."

The "pibble stones" were the huge sea rounded rocks of the shore, split by fire (you can't build smooth round stones without mortar), and the "doors" and unglazed windows were curtained with goatskins, or shutters of the skin stretched on rough frames. These people used no money, they lived on the land and off the land, and their "king" had been the chieftain when the old northern invaders came. In many cases the main "hall" had been taken over many times since by subsequent conquerors, but these small independent communities continued their quiet lives hidden in unexplored crannies of mountain, or on isles; and knew as little as they cared about who troubled England. They were entirely self-supporting, and their food simple but good and well cooked. St. Kildas is an example of an island where the population has removed to the mainland. The Blaskets continue occupied. Aeroplane and wireless have brought most of these isolated communities into communication, but for many centuries you must picture Britain as still superimposed upon quite a large population of people, who had missed, rather than evaded, any definite government, and lived their quiet lives, vastly content, and troubling nobody. Domesday Book was (for its date) an extraordinarily efficient census of population, but these people slipped from between the leaves of the parchment. And it was through these independent people that much of the valuable Saxon and Danish lore was preserved. The vagrancy laws, in the later part of Elizabeth's reign, seldom had to deal with these people; it was returned sailors, discharged soldiers, and the mass of derelict monastery dependants, that made that problem.

A CHILD'S DAY

" Letters of Instructions from King Edward IV to the Earl of Rivers and John Russell, Bishop of Rochester, for the education of his son, Edward, Prince of Wales (1473).

An Elizabethan farmhouse

Item. We will that our said son have his breakfast immediately
after his Mass; and between that and his meat, to be occupied
in such virtuous learning as his age shall suffer to receive, and
that he be at his dinner at a convenient hour, and thereat to be
honourably served and his dishes to be borne by worshipful folks
and squires, having had our livery; and that all other officers
and servants give their due attendance according to this offices.
Item. That no man sit at his board, but such as shall be thought
fit by the discretion of the Earl Rivers; and that then he read
before him such noble stories as behoveth to a prince to understand and know. . . .
Item. We will that after his meat, in eschewing of idleness, he be
occupied about his learning; and after, in his presence, be of

such convenient disports and exercise as behoveth his estate to have experience in.

Item. We will that our son go to his even-song at a convenient hour; and that soon after done, to be at his supper and thereat to be served according as before.

Item. We will that after his supper he have all such honest disports as may be conveniently advised for his recreation.

Item. We will that our said son be in his Chamber, and for all night livery to be set, the travers drawn anon upon eight of the clock."

KING'S LETTERS.

A WOMMANS DAY

"First in the morning when thou art waked and purporest to ryse, lyft up thy hands and bless thee and make a sign of holy cross and if thou says a Paternoster and Ave and a Crede and remember thy maker, thou shalt speed moche the better. And whan thou arte up and redy, then first swepe thy house, dress up thy dysshe borde, and sett all thynge in good order within thy house. Milk thy kyne, scokle thy calves, sye up thy mylke, take uppe thy chyldre, and arraye them, and proudye for thy husbandes brekefaste, dyher, souper and for thy chyldren, and seruantes; and take thy part with them. And orderyne corne and malte to the myll, and bake and brue withall, when need is. And meete it to the myll and fro the myll and se that thou have thy meas re agayne besyde the tolle—or else the myller dealeth not truly with the, or else thy corne is not dye as it should be. Thou must make butter and chese whan thy mayst, serve thy swyne bothe morning and evening, and give thy poleyn [poultry] meate in the mornynge and evening, and whan the tyme of the yere cometh thou must take hede to hale thy hennes and dukes and gese do ley—and to gether up their egges, and whan thyey waxe brodye to sette thei there, as noo beastes swyne or other verymyn-hurte them.

And tho muste know the whole footed foul will sit a month and all cloven footed will sit 3 weeks, except a peyhenne and grete fowles as cranes bustards and such other. And whan they have bough forth their byrdes, to see that they are well kept from the gleyd, crowes, fully marten, and other vermyne. And the beguning of March or a lyttle before is time for a wife to make her garden and to gette as many good seeds and herbes as she can, and speacly much as be good for the pot and to eat, and as need shall require it must be weeded, or else the weeds will overgrow the herbs and also in March is tyme to sowe flax and hempe, for I have heard old housewives say that better is March herdes than April flax. The season offereth, but how it should be sowen weded pulled repeyled watred wasshed dryed beaten braked tawed heckled spon wounden wrapped and woven, it nedeth not for me to show—for they be wise enough, and thereof may they make shetes smokes and much other necessaryes and therefore let thy dystaffe be always redy for a pastyme, and thou be not idle. And undoubted a womman can not get a lynynge honestely with skynnynge on the distaffe, but it stoppeth a gap, and must needs be had. The bolles of flax whan they be repeled of must be rideled from the wedes and made dry with the sun to set out the sedes. The female hempe must be pulled from the churle hempe, for that bearth no sede and thou must do by it as thou dydst by the flax. The churle hempe bearten for seed, and byware that birdes eate it not as it growthe. The hemp thereof is not so good as the female hempe but yet it will do good service.

My fortune! sometime that thou shalt have so many thynges to do that thou shalt not well knowe where is best to begyn. . . .

It is conveyant for a housbande to have shepe of his owne for many causes, and than may his wyf have parte of his woll—to make her husband and herself some clothes—And at the beste may she have the locks of the shepe either to make clothes or blankets or coverletts or both. And if she have no woll of her owne she may take wol to spinn of cloth makers, and by that means she may have a convient lyunge and many times do other works.

It is a wyues occupation to wynoue all manner of cornes, to make malt, and wasshe and wrynge to make hay, shere corne and in tyme of nede to help her husbande to fyll the muck wayne or dounge cart, drue the plough to loode corne and such other. And to go ride to market to sel butter shese mylke eggs chekyns capons hennes pygyes gese and all mannere of cornes and also to bye all manner of necessaye thynges belongyng to house-holde and to make a trewe reckenyne and a compte to her hus-bande what she hath payd. And if the husband go to the market to bye and sell as they ofte do, he than to shew his wife in like mane—for if one of them should use to deceyne the other he deceyveth hymself and he is not like to thrive. And therefore they must be true either to other."

FITZHERBERT.

Distaff and spindle. Where French folk settled called a rock and reel, and used with a different movement, the spindle being run down a trip skin attached to the thigh.

A FARMER'S YEAR

A calendar of the land was written by a farmer called Tusser (1477). His book is overflowing with country fare, and he treats his wife as a complete partner.

From the spring, when he makes a nest for the swan, to the winter, "when pastures be gone and the fields mire and wet", he lives and sings every day—almost every hour of the farmwife's day. He notes that in a litter of pigs it's the pink one who suckles the front teat gets most milk! And he remembers pancake day, and the Christmas log.

Tusser arranges for his farmworkers to bring in kindling daily for his wife's cooking fire, and bracken and furze for her brewing and baking ovens. When the ground is iron hard with frost, he splits timber; "when frost will not suffer to dyke or to hedge", "Then get thee a heat with thy breetle and wedge". A "breetle" being the heavy wooden mallet used for driving in the wedges that split the logs.

Cattle are warmly bedded: "get home with thy brakes [bracken] before summer is gone, for cattle in winter to sit down upon". He gives out gloves for reapers when thistles are in the corn, and helps his wife plant raspberries, and is sympathetic about the difficult training of dairy maids.

In winter, after dark has fallen on the fields, they all sit by the farm-house fire and the women spin and talk; and the men set their drinks to warm on the hearthstone as they mend tools and whittle wooden teeth for rakes and wooden spoons for their darlings.

Every day throughout the winter the few remaining cattle must be set free "to rove and rub themselves and take exercise". His duties are as varied and endless as those of the women—for he must climb the ladder to the loft and see if the stock fish and fruit are keeping well—and he must take his wife to market in good time to buy what she needs for her Christmas shopping.

The days of slave labour are over; the black death and famine years have given the labourer power to bargain for his work—now a farmer must pay the servants well, and see they have a good fire in the hall, and good food and a good holiday with games and fun and lovemaking.

And seed cake, furmenty, pease pudding, beans and bacon, buttered leeks, soused herrings, strawberries and cream, and a dozen other recipes belonging to this household of 1477.

He finished his book of beautiful simplicity by saying that the noblest thing a farmer can have is a good wife to work with him, and strong children to follow him.

FARMWORK CALENDAR 1559

January: wean home calves; cart out the dung in frost; feed cattle and see they sleep warm.

February: plough stubble; harrow winter-sown; stick peas; set melons; sow mustard; where you want to kill nettles, cut; plough, and sow hemp seed.

March: "look twice a day lest lambs decay". See off the droves; rear goose and duck; sow barley; and spare pasture as early as you can.

April: kill a beef, and with that and pork, your people will stay fat till the grass meat comes in; don't feed them dry fish now you can get fresh.

May: sow buck after barley; attend to the hop yard; weed; put calves to grass; bargain *now* for winter fuel!

June: see to the harvest carts, repair; wash sheep, and shear them kindly.

July: pluck flax and get ahead with the miller; "for the harvest—be Captain and work hard thyself and provide bottles and wallets and food in the field for the reapers—good wife see to this!"

August: corn harvest, and let the stubble stand for the oxen to feed on and the goose to glean!

September: thresh corn, gather fruit, and

> " Come home loud singing!
> Come home corn bringing!"

October: sow greens; set hedges and clean the land.

November: keep the hog fat till he is killed; kill off all animals in turn, keeping only those you can support through the winter for breeding next spring.

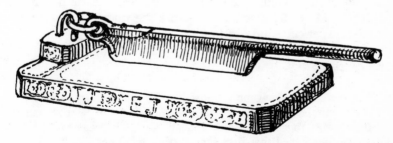

A breaker (mentioned in old recipes). This was used for "working" dough, or sometimes for butter. In some districts it was used for "hackling" flax. In all cases the material was pushed to and fro with the left hand while the "breaker" was banged up and down with the right.

THE NEW WORLD AND THE SAILORS' COOK

The discovery of the New World set new problems in the kitchen. The mediaeval cook had been ahead of the scientists in providing preserved food for winter use (killing the cattle in autumn, and lack of winter provender, had far-reaching effects in the arts of drying and salting and smoking). Now cooks are called upon to invent closer packs, and provide for longer voyages, and a perfect wave of preservation recipes—for pickling, potting, and spicing—washes over the cookery of the sixteenth century.

The melted butter we pour over potted meat tops is the last faint reminder of the thick, airtight suet seal put over the potted meat for sailors.

The clotted cream of Devon, preserved with sugar, was the prototype of our sweetened condensed milk. The folk around Plymouth and the West Ports baked the cream and bottled it to send to sea. Honey, salt, juniper, pine tar and dear knows what preservatives were used on the hams and bacon that was smoke-dried for the tropic seas. Realise that the enterprise and care of the Elizabethan cooks stood firmly behind their sailors. They studied the medical side of food, and here the older mediaeval reasoning merges with half-sensed new truths. For example, black hogs' lard was advised for salves—as if the cook *felt* that the sun's rays could be absorbed by a fat grown in the dark.

The cod lived in cold water—so cod's oil made warmth. The Elizabethan cook did not think any less because she studied less science—she learnt from experience and observation.

The dread scourge of sailors on long voyages was an "unaccountable" disease called scurvy.

> " By reason of Navigation, the sailors fall with sundry diseases; their gummes waxe great and swell, so they are faine to cut them away, their leggs swell, and all the body becometh sore, and so benumned that they cannot stirre hand nor foot."
>
> HAKLUYT, 1579.

This was, we now know, a deficiency disease, and destroyed more men than battles or tempest. The captains discovered that fresh fruit, especially lime and lemon, cured it like a miracle! Then came the difficulty of getting the fruit to keep—for, behold! when boiled, the lemons ceased to work! The returned sailor and his womenfolk must have gathered by the fireside and talked and puzzled over all this. One can picture some capable cook seeing the glimmering of a great truth, though the word "vitamins" was yet unknown. Watercress was sent out growing in jars, live goats skidded on the wet decks, eggs were waxed and packed, butter salted down. Old recipes were hunted up. Broom buds (that were in use for centuries as sheep salve) were tried. All the skill of the old Elizabethan cooks went behind Drake as he sailed off around the world!

We have special interest in the share womenfolk had in providing food for long voyages, because an aunt was one of the first women travelling to the West Indies in sailing ships. She had the minute memory and zestful interest of her period and remembered voyages of several months' duration: "We took goats for milk and hens for eggs, and pigs and sheep, the butcher looked after all animals and they were all eaten by the end of the voyage. Regular diet was salt meat, dried peas and beans, and forms of beans and bacon. We also had boiled salt beef with dumplings, carrots, and root vegetables. Cabin passengers used to take watercress growing in jars, and a few dozen new-laid eggs greased with hot lard and packed in sawdust. The ship provided lemons—against scurvy, and for 'punch'. We took eating apples and conserves in jars. I remember cook used to make a most delicious conserve of fresh apricots and red-currant juice, and we took black-currant cordial. Salves and ointments we always took. I always took a ham as a present to the Captain, as we sat at his table; we cooked it specially with cider and cloves. The cloves helped to keep it. We used to take poultry, potted in tubs and potted trout and salmon done in vinegar, and potted meat in jars. We grew to be very clever! It was our pride. We had apple sauce and onion with the pork. The pig was first to go—the goats and hens last. Cream we boiled with sugar till it was quite stiff; it kept excellently."

On page 344 is her diagram of how the poultry were packed and preserved—using the bread oven—and the legs were made into soup squares for the seasick!

The watercress roots, carried out by the settlers, proved a curse, as they choked up the river estuaries, and, like the Australian rabbits, upset the balance of nature.

But though we forget the part played by the seaman's cook, it's good to read in a hundred log books that the sailors themselves thought the world and all of her.

"SPECIAL SAILORS' FOOD TO BE TAKEN ON VOYAGES FOR THE

'banketting on shipboard of persons of credite'

First the sweetest perfumes to set under hatches to make ye place sweet against their coming aboord.

Marmalade   [Figs barrelled]

Sucket   [Raisins of the sunne]

Comfets of divers kinds *made of puporse* by him, that is most excellent, that shall not dissolve.

Prunes Damaske   [Walnuts]

Dried Peares   [Almonds]

Olives to make them taste their wine.

The apple John, that dureth two yeeres, to make shew of our fruits.

Hullocke   [Sacke]

Vials of good sweet waters, and casting bottels of glasses to bespringkle the guests withall, after their comming aboard.

Sugar to use with their wine if they will.

Excellent French vinegar, and a fine kind of Bisket stieped in the same do make a banketting dish, and a little suger cast in it cooleth and comforteth, and refresheth the spirits of man.

Cynamon water ⎧ is to be had with you to make a shew of by
Imperial water ⎨ taste, and also to comfort your sick in the
                   ⎩ voyage.

With these and such like, you may banket where you arrive the greater and best persons.

Or with the gift of these Marmelades in small boxes, or small vials of sweet waters you may gratifie by way of gift, or you may make a merchandize of them."

NOTE TO TRADING CAPTAIN AT END OF SIXTEENTH CENTURY,

HAYCLUTT.

EXPORT DRIVE IN QUEEN ELIZABETH I'S TIME

" Karsies of all orient colours, specially of stamell, broadcloth of orient colours also. Frizadoes, Motlies, Bristow friezes, Spanish blankets, Baies of all colours, specially with Stamel, Worsteds, Carels, Saies, Woadmols, Flanels, Rash, etc. Felts of divers colours. Taffeta hats. Deepe caps for Mariners' coloured in Stamel, whereof if ample vent may be found, it would turne to an infinite commoditie of the common poore people by knitting. Quilted caps of Levant taffeta of divers colours, for the night. Knit stocks of silke of orient colours. Knit stocks of Jerzie yarn of orient colours, whereof if ample vent might folow the poor multitude should be set in worke. Stocks of karsie of divers colours for men and for women. Garters of silke of severall kinds, and of colours divers. Girdles of Buffe and all other leather, with gilt and ungilt buckles, specially waste girdles, waste girdles of velvet. Gloves of all sorts knit and of leather. Gloves perfumed. Points of all sorts of silke, threed, and leather, of all manner cut and uncut. Shooes of other leather. Velvet shooes and pantophles. These shoes and pantophles to be sent this time, rather for a shew then for any other cause. Purses knit, and of leather. Nightcaps knit, and other. A garnish of pewter for a shew of a vent of that English commoditie, bottles flagons, spoones &c. of that mettall. Glasses of English making. Venice glasses. Looking glasses for women, great and faire. Small dials a few for proofs, although there they will not hold the order they do here. Spectacles of the common sort. Others of Christall trimmed with silver, and otherwise. Hower glasses. Combes of boxe. Combs of ivory. Combes of horne. Linen of divers sorts.

Handkerchiefs with silke of severall colours wrought. Glazen eyes to ride with against dust. Knives in sheaths both single and double, of good edge. Needles great and small of every kind. Buttons greater and smaller, with moulds of leather and not of wood, and such as be durable of double silke, and that of sundry colours. Boxes with weights for gold, and of every kind of the coine of gold, good and bad, to shew that the people here use weight and measure, which is a certaine shew of wisedom and of certaine government settled here. All the severall silver coynes of our English monies to be caried with you to be shewed to the governours at Cambalu, which is a thing that shall in silence speake to wise men more than you imagine. Lockes and keyes, hinges, bolts, haspes, &c., great and small of excellent workmanship, whereof if vent may be, hereafter we shall set our subjects in worke, which you must have in great regard. For in finding ample vent of anything that is to be wrought in this realme, is more woorth to our people besides the gaine of the merchant, then Christchurch, Bridewell, the Savoy, and all the Hospitals of England.

Take also the large mappe of London to make shew of your Citie. And let the river be drawen full of Ships of all sorts, to make the more shew of your great trade and traffike in trade of merchandize.

Rowles of parchment for that we may vent much without hurt to the Realme and it lieth in small roume.

Glew, for that we have plentie and want vent.

Sope of both kindes to try what vent it may have, for that we make of both kinds, and may perhaps make more.

Saffron to try what vent you may have of Saffron, because this realme yeelds the best of the world, and for the tillage and other labours may set the poore greatly in worke to their reliefe.

Black Conies Skins to try the vent at Cambalu, for that it

lieth towards the North and for that we abound with the commoditie and may spare it.

Candles of Waxe to Light. A pot of cast iron to try the sale,
for that is a naturall commoditie of this Realme.

All manner of edge tooles to be sold there or to the lesse civil
people by the way where you shall touch.

To take with you for your owne use. All maner of engines to
take fish and foule. To take with you those things that be in
perfection of goodnesse. For as the goodnesse now at the first may
make your commodities in credite in time to come! so false and
Sophisticate commodities shall drawe you and all your commodities into contempt and ill opinion."

HYCLUTT.

HOME PORTS

The west-coast ports—Bristol, Plymouth and Liverpool, became so
important after the discovery of the New World, that for a time the home
trade up the east coast was neglected. Newcastle coal was not yet much
used, and Scotland was not joined in trade to England so, provincially
speaking, this note on home produce is reassuring.

" I am sure that you may have better cheap freight, of Hull or
Newcastle, then here at London. Besides all this, one may have
such men as wil take paines for their merchants. And further-
more when it shal please God that the ship shal returne to come
to discharge at Hul, for your profit for the sales of fish, cyle,
and Salmon chiefly, hee that will seeke a better market for the
sales then at Hull, he must seeke it out of England! "

TRADE NOTE, 1600.

SLAVE LABOUR AND NEW MATERIALS

Hitherto all luxury imports reached English kitchens from the East,
and coming from ancient civilisations, brought their usage with them.
Now new and untried materials come from the West, not only potatoes
but sugars, treacles, and chocolate came into the kitchen in the sixteenth
and seventeenth centuries from "plantations" which were worked by slave
labour. The Negroes were "persuaded" or "caught" on the west coast
of Africa and taken across to supply labour for the new settlements in
America—chiefly in the south (as they died too soon in the cold north).

The conditions of the slaves, packed below decks during the long
Atlantic crossing, were horrible. After a storm the slave boats used to
heave-to while the dead were hauled out and dropped overboard, and
after a delayed voyage the "waste" in slaves was heavy.

Those in England who knew the conditions of the "blackbirding"
trade deplored it, but in the sixteenth century (as in ours) some wives

troubled little how their husbands made money, provided they made enough!

Here is the description, at random, of a "blackbird boat" taken by pirates—the pirates at least set to work to *feed* their captives. (The "furnace" would be a "built-in" cauldron!)

> " The pirate Captain ordered them to dress a quantity of victuals—so they took geese, turkeys, fowls and ducks, making our people cut their heads off, and pull the great feathers out of their wings, but they would not wait till the other feathers were plucked off. All these they put into a great furnace (which would boil victuals for 500 Negroes) together with several Wesphalian hams and a large sow with pig! which they only disembowled, leaving the hide and hair on. This strange medley filled the furnace and the ship cook was ordered to boil all out of hand."
>
> W. SNELGRAVE.

THE "LITTLE BLACK BOY" IN ENGLAND

Curious and lovely of Shakespeare to make Titania adopt a little Indian baby boy? But later, stories of natives brought back to European courts usually end sadly. Granualle, the wild Irish queen (whose western pirate ships were tied up to her own bedpost, through a hole in the wall in correct classic manner), came to visit Queen Elizabeth, and the two great queens admired each other very much; but the earliest imported "Native Princes" brought home to England usually died—of the climate or the civilisation. There were exceptions, but it is not till the late seventeenth and eighteenth centuries that pictures show the popular little "black slave boys" as foils to their owner's fair pale beauty. These brightly bedecked black slave boys trotted after the sedan chairs around gay London, or followed their patrons to fashionable Bath. They are shown holding the tobacco, or serving the rich chocolate (much as for effect the "Turkish" or "Arab" waiters serve coffee today); but we cannot find that they did any housework or had anything to do with the cooking.

AN AMBASSADOR TO RUSSIA, 1583

The Russian Emperor Ivan Vasiliwich does the English Ambassador proud! In fact "the ambassadour often times sought to have it lessened, but the Emperour would not."

> " One bushell of fine meale for three dayes.
>   One bushell of wheate meale for a day and a halfe.
>   Two live geese for one day.
>   Twenty hennes for the day.
>   Seven sheepe for a day.
>   One oxe for three dayes.
>   One side of porke for a day.
>   Seventie egges for a day.
>   Ten pound of butter.
>   Seventy peny white loaves of bread.
>   Twelve peny loaves of bread.
>   One veather or gallon of vinegar.
>   Two veathers of salt cabiges.
>   One pecke of onions.
>   Ten pound of salt.
>   One altine, or sixe peny worth of waxe candles.
>   Two altines of tallow candles.
>   One fourth part of a veather of cherrie mead.
>   As much of Mallynovomead.
>   Halfe o veather of burnt wine.
>   One veather of sodden mead called Obarni.
>   Three veathers of sweet mead.
>   Ten veathers of white mead.
>   Fifteene veathers of ordinary mead.
>   Foure veathers of sweet beere.
>   Fifteene veathers of beere.
>   Half a pound of pepper.
>   Three sollitinckes[1] of saffron.
>   One sollitincke of mase.
>   One sollitincke of nutmegs.
>   Two sollitinckes of cloves.
>   Three sollitinckes of cinamon."

[1] A Sollitincke is about an ounce.

SALTING, DRYING AND PRESERVING

"Three enormous hogs, which had been killed the day before, lay in different parts of the room, a fourth lay stretched upon his back on the kitchen table, which was drawn out into the middle of the floor. . . .

'Are these the same pigs I used to see you feeding, Mr. Van Brunt?'

'The identical same ones,' replied that gentleman, as, laying hold of the head of the one on the table, and applying his long sharp knife with the other hand, he severed it neatly and quickly from the trunk. 'And very fine porkers they are; I ain't ashamed of 'em.'

'And what's going to be done with them now?' said Ellen.

'I am just going to cut them up and lay them down . . . in salt for pork and hams . . .' And he went on cutting up the pork.

When the cutting up was all done, the hams and shoulders were put in a cask by themselves, and Mr. Van Brunt began to pack the other pieces in the kits, strewing them with an abundance of salt.

'Will the salt make it keep?'

'All the year round—as sweet as a nut . . . it will keep everything in the world if it only has enough of it, and if it is kept dry and cool.'"

ELIZABETH WETHERALL, *The Wide, Wide World.*

GENERAL NOTES ON STORAGE

THERE IS still the big divide between town dwellers, who buy daily from shops, and for whom a refrigerator is ample, and country houses where they grow their own supplies yearly and need store space. Our present dehydrated, frozen, canned, and bottled stores are all evolved from earlier efforts. The "Kilner" jar, with its glass top, rubber ring, and metal tightener, is a direct descendant of the old "Glasse botel" stoppered with a waxed cork, and set to sterilise in the bread oven. And the most modern plastic covers revert cheerfully to the old "scere-cloth", when the fruit, well boiled in its jar, was tied down with the strong waxed cloth.

If the top of the jar was wide, the vacuum sucked the wax cloth inwards; this depression was filled by melted wax or pitch, making a solid, smooth cap. The wax was not lost, being later melted down and strained clean for next fruit season.

The paraffin-wax method of American housewives follows the clarified fat method of the Elizabethan store jars. The boiling-hot food was

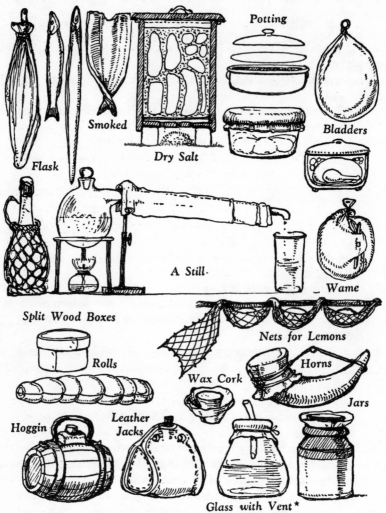

Potting

Smoked

Dry Salt

Flask

Bladders

A Still.

Wame

Split Wood Boxes

Rolls

Nets for Lemons

Horns

Wax Cork

Jars

Hoggin

Leather Jacks

Glass with Vent*

* A Hollow Bone or Quill inserted for ferments

Various storage methods. Many old methods of preservation remain in use to-day. Others have led to the invention of modern substitutes. Wood kept things cool in summer and was used for field drinks. As we use porus coolers. Leather bottles did not break, and now we have plastic bottles.

"swum-over" with an inch depth of boiling clarified fat (usually mutton fat). Provided contact was made around the sides of the pot, the seal when cold was perfect, but the disadvantage of this method was immobility— it could only be used for static jars as movement of the container broke away the seal from the surface of the liquid.

Ferments, like yeast or wine lees (often kept because of their spice content), were covered with damp bladder skins, as these would "give" to the expansion of the gas. These covers also gave the change of humidity, and the drum-tap sound of the tight dry parchment, contrasting with the dull sound of the same covers in damp weather, formed a farmhouse barometer.

Where constant ferment was expected, the bladder was pierced by a hollow quill, or bone (any scientist will appreciate this device). Cooling by evaporation was known, and porous earthenware used for the base of wine jars (where the liquid was needed cool), and glazing used near the top (where floated the yeast, that required slight warmth).

The womenfolk had no "Thermos" but used non-conducting wood hoggins for cold drinks taken to the harvest field, or hot broth to the shepherd's night fold. Grease, salves, or ointments were stored in horns. Lanoline from the sheep, marking raddle (which was a mixture of tallow fat and red earth), soft fats, such as the semi-liquid goose grease, could be pushed in at the large end of the horn, tied over with pliant bladder, and the tip of the horn sawn off, making a primitive "drop bottle", very useful for pushing along the shed lines of a sheep's fleece, and leaving a trail of lubricant as it went along, or would release a spot of oil on to some farm implement. Drenching horns are still used for slipping into an animal's mouth to give medicine. The littlest lambs and babies were fed through shaped horns or thick quills.

Storing of lemons, oranges, pumpkins, onions, etc., was done in nets. Dried roots of all sorts were bundled in old linen—walnuts were husked by rolling up and down in a sack and were stored in wet salt.

Dried stock-fish, or smoked herrings, were hung up in a dry attic; salted herrings hung, like a stiff gold fringe, threaded along fine sticks; eels and salmon, smoked and dried, hung side by side; small, delicately cured pieces of ham, bath chaps, etc., were often buried in a keg of saw-dust. Dried beef was called "hung beef", and hung by the smoke hole.

The "after use" of the old brick bread oven was reflected in the store-house. Nowadays we notice how cereals tend to "dust" and "cling" in ordinary store glasses, and the old shipmen accepted weevils in the biscuits as inevitable. Therefore housekeepers used periodically to "dry off" oatmeal and flour, etc., by spreading it out on the hot floor of the brick oven, after the baking was drawn. Wooden bins were used for cereals—raised from the floor on mouse-proof tiles (little glazed hollow

pots with an overhang, just higher than a mouse). Scents, flavourings, and essences were distilled and stored in small flasks. Soap, candles, and oils had places of their own. Cheeses were in the cheese room or suitably wrapped up to preserve their moisture and aroma (the napkin around the Stilton is a relic of this tenderness). Beans were dried, hazel nuts husked and buried in dry earth. Roots were also buried, in clamps. Apples were dried whole, cored, and strung to the ceiling; pears were usually "smothered" in a warm cupboard. Eggs were oiled—waxed—and buried in sawdust. Oatchaff and wheat straw were used to pack Dutch beef and other dried meats, and vanilla pods were put in sugar. Parkin was stored in boxes.[1]

Near brickyards, cooking in clay was prevalent, and we have shown how it led to the "huff" covering of baking paste; it also accounts for another item that extended to the china clay and "whitewash districts". This was, to cover the smoked hams with muslin, sewn on neatly, and then to whitewash over the muslin—several coats, each dried, atop each other—till the ham was neatly encased in a white crust that effectively kept out flies and dust, and kept in the natural moisture.

Lacking refrigerators or any freezing plant, the old stone larders were well designed to remain cold in the hottest weather. The slate and marble slabs were often two or three inches thick and wedged deep into thick stone walls, and fish or vegetables were laid direct "on the slabs" with no more than a muslin cover over, or a handful of wet rushes sprinkled around and under benches.

In the early nineteenth century one reads "Chloride of lime is helpful", and today, for cleaning the old-fashioned "stone larders", soda to dissolve the grease, followed by a rinse of chloride of lime solution, is better than soap (which clogs the porous stoneware and makes tiles slippery).

Woodwork and shelves are scrubbed and rinsed with the chloride solution and set to dry in a draught.

Modern food is often said "to have kept all right"—but the temperature which will keep butter and salads fresh is utterly inadequate to freeze meat and fish, so study the usage of your modern refrigerator as seriously as your grandmother studied her store cupboards.

[1] Genuine parkin should never be eaten under three weeks old (*see* recipe).

GENERAL NOTES ON CURING

DIVERSE PIGS FOR DIVERSE PURPOSES

Old English custom of killing off all possible stock before the winter did an enormous amount of good in refining the different breeds, and keeping up the standard. Thus the shepherd watched his ewes at dawn, and saved those "upon whos fleeces the hoar frost first melted" as likely to have the greatest vitality. The best cow, the noblest bull, and, not the fattest, but the "best Bonned" and strongest hog survived, and the most prolific sows.

Also, as fresh meat was the first spring need, the farmers early learnt to breed for porkers, as distinct from bacon pigs. Today we are deeply indebted to the mediaeval housewives and farmers for our modern all-purpose pig, which is the result of crossing the best from both types.

The methods of curing and salting varied locally—some districts dry-salting and some brine-salting, some using sugar and treacle (the old replacements of the original honey), some juniper berries, and others gale and sundry herbs, so that diversity of pig and diversity of method interlocked and produced our present diversity of ham and bacon. In the pictures you see the varied characters of the orchard pig, the moorland pig, the wheat-land pig, and the forager pig. These pigs had character before they were pork. Thus we get the Wiltshire bacon, the York ham, the Devon and Somerset bacons, the Suffolk flitch, the Norfolk, and Lancashire, and Durham bacons. All these pigs had some definite *reason* for their diversity.

SINGEING AND SCALDING

The very method of singeing a pig differs in each locality. On the Wyre border, the houses being low and the pigs long, they were slaughtered in the open air, and then (after singeing) hung on the boughs of a tree, high up, out of reach of the wolves from the Wyre forest. (Tradition confirms this cause, for it is still the custom to invite a neighbour to drink with you and "keep an eye on the pig" overnight.) No one in that district thinks it strange to see a cold pink pig swinging high in the orchard, or from the church porch.

Here a pile of straw is built over the dead pig like a thatch, and his hair is burnt off, and later scraped and soused with cold water, the local opinion being that "it does tighten the texture of the fat" (by the shrinking action on the hide?). In other districts boiling water is poured over, and then the pig is scraped with a knife. In other districts the pig is immersed bodily in a vat of boiling water.

Scalding the Pig (down West):

" O dear heart alive! She never belong to take a knife to he! Tes a
brass candlestick she belong to take to he, surely! Her'd take all the
hair of he with she, wityout breaking the skin of he. Mother, shed fley
us alive if she catched us taking the knife to he! Skin of he been tender
after the hot water—oh, NO! dear sakes! she never belong to take a
knife to he; Candlestick, she give a good grip, and she take all the
hair off he and never hurt he! "

Elizabeth Cardynham, Devon.

SMOKING

Smoking, originally done out-of-doors over a smudge fire of wood and
trash, was later done in the chimney (the first hanging in the smoke-hole
of the central fire was probably to keep the flies off—and the dogs).
Smoke-holes and bacon shelves in the farmhouse chimney are often mistaken for priest-holes. A separate smoke-house was very common, and
is still used in some districts.

The type of fuel used gave distinctive flavour to the meat, and often
a short smoking of some resinous wood was used to give a dark fly-proof
finish.

Smoking is now done chemically—using a liquid. Pyroligneous acid is
the active agent in smoke, which preserves and cures meat. This acid is
now sold in bottles—and can be painted over the meat to give it the
smoked flavour. Smoking and curing are also done by injection, but this
method is expert butchers' work, and should not be attempted by
amateurs; nor are we convinced that the injection method of curing
(though obviously quick and an easy way to get the curing liquid dispersed throughout the animal) can be guaranteed. To work from the
inside outwards would seem the most scientific method, for in life the
heart will drive poison from a snake-bite all over the body rapidly, but
in death the syringe drives only one way, without the return suction, and
there is no movement to help the distribution. The method is used in
commercial curing, but as yet it forms no part of plain English usage.

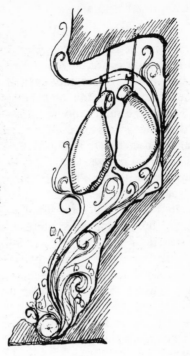

Two hams smoking together. These recesses in old chimneys are often mistaken for "priest-holes".

TIMES AND SEASONS

"When the moon is in the wane." The old idea of killing at the wane of the moon had more in it than superstition. It has been worked out in weights, that animals which graze by moonlight do eat more, and are heavier at the end of a period of moonlight nights.

Another curious old belief (unaccounted for) is that no woman at her monthly period, nor any woman just recovered from childbed, should handle any form of salting.

This is a firm belief in many farms, and they will go to much trouble and expense to bring another hand to carry on the work if the mother of the house cannot. Some of the old women workers may have fostered the belief in order to make themselves indispensable to the younger women—but some put it down to the woman having a slight temperature at the time, as all such work should have a cool hand. (There is so much medical knowledge obscured by superstition, and so much superstition turns out to have a scientific cause, that this is worth reporting.)[1]

[1] An outbreak of difficulty in delivery among parturient mothers was thought to synchronise with the period during which "lions were breeding in Africa". Whether this connected with the constellation of "Leo" or had anthropological interest, I do not know.

SALTS USED IN CURING MEATS

Sal prunella is not the same as saltpetre.

It is a form of saltpetre in which minute quantities of the potassium nitrate is already converted into nitrites, and thus starts the working of the salting process more rapidly. Sal prunella should be used in very small quantities, where the job is being done for the first time. In country places, where the same wooden tubs—the same panshons, and the same old cold salting larders are used over and over again, the nitrites produced by means of bacteria are strongly developed (as with the spores of cheese fungus in an old cheese farm). These bacteria explain the remark "Well, miss, my bacon has took the salt champion—and it was put in the same day as yours, and same pickle."

Prunella balls are saltpetre fused and cast into the shape of balls, and are bought through some drugstores. Sal prunella starts a quicker action, as the fusion of the saltpetre (which is potassium nitrate) converts a minute quantity of this nitrate into the nitrite. It is this latter substance which reacts with the blood of the meat, giving the red colour after cooking.

It has definite value to colonists in hot climates, but see that it is handled cautiously.

About half an ounce should be ample for 100 lb. of meat. Excess of nitrite turns the pickle green and gives a dark colour and hard texture to the meat.

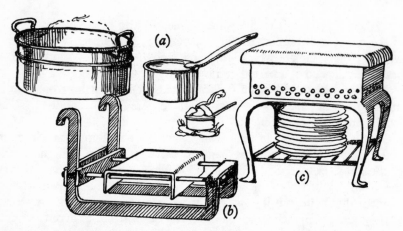

Braising pans for peat or wood fuel. Slide trivets and steel plate warmers. (*a*) Braising pans with sunk lids to take fuel piled on top. (*b*) A slide trivet, hung from the bars of the grate, that could slide the ham (or roast) to or from the fire front. (*c*) The steel 'fire stand' plate warmer, or footman, often very handsomely made. Both these could be used to hold a blistering ham before the fire. The ham was never put in the oven to blister, as it was not required to dry, or cook it, only toast the outside.

THE BOILING AND BAKING CURED MEATS

In boiling, all manner of things are put in the water—hay, cider, beer, treacle, juniper berries, apple pulp, etc. Hams were often baked in the bread oven, crust-wrapped, and always, baked or boiled, the ham was allowed to go cold in the water or crust before being blistered.

BLISTERING AND GLAZING

To prepare, after cooking, the usual way is to skin it while hot, coat thick with crumbs, and then blister before the fire till brown and crisp; the melting fat holds the crumbs, and sets them firmly when cold.

Another method is to glaze the ham with a caramel of spiced sugar, and stick it with cloves.

For blistering hams, old kitchen ranges used to have sliding stands, that drew out in front of the fire-face (to hold the dutch oven or toasting-stand). Trivets were also used. Curiously, the war years brought back much of the old skill in home-curing, as so many people kept pigs. Old country folk, who had not done the work for years, came forward and taught their old skill, and if any new cook has a "share of pig" to dispose of, I suggest that she enquire at her local Women's Institute, or from some farm near, for help in "doing the pig" in the *local* tradition—*for it's sure to be the most suitable to the district.*

PICKLING

Salting a wet pickle

A Wet Pickle

" ' Are you going to do the hams in the same way ? '
' No—they're to go in that pickle.'
' What is in it ? ' said Ellen.
' Sugar and salt and saltpetre, and molasses, and I don't know
   what all.' "

Wide, Wide World.

This "wet pickle" having crossed the salt Atlantic, it became known as the "American wet pickle" but it originally came from Bristol and the west of England ports in the sixteenth century. This is probably the identical recipe used in New England by the Dutchman Van Brunt (though Aunt Fortune may have used honey and saved her sugar—we know she kept bees).

Take 8 lb. of salt, 8 lb. of brown sugar, 4 lb. of bay-salt, 4 gallons of water, $\frac{1}{4}$ lb. saltpetre, and 2 oz. of sal prunella. Boil all together for $\frac{1}{4}$ hour; when cold, pour into the tub and set the hams therein for at least four weeks, better longer. Drain, wipe dry, and smoke thoroughly.

This "wet pickle" was later called "barrel pork" and disparaged by Cobbett.

A Dry-Salt (according to Cobbett)

Cobbett approves the dry salting method; he advises:

"A salting trough which has a gutter round its edges to drain away the brine, for to have sweet and fine bacon the fitches must not be sopping in brine, which gives it the sort of taste that barrel pork and sea junk have, than which there is nothing more villainous. Therefore change salt often and let it melt and sink in, but let it not lie too long.

Before smoking lay the fitch on the floor, and scatter the flesh side thickly with bran or sawdust (not deal or fir). Rub it on, and pat it well down upon it. This keeps the smoke from getting into the little openings, and makes a sort of crust to be dried on. To keep the bacon sweet and good and free from hoppers, sift some fine clean dry wood ash, and put some at the bottom of a chest, long enough to hold the fitch, and lay ashes between and over, and kept dry, the bacon will be as good at the end of the year."

The slate slabs of old larders were arranged for dry salting. Old marble washstands are sometimes used today by enterprising country cooks.

A Spice Pickle (using Juniper)

1 lb. of baysalt, 1 lb. of common salt, 2 lb. of sugar, 4 oz. of saltpetre, 2 oz. of sal prunella, ¼ lb. of juniper berries, a bunch of herbs, including bay leaves, thyme, sweet basil, marjoram, sweet briar, taragon, and a small clove of garlic, spice (including allspice and cloves) about 1 tablespoonful, and 1 quart of strong old ale.

Salt the hams with common salt; first rub the salt on dry several times during the first 24 hours, keeping the ham under pressure between times by balancing a board with weights on top of it, the whole sloping so that it drains as thoroughly as possible, thus extracting the blood and juice. After the 24 hours' salting and draining, let the hams be lifted from under the weight immediately into the pickle.

It is important that the ham, cold and compressed from the first salting, should be put quickly into the pickle just slightly warmer; if the pickle were colder than the ham it would continue the extracting process, rather than begin the permeating one.

To make the pickle, bruise the juniper berries and seethe them with the spices and the beer for 20 minutes, then add the sugar and other ingredients, and stir till dissolved; bring to the boil again, then take it off,

A simple "smoke house" made by inverting a large hogshead. Tenterhooks driven through the bottom suspend the hams and chaps, etc. The bung hole serves as smoke vent. A red-hot horseshoe was handy for starting the sawdust and stick fire, as it could be hooked out for reheating if the fire died down. A bucket of water should be kept handy to damp the hogshead in case the heat shrinks the wood and starts the hoops.

putting in the herbs, and let it cool slowly; when almost cold pour it over the ham, and thereafter turn and rub the ham in this pickle every day for a month. Lift it out, drain, dry and smoke it over a wood fire, upon which juniper berries and herbs are thrown.

Old-fashioned Sugar-cured or "Honey" Hams

For centuries before sugar was cheap wild honey was the chief ingredient. The oldest farmhouse facilities were open sheds and open wood smoking, so that this old method is particularly adaptable to present-day Colonial conditions.

The wild tree honey of Northern Rhodesia seems specially preservative; though usually full of pieces of bark and "honey bread", it needs no more preparation than warming and straining.

The property of honey to "strike in" quickly, and permeate the skin, is well-known to every woman who uses a honey-and-lemon lotion for her hands. It is this permeating property that makes the early stages of curing so much more rapid with honey than with the heavier sugar-and-salt solutions.

Take away the bone from the inner cut side, as the ham will keep better without it. Weigh the ham after trimming, and for each 14 lb. weight allow 1 lb. of salt, ¾ oz. of saltpetre, less than ½ oz. of sal prunella, both lightly crushed, or any local spice, 3 oz. of black pepper, 1 oz. of allspice, ½ lb. of honey and ½ lb. of treacle.

Measure these ingredients into an iron pan and add three times the amount of water. Bring to the boil, and cover closely till cold.

According to the shape of your pickling pot, you may have to make more or less of this liquid pickle; it is better to brew more pickle than risk any part of the meat sticking up above the surface.

Have this pickle made before you kill the pig, and have the dry salt ready.

Take a trough, of wood or stoneware, with some clean sticks across the bottom, and, laying the hams on this, rub the dry salt thoroughly into them. If the weather be cool let the hams lie and drain, under a snow of dry salt, for several days—rubbing and salting them twice daily, till most of the lymph has drained away into the brine below. In hot weather the meat must be put direct from the first rubbing into the pickle. The disadvantage being that the natural liquid draining out dilutes the pickle, so, if you can, keep for 24 hours under dry salt before immersing in the pickle. When the ham is in the pickle, cover lightly, and leave in a cool place all day. In the evening, lift the hams from the pickle, drain, and put them under a snow of dry salt in the salt trencher while you boil up the pickle. In the morning, when the pickle is cold again, replace the hams in it, and boil the salt brine. This need only be done for the first night or so—once the pickle has struck well in the hams are safe, there is no need to reboil the liquids, and the hams may be safely left pickling for three weeks, frequently turning and changing the position. When cured— take up, drain, wipe, and smoke thoroughly at once.

Oak sawdust makes a good cool smoke, so use the nearest equivalent wood. When quite dried a good finish of pine smoking gives a dark, slightly resinous, cover that is very good against flies; but don't smoke with the pine knots till after the first smoking and drying is done, or you may taste the pine too strongly.

Wrap lightly and hang up and dry.

Note. This old honey recipe was experimented on by Rhodesian farmers in 1930, and proved so useful and good that the recipe was given by request to the Bullawayo Farmer's Union.

To Boil a Sugar-cured Ham

Brush and wipe, put to soak in soft water about 2 hours (changing the water if the ham is inclined to be salt). Put to boil with 1 cup of brown sugar, 1 cup of cider, or vinegar, and ¼ oz. of allspice (crushed), boil for half an hour, and then draw aside and simmer for 4 hours. Cover closely and leave the ham to get cold in the water in which it was boiled.

When cold, wipe, skin, cover with raspings and blister before a clear fire.

Kentish Mode for a Whole Pig

This combines the dry salting with barrel salting (land and sea usage). I think that in this method we can trace the very old usages of the ships of the Cinque Ports, and probably the influence of the coastal shipping in the Thames estuary. In coastal vessels it was possible to replenish the pickled-pork barrel at ports of call. It was the long-distance western voyages which developed the dried technique, on account of stowage, as well as tropic conditions.

Therefore the Kentish mode of curing a pig is as follows:

For a porker of 16 st. Kentish weight (that is 8 lb. to the stone, or 9 st. 2 lb. of common weight) allow 2 gall. of salt and 2 lb. of saltpetre, 1 lb. of coarse sugar, and 2 lb. of bay-salt, all well dried and powdered.

"First put hams and cheeks aside to be cured by themselves as sugar-cured hams—then the feet, ears, top of the head, and the tail were brine-salted, for immediate use in making brawns (*see* recipes). Reserve the blade bones, the ends of the loins and spare trimmings for sausage-meat, putting the meat from the bones into a dish for chopping, and the bones

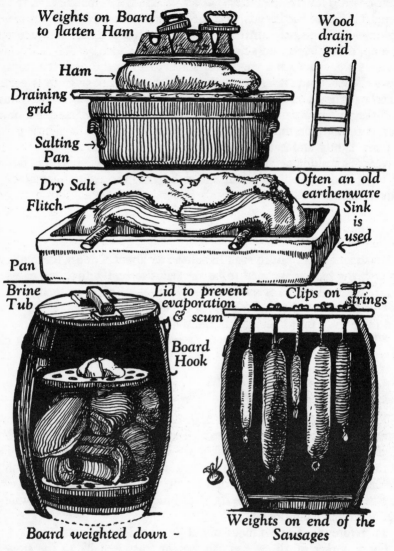

Weights on Board to flatten Ham

Wood drain grid

Ham →

Draining grid

Salting Pan →

Dry Salt

Flitch

Often an old earthenware Sink is used

Pan

Brine Tub

Lid to prevent evaporation & scum

Clips on strings

Board Hook

Board weighted down -

Weights on end of the Sausages

The weights also help to draw out the lymph before penetration by the salt.
Old sinks make good salting pans.
Wet salt pickle now spoken of as "American pickle" was the old "sea pickle"
of Elizabethan sailors.

into an iron pot for stewing. The loin and spare rib should be hung up in the meat larder for roasting after the soft meat is eaten up.

"You now have left the two sides of bacon and the ready-powdered pickling salts. Mix together the saltpetre, bay-salt, and the sugar, and rub the pork with it in every part, paying special attention to folds, and bone ends.

"Cover the bottom of the pickling tub with salt and pack in the pork as closely as possible with portions of the remaining salt between the layers. In ordinary damp weather the salt will draw the meat (see note on curing), and in a fortnight the brine will have risen to almost cover the pork. If, by reason of the shape of the dish or very dry pork, the brine seems insufficient, add more brine." (This is interesting, as the custom of keeping the brine from one curing to the next accounts for the swift action in some cases—and slow in others. In the same way, old wooden tubs in which the bacteria remained active from one curing to the next were much preferred to new ones.)

A board with a stone tied atop was floated in the pork tub to keep the meat under surface. "In three or four months' time the pork will be fit for table, and can be dried off and smoked as bacon, or used as pickled pork."

Yorkshire Method

The original York hams were reputed to take flavour from the oak sawdust from the building of York Minster.

Home-fed pork is cut according to the requirements of the owner. If the family is large, they may cure all as bacon and ham; if small, it may be cut to give one leg of roasting pork, one ham, one shoulder, and two joints, besides the side bacon. People home-curing usually keep both sides of bacon, as they pack better in the salt, though one side may be finished "rolled" and the other flat.

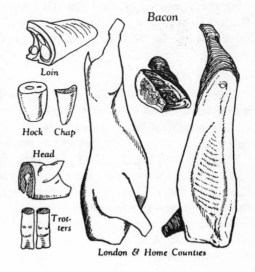

Bacon

Loin

Hock   Chap

Head

Trot-
ters

London & Home Counties

"After scalding, let the pig hang twelve hours before it is cut up, then for every stone (14 lb.) of meat take 1 lb. of salt, $1\frac{1}{4}$ oz. of saltpetre, and $\frac{1}{2}$ oz. of coarse brown sugar. Rub the sugar and saltpetre in first, wiping the meat dry as you work, and rubbing the saltpetre especially well into any bone ends.

"Keep the meat lying on clean dry straw on a well-drained brick or stone floor, and next day wipe dry, and rub with the salt—which should have been warmed and well dried before use. Keep the meat drained and dry, and well rubbed with dry fresh salt, and at the end of three weeks the curing should be complete. Hang in a cool dry place where there is a through current of air, and smoke with oak sawdust. The salt when dried out will crystallise and sparkle on the crust.

"When dry the bacon may be packed in a close chest with dry oak sawdust.

"If very large, the hams will not be in perfection in less than three months' time."

Between the lines of this old recipe one can visualise the stacks of thatching straw (walls were temporarily thatched even during building), the piles of accumulated oak sawdust on the brick and tile floor, the salt, dried in a sack by the workman's fire; even the line "as you work" sounds like some old labourer "attending to" an "acquired" pig, in the blue smoked evening, after benediction.

A Simple Recipe from Leicestershire

1 lb. of bay-salt, 2 oz. of saltpetre, 1 oz. of black pepper, $\frac{1}{2}$ lb. of common salt. Mix all together and rub your hams well; let them lie four days, rubbing them well every way. On the fourth day pour $1\frac{1}{2}$ lb. treacle over them, and turn and rub them twice a week, for a month; then lay them in cold water for 24 hours, and hang them up to dry.

To Boil a Ham

Even a "plain salted" ham comes up wonderfully in this bath, and for a rich home-cured it is the apotheosis.

Take a ham; if large and strongly salted, scrub it under running water and soak for 24 hours, changing the water several times.

Take up—wipe and rub off any "rust" or crusted salt. Make a bed at the bottom of the iron pot of evenly chopped vegetables. Several onions— the golden outer skins included, as they give a golden colour to the fat of the ham—roots and leaves of celery, the hollow tops of parsnips and outer skins of turnips, etc. (the rough tops and skins of vegetables have most flavour). Add a sprinkling of pot herbs and a few peppercorns, put in the ham, pour over 1 pint of sour cider, add 1 cupful of sugar,

A ham boiling in comfort on a bed of vegetable trimmings
with a bag of spice and a mug of cider

1lb. of black treacle, and cover over with a good stack of apple peelings.
Pour in water just to cover the ham (remember the vegetables will make
more juice) and simmer steadily for 4 or 5 hours. Let the ham grow cold
in the liquid. (This is important; all boiled or stewed meats, from fowls
to hams, should be left to grow cold in their broth so that they remain
juicy.) Next day lift out the ham, dry it, remove the rind, and finish it
before the fire, either glazing with brown sugar and sticking with
cloves, or blistering under crumbs. Finish with a sensible, good-looking
hand frill.

Bath Chaps

The cheek pieces of the pig can be cured as "chaps" and make very
good little cold joints for a small family. The type of pig is important for
this joint—some of the flat-headed pigs being quite unsuitable.

Bath chaps began on the local long-jawed, fruit-fed pigs, were cured
by expert cooks, and took their reputation from that elegant eighteenth-
century spa.

The butcher will cut the chap for you. It is customary to leave a piece
of the jawbone and tongue in it (but if the chap is very thick, bone it
completely).

Dry-salt the chaps for 2 or 3 days according to thickness, and then put
them into a cold pickle made with 1 pint bay-salt, 1 quart of common
salt, ½ oz. of saltpetre and ½ lb. of sugar stirred in 3 quarts of water till

A Bath chap. Very useful for a small household.

dissolved; let the chaps lie in the pickle a fortnight, stirring daily. Drain well and smoke strongly. When wanted, soak, boil, skin, and blister with rasps like a small ham. They are carved across and across, and being rather fat are good accompaniment to brawn or tongue.

Bath chaps are also excellent hot, with broad beans, or pease-pudding (the latter boiled with the chap) and parsley sauce. Fresh mustard and baked potatoes complete a perfect winter dinner.

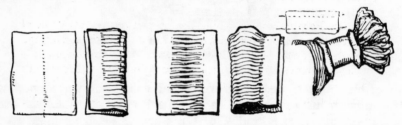

Ham frills (the old carving grip). Fold a sheet of crisp paper in two, cut inwards from the fold. Open out flat, and bend over against the previous fold. Wrap this bunch of frill round the bone, to cover the greasy end. Now fit the small linen band or 'grip piece' over the base of the frill. These little hemmed strips, were made, like pudding basin tops, and dish mats, from odd scraps of table linen. Various qualities of kitchen paper have taken over many of these small household jobs.

The paper frill that adorns the ham bone used to be the folded napkin that gave a good grip for the carver; and a ham with this napkin to hold, and set upon a spiked plank, is far easier to cut than one sliding about on a dish.

COOKING BACON

Pork Slices in White Froth

Thick slices of home-cured pork are very good done by this method:

" Before a good fire stood Miss Fortune, holding the end of a very long iron handle by which she was kept in communication with a flat vessel sitting on the fire, in which Ellen soon discovered all this noisy and odorous cooking was going on.

A tall tin coffee-pot stood on some coals in the corner of the fireplace, and another little iron vessel in front also claimed a share in Miss Fortune's attention, for she every now and then leaned forward to give a stir to whatever was in it, making each time a spasmodic effort to do so without quitting her hold of the end of the long handle. Ellen drew near and looked on with great curiosity, and not a little appetite; but Miss Fortune was far too busy to give her more than a passing glance. At length the hissing

A long handle for solid fuel cooking

pan was brought to the hearth for some new arrangement of its contents.

Miss Fortune was crouching by the pan turning her slices of pork . . . she set the pan back on the fire . . . and the hissing and spluttering began again as loud as ever. . . . In a few minutes the pan was removed from the fire, and Miss Fortune went on to take out the brown slices of nicely-fried pork and arrange them in a deep dish, leaving a small quantity of clear fat in the pan. Ellen, who was greatly interested, and observing every step most attentively settled in her own mind that certainly this would be thrown away being fit for nothing but the pigs. But Miss Fortune didn't think so, for she darted into some pantry close by, and returning with a cup of cream in her hand, emptied it all into the pork fat. Then she ran into the pantry again for a little round tin box, with a cover full of holes, and shaking this gently over the pan, a fine white shower of flour fell upon the cream. The pan was then replaced on the fire and stirred; and, to Ellen's astonishment, the whole changed, as if by magic, to a thick, stiff white froth. It was not till Miss Fortune was carefully pouring this over the fried slices in the dish, that Ellen suddenly realised that breakfast was ready, and she was not."

ELIZABETH WETHERALL, *The Wide, Wide World.*

This recipe went from Elizabethan England to America, and came back in the 1800s. The frying must be done carefully so as to avoid the least burning, and the subsequent cooking of the flour, and turning it into white sauce, must be done thoroughly well. We prefer to pour the white sauce round, not over the slices. As a dish, with boiled broad beans, it is extremely good.

Eggs and Bacon

" To have the best collops and eggs you shall take the bacon, cutting away the rind, cut the collops into thin slices lay them on a dish and put hot water on them, so let it stand for an howere or two. Then drain away the water clean, and pat them dry, and lay them one by one on a dish and set before the fire, so they may toast, and turn them so they may toast throwe and throwe, which done, take your eggs and breake into a dish and put a spoonful of vinegar with them and set with water on the fire and let them take a boyle or two, then take up and trim, and drie them, and dishing up the collops lay the eggs upon them, and this way is the best way and most wholesome."

1615.

Beans and Bacon

A fourteenth-century cookery book says: "Take benes and drye hem in an oven and grynde hom and winnow oute the hulles, and take and wash hom clene and do hom in a pot and seth hom and do thereto gode broth and ete hom wyth bacon."

The small field beans of this recipe are now coming back into favour, and being grown in modern gardens.

Gather the pods. Dry, and winnow the beans out, to be dried and stored for winter use. To cook—tie the beans loosely in a cloth, and put them to boil in the broth when you are boiling bacon. When soft, lift out the bag, drain well, and stir about with a lump of butter or bacon fat, and a dust of pepper. Tilt out smoking-hot on to a deep dish and serve with the bacon.

Peas and No Bacon

"We heard the boatswain's pipe to dinner, and immediately the boy . . . ran . . . in a few moments returned with a large wooden platter full of boiled peas . . . crying ' scaldings ', all the way as he came. The cloth, of a piece of old sail, was instantly laid, covered with three plates . . . and as many spoons. . . . Mr. Morgan himself enriched the mess with a lump of salt butter scooped from an old gallipot, and a handful of onion shorn [chopped] with some pounded pepper. . . . My messmates ate heartily . . . they told me that Wednesdays and Fridays the ship's company had no meat and that these meagre days were called Banyan days."

RODERICK RANDOM.

Tonbridge Brawn

This speciality was probably the result of the amount of bacon cured hereabouts, pigs being a by-product of the Kentish cherry orchards. It was also a posting district (see history note). Split the head and remove brains and bone, also the ears. Strew the inside cavity with salt, and treat the ears and feet in the same way; leave to drain for 24 hours.

Next morning wipe off the brine, and rub well with $1\frac{1}{2}$ oz. of saltpetre and 6 oz. of sugar, and in the evening add 6 oz. of salt. Next day fill up the salting trough with good vinegar and keep all turned about in the pickle for a week.

When ready to make the brawn, wash off the pickle and set feet and ears to boil. When the bones can be withdrawn, lift them out and lay the head flat, cutting the thick fat parts (cheeks, etc.) to lay on the thin lean parts, add the sliced skinned tongue and sprinkle all as you work with a nutmeg grated or 2 small spoonfuls of mace, a very small spoonful of cayenne, and a very little pounded cloves. When all is arranged to your satisfaction, in layers, roll the whole up tightly, bind with a strong cloth and secure with tapes and put it into the oval iron pot in which you are boiling the feet and ears. Add a large bunch of herbs, an onion, celery, and pickling spice. Simmer for 4 or 5 hours. Let it grow almost cold in the broth, then take up and put under pressure.

When cold, turn it out of its cloth and rasp it outside with fine crumbs.

This is less like ordinary brawn than a roll of cold boiled bacon, well spiced, and solid.

SALTING AND SMOKING FISH

" Both salt fish and ling fish if any ye have
   Through shifting and drying from rotting go save,
   Lest winter with moistness do make it relent,
   And put it in hazard before it be spent."

TUSSER.

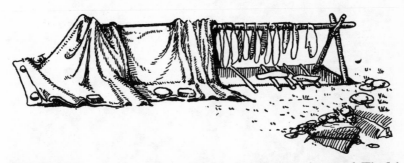

A pit in the ground is filled with a smoke fire of wood peat and seaweed. The fish hang over this and are covered by an old sail to keep in the smoke and keep out the rain. The sail is opened or "set" at the end to catch the wind and blow up the smouldering embers.

GENERAL NOTES ON SALTING AND CURRYING FISH

Up north, at Arbroath, one can still buy smokies—made just like they were made centuries ago. There is this difference: that they are now smoked over wood fuel, not peat; but the product is excellent.

Long ago, when transport was so much more difficult, the curative

properties of peat were valuable. Nowadays, the salting is used for preserving, and the smoking chiefly to give a flavour. The old smoking took
place in the farmhouse chimney or a specially built smoke-house. Frequently
fir boughs and resinous woods were thrown on last to give a "tar" coating
that would deter flies, and the open smoke-hold in the roof was the natural
fly-proof flume.

The salt was mined or dried (in salt pans).

In the north, where they had salt as well as peat, curing was very
thoroughly carried out. Along the rocky coast the sea-salt, crusting in the
crevices, is brownish-grey, roughly crystallised, and has a soft and slightly
bitter tang compared with the sharp salt from Droitwich or Nantwich.

This sea-salt is still in use among hundreds of folk in the British Isles.
Wooden boxes of it, dirty-looking, but of adequate savour, hang by the
open fireplaces, ready to take a spoonful for the cooking-pot, and at meal-
times a small crock is placed on the board—the whiteness of the pot
showing up the greyness of the salt. This salt, and a coarse-ground mixed
pepper, were staple on all the tables of the western seaboard and island
people.

Of course, this salt is not used where they can get the cheap white salt
of commerce, and most smokies, nowadays, are cured in land salt.

(It was over an open hearth on the moors that I first saw smokies, ranged

Drawn at Laxford Bridge, North Scotland, 1920.
Simplicity and comfort—from left to right: food cupboard over working table
with drawer for cutlery, pots above; herrings in rack under thatch; peats, peat
cutter; saucepan and kettle; sheepskin hearth rug; book rest; plaid (this is
wrapped around when needful to go outside; whisky bottle, books, paper
rack; locker for peats and wood; lamp.

in rows, where the open rafters came down against the wall. Here the low roof made a natural fish rack, and against the dark-tinted thatch the gold-smoked fish were thrust endways, in rows, like pegs; when the wind came howling through the open door and set the lamp flame aswing, the live shadow would roll around their gold eye-discs, and the light, flickering along their gold-twisted sides, would set them to a ghostly swim in the dry tide of the peat smoke. Then when the girdle was hot upon the hearth, Robbie would reach up with his hand and pluck down a line of smokies and rub a wee scrap of butter on the pan; he turned them with his long-pointed belt knife.)

Herrings are usually dried folded. Stock fish, white as crusted bone, are split open, flattened, and dried in the open.

All salted fish were washed in peat water in which "racken" (a lichen) had been stewed—this tanned them golden yellow.

The peat fire was damped down, and built so that no heat but a great smoke circled around the fish. It was a slow process. Hour after hour I have sat, watching the blue smoke rise up steadily, weaving endlessly—up and up—bending to the cry of the wind outside, or breaking to the down-draught of the sea-crashed gale. . . . Then, as the gust died away, creeping softly up, against the black feathery soot of the backstone—peat smoke, grey as mist, deep-shadowed as purple heather, curling and winding around the gold bronzed fish, till they were redolent with peat.

Stock Fish, Haberden, or "Yardarm Fish"

> " Broom faggot is best to dry haberden [haddocks] on,
> Lay board upon ladder if faggots be gone,
> For breaking in turning have very good eye
> And blame not the wind so the weather be dry."
>
> TUSSER.

The broom faggot used for heating the bread oven was piled up by the side of the house or shed, and made a good drying-rack; otherwise, as Tusser says, fix up a ladder; but they must lie, not hang, because of the brittle nature of fish. The roof of the house (when thatched) was also used. Of sun there was little, and plenty of rain—yet, somehow, in the wind, those fish did get dry, and hard as boards!

This is the dried stock fish of the northern isles which is salted and dried, on ladder-like racks, in the sun and wind.

This dried fish, and salt bacon, used to be swung at the yardarm of sailing boats putting out to sea. It kept it under much the same conditions that made it (and proved that there was some food aboard anyhow!).

(For recipes for cooking dried stock fish, see Ling, etc.)

To Pot Salmon as at Newcastle

"Take a side of salmon, scale and wipe it and clean it, but do not wash it. Salt it very thickly on a board and let it lie till the salt be all melted and drained off. Now season it in and out 'with beaten mace, a little clove, and a well of pepper', lay bay leaves along it in line and cover it well with butter [mutton fat was used in the Isles], and bake it flat in a dish. When cold, lift it in pieces and lay in a pot, pack close (take out any bones), and fill with a little only of the gravy from the cooking; cover with butter (or more clarified fat) and set back in the oven till hot through, and then withdraw and cover and cool. Thus you may do carp and tench and trout, or any fine fish, and it will keep good some time in a cold place." It is excellent, and a good way to keep salmon after a heavy catch, as it will lose flavour in the refrigerator.

To Pickle Mackerel (a very good, old recipe)

> " When mackrell ceaseth from the seas
> John Baptist brings grass beef and peas."
>
> TUSSER.

Mackerel was the only fish permitted to be sold on the Sunday in Scotland as it should be used very fresh, before the rainbow upon it fades.

To 6 large fish, take pepper and nutmeg and mace and salt, enough to fill, and lay it within (after cleaning, of course). Remove head and tail, lay end to end (that is, pack them like sardines, three heads one end and three heads the other), cover with vinegar and bake till done, and leave till cold.

Soused Herrings

Split and pull out the backbone, removing head and tail, and lay the fish out flat. Dust over with a mixture of dry mustard, salt, ground mixed spice, and a small spoonful of sugar. Roll up lengthways, beginning from the tail end, and as you reach the top insert a bay leaf.

Pack these rolls closely into an earthenware dish with straight sides; there should be enough to fill the dish to prevent the herrings unrolling. Shred an onion over the whole, and fill up the dish with good vinegar. Cover, and bake gently till the fish seems cooked through (about an hour should do a good dishful), and leave to get cold.

The vinegar should set into a jelly around the fish, and the bones will have dissolved away.

They are best served in the earthenware pan in which they are baked, and are a good meal with roasted potatoes and watercress.

> " On potted meats and princely wines
> Not wisely but too well he dines—
> And breathing forth a pious wish
> He fills his belly full of Fish."
>
> R. L. STEVENSON.

POTTING AND PRESERVING POULTRY

Poultry for Export

This is a sixteenth-century recipe for shipload storage.

"Take a good Company of Duck or Mallards. Pull and draw them and lay them in a tub with a little pepper and much salt for twenty-four hours. Then truss and roast them and when they are roasted let them drain from the gravy (for that will make them corrupt) and put them handsomely into a pot and take the fat that came from the roasting and a good store of butter [this would be salt butter] and set it in a kettle of boiling water with a good store of cloves bruised and sliced mace, nutmeg, bay leaves and bay-salt, and let it stew. And while hot pour it over your fowls in the Pot and let the Pot be filled so that the fowls be covered. Lay a Trencher on them to keep them down till cold. And take some of the same kind of spices and bay leaves and lay them on top, and so cover it. It will keep for a good while."

I was able to confirm this recipe, as my aunt sailed to West Africa about 1850 and used it. She told me how they took condensed cream, lemons, "watercress to grow in our cabins", "soup squares for while we were seasick", and "a little kit of chickens". These were all prepared in her own Welsh kitchen, and gave an astonishing sidelight on the active part played by the household cooks in overseas exploration.

My old aunt " managed " to take cold roast fowls to sea for a long voyage. I questioned that the wooden kit would burn in the oven, but she was sure it " only charred a little "; it was probably an old " powdering " kit, and well salted. Earthenware was as good, but heavy.

Soup Squares from the Legs

It was an interesting by-product of the seafarers' poultry that the legs were boiled down with veal trimmings to make soup squares for the voyage.

There would be quite a lot of legs (after preparing such a tubful of potted fowl as already described), so it would be natural to use them up. It is not likely that many modern readers will have "2 dozen fowls' feet" simultaneously. However, the recipe may be useful to some hotel, or farmer's wife; and the whole process is interesting.

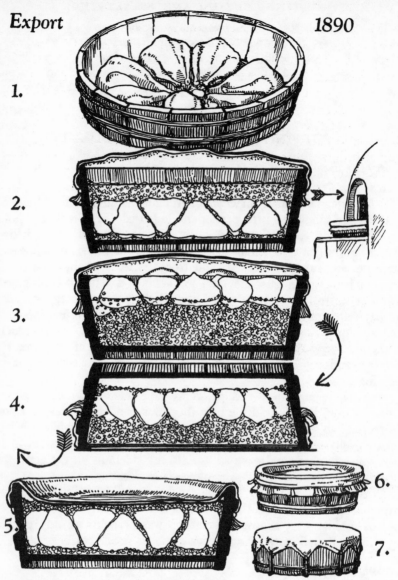

(1) The previously cooked and prepared birds are close-packed in a kit, and covered with shredded suet. (2) The kit is wetted, close-covered, and the whole slid into the oven. (3) The suet melts and floats the birds; the kit is withdrawn, and allowed to cool. (4) When still soft, the kit is turned upside down, and the birds rise through the soft suet towards the bottom of the kit. (5) This leaves a vacuum, so the now cooled and solid kit is once more turned over, and reheated, just enough to make the packed filling fall down again, and in so doing sucks inwards the now well-greased and airtight cover. (6) The kit is now solid, with a concave top; this top is covered with sailcloth and tied down.

Take the poultry legs and any skin or bones of veal or beef. Break all up and put to stew for 8 hours in 4 gallons of water. After 8 hours, try the liquid, and if a little of it sets on cooling, strain off the stock and let it grow cold. Next day skim off fat and sediment and boil again till reduced to glue consistency. Pour out into small cups, and when set turn out onto a strip of flannel; keep turning them on to dry flannel over a warm dry place till the cakes of jelly become quite hard. Put them into a canister. When broth is required, the squares are broken, and a piece the size of a walnut dissolved in hot water and seasoned with pepper and salt, making 1 pint of broth to be served with dry biscuits.

Close-Packing (a device)

It was a device—and amusement—to take a goose or swan, bone it, and stuff it with a boned capon, the capon with a fowl, the fowl with a pigeon, and the pigeon with a lark, and probably insert a little saint token, or a piece of gold for fun; the whole would cut solid bird-meat in firm slices. But was there not more to this idea than amusements for lords and ladies banqueting? Was not this device some attempt by sweethearts and wives to send their menfolk away with as much good food as was possible?

Pickled Eggs (1700)

"When eggs are plentiful, farmers' wives take four or six dozen newly laid, and boil them hard; then, taking off the shells, they place them in earthenware jars and pour upon them scalding vinegar well seasoned with pepper, allspice, ginger, and garlic. The eggs are fit to use after a month."

Eggs thus treated are held in high esteem by all farmhouse epicures. *Dried egg* was made and sold in 1850.

POTTED AND PRESSED MEATS

" The howling desert miles around,
  The tinkling brook the only sound—
  Wearied with all his toils and feats,
  The traveller dines on potted meats;
  On potted meats and princely wines,
  Not wisely but too well he dines."
                                    R. L. STEVENSON.

As to the mediaeval custom of killing stock before winter we owe our knowledge of salting and curing, so to the early sailing ships we owe our knowledge of potted and dried meats.

Pressed Beef

This recipe was evidently used by a sailor's wife for it adds:

"N.B. If you send it to sea, add bay-salt when you boil, and put no green herbs, and season high, and put it in a pot and cover with melted beef suet."

Take a flank of beef and trim, 2 oz. of saltpetre, 3 oz. of bay-salt, $\frac{1}{2}$ lb. of common salt, $\frac{1}{4}$ lb. of brown sugar, and rub the beef well. Then put all into a quart of spring water and turn and rub every day.

Take it out and see that the fat and lean lie equal; take pepper, cloves, parsley, sweet marjoram shredded small, and some bacon fat cut very small; spread inside the beef, roll it hard in a cloth, sew it up, and boil in a pan of spring water with some claret or strong beer; cover, and simmer gently all night (*see* note on wood and peat fires). Dry and press it, and eat with mustard. Enough for 16 lb. of meat.

Potted Meat

Originally "potted meats" were meats cooked and preserved in pots. The top of butter with which we now perfunctorily run over our small pots of paste was a thick layer of suet or butter set stiffly over the meat to exclude the air, and the sprig of parsley laid atop is no less than the boughs of aromatic herbs laid across the old potted meats to keep away the flies and help preserve the contents under the airtight surface.

The best parts of the meat were cooked in the pots; it was essentially a condensing process used to compress extra food value for seamen and travellers—and it is significant that the luxury potted meats, the luxury potted salmon, potted hare, and so forth, are still found around the old sea-port towns and posting inns.

Beef Cheese

This was ship's store—it probably went to America on the *Mayflower*.

It is better to bake it in earthenware for household use, and block tin for packing. As the long cooking under the sealed crust is preservative, it should not be opened or turned out till wanted.

Take three parts lean beef to one part bacon or ham and half a part good rendered beef suet. Mince all these together, mixing well, and seasoning strongly with black pepper, salt, a little powdered clove, and some well-dried thyme (this last is important for the flavour, but it should be well dried and powdered; no green herbs should be used). The old recipes instruct you to well moisten the whole with good brandy (which dates the dish from sailing-ship days), yet for modern usage substitute Worcestershire sauce, but keep the mixture very dry as the suet and fat from the ham will bind sufficiently when heated. Now rub the tin over with cut garlic, and grease it; then take a few rashers of fat bacon and cut them into strips with which interlace the sides and bottom of the baking tin; press the mixture into it (taking care not to disturb the lattice of bacon strips), pack it down tightly, and cover closely with a paste made of flour and water, sealing the edges. Bake it steadily for 5 or 6 hours, and allow it to grow cold in the oven. Of old it was put into the brick bread ovens and left there overnight, being taken out cold next day.

With a gas oven it is simple to turn off the heat—the point is not to move or stir the dish till it has set cold and sealed itself in the sterile air of the oven, thus preventing any bacteria getting under the crust while soft and porous.

When withdrawn cold, the sealing crust will have sunk down close over the meat and any interstices will be closed with clarified suet melted into them.

The "huff" or sealing paste should be removed and the beef inverted for serving—the lattice of bacon strips is very decorative and the "cheese" cuts in firm slices.

Hung Beef

> " Dr. Cairns' cheese was excellent, his hung beef was of prime
> quality."   *The Old Helmet*, 1880.

This way of dealing with "navel piece" or "flaps of beef" is good, and makes these rather difficult pieces into excellent cold luncheon fare.

Take the navel piece—that is, the thin belly flap of the beef where the layers of meat and fat lie divided by layers of skin.

Pull and cut the piece into three layers along one of these divisions (if there is any hard skin or gristle, remove it as you do so).

Wash the pieces well in strong sugar water (treacle is good), then dry the beef and rub well with a pickle made of 2 lb. of bay-salt, 1 oz. of salt-petre, and 4 large spoonfuls of brown sugar. "Rub your beef every place very well with it", and then take common salt and strew over it, and let it lie till the salt be dissolved—which will be in six or seven days—and then turn it every other day, the undermost uppermost, for a fortnight.

After a fortnight, rinse off the salt, and arrange the layers evenly, fat and lean interspersed, strewing between each layer a good seasoning of black pepper, allspice (ground), a little powdered cloves, and a very small quantity of brown sugar. Pack tightly into a flat wedge, and tie up. Set it on to a handful of clean hay, at the bottom of a saucepan, add two or three bay leaves, and a bunch of herbs; fill up with cold water, and bring to the boil very slowly. Simmer a good hour till tender, take up, untie the strings, and wrap in a clean cloth and put it straightway in the cheese press (or under a heavy weight on a strong board). When cold and flat, and quite hard and firm, trim it and glaze it with a well-flavoured brown glaze.

It cuts in square tight slices, marbled lean and fat, and is an excellent spicy cold meat for luncheon or sideboard.

THE HOUSE AND GARDEN IN 1600

"Home is the Sailor! Home from the sea
And the Hunter Home from the hill."

R. L. Stevenson.

HOW PLANTS ARE BROUGHT TO THE GARDEN FROM A NEW WORLD

" It is reported from Saffronwalden that a Pilgrim purposing to do good to his country, stole an head of Saffron, and hid the same in his Palmers staffe, which he had made hollow before of purpose, and so he brought this root into this realme, with venture of his life. If the like love in this our age were in our people that now become great travellers, many knowledges, and many trades, and many herbes and plants might be brought into this realme that might doe the realme good. And if this care had not bene heretofore in our ancestors, then had our life bene savage now, for then we had not had Wheat nor Rie, Peaze nor Beanes, Barley nor Oats, Peare nor Apple, Vine nor many other profitable and pleasant plants, Bull nor Cow, Sheepe nor Swine, Horse nor Mare, Cocke nor Hen, nor a number of other things that we injoy, without which our life were to be sayd barbarous; for these things and a thousand that we use more the first inhabitors of this Island found not here. And in time of memory things have bene brought in that were not here before, as the Damaske rose by Doctour Linaker king Henry the seventh and king Henrie the eights Physician, the Turky cocks and hennes about fifty yeres past, the Artichowe in time of king Henry the eight, and of later time was procured out of Italy, the Muske rose plant, the plumme called the Peridigwene and two kindes more by the Lord Cromwell after his travell, and the Abricot by a French Priest one Wolfe Gardiner to king Henry the eight; and now within these foure yeeres there have beene brought into England from Vienna in Austria divers kinds of flowers called Tulipas, and those and other procured thither a little before from Constantinople by an excellent man called M. Carolus Clusius. And it is sayd that since we traded to Zante that the plant that bearth the Coren is also brought into this realme from thence; and although it bring not fruit to perfection, yet it may serve for pleasure and for some use, like as our vines doe, which we cannot well spare, although the climat so colde will not permit us to have good wines of them. The Archbishop of Canterburie

Edmund Grindall, after he returned out of Germany, brought into this realme the plant of Tamariske from thence, and this plant he hath so increased that there be here thousands of them; and many people have received great health by this plant; and if of things brought in such care were had, then could not the first labour be lost. The seed of Tabacco hath bene brought hither out of the West Indies, it groweth here, and with the herbe many have bene eased of the reumes, &c. Each one of a great number of things were woorthy of a journey to be made into Spaine, Italy, Barberie, Egypt, Zante, Constantinople, the West Indies, and to divers other places neere and further off than any of these, yet forasmuch as the poor are not able, and for that the rich setled at home in quiet will not, therefore we are to make sute to such as repaire to forren kingdomes, for other businesses, to have some care heerein. Thus giving you occasion by way of a little remembrance to have a desire to do your countrey good, you shall, if you have any inclination to such good, do more good to the poore ready to starve for reliefe, then ever any subject did in this realme, by building of almshouses, and by giving of lands and goods to the reliefe of the poore. Thus may you helpe to drive idlenesse the mother of most mischiefs out of the realme, and winne you perpetuall fame, and the prayer of the poore, which is more worth then all the golde of Peru and of all the West Indies."

HYCLUTT

AT HOME

Cider orchards are studied, and research in various types of apple carried on; as a result of orchard grazing, several of the older breeds of pig are revived; these more directly descended from the wild boar stock being better fitted gastronomically to cope with unlimited windfalls.

THE HOUSE OF 1615 HAS A KITCHEN WITH EVERY MODERN CONVENIENCE

" CONO: These buildings severed from the rest do serve as guest chambers! with a chamber for my hothouse. This side you see lieth against the setting of the sunne in Summer, where the sunne may lie from noone till night.

RIGO: But that little Isle, moated about . . . it seemeth more sumptuously built? I take it to be your owne lodging? where your wife and your servants mean to lye safely?

CONO: It is even so—and therefore it is built upon higher ground, both for the better air and fayer prospect, beside my garden and my orchard are adjoining it, with the sweet smell of the flowers for health and pleasure. . . . The windows for the most part open all East and some South, very few West, except for such chambers where I dine and sup. They receive the sunne in winter abundantly, and in summer very little.

RIGO: That is very well.

CONO: Here is my larder built with three rooms, one serving for butter and milk, one for beer and wine and the third to keep flesh of all kinds, poudered [i.e. salted] and unpoudered, and fowles of all sorts, with convenient hooks to hang them up from trouble. Here I have no windows to the South or West, but all North and East. Above is a corn loft, with floor of stone and plaster wall, and an apple close—these we open and receive light through a lattice to the North.

Here is a Bakehouse, and a pantrie with two ovens, one serving for household bread and the other for manchet loaves for my own table, and for tarts and fine bakemetes.

Here are also troughs to keep meale in and troughs to lay leaven in and there is a fair table to mould upon."

MARKHAM.

THE HENPEN OF 1615

" Your henne house would be large and spacious with somewhat a high roofe and walls strong and windowes upon the sunne rising; round about the inside of the walls upon the ground would be built large pens of 3 ft. high for Geese, Ducks and fowle to sit in.

Near to the eavings . . . would be pearches . . . on which should sit your Cocks, Hennes, Capon and Turkies, each on severall Pearches as they are disposed. . . . Let their be pins stucken into the wals so that your Poultry may climbe to their Pearches with ease, let the flore be . . . of earth smooth and easie, let the small foule have a hole at one end of the house to come in and out at when they please . . . this house would be placed . . . neare some Kitchen Brewhouse or else some Kilne where it may have ayre of the fire and be perfumed with smoke which to pullen is delightful.

You shall gather your eggs up once a day and leave in the nest but the nest egge, and no more, and that would ever be in the afternoone when you have seene every Henne come from the nest severally. Some Hennes will by the cackling tell you when they have layd, but some will lay mute, therefore you must let your owne eye be your instruction."

MARKHAM, Perfect Husbandry.

VEGETABLES

"Green herbs, for the service of man."

IT IS very annoying to the historian to hear people speak of the "modern way of cooking vegetables conservatively". They never used to be cooked any other way!

This twelfth-century dish, "Boyl a Flank with worts", has very little flank and is almost a vegetable dish. This one recipe shows the sense and economy of the early English cookery of meat *with* vegetables.

To Boil a Flank with Worts

Take the mutton flank, bone it, and boil the bones (broken) to broth; meanwhile, strew a tablespoonful of salt, a good dust of pepper, and powdered spice, over the mutton, working it well into the spaces; roll up and leave for a day, while the bones are boiling.

Next day, take as many young turnips, parsnips, and young onions as convenient, prepare and slice them, and (after washing off any surplus salt from it) proceed to stuff the flank with the small cut vegetables, pressing them well into the bone spaces, and sprinkling with chopped parsley, thyme, and a suspicion of rosemary or mint. Tie the rolled flank up in a cloth, and put it to simmer in the bone broth to which you have added the trimmings from the vegetables and a little pepper—salt will be supplied out of the meat. Simmer gently till a skewer will pierce the whole easily, showing that the root vegetables are cooked within the meat, which they will have flavoured with their juices (*see* diagram).

Meanwhile shred a spring cabbage finely, and pack it into a deep pan in which you have melted a knob of butter and just enough milk to moisten the whole. Keep the lid closely on the pan, toss about a little to shake

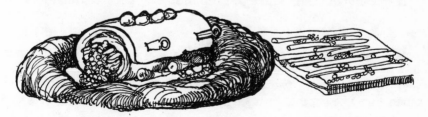

Hedgeroll. Young vegetable in a thin pastry crust.

the cooking liquid well over the cabbage—stir it once or twice to make sure it cooks evenly. 10–15 minutes will cook it.

To serve, roll the flank out on to a hot dish, garnish with the cut vegetables, and put the shredded cabbage around it. Strain a little of the broth into the white gravy left from cooking the cabbage, boil up, and serve as gravy to the dish. It will be very light and sweet and digestible.

ARTICHOKES, JERUSALEM (Helianthus tuberosus)

This has nothing to do with the Holy Land. The word is a corruption of the Italian *girasole*, or sunflower. Artichoke has a very individual flavour, and therefore should always be served alone, and not as a second vegetable at a meat dish. It is extremely useful, coming when other vegetables are scarce. It is much better cooked straight from the ground, when the tubers are full and crisp.

Palestine Soup

The smaller, awkwardly shaped artichokes should be kept for this, sorting out the larger smooth ones for other dishes.

Wash and chop up a large panful of small artichokes, and pack into a saucepan with a very small chopped onion; just cover with water, and cook

Hair sieves should be used instead of metal ones when possible. Now horse-hair is almost unobtainable, they make nylon sieves.

till soft. Then for about two pints of artichoke mush add a knob of butter, a generous pinch of salt, pepper, and a pint of milk. Let all come to the boil again and run through a fine sieve. (The artichokes should be so soft that they rub through without any trouble.) Serve the soup with brown bread cubes that have been fried crisp in bacon fat, and sprinkled with chopped parsley.

A spoonful of cream added just before serving is a great improvement.

Artichoke Hot-pot

Dice some sugar-cured bacon fairly fine and fry till brown and crisp in a fireproof pot. Peel the artichokes, cut them in half, and pack them into the pot. One or two delicately flavoured leeks (on no account use onions) may be cut into inch lengths and cooked with the artichokes, but no other vegetable.

Fill up with white stock and simmer gently till the vegetables are cooked.

Drain off the stock and use it as the basis for a well-flavoured white sauce. Return this to the hot-pot, brown a few crisp rolls of bacon, and lay on top before serving with brown bread and butter.

Fried Crisp Artichokes

A good way of serving artichokes for people who like things crisp. Parboil the artichokes in their skins, and peel when cooked. As peeled, drop into well-seasoned flour and when all are done, coat with a good frying batter, and fry; drain, and serve piping hot, with melted butter. They are delicious like this, being crisp outside, but breaking soft and creamy within.

A dish of such artichoke "rissoles" with a good cheese sauce, served separately, makes a good simple luncheon or supper dish.

BEETROOT

Beetroot bleeds easily, so lift very carefully, brushing off the earth and twisting off the leaves.

Beetroot is round or long rooted

Boiled Beet

Do not peel or scrape. Wash the beet and boil till tender. To test, a skewer should pierce it easily. Leave to grow cool in the water in which it was boiled, then take up and wipe off all the skin, trim and slice into a spicy vinegar, when it can be served at once. If pickling, it is better cut into cubes, as the slices tend to stick together.

Beet is especially good served with cold beef or bread and cheese, or it makes a good garnish for pressed beef, potted hough, etc.

Baked Beet

Excellent served hot with roast mutton or venison. For serving hot, choose small round beets, boil, and skin. Then pile the round red balls, steaming hot, into a brown bake-pan. Just polish them with a spot of dripping from the joint, dust with black pepper, and serve piping hot.

Spinach

Served hot and dry baked, it is dark and spicy, and, being sweet, it serves to bring out the flavour of a savoury roast.

Don't serve beet with boiled meats, or in broth, or with salted meat, or with anything wet. It looks sanguinary, and tastes worse.

Beet

Beets are also good sliced, and served hot, as a base for a pile of spinach. Outline the base with brown crisp potatoes and serve on a hot plate with slices of crisply fried brown bread. It makes a colourful dish of "plain cooked vegetables" from the allotment.

Spinach Beet, and Sea-kale Beet

The talk of "new" vegetables makes some cooks suspicious of "freak foods", but most of the garden vegetables reintroduced since the 1914–18 war are very old ones.

Spinach beet and chard are thus described in the seventeenth century:

"The rib of the white beet being boiled melts, and eats like marrow. . . . The roots of the red beet [our common *betrute* of today] cut into thin slices, after being boiled, when cold, is of itself a grateful winter sallet, being mingled with oil and vingear, salt, etc. There is also a beet growing by the sea [sea-kale], which is the most delicate of all."

CARROTS

These need a sandy soil; gardening catalogues say "any good loam", but they are difficult in some districts, and where they do not grow well, had better be pulled as seedlings.

It is in "thinning out" that the fly goes in, so, when thinning, water well, disturb as little as possible, and use some suitable insecticide. Thinning may be made in three stages. The first thinnings should be only two or three inches long.

Seedling Carrots (first thinning)

Pull, wash, trim off the tops, and boil lightly for a few minutes; drain, toss in butter, and serve hot.

Carrots (second and third thinnings)

When rather larger, pull, wash, trim off the tops, and pack end for end, in a flat pan; dab with butter, season, cover with a little broth, and put on the lid and bake slowly.

Main-crop Carrots

These should be cooked to give the sweetness required in stews and hot-pots, also browned round the joints like potatoes or parsnips (*see also* Boiled Beef and Carrots). As a vegetable, they are best boiled, chopped, and mixed with seasoning and butter. Another method, very excellent, is to grate the carrots into a buttered basin, pressing them lightly down, just cover with water or broth, put the lid on closely, and set in the oven; they will take 15 minutes.

Carrot Puffs

Here is a recipe from the eighteenth century.

"Scrape and boil them and mash them very fine, add to every pint of the pulp about ½ pint of bread crumb, some eggs, four whites to the pint, a nutmeg grated, some orange-flower water, sugar to taste, a little sack, and mix it with thick cream. They must be fried in rendered suet very hot."

I have made the above, using considerably less whites of eggs, and found them very good and light. 1 pint of pulp, ¾ pint of crumb, the grated rind of an orange, the orange juice, and one white of egg, beaten very stiff and folded in.

HORSE-RADISH (Colchlearia, or A. rusticana)

A hardy perennial, and one of our oldest antiscorbutics. It is very tough and hardy, and will grow almost anywhere, though it repays care, and fine long straight roots, very white and juicy, can be got by careful planting of the young shoots in spring.

Horse-radish was made into strong fomentations for both man and beast. Anyone who has wept copiously as they scraped horse-radish, will realise its use as cure for "rhumes in the head", common colds, or neuralgia. Its medical use as embrocation has continued.

Horse-radish with Beef

Wash the roots, scraping them against the grain with a knife, or a coarse grater, until you have a snow-white fluff of the horse-radish. Pile it in little snowy drifts here and there on the beef just before serving. Horse-radish is sometimes made into a sauce.

THE ACCOMPLISH'D GENTLEWOMAN, 1742

Meat and Drink. 1100 gloomily
beats the steak,

1200 surreptitiously samples the cider,

1500 cheerfully salts the pork, 1600 plods home with the bread-oven sticks,
1700 shows a seaside hotel (Bellevue) where they make a notable fish paste.
(This is the jar lid.) Any cook today, can sympathise with these people.

Travel. The country woman rides to market, in 1500 (right) and 1700. Note that cream or milk must be carried on the head (or it churns).

Rowlandson's sketch of a district coach collecting a country passenger (from a wayside Inn).

1200. A Tavern, showing the brush ferment sign (and a thirsty traveller.)

The Tudor traveller returns to the (comfort of) his own fireside.

Soyer's camp kitchen in the Crimea, interesting as the camp boilers have
remained exactly the same till today. The hooked ladles hung overside
reproduce the wooden hooked dippers that for centuries had been used
to hang from barrel rims. *The Elizabethan kitchen* shows spit roasting.
Spare spits are over the mantelpiece, dripping pans below the roasts,
ventilated store cupboards, and wooden trenchers and tubs and high
pewter candlesticks can be seen. The spit seems to be worked by an
early form of weighted clockwork.

Mankind refreshes. 1600. The flagon pours water into a bowl for rinsing the fingers. Chief interest, the wide padded seats, that replace the older benches.

1700. A coffee house, note the churchwarden pipes, card games, news sheets, and most attractive barmaid.

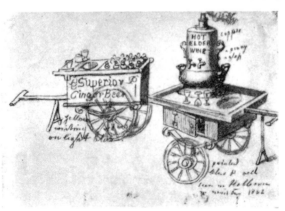

1800. Street vendors' drinks, for working men. Ginger beer kept cool, elderberry wine kept hot.

Early Edwardian kitchen. Note the home cured hams and bacon hung up. The iron fender beneath the table indicates that the roasting jack is already set before the fire. The floor is tiled, and the table legs are set on stone feet, to keep the wood dry when washing the floor. Dishcovers are used in transit from kitchen to dining-room.

Victorian Breakfast. A full description of this is given in the text (p. 598).

Mediaeval banquet and modern banquet of 1953. It was unusual for the mediaeval company to extend around the ends and front of the " High " table, but this picture shows so clearly the musicians' gallery, the huge salt cellar, the squared "trencher bread " and small hand rolls, large chargers of food, and the draught screen behind. The two pages, the gold cups and sideboard display, can all be matched in the modern picture.

"Keep field in the heat"—
Tusser. Mediaeval Flemish 15th
century and 19th century English.
Country women carry out the
meal to harvesters who keep field
through the noonday rest. Notice
the Flemish cut the corn with a
Hainault scythe, and one, using
a hand scythe, cuts the corn high
up. Later the straw will be used
as fodder.

In the 19th century, the corn
is cut close to the ground and
banded by hand. One man
drains a wooden hoggin, but till
this century heavy earthenware
(not tin) was used to carry the
drinks.

It is by thinking in " lifetimes " that one gets the sense of time in history. One's mother is " old-fashioned ", one's grandmother " can remember", but once the direct contact is lost, reports written down become "history", and lumped together as one vague period called " of old. . . ."

The Plague, Fire, revolutions, and troubles of the previous centuries are not enough to account for the strangeness of this period. Their uneasy peace gave time for trade and commerce to begin and there is no lack of money pouring into the country, but this period was drunk with a strange new freedom, more potent than any draught of gold. The heavy clouds of old mediaeval beliefs have lifted, and science sees with fearless eyes. Old dogmatic authorities, whose statements have been taken seriously for centuries, are now suddenly " the classics ", and questioned.

Fetters of an ancient priest-craft have been burnt through in the fires of martyrs burnt at the stake for honesty of thought. It is a freedom that Piers Plowman had visioned through his curbed, restricted world, centuries earlier.

" Relation direct, a record of Truth, following and finding out and strongly standing forth."

In this century all " thought " seems to grow in a new freedom.

The old and lovely English poets learn a new craft; the chuckles and guffaws of the mediaeval period have gone, these new people have learnt to laugh at themselves—and, laughing, have become self-conscious! The depth and brutality of the period is hidden behind pasteboard and wit; and this picture has all the mixed spice of the period. The fireplace is " classical ", the long windows " Georgian ", the sturdy kneeling boy " Elizabethan ". Regard the " stance " of the two ladies—their poise and detachment! How elegant compared with the clumsy Dutch-English cookwoman, who has just rescued the milk from boiling over!—doubtless the milk for the mother and child dimly seen in the room beyond, behind the flurried lackey.

Inconsistent, elegant, intriguing, the atmosphere of the whole picture portrays the period as surely as the incident of the parlour lapdog scrapping with the kitchen cat (and likely to have the worst of the encounter).

The divine domestic is now at hand.

These new ladies of gentility are only granddaughters of that beloved Elizabethan mother who " had so much to do that she did not know where to begin," but are centuries further removed in outlook. Soon they will be out of the kitchen altogether and at the mercy of their own servants; and then, La, my dear! the saucy wenches! The air with which the central figure hands over some product of her still-room already shows a certain diffidence.

This edition of a book, which began in 1600 as the *Complete Cook*, is now called " The Accomplish'd Gentlewoman ". Compare this classical abstraction with the materialist view of " The Complete Cook " in 1800 (*see* p. 400).

Some Common Root Vegetables

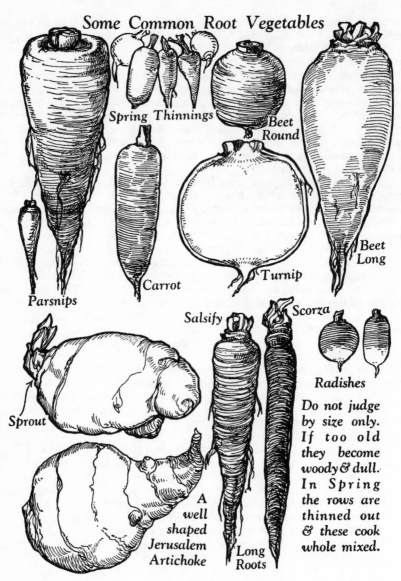

Spring Thinnings

Beet Round

Carrot

Turnip

Beet Long

Parsnips

Salsify

Scorza

Radishes

Sprout

A
well
shaped
Jerusalem
Artichoke

Long
Roots

Do not judge
by size only.
If too old
they become
woody & dull.
In Spring
the rows are
thinned out
& these cook
whole mixed.

The cook and the gardener must work together with understanding

Mild Horse-radish Sauce

Take whipped cream and grate into it as much horse-radish as it will hold. Stir in lightly a spoonful of sugar and just enough mustard to make the sauce a delicate yellow.

Strong Horse-radish Sauce

Some people prefer the horse-radish shredded into white-wine vinegar with a dust of pepper.

Hot Horse-radish Sauce

Make a cream sauce with flour, butter and milk, and let it cook and boil well. Withdraw it from the fire and stir in finely grated horse-radish till stiff. Let it remain just long enough to heat through. Stir in a lump of butter and enough mustard to make a pleasant cream colour, and serve piping hot in a hot tureen with a hot ladle. Good with some sorts of fish—especially the oily kind, or with mackerel—or liked by some with hot boiled pork.

Horse-radish Vinegar

Put a large shallot, cut up, into a pint of mild vinegar, and set the jar on the hob to get hot through. Shred it full of horse-radish, cover the jar tightly and let it stand on the stove, keeping hot, and infuse for a week.

Strain through muslin into an enamel pan and boil once quickly and thoroughly. Bottle and seal down while hot. This is very strong, and you will only need a spot or two when using.

Embrocation for Rheumatism

The expressed juice of horse-radish made into an emulsion with the yolk of an egg is a country embrocation.

Horse-radish Pouring Sauce

All potted hough, pressed beef, and brawn recipes are better with horse-radish sauce poured on. To make this pouring sauce, grate some horse-radish into hot milk, and press it well to get the flavour out. Pour off the milk and thicken it with a knob of butter and fine oatmeal. Boil well, and leave till cold. The sauce should be only as thick as cream.

ONIONS

Bread and cheese and onions were traditional for centuries, carried in bag or pocket to the fields; here the twelfth-century ploughman sets out to walk the country—

" In script he bare both bread and leeks,
He was forewoke and all forsweat,
A man might see through both his cheeks
And everywrang tooth where it sat."

Scallions

Now a name given to bolted onions—but is a perennial plant that grows in clusters, and can be used chopped for all plain cooking purposes; they stay in the ground all the year round. Holtsers are the Welsh version of these, rather smaller, and with a very marked spring growth; these make the best tansy that I've had, made by a farm-hand.

Take holtsers in spring, chop them finely, and fry in bacon fat. When they are soft drain off any fat, and pour on enough beaten egg to cover, and pepper and salt and chase them round—till blended—and then "leave 'em be" till set, "not let 'em boil, mind, or the egg will be all a-whey, just set it nicely". Then turn on to a hot plate, and it is excellent.

Tree Onions, or Egyptians

A perennial, growing nearly four feet high, and with hollow tall stems that rise up and develop a small cluster of baby onions, like a head, on top. These small onions, from five to a dozen in number, swell, become heavy, grow leaf-tops, and a few roots, while still in the air, then the parent stem bends and deposits the young onions, now growing vigorously, onto fresh soil, about a foot or more away from the original root. Therefore a row of these onions is better than a bed, which is apt to become crowded. When you want to make a second row, dig and prepare a line about two feet away from the first row, bend over the onions to that side—and they plant themselves. These small top onions are exactly right for pickling, being round, hard, and of most uniform size (see drawing).

Pickled onions. Pick the largest of the top onions off and pack into wide-mouthed jars, and cover with boiling spiced vinegar. Drain off and boil up once again, and seal down for use in about a month.

Spring Onions

These are grown in masses for the market near Tewkesbury, where they have grown a special red willow for splicing up both onions and celery (the touch of colour makes both vegetables look whiter). In the garden, sow in drills, and pull early. The thinnings from the proper onion bed, pulled later, are not nearly so good.

Large Onions, Baked

Bake in a pan, with knobs of butter, and a spot of broth to start them off (they make their own gravy after that). Cover closely the first part of

Most Common or Garden Onions

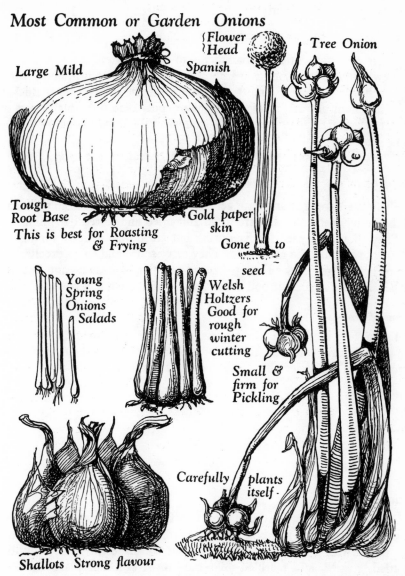

Large Mild

{Flower
{Head

Spanish

Tree Onion

Tough
Root Base
This is best for Roasting
& Frying

Gold paper
skin

Gone to

seed

Young
Spring
Onions
Salads

Welsh
Holtzers
Good for
rough
winter
cutting

Small &
firm for
Pickling

Carefully plants
itself.

Shallots Strong flavour

English cooks are fond of onions but do not care for garlic. Bread and cheese
and onions are spoken of as Field Fare in our earliest manuscripts.

the time, but remove the cover just before serving to let them brown becomingly. Season lightly.

White Onions, Stewed

These are excellent accompaniments to roast mutton.

Stew some large onions in a little milk with a peppercorn, and a clove for each onion. When almost soft, drain off the milky gravy, thicken with fine flour and return over the onions, put some very small spots of butter here and there upon the dish—to make gold drops among the whiteness—and serve hot.

If served with pork, substitute a small sage leaf for the spice.

Shallots

Shallots are tougher and stronger than onions, are grown from the small bulbs rather than seed, and are lifted and dried and stored like onions.

They should be used for flavouring but are not so delicate for dishes where the onion is the main item. They serve soups and stews excellently. If you are obliged to use shallots instead of onions for sauces and delicate dishes, be sure to soak or boil them first to make them less powerful.

Skins of Onions

The papery golden skins of onions should not be thrown away. They are good natural colouring for soups and stews. Broth should always be made golden and delectable *by cooking the skins in it.*

Onion-skin Eggs

For Easter eggs, cut the onion skins tastefully, and wrap them round the eggs with a wet cloth and boil the eggs hard. Let grow cold in cold water and polish with a scrap of grease, and you will have the most beautiful mottled, striped, and marbled gold-and-brown egg. For plain-coloured eggs, boil the skins loose in the water—and you will get a clear yellow.

Chives

Chives, the small purple-flowered onion, is best used for salads, though it can be used chopped with parsley or other herbs where a slight flavour is wanted. It is perennial, pretty, and about a foot high.

Garlic, Wild (Allium sativum)

This grows in parts of Wales to such an extent that we believe it to have been the origin of the national emblem. The white lacy flowers, gathered in shady woods, make a savoury garnish to the spring salad.

Spanish Onions

> " Yet marchaundez of Braban and Selande
> The madre and woode that dyers take a hande
> To dye wyth; Garlicke and onyons
> And salty fysshe als; for husbonds' commons."

Braised Spanish Onions

Choose the largest. Remove only the dry outer skins and rootlets and pack them close together in a bake-pot.

Chop some fat bacon or the trimmings of ham or bacon and pack into the interstices. Season with pepper (salt will scarcely be needed if bacon or ham are used). Add only a spoonful of water (enough to start the steam). Put the lid on tightly and cook in a hot oven till the onions can easily be pierced by a silver skewer.

Serve from the dish with hot buttered toast, on a cold winter evening.

Fried Onions

These should be cut a little time before use, in order to dry out, and fry more crisply. They will fry more crisply and splutter less if they are shaken loosely up and down in a well-floured cloth before putting into the pan. See that the fat is smoking. Leeks, or perpetual, tree, or scallion onions can be made into "rings" by slicing with a slanting cut.

Pickled Onions

These are made in vast quantities by country people. Special small pickling onions are used, the hardest are the small rounded onions from the top of the perennial onion (*see* drawing, p. 361).

Peel and lay them in a strong brine for three days. Take them out, wipe, drain, rinse, and pack the onions into jars, pouring over them a boiling-hot spiced vinegar.

Tie down whilst hot, and they will be ready for use in six months' time.

If you want to make pretty pickles, pick out the small pearly onions and arrange them in the jars with red chillies and one or two green capers. Let the vinegar be clear white-wine vinegar, or tint it golden by boiling the papery outer skins of onions in it.

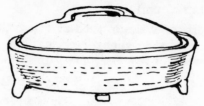

The earliest form of braising pan. A Cornish iron roasting pot—the short legs allow the heat from the fire to pass under the pot and the lid can be piled over with burning fuel. Many vegetables are best braised.

Onion and Apple Pie (Cornish)

Line a shallow tin with thin short crust, and cover the bottom with a layer of peeled, cored and finely sliced apple. Cover this layer with a more chopped layer of onion rings, sprinkle with a teaspoonful of finely chopped sage, pepper, salt, and a pinch of mixed spice. Go on with alternate layers till the top is reached, which pile up fairly high. Moisten the edge of the paste, and put scraps of butter (or Cornish cream) on top of the top layer, cover with a thin crust, and bake in a brisk oven—or under a bake-pot. To be eaten hot. "Some do put a little sugar over the apples if they be very sour—but 'tis better not."

Onion Sauce

Make a good white roux, using fine oatmeal rather than flour. Meanwhile stew some chopped-up onions, and if the onions are strong, throw away the first water and fill up again to make the sauce milder. When the onions have come to the boil for the second time, add an equal quantity of milk, and use the liquid (which will be warm and ready) to complete the roux for the sauce. Chop the onions and return them to the well-boiled sauce and let them cook in it till done. Some people add a clove or sage leaf to the sauce, but onion sauce should be onion only.

Hot onions cooked in milk and butter were a farmhouse remedy for a cold on the chest.

LEEKS

" Now leeks are in season, for pottage full good,
    And spareth the milch-cow, and purgeth the blood,
    These having with peason, for pottage in Lent,
    Thou spareth both oatmeal, and bread to be spent."

                                                        TUSSER.

Leeks. This one was drawn after spring growth had begun.
Leeks should be eaten younger, and should not be too thick,
as then they lose flavour in over-long cooking.

Braised Leeks

Leeks braise better than they boil.

Lay evenly sized leeks flat in a shallow well-buttered dish with a damping of milk or stock. Season lightly, cover closely, and cook in their own juice till tender.

It is a mistake to serve these delicate vegetables with thick sauce; the liquor and butter together in the dish should be sufficient.

Leekie Pie

Thin leeks do well for this. Wash and shred them and set to stew with a little water and a knob of butter. Line a shallow pie-dish with very thin short crust, and pack the leeks (they should not be cooked much, just softened enough to pack closely) into the pie, together with a little finely chopped bacon, and pepper (you will not need salt, the bacon will supply that).

Cover the pie with the rest of the short crust, sealing the edges well, and making a hole in the middle of the cover. Bake till leeks and bacon are done and crust a fine crisp brown. Take out of the oven, have ready an egg beaten in enough seasoned milk to just fill the pie and pour this in through the hole in top. Replace the pie in the oven, just long enough to set this custard, and serve the pie hot or cold. The delicate oniony flavour of the leeks pervades the custard, and this dish makes an excellent meal.

PARSNIPS

The "parsnep" (all roots are "neps"—tur nep, pars nep) was so very well known in England that the potato came into favour chiefly because it was sweet "like a parsnip"—the first potatoes being sweet potatoes.

" The potatoe, a sweet roote which farre exceedeth our English parsnep."

were the words of introduction.

It was the sweet flavour of the parsnip that was so much liked—and also the fact that it could stay in the ground during the winter. It was a most valuable asset to England, and continued to be standard usage long after the Elizabethan age brought the new potato. It often figures in sweet dishes, and the green tops were fed to cows as late as the nineteenth century. Stevens, in his farm book, mentions what good milk the parsnip fodder produces. Also, it is the type of sweetness that mingles with honey and spice, so that some boiled plum and marrowfat puddings, flavoured with spice and sweetened with honey, were made with a parsnip base.

Parsnip Leaves

" In October, the leaves of the parsnips should be given to cows. . . . They will impart much richness to the milk."

LAWSON'S AGRICULTURAL MANUAL, 1858.

Frosted Parsnips are Best

Parsnips as vegetables are not really worth eating till after the first hard frost, when the roots become mellow and golden.

Their first position is with the roast meat. Parsnips browned round the joint of roast beef are at their best.

Parsnip Chips

Parsnips also make good "chips". Scrape the parsnips and cut them into four quarters top to tail; then divide again, and divide again, and then cut the wedges into slices, each about as thick as a lead pencil. Put these "chips" into cold water and boil for a few minutes, drain off the water (use it for some dish you want to sweeten) and dry the chips in a cloth and toss them well in dry flour. Have ready the pan of smoking fat and fry exactly as you would do chipped potatoes. Serve piled up on a hot dish; they should be crisp golden fingers, and with baked autumn tomatoes and dripping toast make a country supper in themselves.

Parsnip Cakes

Boil the parsnips, and, when cooked, mash them very thoroughly, working in a small quantity of flour, a good pinch of mace, pepper and salt, and a large lump of butter or dripping. Form into round flat cakes, about an inch through. Egg and breadcrumb them, pressing well, and fry in smoking fat till brown. They should be crisp outside, and open to a soft golden cream inside.

For a really good winter-evening supper, take a couple of brown and creamy parsnip cakes, a couple of fried tomatoes, hot brown gravy, and brussels sprouts.

Parsnip Pie for February

Boil and drain some parsnips and press through a sieve. To about a pint of this golden mush add a tablespoonful of honey, a strong dash of ginger, and a pinch of spice. Beat in the golden grated rind and juice of two lemons, and the yolk of an egg. Line a flan pan with thin crisp pastry, and fill with the mixture. Lattice across the flan with the cut trimmings of the pastry and bake till golden brown. Pile the beaten white of the egg (sweetened and flavoured with a little of the lemon rind) round the edge, and return to the cool oven to set. Serve cold, garnished with primroses at the cross of the lattices. A very pretty country dish.

POTATOES ARRIVE

" These potatoes be the most delicate rootes that may be eaten, and doe farre exceed our passeneps or carets. Their pines be of the bignes of two fists, the outside whereof is of the making of a pine-apple, but it is soft like the rinde of a Cucomber, and the inside eateth like an apple but it is more delicious than any sweet apple sugred."

DRAKE.

All cooks should grow a few early new potatoes; they need not be large, and should be used straight out of the ground. An old "seed" potato can be cut up provided each piece has one strong "eye". Leave the pieces in the sun and air, till the eye looks green and begins to sprout—then plant in any clean sandy soil.

As soon as potatoes are "lifted" or bought by the sackful, they should be graded according to size. Use any damaged ones at once. The largest bake best. The middle size steam or boil, the smallest are used for pig and hen food.

How to Use New Potatoes

New potatoes (one to two inch). These are so delicious direct from the soil that it is worthwhile for any gardener to grow a few early ones, even if there is no room for a main crop. They will grow well in the sandy soil of seaside bungalows—or any odd scrap of land, as it is not a heavy crop you want, but an early one. For main crop, you need space; but for a few "earliest" you chiefly need enterprise.

Very Small Size "Earlies"

(1) Lift straight from the ground, rub off the skin and cook in boiling salted water to which a sprig of mint has been added; drain, polish in melted butter and serve with green peas.

Medium Size "Earlies"

(2) Lift straight from the ground, rub off the skins, and boil in sea-water. Drain into a bowl lined with a hot cloth; have a pat of butter and a bowl of salt, take a potato, dip it in butter, into salt, and eat it whole. Buttermilk is the correct drink for this meal.

Full-grown potatoes (three-inch; not new). Sort these according to size. The middle-sized ones, of same weight, boil in their skins, after scrubbing well; the smaller ones (less than three-inch) are best washed in a pail in running water. In either case, pack the pan with same-sized potatoes, cover with water, add salt, and bring to the boil, and cook gently till they are just cooked through. Then pour off the water, cover the potatoes with a thick cloth, and leave them to steam till quite dry.

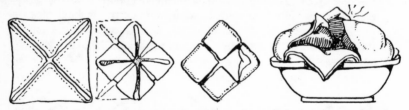

Serve roast potatoes inside a folded napkin or piece of blanket to keep them hot

Very large potatoes (five-inch; old). Bake in their jackets. Scrub, rub with a piece of bacon rind (as that salts and greases simultaneously), put on the hotplate of the oven, and bake till soft. Lift out, crack open, and insert a knob of butter and a pinch of salt. Send to table, crack side up, wrapped in a hot napkin on a hot dish.

Very old potatoes with parsley and egg (potato balls). Peel the potatoes, and cook in boiling salted water with a dash of vinegar. Meanwhile finely chop a large handful of parsley, season with pepper. Drain the potatoes, adding a large lump of bacon fat, and mash them thoroughly, adding the parsley powder. There should be enough parsley to make the potatoes quite green, and enough bacon fat to make the whole translucent. Beat together very well, and work over the heat till the pale-green mass becomes reasonably firm and dry. Flour your hands and form potato balls; egg-and-crumb, and fry them. If you mash some other potatoes, enough egg to make a yellow filling, and fry the green and yellow balls at the same time, you have turned the ugly old potatoes into a very pleasant dish, and added to their value as food.

The holes should be wells of seasoned melted butter or golden bacon fat

Punch-nep (a Welsh dish)

Boil equal quantities of potato and white turnip, separately. Mash both, with butter, and put together, beating well and seasoning rather highly. This extremely simple dish is astonishingly good. It looks like hot alabaster when made well. Pack into a hot bowl, and prod holes, into which you should pour warm cream, but melted butter will do.

Broxty (an Irish dish)

"Broxty in the dish, Broxty in the pan,
If you don't eat Broxty—you'll never get a man."

Stelk. A pool of butter in the centre.

Grate raw potato into enough hot milk to cook the mass; stir till hot, soft and firm, season, pile into a mound on a hot dish; make a deep well in the centre and pour in boiling bacon fat or melted butter. You eat with a fork, taking the dry potato and dipping it into the fat.

Mashed Potatoes (English)

Boil, drain, and dry off thoroughly. Heat some milk and butter in a saucepan and, when boiling, beat it into the potatoes, beating all the time till it's light and white as hot snow.

Fried Potato Plate

Melt some dripping in a deep thick frying-pan and, when smoking-hot, press in the cold cooked potato; as it browns, keep stirring it up from the bottom till the mass is full of fried brown pieces, then press down firmly and leave awhile. When all the round of the bottom is smoothly brown, turn out, upside down. Good under beef rissoles.

Potato-Apple Cake (for an autumn tea)

It is difficult to sort which recipes were taken from Wales to Joyce's country in Ireland, and which brought from Ireland to Wales via Liverpool and Holyhead, but I have found this dish in the Lleyn and in Ireland.

1 lb. of cooked potatoes, mashed while hot with a large knob of butter (1 oz.), a good teaspoonful of sugar, and a little spice of ginger. "Dry off" the mash with about 4 oz. of flour, till it will roll out smoothly on a floured board. Roll it into two thickish rounds (as if making rather thick pastry). Cover one round with an inch layre of sliced apple, damp the edge, and cover with the other round (it is a trick to roll the top crust slightly larger to allow for the piled apple). Nip the edges firmly together, mark a deep "X" on top, and bake in a hot oven till brown outside and the apples soft within.

To serve, make a hole in the top lid (cutting round the edge rather high up, as you do not want to spill any juice), hastily cover the hot apple inside with thin slices of butter, and thickly with sugar; put back the lid, put back into the oven for one minute to melt the butter, and serve instantly.

It is better to "carve" the pudding with two forks, pulling the pudding into four farls (where you marked the X on the top).

It is far more delicious than it sounds, as the butter and sugar melt with the apple juice all over the hot soft crust. It makes a wonderful hot tea dish on a cold evening.

Stelk (onion-potato supper dish)

(Old winter potatoes, cooked with spring onions.)

Take spring onions—(holtzers will serve, but late spring onions are best).

Trim and cut the onions into half-inch lengths—right up the green tops. Set to simmer in a pan of milk. Meanwhile boil the old potatoes and set to

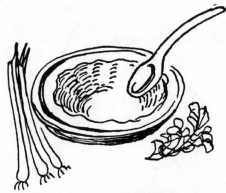

How to form a deep potato lining in a baking pan

keep hot on the stove. When the onions are tender, use the flavoured milk to mash the potatoes, and beat till light; lastly, add the green onion pieces, and as much butter as you can spare, seasoning rather highly as you do so.

It should be a creamy green fluff when done—make a well in the top of each serving and put a lump of butter to melt in it—you eat from the outside—dipping into the pool.

SALSIFY

> " ' Why, it is not dinner-time yet this great while, Margery . . .
> it isn't much after twelve.' ' No, Miss Ellen . . . but by and by
> I'll be busy with the chops and frying the salsify and I couldn't
> leave the kitchen.' "
>
> *The Wide, Wide World.*

A root with a curiously salt, fishy flavour, called also the vegetable oyster. Salsify, with its tall, pinkish-purple flowers, is a very handsome border plant. It is more popular in America than in England. The root should be lifted and scraped with care. It is boiled or steamed, tied together in bundles, and afterwards cut loose and fried an appetising brown. Sometimes the roots are egg-and-breadcrumbed before frying, and served with slices of lemon, like fillets of fish. It is certainly a vegetable to eat by itself, and so like oyster that it takes in the cat!

Salsify, Baked

Boil the salsify till soft, and when cool enough to handle, scrape and
rub off the outer skin. It is then a long, translucent root, a curious fishy
grey colour. Slice it slantingly into oval cuts, laying them in a buttered
piedish. Dredge with crumbs, just moisten with the liquid, and bake till
crisp. Garnish with watercress and serve with anchovy sauce.

Salsify Pie

Prepare the Salsify as above, but the pieces may be larger. Make a white
sauce with butter, flour, pepper, salt and a spot of anchovy sauce (enough
to colour it a delicate pink). Cook this sauce thoroughly. Then take a deep
piedish, pack the cut salsify into it, filling up with sauce and sprinkling
with a little chopped parsley. Cover with a potato crust and bake, like any
other fish pie—or the mixture may be cooked in scallop shells.

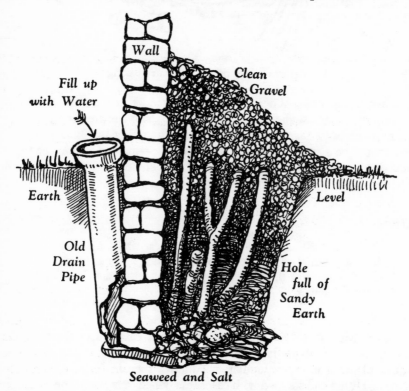

Seaweed and Salt

Sea-kale. Plant the thongs (root cuttings) of sea-kale at the foot of an old
wall on the sunny side. Plant them deeply on to a bed of seaweed and stones
and manure. Sink an old drain-pipe on the other side of the wall and keep it
full of water. When the shoots grow through the gravel cover with clean leaves
or straw or sea-kale pots.

SEA-KALE

The best sea-kale I found was on a beach in the Lleyn. The stalks had forced their way up three feet through hard round pebbles and were blanched to perfection.

This vegetable is best plain with butter, like asparagus. To grow this plant well, remember that it is a hardy sea-coaster. Plant the roots four or five feet deep on rocks, stones, sand and seaweed (which can sometimes be obtained free from your fishmonger, who gets it as packing). Let it grow freely for a year, to establish itself, before cutting.

It can be blanched inside covers, or if you are lucky enough to have basketfuls of dried brown beech leaves, the white shoots will come up through these clean, dry, and white as a mushroom. I am told dried bracken can also be used. Anything is better than earth, as the shoots are so frail.

TURNIPS

Small white turnips (six-week turnip) should be pulled when about two inches across. Trim them, leaving a small tuft of the pale green top leaves. Boil in salted water till tender, drain well and send to table piled on a dish with white pepper and melted butter.

Large golden turnips should be boiled, mashed with bacon fat and pepper, and served piled high with a "well" of gravy in the middle.

SWEDES

Swedes should be boiled and mashed like turnips. Some people like the tall soft sprouts of the swede that grow after it has been lifted and stored. These are boiled and served with butter like asparagus.

Turnips, Carrots and Brown Gravy (a Lancashire dish)

A Lancashire mill-lass made this dish for me when I was a child. It's simple and excellent, but must be made exactly right.

Scrape, slice and *boil together* equal quantities of turnips and carrots, and cook till soft, but not broken, drain off the water, and use it to make some good brown gravy. Add a little pepper to the roots in the saucepan, and chop, chop, chop with a sharp knife till the vegetables are in very small cubes (like crystal sugar). Do not mash them, for that is not the same effect at all. Just *chop* with a sharp knife in the hot saucepan; when fine and dry put into a hot dish; pour the hot brown gravy over them and serve with slices of dripping toast (I hope some other children will enjoy this as much as I did).

Vegetable marrows can also be grown as bush marrows

VEGETABLE MARROW

There are no traditional recipes, as the vegetable marrow came to England towards the end of the nineteenth century. There are many different kinds. Use the young middle-sized ones as vegetables, and old and woody ones can be kept for preserving.

Stuffed Marrow

Cut off the end and scoop out the seeds. Make a filling of tomatoes, brown breadcrumbs, salt and pepper, chopped parsley, and bind with an egg, mix very dryly (for the damp marrow will steam the filling). Fill the marrow, replace the end with four sharpened matches or a skewer, and bake, basting well with butter till the marrow is tender.

Another filling: finely chopped pork, beans, parsley, pepper and salt. Serve with mustard sauce.

Another filling: spring beans, finely sliced and cooked inside the marrow with butter.

Still another filling: the scourings from a ham-bone with spinach.

Serve stuffed marrow on a hot dish, tilting up the open end, on a wedge of bread. Remember the marrow is a very moist vegetable, so you must make the filling appetisingly dry and savoury.

Vegetable Marrow, Cold (salad)

Choose a very small young one, so that there is little centre to remove. Short, almost globular marrows are best for this, as long ones may break.

Hollow, cutting off the end, and steam, standing upright, with a bunch

Serve stuffed marrow on a wedge of bread or folded cloth

of mint inside to flavour it (you will have to cut a small slice off the bottom to make it stand steadily). When just cooked through, let it get cold. Fill well with a mayonnaise mixture of young peas, tiny carrots, and fresh chopped cress. Make the dressing rather stiff and fill the case to over-flowing, arranging the tiny carrots amongst the bunches of watercress sprigs on top of the yellow bowl of the marrow. Serve with brown bread and butter, and hot coffee. It makes a pleasant light lunch. Small young radishes and mustard and cress are another good filling. Cut a few of the radishes rose fashion and arrange cress and roses on top. A very pretty dish.

A cool salad

Vegetable-marrow Jam

For this use old tough marrows with strong, hard rinds. Hack the marrow into cubes, half an inch square, and allow 1 lb. of fruit to 1 lb. of sugar. Spread the cubes over a deep dish, strewing with the sugar. Leave for 24 hours or until the sugar has melted to a golden run of juice and the cubes have a shrunken look. Tilt all into the preserving-pan and boil swiftly to a set. This jam may be made spicy with lemon and ginger if liked. In proportion, the rind and juice of 1 lemon to 2 lb. of marrow is about right. The root of the ginger should be used, boiling it with the jam.

Vegetable-marrow Fritters

Slice a young vegetable marrow into neat slabs, about two by four inches. Steam gently over boiling water till just clear. Lift out and set to drain on a hot dry cloth. Beat up a good batter, previously made with an egg and seasoned flour. Coat the slices in the batter, and fry to a crisp golden brown in deep lard. For a supper or luncheon dish, serve with hot tomato sauce, and finely cut string beans and brown bread and butter.

Marrow Mangoes

This is an East India Dock recipe of 1850. Take a small vegetable marrow that will fit into a stone jam-jar. Cut it in half lengthways, take out the seeds, and lay it in salted water overnight; next day, drain it, and fill the seed space with mustard seed, peeled and chopped shallots (or garlic), scraped horse-radish, and a good amount of pickling spice. Tie the halves together and pack it into the jar and pour over it boiling-hot vinegar; next day, drain off and keep boiling up and pouring on daily, till the marrow looks semi-transparent and dark and soft. Take up, shake out the seeds (you can use them again), slice the "mango" and pack into jars, and boil up the vinegar with some sugar, and pour, boiling-hot, into the hot jar. Tie down, and keep some months before using.

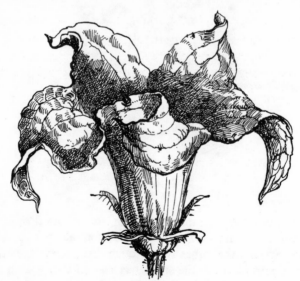

The golden flower drops off as the fruit is formed, so using the flower does not harm the plant.

Vegetable-marrow Flowers (golden pockets)

After the marrow has "set" the golden flower drops off. Collect several of these thick golden flowers, stuff them with a light lemon-flavoured forcemeat, dip in batter, and fry a delicate golden brown. They make a pleasant dish, garnished with the smallest red tomatoes (baked) and bunches of fried parsley.

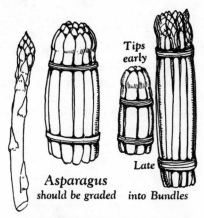

Tips early

Late

Asparagus
should be graded into Bundles

Asparagus is expensive because it monopolises a large bed for many years, s o does not work in with other garden produce.

ASPARAGUS

When gathering, cut all the shoots on the bed and sort into bundles, tying them up according to length and thickness. Cook upright in a tall saucepan so that the thick stumps only stand in the boiling water and the delicate heads are steamed. Drain and serve on slices of toast, dipping each stick into a little pool of just-melted butter.

BROAD BEANS

> " Beans be damned by Pythagoras, for it is said, that by oft use thereof the wits are dulled and cause many dreams, for dead men's souls be therein. Therefore ' Varro ' saith that a bishop should not eat beans."

The broad bean, *Faber vulgaris*, is for early summer use, and duck and green beans are a special English delicacy.

When young, the green beans are as delicious as peas, and should be cooked as simply and speedily, and served with nothing but a pat of butter.

Older beans need a little longer cooking and may be improved by a polish of hot, buttery parsley sauce. When the placenta (i.e. the little

The black spot that marks an old broad bean

hook that fastens the bean to its pod) comes loose easily and leaves a white scar, the bean is still young enough for ordinary cooking, but when the scar becomes black, then the country people call them "blackspotted beans" and reckon them indigestible food, though good enough for a hungry plough-boy—and indeed, some old country folks do not "reckon you get the full flavour of a broad bean till the black spot is come and the grey skin is pretty tough".

If you have some beans too old for your taste, boil them and press them through a sieve. The too-tough skins will be left behind, but the green

When broad-bean skins become tough the green filling makes a good purée spread on hot toast under scrambled egg

hot drift that powders through will be light and well flavoured. Shake a little melted butter over it, and you will find it a delicious dish served with hot buttered toast, or with a scrambled egg, or with small rolls of well-grilled bacon laid on top.

"Beanes and Bakon" served this way will last well into the autumn.

Parsley cooked with beans brings out their aroma, like a sprig of mint cooked with peas.

Bean Butter

> "*Beene butter* is use moche in Lent in dyvers countries—it is good for plowmen to put in their paunches."
>
> BOORDE.

This seems to have been dried winter beans, boiled to mush in mutton broth and used as a thick spread upon coarse oatcake.

Baked Beans and Bacon

"Baked beans" are dried beans and dried bacon cooked together, closely covered, so that the flavour of the pork is absorbed by the swelling beans.

This simple country dish, made for centuries by the country people, is now a commercial commodity canned in vast quantities.

It is only an economical dish where a continuously hot oven is in use, as it takes 24 hours to cook properly.

Put a large bayleaf at the bottom of a 7 lb. jam jar (or deep pot), stand upright in the jar a wedge of sugar-cured ham, or a small "Hock" of bacon. Add a generous spoonful of honey, and some white pepper, pack small dried white beans around the bacon hock, or ham, one third only of the length (as the beans will swell considerably), fill up the jar with water and tie up the top as close as you can (without risking a burst jar) to keep in the aroma and steam. Bake continuously for hours, till the beans are soft and the jar full of juice.

BRUSSELS SPROUTS

> " Sprouts are very delicate, so boiled as to retain their verdure and green colour. . . . The best seed of this plant comes from Denmark and Russia."
>
> 1699.

To "retain their verdure" drop them singly into fast boiling salted water, cook very rapidly, drain thoroughly, and serve hot.

The very small sprouts that do not develop, near the top, are delicious scattered in broth; they only take a few minutes to cook.

Brussels sprouts should be tight and firm

The large head of the sprout can be used for "greens" in a hard winter. Remove all the thick stems, as no amount of boiling will make them edible, and the thick green leaves will cook quickly as cabbage.

CABBAGE

> " 'Tis scarce 100 years since we had Cabbages out of Holland, Sir Arthur Ashley, of Wilburg St. Giles, in Dorsetshire, being the first who planted them in England.
>
> Cabbage is not so greatly magnified by the rest of the doctors, as affording but a gross and melancholy juice. Yet loosening, if moderately boil'd. It is seldom eaten raw, except by the Dutch."
>
> A GARDENER'S BOOK OF 1699.

Spring cabbage

Early spring cabbage, coming when green food is new and pleasant, should be cooked quickly, roughly shredded up, in as small amount of water as possible, chopped, seasoned, and served green.

The large white close cabbage has less novelty of flavour, and can be made into dishes with advantage. Both this cabbage and the winter savoy can be shred and eaten raw as salad.

The mediaeval instructions were curiously modern. "Take a large quantity of the worts—and shred them, and put butter thereto, and seethe them and serve forth—and let nothing else come nigh them." This, in various forms, convinces me that our modern "conservative cooking" is as old as the hills. The "worts" were simply cooked in butter in a closed earthenware pot, set in boiling water. But if you want the fresh crisp taste, cook the cabbage this way:

Savoy or winter cabbage

Have a large pan, the bottom just covered with an inch or so of boiling water, salt the water a little, and shred the cabbage finely and throw it in. Pack it down, put on the lid, and give it 15 minutes' quick boil. Shake the pan sometimes. Turn out into a hot colander to drain, and serve instantly. It should be tender but still crisp.

Cabbage and Milk

Put a cupful of milk and a knob of butter on in a pan, with pepper and salt. Chop the cabbage very finely—and also across and across—and pack it into the milk. Cook close-covered for about 20 minutes, being very careful not to let it burn. Now remove from the fire, and add another knob of butter, and chop and toss in the pan which should have some rich milk gravy in the bottom.

Pile the cabbage on to a hot plate, thicken the milk gravy left in the pan with a beaten egg—on no account let it boil and curdle—and pour this savoury custard gravy over the hot cabbage. Eat with hot buttered toast. Cabbage cooked this way is a light meal—not an accompaniment to a meat dish.

Cabbage Salad

Cabbage *as salad* needs no recipe, except the warning to choose the other ingredients of the same texture—it is a mistake to mix soft things such as tomato or beet with stiff cabbage; they only become messy, and spoil the crispness of the cabbage. Use chopped celery, apple, grated carrot, horse-radish or other equally sturdy winter growths—nothing less hard and crisp than the cabbage itself should be used.

Red pickling cabbage

Red-cabbage Salad (called "Yorkshire Ploughboy")

One red pickling cabbage shred fine as silk, one onion shred as fine. Dressing: 1 tablespoonful of treacle, 2 tablespoonfuls of vinegar, 1 salt-spoonful of black pepper; mix all, and eat with cold meat and jacket potatoes with butter. Also excellent with corned beef.

CAULIFLOWER (Brassica oleracea botrytis cauliflora)

This is believed to be a Mediterranean plant. Centuries of cultivation have produced many varieties.

The outer leaves should curl over, protecting the flower. These leaves are very succulent, and sweeter than cabbage leaves. On account of its intricate shape, cauliflower should be soaked in cold water for at least an hour to get out any lurking insects. Dietetic experts recommend cutting the cauliflower up to cook a little quicker, but there is something very satisfying about a round creamy well-grown cauliflower head.

To cook the cauliflower, trim off the outer leaves, split the thick stem upwards two or three times and steam, or boil, stalk down, in a very little salted water. Drain well. The cauliflower, being a delicate but almost flavourless vegetable, makes a good dish with cheese.

Cauliflower in Gravy

Bolted or ill-shaped cauliflowers can be well used in this way. Break the cauliflower into even-sized sprigs, and dice the stems; seethe the pieces in beef stock till tender, drain, and keep hot, while you use the stock in which they were cooked to make a rich brown gravy, well seasoned. Put the sprigs back into the gravy, and serve with snippets of brown toast. (Diced carrots are good with this dish.) The beef gravy should be very well seasoned.

Cauliflower

Cauliflower Cheese

Steam or boil the cauliflower, drain thoroughly, and put it on a slice of brown toast in a fireproof dish.

Make a cream sauce with 1 tablespoonful of butter, 2 tablespoonfuls of flour, and pepper and salt. Melt the butter, beat in the flour, and cook thoroughly. Then stir in milk till you have a very thick coating sauce, and cook this still more thoroughly. Finally withdraw from the fire and stir in 2 good tablespoonfuls of grated cheese. Let this melt, stirring lightly, but do not let the sauce boil after the cheese is added. Pour it slowly over the hot cauliflower, letting it trickle down well between the sprigs; sprinkle a little extra grated cheese on top, brown for 1 minute, and serve.

Sprigs of cauliflower for pickle

Cauliflower in Pickle

Sprigs of cauliflower are an essential part of a mixed pickle.

Outer Leaves of Cauliflower

The outer leaves of a cauliflower make an excellent dish in themselves. Remove any midribs which seem woody and shred the fleshy blue leaves finely into a thick pan in which you have melted a tablespoonful of butter. Dust with pepper (do not add any salt), add a bay leaf, and let it cook with the lid on till the shreds are quite tender. Take out the bay leaf, add a sprinkle of salt, a small teacupful of milk, a tablespoonful of sugar, and a finely shredded potato. Stir and cook another 15–20 minutes.

Dish up. You should have perfectly cooked, finely shredded green, and about a teacupful of savoury white gravy from the bottom of the saucepan to pour over it.

The Stem for Soup Cubes

The thick stem of the cauliflower, if not woody, can be skinned and diced, and it will be found to cook a clear translucent green, very pleasant as a garnish to white soup.

CELERY (Apium graveolens)

This is grown in trenches in autumn. There used to be a red variety, but now the white is general. There is a special trade of "celery washer" to remove the earth from the ridged stems and pack them for market. Specially grown bright gold, or green, withys are used for tying up the bundle, making the celery stalks look extra white by contrast.

Celery is so good raw, crisp and fresh, with cheese and biscuits, that celery hearts should be served every lunch-time all through the winter. Let the celery be washed in cold running water, then split and stand it upright in a celery glass. It will curl a little, decoratively, and the crisp sticks prodded in salt and snapping clean are most appetising and a sovereign cure for rheumatism.

On no account throw away the root piece. It is the best nutty bite of the whole.

Decorative celery boats with cream cheese and butter cargo, and biscuit sails, upon a green wave of watercress

Four Celery Salads

(1) Celery sticks and cheese straws and salt.

(2) Chopped celery, chopped apple, and a few whole walnuts.

(3) Some raw chopped Jerusalem artichokes (which taste very like Brazil nuts when raw), mustard and cress, or a few nasturtium seeds, piled down the length of the longer, boat-shaped sticks of celery, with cheese biscuit sails and watercress foam.

(4) Chopped celery, chopped apple, cream cheese and a pickled walnut on top are good.

Baked Celery

Take a shallow earthenware dish with a lid, grease it well with good dripping, pepper and salt it, and lay the celery sticks end to end in it till full to the top. Pour in a little good stock, cover and set in a hot oven until the sticks are tender. Do not open to let out the aroma, but give it a tilt now and then, to swish the gravy up to baste the top sticks. They will take rather a long time to cook—from 30 to 40 minutes.

Serve as they are, from the hot dish. You can drain off the liquid and use it with fine oatmeal or cornflour to make a brown sauce, but it is really better plain.

Boiled Celery

Tie the celery into bundles with long bacon rinds, and simmer gently in barely enough water to cover (a baking-tin is a better shape than a saucepan), and when done, drain, remove the rinds, and serve like asparagus, flat on hot buttered toast. Again, if sauce is liked you can use the liquid and butter to make it.

Barley Bake, with Celery

The outer, rather tough sticks of celery are best for this, as they and the pearl barley take about the same time to cook. Butter a pan, cover with pearl barley, about as thick as if you were going to make a milk pudding. Add a bay leaf and fill up with celery chopped into half-inch-long pieces. Fill up with mutton broth and set in a very moderate oven to bake patiently for hours. Keep carefully covered and give it a stir occasionally. The barley will absorb the flavour of the celery and the dish should be firm enough to help with a fork but moist enough to need a spoon to scoop up the gravy.

Celery and Windfall Apples, or Jugged Celery (an old country dish)

As much windfallen apple as celery. Wash the apples, but do not peel or core, and stew them with as little water as possible, until a stiff pulp. Add a clove and a spoonful of sugar while cooking, rub through a sieve. Put a slice of bacon at the bottom of a jug, put the apple into it, and pack into it, in an upright position, as many sticks of celery as you can wedge in, until the pot is full (by this time the apple sauce will have risen to the top). Trim off the sticks level, and cover the top with these chopped ends and chopped bacon. It is the flavour running down the fibres that makes this dish. It is not nearly so good if the celery is cooked flat, therefore a deep-sided stew-jar or jug must be used.

CUCUMBER

"Cucumber flower, eke growing on his vine,
  Into some earthern pot, if that ye leade,
  Made like a man, or beaste fearce or benign,
  As man or beaste, as hath the pot in dede.
  It will be tendre if ye set
  A broad flat vessel with water two hands deep
  Under them, whereof up will they be fette
  By routes and in lengths away they creep."

PALLADIUS ON HUSBANDRIE.

Young Cucumber

A fresh crisp cucumber is so delicious that no one wants to do anything but eat it. Some like it finely sliced into vinegar and served in a shallow clear glass dish. Cucumber is utterly spoilt if frozen (in a refrigerator): it is so full of juice that the frost bursts its texture.

Old Cucumber

An old cucumber that has become too seedy and bitter to eat raw can be hollowed out into little cups (about the size and capacity of an egg cup), stewed very gently till soft, and filled with hot peas tossed in butter, a few asparagus tips, or any delicate vegetable filling.

Cucumber Mandram

This is a Victorian recipe. Cut a peeled cucumber from the end downwards in square cuts, so that when sliced across it falls in little square dice. Add an equal quantity of spring onions cut into small round pearls, and an equal quantity of cold cooked pearl barley. Shake together and season with the juice of a lemon, white pepper and a pinch of salt, and serve in crisp lettuce leaves. Excellent with salmon or pickled fish.

LETTUCE

Sydney Smith's well-known recipe for salad.

> " Two boiled potatoes passed through kitchen sieve,
>   Softeness and smoothness to the salad give
> Of mordant mustard add a single spoon,
> Distrust the condiment that bites too soon
> Yet deem it not thou man of tast, a fault
> To add a double quantity of salt—
> Four times the spoon with oil of Lucca crown
> And twice, with vinegar procured from Town;
> The flavour needs it, and your poet begs
> The pounded yellow of two well boiled eggs;
> Let onions atoms lurk within the bowl
> And, scarce suspected, animate the whole;
> And, lastly, in the flavoured compound toss
> A magic tea spoon of anchovy sauce. . . ."

Lettuce Stalks (from bolted lettuce)

The tall "run to seed" lettuce stalks make a candied preserve, very like root ginger.

Strip the stalks and peel them clear of the fibrous outside part (it is the soft-textured core, or pith, that you want). Cut this inside part into lumps; weigh, and to every pound, allow a pound of sugar and a "knob" of ginger root.

Boil sugar and ginger in enough water to cover the lettuce stems, and when quite boiling drop them in, and leave till next day. Next day drain off the syrup and boil up and pour over the stems, and keep on doing this till the stems look quite clear and the liquid is reduced to a thick syrup.

At the last boiling add a pinch of citric acid and bottle the stems in jars—like Chinese ginger, which it closely resembles.[1]

---

[1] The expressed juice of the lettuce is one of the oldest soporifics. The juice was dried on plates, and afterwards bound into white cakes. It was given to patients before and after surgical operations in conjunction with poppy seed.

ENDIVE (Cichorium endivia)

A native of north-east China, of use to us as salading in winter, bleached for use under any dark cover.

NETTLES AS SPINACH

Young nettle-tops come in useful at a time when green vegetables are scarce.

Gather a large basketful (a glove is necessary). Wash and press down damp into a deep pan with barely enough water to cover the bottom of the pan and prevent burning. Cover closely and cook rapidly, stirring occasionally till a green mush, usually about 20 minutes. Then add a generous spoonful of butter, and salt and pepper, and chop well, mixing thoroughly. Be very careful not to incorporate any of the nettle stems, which are invariably tough.

PEAS

> " Q. How do you boil peas?
> A. Briskly, ma'am."
> FINCHLEY MANUAL FOR THE TRAINING OF SERVANTS, 1800.

Green Peas

Green peas were traditionally served with spring chicken on Easter Sunday, and duck and green beans for Whit Sunday.

Young Peas should be cooked a few minutes in quickly boiling water with a sprig of mint and a small spoonful of sugar. Drain and eat at once.

Cold, they provide a perfect garnish for salads or for light summer moulds.

Older peas require more cooking, and a pat of butter in the dish improves them. Very old peas are only good in stews or hot-pots.

"Old Peson wyth Bacon

"Take old peson and boyle hom in gode flesh broth that bacon is soden in, then take hom and bray hom in a morter and temper hom wyth the broth and strayne hom thrugh a strayner and do hom in the pot ande let hom boyle. Serve forth wyth Bacon."

Dried peas can be kept for the winter. When re-cooking, dried peas should have a little milk added to the water in which they are soaked and boiled.

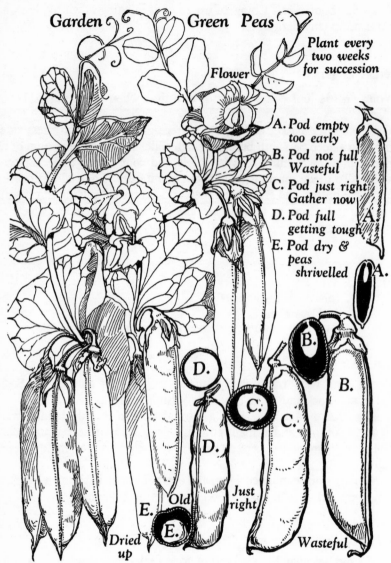

Garden Green Peas

Flower

Plant every
two weeks
for succession

A. Pod empty
too early

B. Pod not full
Wasteful

C. Pod just right
Gather now

D. Pod full
getting tough

E. Pod dry &
peas
shrivelled

A.

A.

B.

B.

C.

C.

D.

D.

E.

E.

Old

Just
right

Dried
up

Wasteful

Careful selection should ensure fresh young peas for a long season

Pea Pods

It is not generally known that pea-pods make a good pea soup, as they have all the flavour of the pea, though the texture is uneatable. Wash the pods, throwing out any hard ones, and boil them for an hour in a closely lidded pan, with just enough water to cover. Drain off the liquid, pressing the pods well, and this sweet juice can be made the basis of a delicious clear green-pea soup.

Pease Pudding

" Good peason and leekes, to make poredge in Lent
And pescods in July, save fish to be spent.
Those having, with other things, plentifull then
Thou winnest the love of the labouring men."

TUSSER.

Pease-pudding is made with the old mealy peas, and peas and bacon and pease pudding are two of the oldest of English dishes.

Pease-pudding is served with boiled bacon and is a solid, satisfying winter dish. For four people take a double handful of peas (if dried, set them to soak overnight) and put them with some shredded mint and a little sugar and pepper (no salt: the bacon will supply that) into a well-greased pudding-cloth.

Tie it up, leaving a little room for the peas to swell, but not too much (for the peas are already soft), and suspend the bag of peas beside the simmering pork. Arrange that peas and pork be done about the same time. A pease-pudding this size should take about 2 hours.

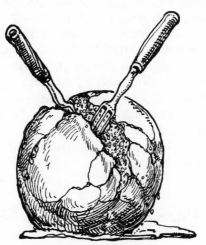

Split and pull apart with two forks

When done, lift out both pork and the pudding, dish the pork and lift out the solid green cannon-ball on to a hot dish. Set two forks back to back in the middle of the pudding and pull the pudding apart. It should fall into crumbly lumps.

Put a generous spoonful of the bacon broth, hot from the dish, over each piece of pudding, dust it with fine white pepper and serve it hot with the bacon instead of potatoes.

To Keep Green Peas till Christmas

Though the essential goodness of English usage is to enjoy things in their natural season, this way of keeping peas is interesting, as being one of the sailing-boat methods. (I abbreviate from the original.)

"Shell what quantity of peas you please, and put them into boiling water and give them four or five 'walms' (boil them up five times). Then strain them into a well-boiled clean cloth, and when dry, pack them into clean dry bottles. Pour over them clarified mutton-fat, to 'fill the necks', cork them down close, and set them in your cellar. When you use them, melt them out gently, and boil with some fine sugar and mint and butter."

RADISH

Radish Pods

Radishes run to seed rapidly, and the pods make a good lively winter pickle.

Pick the pods when the seeds inside are like soft seed pearls, drop the pods into boiling brine, and let it grow cold—if they are now bright green you can pickle at once, but if dull, boil up the brine and pour it back over the pods once or twice till they are bright as emeralds. Drain, rinse clear of salt, pack the pods into glass bottles, with one or two scarlet peppers, cover with white clear vinegar, and cork down for winter use. They are a very pretty garnish to winter's potato salad.

The clear green pods in a dish of pellucid pickled onions make a jade and pearl symphony that belies its potency.

They are also delicious (and most decorative) with cream cheese.

TOMATOES

To skin easily, dip them into boiling water for about 1 minute. Slice *with* the core to keep in the juice for sandwiches, and *against* the core to loosen the juice for chopping up and cooking.

Tomatoes Stuffed

These are very simple and easy. The filling can be anything suitable. Chopped ham, cheese, etc., are good, or an egg, beaten till custard, with a little milk, and seasoned with herbs. This will set nicely in tomato cups in a cool oven. Garnish this pretty red and gold dish with sprigs of land-cress and make the extracted pulp into a hot sauce, with a bay leaf and a suspicion of garlic, to hand with them.

Tomato Pie

Butter a piedish and line it with breadcrumbs. Fill the centre with burst tomatoes—tinned or bottled tomatoes are excellent for this—sprinkle with pepper, salt, and a little parsley, cover with more crumbs, and dabs of butter. Let the dish stand about an hour before you put it in the oven.

WATERCRESS

" They reckon it is a good thing to eat in the spring. They
prophesy it purifies the blood."

E. C.

This favourite old English salad is not understood by the cook who thinks of it as sprigs of garnish.

The eighteenth-century advance in science realised the value of this iron-rich green stuff, and the best is now grown under ideal conditions, where ice-cold springs, clear and clean, specially bored through the solid chalk, gush gallons of fine fresh water over the beds.

Very young cress is light bright green, but the knowledgeable prefer

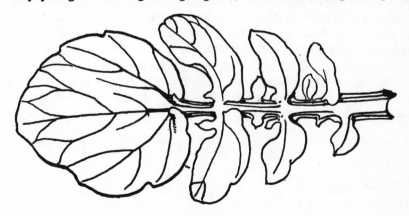

Landcress

their cress "sunburnt"—that is slightly older—when the leaves have acquired a delicate bronze.

The leaf has then more crispness and "bite", and is the perfect accompaniment to cheese and biscuits—especially the firm white Caerphilly—mild summer Cheddar, Wensleydale and single Gloucester. (The peppery Cheddar and hotter types of Cheshire provide their own "bite" and most of the blue mature cheeses of winter are better with celery.)

Watercress should *never* be put in a refrigerator—a shallow bowl of water standing in a cool place is sufficient. The texture is lost in frost.

Watercress Salad

Dice even waxey new potatoes and drop into a very little salted cream. Cover the bottom of a flat dish with sliced tomatoes. Take a small bunch of parsley and shred finely over the tomatoes. On this green bed lay a layer of the white potatoes, and finally cover the whole with watercress sprigs. Serve dry, and hand oil and vinegar separately. Do not use pepper with this salad.

Watercress for Teatime

Watercress for tea is essentially English. You get it in most unexpected places! I have had it in country cottages, in cathedral city tea-rooms, and the British Museum.

A *good* cress sandwich:

Cut brown bread and butter it; lay the slices around; dip each sprig of cress in kitchen salt (the crunchy type, not the powdered), pack closely all over half the slices; press the top slices *firmly* down upon the under slices and stack the sandwiches one on top of another and serve at once. Do not trim off the characteristic little frill of green leaflets that escape beyond the brown edge of the sandwich; their stiff green border prove the freshness of the sandwich, and add to its enjoyment.

A delicious sandwich is fresh brown bread and cress alternated with white bread sandwiches of pink shrimps.

An appetising country device is to use a large square of fresh bread cut twice diagonally—and replaced with the pink and white, brown and green squares alternately opposite. A suitably decorative way of indicating that they should be eaten two together.

Freshly cut thin sandwiches decorate country tea-parties; brown and white bread and butter, cut diagonally, and arranged alternately, is a pleasant device

CRESS (Lepidium sativum)

This is usually grown in conjunction with mustard—the "mustard and cress" of childhood's garden makes particularly good sandwich filling with meat or fish pastes. Bloater paste, creamed up with butter, and served with chopped cress between brown bread slices, is specially good—children like cress also with chopped egg. Salt cress, but if served with the "mustard" it does not need pepper.

The long-drawn-up cress of the market gardener, grown in water only, is usually too "white whiskery" and has less flavour than the common or garden growth.

BRACKEN

The bracken increase that destroys so much of our land comes from many causes. Bracken used to be cut for bedding for farm animals, for covering-in root crops, and for weaving into shelters and hurdles, and trusses of it were burnt in the ovens and used to light the open hearths. Quantities were used by the slate and heavy earthenware workers to pack their wares for road transport. The invention of the pneumatic tyre on the lorry caused much bracken to remain uncut, as less packing was needed. The sheep were on the hills so early that they ate young shoots for lack of other grazing—and where the bracken was not brought down for use about the steading, the shepherd would cut it all over his sheep walk because, growing high, it hid the sheep, induced fly, and spoilt the fine grass "bite". All these reasons combined to keep the growth of the bracken within bounds. Now it is not cut and has become a desperate weed instead of a useful growth.

Young bracken fronds are edible when about three inches high and still tightly curled; they should be so young that they snap off.

Tie in loose bundles and cook like asparagus—only longer, and serve with melted bacon-fat. They have a distinctive smoky flavour—rather like the smell of Darjeeling tea. Brown bread and butter is the best accompaniment. You either like them very much or not at all.

SORREL (Sorrel antiscorbutic)

" Two afternoons in each week . . . occupied by all hands in collecting the leaves . . . to be served in lieu of lemon juice, pickles and dried herbs . . . a part of the leaves was served to the messes . . . as puddings, salads, pickles or boiled greens. . . . It is well known to be a never failing specific for scorbutic affections."

Parry's Voyages in the Arctic, 1819.

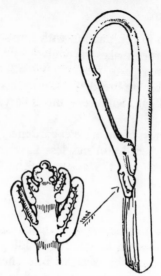

Bracken. The bent frond slides up the flattened stem till free of the earth

The use of this astringent herb is, I believe, a French importation. I had white soup made with sorrel at a French convent in Yorkshire, and among the French traditional usages near Nottingham was a sauce for veal made of sorrel.

Where the French element predominates in Britain, sorrel is used in soup and salad, especially in spring.

It is strongly acid, but has a fresh sharp bite that is lively and refreshing, and the young leaves are available early in spring when green stuff is scarce, so try it these ways.

Buttered Sorrel Sauce for Veal

Beat and chop finely with a little vinegar, add a piece of butter, and set on the fire till hot, and the butter well melted in.

Sorrel Sandwiches

(1) Cut thin slices of brown bread and butter and spread with cream cheese—shred the young green leaves and "stack" them across the white cheese, letting the loose green fringe stick out a little all round. Press together. (The idea of the fringe is to give you a small foretaste of sorrel before you bite into the cheese.)

(2) Dry biscuits stuck together with the least scrap of home-cured bacon dripping and a leaf of sorrel.

Sorrel as Vegetable

Gather a large basketful of sorrel leaves, young and fresh, wash them, and put them damp into a jar with a knob of butter and a very small onion. Cover closely and stand in the oven or in boiling water till the leaves are soft and tender (an hour or less). Chop and chop with a knife, like spinach, adding pepper and salt as you do so, and serve like spinach (it is very pungent).

Sorrel Soup

Prepare as above and stir into a good white stock. Serve with fried bread cubes.

Sorrel Sauce

> " Stamp sorrel, wheat bread, and slices of hard apple, with a little vinegar, and sugar, press well and put the liquid into a sauce pot. Garnish with marigold flowers and some slices of oranges and lemons."
>
> 1700.

I tried this "alle manner waies", but could get nothing but an acid greenish mass. When, however, the bread, apple, vinegar and sugar are boiled together first, and then filled with stamped and sieved sorrel, and strained, it became a clear thick green juice, which looks beautiful flaked with orange marigold petals, and has a fine pungent taste. (It would, of course, be used sparingly, like mint sauce.)

Scurvy Grass

> " A number of men employed all day in picking [scurvy grass] for purpose of boiling with our pea soup. The taste . . . somewhat resembled turnip tops . . . but whatever may be its anti-scorbutic qualities, it has little or nothing to recommend it to the palate."
>
> CAPTAIN PARRY.

MISCELLANEOUS PLANTS OF USE IN THE KITCHEN

Alliaria, "*Jack-by-the-hedge*", "*Sauce Alone*", "*Onion Nettle*": This soft green herb, about twelve inches tall, with small white flowers, has a great flavour of onion, and the edible green leaves can be shred fine in salad, to give the onion flavour—it can be used in stuffings, but is best raw, as its onion aroma is much lost in cooking. Useful in sandwiches, for cheese or potted meat spreads. The small white flower clusters make a pleasant garnish.

Clary: "When tender is not to be rejected in omelets; made up with cream fried in sweet butter, and eaten with sugar and juice of orange or lemon." (Acetarier, 1699.)

Clavers: "Follow-me-lad, the tendre winders with young nettle tops are used in Lenten pottages." (Acetarier, 1699.) An interesting use for this weed was to top the brass pins of the pillow lace makers: the small round seeds were pushed on to the pins while green and made padded heads.

Corn sallet: "The tops and leaves are a sallet in themselves, seasonably eaten with other salleting the whole winter long and early spring. The French call them Salad de Peter, for being eaten in Lent." (Acetarier, 1699.)

Hop tops: Cut in spring, they are boiled in broth and eaten like asparagus with butter toast—a Kentish dish.

Anyone who considers that English cookery must have been flavourless before foreign spices were imported should try some of the aromatic English plants listed by Tusser, an East Anglian farmer of 1557. These are some he considers necessary "for the kitchen garden":

(1) Avens, (2) Betony, (3) Bleete, (4) Bloodwort, (5) Buglas, (6) Burnet, (7) Burrage, (8) Cabbage, (9) Clarye, (10) Coleworts, (11) Cresses, (12) Endive, (13) Fennel, (14) Mallowes, (15) Saffron, (16) Lang de Befe, (17) Leekes, (18) Lettis, (19) Longwort, (20) Liverwort, (21) Marygold, (22) Mercury, (23) Mintes of all sorts, (24) Neps of all sorts, (25) Onions, (26) Orach (arach? red dye for cheese?), (27) Patience, (28) Perceley, (29) Penerial (Penny Royal), (30) Primrose, (31) Poset, (32) Rosemary, (33) Sage, (34) Saffron, (35) Summer Savory, (36) Sorrel, (37) Spinnage, (38) Suckery, (39) Siethes, (40) Tansie, (41) Tymme and Tinne (?), (42) Viollettes of all sorts.

These he recommends buttered (rightly):

(1) Beanes, (2) Cabbegis, (3) Carrets, (4) Cytrons, (5) Gourdes, (6) Nawues (?), (7) Pompions, (8) Parsneps (we still say "Kind words butter no parsneps"), (9) Poncevall peas (large ones), (10) Rapes, (11) Turneps.

Tusser's medical herbs include:

(1) Anniseed, (2) Archangel (Angelica?), (3) Betony, (4) Chargule, (5) Cinquefoile, (6) Cummin, (7) Dragons, (8) Detany, (9) Gromwell, (10) Hartstongues, (11) Horehound, (12) Lovage, (13) Lychoras, (14) Mandrake (some English version? Cumphrey?), (15) Mogwort, (16) Oyonnes, (17) Poppye, (18) Rue, (19) Rhubarb (early importation used for medicine only), (20) Smal ache, (21) Sarefradge, (22) Savin, for botts, (23) Stitchwort, (24) Valerian, (25) Woodbine.

Other useful Cooks' Plants

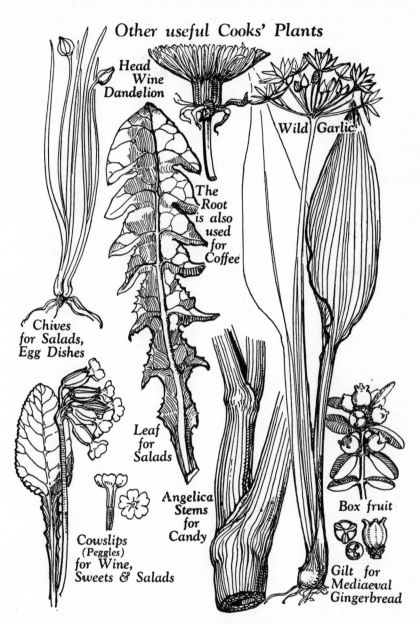

Head
Wine
Dandelion

Wild Garlic

The
Root
is also
used
for
Coffee

Chives
for Salads,
Egg Dishes

Leaf
for
Salads

Cowslips
(Peggles)
for Wine,
Sweets & Salads

Angelica
Stems
for
Candy

Box fruit

Gilt for
Mediaeval
Gingerbread

Various plants mentioned in the text

Tusser also gives Dill, Fumetorie, Eyebright, and about twenty others for distilling. Woodruff he specially notes for flavouring sweet (it's very delicate) basil, a pot plant, and finishes a list of three hundred herbs with the rhyme:

"Thus ends in brief, of herbs the chief—
Who more would have—of field go crave—"

NEW FREEDOM

THE EAST INDIA COMPANY

THE AMERICAN WAR OF INDEPENDENCE

DUTCH INFLUENCE

OTHER INFLUENCES

INFLUENCE OF THE ENGLISH FARM

The Complete British Cook.

There is a confident poise in the poker that portrays a master mind. The sugarloaves hung aloft; sugar is still wrapped in blue paper, but "sifter" sugar spoons are still needed to sift out the small lumps of broken-up sugarloaf. The hams, herbs, and onions, the little anchovy barrel, are the same today. The three jars on the shelf probably held rennets or yeasts; being fitted with bladder covers and quill "gas escape" stoppers.

Below on the wall hang steak tongs, beside them a tinderbox on its chain. The metal pestle and mortar remind one that most spices were bought whole, and pounded in the mortar just before use so that the aroma was always fresh. The largest canister would hold cocoa nibs, for the popular chocolate (these took up a lot of room compared with modern cocoa powder), the smaller sized canister would hold coffee; tea would be locked away in a small teacaddy; and the cups would be tiny, with no handles—they would be "dishes of tea".

Next to the canisters is a dredger for flour or powdered herbs (see Dredgings). The candlestick has a "lift" that runs up a side slot, to raise the sunk candle as it burns down. This candlestick upon the mantelpiece was constantly needed for sudden excursions into dark cellars and larders. The "straynor" was probably of "milk style pattern"; made to take different thicknesses of tammy cloth over a movable base. The wooden spoons in their rack were a usual gift to a country girl from her lad, often carved with her name and his love.

The game larder is seen through a doorway. Turkey, hare and small birds, below rows of jars and bottles. Behind the cook is the side oven, or hot plate.

The fireplace has movable bars, but the shape is still like the long narrow fires of the previous century. The pot crane over it might be of any century, but the spit (by its light construction) is being turned by one of the new-fashioned heat vanes, set up inside the chimney. The hot draught rushing up from the roaring fire spins a rotary propeller set across the chimney, the axle of which, being fitted with a worm-wheel coupling, is geared down to the spit wheel by a light brass chain. The beauty of this arrangement is that the hotter the fire, the quicker must the spit turn. This was a really brainy invention, and important, for it marks the first step in utilising the "wasted chimney heat". Near the cook are the hand-picked coals ready for adding to the roaring fire. These coal baskets would not spill dust, being woven of close fenland reed-leaves.

The dripping pan and basting spoon show, as the cook has drawn back the roasting screen (one thick leg of it shows on the right) because the joint is almost ready, and is now being "finished" to a crisp froth before serving; also, she is poking a hole in the fire to take the small gravy saucepan.

Note that the spit is run through the fat of the joint, and is of the flat "sword" type. A fine round one suitable for birds, and other spits are on a rack over the mantelpiece (these racks, often found in old houses, are sometimes confused with the shorter, heavier gun racks). The last-minute "glazing" egg, knife, and platter are on the table.

The kitchen floor tiles are unglazed earthenware (scrubbed with sand, soda, and occasional applications of red raddle).

This new edition of the *Complete British Cook* was published in January 1800 and therefore portrays a kitchen towards the end of the century. Contrast this "Complete Cook" with the classical "Accomplish'd Gentlewoman" of 1742 (*see* p. 356).

NEW FREEDOM

THE EAST INDIA COMPANY

TRADE with India still needed a year's voyage around the Cape of Good Hope—a route disputed by the Portuguese, who expelled the English from the Spice Islands, fought them in Persia and killed the traders there in 1623—so that the long overland route of the fourteenth century was still in use, and freights—packed on camels' backs—of spice drugs and Indian produce, light-weight, dry and dusty, reached the English kitchens.

This "Levant Company" overland route continued after the sea route was opened. Tea was sent overland, as the damp of the long salt sea voyage spoilt the flavour; nor was it possible to keep spice, salt, or gum dry in the ship's wooden hold. The silver wrapping of modern tea is a remnant of the heavy lead casing once used to keep out the damp, and tea chests are foil lined today.

The East India Company evolved from stocks supplied by adventurers who had shares in the ships.

Later the Company had a fleet of swift "Indiamen" and complete trading stations in India, and paid enormous profits, so that the effect of the East India Company can be seen in all the household life of the period.

The extravagant social life among the new "Company's Agents in India" is soon reflected brightly at home, and anyone who could boast of friends or relatives *in* the Company was proud! The returned travellers brought home gifts that set new fashions—turbans with paradise plumes, fine Indian muslins, cashmere shawls. Chinese Chippendale became the fashion, delicate fine porcelain and china tea cups. Yellow chintz and black lacquer—the fashions carry on into the eighteenth century.

There are many small details that bring the "Indiamen" trade very close. The tall old English grandfather clock was about the size and shape of the narrow cabin lockers, and sailors, waiting the "turn around" of their ships out East, would get some native craftsman to lacquer the long narrow locker lid and bring it home next voyage—so that many an old oak Grandfather clock case was repainted by an English hand, to make it match the new lacquered door in front. The cookery in the kitchen has many new light dishes with new spices—ginger now comes, not dried over the desert, but in succulent lumps, dripping syrup from stone jars heavy in a ship's hold.

Also, the heavy meat meals of England, and extremely high game, were disliked by returned voyagers sick of goat's flesh, and cooks made light rice and spiced fruit dishes. China Chilo is a good example.

THE AMERICAN WAR OF INDEPENDENCE

New England and the southern states were only a generation removed from being "plain English settlers" and the military use of the "Red Skin Indian" against our own white descendant was bitterly disapproved. Taxation (cause of the trouble) had been dropped for all goods except tea, and the Boston Tea Party (catch name for the Transatlantic riot which emptied a cargo of tea into the salt water of Boston harbour) proved the last straw. Financially, the tea trade was involved with our new East Indian economics, but psychologically, the wanton destruction of "all that good tea" excused a climax! so that once again housewives studied condensing and preserving for shipboard. When Ireland joined the western complications, Liverpool became important and soon the Liverpool–Manchester canal was built, making transport of heavy kitchen goods and stores possible.

DUTCH INFLUENCE

Marlborough's war in Flanders makes a difference to the English housekeeper because Dutch influence flows into our kitchens; the old-fashioned "wafers" went out of favour with the Reformation (they were too like the Holy Wafer of the Mass), but now, printed alongside the "old English recipy" are instructions "How to make a new Dutch waffer", Dutch eatables are popular in our kitchens, and Holland's cheap gin soaks into our southern and eastern counties. In London one can "get drunk for 1d. or dead drunk for 2d." (and one frequently did so).

THE NEW DINING TABLE

The "platt" of a laid table opposite (two of four courses) shows the new eighteenth-century character. Contrast it with the previous centuries, and note that it is the first genuine dining *table*. Till this date they have been "boards".

The early mediaeval "board" was a board set upon movable trestles. It was draped with layers of fine linen, but its only static decoration was the enormous salt cellar, the ewer and basin and plates were laid out upon the "side" board.

Not till the guests came in was the dining board made gay with their privately owned "nefs" and drinking cups; the platters might be of bread, treen, or silver and gold, according to the household, and napkins and bread rolls were supplied—but the single long mediaeval "board" was characteristically "laid bare". Courses might be elaborate; trumpets herald flaming peacocks; carols bring in the boar's head; or pages could carry round meat hot on the spit. But though a dish might be carried to the table to serve, the long narrow "board" and the processional procedure were characteristic right up to the fourteenth or fifteenth centuries.

The breakaway from Hall to small cosy dinners by the fireside (shown in so many Tudor MS.) for a man and wife and their household cat or dog (prevalent during the reign of Henry VIII) seems tactless. But the characteristic Elizabethan table was still a "board". It was sometimes two or three boards wide now; the trestle legs were fixed solidly, the benches were wide and some had hinged "backs" (so that you could turn from the table and sit facing the fire), but it was still a "long board". The handsome gold and silver platters had been the pride of the mediaeval side board, now the Elizabethan pride was shown in pewter—and the side board rose in shelves, becoming a "dresser" to display complete dressing (a "garnish") of pewter. English pewter was lovely in design and texture, and the board was laid with large and small plates, tankards, goblets, saucers (small bowls to hold individual choice of sauce, while you shared a central platter), salt cellars, and even a few spoons were made to match, and shone upon the linen table cloths with a moonlight lustre.

People still carried their own "nef" (and today a child's christening gift of knife, fork and spoon recalls the "nef" that was given to the mediaeval child as soon as he was old enough to come to the lord's table); so, though the board was no longer "laid bare", it was only laid for eating at, not for the display of food.

The long wide tables of the sixteenth to seventeenth centuries (so generally called "refectory tables") were sometimes three or four boards wide, and had four legs set in from the ends and joined at floor level by stretchers that held down the rampart floor rushes.

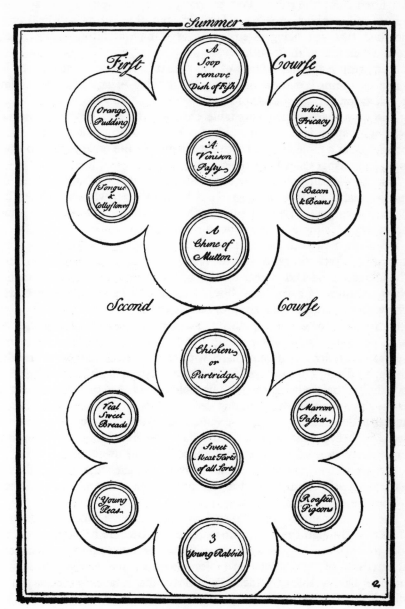

The new dining table

Chairs were set at the ends, and sometimes stools replaced the benches that fitted along the sides. Pewter, glass, horn, and leather, and spoons, knives and napkins, etc., were laid out, but the boards still held only the food that was being eaten, and everything was within arm's reach from either side of the board.

Now, realise the importance of this "platt". It is the first century in which the dining board has become a dining table—shaped for the display as well as for the assimilation of food.

The very shape of the new table changes; the legs become a central pillar with splay feet, and instead of one or two people accommodating themselves at a table large enough for a banquet, the table accommodates itself, and changes size to fit the guests.

The new dining table is finely made by skilled craftsmen (often of Spanish mahogany) and the garnish of Elizabethan pewter is replaced by the new Georgian service of silver, and Georgian silver enjoys the same reputation for simple beauty of texture and design.

Upon this new wide dining table is lavish display. Cookery books are now full of "set" dishes, elaborate creams and jellies, handsome pies, etc. The lovingly-modelled copper moulds of this period are a study in themselves. Sheaves of corn, lions, birds, fruit and flowers, and architectural achievements, all show the artist in service of the cook.

Instructions for garnishing dishes are often as long as for the making of them. The legs and wings of poultry and the heads and tails of fishes are used as decoration. Gruesome hares with ears set erect, and calves' heads, with grim detail, are displayed on decorated dishes; for all are to be seen and admired before being eaten. The table is loaded with food, and extra plates, glasses and the dull standing dishes are set on the side board. Some carving is done on the table, wines and flagons are now carried round, or placed in heavy wine coolers on the floor (where, during the Georgian period, they were often regrettably joined by their owners).

The use of food as decoration has arrived, and the wide dining table is as characteristic of this period as the processional "board" was characteristic of the mediaeval period.

The development from this "platt" carries us through to our own period. Gradually, through the Victorian reign, tables become heavier, solid oak tends to replace mahogany, and some of the workmanship in the mechanical extension of these Victorian tables shows our national genius. (We ourselves have a table of golden oak so heavy that it takes four strong men to lift it, but it winds out to a prodigious length on a screw that can be turned by one hand, and the slides pass their polished and fitted sides with the smoothness of oiled silk.) The simple lovely Georgian silver became ornate in Victoria's reign, the great salt cellar became dozens of silver or crystal "sets" between guests—the cruet had arrived—and damask patterns shone under the elaborate silver dishes. Saucers came off the table and went under the new tea cups. Electro-plate was invented, and gas replaced candelabra. Gradually decoration by food was replaced by decorations of flowers and fruit; then, at the turn of the century, for the dinner (so called à la Russe) the table is cleared again, and menus recall a little the old processional courses. Gradually the table decorations become almost as important as the dinner, and the table space is set out in ornamental designs on looking-glass—small statues, fountains, patterns of flowers laid out like a garden. The Edwardians had centre-pieces of silver stag tiered dessert dishes and the tall glass flower-stands (that so effectively hid one's opposite neighbour); we have now returned to the low setting of individual flowers and candles.

All this short history, showing the changeover from the "board" to the table, can be understood in this eighteenth-century "platt".

OTHER INFLUENCES

Though the East India Company already brought to our cupboards all manner of spicery, root ginger, fine teas, and gums, Captain Cook's voyages to New Zealand and Australia had not yet much effect in the English kitchen, though his study of diet for sailors altered the diet of the Navy (which was then very bad, being largely a matter of pillage and dishonesty). The only cheerful point then was the Navy ration of rum! It is a firm belief among all ratings that Nelson's body was brought home pickled in the ship's rum barrel, hence the name "Nelson's blood".

At the end of the century the French Revolution and the coming of many French refugees and prisoners brought much French influence into our cookery and clothing. Around Nottingham where the lace trade flourished are many French Huguenot names—Cattel, De Lacy and Voce (Voiser)—and local people have a strong tradition of wine making. (The spinners thereabouts used the trip skin instead of the spindle.) Centuries before, the English ploughman had known "no French save from Norfolk"; and on the east coast today the notices are sometimes in Dutch and French because of the foreign workmen on the dykes!

The Union with Scotland had given a market for industries, but its chief influence in English kitchens came through the enormous advance in agriculture made by Scottish farmers. This is touched upon in the next chapter.

INFLUENCE OF THE ENGLISH FARM

" Men of the greatest learning have spent time in contriving instruments to measure the Stars. . . . They think it more eligible to study the Art of Ploughing the Sea with ships, than

Tilling the Land with Ploughs. They bestow the utmost of their
skill learnedly to pervert the National use of all the Ellements
for the Destruction of their own species by the Bloody Art of
War . . . they invent an Infinite Variety of Slaughter . . . but
think it beneath a Man of Learning to employ his Labour in the
Invention of a new instrument for increasing Bread."

JETHRO TULL.

With the eighteenth century comes the best English farming. Towns
were large enough to form a good market, but their industries had not
yet depleted the land of its workers, who could still live in comfort on
their own produce. Jethro Tull was the leader of market gardening, "by
our Houghing [horse ploughing] we can raise as good cabbages and
carrots in a field as we used to grow in a garden". The east coasting
trade—declined since the New World developed the western seaports
—developed a Scotch trade. The Firth of Forth and Fifeshire (that
beggar's mantle with a fringe of gold) had a rich alluvial coastal plain
to the south called the Carse of Gowrie, and there agricultural history
was made by farmers who were the grandsons of the Gentlemen Adventurers of Elizabethan days. By this period were discovered the root
crops and feeding stuffs that made winter feeding of cattle possible, so
that the killing of stock in autumn ceased, and fresh meat was available
in winter. Jethro Tull invented agricultural machinery, and in this
century there rose an "aliveness" and enterprise among the quiet farming
folk.

For a small example: Farmers returning from Flanders brought word
of a swinging scythe called the "Hainault cutter", and as it was thought it
might speed up the cutting of barley, they brought over some men from
Flanders to give a demonstration in Scotland! After trial they decided
the Scotch straw was too weak to stand against the swinging stroke, and
the modest skirts of the woman field-workers got in the way. So the
Hainault scythe was not adopted. (*Proceedings of Scottish Agricultural
Society*).

But note that the *whole research is done privately by the farmers themselves. There is no Government support, nor pay.* The same "enquiry" today
would probably involve a Special Commission and subsidy, but then,
three or four farmers club together, cross to Flanders in a coasting boat,
a few foreigners are brought back and lodged on local farms, and some
keen, quiet man (by lamplight, with his quill pen scratching gently) writes
out the "Result of the Investigation" for the public newspapers. This is
itself an agricultural revolution; the farmer has his weekly paper! only
a news-sheet at first, but it is a newspaper, and the grandson of Cono
(who now lives in that country residence of 1615) is an influential person,
with a sense of humour:

" Animals will scratch! and scrape themselves, and if your cow has nothing else to rub on—away goes your gate! and your fence heaves up to the pleasure of your pig. So I have built a scratching post of rough pine across a corner of the field, at a steep slant, so that now every animal on the farm, from the tallest mare to the smallest lamb may scratch himself to his satisfaction, ' Even the Edinburgh Reviewer may take his turn ' and ' Bless the Duke of Argyle in comfort' ."

A new crop, Saint Foin, is grown, and pleases the bees as much as it feeds the beast. Churns go round and round instead of up and down, a dozen new discoveries and inventions show the genius of the period.

Probably Scottish influence (where women have always taken full share of responsibility) backed up the woman's side of farming, for the poultry and dairy work were superb. Eggs were forty for 1s., there were cream and milk dishes, and at least forty sorts of English cheeses.

On the farm there was both old and new; old Saxon forms of mead and corn foods, and the Souse and Lunt of the Highland shepherd, together with most delicate possets and tansies and junkets. The still-room becomes a "Ladies' Delight", and by all records, the cook seems to have had more sense than the doctors of the period (£1,000 reward was paid for one "cure" of baked and powdered snail shells!).

Towards the end of the century comes the classical cult of "Rural Delights" and "Fair Milkmaids" and Bath, of the eighteenth century, insists on the best of both worlds, rural and urban.

BATH—AND THE BEST OF EVERYTHING IN ENGLAND

The eighteenth century enjoyed a popular spa; London was spreading; and the large country estates of the seventeenth century had produced a society of "country houses", (with a "house in town") where people exchanged hospitality and "travelled for pleasure" in a way quite new; certainly quite a different way from the "family business", or "need to visit my daughter", that upheaved the Elizabethan household. The song of spring birds, that made Chaucer's folk "long to go on pilgrimages", has a curious echo in the urge of mating that sent the eighteenth-century matrons migrating to Bath "in the Season". On medical grounds, all the various mineral springs—Droitwich, Tunbridge Wells, Harrogate, Malvern Wells, Llandrindod Wells, and hundreds of others—were listed and studied, and the treatment at most of them (by enforcing the drinking of pure water) did counteract the drunkenness and overeating of the period. But Bath was fashionable! The Pump Rooms were the delightful meeting places for the gayest Londoners, and thereto came the freshest and most charming young daughters from the country houses in England. Everything in Bath was the best of its kind—even Bath buns were superior to all other buns!

Reason? Bath stands on the direct route, worn by centuries of travel, to Ireland; it is within coaching distance of London and the West, where the golden glory of Plymouth, Bristol, and the Elizabethan ports, was still reflected in the rich estates of the "west countree". You must remember that railways have not been made, and think along coach roads (later by canal transport), to realise the position of Bath in the eighteenth century. It was "a wonderful centre for travel".

It was this position which helped to make the food of Bath so excellent. Bath stands where the west drover-roads brought the finest meat down from the Welsh grazing grounds to the Bristol and Gloucester markets. The finest beef from the mountains, fattened as they slowly grazed down along the lush Severn valleys. It was at the end of the "golden valley", where fruit and vegetables spill their richness down the vale of Tewkesbury. The apples of Glastonbury brought great flagons of cider, and from the warm yellow Cotswold walls came apricots, hot from the sun, and cherries, and plums. Up from Devon and Somerset came the richest cream, bowls of fermenty, and junket rennets (Bristol and Gloucester made polished-horn drinking cups, and the horn spoons which "are the best spoon to eat fermenty withall"). Up the Severn river came the finest fish, and along the shallow streams in spring the shoals of elvers, to make elvercake. Salmon and fresh river trout, and (by fishing boat) pilchards and sea fish from the Cornwall coasts.

On the long salt marshes to the south grazed the small fine "salt mutton" (the *pres sale* of France) that the shepherds brought to market, and sold with the dark green laver weed, sauce always eaten with "marsh mutton". Also, from Bristol way (where the rich soap boilers made their money from the refuse fat from the tanners' yards) came scents and spices and fine imported wines—brought by cargo boat from overseas. And besides the legal trade, almost any smuggled French brandy or Spanish wine.

The delicious food of Bath was not only rich and elaborate, it had that perfection of simplicity which takes the very best materials, and uses them with that exquisite care which is English cooking at its best.

We have given many Bath recipes in this book—but for one example— here is a junket—Junkets were made everywhere—but here is a Bath junket called "Damask Cream".

Cook cream gently with some mace and cracked cinnamon till delicately flavoured. Add sugar and rosewater, and set it with fine rennet. When cold, flood over it soft cream flavoured with rosewater and lightly strewn with powdered sugar. Serve surrounded by deep damask rose petals. That was a junket—at Bath!

COACHING DAYS

ROADS WERE a belated development from any woman's point of view. Mankind could go off on a good horse, with a pack-horse for luggage, and put up at inns.

Goods and merchandise could go slowly by waggon, or be carried around the coast, popping in and out of seaports like pigeons. There were regular pack-trains of carrier horses, and towards the end of the century the men provided canals and waterways for the transport of their goods—but not for her comfort!

The country housewife travelled in a solid-tyred, badly sprung coach, and the roads were awful. However, it was surprising how much travelling was done by private coach and through the fixed "posts". These "posts" or regular stopping places on main roads were able to anticipate the number of guests they would have to feed, and know the time of their arrival, but the smaller inns on less regular routes had most difficult housekeeping.

Around the fixed "post houses" the country people had a good market for their produce, and quite a lot of unofficial trading was done. Stilton and Cheshire cheeses and Mowbray pies are examples of eatables whose reputations were made by posting travellers.

In the eighteenth century an inn was, basically, a farmhouse set by the roadside, and as such was self-supporting, growing its own corn and keeping its own cattle, sheep, pigs and hens.

The owner had to cope with the ordinary work of a farm, therefore, besides a garden for vegetables. An orchard, with bees (both for sweet cooking and honey for curing hams, and wax for furniture polish).

All these products must be preserved for use in winter. The summer milk must be turned into cheese, and butter must be salted down for the winter. The innkeeper's wife must be expert in storing, preserving, salting, drying, smoking, curing of meats, bacon, hams, and all pressed and preserved meat, glazed tongues, brawns, and potted meats.

Fruit was preserved in honey, or spiced in vinegar, and soft fruits candied and jellied. (A note on store jars will be found on p. 319.) Eggs had to be pickled, or waxed, and winter packed, and fish had to be pickled, or soused, or salted and dried.

Besides all this ordinary farm household work was the extra amount of ale and beer brewing (for all brewing was done on the premises). Also, at the best inns, the wife usually made wines—and was expert in stirrup cups, possets, and caudels needed by belated horsemen or cheerful revellers.

A certain amount of invalid diet had to be kept handy, and remedies for the accidents of the road (anything from a broken collar-bone to a miscarriage). Ostlers and grooms were always wanting hot mashes, special poultices, and all the "bucket cooking" horses always seem to require at inopportune hours. She probably had her own children and babies to attend to—besides the welfare of her "outside servants" and, probably, aged relatives!

On top of all this work was the daily round of a large house. Fires must be made in empty rooms to keep them aired. Linen and blankets and bedding must be turned and dried. Windows and shutters, and candles and oil lights kept clean and bright for the influx of travellers, who would come in a bunch—suddenly—without warning.

In ordinary times an inn had to be ready, any night, to supply fifty people with a square meal, and about twenty-five of them with beds. The arriving and departing travellers would meet for the meal, and the new arrivals stay on overnight. Though, English weather being as usual, a sudden snow or flood might prevent departure, and all fifty travellers be pent up together for a full week.

Many of the dishes that could be "kept hot" as well as the "cold stands", such as hams, pressed beefs, brawns, and potted cheese and dried biscuits, come from English inns. Also the more solid preserves, the lemon curds, and almond fillings; for with a supply of these, a hurriedly made tart or pie could be filled and cooked while the travellers ate their first course. Because many of these standing dishes would be repeated at scores of inns on the same road, an individual variety of bottled sauces and pickles had to be on the table, and these were made at home (Worcestershire sauce and Yorkshire relish were so invented).

Also there was the ever-present domestic problem! for if one employed an ugly ill-favoured wench to serve, the travellers grumbled; and if one employed a pretty, lively wench, she got married!

So—having seen the innkeeper's side of the housekeeping, here is the traveller's point of view.

WHAT IT WAS LIKE TO BE A TRAVELLER

"The diary of Mr. Young, traveling in the North."

Rotherham (*Crown*). Very disagreeable and dirty. Hashed venison, potted mackerel, cold ham, cheese and melon. 1s.

Leeds (*King's Arms*). Cook dirty. Veal cutlets, tart and cheese. 8d. No beer.

Driffield (*Nag's Head*). Civil and cheap. Mutton steaks, ducks, tarts, cheese, mushrooms, capers, walnuts, gherkins, and other pickles. 2s.

Scarborough (*New Inn*). Cheap but dirty. Cold ham. Supper: chicken, lobster, anchovie, cheese. 1s. 4d. (Coffee and tea, 6d.)

Castle Howard (*outside Carlisle*). Excellent house, but dear—and a saucy landlady. (He does not mention what she charged him.)

Stokesay-in-Cleveland. Civil but shabby.

Richmond. Brace of partridge, leesh of trout, cheese. 1s.

Greta Bridge. Middling.

Bowland. Civil but not cheap.

Newcastle. Extravagantly dear! Boiled fowl and oysters and one woodcock. 2s. 6d. Next day: roast fowl and one small haddock with 10 smelts on it. 2s. 6d.

Glenwele. Boiled fowl, catchup sauce, roast potatoes. 8d.

Carlisle. Good. Broiled chicken with mushrooms, plover, plate of sturgeon, tart, mince pies and jellies. 1s. 6d.

Penrith. Roast beef, apple pudding, potatoes, celery and potted trout. 1s.

Kendal. Civil and cheap. Brace of woodcock, veal cutlets. 1s. Next day: boiled fowl and sauce, roast partridge, potted char, cold ham, tarts.

("Foreign sweetmeats" were 8d., and a cup of tea or coffee, 6d.)

One can picture that cheerful traveller sitting by the fire in his room, boots off, slippered feet before the blaze, writing up his diary and then getting into his fourposter bed.

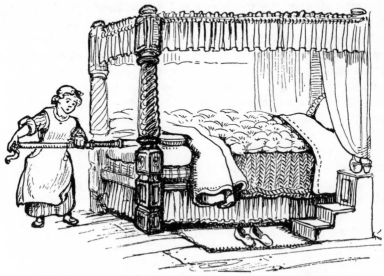

The warming pan, full of hot charcoal from the wood fire, was run up and down in the bed before you got into it

FRUITS, HERBS, SEEDS AND FLOWERS

" September blow soft 'til the fruit's in the loft."

TUSSER.

APPLES

Storing Apples

" Lay them dark as wind may not come near,
And do fair straw upon them, fleyke them under,
Or in heaps save, a little space asunder.
These heaps must ye now and now divide,
Yet be there divers folk say diverse wise,
And all in pitched potts will they hide,
Another of clay, another grease.
Yet hath a third for them a fresh devise,
Only the little feet to cleme in clay
And on a floor with chaff bestrewn to lay.
And other dip her little feet in pitch all warme.
And so in order lay them on a form."

PALLADIUS ON HUSBANDRY.

ACCURATE AS when the Colchester monk translated the original in the twelfth century. Apples must be kept from all sudden changes of wind temperature, and with a little light straw over them, and openwork "Fleyke" or planks under. They may be sweated in heaps, but the heaps must be watched and cleared often. Yet some do bottle apples, then (of old) cork, and pitch, or sealing wax must serve. The stopping of the stems with pitch seems the only thing we do not continue, though specimen apples are sometimes hung up by the peduncle.

Bottling Apples

Peel, quarter, core, and drop at once into clear water with a squeeze of lemon juice in it. Pack into the jars, fill up with syrup and proceed as usual. A pleasant change is made by cooking blackberries in a jar until the juice runs, and using this to fill up the apple jars. Another is made by adding a quince, or some quince seeds may be put into the jars.

Norfolk Biffins

A hard sweet apple of rosy colour and firm skin—they were slowly dried in the old bread ovens and packed down flat in layers as they dried—

so that they were red, round, wrinkled "biffins". If the skin burst, they were spoilt, as it was the slowly cooked juice converted within the apple which gave the biffin the advantage over modern apple "rings".

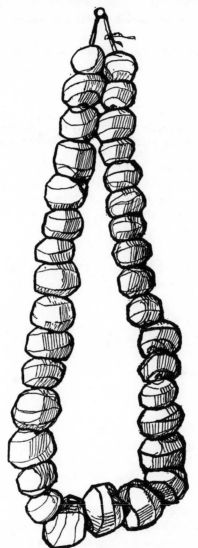

Apples were dried whole, peeled and cored,
and threaded onto strings

Dried Apples

Nowadays the custom is to cut the apples across, and dry in rings, but the older way cored them, with a bone-corer, and strung them up to the ceiling in long lines. If you have a good drying-room, with a current of air, and warm and dry, then the apples will keep well whole; otherwise, pack and store, sliced, in flat wood boxes.

Apple sauce for pork can be made with dried apples very well, if they are put into plenty of water and a closed pot and put into the oven while the meat is cooking.

Dried apples, not soaked, but chopped up with the currants and raisins, etc., make the fruit mixture for a cake go farther.

Roast Apples

Some sorts of apples roast better than others; the best should burst into a juicy fluff in about 10–20 minutes, according to size.

When the cores are left in, the pips give a pleasant aroma to the fruit, so well-flavoured apples should be roasted whole. Later in the year the core may be withdrawn with a scoop, and the space filled with sugar and spice, honey and ginger, or mincemeat, or candied peel and syrup, or any stuffing that will cook with the apple.

An Apple Scoop

The shank bone of a sheep, cut slanting and filed smooth, makes the best apple scoop. It doesn't rust, bend, or discolour the fruit.

An apple scoop made from a sheep's shank bone

Chaucer's Roast Apples

Apples roasted with sugar candy and galingale syrup (a very delicate dish). Galingale is a lumpy spice, with the aroma of damask roses, usually to be got through a wine spicery. Peel the apples finely and set level on a platter. Stew the galingale root in enough water and honey to fill the platter. Drain over the apples, and bake gently; withdraw from the oven, and serve cold, scattered with crushed white sugar candy. They should look like frosted pink roses, in a syrup the colour of rose quartz.

Nursery Apples

Core the apples and fill with brown sugar. Pack into a platter, just fill with water, and bake till the apples are fluffy and soft and the sugar has boiled to toffee.

Buttered Apple Dice

We know that buttered apples is a dish which dates from 1700, maybe earlier.

Peel, core, and chop the apples and drop into the sugar bowl as done. Meanwhile cut a slice of stale bread into cubes, the same size as the pieces of apple. Melt just enough butter in the thickest frying pan to fry the sugared apples; keep them well stirred around till they go a golden sticky brown, then toss out, add a little more butter and fry the bread cubes so that they mop up the juice and caramel left from the apples. When quite crisp, toss both together and serve instantly, with crushed sugar strewn over. This dish should be very crisp and crunchy, with soft pieces of buttered apple in it. It was probably laced with sack or hot cider; but is good with cream.

Apple Pudding, 1700 (now called apple amber)

"Peel and quarter eight gold-runnets, or twelve golden-pippins; cast them into water, in which boil them as you do for Apple sauce; sweeten them with loaf sugar, squeeze in them two lemons, and grate in their peels; beat eight eggs, and beat them all well together; pour it into a dish, cover with puff-paste, and bake it an hour in a slow oven."

Apple Charlotte

Butter a piedish and cover thickly with crumbs of stale bread, dust with nutmeg or spice. Peel, core, and chop up enough windfall apples to fill the dish to overflowing, and pack them in with a few crumbs, sugar, dots of butter, and, if possible, scraps of candied lemon peel. Cover the top thickly with more crumbs and dot with butter, and bake, covered the first part of the time; when the apples soften, remove the cover and let the crumbs crisp and brown. This dish should turn out a neat spicy brown loaf full of apple pulp. It is impossible to time exactly, as so much depends on the apples' cooking qualities; dried apple pulp takes about 30 minutes. Served with hot chocolate sauce.

Apple Soup (a manuscript recipe of 1400)

"Nym appeles sethe hem frete hem throue an her [hair] sieve—cast it on a pot and caste thereto good fat broth, and sugar and safron (and on Fisshe days almond mylke and oile of olive), and boile hit mease and caste onto good pouder [seasoning] and gif forth."

MS. of 1800

"Five pints of mutton broth, three or four pounds of windfall apples, cut up but not peeled or cored. Simmer the apples in the broth till soft, and press all through a strainer; season with a very small pinch of ginger [better in this than pepper], salt and reheat with a handful of pearl barley and cook gently till the barley is soft."

This is an excellent winter night soup.

Apple Pie (1767)

"Make a good Puff paste crust and lay some round the sides of the dish, quarter the apples thick, throw in some sugar with a little lemon peel minced fine, and a clove here and there, and then the rest of the apples. Boil the cores and peel, with a blade of mace, and some more sugar till it be very good [i.e., a thick syrup], pour over so that the dish is full, put on your upper crust and bake. Serve it smoking hot, with sugar dredged upon it and cream with it."

Mice and rats will also core apples to their own satisfaction

Apple Butter

" They are employed today, making a delection they call Apple Butter."

NOBODY, 1850, NEW ENGLAND.

In its stiffest form this was sometimes called apple cheese. Then it was almost candied, and turned out as a dessert dish, at Christmas, apple cheese was set at one end of the table, amber golden, and garnished with hazel nuts and whipped cream, and Damson cheese, ruby dark, garnished with white almonds, and with port wine poured over, at the other end of the table. It was made in all country houses at windfall apple time. The best was made of all one type of apple, but mixed apples, of all sorts, with a quince or two, made a delectable apple butter.

Take all the windfall apples, wash them, but do not peel or core, and cut them across the core so as to cut through the pips—this is important for the flavour. Put into a deep preserving pan, start with a cup of cider or water, and cook slowly, covered closely, till all are a soft mush. Now press it through a coarse sieve; if sufficiently cooked, you will see the small white kernels of the pips going through the sieve with the apple pulp; nothing should be left in the sieve but the peels, and empty cores, and pips. Measure the pulp and add 1 lb. of sugar for each pint of pulp, and 1 clove to each 4 pints. Stir sugar into the pulp till dissolved, and cook slowly till clear, then boil till the stiff mixture coats the back of the spoon with golden gum.

Pot into wide-mouthed jars and tie down. It improves with keeping up to a year. It should turn out firmly, with a very slight crystallising on the crust, but mellow, soft amber juice within.

Rats and mice will eat into apples to reach the pips

Ancestral Apple Pie

" Of all the delicates which Britons try
To please the palate or delight the eye,
Of all the sev'ral kinds of sumptuous fare,
There is none that can with applepie compare.

Ranged in thick order let your Quinces lie,
They give a charming relish to the Pie.
If you are wise you'll not brown sugar slight,
The browner (if I form my judgment right)
A deep vermilion tincture will dispense,
And make your Pippin redder than the Quince.

When this is done there will be wanting still
The just reserve of cloves and candied peel;
Nor can I blame you, if a drop you take
Of orangewater for perfuming's sake.
But here the nicety of art is such.
There must not be too little nor too much.

O be not, be not tempted, lovely Nell !
While the hot-piping odours strongly smell,
While the delicious fume creates a gust,
To lick the o'erflowing juice or bite the crust.
You'll rather stay (if my advice may rule)
Until the hot is corrected by the cool;
Till you've infused a luscious store of cream,
And changed the purple for a silver stream.

Till that smooth viand its mild force produce
And give a softness to the tarter juice.
Then shall thou pleased the noble fabric view,
And have a slice into the bargain too;
Honour and fame alike we will partake
So well I'll eat what you so richly make."

KING.

Friar's Omelet

This was probably *Froise Omelette.*

"Put a knob of butter in a frying pan, and when smoking hot, slice into it 2 or 3 good cooking apples (as many as the butter will fry). Let the apples become soft, lift out, and keep hot. Into the pan pour a shallow covering of good batter; let it cook till set, toss over and, while the underside is browning, lay the hot apples gently on top. Sprinkle with sugar, and as the batter finishes, fold it over (like an omelette) and slice on to a hot dish."

A good batter for the froise: 1 egg yolk, nearly $\frac{1}{2}$ pint of milk, beaten with 4 oz. of flour, 1 spoonful of sugar, and a dash of spice. Beat 10 minutes and fold the stiffly whipped whites into it just before use. Serve this apple pancake with a few drops of cider and crushed sugar.

Apple Pasties, Fried (1600)

Cook the quartered apples with sugar and a stick of cinnamon, add a piece of fresh butter, some lemon juice and orange-flower water. Put the mixture into thin pastry cases, seal well, and fry them. Dredge sugar and serve hot.

Apple Tansy (medicinal)

" A Tansey is good hoot, ele cast it not in youre clowche."

1400 MS.

The early tansies (tenth to fourteenth centuries) seem to have been a hot purgative porridge, made of worts (tansy), rough grains (barley or bran?) and fats (marrow or suet?). The purgative action was mechanical rather than chemical. The softly solid substance must be eaten much hotter than the body's heat, and the overcharged fat, being thrown outwards, lubricates, while the bulky mass distends. The mass was frequently followed by some hot herb teas, the complete action being calculated to "sweep all before it". By the sixteenth century this homely mechanical laxative was superseded by terrific chemical pills, and by the time of Izaak Walton his "minnow tansies" were a fishy type of scrambled egg.

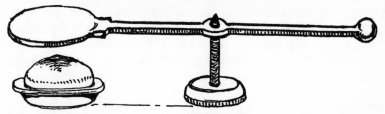

The old-fashioned "salamander" or red-hot "top" cooker. Its ancestor was the waffle iron and it is now reproduced in the most modern electric "invented cooker" which is held *óver* the dish in the same way.

It's nothing to do with cooking, but an amusing shepherd's trick was to heat a shovel in the fire, and use it like a salamander to smooth out his sheep's woollen fleece, to make them broad-backed, and square, and good-looking for a Show.

Apple Tansy (1760?)

"Three or four apples pare and slice and fry in a little of butter till soft, take the yolks of 4 eggs and 4 spoonfuls of water, and rose-water, and nut-meg and sugar and beat well together, and whip the whites of the eggs to sno' and stir it in, and pour over the soft apples in the pan, and let it cook till set, brown the top side before the fire [under the grill in a modern stove] and fold with the apple pulp inside and dredge sugar and serve."

This is the lightest type of tansy we have found.

A later form of custard tansy. Three large apples, sliced thinly in rounds and fried in butter till soft; mash up, and sweeten, and put at the bottom of a buttered dish. Take three eggs, beat them well with as much good milk as they will set, adding the apples' bulk of fine crumbs, nutmeg, sugar or spice to taste. Pour the custard gently over the apple pulp and put into a cool oven and bake very slowly till set. Reserve a little of the cooked apple pulp to place on top; sprinkle with sugar, and serve hot.

Toffee Apples

Before the general importation of plantation sugar—they would be quite expensive. Probably small windfall apples dipped in a toffee of honey and beeswax bedabbled the fairs of St. Bartholomew even before sugar, as we know it, came into general use.

Only small apples must be used; and toffee of the right consistency to coat deeply, with that iridescent, luscious gold that crackles.

Take $\frac{1}{4}$ lb. of butter and melt it; add to it $\frac{1}{2}$ lb. of treacle, 1 lb. of brown sugar, and 1 tablespoonful of vinegar. Boil 20 minutes and dip quickly.

Verjuice of Apples

" Be suer of vergis (a gallon at least),
   so good for the kitchen, so needfull for beast."

TUSSER.

Verjuice was in constant use till the last century, when its place was taken by the squeeze of lemon juice. It is really a very sharp cider—not a vinegar. The distilling was of interest, for it would account for the apparent mildness of some of the pickles made. In copying old recipes, very often a sharp cider is much nearer the original than modern vinegar.

To distil verjuice for pickles. "Take three quarts of the sharpest verjuice and put in a cold still and distil it off very softly; the sooner it is distilled in the spring the better for use." (*Compleat Housewife*, eighteenth century.)

Verjuice of Crab Apples (this was the best verjuice)

"Verjuice: gather crabbs as soon as the kernels turn blacke, and lay they in a heap to sweat and take them into troughs and crush with beetles. Make a bagge of coarse hair-cloth and fill it with the crabbes, and presse and run the liquor into Hogsheads."

A "beetle" is a heavy wooden mallet, and the method is exactly the same as making Monmouth Cider (which see)

The quince is hard and pear shaped, bright yellow when ripe and red when cooked. It has a most delicious aroma.

QUINCES

" Take quynces ripe and pare and heue hem smal,
And al for smal, but kest away the core,
In honey thene upboile hem, lese and more
De pepur (or ginger) with yt boyling, smalest grounds,
This is the first mannere, the seconds . . .
is to boil with honey till well thicke . . ."

PALLADIUS.

Quince Honey

This is a very early (twelfth-century) translation from the Greek, and is typically early-English cooking King Edgar is reputed to have imported quinces). If you have quinces it is a good way to use them. I used the strong honey water from washing out the combs and honey separator, knives, etc. (as they would of old when making mead). This honey syrup I filled with as many quinces as I could cut up into it, "al for smal", and boiled all till soft, rubbed through a sieve, and reboiled again, slowly, till the resultant quince puree was a clear dark rose-coloured honey. The flavour was delicious. I experimented, adding a little ginger and "pepur", as I believe the old English cook was trying to imitate one of the dark aromatic Greek (?) or Spanish (?) honeys? Some Crete honey may have reached England, with its strange rosemary tang, or the Trebizond honey, which had medicinal properties. During the war people made parsley honey, so this is an interesting survival.

Quince Marmalade [1]

A very old and delicious recipe.

Collect your quinces, and pare and chop up at least half of them, including the least ripe, just cover with water, and set to boil to pulp. When soft rub all through a sieve. To this golden red thickness now add the remainder of the quinces, pared, cored, and cut into neat sections. Set the pan back to simmer gently and steadily, till the whole quinces are almost soft, and the pulp pretty thick (stir well, or it will burn). Now add sugar, 3 lb. to a quart of the pulp. When the sugar has dissolved, boil fast till it sets when tried. It should be very firm, and a dark bright-red colour. Slices cut from it make good garnishes for plain white "creams" or it can be melted and used as a sauce over blancmanges.

Quince Mould

Cut up 3 lb. of quinces and simmer in enough water to cover till they are all pink mush, and leave overnight (as the seeds give out a lot of "jelly"). Next day, add just enough dissolved gelatine to ensure a firm "set", and, warming all together, rub the pulp through a sieve, sweeten to taste and, just before setting, stir in a cupful of firmly whipped cream. Chill and turn out. This is a beautiful and unusual rose-pink cream.

Quince Custards (1742)

" Take quinces and scald them till they are soft; pare them and mash and pulp through a sieve. Take an equal weight of quince and double refined sugar and the whites of eggs and beat it till it is as white as snow, then put it in your dishes, and pour custard around."

Quince Roast (1700)

" Quinces roasted over hot ashes—scraped out of their skins and mixed with cream and a little sugar and ginger make a dish for children."

[1]Rather resembles guava jelly.

Quinces in Paaste (quince pie, fourteenth century)

"Make amends coffyrs of paaste and take quynces and pare and take out the core and take sugar ynough (or ellse take hony in stede if thou maest more sugar) and if thou takest honey put thereto poudre, pepor and ginger and fill the quynces and bake them ynugh."

"Coffyrs of paaste", were small tartlet cases, and the quinces had to be cooked, with sugar or honey, before filling the cases and baking.

Quince Comfits (1700)

Stew the quinces (cut up but *not* cored, as the quince seeds have much mucilage), rub through the sieve, and put the thick pulp with an equal quantity of sugar into a thick pan and stir it over a gentle heat till it "dries up", leaving the sides of the pan clean. Roll it out half an inch thick, stamp into rounds, and go on turning them and drying till stiff as candied fruit leather. The pices are then dusted with powdered sugar and stored in tins. The same recipe can be used with dried apricots.

This resembles the peach meibos made by the Dutch at the Cape of Good Hope, and was probably learnt from the Low Countries. (*See* Wafers, for Dutch influence.)

MELONS

Small good melons may be grown well in an ordinary garden with a frame to start them. They became popular in England in the seventeenth century.

> " Every gardner nowadays knows how to raise melons, but few to govern them; when you would gather a *ripe* melon, you will notice its turning a little yellow, for that time it does ordinarily ripen . . . the gardner must therefore not fail of visiting the Melonière at the least three times a day, for this critical time. After twenty-four hours' keeping; for Contrary to the Vulgar Opinion, it should be preserved in some sweet dry place and *not* eaten immediately it comes from the garden. A perfect Transcendent Melon will be Full, Juicy, and without vacuity. . . ."
>
> 1699.

Melon Salad

A good melon, sunripe, reddish by the seeds, and spilling gold juice, needs nothing but a dust of sugar. A large melon makes a good fruit salad bowl. Cut off the top, lidwise, and skim just enough off the wider end to make it stand firm. Scoop out the seeds (and set them to drain off for the juice), with a sharp silver spoon scrape out the melon meat down to the thin inner rind, and slice, season with sugar, lemon juice (one lemon to a large melon), a shred mint leaf, and either white-pipped grapes, or thinly sliced ripe pears, or some other soft, lightly flavoured fruit. A few small wild strawberries, or halved greengages, may be added as garnish and variety, but do not use strongly flavoured fruits, as they will swamp the delicate melon flavour.

Pour over the juice drained off the seeds, sweetened with honey. This salad should be characteristically soft and honey-coloured and should not be frozen, but rather sun warmed, before serving direct from the melon bowl.

Melon Mangoes (1700 (?))

Mangoes were evidently "news" after their discovery. Here is a contemporary effort to copy them. "Take small melons and cut a snip out of them and take out the inside, beat mustard seeds and shred garlick, and mix and put *into* the melons, and put the pieces you cut back in their places and tie them on, and put in your pot and boil in some vinegar [as much as will cover] with whole pepper, and salt, and jamaica pepper, and pour it scalding hot over, and cover them close, and do this nine times for a week and when they are cold cover with a bladder." (*See also* Marrows.)

APRICOTS

Apricot Stuffing for Hams

This is erroneously considered an American innovation; it is certainly Cape Dutch, but we think it originated in Oxfordshire contemporarily with the growing of Moor Park apricots, which hang so golden against the Cotswold stone walls. The rather hard "thinning apricots" are to be preferred for this stuffing (though it may be made very well with dried apricots).

Fruit-stuffed hams were baked wrapped in crust in the brick bake-ovens, and made only for special occasions, such as the Wool Fair, as they did not keep "in cut" like ordinary bone hams. The apricots are roughly chopped to get the stones out, and put with an equal quantity of fine white breadcrumbs and a little salt and pepper into a pot with just enough water to prevent them burning until the juice runs (there should be just enough juice to soak the crumbs). If the apricots are juicy enough, there is no need to pre-cook the stuffing at all, and it can, with advantage, be packed in raw. (The point is that you want the apricot juice to soak the crumbs before they are rendered waterproof by the melting lard in the ham.)

Press the stuffing into the hambone hole, wrap the ham in its paste cover, and bake, letting it grow cold before cracking off the crust (*see*

Ham *wrapped in Paste for Baking*

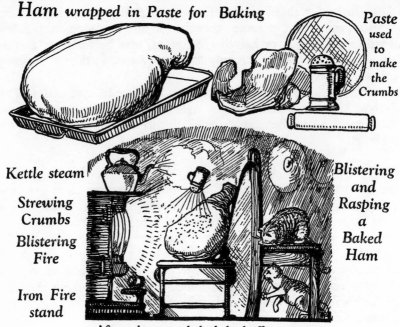

Paste used to make the Crumbs

Kettle steam

Strewing Crumbs

Blistering Fire

Iron Fire stand

Blistering and Rasping a Baked Ham

After a ham was baked the huff crust was
used for the crumb-rasping

diagram). As a refinement, the apricot kernels are cracked and splintered over the sugar-glazed ham in place of blistering.

This is probably a Cotes Wold recipe, as the Moor Park apricots would be thinned about the time of sheep-shearing suppers, for which the hams would be cooked.

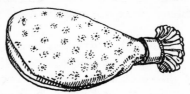

A glazed ham studded with cloves, and cooked with apricots

BLACKBERRIES

" The running blackberry would adorn the parlors of heaven."

W. WHITMAN.

Blackberry Pie

Use a deep earthenware piedish and pack it full, sprinkling sugar between the layers. Fill up (there should be very little room if well packed down) with the very moist pulp of cooked apples.

Wild Blackberry Bramble
(October)

3. 4. Late
        no use

3. 3. Second
        small firm
3.   Good for
        jam
2.   (See Note in text)

1.

First Large juicy Eat
                    raw

Tea
Tips.

In September the lowest berry of each cluster swells and ripens alone. These are the largest and sweetest and best fruit; they should be eaten raw, being soft and full of juice.

Late in September the secondary berries ripen; these are less juicy but good for pies and puddings and jam-making.

In October the last blackberries are smaller and there is more seed in proportion to pulp, so mix with apples when cooking.

Blackberry Pudding

Because it is a mistake to overcook blackberries, the pudding should be given the thinnest possible crust, and apple pulp used for filling the interstices between the tight-packed berries. A knob of butter inside is a great improvement. Late in the season it is good to add a pinch of spice.

Blackberry Cordial

Take new cider straight from the press and equal parts of blackberry juice. Strain both together and mix with as much honey as will float an egg. Boil gently 15 minutes in an earthenware pot. When cool, barrel it, but do not fill the barrel. In March bottle it; it will be fit for use six weeks after bottling.

Blackberry Junket (very delicate)

This is a very old recipe, and if you have any people in your household who cannot eat the seeds, make this. Take a square of coarse strong cheese cloth, and pile it full of the ripest blackberries you can find. Knot the four corners, slip a stick under them and twist, over a china bowl, pressing the bag with a wooden spoon, till you have a bowl full of rich thick blackberry. Don't add anything to it; it should set solid in about 2 hours if left undisturbed in a warm room. It will be of the consistency of junket, and is delicious served from the bowl with thin rolled brown bread and butter, or sponge fingers (and, of course, Devonshire cream if possible). I have never met an old lady or gentleman who did not appreciate this dish made specially for them.

Blackberry Salad

Gather the first large ripe blackberries, very ripe. Stand them in a glass bowl in the hot sun (or in a greenhouse) till hot through, then crush lightly with rough sugar and serve with a little red wine poured over.

Blackberry Fool

Bake the blackberries in a covered jar till the juice runs. Rub through a sieve and when cold mix the resultant pulp with an equal quantity of whipped cream. Serve whipped high in pale lavender-coloured whirls, in glasses. When cream is not available, use an equal quantity of fine cornflour cream (rather thinner than for a blancmange, but slightly thicker than custard).

Blackberry Wine (1700)

Take your berries full ripe, and fill a large wood or stone vessel with a spicket in it, and pour on as much boiling water as will just appear at the top of the vessel, and as soon as cool enough to bear your hand, reach in and bruise well (as if you were breaking curd) till all the berries be broke. Then let it stand covered till the berries be well wrought to the top, usually three or four days. Then draw off the juice through the spicket into another vessel, wash out the cask and replace the spicket, and pour back the juice, adding to every 10 quarts 1 lb. of sugar. Let it stand and work (with yeast floating on a slice of toast) for a week, then again draw off and clear it with 4 oz. of isinglass (which has been steeped 12 hours in a pint of good white wine, and next morning melted over a slow fire and added to the blackberry juice). Stir the isinglass till it mixes well, strain into a barrel, bung it up and bottle late next spring.

Blackberries, Other Uses

Blackberries used to be collected by the country people and sold for dyes; navy blue and indigo were originally blackberry juice. It was also used to dye black woollen stockings, and re-dip black silk that had become green (mixed with ivy leaves it gave a heavy black). The seventeenth and eighteenth centuries speak of the maids wearing "pale lavender ribbons". These lavender ribbons took their delicate tint from the same laundry sleight. The tips of the growing leaves were dried and rubbed down to make "black tea". The trade in old tea leaves (when real tea was 18s. a lb.) was made by adding these old leaves, re-dried, to blackberry leaves. Blackberry and honey is still used for sore throats, and hot blackberry juice and honey for a chest cold.

Blackberries were put into buns instead of currants during the hungry times of the Industrial Revolution; poor people cooked parsnips and beetroot with their blackberries to sweeten them.

Cloudberries

" Mwyar Berwyn—or cloudberries are considered by the natives
as anti scorentie and held in high esteem for tarts."
                                                    EVANS, 1798.

They are the blue-black berries, on rough, vivid green short stalks, that one finds when gathering bilberries on the Berwyn mountains (and elsewhere). They are nowadays usually gathered in with the true bilberries, which they so much resemble.

BILBERRIES

Other names are wortleberry, hurtleberry, "hurts", blaeberry. Bilberries take a long time to pick and on some moors there are bilberry "rights" and large parties of gypsies or villagers go "up on the mountain" for a day,

Bilberry flowers

arranging to be met by some farm lorry to bring home the baskets in the evening.

The berries are damson blue, with a fragile peachlike bloom, the colour of a mountain mist. Hand-picked ones are piled into bowls and eaten with cream and sugar, but some pickers "scrabble" them out with a rake, and these are full of fine leaves and chips. To wash them, turn the berries into a deep jar and swish the water lightly from above. Leaves and twigs will float up, and can be skimmed off.

Bilberry Tarts

Are the best on earth! For tarts (as the berries "go down" so much, being so juicy), it is permissible to put the white fluff of roast apples into the dish, under the bilberries, to sop up the juice and give the tart a little more substance.

In Lancashire, where they make "fruit between two skins" they sometimes put a mint leaf here and there on top of the bilberry layer.

GOOSEBERRIES

" . . . Chrystal gooseberries.
   Are piled on heaps, in vain the parent tree
   Defends her luscious fruit with pointed spears! "
                                             HOBBINAL.

The great gooseberries, yellow and red, are dessert fruit, let them lie in the hottest sunshine till warm through before serving—it brings out the sweetness and flavour.

Gooseberry Tart

Should not be made too soon, the smallest green berries have not developed full flavour and are very sour.

The raised crust should be made like pork-pie crust, but lightly sweetened (instead of salt and pepper seasonings)

Gooseberry Raised Pie

Nottinghamshire used to make a pie, raised like a pork-pie crust, but filled with green gooseberries, and after baking, melted apple jelly was poured in through a slit in the lid, the pie was served cold always, as it cut like a pork pie, solid, with firm-set jelly between the green gooseberry centre and the white firm crust.

Gooseberry Fool

This old English sweet was made with whipped cream, but nowadays we compromise on custard. Put the green gooseberries into a jar and bake (covered closely) till soft pulp; while still hot, stir in a spoonful of butter and enough sugar to sweeten; and let cool (you may rub through a sieve, but this is not necessary unless the skins are tough). When cold, fold into an equal quantity of cold whipped cream, or cold stiff custard. It is important that the gooseberry pulp and the cream be exactly the same consistency so that they combine as a soft green cloud.

Gooseberry Tansy (about 1700)

Cook a quart of gooseberries with some butter in a covered jar till quite soft, beat 4 eggs and fill them with a double handful of fine white breadcrumbs and a cupful of sugar. Blend this into a gooseberry pulp over a slow heat, stirring gently till the mass is cooked firm (on no account let it get too hot or the custard will curdle).

Turn out onto a hot dish, sprinkle with crushed sugar, and serve with hot cider or melted apple jelly.

It is a little tricky to make a really good tansy, the nicety of skill being to use only just as much breadcrumb and egg as will take up the buttery liquid from the cooked fruit, and make the same "bind". It may be found necessary to add another piece of butter if the fruit is very dry, or more crumbs if it is late soft fruit. The completed dish should be the consistency of a "solid omelette". Raspberries make a good tansy, so do mulberries and loganberries. Strawberries are delicious, and should be laced with a little white wine before serving. Apple is good served with blackberry syrup.

MULBERRIES (*Morus nigra*)

> " Glasses they'll blow you crystal clear
> where just a faint cloud of rose shall appear
> As if in pure water you dropped and let die
> A bruised black-blooded Mulberry."
>
> BROWNING.

The mulberry has an interesting history involved with the silk trade.

Quantities were planted to feed the silkworms, and thus mulberry trees in England often denote an earlier "silk" settlement. The number around London are specially noteworthy.

When ripe, the fruit falls, so it is best gathered from the ground (for which reason all mulberry trees should be grown on a grass plot). If you have a tree unfortunately placed where grass is impossible, spread clean hay, straw, or even sheets of paper below the tree during the season.

Use the fruit in every recipe given for raspberries or loganberries. Mulberry pie, cold, with junket, is excellent. Like raspberries, mulberries are not successful in a boiled pudding, unless mixed with apple, to give substance.

Mulberries can be served piled in pyramid form on a deep dish, strewn with sugar, and lightly baked in a hot oven, just long enough to burst them, and make the juice run. On a chilly autumn day serve hot with a hot milk pudding. The expressed juice also mulls well in wine.

A word of warning: mulberry juice stains very badly, so beware of white linen.

STRAWBERRIES

> " Rawe crayme undecocted, eaten with strawberys or hurtes is a rurall mannes banket.
> " I have knowne such bankettes hath put men in jeopardy of they lyves."
>
> BOORDE.

Real Strawberries and Cream

Take a deep cold bowl half full of cream (an old punch-bowl is excellent for this purpose). Whip the cream slightly, but do not make it too stiff.

Then drop into it as many strawberries as it will hold, the smaller ones being put in whole, the larger cut up. Stir as you go, mashing slightly, and when the cream really won't cover another strawberry, leave it to stand for an hour. It will then be a cold level pale-pink cream. Crust it over with dredged white sugar and serve forth, in June, on a green lawn, under shady trees by the river.

Serve cream with fruit fillings in sponge cakes

RASPBERRIES

" Wife, into thy garden, and set me a plot,
With strawberry roots, of the best to be got:
Such growing abroad, among thorns in the wood,
Well chosen and picked, prove excellent good.

The barberry, raspberry and gooseberry too,
Look now to be planted, as other things do:
The gooseberry, raspberry and roses all three,
With strawberries under them, trimly agree."

TUSSER.

The wild raspberry still grows in parts of England. It was a pilgrim plant, and the homesick English, plodding along to the crusades to Jerusalem, write that the way is "very hard and stoney and maketh pilgrims very boney" but "Raspberries grow by the way, with pleasure you may assay". The small wild raspberries have a special flavour, and a few canes brought in and cultivated soon make larger fruit and are very healthy stock.

Raspberry Jam

Put the berries and an equal weight of sugar together, on a dish, in the sun till hot, then tilt into a pan, bring to the boil, and cook rapidly 3 minutes; pot while hot and close down.

Raspberry Jelly (1600 dish garnish)

Wring out a strong linen bag in boiling water and fill with bruised berries. Hang it in a hot oven or before the fire till the juice runs, and then press (in the cider press). To each 4 lb. of juice add 5 lb. of hot crushed sugar and boil 5 minutes (it should set when cold). Pour into straight gallipots, so that the red jelly may be turned out and cut into thin slices, with which to garnish your white creams at Christmas time.

Thin round slices of this jelly, laid at the bottom of round cups, and filled in with cool ivory creams, turned out in clusters on a silver dish, and garnished with green angelica leaves, were characteristic "pretty" side dishes till the eighteenth century.

Raspberry Cream (about 1700)

Of old, "creams" were in most cases a basis of plain whipped cream, sometimes enlightened with white of egg, and sometimes enriched with yolks before being flavoured and sweetened. Do not altogether disregard cream recipes nowadays, as often the dish can be prepared with a custard cream, or a light blancmange base. They will not be such good "creams", but they will serve our present purpose.

> "When you have whipt your cream, sweeten it, *and take two ladlefulls*, [only] and bruise the raspberries into it, and season with rosewater, and again whip it well, *and then put it to your* [*main*] *cream*, and, stiring all together, dish it up."
>
> 1700 MS.

This is the best method, as it flattens your cream much less than if you bruise the raspberries into the whole whipping at once. Also, the colour is better, giving a clearer "apple-blossom effect". The rosewater makes it delicious.

DAMSONS

The small hard damsons from the grey twisted trees in old gardens are best. The new rounded damsons, and "plum damsons" may be larger fruit, but they are not so firm and spicy as the old-fashioned, small, oval damson with the black, bloomy skin and green flesh.

Damson Cheese

Damson cheese is one of the oldest country recipes. The cheese, if properly made, is almost black, cutting a deep purple, and should keep for years.

Set the damsons in a stone jar and put them "in the bread oven when the loaves are drawn", (or in the modern oven, cook slowly, till the juice runs freely, and the stones are loose). Then stir the fruit well and rub it through a sieve. Crack the stones, take out the kernels, and add them to the pulp. This is important, as they give their strong almond flavour to the juice.

Put the pulp back on the fire, adding for 1 lb. of pulp, 1 lb. of sugar which has been allowed to get hot in the oven while the damsons were having their final baking. Boil well till it jellies and then put the cheese in straight-sided jars, covering closely. Put brandied paper over the top before closing it down.

It should not be used for six months, and improves up to two years. It is at its best when it has shrunk a little from the sides of the jar and the top is just beginning to crust with sugar. Then it can be turned out onto a plate, stuck with split almonds, and served, with port wine poured over it, as a dessert.

The cheeses were sometimes poured out onto deep old dinner plates and after some days in a dry store cupboard, were turned out and stacked one atop the other with spice and bay leaves between, and the whole pile covered over from dust and kept in the warm dry cupboard till shrunk and crusty with candied sugar. Such an old damson cheese was a foot high, a foot across, and quite hard (*see* p. 16).

A well-risen boiled fruit pudding takes a lot of beating

Damson Pie and Pudding

Be sure to cook damson pie in a very deep piedish, as it requires much juice. For damson pudding, make the crust thin, and use plenty of damsons.

Baked Damsons

For "baked damsons", pack them into an earthenware dish, cover with sugar, and fill to the level of the damsons with water. Cover closely and bake till the fruit is soft. Leave it covered-close till cold to preserve the aroma.

BULLACES

Bolas, or (modern) bullaces, are as old as damsons; they are a rounder shape, and have not the same rich syrup as real damsons.

For damson cheese, or damson wine, or bottled damsons, it is very essential to be sure you get the long-shaped, narrow-stoned damson.

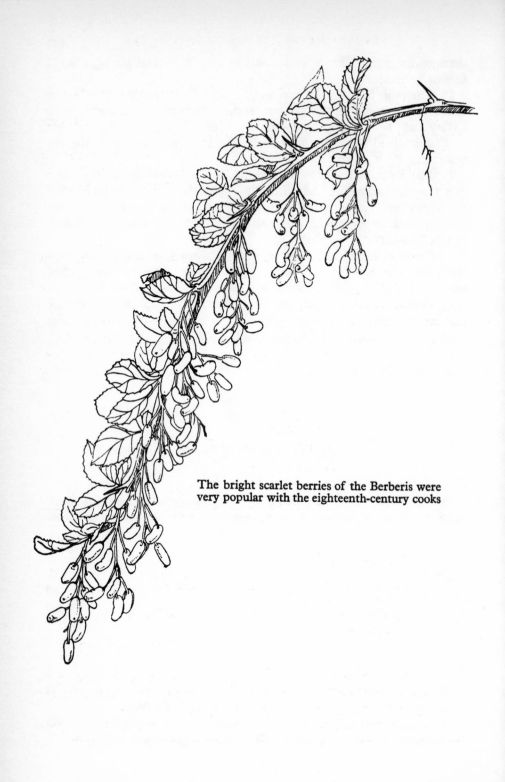

The bright scarlet berries of the Berberis were
very popular with the eighteenth-century cooks

BARBERRIES

These are made into a red jelly for eating with mutton. This was the scarlet jelly poured on top of the little mutton pies.

The tree on which the barberry clusters grow is sharply stuck with thorns so they are most easily picked with scissors, direct into a jar.

Set the barberries in the jar on a hot stove till the juice runs; strain off the juice, and for 1 pint of juice add 1 lb. of sugar. Boil rapidly until it jellies, and tie down in small pots. It is slightly more tart than red-currant jelly, and a beautiful amber red.

Barberries, Candied

Barberries were candied for decoration on sweet dishes. Sugar was boiled to syrup point, and the bunches were dipped carefully into the sugar, and left there several hours. They were then lifted out, the sugar reboiled to candy point, and the berries put back and left to candy.

For ordinary meat dishes the berries were simply pickled in strong brine with a lump of alum in it (to preserve the colour) and lifted out, rinsed, dried before the fire, and used at once. The bright red colour is very decorative, and the tart taste goes well with winter dishes when fruit is lacking.

Medlars

MEDLARS (*Mespilus germanica*)

> " Medlars are a native English fruit which grow wild in the
>   hedges about Minishall in Cheshire.
> " They are kept in moist bran for a fortnight before being rotten
>   enough to eat."
>
> *Child's Guide*, 1850.

A central-European tree, long native to England, and found wild, especially in the south and west. The fruit is shaped like a large rounded rose hip and is the colour of unripe russet apples and hard as bricks.

They should be gathered and kept some weeks until they have gone soft ("bletted" is the old term). Some people like them thus for dessert, or the brown squash within the rough skin is scraped out and mixed with cream and brown sugar.

Or arrange the medlars on a shallow dish with butter and cloves, and bake them a few minutes; serve like roasted apples.

CRANBERRIES

> " Cranberries are grown in the fens, but Longtown in Cumber-
> land grows the most richly flavoured."
>
> *Child's Guide*, 1850.

Curiously, this very specialised wild berry is little known in England outside its few natural growing places. In fact, it is one of the plants whose goodness has been preserved by the English in America, and brought back to us as something new. It is indispensable for turkey sauce, cooked till soft and well sweetened.

WHITE CURRANTS

A Delicate White-Currant Preserve

> " Boil together for seven minutes, an equal weight of white
> currants, picked with the greatest nicety, and finest white pre-
> serving sugar. Stir the preserve gently the whole time, boil
> rapidly, skim thoroughly, and just before taking off the fire,
> strain in the clear juice of one lemon to each four pounds of
> fruit."
>
> ELIZABETH ACTON, 1840.

ROWAN BERRIES

> " Rown Berries are not botanically berries, but pomes, being
> like tiny dry apples clustered together."

Rowan Jelly

This is made from the scarlet fruit of the mountain ash or rowan tree. The soft, creamy, fluffy blossoms are very sweetly scented. The berries are rather dry, so that it is a good thing to put a few of the mountain crab apples with them to help the juice. Set the berries and cut up "crabs" into a large pan, with water to prevent burning. Then cover the pan closely, cooking till the fruit is soft; press it through a bag to extract the juice, measuring 1 pint of juice to 1 lb. of sugar, and boil till it jellies. It is a beautiful dark red with a faintly smoky aroma, and should be served with mountain mutton, game, etc., just as you would serve red-currant jelly with valley meat.

(Witches were powerless to work harm against anyone sheltered under the rowan tree.)

Hawthorn
The haws are very dry fruit (and to my mind are better left for the birds in winter)

HAWTHORN

Hawthorn Buds

The leaf buds are called by the children "bread and cheese"—in Welsh, "Barra cause". Pick and use as "salading", between bread and butter. The small tight green buds before they open, can also be used to enliven the potato and beetroot salads of winter. Take about 1 teacupful of the buds, to 4 teacupfuls of the prepared potato salad.

Hawthorn Buds and a Spring Dinner

This was taught to me years ago, in Wymeswold in Leicestershire, by an old woman who could not read or write. She had brought up five children in a little thatched cottage on her husband's wages as a farm labourer (then about 12s. a week). They had their milk free, and meal, and a little pig, which was their bacon for the year, and winter lard supply: they also kept hens, free upon the stubble, and "gleanings" for the winter porridge.

This "spring dinner" had been her childhood event every year; and her children had it for their children, so "that was four generations".

Make a good light suet crust, season it well with salt and pepper, and roll it out rather more thinly than for a jam roly-poly, and as long in shape as possible. Cover the surface smoothly with the green buds, patting them

The hawthorn buds called "bread and cheese"

down lightly. Now take a rasher of bacon and cut it into very, *very* fine strips, and lay them over the green. Moisten the edges of the crust, and roll it up tightly, sealing the edges as you go. Tie it in a floured cloth and boil or steam it for at least an hour, longer if very large. Unroll it on to a hot plate and serve it with gravy. Like all very simple dishes, it must be made very nicely, seasoned with care, and the crust fine and light, then I think you will be surprised how good it is.

Hawthorn-Flower Liqueur

The strong almond-scented may blossom makes a good liqueur. Gather the flowers when in full scent, using scissors, and taking the flower heads only, not the tiny stems. Pack them into a bottle with a wide mouth, shaking them down loosely, but do not bruise them or ram them in hard. Shake a very little crushed sugar candy over the flowers (2 tablespoonfuls to a pint bottle would be ample). Fill up with brandy, and cork tightly. Put the bottle into full sunshine till warmed through, then store in a dark, warm cupboard, and shake it up and down gently, several times, during the first few weeks (so that the candy is evenly dissolved and distributed) After that, let it stand unmoved for at least three months. Decant very gently into a small flask and cork securely, sealing closely.

Hawthorn Fruit

The ripe red haws make jelly. Wash them, and for every 1 lb. of fruit add $\frac{1}{2}$ pint of water (rather more if the season has been dry); simmer very gently, mashing them down often. If you have any windfall apples, or red apple parings, they may be added with advantage, but not enough to swamp the flavour of the haws, only to help out the juice, as they are rather a dry fruit. When all is soft, put into a jelly bag and hang up to drip overnight. Measure the juice, and add 1 lb. of preserving sugar to every pint of juice. Put into a preserving pan over gentle heat till the sugar is melted, then boil rapidly till the jelly sets. Put into pots and tie down: is specially good with cream cheese.

SLOES

" Seeth water, and plump therein plenty of sloes,
Mix chalk that is dried, in powder with those;
Which so, if ye give, with the water and chalk,[1]
thou makest the lax fro thy cow away walk."

TUSSER.

[1] Alabaster was even better than chalk, the noses of many carved effigies may have been powdered for cows, and babies (today we give milk of magnesia).

Sloes used to be standard medicine for cow flux, and to suck a sloe cured "mouth hills" (gumboils?). The astringent wrinkling the mouth may have had some effect on the trouble; and the mechanical action of sucking probably had something to do with it.

In some years the dark purple sloes are almost as large as damsons. The dusty black bark of the tree was the basis of a mediaeval ink.

Sloe Gin

" Many sloes—many cold toes."
PROVERB.

Sloes are best preserved in gin. *After the first frost* (which bursts the texture slightly, making it more easily penetrated) gather the sloes direct into the sloe-jar, and fill the interstices with gin. Cork securely, and set away in a warm, dark cupboard. By Christmas-time it may be poured off and used, but may stand longer with advantage.

Sloe gin is a recent adoption into modern cocktails. Previously, blended with penny royal and valerian, it had long been used by old-fashioned country wives in connubial emergencies—hence the nickname "Mother's Ruin".

PEACHES

Peaches were grown in the Victorian hothouses, trained against the walls. For dessert, they were sometimes made into a salad. A thick glass bowl was rinsed round with a little brandy, the fruit sliced into it, and barely covered with champagne and crushed white sugar candy. It was made at the sideboard, and served instantly.

MIXED FRUITS

Baked Fruits, in a Cooked Salad

Strawberries, raspberries, cherries, white currants and later plums, blackberries, apples, apricots, pears, and other fruit, alone or blended, may be cooked thus. Boil sugar and water to a strong syrup, with a pod of vanilla or a stick of cinnamon (according to the fruit used), and placing the fruit in a hot earthenware dish, pour the boiling syrup over and *then keep it hot till the fruit is cooked.* The fruit should never boil, or be broken, but kept lying in the scalding hot syrup till quite soft. If some fruits cook more quickly than others, then should be put in later. Very soft fruit, such as strawberries, may be slipped in just before the dish is removed from the stove. It can be served hot with baked custard or chilled with boiled custard. It is a great improvement on boiled or stewed fruit.

Sea Holly

EYRINGO ROOT (Eryngium maritmus sea holly)

This is often mentioned in old recipes, the blue-grey, thistle-looking plant, with spiky leaves, common on level places above the tide-line. Markham (1616) writes that "It Groweth in untilled rough and drie ground ", and a contemporary survey of Devon mentions it as that plant "Whos rootes are called eringo". It was a staple product, harvested and sent inland from several places. Old records of Colchester note that the town is famous for "oysters and eringo root".

Unfortunately, it is one of the plants that have suffered much from holiday-makers, who carry it home to dry in vases for winter decoration and acres of it have been buried under the cement promenades of seaside watering places. As it will grow in "rough untilled ground" it would make a sensible crop behind many seaside bungalows.

Lift the roots, either in spring, when ready to burst up, or after seeding (which is best depending on the locality), and prepare by washing and parboiling. Then slice thickly and candy like angelica. When candied, it is golden brown. The woody portions used to be dried for flavouring, like cinnamon sticks.

Eyringo Conserve (a very old recipe)

"Take Eringo roots (Sea Holly), fair and not knotty—1 lb. and wash them clean, and boil them very tender—pull off their outermost skin, but see you break not. Put into cold water and let remain till all be finished and to every 1 lb. of roots ¾ lb. of sugar, and boil to height of a sirrup and cook your roots—(but very gently lest they break) until they be enough, and when cold, put up and keep[1] them".

Eyringo jelly[2]

1 oz. each of sago, hartstrom shavings, eyringo root, and pearl barley; put into a pan with 2 quarts water, and boil till reduced to 1 quart.

Strain and let it set—it should be stiff.

Slices of it should be put into invalid drinks—or it may be flavoured and sweetened and eaten as a jelly (see Sago).

Eyringo Toffee

Boil some of the sliced root in a little water till well flavoured, and add this water to the sugar and butter with which you make the toffee: just as it is ready to set, drop the softened root chips into it. Excellent.

BORAGE

> "The sprigs of borage in wine are of known virtue to revive the hypochondriac and cheer the hard student."
>
> EVELYN, Acetaria.

Borage for Claret Cup (a Victorian Magazine)

"1 large teaspoonful of white sugar dissolved in boiling water, 1 glass of sherry, ½ glass of brandy, ½ glass of maraschino, a thin rind of lemon and a strip of cucumber rind, 1 large bottle of claret. Let all stand for an hour. Carry to the picnic, packed in ice, and laying a sprig of borage in the cup, add seltzer water when serving. The borage should not be allowed to remain in the cup, but it will impart an aroma that nothing else can. On this account the pretty blue flowers can be had of every gardener during the picnic season, and it is grown under glass all the year round for the express purpose of flavouring claret cup."

The bright clear blue flowers make a beautiful garnish for a salad, together with the scarlet nasturtium flowers. Only the petals of each should be used.

[1] Keep—an old word for "store".
[2] Sometimes called Gloucester jelly—as sea holly grew up the estuary.

ROSES

Rose Flowers

Rose petals make a pleasant jam. Damask roses have the most aroma. Cook, with as little water as possible, then measure 1 lb. of pulp to 1 lb. of sugar and finish as usual. If liked, half apple jelly and half rose pulp may be "set" together, but this mixture will not keep so long.

Rose Hips

It is rather interesting, in the light of the "modern" rose-hip syrup for babies, to know that hips were preserved—vitamin complete—in 1730.

"Gather the hips before they grow soft, slit them in halves and take out all the seed and white that is in them very clean; then put them in an earthen pan, and stir them every day . . . till they are soft enough to rub through a coarse hair sieve. As the pulp comes, take it off the sieve. They are a dry berry, and will require pains to rub it through, then add its weight in sugar and mix it well together *without boiling*, keeping it in deep gallipots for use."

These were also called "Shrouts" or "Rose Shrouts".

VIOLETS

A Very Old Violet Sweet (14th century)

"Take flourys of vyolet and boyle them, presse them, bray them smal, tempre them uppe wyth almaunds mylke or gode cowe mylke and byl yt wyth amonds flor and flore of rys. Sygre yt enow and putte cream thereto, color yt wyth the same that flouers be on aboue."

This is one of the many recipes that leads me to believe that "almond mylk" is not pure almond oil, but skinned and pounded almonds blended with milk or water. This old sweet is a delicate ground rice pudding enriched with ground almonds and thick cream, and garnished with fresh violets. I have made it also with damask rose petals, using a spot of rosewater, and sweet almonds, and candied rose petals on top.

Recipe (modern). To a tablespoonful of ground rice, allow a teaspoonful of ground almonds, and a few whole sweet almonds chopped lengthways; make with milk, rather softer than usual, and boil extra well, before sweetening and flavouring, with either violet flavour, or triple rosewater (the latter more easily obtained from a chemist). Pour into shallow glass bowls and chill, then cover with flavoured sweetened cream whipped stiffly and covered with crystallised violets, (or rose leaves, whichever you have used), strew with crushed sugar; a very pretty, delicate dish.

Violet Ice Cream

A delightful uncommon ice cream is made by filling whipped cream with as much fine *fresh* brown breadcrumbs as it will carry. Freeze lightly, beat in coarse crystallised sugar, or crushed sugar candy, and chill again. Finally cover lavishly with crystallised violets. The crumbs must be fine and fresh and brown, and the sugar as coarse as fine crushed ice; the texture is delicious.

COWSLIPS (*see* Cowslip Wine)

Candied Cowslips (1700)

"Gather the flowers, when the dew is off, and pluck off leaving none but the yellow blossoms and weigh 10 oz. of yellow pips. Take 8 oz. of sugar and put the sugar into a pan and candy it with as little spot of water as you can and take off the fire and shake in the flowers—little by little, never ceasing to stir till they be dry enough to put into glasses or gallypot. They are rather candied than conserved. A scabious flower done so cleans the heart and lungs."

ELDER FLOWERS

The aroma is so strong that a bunch of the flowers, drawn through any fine jam just before bottling, will scent it deliciously.

Elder Flower Wine

This is a pleasant light summer wine, very clear and sparkling. It had great popularity among country people about 1920. It is extremely simple to make:

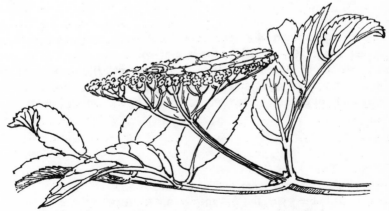

The flat cream blooms of elder, called "slices of bread"

Put several freshly gathered heads of elder flowers into a deep jar. Pour over them 1 gallon of cold spring water. 1¼ lbs. of sugar, 2 table-spoonfuls of white-wine vinegar and (if liked) the juice and rind of one lemon. Stir till the sugar is dissolved, cover and leave to stand in a cool place for 24 hours. Strain off and bottle. It may be drunk in two weeks' time, but improves up to six months. It foams deliciously.

Elder Flower Flavouring

A little of the above wine makes a delightful flavouring essence for junkets, cakes, or any light sweets. Also as a substitute for lemon juice in icing.

ELDERBERRIES

The fruit is ripe when it turns and hangs down in tassels.

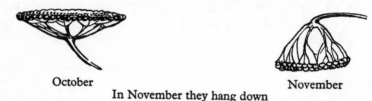

October   November

In November they hang down

Elderberry Sauce

Take 2 pints of berries, picked from the stalk, and bake them in a covered jar with ½ pint of vinegar. Next day strain the juice into an enamel pan with a good lid, add a shallot minced, a piece of root ginger bruised, a teaspoonful of cloves, and a few peppercorns. Boil up well, pour into a hot bottle, and cork securely.

Elderberry Rob

The extracted juice of elderberries baked to a syrup with sugar and spice and stored for hot drinks for winter colds.

Put a jar full of elderberries into a hot oven until the juice runs; strain off and to 1 pint of juice add ½ lb. of sugar and ¼ teaspoonful (or large broken stick) of ground cinnamon; cover and boil slowly till thick.

SQUILLS

Sirop of Squil

" . . . Garlande them, and so depende
Into the wyne, tho that they go not too depe.
And take hem oute at xx dayes ende.

The wyne is goode the cough away to kepe,
All ill oute of the wombe it maketh lepe,
It solveth flewme, and helpeth spenetye
Dygestion it maketh to been quyk."

PALLADIUS.

The large juicy bulb of the common blue and white squill was made into vinegar. It continues in use as a medicine today.

PEARS

Hard Windfall Pears

" Fruit gathered too timely will taste of the wood,
    will shrink and be bitter; and seldom prove good:
So fruit that is shaken, and beat off a tree,
    with bruising in falling, soon faulty will be."

TUSSER, 1477.

"Peris in Syrippe" (probably the twelfth-century original of the 1850 recipe)

"Take Wardons and pare hem and caste hem in a potte and boile hem til thei ben tendre. Cutt hem in two or three. Take poudered canell [cinnamon] and caste it in gode red wyne and sugar therto, and put in an earthern potte and lat boyle and caste the peris thereto and take pouder ginger and litul saffron to colour hit, and loke that it be poynante and also doucet [i.e., sharp with vinegar and sweet with sugar]." Spiced pears are mentioned in early American households.

Pears and Vine Leaves (16th century)

(An older version of this recipe gives "wine lees" in place of "Gode red wyne".)

"Lay a layer of vine leaves in an earthern pot, and over them peeled and halved pears, and then leaves and then pears again, till the pot be full, and putting some fine sliced gynger, and a few cloves between each layer. (Put not too many cloves, one to each dozen pears unless they be very large). Fill up the pot with as much [cider] as the pot will hold, and lay some dish or board upon the pears that they do not swim, and cover the pot closely, and stew it all night when the fire be low—or in the oven after the bread be drawn."

Let the pears grow cold in the pot; they will be soft, golden brown, and should be served cold with whipped cream, or custard and sugar.

Pears in Syrup (this recipe came from Cambridge about 1850)

Take the firm ones that will not ripen, pare them (and if large, cut in half). Lay them in an earthen pot, with ½ cup of vinegar, 1 pint of water, 1 lb. of sugar (or the wash from bee sections), 2 cloves, and a small piece of bruised ginger root; just bring to boiling point, and then the jar, covered, may be set to simmer till the pears become quite dark, and the juice rich and syrupy. They are done when they can be easily pierced with a silver fork. Strain the juice and pour it over the pears piled in a deep dish, and garnish with whipped cream.

BROOM

> " To make broome salve take a sheet full of broome crops, leaves, blossoms and all, and chop them very small, and then sethe them in a pann of 20 gallons of running water till it waxe thicke like a Jelly, then take 2 lbs. of sheep's suet molten and a pottle of olde pisse, and as much brine made with salt and put all in and stirre about and then straine . . . but the best grease that mey be given to sheepe is grease him in the mouth with goode meate."
>
> FITZHERBERT.

Broom Salve

As made for the fishermen of Whitby.

Take a crock of pure hog's lard and, when melted, fill it full of broom and gorse blossom, leave overnight—strain and press out the flowers and refill the lard with fresh blossoms till the salve becomes yellow.

Fish bone cuts and "sailors' sore hands" were well bathed with hot, boiled watercress water. Then the salve was used to heal them up. Copious draughts of green herb teas "for the blood" were firmly administered at the same treatment.

WORMWOOD AGAINST FLEAS

> " While wormwood hath seed, get a bundle or twain,
>   to save against March, to make flea to refrain:
> Where chamber is sweept, and wormwood is strown,
>   no flea, for his life, dare abide to be known."
>
> TUSSER.

MARIGOLDS

The common marigold with the pungent scent is a most useful cookery plant.

Marigold Cheese

Marigold cheese was made in August or September (*see* Cheeses). The heads of the flowers were bruised into a little cream or butter (to extract the essence) and the mass then stirred into enough scalding hot water to dissolve off the scented grease. This water was strained into the tub of milk and cream, and the whole curdled with rennet. For those who only make small milk cheese, it is not possible to do this with sour milk, as the acid change which has already taken place in the milk would prevent it taking up the flavour.

Marigold Salad

Take 4 cupfuls of cold, waxy, diced potatoes, 1 cupful of watercress leaves, and a very small bunch of chives; mix together with a cupful of good dressing and stir in 1 cupful of picked marigold petals, using a few loose on top in lieu of the usual yolk of egg.

ASHEN KEYS

Pick them while young and tender. Boil them till soft, throwing away the water if it tastes bitter at the first boiling. Drain the keys and cover with boiling, well-spiced vinegar poured on while the keys are also boiling hot.

LIME

Lime Leaves in Spring

While the shell-pink scale leaves still cling to the opened leaf buds, the new soft leaves of the lime tree make a most delicate sandwich filling. Gather with scissors, cutting off the stalks; rinse under running water. The leaves are too soft and lack the essential crispness for salad, but the flavour is delicious as sandwich spread. (1) White bread and butter, spread with lime leaves, sprinkled with lemon juice. (2) Brown bread and butter, cream cheese, and lime leaves. (3) White bread and butter, lime leaves shredded up and sprinkled with pepper and salt, and a moistening of cream.

Lime Blossom in Summer [1]

The blossoms, gathered in July and lightly dried, make a delicious, pale "China" tea, very fragrant and refreshing. A small handful of the dried blossom to a medium-sized pot, and infuse with boiling water.

[1] Also used to induce sweat in fevers.

COLTSFOOT

That deep rooting weed, whose yellow flowers are so pretty in spring, has later a wide grey-green leaf, springing from a whitish pink-tinged stalk. Both flowers and leaf have many uses. The flowers are used to make wine (use the dandelion recipe). The liquid extracted by chopping and boiling the leaves and stems is used with sugar to boil into coltsfoot candy for coughs (*see* Barley Sugar). The leaves themselves, dried, "pickled" with a little brandy, and shred finely, make a smoking mixture.

Coltsfoot Candy

Chop and bruise a pailful of coltsfoot leaves, and stew in 1 pint of water. Strain off the liquid, pressing the leaves well. Make a toffee of 1 lb. of sugar, 1 lb. of treacle, and a knob of butter, using the hot coltsfoot liquid to melt the sugar. Let the ingredients melt together, then boil rapidly till it "crisps" when tested in cold water. Lift off the fire, stir in ½ teaspoonful of bicarbonate of soda (it will foam up). Pour it out and whip it till almost stiff, then twist it into sticks.

Coltsfoot Syrup (MS. book of 1850)

"Wash the leaves and pound with sugar and cook gently and pour into a bag with a sprig of rosemary in it—and let it drain through—boil the juice till it thickens and it cureth old coughes."

Coltsfoot Tobacco

" Look you! that I have no smells about me, but such as a Christian ought to have, except it be the effluvia of tobacco, which is cephalic odoriferious aromatic herbe, and he is the son of a mountain goat who says otherwise."

SMOLLETT, *Roderick Random.*

Most old country men have their own ways of making "smoking mixtures". Coltsfoot leaves form the basis, but woodruff, comfrey leaves, and chestnut and beech leaves are sometimes added. The general method is to gather the coltsfoot leaves and dry (hanging down in bunches in an airy shed) till soft and yellowish; they are then packed down in a wooden box (or a small old brandy cask) ripping out the midrib of the leaves, and lacing with brandy. The drying is continued on the kitchen mantelpiece, and the completed job rolled up damp, so as to get an even texture; it is pressed under a weight, and can then be sliced or cut like a Navy roll.

Note. The coltsfoot leaves must not be gathered till *all* the flowers have disappeared.

NASTURTIUM SEEDS AS CAPERS

Gather and put them in cold water and salt for three days; then make a pickle of some white-wine vinegar, shallot, horse-radish, pepper, salt, cloves, mace and nutmeg quartered; put in your seeds and stop them close; they are cooked as capers.

RAPE

Rape seed used to be grown in England. Colza oil comes from rape.

LINSEED FOR CATTLE

> " Jelly from linseed is easily made by boiling good linseed in
> water and while in a hot state, pouring it into a vessel to cool,
> where it becomes a firm jelly, a proportion of which is taken at
> every meal or bruised down in a tubful of warm milk and distri-
> buted to the calves."
>
> STEVENS, *Book of the Farm.*

Linseed Cake

This is the direct result of the enterprise of these old farmers. The things they tried out for themselves, because of local shortages or need, were tested and found good, and became a commercial affair. In this case the packing material already at the port where the linseed came in was the dust from peat moss packing (*see* Peat). It was combined into the cow-cake, as dry fodder was easier to transport.

Linseed Meal

Makes an old-fashioned poultice, still valued for its comforting warmth, by country mothers who have to deal with emergencies and "get the patient relieved and able to sleep, till the doctor comes next day". Be sure to remove the poultice gently, and replace with warmed wool or covering of flannel.

Cough Mixture

1 stick of hard "spanish juice" to 1 piled tablespoonful of linseed. Boil the crushed stick in 2 pints of water till dissolved, add the linseed, and boil well. A jelly is formed when cold. Sweeten with a little honey. A spoonful or two is a harmless cough mixture for children.

DILL (a novel use)

Dill, to keep awake in church.

> " ' Haven't I eaten quantities of dill in the course of the summer, trying to keep myself awake. . . .'
> ' Cloves is better—but when we had good Dr. Dardenburgh he put us all to sleep. . . .' "
>
> SUSAN WARNER, novelist of 1850.

SAFFRON

> " The Saffron of England is the most excellent of all other. . . . A certain young gentleman called Crocus went to playe at coytes (quoits) in the field with Mercury, and Mercuries coite happened . . . to hit him on the heade . . . and ere long killed him, to the great discomfort of his friends . . . in the place where he bled Saffron was found to grow."
>
> HOLINSHED.

Saffron has a deep yellow stain, and pleasant honey aroma. In mediaeval cookery it is sometimes put in stews, and made dishes, where its flavour must have been entirely drawed, and only its colour wanted. It is characteristic that in the thirteenth century they prefer gravy from the pork bright yellow with green spots! whereas we serve a decorous "brown". Saffron was used to increase the golden colour of cakes, which had other flavours; and gradually saffron went through cordials and possets, till it becomes definitely medical (*see* Saffron in bread).

Spirit of Saffron for the Consumptive Cough (1700)

"Take four drams of the best saffron, open and pull asunder, and put in a quart bottle and pour on one pint of the ordinary spirit of wine" (that, says the economical housewife, "at twelve pence a quart" is quite good enough), half a pound of white sugar candy beaten small; stop it with a cork and set it in the sun and shake it twice a day till the candy is dissolved and the spirit a deep orange colour. Let it then stand to settle and clear it off into another bottle, and keep it for use. A small spoonful for a child or large for a man, is excellent for the consumptive cough."

MUSTARD

> " For scyatica, use a plaster of mustard." 1615.
> " Mustard seed is very apt to shed, and therefore must not stand until it is too ripe; it is best cut in a morning when the Dew is yet on it, when dry, house it with a Sheet carried between two, with a Pole on each side: When strip'd . . . beating it on a Hurdle, the seed will come out, the light seed will come after and must be well winnow'd off."
>
> MAVER.

Mustard

" Take the mustard seed, and grind one and a half pints of it with honey, and Spanish oil, and make it into a liquid sauce with vinegar."

" *Mustard*. Wash the seed till the husks be floated off, dry the sorted seed and stamp it fine and sieve it through a cloth to make mustard *flour*.

To make mustard for the pot, slice some horse-radish, and lay it to soak in vinegar, squeezing it well, and add a lump of sugar and an onion chopt. Use the vinegar from this mixture to mix the mustard."

ACETARIA, 1699.

(*See* recipe for Mustard Sauce with Brawn.)

MARJORAM

This herb was used to flavour milk and curd dishes in the excellent farmhouse cooking of the fifteenth and sixteenth centuries. These recipes, infiltrating into the aristocratic circles of the eighteenth century, are often over-elaborately misused. Thus we find a pudding of which the basis is curd, marjoram-flavoured, followed by the remark, "old-fashioned and not good". Marjoram does, however, flavour milk dishes very pleasantly.

Wild Marjoram (Origanum vulgae)

In the mountain villages so many small cottages have perished, and their gardens run wild, that the small wiry plant which gardeners now call "pot marjoram" seems to be wild. Tame or wild, it is certainly one of the most aromatic of our herbs, and of great use in dry cooking—such as stuffing for fowls, or forcemeat of any kind, where its permeating aroma is preserved. It is less successful in wet cooking such as soups or stews, as the aroma is fugitive.

BALM (or Lemon Balm, or Balm of Gilead)

" The tender leaves . . . and sprigs fresh gathered put into wine or other drinks, during the heat of summer give a marvellous quickness. This noble plant yields an incomparable wine, made as is that of cowslip flowers."

HERBAL, SEVENTEENTH CENTURY.

The plant, common enough in old-fashioned gardens, grows into a huge soft bush of lush green leaves. The flower is inconspicuous, but the lemon scent delicious. It was strewn over the wooden floors in summer apartments in the Middle Ages, and, when trodden, gave a sweet, refreshing perfume. It is best used fresh, as it does not dry well. It will replace lemon-juice in making forcemeats and stuffings. A few leaves are pleasant in a salad, and give aroma to summer drinks.

ANGELICA

Candied angelica is mentioned specially as a home-made product up to 1860, as "it can seldom be bought in market".

Angelica grows by most brooks in England. Cut the thickest stems while still young and crisp. Slice into lengths to fit your pan; about four inches is long enough, scrape to remove any coarse outer fibres, and then let it simmer in strong sugar syrup till tender. Drain till almost dry, and then strew crushed sugar over it and let it cook gently in this thickened syrup till clear and bright. Lift the hollow stems on to a tray, boil the syrup to sugar point again, and pour over the angelica, draining off, and reboiling, till the angelica can be dried off into stiff candied lengths. Store in a dry cupboard, with layers of grease paper between.

FENNEL

> " The Fennel, with its yellow flowers,
> In an earlier age than ours,
> Was gifted with the wondrous powers
> Lost vision to restore. . . .
> I pledge you in this cup of grief,
> Where floats the fennels bitter leaf,
> The battle of our life is brief."
>
> LONGFELLOW.

Its chief use is flavouring sauce for fish. The oldest recipe I can find is:
"Melt butter in skillet, chop fennel till mist, stir into butter when it boils, cook two minutes, and serve."

HOPS

> " Turkeys, heresies, hops and beer
> All came to England in one year."

Buttered Hop Tops

Gather the young shoots (not later than May), only about four leaves down, and lay to soak in cold water with a handful of salt. Drain, plunge into boiling water enough to cover easily, and boil rapidly till tender. Drain the water off instantly, and chop up in the hot pan with pepper, salt, and a lump of butter. Serve hot.

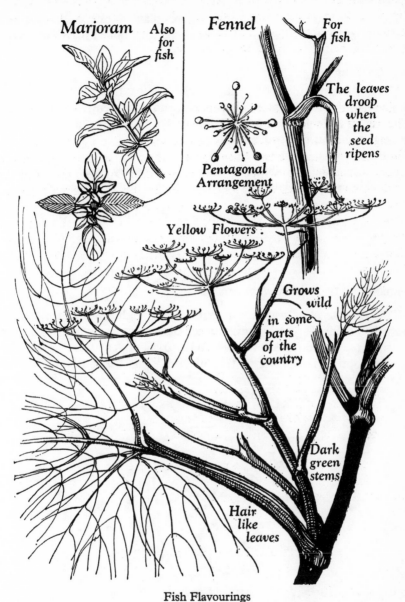

Marjoram Also for fish

Fennel For fish

The leaves droop when the seed ripens

Pentagonal Arrangement

Yellow Flowers

Grows wild in some parts of the country

Dark green stems

Hair like leaves

Fish Flavourings
Fennel grows wild along many estuaries where the salmon run.
Marjoram grows wild by hill streams.

Hop Sauce

Prepare as above, but chop into a good plain butter sauce, and serve with fish, chicken, or instead of caper sauce with boiled marsh mutton.

Hop-top Soup

Using the dried peas of winter, make a good thick peasoup. Take a double handful of hop tops; chop finely, and cook gently in the soup till soft; add a little scraped onion, some pepper and salt, and, just before serving, a cupful of good milk.

> "Artemisia Absinthium is used by the country people instead of hops . . . for destroying acescency in beer grown hard for want of them.
> The leaves steeped in boiling water, applied to a bruise removes pain."
>
> EVANS, 1798

MAIDENHAIR FERN (*Adiantum capillus*)

This delicate plant was very popular in the eighteenth and nineteenth centuries, being used to garnish sweet dishes, much as parsley is used to garnish savouries today. It was also the basis of "capillaire", which was a most popular flavouring in the 'nineties. The black ribs of the fern

Maidenhair Fern

make a mucilaginous syrup, with sugar, that has a distinct aromatic flavour. It was usually "improved" with orange-flower water, and (relics of the earlier ingredients) sometimes coloured with saffron. Quantities of this fern used to be imported from Ireland.

"*Capillaire*"

Stew 2 oz. of freshly gathered fern in gentle heat for several hours—strain and boil with sugar (proportion 1lb. to 1 pint of juice). When thick (it will turn to jelly), add a spoonful of orange-flower water and cork securely.

In the nineties capillaire was considered mildly tonic and very refreshing, and was the basis of many soft drinks. It was also added to barley water, and "Taken on rising". Magazines of the period state that it was "Often prefered to wine by Young Ladies". Here is one representative mixture.

Cherry water and Capillaire

Pound a dozen cherries so as to break the kernels and put into a large glass with crushed ice, add a wineglass of capillaire and fill up with iced water. Serve with light crisp biscuits.

PARSLEY

Parsley Honey

Large parsley that has gone to seed will do for this. Pack an enamel saucepan full of wet washed parsley, and just cover with water. Boil 30 minutes. Strain through a jelly bag. Measure, and for every pint of juice, use 1 lb. of sugar. Boil the sugar in the juice very rapidly till it begins to set, then cool and cover. Some cooks like to add the juice of a small lemon with the sugar. It is like thin honey.

COMFREY

" Cumphery roots, roasted in the hot embers."
                                        ACETARIA 1699.

(*Boneset, knit bene, consound, wound wort, Symphytum officiale*)

This large bushy weed (three feet high) has coarse green leaves and small white or purple flowers.

The whole plant is intensely interesting.

In Scotland, still called "boneset"—it has been used for centuries as a medium for setting broken bones—and as a plaster to prevent wounds warping in healing. It has never been taken from the *British Pharmacopoeia*.

The root lifted in March is found to contain a well of clear watery juice, and has a glutinous slimy texture. In this root, grated up, the broken limb was set, and the mash used as surgeons today use plaster. It had the advantage over plaster that it held within itself an agent for promoting growth, so that the slowly setting mash also acted as a healing poultice for compound fractures. Once set, the mash became as hard and firm as plastic wood, and remained so till it was sawn through at some prearranged "join" in the cast.

Recent research[1] gives the curative property of the plant as "allantoin" which "acting like a hormone, sets going proliferations of considerable magnitude". The country people say "it makes for growth". Therefore, as a substance that will hold a wound from shrinking or set a bone firmly in position (while inducing a rapid growth of new tissue) comfrey is still used with success.

Old herbalists praise the juice as healing for those "bursten within" and country people drink it in bleeding pleurisy, and for gastric ulcer. They also affirm that washings and applications of the fresh juice cause the living flesh to grow up rapidly from the bottom and sides and so push out the foul or dead flesh and fill in the gap in the wound. Like most plants, the chemical contents vary in position, during time of growth. The root should be lifted in early March, when it is full charged, waiting to burst into growth. Later in summer the leaf tops and flowers are full charged and the root almost empty.

Therefore in winter poultices of the soft mashed root pulp are used; in summer, dressings of the leaves.

Cumphray is one of the plants invariably found around mediaeval hostels, landing places, or fords, anywhere that horse travellers were likely to arrive with broken bones!

To make a comfrey dressing, lift, wash, and clean a root (large as a swede, but shaped like a hollow-crowned parsnip); grate the golden flesh on to gauze laid in a clean bowl (it has a soft, glutinous texture); lift the gauze, keeping in as much juice as possible, and use as a cooling, healing poultice.

Washes of the expressed juice are used to promote quick growth of skin over an abrasion, or hurry a broken nail.

In summer, an infusion of the leaves and flowers replaces the root juice (using hot, not boiling water).

ACORNS

> " Though good store of acorns the porkling do fat
> Not taken in season may perish of that,
> If pig do start rattling and choking in throat
> Thou loosest thy porkling—a pig to a groat! "

These have been used ground up to supplement bread flour in times of need, but as far back as records go in England, seem to have been used

[1] " *Symphytum officiale*, and its contained Allantoin ", by Charles J. Macalister M.D., F.R.C.P., gives the medical explanation of this plant's properties, corroborating the above findings.

Acorns

mostly for pig feed. Modern pigs are supposed to choke upon them, but the mediaeval pigs probably ate a lot of earth and pignuts, etc., at the same time. Acorns can be roasted to make a miserable coffee and are being tried out for hen feed—but only experimentally as yet.

HAZEL NUTS

These are the hedgerow nuts of England. Old books describe how the nutmeg nestles within its mace "as the hazel in its green case". They should not be gathered till so ripe that they begin to fall from their cases, and they should be stored *in* the cases, as it keeps them moist till wanted. Kentish cobs, in which the shells are longer and softer, are the best type of this nut.

Walnuts

WALNUTS

> " A woman, a steak and a walnut tree,
> The more you beat 'em, the better they be."

The custom has its adherents to this day, and anyone who has a walnut tree that does not bear might try it—early in March while the sap is rising. A bill-hook is the usual weapon to beat with, and the soft green bark of many old trees shows the marks of past treatment. The sweet-smelling walnut leaves are sometimes used to make a type of pot-pourri, with tonquin beans and spices; this has a warm pleasant smell like the colour of a Persian carpet.

Pickled Walnuts

The nuts are first picked, being taken while full grown, but quite green and still soft right through. The test is to run the *head* of a needle through them. At this state, they are put out for sale in country markets to make into pickles.

This is an eighteenth-century recipe (very like earlier ones).

"In July gather the nuts and let them lie in strong salt water for a week till black, then put them into a colander and pour hot water over and through them till the salt is washed off. Drain, and pack them into a jar, packing some cloves of garlic and a few cloves and whole peppers among them. Boil some vinegar with spice [nutmeg, jamaica pepper, and allspice] and pour it over the walnuts boiling hot. Let stand that night, drain off and boil up and do the same again next day. Then cover the jar closely and tie down." The old recipe gives for every 50 nuts 3 spoonfuls of mustard seed, but we find this too much; I ordinary tablespoonful of mixed pickling spice and 2 whole nutmegs, chopped up, is enough to spice vinegar for a hundred nuts or more. Other recipes insist on the nuts being pricked all over to let the pickle penetrate, but such pricking tends to break the skin and make the nuts ragged-looking.

Ripe Walnuts

They fall when ripe, and lie, like small white bones, very bright on their broken husks, and yellow leaves. Pick them up daily, before the thick-falling leaves cover them up. Never wash them. If the husks adhere to some, lay those aside (some trees seem to drop cleaner than others, and the weather also makes a difference). Keep the clean nuts separate from the husky ones, as the clean ones will always be whiter and fresher-looking for dessert. Put the husky ones into a long coarse sack and let two people take an end each and shake the nuts from end to end with a rolling movement, backwards and forwards. Throw them out on to clean grass, and you should be able to pick them up fairly clean. If not, leave till dry and do it again. Walnuts should be stored buried in salt or sand to keep them fresh.

ALMONDS

> " Almond butter made with fine sugar and rosewater and eaten with the flower of many violets is a commendable dyshe—specially in lent when Vyolets be fragrant."
>
> 1700 MS.

More common in England of old than now; they were grown for the nuts, which were popular in English cooking. Peach kernels are sold for almonds commercially; they are much more rounded in shape.

Note. The stones of all stoned fruit should be cracked and the kernels added to the jam when cooking. The exception is peach jam, or apricot jam when made of dried or preserved apricots; to this custom decrees that a few almonds take the place of the missing apricot kernels. If making this jam in any quantity, buy peach kernels rather than almonds.

Almond Milk (mediaeval)

In the old recipes of the fourteenth century (and earlier), much cooking is done with "milk of almonds". This is not (by context) almond oil, nor any liquid that would mean great quantities of the almond being used. (As one would say "cook in lemon juice" when one meant "cook with lemon in the water".) Orgeat (the French barley water) was flavoured with almonds, and from experiment I think a similar "syrup of almonds" is *probably* what the mediaeval cooks meant by milk of almonds.

One pound of sweet almonds and a few bitter ones among them. Pound them up, adding water up to 3 pints. Stir this into about a gallon of thick barley water, sweeten, and boil. This thick creamy almond fluid is, I believe, the early "almond milk". It can be used in milk puddings.

Chestnut Roaster

CHESTNUTS

Chestnut roasters can sometimes be bought in antique shops, or country markets. The nut bursts with a loud pop, and, if loose, flies off the hot hob, so these small boxes, full of airholes, are sensible fireside cookers for winter evenings. It was a fortune-telling trick to name the row of chestnuts set along the top bar of the hot gate, and the first "name" to pop was the first lover to pop the question. If he jumped into your lap, you had him; if he popped into the fire and was burnt up . . . well, you didn't.

COCONUTS ARRIVE

"The said cochos hath a hard shell and a green huske over it, as hath our walnut, but it farre exceedeth in greatnesse for this cochos in his green huske is bigger than any mans two fistes; of the hard shell many drinking cups are made here in England, and set in silver as I have often seene.

"Next within this hard shell is a white rine resembling in shewe very much even as any thing may do, to the white of an egge when it is hard boyled. And within this white of the nut lyeth a water, which is whitish and very cleere, to the quantitie of halfe a pynt or thereabouts, which water and white rine before spoken of, are both of a very coole fresh taste, and as pleasing as any thing may be. I have heard some hold opinion that it is very restorative."—SIR FRANCIS DRAKE.

Leaves of Sweet Gale

MYRICA GALE

(*See* Drinks, for Gale Beer.)
" Bog myrtile or Sweet Gale.
The poor inhabitants [Welsh] term it BWRLI or the emetic plant and use an infusion as tea. . . .
A decoction is used in the morlus fredicularis and in the common species of herbs.
[It is astringent and brews a tannin.]
The plant also furnishes a yellow dye for woollen cloth which, by its powerful odour, is fatal to moth and discourages bugs.
Linnaeus suggests that camphor might be procured from it.
The cones, boiled in water, yield a scum, similar to beeswax—capable of being made into candles [like those made in America from another species, Myrica cerifera]."
Tour of Wales, 1798.

SUNFLOWER

" 30 to 40 bushels of seed to the acre is a fair crop, and should yield 40 to 50 galls. of oil."
LAWSON.

The sunflower cultivated in our flower gardens has been cultivated for food by a few special communities, usually of French extraction. The oil extracted from the seeds is used in cooking, and the roast seeds, ground, blended with coffee. The same French communities used the stripped leaves as cow fodder, and the dried stems as oven fuel. In our gardens, the giant sunflower (Helianthus annuns) was often grown as a wind-break with Jerusalem artichokes (they did not improve the artichokes, but looked handsome). The heads are usually hung up in the pen and left to the hens to pluck bare.

CORIANDER

(*See* Bread.)

> " Coriander is much grown in Essex and Kent. It is used by distillers and druggists and confectioners."
>
> *Child's Guide*, 1840.

BASIL

> " Basill is sowen in gardens in earthen pots . . . it is good for the hart and for the head. The seede cureth the infirmities of the hart, taketh away sorrowfulnesses which cometh of melan-cholie, and maketh a man merrie and glad."
>
> GARDEN HERBAL.

> " Fine basil desireth it may be her lot,
>   to grow as the gelliflower, trim in a pot;
>   That ladies and gentles, to whom ye do serve,
>   may help her, as needeth, poor life to preserve."
>
> TUSSER.

At the end of August, fill a wide-necked bottle with basil and cover with sherry. Cork and stand for ten days, drain off the sherry, and refill the bottle with fresh basil till the sherry is well impregnated. A spoonful of this sherry should be put into mock turtle soup just before serving. (*See* Soups and Sausages.)

CARAWAY

(*See* Cakes.)

> " Carraway seed is much used by pastrycooks; it grows wild in many parts of England, particularly around Bury St. Edmunds in Suffolk, and also in Essex and Kent. It is threshed in the fields in a cloth in the manner of rape seed."
>
> *Child's Guide*, 1850.

GRAINS OF PARADISE (*Amomum granium paradise*)

These are a small spice, very hot and much liked in early English cookery. They are still obtainable, being used by wine merchants to "produce" different flavoured wines from the basic grape juice. It also livens up flat wine.

BUNIUN FLEXUOUSUM

EARTH NUT

EARTH NUTS (or Pig Nuts)

These small forms of truffles are common enough everywhere, in woody places. At one time they were studied in Ireland as a source of food, but though thick enough in places, are very small. The leaf (when the nut is ripe) is fine, hairy, and light green, and the long white thread of them goes deep into the earth.) The nut at the end is about the size and somewhat the shape of a hazel; it will require washing and is then eaten raw.

LICHEN "Lichen Amphalodes.

The island dyers steep this in urine till it forms a paste, which they dry in the sun and with the addition of alum, make a brown dye for their wool.

Both L. Amphalodes and L. Tartarives are so abundant that the poor people employ themselves in gathering them for the use of the dry salters—at 1*d.* lb. and 30 lb. a day a whole families work.

From these lichens the dye called arcell or archil is prepared."

EVANS, 1798.

The old stone querns or old millstones were often used to pulverise the lichen, which was then stirred into vats or cauldrons with lime and urine, and left till thick. It is the basis of many colours and gives the characteristic smell to the tweeds dyed with the lichens.

PINE NUTS (Pynotys or Pine Nuts) [1]

These appear often in early recipes. They were probably the small seeds from the pine cones, used as a spice. They have a pungent turpentine

[1] The pine nuts of commerce today are imported.

flavour; also I believe the sticky pink aromatic ends of the common fir were cooked in a mixture till it is "charged with the flavour y nough". The "fir end" was then taken out (as one withdraws a bay leaf or vanilla pod). The pine flavouring would then be accentuated by the small pine seeds strewn on top as a garnish.

Pokerounce

This seems to be a delicious hot, spiced toast, spread with pine nuts.

"Take hony and caste it in a potte till it wexe chargeaunt y now. Take gyngere and canel and galyngale[1] and caste thereto. Take whyte brede and kyt into trencherous and toast and take the paste [i.e. boiled and flavoured honey] whyle hot and spread it upon them with a spoine and plante it with pynes and serve."

Modern recipe: take a gallipotful of honey with a large sticky pink end from a fir branch submerged in it, cover, and put on the stove to bake slowly. When the honey is strongly flavoured, add a pinch of mixed sweet spice and spread it hot on hot buttered toast garnished with pine kernels.

BED STRAW

Ladies' yellow bed straw—the wild flower of the hedge—is often found near dairy farms, and is said to act as rennet in setting milk.

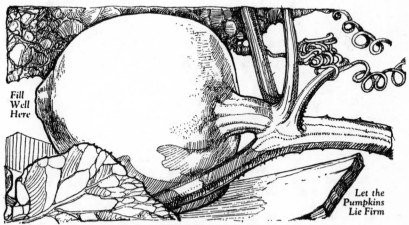

Pumpkins and all gourds should lie firm and dry

---

[1] Galingale, a mediaeval spice root; now difficult to obtain, it cooks a faint pinkish colour and smells of roses.

THE PUMPKIN (supposed to have been the first thanksgiving dinner, with
 wild turkey and cranberries, of the American Pilgrim Fathers).

Never very popular in England, I can find no good English dishes, so add
two American, from a book of 1870.

Pumpkin soup : Steam, the seeded and peeled pumpkin slabs, till soft,
rub through a coarse sieve, and reheat with pepper, salt, and enough milk
to make a thick soup, butter and egg yolk are added to make a richer soup.

Pumpkin pie: Cook the pumpkin till soft enough to beat to a pulp, then
beat in (to a quart of pulp) 1 teacupful sugar, the rind of a lemon, a grate
of nutmeg, and (if liked) a pinch of ginger, bake in a pie crust. This is a
standard "plain filling" but melted butter and eggs and spice may be
added to the pumpkin mash, and there is no question that the pumpkin
is a very worthy vegetable; but the Marrow takes its place in English
gardens.

Several varieties of both filberts and cobs are grown in England, mainly in
Kent, which has given its name to the Kentish cob, an extremely large round
nut with woody shell and short husks. The filbert, which ripens earlier than
the cob, is said to take its name from St. Philbert's feast day on August 22nd.
The shell is thinner and longer in shape, and the long, graceful husks entirely
enclose the nut. Some confusion arises in marketing, as an excellent large
variety of Kentish cob is called Lambert's filbert, after the cultivator, Mr.
Lambert of Kent; but for ordinary purposes the rounded hard shell is the
cob and the thin long-shaped shell contains the filbert.

THE HAFOD

THE HAFOD, OR SUMMER FARM IN EARLY TIMES

SUMMER AND winter farms are common to all mountain countries. There are old people in the principality, who can remember this usage in Wales. And the extract from a Scottish letter, sent from one of the lower winter farms to their hill farm, is as late as the eighteenth century.

A hafod is a household entirely dependent on mountain weather. Snow-bound hills are uninhabitable, but in spring the grass bursts out from under the melted snow, and with the first green a few workers go up and open the small shelter of the "summer farm", which is the centre for the herds of cows and sheep and goats all summer. This hafod had usually a large common room with a central fire, and over it two rooms where workers slept. The herds came up from the valley and were milked on the mountain pastures all through the bearing season. As the flow of milk increased, workers, idle (after spring sowing) on the farm below, came up and joined the mountain dwellers in making cheese and churning, washing and salting down of butter. They harnessed the waterpower of some mountain stream, and used it also for the washing of troughs, etc. Probably the distilling of a whey spirit was general.

The farm workers brought up from below round wooden tubs packed full of dried oatcakes (bread would not have kept fresh). These oatcakes exactly filled the tubs (which went back full of butter), and the Welsh *barra cierch* are still as far round as the base of an old butter tub. The mountain workers lived on this oatbread and butter and cheese and curd dishes all summer, learning the variety of mountain herbs that they watched the beasts relishing; and the spice of the wild thyme, the aroma of sweet gale, and many other herbs flavoured their monotonous diet. They would work with the milk all day, and in the evening make up the slow peat fire that burnt under the cauldrons of whey, heat the stones used for scalding the tubs,[1] and smoke the ewe milk cheeses. Over the same central fire they warmed icy fingers, perhaps occasionally they cooked the small lamb that could not be reared, or made veal broth with barley, or the oldest "lobscouse" of sheep's head, cereals and wild garlic; but the main diet was oatbread and butter and whey, and curd dishes. They used

---

[1] A trick common also to sea-coast workers. To save boiling quantities of water, tubs are filled with water (salt water if by the sea) and red-hot stones from under the fire are flung in till the water boils. Fish is sometimes cooked this way. An early prototype of the immersion heater.

wooden bowls and horn spoons and, afterwards, sat around in the firelight and spun wool and sang; while the wind howled through the rocks above and the stream piped below.

When the spate of milk slowed down, the young men and strong women (who were needed to harvest in the fields below), went down on ponies, laden with purple bilberries and heather honey; and only the very old or very young stayed at the hafod till the winds of autumn blew cold; then the last old men, and the old crones, came down behind the slowly driven herds, back to the lowland farm and winter sleep.[1]

A FARMER'S WIFE'S DAY—DEALING WITH THE "SUMMER FARMS" OR "HAFOD"

" I sketch out," says the writer of a diary in 1806, " a Monday, being the day when all the remote dwellers in glens come down for supplies. . . .

Item at 4 a.m. Donald arrives with a horse loaded with butter cheese and milk. The former I must weigh instantly. He only asks to take back, an additional blanket, for the children, a covering for himself, 2 milk tubs, a cog, and another spoon, (because little Peter threw one of the set in the burn). 2 stone of meal, a quart of salt, 2 lbs. of flax for the spinners, for the grass continues so good they will stay a week longer. He brings intelligence of the sow being a joyful mother of a dozen pigs and requests ' something to feed her with'. All this must be ready in an hour! and before the conclusion, comes Ronald from the high hills where our sheep and young horses are all summer, he only desires meal, salt, and women with shears to clip the lambs, and tar to smear them with. He informs me the black mare has a foal, a fine one, but she is very low, and I must bring her to the low meadows before he departs. The tennants who do us service come, they are going to stay 2 days and cut wood for our new byre, and they must have a competent provision of bread cheese and ale for the time they stay. Then I have Caros breakfast to get, Janets hank to reel, and a basket of clues to dispatch to the weavers, K's lesson to hear, her sampler to rectify, and all must be over by 11 o'clock, while his Reverence, calm and regardless of the bustle, wonders what has detained me? and urges me to go out for a walk! . . ."

This extract is of a late date, as the hafod was continued throughout the centuries—and its effects on the food and working of the country people show strongly during the Industrial Revolution.

[1] Crones, experienced old ewes, past breeding, hence " old cronies."

DAIRY PRODUCE

" It is within the power of every farmer to furnish his table at all seasons, and particularly in summer with very pleasant and wholesome dishes from his dairy."

STEVENS, *Book of the Farm*, 1800.

It is surprising to realise how general "a dairy" was in an English house. Not farmers only, or large country houses with a home farm; but ordinary small householders with children usually "kept a cow near the stables". Often it was supplied by the local farmer and returned to him when dry. In some districts the labourer's cow was definitely part of his wages.

The difficulty with a one-cow dairy is the period when she is dry before calving, so that a usual method was to keep one cow and a goat. Goat's milk was considered good for babies, not that the Victorian nurses studied the "content" much, but doctors knew that goats were usually very healthy and tuberculin-free, and nurses could see they were sturdy, so a billy drew the goat cart, and nannie was milked.

Cows were kept in London until a few years ago, and as late as the nineteenth century were milked in the streets to prove there was no adulteration with water. Milk "warm from the cow" was considered specially nourishing and was sent to invalids and sick children.

" From April beginning, till Andrew be past,
 so long with good huswife her dairy doth last;
 Good milch-cow and pasture, good husbands provide,
 the res'due, good huswives know best how to guide."

This "residue" was the butter, cream cheeses, skim milk and thick cream, and curds and whey and butter milk, etc., all of which the "good huswife" had to deal with (as she also dealt with baking and brewing and washing). Ewes were milked on most mixed farms.

" At Philip and Jacob, away with the Lambs,
   that thinkest to have any milk of their dams:
   At Lammas leave milking, for fear of a thing,
   lest (requiem aeternam) in winter they sing.
   Yet many by milking (such heed do they take:
   not hurting their bodies, much profit do make."

The ewe had to bring up her lambs, but as Tusser says, if the matter
was managed well the extra milking did not hurt the ewe and was profitable.
Ewe-milk cheese was made on hill farms.

Goat-milk cheese was usually very strong.

Buttermilk is the liquid left in the churn after the butter is made. It is
slightly acid, and when well threshed about in the churn has a foamy,
mildly fermented quality. When fresh and icy cold it is delicious, but
soon becomes sour and flat. There should be a distinct aroma of peat, bog
myrtle, meadow grass, or alder, according to the pasturage. Buttermilk
from hay or cowcake lacks this, and is no use for drinking, though it
serves to mix scones and oatcakes, etc. Scraps of butter floating in the
buttermilk show a careless, generous nature! and today there is such
definite courtesy in the offer of buttermilk to travellers, that its refusal
is a subtle offence, implying a slight "snub"—or confessing to a weak
stomach!

This quotation holds a truth at least two centuries old.

" In the quarry districts of N. Wales, persons collect it from
farm houses and bring it in pots in panniers on ponies—and
retail this useful article at 1d. a quart. On my wishing to be
informed if it was substituted for beer at meals? I received the
indignant reply ' Aye sure indeed ! and cood enough God knows.'
So I perceived I had inadvertently touched upon a tender string."

Tour of Wales, 1798.

In lowland Scotland milk is "dour", "sweet", or "scum", i.e. buttermilk, ordinary milk sweet from the cow or skimmed milk.

Irish "two-milk whey" is made of two-thirds sweet milk "turned" with
one-third buttermilk, the whey drained off and flavoured, and drunk fresh.

Cream is now (1951) so forgotten that children of ten would not think
this a "suitable reply":

" Plain cream is an excellent accompaniment to oatmeal or barley
porridge. Without cream, tea or coffee would lose much of their
relish, and so would pastry and jellies and fruits. White flour
bread, eaten with thick cream, makes a wholesome dessert."

VICTORIAN *Child's Guide.*

Devon and Cornish creams, cooked slowly over the soft peat fires, probably led to the making of condensed cream. I know the following recipe was in use in 1880—and probably much earlier.

"Condensed cream or how to preserve cream for sea store.

Put one pound of sugar in a quart bottle of earthenware. Fill it up with fresh cream, and see the cork fits well, but do not drive it home yet. Wrap the bottle in a cloth and stand it upright in a deep pan of cold water then let it simmer, and boil, till the sugar is all dissolved and incorporated. Give it a final good boil, and then let it cool, driving home the cork as it does so."

Before the war milk was "separated" by centrifugal force by a machine, and cream dripped out at one pipe while the skim milk foamed out at another—the whole process being carried out inside the "separator machine" which made a fine high-pitched whistle as it worked.

But now milk is "sold away" and the old churns fall to pieces, and the separators rust, and only a few special farms have working dairies.

> " Good servant in dayry that needs not be tolde,[1]
> deserveth her fee to be paid her in golde."
>
> TUSSER.

BEISTYN

> " The first food the calf receives is the beistyn. Being of the consistence of the yolk of the egg, it seems an appropriate food for a young calf."
>
> STEVENS, *Book of the Farm.*

This thick yellow substance is the first milking of the cow after calving. The first liquid that all mammals give their young is designed to clear the newborn babies' inside tracts. Nothing will do it so well as this first milk that is timed by Nature to meet the time of birth—so that, by law, beistyn must not be sold, nor the calf deprived of this first natural aperitive; but with cows there is usually so much beistyn that the creature would be unable to cope with it, unless some was taken away, and so custom decrees that it is given away in a jug to friends, and custom also decrees that the jug must never be returned empty. (To lend or send a cradle empty, is the worst bad luck in the world, and to return an empty beistyn jug bodes no good for the calf!)

"Bestys", or "Beastlyns" or "Firstings" is golden yellow, and thick as double cream; it should be thinned down with four times its quantity of plain milk, sweetened, and set in a cool oven with some simple flavouring—a vanilla pod, or cinnamon stick. It will set exactly like the richest

[1] We still say " she's a good worker, she doesn't need ' telling ' " and you give people a " telling off ".

egg custard. A good finish is to cover the top with damp sugar, and crisp it under the grill or before the fire; the sweet caramel crust, in contrast to the smooth custard, is pleasant.

WHEY

> " Water and Whey of drinks are first
> They cool, dilute, and quench the thirst."
>
> POPE.

Whey is the liquid drained away from curds or junket. It looks like barley water and the flavour depends entirely on the curd formation from which it is drained.

Curds and Whey

> " Little Miss Muffet sat on a tuffet, eating her curds and
> whey . . ."

Sometimes the whey is sweetened and flavoured and poured back over the dried curds (curds and whey). There are hundreds of dishes made thus of coagulated milk.

RENNET

> " If through the industry of the chemists we are able to rescue
> the manufacture of Rennet from the mysterious and empirical
> hands of the dairymaid . . ."
>
> *Proceedings of the Scottish Agricultural Society*, 1820.

It is not generally realised that many sorts of rennet are made according to the coagulating principle required. There is a rennet made for turning milk for cheese, and another type that makes the softer junket; one rennet can take the place of another, but the results are not so good.

How Rennet was Prepared (a sixteenth-century flavoured rennet)

"Let the calf suck as much as he will, just before he is killed, then take the milk bag out of the calf and let it lie twelve hours covered in stinging nettles till it is red. Then take out your curd and wash the bag clean and salt it inside and out and let it lie in salt for twenty-four hours. Wash your curd in new milk and clean it and put it back in the bag with three or four streakings [the last milk from the cow], a beaten egg or so, twelve cloves, a blade of mace, and skewer the bag shut and hang it in a pot.

"In another pot put half a pint salted water, six tops of the reddish of blackthorn, as many of burnet, and two of sweet marjoram, and boil all together and let it cool and put some of this flavoured water into the bag with the egg and thick milk and let the bag soak in the rest of it.

"This water in which the bag lies [and into which the heavier liquid from inside the bag exudes by osmosis] is the rennet, and so strong that the bag can be refilled and left to exude more than six or seven times before the curdling action of the stomachic juice is exhausted."

The recipe is interesting for the *thought* of the cook behind it—she realised that the stomach would begin to water in expectation of the meal, and feeds the calf, before killing, so that the coats of the stomach would be full of the rennet juices she wanted. To keep the bag active, she leaves the lump of curd within it, but the nettles (which she thinks may sting the blood from the inner coats out to the surface, and so cause the bag to contract slightly) probably had no effect at all—the action of the blood being quite mechanical in the texture of the bag. Again, she wastes a perfectly good egg and the strokings,[1] in her feeling that the bag would go on producing rennet better "if it had a meal inside that needed the rennet juice to digest it". And her thought results in making the inside liquid heavier than the outer liquid, and so setting up a system of osmosis through the porous bag, rectifying her wrong belief. That is why I am convinced this is an older recipe elaborated, because mediaeval people had just this way of holding firmly on to the wrong end of the right stick.

Junkets, Curds and Whey or Creams

Junkets are made best in the peat country in the west of England.

In modern making, the milk is heated blood-warm and set with rennet. Rum is a usual flavouring, and clotted cream a usual accompaniment; often a powdering of nutmeg or cinnamon, covers the top.

The older junkets were usually made with the milk warm from the cow, and apparently curds and whey were sometimes listed as "junkets" in old cookery books. Sometimes curds are listed as creams.

Hatted Kit (a "curd cream"; a kit is a wooden milk pail).

" Make two quarts of new milk scalding hot and mix quickly with four quarts of fresh cold buttermilk; let it stand undisturbed till cold and firm. Skin the ' hat ' off and set it to drain, then press it into a mould, turn out; and serve with cream and sugar. The slight acidity of the dish, with the richness of the cream and the sweetness of the sugar, make this a very delicious desert."

ABOUT 1700.

---

[1] Strokings are the last milk "stroked" from the cow's udder; the action being lighter than milking out the main flow.

Note. This is made commonly in Scotland today, but sometimes a curd called "croudie" is served; and the name "Hatted Kit" given to a foaming posset drink. All these terms are very confusing, so we will deal with *cream* and *milk* first.

CLOTTED CREAM

" Clowtyd crayme and nawe crayme put together, is eaten more
for a sensuall appetyte than for any good nouryshement."
BOORDE.

Clotted cream is still a speciality of Devon and Cornwall.

The origin of the name is disputed, but a "clout" is a thick patch, presumably of leather, since you have "old shoes unclouted"—and the cream wrinkles up into thick leathery folds. "Cloutynge" was also a wrapping. "Cristie clene religioun, withoute cloutynge of sinfulle mennis errours."

The old spellings give "clowtyd, clouted, clowted, clawted, clotted", we presume the cream was the same thick, wrinkled, folded, yellow, crusted cream as made by the country people today.

To make Clotted Cream.

"Take the night's milk and put into a broad earthenware pan and in the morning set over a slow fire, letting it stand there from morning till night, suffering it not to boil, only heat.

"Then take off the fire and set in some place to cool all night and next morning dish off your cream and it will be very thick."

(The flat sides of the scallop shell-fish that abound on the Devon coast make good cream "lifters". They are naturally grooved.)

At the farm near South Molton in Devon, where I saw Devon cream being made, the maker used the old Devon earthenware panshons. As they are heavy, they are being superseded by enamelware and metal pans, but this expert assured me that the more steady heat of the thick earthenware was worth the weight of lifting it—in cream! Her cream pans cooled equally slowly on the stone-flagged floor in her dairy, and her cream was accounted some of the best in the west country.

Peat and wood fires make excellent clotted cream, as the heat is gentle.

Cream Custards

Custards overlap into the cream section in this book. (Today to warn against using "too many eggs" sounds foolish) but 1 egg to a pint of milk is sufficient. Beat the yolk and white separately, blend together and beat again into the milk. Sweeten and flavour very delicately and set all custards to cook as slowly as possible. A full hour in the oven at Regulo $\frac{1}{4}$ will give a much creamier custard than half the time with twice the heat. Watery custards are the result of too hot cooking.

These days when making boiled custards it is sensible to use a fine corn-flour foundation. Boil this thoroughly first, then beat in butter, sweetening and flavouring, take from the fire and, lastly, blend in your precious well-beaten raw eggs. The cornflour mixture will still be hot enough to cook the egg sufficiently. This way you will get the best value from your expensive eggs.

Sweet Creams in Early Recipes

The method of scalding cream was used also for making rich "creams" with soft fruit. The cream was "boyled"—i.e., heated with spice, sugar, and a dash of rose, elder flower, or orange-flower water. "When you have boyled your cream take two ladlesful of it, being almost cold, bruise the soft fruit together, with it, and season with sugar rosewater, and put it to your cream, stirring all together and so dish it up."

"Cream" was not always plain cream from the milk; it was the name given to other soft mixtures, such as we should now call custards, or "fools". For example, here is a simple white-crumb custard, in which the cream need be no more than good milk—the whole point in this recipe being that the milk would be heated in an earthenware panshon over very soft wood or peat ash, and the eggs (note) are stirred into the hot milk *after* it is taken off the fire, so that it could not boil and curdle, *but the earthenware panshon would stay hot long enough to thicken the mixture.* "Take a quantity of cream [milk] and set it to boyl with a large mace or two, and while it is boyling cut some thick snippets of bread, and lay them in a very fine clean dish, and have six yolks of eggs strained with rosewater and sugar. Then taken the milk off the fire and put in the eggs and stir all together, and pour on the slices of bread [fine manchet bread], and being cold scrape on sugar, and serve." A very simple custard, but very good.

Temperatures for Creams

Creams, blancmanges and jellies were always set stone-cold, being kept on the stone floor of the cold underground cellar, till served; custards were only ordinarily cold; milk dishes, fermenties, junkets, etc., were only dairy-cold. This was a subtle distinction, and flavoured for ac-cordingly, *as freezing tends to subdue flavour and destroy aroma completely.*

Old-fashioned Garnishes

In the garnishing of plain blancmanges there was far more enterprise. A perfectly plain white shape would be turned out on to a dish as white, and garnished with scarlet geranium. Maidenhair fern was popular for jellies (being very light and trembling appropriately). A sturdy brown chocolate mould would have queer little sticks of cinnamon stuck into it with bay leaves at their ends. Virginal junkets were never garnished, beyond a bronzing of nutmeg atop. "Dish creams" (i.e., soft creams that had to be ladled out with a spoon) would be poured into a glass dish, which was set down on a circle of tiny flowers or bright leaves. The "candied damask rose leaves", or "candied cowslip pips", served with appropriate creams, were edible, as were the bright red barberries and red-currant jelly.

Rosemary, leaves of scented geranium, thin slices of black prunes, angelica and cherries were used to decorate boiled puddings, and the jelly mould shapes were the work of artists. Wedgwood designed some beautiful shapes.

Orange-flower Cream

This was a luscious dish of the 1700s.

Boil 3 quarts of clear sweetened water with the zest (yellow rind) of 2 lemons, and the juice. Beat 8 eggs into 1 quart of cream, and pour it in. Stir it very slowly one way and then let it stand. Then skim off the curd into a pierced dish to drain, and when set, turn it out and pour round it whipped cream sweetened and flavoured with orange-flower water.

These curd creams of the eighteenth century seem to be the counterpart of the "Leche of cream" in the fourteenth and fifteenth centuries, and probably earlier.

Almond Blancmanges

> " Perhaps no form of cream is more agreeable or more generally admired than blancmange flavoured with almonds."
>
> VICTORIAN COOKERY BOOK.

Cook 1 pint of milk with 2 laurel leaves till well flavoured, and use to make a smooth blancmange with 3 dessertspoonfuls of best cornflour and sugar to taste. While still boiling, beat in 1 tablespoonful of almond oil. Pour out into a mould previously soaked, and when cold, stick with split blanched almonds (*see* Dublin Rock).

"Finis"

Bread and Milk of the Victorians (Soyer's recipe)

Boil 1 pint of milk with ¼ oz. of sugar. Cut *crusts* into small pieces and put into a *hot* bowl.

Put on top of the crusts 2 very small pieces of butter, a grate of nutmeg, and a pinch of cinnamon.

At once, pour over the boiling milk and cover closely. Keep hot.

In 5 minutes the bread will be soaked and soft; it should not be touched or stirred in any way to break the texture.

It will be very light served thus.

GENERAL NOTES ON BUTTER

" Butter of the richest quality and flavour and appearance can be made from sweet cream. Were such butter not super-excellent, would noblemen have it on their tables every morning? I consider butter out of the churn from sweet cream, and before it is handled, the most delicious. For my own use I would never desire better butter all the year round than that churned every morning from sweet cream. Such butter on a new cool baked oatcake, sweetened with flower virgin honey, accompanied with a cup of hot, strong coffee, modified with crystallised sugar and fresh cream, is a breakfast worth partaking of."

STEVENS, 1870.

In all England I hardly know a craft that varies more than making butter. It was made from milk cooled in round flat milk pans, the cream taken off with a skimmer of porcelain or a shell.

Some block-tin milk pans are in use now, there are a few earthenware ones and glass ones may be found with luck; and there's many a bird-bath in a country garden that was once a square, built-in marble milk-cooler, and the pride of the dairy.

Of the old tall plunge churns there is nothing left but their shape and name in the present-day iron milk "churns", of railway and lorry.

There's a derelict specimen to be found in England of almost every

Butter Hands

churn that was ever invented. And as for labour-saving contrivances, I have known water-wheels, donkeys, and dogs, all used for the monotonous labour of churning.

There is much "traditional" usage involved with the "practical" in dairy work. Wool and cloth must not come into the dairy; old linen for the wood; and scouring sack (hempen) for the floor. White sand from the brook to scour the floor with, and lime "set" with skim milk to whiten the walls. Theoretically, soap ought not to be used at all, but if you must use it, the best dairymaids will make a fine jelly of it, and use it with cold water only, so that it will not stick in the wood, and they rinse off very fine. A dairywoman's hands should be smooth as butter, white as milk, and cool as spring water.

The milk utensils must be scalded with boiling salted water, and get a very clean rinse, and the tubs and jars should not be dried, but set to drip and drain in the wind until they bleach white as snow.

In old hafods, or hill dairies, the scalding was done by throwing red hot stones into the pails full of water.

The fashion for salt butter has changed: butter when it was plentiful from the summer grass used to be pounded into wooden kits, with finely powdered salt. There was much controversy over the delicacy of this salt, our only rivals being the Dutch, who "made a very refined form of salt". But there were those in England who considered the best Droitwich salt equally good.

Salt butter put down at the best time of the year was preferred for use on oatcake, or with cheese, and meat dishes, and a few of us miss the cold fresh tang of the rather hard salt butter.

Butter used to be sold in round "pats", formed in a wooden mould (that also measured out the weight). Each portion was stamped with the pattern of the farms where the butter was made. Some of these old butter stamps were very finely carved, and the design, as a rule, showed the type of farm. Thus the "swan" means a farm with water meadows; sprays of bog myrtle, a hill farm; corn sheafs, a corn-growing farm; or, sometimes, a prize cow or bull set its portrait upon the produce of that dairy. Nowadays the designs are bought at random, and most of the butter is now sold in squares, for easier packing and transport. Cambridge districts used to measure its butter by the yard—selling it in lengths something like long french bread, with a "ring gauge" for size.

I have drawn the dog churn—this is funny-looking, but I've never known it get out of order (though a passing rat once threw it out of gear!). It is a large wooden wheel or circular platform on which the dogs run—their weight keeps the wheel turning, and the wheel is geared to the dasher[1]

[1] These old "paddle dashers" have recently been bought up by clever antique dealers who sell them as newspaper or folio stands.

Some Old Types of Churns

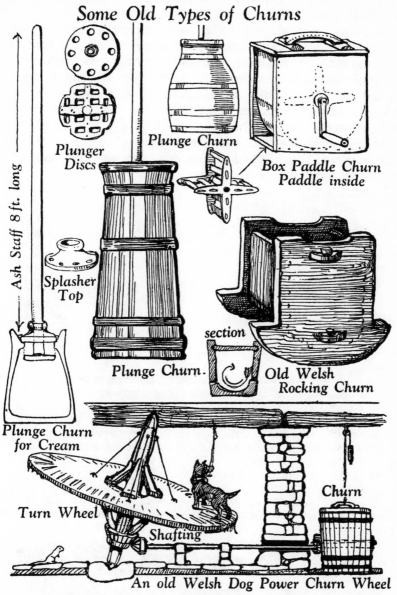

Ash Staff 8 ft. long

Plunger Discs

Plunge Churn

Box Paddle Churn
Paddle inside

Splasher Top

Plunge Churn.

section

Old Welsh Rocking Churn

Plunge Churn for Cream

Turn Wheel

Shafting

Churn

An old Welsh Dog Power Churn Wheel

Most hill farms used water power for churning. The collecting of mountain streams to form city reservoirs has altered many old useful water courses in country places.

which revolves in the churn. It is no hardship, the dogs turn up to their job as gladly as their fellows turn up for their job with the sheep.

It was funny to watch the knowing way they run the wheel up to its full spin, and then, with a funny little hop and change of legs, they settle down to a steady canter till half-time, when they stop, and get a drink of butter-milk while the dairymaid cleans the churn; then on they go again till they feel the wheel trundle unevenly, and the butter coming; a few more turns, and down they sit, well satisfied, and are "paid off" with a well-deserved dinner.

They use water-wheels in some farms.

If I tried to tell you all the different ways butter was made in England, there would be room for nothing else in this book.

Dairymaids' masterpieces

These fancy pieces in butter were made large in shops, or on stalls, by dairy-maids, or small for tables by tablemaids. They were tests of skill. The tower showed a very nice judgment in picking up exactly the right amount and duplicating it exactly. The sections were *not* weighed and measured beforehand, a roll was made—cut into the three or four equal length pillars—another round flattened for a pat above them, another roll cut for smaller pillars made above that, till the tall balanced tower attested to the makers' judgment and skill.

The basket is easier, needing less exact weight judgment, but a " pretty eye ". The whole is built up from pat and roll units, bent and flicked together, and nothing is touched, except by the wooden butter hands, from start to finish.

These efforts used to be competitions between dairymaids in small country fairs.

Butter balls

SALTED-DOWN BUTTER

To preserve for winter, butter was extra well washed, pressed dry, and packed into clean well-scalded " kits " (small kegs or tubs). The butter was taken up in the hand and *flung hard* into the kit, to get a close pack; when the base was covered, the packing rose up the sides, in pressed down lyers, salt strewn between, the knuckles of the closed fist being rammed down around the sides, and every care taken to exclude air pockets. The top layer was kept slightly raised, the cover rammed down, and the top of the kit ringed on securely. This salt butter was delicious with oatcake, or for the bread and butter served with cold meats; for sweet dishes, cakes, or " tea " bread, the salt was " washed " out before use.

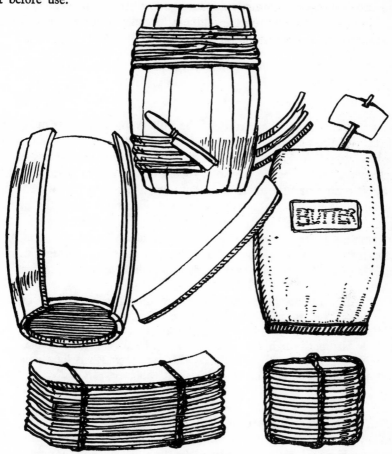

BUTTER TUBS

The big barrels of butter that used to come from Denmark or Ireland were bound with withy bands, *never metal*, these bands were cut loose and the staves removed, leaving a barrel-mould shape of butter. The staves were packed for return, so you often saw very old tubs with brand new withys—they were a very buoyant cargo on the return voyage.

GENERAL NOTES ON CHEESE

" Cheese is made of mylke, yet there is sortes of cheese, which is to say, grene chese, softe chese, harde chese, and spermyse. Grene chese is not called grene by the reason of colour, but for the newness of it, for the whey is not halfe pressed out of it.

Softe chese, not new nor to olde, is best. Harde chese, is hot and dry and wyll to dygest. Spermyse is a chese the which is made with curdes and with the juce of herbes. To tell the nature of it (Spermyse) I can not, consyderynge that every mile-wyfe may put many juces or herbes . . . not one agreynge with another. . . .

Chese . . . oughte not to be tough nor bruttel; it ought not to be swete nor sowre, nor tarte, nor salt, nor to fresshe . . . it must be of good savour and taledge, nor full of iyes, nor myters, nor magottes."

MARKHAM.

Cheese depends on the quality of the milk from which it is made; that depends on the pasture the cow feeds on; and that depends on its geographical position. Cheese also depends on the type of farming locally, whether the farm specialises in dairy work or is a mixed farm, and if the cheese is made for their own use or produced for industry (which needs a more staple produce). Crossing these considerations come the material considerations of the land: whether the land will support large farms or only small scattered ones. These considerations *all alter the form of the cheese*, for the number of cows to a milking dictates the "number of milkings to a cheese", and that alters the *type* of cheese, as well as its *size*.

" Although the lowe meddowes doe abound in the plenty of grasse, yet the higher grounds even bearth the sweeter grasse, and it is a rule amongst Husbandmen, that the low meddowes do fill, but the high meddowes do feede. The low are for the stable, but the high are for the Cattle, that [grass] which is long will maintaine life, but that which is short will breede milke."

MARKHAM.

This means that some milk is "thick" in itself, from compact high feeding, and some "light" or wet from lush meadows; and the "fat" content varies with the type of cow. *Also, from the air, and the utensils used, come the bacteria; the airborne cultures that make the type of cheese.* It is now possible to buy this "culture" (for almost any cheese!) by name, and inject it into any sort of matrix of curd! but though this culture is true to type, it does *not* make the same type of cheese in a different type of matrix— or under different conditions.

The following trade letter is interesting.

" Dear Madam,

In reply to your letter of the 27th May, the addition of suitable organisms is now a regular practice in the cheese-making industry.

In the case of hard cheese such as Cheddar, Cheshire and Caerphilly, the main bacteria concerned are strains of Lactic Streptococci, chiefly Streptococcus Lactis. These organisms are artificially cultivated and added to every batch of milk which is made into cheese.

These particular bacteria are not in fact the whole story, and some other species are concerned in the later stages of ripening when the cheese exceeds two months in age. These organisms are known and have been isolated, but the practical difficulties of adding them have not yet been solved, although there seems little doubt that these organisms will also be added artificially in the near future.

The green mould cheese such as Stilton is of course particularly dependent upon the action of the mould Penicillium Roqueforti for the special flavour. It is not normally necessary to add the mould artificially in premises where the cheese is regularly made since the buildings themselves become more or less permanently infected.

When Stilton cheese is made in a new location, however, it is a great advantage to add a culture of the mould during the first few weeks of manufacture. We ourselves decided to manufacture Stilton cheese in Somerset and were told that it would be quite impossible to do so outside the Stilton district of Leicestershire. We adopted the expedient, however, of artificially adding a suitable mould culture at first and were completely successful in making first-grade Stilton.

The other organism you mention, namely P. Camemberti, is of course the characteristic mould of Camembert cheese. This is not made on any scale in Britain but is manufactured quite widely in the United States, and there the same method has been followed, namely, addition of a culture at first to get the process started in the particular location.

Yours faithfully,

APLIN AND BARRETT LIMITED."

I do hope this very untechnical exposition of the situation describes the problem to ordinary readers, for the subject is very interesting.

The end of individual localised cheese came with the development of motor transport. Milk collecting by motor became easy, so the makers in large cheese centres took over the small local trade, and closed down the local cheese-making, and in about fifty years over fifty different types of

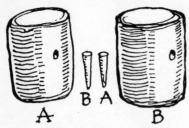

A   B

How a culture from one cheese
can be introduced into another

CHEESE SCOOP

Cheese scoop or cheese peg. For
sampling cheese (*see* "Checky Pig"
in pastry section)

English cheese had ceased to exist! The milk-marketing scheme completed
what was already begun. What human being is going to work hard making
butter and cheese, when he can get the same price selling milk direct? the
cheese presses were sold off, the dairy closed, and an English industry ended.

In districts where the local reputation warranted the enterprise, new
local factories were set up; they bought the milk wholesale and made the
cheese (quite good cheese), and the farmers' daughters, instead of working
in hard conditions at home, motored down with the milk lorry to the
factory where, in good company, and well paid, they did what they had
done, for less money, at home!

Note now the result. All milk varies during the year, and in most of
the individual cheeses there was some definite *seasonal reason* for the
excellence of the cheese. For example a "moorland" cheese was only made
in spring, when the winter, hay-fed cattle went out and grazed the scented
alder and new grass on the mountains; this diet cleared their blood, made
delicious milk (full of the casein and flavours that make for the best cheeses),
and the cheese made from this special milk was "moorland"—it was blue
moulded and light in texture, and had a delicious aroma. The moorland
farms never bothered to make cheese *except while the cows were on this
fresh grass:* they might make an odd cheese or so in winter (if the snow
prevented getting the milk away, or they wanted a cheese to sell to the
Lancashire cooks for welsh rabbit!), but they never considered that "hay
cheese" was "moorland" or "dale" cheese.

Now, cheese factories *have* to run all the year round, and therefore they
must continue to make cheese (even when they know it's not worth making).
The summer cheese is good, but the cheese made the rest of the year is
worth nought! The texture is rubbery, the cream content lower, and yet it
is still retailed as the standard product.

Now comes retribution: the sub-standard cheese is so poor that it
invites contrast; so the good cheese standard must be lowered till both are
"standard mediocre". The industrial revolution of the dairy is complete!
And our really fine cheeses are lost to England.

THE VEINING OF CHEESES

There is a curious belief among miners that the metals in the soil affect the milk and thus the cheese (the use of a copper curd breaker is believed to foster the green mould). The old people contend that "this mould started when the cows grazed around the old copper-mines". There is enough metallic taste to some of the streams coming from such coppered earths as Parry's Mountain to make the idea plausible; it is generally known now that all this veining is the result of spores contained and preserved in the old wood and buildings where the cheeses are made. All cheese utensils of wood are scrubbed and scalded, but it would take stringent septic treatment to do away with the infection in old farms.

The unexpected squareness of "brick" cheese in some parts resulted from laying the cheeses on straw to drain—the hollow straws made a natural drainboard, and many soft cheeses were made on straw—and pressed under a board. Another consideration for cheese shape was the possible use of old querns (out of service since the corn-mills came

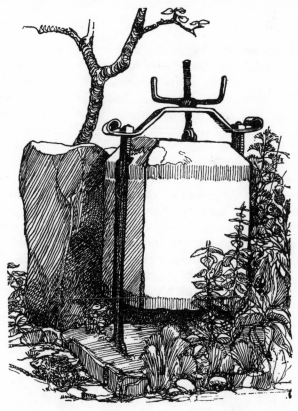

The sad sight outside the farmhouse door. The old disused cheese pres

into use). I believe that many old querns ended up as small cheese weights, and may account for the accepted size and weight of some of the smaller cheeses.

The old stone cheese-presses can often be seen outside the farm-buildings today. If you look, you will see the two grooves, one each side, that slid in the press (*see* illustration).

I should like to research and write an entire book on our lost English cheeses, but can only tell you how to make a few from an infinite variety.

TYPES OF CHEESE

Cheshire Cheese[1]

> " O Mary, go and call the cattle home—Call the cattle home—
>> Call the cattle home. . . .
>>> across the sands of Dee!
> The rising tide was cold and dank with foam—and all alone
>> went she! "
>
> OLD SONG.

The rich Cheshire pastures accounted for the excellence of the Cheshire cheese. The original Cheshire cheese was a pale golden colour—and its reputation was so good that it was imitated by Welsh farmers. The cattle grazed on the pastures of the Dee sands (hence the song of Mary, who was overtaken by the tide, drowned, and whose voice still haunts the estuary). Welsh cheeses, which had an admixture of goat's milk (and certainly were completely different in flavour), were sold in the open market to the coach passengers (through which transport they even reached London). These Welsh cheeses were bringing the Cheshire cheeses into disrepute, so the Welsh cheeses were obliged to be coloured, with annato, to distinguish them. Then (by that cussedness that haunts such arrangements) the Cheshire cheeses began to be lightly coloured also; perhaps the Holyhead passengers having called the red cheese "Cheshire", would not believe the pale colour was really Cheshire cheese; anyhow, the Cheshire cheese became reddish. Now these last ten years has seen the old Cheshire cheese turning pale again, and the Flint border cheese a bright red!

Essex Cheese

> " Those that made me were uncivil,
> They made me harder than the devil.
> Knives can't cut me, fire won't light me,
> Dogs bark at me but can't bite me."

---

[1] A Cheshire *cat* was an old cheese measure.

Stilton Cheese (1600)

"The first Stilton ('The Times') as far as my present
research work carries me, was being made in the early part
of the eighteenth century in the dairy at Quenby Hall, a fine old
Elizabethan mansion, about seven miles from Leicester.

At that period one Elizabeth Scarbrow was making there a
famous cheese known as Lady Beaumont's cheese. When she
married she took the recipe with her and made it in her own
dairy at Little Dalby. It was then called Quenby cheese.

In time her two daughters married, one to Cooper Thornhill,
landlord of Bell Inn at Stilton, in Huntingdonshire, and the
other to a farmer named Paulet, of Wymondham. The farmer's

Chloride of lime was
used to prevent mice
where cats were not
permitted

wife continued to make Quenby cheese, and one Christmas
she sent one as a present to her brother-in-law at Stilton.

Now the Bell Inn at Stilton was a stage on the great North
Road from Aldersgate Street to Glasgow, and when the passengers got out there, the cheese was put before them. So much was
it appreciated that the landlord told his sister-in-law he would
take every cheese she could make. From that time it came to be
called Stilton cheese, though it was not made there."

F. WHITE, *Letters*, 1930.

Somerset. Some of the richest cheeses are made down west, and the
agricultural colleges are doing excellent research on the old makes of cheese.

Somerset also made the largest cheese on record:

"A huge cheese was made nine feet in circumference in 1841 for Queen
Victoria from 737 cows. That is one milking from all the cows in the entire
parish of West Pennard, Glastonbury, Somerset. The milk was collected
and made all in one day and the cheese when done was probably pressed
under a mill-stone—though it is interesting that some very elaborate and
beautiful German ironwork cheese-presses are still to be found (unless
they went for salvage) near Wookey Hole.

The Queen's Cheese (1600)

"Six quarts of the best stroakings and let them stand till cool, and set two quarts of cream on the fire till they are hot. And take two quarts of water hot and two yolks of eggs and one spoonful of sugar and two spoonfuls of rennet and mingle all together and stir" (note six quarts cold and four quarts hot, makes a blood-heat mixture). The rennet should not be put into the hot water, but, as the recipe says "mingled together". When the cheese has come "use it as other cheese" (i.e., drain the whey out and press), and then "set it on the leaves of nettles, and it must be turned and wiped dry, and new nettles every day and in three weeks it will be fit to eat. This cheese must be made between Michaelmas and Alhallowtide".

Cheddar Cheese (1700)

This recipe is easy to follow, and old enough to give a fair idea of the process.

"Take the milk of twelve cows in the morning and the evening cream of twelve cows, and put to it three spoonsful of rennet, and when it is come [i.e. the curd] break it, and whey it, and when it is well wheyed break it again, and work into the curd three lb. of fresh butter, and put it in your press, and turn it in the press for an hour, or more, and change the cloths and wash them every time you change them; you may put wet cloths at first on to them, but towards the last put two or three fine dry cloths to them. Let it lie thirty or forty hours in the press, according to the thickness of the cheese; then take it out and wash it in whey, and lay it in a dry cloth till it is dry, then lay it on your shelf, and turn it often."

Note that twenty-four milkings must be used for the above—twelve morning milks and twelve panfuls set the night before, in order that the cream may be risen in time to add to the morning milk. (Because separators were not in use then, you had to wait 12 hours to get cream risen.)

Newmarket Cheese (to cut at two years old, a slow cheese—1800)

"Any morning in September take twenty quarts of new milk warm from cow and colour it with marigolds; when this is done get ready a quart of cream in a quart of fresh water stirred over the fire till scalding hot. Then stir it into the milk and do it with rennet, and when it is come [i.e. the curd set], lay your cheese-cloths *over* it as it lies in the milk-trough, and settle it [i.e. press down] with your hands, the more hands the better [for the same type of work now they use a special lid in the cheese-trough], and as the whey rises take it away, and when it is all cut, put the curd in your cheese-vat, breaking it as little as you can, and put it in the press and press it gently an hour. Take it out and wipe it and cut it in thin slices, and lay them singly on a cloth and wipe dry. Then put in a tub and with your hands break it as small as you can, and mix it with a good handful of salt, and a quart of cold cream; put it in the vat and lay one pound on it till next day [too much pressure now would only drive out the cream which must be absorbed], and next day, press it and order it as other cheese [i.e., get it dry]."

Newport Cheese (about 1890–1900)

"To make the thick square cream cheese as at Newport (Mon.) you must get a vat made a quartern and a half high [?], the bottom nor the top must be fastened in and it must be four-square with holes all over. This cheese must be made in May."

Dunlop and Cheddar Cheeses were very rich in butter.

Suffolk Cheese (this was tough)

> " Then Cheese was brought. Says Slouch, ' This e'en shall roll
> I'm sure it's hard enough to make a bowl;
> This is skimmilk, and therefore it shall go,
> And this because it is Suffolk follow too."
>
> KING.

Another name for Suffolk cheese was a "Suffolk bang". Being made after selling the butter off it, only the casein was left.

Wiltshire makes a lovely cheese. The story goes that they tried to rake the moon out of a pond down there, believing it to be a cheese drowning.

Devon makes some of the best cream cheeses—though some were only an excuse for using up clotted cream that had soured. These are *not* cheese (though good).

Glamorgan made fine cheeses. There is a district down there called Gwent—white—where a breed of white cattle were kept especially against urgent need of the King. There was a regular route there, across by St. David's, to Ireland, and an estate in that district had to be able to send its pepper corn rent across to London by a team of eight white oxen, thus very cleverly ensuring that a large herd of white oxen were always kept thereabouts for sudden need. A great many cows must have been milked around Glamorgan to breed those white herds, and plenty of cause for good cheese on such a busy thoroughfare in those days.

Note. The Welsh cattle were black, hence the choice of white oxen.

Caerphilly Cheese is very good, and is obtainable at Welsh dairies in London.

Labourer's or a "Poor Man's" Cheese

"The contents of my churn I put in an iron pot over a slow fire, as the buttermilk curdles, the curd sinks, and next morning, when cool, I pour off the whey, and work the curd as any other cheese, giving it a little salt to taste. The curd is then put in a strong linen cloth, tied tightly, and hung for the remainder of the day to drip, and then retied, and hung up to dry for four weeks, when the cheese is fit for use. If the folded linen cloth is hung in a net, it gives a pleasing appearance to the cheese. If a little bit of butter be worked into the curd, and the cheese kept for three or four months, it will be very good; at least it will taste like ewe-milk cheese, and it can be made with only one cow."

MISS NEILSON, OF KIRKINTILLOCH, 1820.

Potato Cheese (another poor man's cheese)

An attempt from the hungry days of the Industrial Revolution.

5 lb. of potatoes boiled and pulped; 1 lb. of solid sour milk. Knead together and leave for three or four days, according to the season, in an old wooden cheese kit. Knead again, and press into small square rush baskets, and pack them together and leave in a cool shady place for fifteen days. The cheese will then be ready and keep some time.

Note. We are told on good authority that this makes a rather soft white cheese, but that its type depends entirely upon the culture present in the "old cheese kit". We have been unable to make it ourselves (to date), but include it as an interesting corollary to the potato-fed yeast (*see* bread).

Sage Cheese

" The juice of spinnage and sage, pounded and put to the cheese, and sage pressed into it. Press, mound, and it will eat very agreeably in six months."

1700.

Slipcote, or Slipcoat Cheese (a quick cheese)

This name is *also* given to the Stilton cheese that bursts its shape after moulding, and spills down in a soft mass; these cheeses were taken from the shelves and eaten straight away without waiting to ripen and were nicknamed "Slip coats".

"Take new milk and put rennet, and let it get cold and break it as little as you can in putting it into the cheese vat, and there let it stand and whey itself some time [the wooden cheese vats are full of drain-holes at the bottom]. Then cover it and set a two pound weight on it [very light], and when it will hold together [under this light pressure] turn it out of that cheese vat and keep turning it into dry vats for a few days till it has done wetting, and then lay it on sharp-pointed dock-leaves till it is ripe."

This, you see, was a light-textured cheese to be eaten quickly. Much of the moisture would remain in its texture; it was never under heavy pressure.

Green Cheese

" But two grene cheses A fewe cruddes and creem, and a hauer cake, and two loues of benes and bran."

The Vision of Piers Plowman.

"Two grene cheses" Probably meant two cheeses not yet ripe (as today a butcher speaks of a green tongue meaning one not yet pickled).

Cream Cheese (1820 or earlier)

"One pint cream, twelve pints milk warm from the cow. Turn with rennet and let out the whey through a spigot at the base of the wooden milk-pan. Let it drain awhile, and then turn out on to a cloth, fold the corners of the cloth over and set a light board atop and leave for twenty-four hours, on a draining-board. Turn over on to a dry cloth, and turn back on to a platter set with vine-leaves. It will only keep properly good for one day."

A very delicious cheese used to be made on the Leicester wolds and sold in Loughborough market-place. It was a milk cheese, with a cream cheese set in the centre of it.

Cheesecakes

" Take new cheese, and grynde hit fayne, in mortar with eggs. . . . . Put powder thereto of sugar coloure hit with Safrone. Put hit in cofyns [pie crust cases] that be fayre, and bake it forthe."

BOORDE.

This is the cheesecake still made in Yorkshire. It is the new cheese curd rubbed down into a custard with milk and eggs and baked in a pastry case. Currants are sometimes added.

Potted Cheese

Take 1 lb. of old Cheshire cheese, shave it very thin into a mortar, and put to it 1 oz. of beaten mace, $\frac{1}{2}$ pound of butter, and a glass of sack; beat and grind all together, put it into a pot, leave it awhile, and cut it in slices for cream cheese.

This is the eighteenth-century recipe. Stilton and many other cheeses were potted with spices in this way.

Welsh Rabbit (rare-bit)

Put a lump of butter into a saucepan and melt, add twice as much ale, a pinch of salt and 2 pinches of pepper. When just about to boil, grate in enough cheese to make a thick cream (stir only just lightly enough to dissolve the cheese-flakes). On no account let the mixture boil after the cheese is in—and cook it only just long enough to blend it.

Have ready a slice of hot buttered toast, pour the rabbit quickly over it, give it 1 second under the grill (or hold the red-hot fire shovel over it).

For a rich rabbit, *fry* the toast in bacon fat.

Beer is the best drink with Welsh Rabbit.

" Tamaid Anghyffredin Cymreig

Llond llwy de o wenith yr India; dwy wns a gaws.
Llond cwpan de o lefrith, un wns o ymenyn.
Chwarter llond llwy de o geddw (mwstardd), halen
A phupyr wedi eu cymysgu, i dymmeru.

Modd

Tafeller y caws, todder yr ymenyn a'i gymysgu a'r gwenith India, yna rhodder y llefrith a'r caws a'r tymmerydd atto, troer uwchben gwres cymmedrol, nes y byddo'n feddal, ac yn tewhau: tywallter ar farra wedi ei grasu, gydag ymenyn arne, heilier yn boeth."

MRS. JONES.

Toasted Cheese and St. Peter

"Fynde wryten amonge olde jestes how God made St. Peter porter of heven. And that God of his goodness suffred many men to come to the kyngdome with small deservyng. At which tyme, there was in heven a grete company of Welchmen which with they rekrakynge and babelynge trobelyd all the others. Wherefore God says to St. Peter that he was wery of them and he would fayne have them out of heven. To whome St. Peter sayde, ' Good Lorde, I warrent you that shall be shortly done '. Wherefore St. Peter went outside of heven gayts and cryd with a loude voyce, ' Cause Babe! Cause Babe ', that is as moche as to say ' Rosty'd chese! ' Which thynge the Welchmen herying ran out of heven a grete pace . . . . And when St. Peter sawe them all out he sodenly went into Heven and lokkyd the dore! and so aparyd all the Welchmen out! "

BOORDE, FOURTEENTH CENTURY.

BREAD

" GIF US TO DEI URE DAIFS BRED "

CORN IN ENGLAND

" All corns fair and clean
That groweth on ridges out of the rean.[1]"

CHIEF CORN crops of England have always been wheat, oats, barley, and rye. Wheat still grows chiefly in the south, and oats are more northerly. Rye is less common. The wide drained acres of East Anglia now produce corn where, in the Middle Ages, were wild fowl, and reeds, and fish; and since the war corn has been grown on mountains, on leas that had not been broken for centuries.

"To break a lea, makes a man, and to make a lea, breaks a man" means that years of saving are needed before a farmer can afford sufficient lea grass to keep his stock (without buying feeding stuffs from outside), whereas if he sells off his animal stocks and then ploughs their well-manured leas, in one year he has made himself in *cash*. But where has the farm economy gone? He must now buy his foodstuffs, as he has no lea.

Thus there has always been overlapping between the corn bin and the stock yard, and the balance still swings between animal manure and corn prices. It is not a simple question of importing corn or meat, or home-growing meat or corn, but a problem of balanced farming on well-manured land in good heart. On the whole it is sensible to use the imported corns for mass production of bread flour, and the home-grown crops where their delicate fugitive aromas can be appreciated. Scotch porridge oats are an example, and some types of barley for brewing.

Some of the feast days connected with "corn" still exist. Plough Monday was the first day out with the plough in the New Year. All the boys who "lead plough" get together, and go in parties to call at front doors, dragging with them a plough, and singing and begging. If the owners paid up handsomely, in food, wine, or money gifts—the boys would cheer, and scratch lightly in front of the door (as a sign to other parties that they had been). But if the owner was mean, they would plough up the earth before his door into a dreadful mess. When all was collected,

---

[1] *Rean*—the central furrows, to either side of which are turned the sets of furrow lines in planning a ploughed field.

Bread Shapes

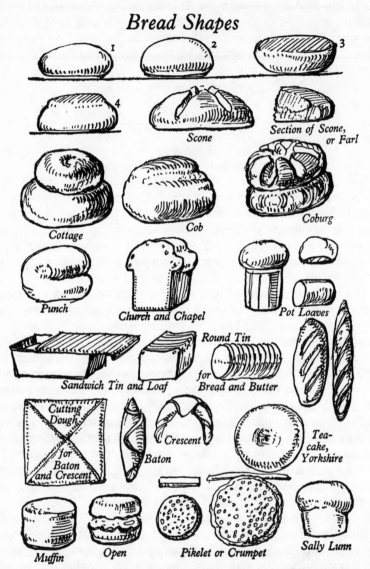

1, 2, 3, 4: The bakestone is an early form. It is cooked till it rises; then turned to complete baking. Therefore the top crust is smaller than the lower. It was this type of "trencher bread" that was cut to provide two "plates" for the mediaeval dinner table.

the lads had a jolly good dinner at the local. When the first rean is cut across the field the ploughman still sets a mark towards which to steer straight across the field, and in olden days it was the custom to set up a special mark. Religious houses would make a ceremony, and hold the church cross for guidance. The lord of the manor might hold firm the cross of his sword hilt to guide his man.

CORN MEASURES

" Would a bushel of evil all excusen,
    for that a grain of love is on it shove."

CHAUCER.

Just as the long measures of England are based on material things—the barley corn, the thumb, the arrow (a yard) of the archer, the foot, or the hide of land, so the quantitative measures are puzzling to the foreigner and deserve a word of interest. The bushel is a good example. There were several bushel measures all different in England—the Winchester bushel of Henry VIII's time being definitely smaller than the official version, which, by Henry VIII law, had been fixed "that the measure for a bushel contain VIII gallons of wheat". In 1826 the Imperial bushel was established by law as 192 cubic inches, and all measures marked as Imperial bushel are that amount.

This measure is (for dry things such as corn) spoken of as a strike because the measure was filled, and the top levelled off with a true stick or rod, which struck off the surplus. Anyone who has to count measurefuls knows the confusion or "did you count the first one?" or "is that the seventh?" or "have we had seven and that's the eighth?" Now the bushel was filled and it was levelled off with one stroke of the stick—that was one strike— and the last measureful was the last strike. If it was not full to the top it could not be struck nor counted.

Today the country people often use a temporary "strike", or "peck", or "bushel", meaning the handy basket or mug which they strike off level and sell at so much a time. Thus the country housewife may say "Hum? 1s. a peck? Just see how big his pecks are this week before you buy the peas!" The man brings one peck to show; and she will say "Oh well, bring three pecks," knowing she will get three times that same measure. *But they will not be any known official quantity.*

A bushel = 4 pecks, or 8 gallons.

The old "Winchester bushel" which continued till Henry VIII's time, was taken to the New World, and is still in use in the United States and Canada. Fitzherbert, in 1523, speaks of the "London bushel", and there are many more measures, till the "Imperial bushel" was established in 1826.

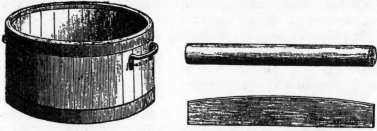

A Bushel measure and Scotch and English "strikes"

The stick drawn across the top of the bushel was square in England—but rounded in Scotland. The rounded was supposed to press down a few extra grains into the bushel as it rolled across the top—but the matter was controversial. The thick round boxwood rulers still in the desks in some rural offices began life as "strikes". The *bushel* is fixed, the *strike* is adjustable.

The graphic saying "To measure our corn by their bushel" thus explains itself; and, like most country analogies, has considerable hard fought controversy behind it.

BREAD OF WHEAT

"Wete the loveliest corn men eat."

Being rich in gluten, wheat flour makes the best type of white bread. Up to the sixteenth century it was usually spoken of as "bread of wheat" because the average bread was of mixed flour. In earlier mediaeval times so much respect and value was set upon this "fine white bread", served only at the high table, that it became a symbol of regal riches.

Probably in pre-Reformation days, the fine white wafer of the Mass bread had something to do with this feeling, and so white bread had almost magic properties for centuries. This makes understandable the aversion to "a dark loaf" among the workers of today. It has nothing to do with diet—it's the feeling that their children should have *the best*; and the best has always been the Whitest. Thus in the nineteenth century

" There is another cause for starvations amongst us, which should move every mother's heart . . . little children dying for want of bread, mothers who spent their last penny for that which is no bread—man's deceptive innutritious constipating white loaf . . ."

Food Reform, 1882.

The rich or intellectual will eat and enjoy all types of brown, oat, wholemeal, rye, and malted loaves, but the poorer the district, the more firmly it will insist upon *their right to a white loaf*. The Government's problem was always how to combine old tradition with new dietetic discoveries.

Holy Bread

" The paste of the uble, not ne ogh
  Be made of any maner of soure dogh
  For the soure dogh maketh alle soure
  The swetnes that cumth of the floure
  By thys soure dogh ys tokenyng
  That enuye ys a wykked thyn."

Translation

The paste of the humble not the high
  Be made in a manner of sour dough
  For the sour dough maketh all sour,
  The sweetness that was in the flour,
  Betoken by this sour dough's working,
  That evil is a wicked thing.

Thirteenth-Century Sermon.

A sourdough was the name given to an old pioneer—as he made his own bread by keeping a piece over each time to go "sour" and start the next ferment.

Surleas was the flat loaf (like mediaeval trencher bread), made by Norman-French pioneers, which was set to "prove" under the warm bedding—"*sur lit*". The old Cape-Dutch voortreckers used the same method while travelling by waggon.

Magic Bread

The bread for the Mass in pre-Reformation days was made of most precious and best wheat flour, fashioned and stamped in the form of a special wafer—wafers being made of fine flour, in a sort of pancake between hot irons (*see* Wafers). That is why we find Huck Finn properly impressed by the fact that best white bread—"such as a quality eat"—had been set afloat to find their murdered corpses.

> " I took out a plug, and shook out a little dab of quicksilver and set my teeth in. It was real baker's bread—what the quality eat—none of your low-down corn pone. . . . I says I reckon the Widow or Parson, or somebody prayed that this bread would find me, ... and it has done . . . so there ain't doubt but there is something in it, when a body like the Widow or the Parson prays, but it don't work for me."

Huckleberry Finn.

American superstition of English origin, for it went to America as a relic of the pre-Reformation belief in the power of consecrated bread; the old mediaeval stores are full of the wonder-working "host" leading to the avenging of murder. (In this case you will remember the boys were supposed murdered and drowned and the bread floated to find them.)

Good Bread (and a note on crusts)

" God may send a man good meate but the devyll sende an evyll cooke. Wherefore gentyll bakers sophystycate not your breade made of fine whete. Gentyll bakers make good breade—for good breade doth comfort a mannes herte. Hote bread is unholesome for any man for it doth lye in the stomache like a sponge—yet the smel of newe breade is comfortable to the heade and to the herte. Sodon breade and breade baken upon a stone or yron is not laudable. Burnt breade and harde crustes and pastry crustes doth ingendre melocoly humours.

Wherefore dyp[1] the upper crust of your bread and whoso doth use to eate the second cryste after the meate it maketh a man leane. Bread which is nututyne and praysed should have these properties. Fyrst it must not be newe but a daye and nyght olde. Nor is it good past 4 or 5 days olde—(except the loaves be great). It must be well muldyd [moulded? kneaded?] and thorowe bake it must be lyght and not hevye and temporately salted."

1400.

Wasted Bread

" The waste of bread in England impresses thoughtful observers and foreigners express the most painful astonishment. It is not solely the fragments of it swept daily from the table of the wealthy and thrown away by pampered and careless servants, or those crusts which ill-trained children are allowed to leave at all their meals."

ACTON, 1850.

YEAST

" Few people know that ABC stands for Aerated Bread Company, because the original firm made bread by a patent process, mixing it inside an iron box with aerated water [carbonic acid gas] which lightened the dough, without yeast."

ANSWERS TO CORRESPONDENCE IN A NEWSPAPER, 1880.

Brewer's yeast. Yeast was one of the perquisites of the brewer's wife; and sold to the farmer's wife at market, to which it was carried in earthenware jars, covered with a cloth. For safety, these were placed overhead on the top shelves of the carrier's cart, above the benches on which the passengers sat. A contemporary sketch mentions the indignation of the market women when the jerking and shaking and heat of the enclosed cart, sets the yeast working, and, despite the cloths, the jars froth over and drip down onto their best bonnets!

[1] Dunking (modern).

A farm bakehouse and some of the equipment. Construction of
the dough trough was very subtle.

Dry yeast—for shipboard, or store—was made by spreading the yeast out on a wide board, and more on top, over and over, as it dried, till it was a couple of inches thick. It was then cut up, prised off the board, and stored in canisters. When wanted for use, a piece was broken off and crumbled into warm water—and set growing again (*see also* Wine Bush).

Potato yeast. Mealy potatoes boiled, and pounded up with some treacle and their own boiled water till the mass was just warm, was also used to feed the yeast. A small piece of growing yeast was started on this, and with the help of a little additional sugar would make enough for a baking within the week.

German yeast came chiefly from Hamburg, and later from Holland. It was introduced about 1850, and by 1866 we imported 5,735 tons in a year.

Modern yeast obtained from a grocer will have a clean fresh smell, and be cool and firm. To start the plant growing, put 1 teaspoonful of sugar to 2 large tablespoonfuls of yeast and break it up gently in a cupful of warm water; add a little more water, and set it in a jar in a warm place to work. It should froth up and fill a 2-lb. jam-jar within an hour or so.

DOUGH (1200)

How a Lady Embraced her Uncle with her hands "all paste and flour!"

> " There was a Knight and he had two fair nieces . . . And coming home from his voyages he brought for each of them a gown of the best and godliest shape and devise as at that time.
>
> And it happened he came late unto the Manor of one niece, and called for her . . . and she went to her chamber for to array herself . . . and sent word she ' would come '; . . . and again he sent . . . and she prayed he ' would not think it long '—she'd come anon . . . So, the Knight disdained that his niece tarried and rode his way ! But, the other niece—when she heard him, notwithstanding she had took upon her to make leaven [dough] and withall had her hands all pasted and floury—As she was; she cometh ! freely and with great voice ! and embraced him pleasantly between her two arms, and said ' Dear Lord ye be right welcome, I come as I am ! for gladness of your coming ! so—please you to forgive me !' And the Knight (within himself) praised her greatly ! and loved her more and gave her the TWO Gowns !"
>
> *The Knight of "la Tour Landry."*

BAKEHOUSE MATTERS

> " I do love manchet breade, and great loaves the whiche be well mowlded and thorowe baken."
>
> BOORDE.

TYPICAL
FARMHOUSE
BREADOVEN.

Note the "bat" for placing the loaves; the slot in front of the door to take the
brushed-out wood ash; the brush, rake, and mop with which the oven is swept
clear before use.

Bread troughs. The trough is waist-high, of thick wood or slate, bolted
together with wooden pine, and secured on a thick base, which forms the
top of a firm-legged stand. It slants pretty finely, and the inside is smooth
and has a sweet yeasty smell; probably the thick wood is impregnated
with ferments, somewhat as the wooden troughs that are used in bacon
and ham curing are impregnated with their own nitrates and add to the
quick action of curing. Unlike dairy utensils this bread trough is not
scalded after each use, but wiped clear, any dough sticking to the sides
"crumbed off" with a rough dry cloth; and cloths, bake tins and flour pots
are usually stowed in it till next baking day. The lid serves as a table when

not in use. If you ever find one, look inside for the tiny "tally marks" cut by the farmer's wife, to show her measure, as we use measuring bowls today.

The trough lid may have a rim, which turns into a baker's tray, to hold the lines of loaves during transit to and from the oven—the other side being used as a flat board or "top" to roll out and handle the dough.

Altogether a good piece of furniture well designed for its purpose.

Bread panshon. If not made in a trough, a panshon is used; it is of thick earthenware, that will not scorch when set down before the fire "to rise the bread". Tins do not distribute their warmth so evenly as earthenware, so the bread set to rise in a tin rises too much on the hot side, and chills on the side away from the fire.

Other Bread Utensils

Yeast jar. It is necessary that the country woman considers these details. The yeast is usually kept in a jar, made thick enough to stand on the back of the stove, a dipper used to carry in the buttermilk or water from the boiler, fits into the jar.

The salt-box is kept in a dry place by the kitchen stove. The salt-box cannot have a metal hinge as it would rust—or verdigris—so it is secured by a leather hinge strip, and the oak must be sufficiently thick to prevent the securing nails from penetrating to the salt, or sometimes the box sides are secured by oak pins, and the lid grooved in.

Knife. A long knife is required to cut the dough, and to put the cross cut to keep the devil out. Good dough at this stage should be smooth and soft, and firmly elastic; it should feel as if it had a life of its own. There are few things more delightful.

Bread Shapes in England (see p. 494)

The Cottage. The piece of dough is lightly rolled out, a division is rolled with the edge of the hand, the whole then lifted and set on end, and in the lifting the top bit is twisted slightly to make the divide more marked. Top and bottom sections are then let down into each other, and a central punch secures them, and there is the familiar cottage loaf ready to slide into the oven. Sometimes the top is scored around with a knife, which makes it more crusty, and tends to spread it out more evenly—"tis all as you fancy and custom dictates".

The Round or Cob. The plain round loaf usually has a cross cut on top to let the dough rise more easily (or to let the devil out?).

Tin loaves. The loaf that is baked in a tin is perhaps more favoured in mechanical districts, and the round loaf in the agricultural. The closed tin that makes a square loaf is only ordered in country districts for sandwiches, and the round shape for thin bread and butter.[1]

Pot Loaves. There used to be a loaf baked in Lancashire in a thick jampot. It cut nice thin bread and butter for tea from the round part, and the top cob was handy for the man's dinner pail.

Batches. Batch or scone-shaped loaves are rather arty, and usually made of very brown bread for country visitors; they are not scones except in shape, and are not baked quite like plain bread.

A Punch is a loaf just punched round and baked that shape. Coburgs and Pones are their own shapes (Mark Twain says all American corn bread is made in a pone shape).

RECIPES

> " 'Twas beautiful dough, like a milking breast it was."
>
> A COUNTRYWOMAN.

A Simple Home-made Bread of Wheat Flour

These very plain directions to a learner are by Elizabeth Acton (1857): "To make two loaves of crusty fresh bread."

Take 1 quartern of flour, (3½ lb.), 1 large tablespoonful of brewer's yeast, 1 teaspoonful of salt, and about 1½ pints of water.

You will need a deep panshon to knead the dough in, a jug to mix the yeast, a knife and clean teacloths, a piece of old clean blanket or sacking, and a couple of bake-pans (I like earthenware bake-pans, myself, rather than tin; they seem to distribute the heat better, though tin ones pack closer, being square). Fit the pans into the oven and see they are right, with plenty of room for the bread to rise, and grease them a little, and have the table top clear, and your oven laid (or lit).

Put the flour into the bowl and make a well in the centre not right down, just a "pokehole amidst". Take the yeast and rub it gently down into about 1 pint of warm water. If it is tired yeast, a little sugar livens it up, if fresh it should not need any encouragement. Pour this yeast cream into the flour hole, and rock it a little gently with your hand, or a *warm* wooden spoon, so that some of the flour falls down into it, and shake an equal thickness of flour over the top, so that the yeast is embedded warmly in the midst of the bowl of flour. Put a clean cloth over the bowl, and for fear of draughts a piece of blanket over that, and set it to stand undisturbed in a warm place for an hour or little more to prove. After an hour the yeast should have grown and permeated the

---

[1] In the colonies I found a bread baked in half petrol-tins, each second loaf had a wart on one side where the stopper used to be.

flour, and risen up through it in bubbling cracks (this *proving* the yeast alive). Now place the panshon on a chair or low bench, and pour in about ½ pint more warm water, and gently mix in the flour surrounding the yeasty part, and go on doing this, sides to middle, with a happy pawing action, like a contented cat, till the dough is all one even mass of warm soft resilience. It will be sticky at first and the moist parts will stick to your fingers, so keep dipping your hands in the dry part of the flour, and sprinkling dry flour on the damp places, your skill being to bring the whole of the dough to one consistency throughout.

As a test of your skill, the panshon should never be sticky, but be dry and floury to the end, because the action is more a centralising rocking motion, a very gentle but brisk roll-and-press action, in no sense a stir around.

You may, while working, have to add a little more warm water, but do it gradually, as you can't take it out again, and to add more dry flour spoils the consistency of the whole. Now you have your dough —knead it.

Turn the whole ball out on to the table and press the middle with your folded fist and work it round and round, sides to middle, folding it in and kneading it down till all is one spongy elastic lump of resilience—no dry lumps of flour, no damp spots of yeast, but an even texture—with a lovely alive elasticity that seems to spring back against your fists.

Round it up now, and put it back into your pan, and cut a deep cross over it (the cross should burst open even as you cut it), cover all with the warm cloths again, and set it back to rise again for another hour, or till it seems to have stopped swelling up, and is as large as it's going to be. The cross will be wide-open gashes now, with the sides glistening and showing the spongy texture within.

Take it up on to the table and cut into two loaves, and shape as you have a mind to do. Put them roundly into the warm bake-pans and set near the stove for another half-hour to plump up even more, and then bake them.

If you want a very crusty loaf, score one loaf criss-cross so as to get as much crust as possible, bake one smooth and plain to keep longest, and if you have enough dough, keep a little to make a dough cake, with currants and sugar, or a doughboy for a child, and these you may keep covered with a cloth, till the bread is drawn out of the oven, and bake anon.

Baking

To tell if a loaf is done, tap it on the underside, and it will sound hollow and dry; the dull thump of a loaf which is still moist in the middle is quite different.

If you want a loaf to have a crisp crust, dry it quickly in a hot place; if you want a soft crust, wrap it in a blanket while warm. If you want a shining crust, brush it over with a glass of milk, or sugar and water, or egg-white and water, and return it to the oven for a final polish. When you want breads strewn with seeds or crushed sugar and spice it is better stuck on top last, as some seeds lose their pungency in the long baking it takes to cook the loaf. When done, cool all bread before putting away.

"All loaves that are not baked in an oven but uppon irons or hotte stones or upon the earth or under hotte ashes are unwholesome because they are not equally baked but burned withoute and rawe within. And such loaves as are baken in an oven the greatest loaves do nourish most . . . but whether breade be made in forme of Manchet, as is used of the gentilities, or in great Loaves as is used among the Yeomanrie, or between both, as with the frankelinger, it is no matter, *it must be well baked.*"

MARKHAM.

Fancy Breads

The farmhouse cook usually keeps one small piece of dough separate, and adds eggs, sugar, spice and fruit and makes a bunloaf—or currant loaf—for tea. The Barra Brieth of Wales is this type of loaf, so is the Yorkshire tea bread, also the saffron cake of Devon, and the London currant loaf. In all its forms (and it can become an elaborate yeast cake) it is the family dough which the cook has glorified. Most of the seed and spice cakes, and the gingerbreads, were copies, made in the farmhouse dough, of the smaller elaborate sweetcakes, that had quite different foundations. (These light breads are dealt with in another chapter.)

VARIOUS COUNTRY BREADS

Nearly all counties of England have their own special type of bread.

"Devonshire is celebrated for the excellence of its bread, in Suffolk almost every cottager wife knows how to make it well, and in the North where large dairy farms are numerous. But in Kent, Sussex, Surrey, Middlesex, and many other parts of the Kingdom, not one woman in twenty is capable of making a loaf."

ACTON, 1857.

Surrey Bread

Made with $5\frac{1}{2}$ gallons flour, 1 teaspoonful of salt, 1 pint of yeast, 1 gallon of warm water—and the whole of the flour is mixed in at once with the warm yeast and water; it is then left to rise for 2 hours, and then kneaded and baked in rather large loaves.

Bara Brieth (the Welsh currant bread)

This recipe was made by Mrs. Jones, who for long kept the old Welsh Temperance Inn at Llanrhaiadr-y-Mochnant.

The bread is brown and close, and the loaves large. It should be spread with butter.

2 lb. of flour (half oat and half wheat), $\frac{1}{2}$ lb. of lard, $\frac{3}{4}$ lb. of fruit (sultanas, etc.), $\frac{1}{4}$ lb. of candied peel, $\frac{1}{2}$ lb. of sugar (brown, demerara), a pinch of salt, 2 eggs, $\frac{1}{2}$ teaspoonful of mixed sweet spice, and 2 oz. of real brewer's yeast.

Make the dough—after putting the fruit and spice to soak in a jar of hot water on the back of the stove. Use the warm spicy water from the soaked fruit to mix the dough, after yeasting it, and add the fruit (still warm), last, before shaping into loaves. Of old it had currants or blackberries in it, and was very suitable for shepherds, and children walking a long way to school, as the fruit kept it moist.

Yorkshire Breakfast Bread

Take 2 lb. of flour, salt, 1 teaspoonful of yeast in 1 pint of milk, and a little sugar. Warm everything, and make and knead up as you would bread, but do not set it to rise till you finally tuck it down again in the panshon, then cover it, and leave it overnight in the warm kitchen. Next morning (not later than six o'clock) work it up into rolls and leave them to rise on the baking sheet near the stove till half an hour before breakfast, then bake in a hot oven, and serve hot, wrapped up in a warm napkin on a hot earthenware dish.

Newcastle Bread

This was brown, and had carraway seeds in it.

Drover's Bread (sometimes called "Travellers' Bread")

> " He should carry provision with him, *such as bread and meat* and cheese, or butter so that he may take luncheon quietly beside his flock while resting in a sequestered part of the road. . . . The injunction to refrain from spirits will sound odd to the ear of a Highland drover; but though a dram may do him good in his mountain air, and while taking active exercise, it will not do him good while walking at a slow pace in low country. Much rather drink ale or porter during the day, and reserve the spirits till evening when he can enjoy a tumbler of warm toddy beside a comfortable fire before retiring to rest for the night."
>
>   *Book of the Farm* (from " Cattle Drovers' instructions "),

Take about 2 lb. of steak, lean and fat; cut it small as fingers, add pepper, salt, and a pinch of mustard. Knead the dough, working in a little seasoning and dry mustard (only a pinch), roll out, and, using the pieces of beef as filling, make what I can only describe as an outsize sausage roll—packing the fat and lean pieces of meat alternately. Bake with the other bread and wrap in a clean napkin until cold.

Mutton can take the place of beef (add with mint, pepper, and salt in the dough) or lean bacon (dry mustard in the dough).

Be sure the bread is wide and thick enough to wrap the meat entirely, to seal the roll and keep in the gravy. Do *not* use vegetables, they will cook soft before the bread is done, and make the dough heavy (*see also* Bread Pies).

Thumb Bread

Piecing and thumb-pieces. The American word "piecing" for a snack taken in the hand, has been preserved since it left England with the Pilgrim Fathers. In Yorkshire they still speak of a "piece poke" for a dinner bag. A thumb-piece was the name given to a piece eaten out of hand and the dirty thumb of the workman caused the piece left over to be called the "thumb-piece". Hence an *extra* piece was packed up to allow for this thumb-piece—or to have a little extra to give away.

Bran Bread (use of bran as aperient in the fourteenth century)

" Browne breade made of the coarsest of wheat having in it much branne, filleth the belly with excrements . . . and besides that, it is good for labourers, I have known that such as have been used to fine bread, *when they have been costive, by eating browne bread and butter have been made soluble.*"

For your browne bread for your hinds [servants] which is the coarsest bread for men's use, you shall take of barley 2 bushels and pease 3 pecks, of wheat rye 1 peck, and 1 peck of mault. These you shall grinde together and dress through a meal sieve. Then putting it in a flour trough, set liquor on the fire, and when it boils let one pour on the water, and another with a mash rudder stir some of the flour into it, season with salt, and so let it lie till next day. Then putting in the rest of the flour, work it up to a stiff leaven, and then mould it and bake it in great loaves with a very strong heat.

If your trough be not sour enough to sower your loaves, you shall either let it lie longer in the trough, or else take the help of a sower leven, with your boiling water."

Rye Bread

Rye was used in England up to 1700, but is not a typical English corn. The earliest records give mixtures of other grain to help out the glutten. Here is a rye-bread recipe.

"Late after sunset put a quart of warm water on the banked down fire with enough oat and wheat meal to make a batter and a little salt and yeast. Let it 'work' all night when it should be a soft sponge. Dry this off with rye flour, kneading to a dough and adding more warm water if it will take it up.

Let the dough rise again by the raised fire till midday, then knead it again and make into loaves and let them prove [i.e. go on rising if they will] and bake on your hearthstone when you sweep back the fire."

Eighteenth-century Coconut Bread

It is curious to find coconut bread popular in the eighteenth century. Grate a fresh coconut, brown rind and all, into a pint of milk, and let it cook very gently without ever boiling till the flavour is well incorporated; cool slightly, and use this milk to mix the yeast and dough, adding the coco-nut, together with a little sugar. (One nut to $3\frac{1}{2}$ lb. of flour.)

Bread in Store and Cut. Store bread in wooden bins, or in an earthenware crock with a fitting lid. Bread kept in tins goes stale sooner than bread kept in the porous earthenware or wood.

To freshen stale bread; dip it in water and put for a few minutes into a hot oven. The crust may become rather brittle but the bread will be as spongy as when new.

Saffron "Cake" Bread

Originally a saffron bread or dough cake. The saffron stamens were steeped in warm water in a covered jar. The water drained off was used to mix the yeast and dough, which took on a fine golden colour.

Sometimes cream (or butter) was added to preserve the aroma, or honey or sugar to liven the yeast; but the original saffron cake was not sweet though strongly aromatic.

FAMINE BREAD

" Let her gouerne her bread so well as that no one be suffered to use it otherwise than in temperate sort . . . and in time of derth, let her cause to be ground awong her corne, Beanes, Pease, Fetches or Sarrasins corne,[1] in some small quantities for this mingling of the lowers raiseth the paste maketh the bread light and to be of a greater bulk."

MARKHAM.

[1] Saracen's corn (*Sorghum vulgare*)—sometimes the name given to common buckwheat.

TEACAKES AND BREAD OF WHEAT

Manchet Bread (Manche—hand bread)

An old writer says:

> " Your best and principal bread is Manchet, which you shall bake in this manner. First your meal, ground and boulted through the finest cloth, you shall put into a clean kimmel [kneading-tub] and opening the flour hollow in the midst, put into it the best ale barme, three pints to a bushel of meal, and some salt to season it with. Then put in your liquor reasonably warm, and kneade it very well together, both with your hands and putting it through the brake—or for want of a brake [*see* p. 311], put it in a cloth, and with your feet tread it a good space together. Then let it lie an hour, so as to swell, take it forth and mould it into manchets, round and flat, scorch it about the waiste to give it leave to rise, and prick it with your knife on the top, and so put it into your oven and bake it with a gentle heat."

FOURTEENTH CENTURY.

Yorkshire Teacakes

> " Q. How do you make Yorkshire tea cakes?
>
> A. Mix 2 lb. of flour with $\frac{1}{4}$ lb. of butter melted in 1 pint of milk, 2 eggs well beaten and 3 tablespoonfuls of fresh yeast. Having left the mixture to rise I knead it, and make 4 or 5 cakes. These cakes I place on a tin, and leave to rise fully. When risen, I put them in a slow oven and bake them.
>
> Q. Would they not be lighter made without butter?
>
> A. Yes ma'am, but most prefer them made with butter as they eat shorter.
>
> Q. How do you send them to table?
>
> A. They should be buttered hot, or if cold cut in two and toasted brown and buttered."

Finchley Manual.

Yorkshire recipe.

Warm a big earthenware panshon, rub 2 oz. of butter and lard mixed into 2 lb. of flour; mix 1 oz. of yeast with $\frac{1}{2}$ pint warm water, make a well in the flour, and pour this in, cover the surface of the yeast pool with flour lightly brushed in from the sides. Cover with a warm cloth, and stand the bowl before the kitchen fire for 1 hour. If the yeast has risen enough it will have boiled over and be full of bubbles. Add a well-beaten egg, a spoonful of salt, and just a little warm milk (all should be the same mild temperature). Knead and knead till the dough is smooth and leaves the panshon clean. When all has become one smooth pumpkin shape of dough, leave it alone; cut a deep cross over the top, cover and leave it to rise once more until it is as high as it will go—about 1 hour. Now divide into twelve pieces, and shape them into round flat cakes on a warm tray and again give them a little time to rise under the warm cover.

Then bake in a moderate oven—probably for 30–40 minutes, but do not let them get too brown.

These Yorkshire teacakes are so important in the West Riding that no table seems "laid" without them. They are a direct descendant of the manchet bread laid for each person on mediaeval tables. In "allowancing" a Yorkshire tea, two plain teacakes are counted for each place, one teacake cut in slices and buttered between each pair, and split and toasted teacakes brought in hot for everyone at intervals.

The right way to butter toasted teacakes (IMPORTANT). Toast bottoms and tops first; split and toast insides; *lay* (do not poke or spread) bits of butter on the lower half; cover with the top half; and invert. Keep hot for 3 minutes, then turn right side up, polish the top with a suspicion of butter, cut in quarters, and send to table. In this way the butter is evenly distributed and does not all soak down into the bottom crust.

Roehampton Rolls

Take 1 lb. of flour, whites of 3 eggs, 3 oz. of butter, 1 spoonful of yeast, Make a dough of the flour and butter and yeast, whip the whites till stiff, and fold in lightly. Let it rise in a rather warm place for 1 hour, form into small rolls, and bake 10 minutes.

Lardy Cakes from Oxfordshire

These seem to crop up on the borders of the chalk line that runs across England from Wiltshire, through Oxfordshire to Cambridge. The best I ever ate were made by Mrs. Martin's Susan at Adderbury, near Banbury. This is her recipe.

Take some of the dough from the bread. Roll it out a quarter of an inch thick, dot with dabs of cold stiff lard about the size of half walnuts, sprinkle with crystallised sugar, and fold the dough into three, or end to end, pinching the sides together to keep in the air. Fold it over once more from the side and roll again—beginning to roll from the open end, so as to imprison the little pockets of air within the dough. Do this three times, putting the dabs of lard between the bubbles showing through where the first dabs were imprisoned. The last time strew very lightly (over the sugar and lard) with spice—barely a breath of nutmeg or a suspicion of cinnamon or allspice (spice very delicately indeed, as the lard takes up the aroma strongly).

Roll out to the size of the baking-tin, marking it across and across, for lardy cakes should be broken down their cracks, never cut. Bake in a hot oven.

London Buns

These plain long-fingered buns with white sugar icing, are now called London buns, but this old recipe is richer. 3 lb. of flour, with 8 oz. of lard rubbed in; 1 oz. of fresh yeast mixed with a tablespoonful of moist sugar and a little milk, and left to become liquid. Then add 1–1½ pints of warm water to the working yeast, and pour it into the middle of the flour and lard, working it together to a soft batter. Cover and leave to rise in a warm place for about 2 hours. Knead well, working in ½ lb. of washed, dried currants, a teaspoonful of carraway seeds (optional), and a teaspoonful of powdered nutmeg mixed in with ½ lb. of sugar. Form oval buns, and let them rise well before baking.

Hot Cross Buns

I have found the same recipe used for hot cross buns, the Good Friday bun having yellow candied peel substituted for the currants, and beaten eggs added to the dough, so that the buns were hot and golden under the cross. "Spice" and "the cross" are important things in all hot cross buns.

Bath Buns

Make a light dough with ½ lb. of flour, ¼ lb. of butter or lard, 1 oz. of castor sugar, 2 eggs, ½ pint of lukewarm milk, and about ½ oz. of yeast. Rub butter into flour; blend milk, yeast, sugar, and beaten egg together (keeping out a spoonful of egg), make a well in the flour, pour in the yeast mixture, and mix your dough lightly. Set it to rise in a warm place, then knead again, and add 2 oz. of candied peel chopped, and the sugar candied in the peel also chopped up. Knead, shape into buns (pretty big ones), brush the reserved egg over them, and cover with crushed-up lump sugar. This is the special part of Bath buns, and soft sugar does *not* give the same effect. Bake lightly and thoroughly till golden brown. Do not put currants in Bath buns.

Wigs

> "And we had the most delightful things for tea, and some things—cakes—Mrs. Wishart calls wigs, the best things you ever saw in your life."
>
> SUSAN WARNER, *Nobody*, 1832.

Wigs are called whigs in a text of 1826.

To make a plain wig. "Take 1¼ lb. of flour and ½ pint of milk made warm, mix these together and cover it up, and let it lie by the fire half an hour;

then take ½ lb. of sugar and ½ lb. of butter and work these into the paste and make it into wigs with as little flour as possible. Let the oven be pretty quick, and they will rise very much." 1700.

To make very good wigs. "Take ¼ peck of finest flour and rub into it ¾ lb. of fresh butter till it is like grated bread, something more than ½ lb. of sugar, half a nutmeg and half a race of ginger grated, three eggs, beaten, and to them put ½ pt. of thick ale yeast, and three or four spoonfuls of sack [or white wine]. Make a hole in your flour and pour in your yeast mixture with as much warm milk as will make it into a light paste—let it stand before the fire to rise half an hour; then make it into a dozen and a half of wigs. Wash them over with eggs just as they go into the oven—a quick oven and an hour will bake them." About 1700.

A rich wig. "Take 3 lb. of fine flour and ¾ lb. of butter and rub it into the flour till none be seen, then take a pint or more of new warm milk and ¾ pt. of ale yeast and with these make a light paste and put in carraway seeds or what spice you please and set it before the fire to rise—and then mix in ¾ lb. of sugar. Then roll them out pretty thin and put them on plates and set them to rise before the fire, and let your oven be pretty quick and they will soon be bak'd."

Whigs, 1900, *as made by Mrs. Stubbs, near Loughborough.* 1 lb. of flour, 6 oz. of butter (or lard), 1 oz. of sugar, 2 teaspoonfuls of baking powder, 2 oz. of currants, 1 tablespoonful of chopped candied lemon peel, a little angelica, and a few chopped candied cherries; mix with 1 egg and a little milk, and bake in hot saucers for about 20 minutes, candy the top when done with white of egg and sugar crumbled on. Split and butter, and eat hot.

Sally Lun Buns

These have been supposed to be called after a buxom Sally Lun who lived in Bath and "cried" them in the streets. A not too reliable writer half a century later states this, and adds that a baker called Delmar bought the recipe and made his fortune with the buns. We do not dispute the existence of the cook, nor the baker, but the "cry" she yelled in good west-country French was "Solet Lune! Soleilune!" An appropriate name for a round bun, flat gold on top, and flat white below.

This yellow-white bun was an infernal trouble to make, taking from sunrise to sunset to "raise", was made gold on top with the beaten yolks of eggs, and split hot and embosomed in clouds of cream.

Various early spellings are "Soli lume", "Solileme" and "Sollylum".

Take ¾ lb. of fine wheat flour, and ¼ lb. to mix separately with ½ oz. of yeast. Add enough new warm milk to make it liquid. Set this to work by the warm hearth. Meanwhile mix the ¾ lb. of flour with salt, sugar and spice, and at evening time knead this out with new warm milk—work it till flat on a board and spread the leaven over it—folding it in lightly. Set it to rise again overnight in a warm place and next morning shape pieces of the dough very lightly into round baking rings and let rise again till the rings are full. Now bake delicately and beat the *yolks* only of some eggs and brush over the tops of the buns and set a fine gold colour. Slip off the rings, and when you eat the buns slit them open and fill with cream whipped to snow (using the white of the eggs) and sweetened, and strew with crushed sugar.

This recipe is taken from Acton, 1855, who in turn spells it "Solemena" or "Soel Leme".

Muffins and Crumpets

These are usually obtained from the bakehouse.

Crumpets vary locally from large brownish dinner-plate size made with an admixture of brown flour in some mountain districts, to small, rather thick, very holey crumpets made in the Midlands. The pikelet is the Lancashire-Yorkshire crumpet of medium size. All crumpets should be toasted on both sides, the smooth side first, the holey side last, as this produces a suitable concavity for the butter. Crumpets a day old should be dipped in milk and placed in a hot oven to freshen before being toasted.

Muffins must be fresh. Never cut a muffin, snip round the curved sides and pull top and bottom apart and insert the butter in thin slices, do not attempt to spread it.

A note by Soyer (who did much to improve our soldier's diet in the Crimea, and afterwards) assures cooks that "half an ounce of butter *to each* crumpet is quite sufficient."

A pudding made from muffins will be found in Puddings.

Bread Pies, Baked

Sometimes called "bread roasts". Good for making a little meat go a long way.

Take a square sandwich loaf, and cut off one long side. Run a sharp knife around the four sides of the exposed crumb, leaving a half-inch crust. Cut out a piece at the end and pull up the white entirely in one piece (this can be sliced for toast, or cut and dried in the oven to make rusks to eat with cheese). Brush over the crust "case" inside and out with melted butter, or dripping, or bacon fat, according to the filling for which you require it, and set it in the oven for 5–10 minutes till crisp and brown (put the lid piece in also).

Fill the crisp case with piping-hot savoury meat, crisped vegetables, the remains of a cold joint tossed hot in well-flavoured sauce, with fried mushrooms and grilled bacon. In fact, any pleasantly blended crisp, rather dry ingredients can be packed in, the lid put on, and the whole given a few minutes for the aroma to penetrate the crust. Send to table with a separate clear sauce, such as tomato or apple, according to the filling of the crust.

Bread, Fried

This is the "pain perdue" of the Norman-French cooks.

The recipes begin in the earliest cook-books, and continue, almost unchanged, except for flavouring, right down to the modern time.

The fine wheat bread (in the earliest centuries) made it a comparatively rare and expensive dish, and in the early recipes the "eyroun" are "mellied" with "gynger" or "honny", later the "eggs are mixed with milk and sugar".

It's one of these simple basic recipes, in which you can tell the century by the contents! This recipe is chosen because the lavish eggs and cream, and the sack, mark it as typical eighteenth century, but the careful mention of "manchet", and "cutting it round ways" sounds as if it had been copied (for centuries) from earlier versions.

To make fried toasts. "Chip a manchet very well, and cut it round ways into toasts; and then take cream and eight eggs, seasoned with sack, and sugar, and nutmeg; and let these toasts steep in it about an hour; then fry them in sweet butter, serve them up with plain melted butter, or with butter, sack, and sugar, as you please." 1700.

Fried Bread, 1951. Cut slices half an inch thick from a stale loaf, soak well in egg, well-beaten with milk, sugar, and flavouring, drain, and fry till crisp. Hot jam may be put on the slices, or cinnamon and honey (in this case omit the sugar with the egg mixture). The sweet is so well known and simple that its interest is its antiquity.

Buttered Crumbs

These are now served with game, a custom derived from the earlier form, which was a loose forcemeat served with meat. The eggs and spice were gradually omitted till the plain version—"buttered crumbs"—figured as a side dish in the eighteenth century. We give two forms, both adapted from the early English

Crumbs, savoury (very useful for making cheese dishes, or making the "bacon and tomatoes" a suitable solidity). Heat a large spoonful of bacon-fat till smoking hot, and shake into it slowly enough rough fresh bread-crumbs to fill the pan. Stir continuously with a fork till the pan is full of crisp brown crumbs. Give a moment to brown evenly, toss on to hot draining-paper, sprinkle with chopped fresh herbs (parsley, thyme, etc. according to the dish it accompanies), pepper lightly, pile the crumbs up lightly, and serve swiftly.

Crumbs, sweet. Melt lard or butter till smoking hot, fry the crumbs, serve with sugar and spice, or hot fruit syrup. In winter, serve with honey and a pat of butter, or a spoonful of hot cider and sugar.

This simple dish is usually liked by children, who enjoy the crunch, and is a good way of giving them extra fat.

Bread Jelly

" Mrs. Forrester made some of the bread jelly for which she
was so famous. . . . A present of this bread jelly was the highest
mark of favour dear Mrs. Forrester could confer . . . and a
mould of this admirable, digestable, unique bread jelly was sent
to our poor sick conjuror! Who says the aristocracy are proud? "

Cranford.

Take a large bread roll, pare off the crust thinly, slice, and lightly toast
the crumbs. Cover with 1 quart of water, and boil gently till it becomes
almost clear and will set on a cold plate. Flavour with a little cinnamon
stick, or thin yellow rind of lemon. The jelly should be sprinkled with
sugar and served with cream in a saucer.

It may also be reheated, with milk or wine as a drink.

Cider Meat

Cut bread into a hot basin (as for bread and milk), add a spoonful of
honey, and enough cider to wet all thoroughly.

Fill up with boiling water, and eat as hot as possible before going to
bed. This (which I believe to be a Somerset recipe) is very soothing for
bronchitis.

Pananda

" I get so tired of gruel, and pananda I cannot bear."

Wide, Wide World.

" Put the crumb of a penny loaf into a quart of cold water, and
a blade of mace, and boil it till 'tis boiled smooth. Take it off the
fire, and put on a bit of lemon peel, and the juice of a lemon, and a
glass of sac and sugar to your taste. This is very nourishing and
never offends the stomach. Some serve it with butter and sugar,
adding currants, which on some occasions are proper but the
first is the most grateful and innocent."

VICTORIAN COOK-BOOK.

OATCAKES AND "DRY" BREADS

" ' Do not the people in the North of England, Scotland and
Wales live even now upon oaten cakes? '
' Yes, and from habit prefer them to bread made of wheat.' "

" MANGALS QUESTIONS ", 1850.

Unleavened Bread

" Breade without leaven is good for no man. Howbeit in England our finest manchet is made without leaven."

1500.

" In Lincolnshire, my native county, unleaven bread or cakes are common. In the mowing season, and during harvest, the labourer's wife would be up at four or five in the morning to bake them. They were eaten hot, split and buttered, or with slices of cold boiled bacon. A goodly pile of these bacon sandwiches, prepared while hot, would be packed up for the men's refreshment while afield. I asked her why she baked every morning, and she said they stay on the stomach longer, and a man can work far better on them than on light bread. He'd feel empty and hungry directly on light bread, unleaven is best for working men afield."

Girls' Own Paper, 1880.

" They carry with them none other pervayance but on the horse, between the sadle and the panel, they truss a broad plate of metal, and behind the sadle they will have a little sack full of oatmeal . . . and they lay the plate on the fire, and temper a little of the oatmeal and when the plate is hot they cast the thin paste thereon, and make a little cake, in manner of a cracknel or biscuit, and that they eat to the comfort of their stomacs . . . wherfore it is no marvel they make greater journeys than other people do."

FROISSART.

Scotch Oatcake

This recipe, fundamentally the same as described by Froissart, is still the standard usage for the Scottish Educational Department of Cookery. The Scotch soldiers probably used some of the greasy water from the army cauldrons, as a small amount of fat is needed to make the oatmeal cakes "bind". They can be made with water only, but are too brittle.

1 lb. of medium oatmeal, 2 tablespoonfuls of melted bacon fat, 1 teaspoonful of salt (Scottish teaspoons are large), boiling water. Mix salt and oatmeal, pour in the fat (stirred into some of the boiling water) and work and knead, adding more water to get a rather soft dough. Work and knead well, roll out as thinly as possible on a board sprinkled with fine oatmeal. Cut into squares or triangles, and bake in a cool oven or on a girdle till they begin to curl. Finish drying them out before a hot fire or in a cool oven, with the door open.

Welsh Oatcake

This is the Welsh oatcake made in all hill farms. It is thinner than the Scotch, and thicker than the West Riding. It is baked on a very characteristic round girdle over a wood fire. As this Welsh oatcake has interesting historical connections with the Hafod we give this demonstration by Mrs. Jones in detail, for the method of making has remained unchanged for centuries. There is an open wood fire under a flat round iron baker ("Plank", in Welsh), on the table are oatmeal, water, and butter and a round basin.

A double handful of oatmeal goes into the big brown basin, a piece ("see you it iss only a little piece") of butter into the warm water, and the warm water is then poured into the oatmeal and beaten with a wooden spoon. The mass is then divided and set out in a row of lumps.

"Now we must be quick—while they are still warm," and pressing a lump flat with one hand and "rounding" with the other the first lump flattens out meekly into a brown round oatmeal moon about as big as a dinner plate.

"It iss quick now." And a small Welsh rolling-pin fairly hops into play, rolling this way and that way actively.

"It iss so that you get it smooth. Now I will show you how we make it very nice." Plate off the dresser is brought down, and the moon is trimmed "very round", "but when we make many it takes too long—there!" and the first Bara Ceirch lies before us, thin as a penny, and round as a dinner-plate (or the bottom of an old milk tub).

It is skilfully slipped onto the hot gridiron.

Now Mrs. Jones fairly flies round.

Browning one cake, beating down the next one, a few more sticks on the fire, a drop more hot water. . . .

When they are made at harvest time on the big farms, one woman mixes, one rolls them flat, and one sits always by four girdles, turning the browning oatcakes and mending the fire, and all are kept busy, and the round brown moons slide off the girdle at the rate of almost one a minute (4 minutes is the average time on the girdle).

As soon as one cake is brown, it is lifted ("stiff now!") up off the grid, and laid flat on the table a moment to steam. It is then propped on the iron fender to dry.

The cooling cakes bend themselves up in the middle so that they look like flat, shallow saucers.

As Mrs. Jones says, "All men, they do like the Bara Ceirch, to work on, yess—indeed they will have it, for a harvest, it iss better than bread."

So this genuine Welsh oatcake is still made in farms in the hills.

A commercial imitation can be bought, but it has not the coarse-grained brittle roughness of the genuine article, as commercially it is made thicker for packing purposes.

West-Riding Oatcake (haver, or clapper)

The former is the correct word, as this type of thin oatbread was introduced into the north-west districts by the armies of John of Hainault in the twelfth century.

Froissart comments upon the crude barren land which is nevertheless more rich than it appears—and the honesty of the type of native, who "always served one pennyworth of hay for one penny, whether it was bought by lord or knave".

All the stone cottages used to be built with a bakestone at the side of the fireplace, and racks for the haverbread hung across the ceilings.

Edwin Waugh, in *Ben and Bantam*, 1866, refers to

"A bread fleigh, or rack, suspended from the ceiling like a great square harp."

John Leech, of Hard-by-the-Castle Yard, in Skipton-in-Craven, for many years supplied Simpsons and London clubs with a weekly supply.

Some makers "throw" onto the hot iron slab from a cloth; and some from a shallow bowl—it is a matter of knack. Originally the haver would be cooked on the flat hearthstone, from which the hot embers would be brushed back, and the place changed, as the stone grew cold. The name "clapper" was an importation from the south and west, perhaps, where there is a type of oatcake, made very thin by clapping it between the two hands (or perhaps from "clapper stone"?), but these are smaller cakes, roughly round, and altogether different from haver.

This description of haverbread-making is from a magazine of 1880; the method is still unchanged, and so is the recipe, but stone was used instead of iron in earlier times.

> "We found Mrs. Marsden in full swing with her oatcake. Her stove was a thick plate of iron 2 feet long set on brickwork, and heated by a fire below. Beside her a wooden vessel [an old barrel churn] containing the batter made of oatmeal salt and water. I am inclined to think some yeast was used, as bubbles kept rising to the surface.[1] A bowl of dry meal, a pasteboard scored into diamonds, instead of being quite smooth, a wooden ladle, and an oblong piece of coarse linen.
>
> First throwing a handful of dry meal on to the board, she stroked it into an even oblong, she next poured on a ladleful of batter. She then dexterously transferred the batter from the board to the cloth, which was well mealed over, and which she lifted with both hands holding opposite corners.
>
> Then with a rapid movement, she threw the batter in a longer oblong straight on to the heated iron plate, dropping the lower corner of the cloth as she did so.
>
> [1] See end of recipe, where this binding mixture is given.

In less than half a minute the oatcake was ready to be skinned up with a spatula and hung across a wooden rail. The rapidity with which the operation was performed showed the fruits of long practice.

The stream of batter ran along the iron plate almost from edge to edge, and was so thinly spread out that it was absolutely in small holes; yet without being broken. To throw oatcake so thin is deemed a mark of the accomplished hand.

The newly baked and still perfectly soft and pliant cakes were brought away by the cottagers. Each had a towel folded length-ways. This was opened across one arm, the dozen or so oatcakes placed over the arm, and covered with the other fold, and so carried home, to be hung on the rack from the kitchen ceiling. In a few hours the clapper would be perfectly crisp and brittle as glass."

1880 NEWSPAPER.

The binding mixture. 1 quart of warm water, 1 oz. of German yeast (bread yeast) and about 3 lb. of *fine* oatmeal (dust meal is good as the finer the particles the better); stir all together, gently working by hand till smooth; cover, and set to rise. Use this liquid (if necessary thinned with more warm water) to bind the rougher oats for haver-cake baking.

In 1938 Mr. Leech did not use a cloth, but threw direct from a thin light board. Also he had a second hot plate, onto which he turned over the oatcakes, and his assistant took them from this hot plate and folded them up exactly as if they had been pieces of thin cloth. Cool, but still pliant, they were thus wrapped in brown paper, and despatched by post—or sent on to the retailers in the town, or customers. They would stay pliant for several days.

The Lancashire Regiment were known as the "Havercake lads".

OATMEAL

Corn Grains

> " HE had a thumb of gold parde! "
> CHAUCER.

A miller can tell, by the feel of the flour between finger and thumb, exactly how the grinding stones are set for the corn,—so that the "Miller's thumb" was a real asset, as well as a pun on his thieving!

The more northerly grown oats have a finer flavour, for oats have a very distinctive flavour and aroma.

Few people realise the variety of oatmeals and their many uses. Rough cut or rough ground oatmeal is hard and crisp and nutty in texture. This is best for solid food and is put into meat dishes and broths, and oatcakes. Medium oatmeal is used for bannocks and for mixing with other flours. The fine oatmeal is used for bannocks, scones with butter-milk or pancakes, for flouring herrings, thickening soups and broths, or to boil, with butter, into a delicate warming gruel.

Porridge

Take a thick saucepan one-third full of boiling salted water, "bubbling fast as galloping", and have your coarse oatmeal dry and convenient by your left hand. Then with the left hand sprinkle the oatmeal very lightly down on to the bubbling boiling water, so that every grain falls separately into the boiling water, is instantly sealed up, and so stays crisp, and no grain ever softens to slime.

Never scatter fast enough to stop the water bubbling, never stop sprinkling and stirring till the last handful of meal is in, then seize the spurtle (stirrer) and drive all vigorously round and round till the porridge suddenly thickens; clap on the lid and 20 minutes later it is exactly ready.

Quantities vary with the age of the meal and individual taste. We use roughly a small cupful of oatmeal to two large cupfuls of water and a teaspoonful of salt to a cupful of oats we think not too much.

To serve Scotch fashion. The porridge is poured smoking hot direct into a bowl, set by a mug of cold milk, then with a spoon you take up some porridge, dip up the cold milk into the spoon and so get a good hot mouthful, solid enough to chew, and yet fresh and cool with the milk. This is the test of good oatmeal porridge: each grain is distinct, though soft enough to lie level in the bowl; it "cuts" cleanly, and never clings to dish or spoon.

Porridge on the Farm (eighteenth century)

" Considerable trouble is imposed on the inmates of a farmhouse in providing and cooking food every day for a large number of reapers. Complaints are made that the porridge is too thin, not enough boiled, that the milk is skimmed or sour . . . the farmer has control over the porridge [and should see] that the porridge is properly cooked and the milk in a sweet state.

Taking the price of bread at 1d. for 1 lb. for oatmeal and 1¼d. for 1 lb. for white wheaten bread, the cost of the food of harvesters is: 10 loaves out of 1 peck of oatmeal gives a weight 1 loaf of 11.2 oz., and oatmeal at 1d. for 1 lb. fixed the value of the loaf at 2.8 farthings, the cost of baking with yeast being 1 farthing for 1 lb. of oatmeal including yeast and salt, the baking of 1 loaf of 11.2 oz. increased with yeast, salt and water to 14 oz. will be 0.7 farthing; 1 oatmeal loaf baked with yeast will thus cost 2.5 farthings—2½ farthings."

      STEVENS, *Book of the Farm.*

Flummery (made of oatmeal)

> " To make a pretty sort of Flummery. Put three handfuls of
> fine oatmeal into two quarts of water, let it steep a day and night,
> then pour off the clear water through a fine sieve, and boil it down
> till it is as thick as hasty pudding. Put in sugar to taste and a
> spoonful of orangeflower water. Pour it into a shallow dish to set
> for your use."

1700.

This is a pleasant light summer substitute for porridge, and pleasant
also with crushed fruit and cream. A fair quantity can be made at once,
as it will keep if boiled daily.

Oatmeal Pudding (English valley recipe)

> " Of Oats decorticated take two poun,
>   And of new milk enough the same to drown;
> Of raisins of the sun, stoned, ounces eight,
>   Of currants cleanly picked, an equal weight;
> Of suet finely sliced an ounce at least,
>   And six eggs newly taken from the nest,
> Season this mixture well with salt and spice
> 'Twill make a Pudding far exceeding rice;
>   And you may safely feed on it like farmers,
> For the recipe is learned Dr. Harmer's."

KING.

Gold Belly (an oatmeal pudding; Scotch mountain recipe)

I had this at Cape Wrath Lighthouse about 1918. It is an excellent
example of the same pudding and same recipe, but with that subtle change
in ingredients that marks the "mountain" cookery from the "valley"
cookery.

Thus buttermilk was used instead of sweet milk, and a little clarified
mutton fat in place of the lowland beef suet. This lack of distributed fat
was compensated by the big lump of butter placed in the middle of the
pudding before boiling, and the rum and butter, or brandy and brown-sugar
sauce, complete an almost diagrammatical contrast due to geographical
influence. The lack of eggs in the northern version is probably less
geographical than calendar, as it was a winter recipe, when northern hens
were not laying. So I have not included the lack of eggs in the difference
between the two recipes.

Northern version. 2 lb. of coarse oatmeal, enough buttermilk to swell it
thoroughly (soaking it overnight), and add raisins, chopped peel, and a few
sliced prunes. If there is not much loose butter (scraps from the churn)
in the buttermilk, add a little shredded mutton fat. Knead up with fine

dry oatmeal to form a ball, putting a lump of butter and a big spoonful of brown sugar in the middle; flour the cloth, and boil (4 hours is not too long). Roll out, smoking hot, into a bowl and eat with melted butter and brown sugar for six o'clock "tea".

It was standard pudding put on when the boys were "out late with the boats", as it could not be overboiled. It is good also for "after footba' " teas.

"*Amendment of Salt Mete*" (oatmeal dumpling)

An oatmeal pudding to eke out the meat ration. This is very good boiled in broth with vegetables.

> " Take a fare lynne clout and do theymme a disshful of otemele, lyne hit and hang it in thy pot down to ye botome. Let it from the fyre and let hit kele—suththe set hit open to yet fyre and drawe out by clout and that is goude."
>
> FOURTEENTH CENTURY.

Excellent. Flour the cloth, pour enough broth onto some oatmeal to wet it well, and then tie up loosely and "hang in thy pot". Split it open when cooked, like a pease pudding (which see). It is better than potatoes or bread to eat with boiled bacon or salt meat of any kind. It is like a very dry, floury brown dumpling.

Wash Brew

Here are two recipes, the first one dating from 1623.

(1) "From small oatmele; by steeping, and then boyling it to a thicke and stiffe; a jelly, is made, which is esteemed in the West parts of this kingdome, which they call Wash Brew (and in Cheshire and Lankeseire they call it Flamerie or Flumeria. . . .) Some eate it with Honie, that is reputed the best sauce."

(2) Take a double handful of fine oatmeal and stir it into about 2 quarts of water, and let it stand overnight. Next day boil it gently till thick, and stir in a good knob of butter and enough milk to make it to the consistency of double cream. Continue to cook it slowly and test a little on a cold plate, and when it "sets" pour it on to shallow bowls. It is a pleasant, roughish brown cream like junket and makes a cool summer breakfast cereal—with cream and sugar.

Oatmeal Caudle

This was a good hot drink, with some substance in it for a cold night, and most deservedly popular with labourers setting out for the long drive home after a winter's market day.

I believe it would be a popular brew today in many country pubs as there is nothing at present that well serves a really hungry man who is too tired to eat.

Take 2 quarts of ale, and 2 quarts of water, and add to them 2 handfuls of oatmeal (fine), 12 cloves, a nutmeg broken, and a small race of well-bruised ginger root. Boil all together carefully for half an hour, stirring well. If it should work up too thick, add a little more ale (or beer, to taste). Pour it out into a hot jar on to a ½ lb. of warm sugar and a bit of lemon peel (or beer gale, or balm). Cover it close with a hot blanket, and serve in hot mugs. It should be middling strong. It goes down well with a bit of bread and cheese, but drunk off quick it will get a man home under his own steam.

Oatmeal Sausages (or white puddings)

These curious cereal sausages from the west country belong to districts where oats are grown rather than wheat. They are popular in the south of Ireland. The proportions are: prepared oatmeal, one measure; lard or mutton flead (see Flead), half a measure; chopped onion, dried herbs and spice, a quarter of a measure. (Actually, you use slightly more than the oat measure, for they must be "dry baked" before use, which reduces bulk and weight.)

Spread the coarse oatmeal out on a tray and dry it very thoroughly. It can be done before the fire or in an oven. To this dried oatmeal add the flead, chopped finely, the chopped onion and the herbs. Add a little pepper and salt. The herbs should be dried parsley, thyme, sage, marjoram, and penny royal, or to your own liking.

Mix all well together and press into sausage skins, leaving plenty of room for the mixture to swell. Put about four inches into the skin, then tie it with thread, tie again, a half-inch from the first knot, fill up another four inches, tie again, and then again, making a dotted line of the sausages. The stuff swells so much in cooking that it is necessary to have this double tie between the sausages, as otherwise you cannot cut them apart without bursting.

Now plunge the sausages into boiling water and let them boil a good 40 minutes, till they have swelled all they have a mind to, and prick them well as they swell so that they don't burst. When thoroughly boiled, hang them up to dry. They will keep some time when they are thoroughly dried out.

Serve as ordinary sausages with bacon; or roast them, basting with bacon fat, and serve with apple sauce or egg-and-breadcrumb; them and roast, basting with mutton fat, and serve with onion sauce.

Note. The oatmeal has the quality of absorbing the flavour of the meat fat with which it is made, therefore in districts where it is made from pork flead the white puddings are seasoned thoroughly with sage and onion, together with pork. Where they are made with mutton flead, parsley, mint, and thyme predominate in the seasoning. They are never made with beef suet.

Special Glamorgan Sausages

> " The breakfast was delicious, consisting of excellent tea, buttered toast and Glamorgan sausages, which I really think are not a whit inferior to those of Epping."
>
> BORROW.

The main ingredient is cheese, and the white of an egg is used to form the skin. The recipe is as follows:

5 oz. of breadcrumbs, 3 oz. of grated cheese, 1 teaspoonful of finely chopped leek or onion, $\frac{1}{2}$ teaspoonful of mixed herbs, $\frac{1}{2}$ teaspoonful of dry mustard, pepper and salt, 1 egg.

Separate yolk of the egg from the white.

Mix together all dry ingredients and bind with the yolk of egg, adding a few drops of water if necessary.

Cut mixture into little portions and roll each, on a floured board, into sausage shapes. Dip each sausage in the white of the egg, which has been slightly beaten. Crumb and fry in fat. These may be served hot or cold.

Parkin

1$\frac{1}{2}$ lb. of medium oatmeal, 1$\frac{1}{2}$ lb. of plain flour, $\frac{3}{4}$ lb. of rough sugar, 1 oz. of powdered ginger, $\frac{1}{2}$ oz. of allspice, 3 oz. of candied peel (cut chunky), and almonds.

Mix all the dry ingredients together in a large basin.

Take 2 lb. of treacle (either the old-fashioned reddish "loose" treacle or equal parts of black treacle and golden syrup mixed) $\frac{1}{2}$ lb. of fat (mutton dripping will do) and about 2 pints of water. Set these to boil together in a large pot.

When the liquid has boiled and mixed well, stir in 1 large teaspoonful of bicarbonate of soda, and as it froths over, stir it quickly into the dry ingredients. Mix well for 2 or 3 minutes (you may have to add a little more liquid)—it should be a very soft dough that will just pour into a well-greased shallow tin. Bake evenly in a slow oven 1 hour or longer. When the middle will not "dint" on pressing, it is done. Let it cool in the tin, as it is very brittle while hot.

Turn out, cut into square slabs, and store in a wooden box—not a tin—as the parkin is best kept a week before use and gets a pleasant moist texture.

Parkin-and-apple Pudding

When making parkin, it was popular in the north country to make an extra panful to serve hot, smothered with apple sauce, at tea-time.

Grasmere Gingerbread

A type of gingerbread known as Grasmere is now made of fine wheat flour, but was originally made with fine oatmeal. $\frac{1}{2}$ lb. of fine oatmeal, $\frac{1}{4}$ lb. of fat, $\frac{1}{2}$ lb. of sugar, 1 spoonful of syrup, 1 teaspoonful of ginger, $\frac{1}{2}$ teaspoonful of cream of tartar and bicarbonate of soda. Mix all the dry things together and beat in the melted fat, sugar and syrup. This should just bind it very dryly. Press into a tin and bake and do not turn out until quite cold.

Sowans

> " Till butter'd so'ns wi fragrant lunt
> Set a' their gabs a-steerin' ;
> Syne, wi a social glass o'strunt,
> They parlted aft careerin'
> Fou-blythe that night."
>
> BURNS, " Halloween".

Sowans, as a dish, has two forms, the first purely cereal, when the grains of flour left within the shell of the oat grain are used as gruel; the second when the liquid from the shell itself forms the basis of a fermented liquor.

(1) The "butter'd so'ns" referred to above, would be the thickened cereal form. To make this, the shells of husked oats are steeped in water, stirring repeatedly for 24 hours. They are then stirred again and strained off into another basin, where the liquid is allowed to stand undisturbed overnight. In the morning there is a clear liquid on top and a cloudy sediment below. The clear is poured away (and, boiled, can form the basis of a drink something like barley water), the thick substance at the bottom is boiled (this will stop any tendency to fermentation), and then cooked slowly till sugar is formed.

This thick gruel is then flavoured, seasoned, buttered, and drunk steaming hot, or poured out and allowed to set, and when cold may be treated like a junket and eaten with sugar and milk, or salt and milk. It is, in fact, a very light, digestible porridge food.

(2) Sowans as a clear liquid is not boiled, but set aside to ferment (an acetous ferment). This fermented liquor was probably an early proto-type of whisky, though rye was used to make a ranker spirit. The sowan type of cereal broth is found in various forms in all mountain rural dis-tricts. (In the plains and wheat-growing districts fermenty, soft fruit, and herb brews tend to replace it.)

Brewis

The tea-kettle broth of Wales was made originally from the same oat shellings as sowans. Later it was made from oat bread, Bara Cierch, and still later with ordinary bread (crusts for choice, as nearer to the original).

In the earliest recipes, oat shells were stirred and soaked (see Sowans), the clear liquid poured off, and the lower thickness boiled till it became a thin broth (not so unpalatable as it sounds). This, with a lump of bacon fat, pepper and salt, made the palatable gruel called "brewis".

In a later form the boiling water was poured on to crumbled oatcake, the dish was covered, and cooked on the peats for 10 minutes or so. Butter, pepper and salt were added and it was eaten hot from the hot basin with a horn spoon (you can eat hot things hotter with a horn spoon).

The brewis made today by old people in the Principality is made of ordinary bread.

For this, take a deep bowl and make it thoroughly hot, and half-fill with finely cut bread crusts. Put a lump of butter and some pepper in the middle of them, and pour boiling water slowly on to the lump of butter, so that it is melted and will run well down into the bread. Cover the basin for five minutes; add a little more salt and eat hot.

Oatmeal Pudding, Baked (using fine oatmeal; 1477)

Mix the oatmeal with milk to a medium cream, and cook; add more milk as it thickens till as thick as very thick cream. Boil very well and sweeten. Now grate into it 3 tablespoonfuls of very finely pounded suet, a whole nutmeg grated, and some chopped peel. Bake in a piedish in a hot oven.

To serve: crush sugar candy on top and set back in the oven till caramel. It needs some topping as it is rather a dull brown colour (that is why the older recipes colour it with saffron).

Oatmeal Gruel for a Cold

> "Grewel made with otmele in to which no herbes be put, can do lytle displeasure except that it doth replete a man with ventosyte [wind] and it relaxeth the belly."
>
> 1400.

Melt a tablespoonful of suet, and cook a finely sliced onion in it till soft but not coloured. Season with pepper, salt and cinnamon, and stir in about a teaspoonful of fine oatmeal, stirring all the time till the mixture is dry and binds on the spoon. Now add milk, gradually, till a thick white sauce results. Boil this well, thinning down with a little more milk if too thick. Check for seasoning, and serve piping hot in a hot bowl wrapped in a napkin. (1800.)

Brose

Scotch brose is traditional; early recipes used only the shellings, or even the husks and waste from the grindstones (or in some cases the dust from the more coarsely cut oatmeal), but nowadays the word has two or three meanings for different types of porridge soup. I believe the earliest brose was the cold preparation of oat or barley meal carried by shepherds and labourers of the hills. In the sixteenth, seventeenth, and eighteenth centuries, leather or wood hoggins were carried by the workmen, and it is more than probable that some bacterial culture in the hoggin assisted fermentation.

To make brose in those days the ground oats, or the shellings, were put into dry hoggins. The shepherd hung his hoggin on his back, and climbed up the mountain. Near the top, he filled it at some brook, again hung it on his back and set out on his long tramp after the sheep. The warmth and the movement (and perhaps the bacteria in the hoggin) set up fermentation and the churning motion over the rough ground speeded up the process. The result, some hours later, was a thick, rather aerated porridge. (When I tried this myself the porridge did not actually ferment, but then my hoggin was clean, but the result after ten miles was like well-beaten batter, full of air bubbles, and slightly sweet.)

Another brose was oatmeal and salt in a bowl, with boiling water poured over it. It was allowed to swell a little (not too long), and this almost raw porridge was called brose.

Brose, nowadays, loosely designates many forms of broth; for example, when oatmeal was stirred into clear mutton broth (from the sheep's head) till it thickened like porridge, it was called brose—as distinct from the same broth with meat scraps and vegetables in it, which was called "broth".

BARLEY, RYE, BRAN AND OTHER CEREALS

Barley Meal

> " Wha in his wae days were loyal to Charlie?
> Wha bit the lads wi' the bannocks of barley."

Though barley was used as flour in the same way as wheat, barley bread was coarse—Piers Plowman has "Two loaves of barley bread", and its denser quality seems to have made it suitable for the round plate bread (the flat loaves that were laid on the table and used as plates). It also cooked better in flat hearth loaves.

Barley meal makes the best milk porridge and pearl barley goes best in broth. Barley water, and many barley recipes, come under their separate headings. Derbyshire "barley bake" is interesting, as the grain was supposed to be good for throats (goitre?).

Pearl Barley

Spring barley is steamed, dried, and ground between high (set high) millstones to take off the husk; the little dark line across pearl barley is this husk, left in the seed furrow.

Scotch pearl barley is very round, and is called "bere" or "brigg". Pearl barley boiled in sweet buttermilk, like porridge, and eaten with treacle on it, is: "Common work food in the Fen districts where the Hollanders settled." (Webster.)

> " The crust of the Christmas Goose Pies of Cumberland was
> compounded of barley meal."
>
> ACTON, 1819.

As a rule pastry is not attempted with barley flour, but it makes a fair boiled crust.

Ale-berry of Barley

Barley berry is made by boiling stale barley bread in mild ale till soft and thick. The resultant "porridge" was sweetened with heather honey and served with thick cream.

For rickets, or "painful legs in children" (rheumatism?), a warm bath, rubbing with goose-grease, feeding with hot aleberry before bed, and wrapping in a blanket, was soporific, nutritive, and effective.

A Note on Rye

> " If soil do desire to have rye with the wheat,
> By growing together, for safety more great;
> Let white-wheat be t'one, be it dear, be it cheap,
> The sooner to ripe, for the sickle to reap."
>
> TUSSER.

We have found the husks of rye grains in the cracks of fourteenth-century oak chests, and its long straw was commonly used for thatch. In old houses near Ludlow I've found it a foot deep on the top ceilings under the roof. Rye straw is very tough, and is still grown in some districts, where coarse pottery and earthenware require packing material for transport. Of old, the broken rye straw left over from thatching was sold for this purpose.

The fungus disease of rye, *Claviceps purpurea*, is retained in the *British Pharmacopoeia*. It was formerly a midwife's parturient; its illegal use as an abortive was sometimes disguised as material for witchcraft. Old volumes of the *Journal of Agriculture* give notes of stock losses through cattle grazing grasses diseased by this fungus. Infectious abortion was sometimes attributed to it, and sometimes to spells. Huge epidemics resultant from using infected rye bread have been common in Europe for centuries; the last small epidemic in England occurred in Manchester in 1927 among the Jewish immigrants from Central Europe.

It is curious how seldom rye bread is mentioned, except unkindly, or as a "mixed corn bread". Like all foreign breads, it can be bought in London and Liverpool, Manchester and big cities, but I've never found it made in the country, and so omit it.

BRAN

Bran Flummery

Bran was much used for washing seventeenth-century chintz, and stuffing upholstery, such as coach and boat cushions, but it is also the basis of a very pleasant summer sweet called variously bran flummery and bran jelly.

Take ½ peck of bran, and let it soak several days in 2 gallons of water. Strain off, pressing hard, and boil down to a third—so that when cold it sets like a jelly—serve it with sugar, rose water, or orange-flower water, and put cream on it, or milk.

This flummery appears in many forms. I have chosen this later period as nearest to modern taste, but the "long boiling" dates from the continuous open fire. For modern usage adapt as follows:

Take ½ peck of bran, and let it soak in 1 gallon of water overnight. Next day let it boil gently till the liquid appears thick; sweeten lightly and stir with a head of fragrant elder flowers, or sweet briar, to give it a slight fragrance. Strain off into shallow bowls, when it will set very quickly. It is a pleasant change from junket, and with crushed fruit makes a simple summer breakfast cereal.

(*See* Oat Chaff.)

SAGO

"He's ill, and Mamma said I might have some jelly and sago for him."

Old Helmet (a novel of 1850).

When a thing is rare it is valuable—and when a thing is valuable all manner of valuable uses are attributed to it with small deserving. In 1850 sago was a rarity, therefore it was "invalid diet". It is interesting to find it becoming cheaper, being adopted by the "poorer classes" and dropped by the "expensive classes" (there is more snobbery about food than anything else).

Sago Jelly

A recipe of 1780 says: "Boil sago till it jellies, a spoonful and a half to a quart of water, then season it as you do salop [*see* Salop], and drink it in chocolate dishes, or you may put in a pint of thick cream, and a stick of cinnamon, and thicken it up with two or three eggs."

Sago Milk

> "You sniftin' and shirking up there among the arreroot and the sago?"
>
> > KIPLING, *Soldiers Three.*

This recipe was used in the Boer War.

1 teaspoonful of sago crushed, 1 pint of milk; stir till it boils, cover closely, and leave to cook very slowly on a hot place for 1 hour. Strain, sweeten, flavour and serve in a glass.

"Ruddy Glue" (*see* Damsons)

Sago was also used to copy the older English wheat flummeries. This excellent dish is liked by people who do not care for milk puddings. Fill a deep saucepan with about 2 pints of damsons, 2 pints of water, and dredge in about 1 pint of crushed sago. Boil altogether until clear and the damson stones float loose, skim them off, break and take out the kernels which are replaced in the pudding, sweeten, pour into a deep earthenware oven dish and bake till all trace of sago is lost in a gorgeous crimson gum. Serve piping hot with cold milk and crushed sugar. It is also good cold. This was learnt in my first Yorkshire kitchen; the English boys gave it its unlovely English name.

(For Portland Sago, *see* Salop.)

RICE

> "If you will sow rice you may doe it, but it is like to prouve a work of curiositie rather than of profit, for rice is a commoditie belonging to growing amongst Indians. . . . Chuse out some field that is bare and foul, . . . that through it you may convey some little brooke of water—sowe your rice therein—after steeping . . . and draw your little brook along through it and suffer it to continue five whole months at the depth of two fingers. . . . If you boyle rice in milk adding thereto sugar and cinnamon, it will provouke into venerie. Many do think it maketh fat; but seemingly that (according to the physitions) it is not digested in the stomach but verie hardly, it must need nourish but little— How can it possibly make one fat? Indeed it may be said to puff up rather than to make fat."
>
> > MARKHAM.

A Mediaeval Rice Pudding (1400)

"Nym ye ris whes hem clene, seethe hem fort til hit breke [till a grain taken in the fingers will break], let it kele, do thereto almand mylke, and of Kyne [cow's milk] colour yt salt, and gif yt forth."

Farmhouse Rice Pudding

Usually made in old houses where it costs nothing to leave the pudding cooking itself slowly on the hob for hours. Use a very slow oven. Wash the rice. Butter the dish, cover the bottom a quarter of an inch thick in rice, and cover that with three to four inches of sweetened milk, put some slow flavouring into it, such as vanilla pod or cinnamon, cover closely and bake slowly, stirring often at first, till the rice has swollen and the milk is thick. If the milk is creamy—that's all. If the milk is not creamy, add a small spoonful of fine oatmeal—or of very fine suet. Raisins may be put in.

The Loose Rice for Curry

This should be dropped slowly into fast-boiling water and kept galloping till done—test by squashing a grain. Drain through a wire sieve, and shake loose before a hot fire for one minute.

East End "Meat" Rice for Mutton

East End women make a rice pudding using broth to cook the rice instead of milk, and pepper and salt and herbs for flavouring. When cooked, it is finished under the joint of mutton (like Yorkshire pudding under beef). Some put chopped onion with the rice, to its improvement.

Thunder and Lightning

Hot plain water-boiled rice (as for curry) served piled high and loose on a hot dish, with golden syrup handed separately.

Ground Rice Pudding at Bath

Here is a rice pudding of old-fashioned opulent date—"as served at Bath" in the 'nineties. Set a pint of thick cream on the fire, put in 3 spoonfuls of flour of rice (ground rice), stir, and when it is pretty thick, pour it on to 1 lb. of fresh butter in a pan. Stir till almost cold, then add grated nutmeg, salt, sugar, 6 beaten eggs with a spoonful or two of sack, and beat and stir all well together, and put a little fine paste at the bottom of your dish and bake it.

Sleepers, or Dormers

These date from Mr. Stephenson's new steam railway.

They are boiled rice, drained, and seasoned with freshly chopped herbs, to which is added an equal quantity of cold minced meat. The whole is pressed while hot into a flat tin and left to set, and when cold cut into slices (sleepers) and egg-and-crumbed and fried. Serve with beef gravy if the meat is beef, or with melted red-currant jelly if mutton, or apple sauce if made with pork scraps. (As a change from the usual rissole they are to be highly recommended.)

SEMOLINA

"Q. What is semolina?
A. A light and wholesome food formed from wheat flour; it makes excellent pudding."

CHILDREN'S EDUCATIONAL QUESTIONS, 1850.

"The best kind of wheat was called in old time Silogo. Whereof was made the finest bread called Panis Siligineus, which wee call Manchet, and was pleantifl among the Romaines. . . and although Plinie preferred the wheate of Italie before all other . . . yet as I think wee have as good wheate in England as many be found in any Countrie in all Europe, and as good bread is made theorof, especially that of Yorke, which they call Maine bread."

LAURENS, 1400.

"Coarse wheat flower is that which to the Latines is called Similago and is made of wheat excellent good, having the greatest bran only lifted from it . . . the french name Semole . . . from the Latine Sinemola. . . . We have not any of the corns in this countrie."

MARKHAM (translated from a French book into English usage).

There are no very noteworthy early semolina recipes, till they were made up with eggs and milk in the lavish eighteenth-century manner. Semolina never seems to have been considered "precious" like sago.

Here is a good 1951 semolina pudding.

Have about 2 pints of water boiling fast, salted, and dribble into it semolina till the water is full and dense (exactly as if making porridge). Do not expect it to get thick at this stage—only "fill" the water, letting each grain of the semolina float free (this gives it a clear texture). Now cook slowly till thick, then beat in as much butter as you can afford; when well cooked in, add cold milk till rather thinner than you want the pudding when done; grease a pudding dish, and put a layer of treacle into it; cover with the semolina, dot the top with butter and sugar, and bake till there is a crisp toffee crust. Serve hot.

The cooking first with water is because a higher temperature is better to burst the starch grains, and the cold milk added later is not "boiled away", and wasted in the previous cooking.

Buckwheat Cakes

Buckwheat is mentioned by Stevens as a crop tried out in Scotland about 1850, but it is too dependent upon the weather for harvesting to have become popular. The buckwheat cakes and maple syrup of New England probably had their Elizabethan prototype in ryecakes with honey.

Mrs. Cobbett says: "Being so much the fashion to eat cakes [rolls] instead of bread [loaves] for breakfast and tea . . . the Americans used to make a great variety, not only sweet kinds, but such as buckwheat cakes and rye cakes which are always eaten hot and which few strangers fail to admire." This is Mrs. Cobbett's own recipe, as made in her house in Kensington in 1846.

"1 lb. buckwheat flour made into a batter with warm water, stir in 2 tablespoonfuls of yeast, cover, and set to rise by the fire. In three hours it will be ready to stir in more warm water or buttermilk, till the consistence of thick batter. Grease the iron ring and girdle, take a cupful of batter and pour it in, letting it spread out to the size of the ring (or without a ring, to a breakfast-plate size). When done one side, turn as you would a pancake and cook the other side, regrease the irons, and when you have put another cake on to cook butter the first one, and put it by the fire to await the second, and so on, to the end. Be not alarmed at the colour—that is always dark, for a pile of hot buckwheat cakes on the breakfast table in the country on a cold frosty morning is not to be despised."

MAIZE

Those old enough to remember the sudden affliction of maize meal that stuffed us during the First World War will realise why this American corn is included in this English book. As green corn, and corn on the cob, it has been popular here since Longfellow wrote the Indian story of Mondamin—golden-haired giant—and is likely to be more grown in future.

Maize-meal Mush

Made like porridge, but with maize meal. It is good eaten like a hasty pudding, with butter, sugar, treacle, or stewed or baked fruit. When cold it is solid like a ground-rice pudding and may be cut in slices and browned in the grid, and eaten with cold meat.

Indian Meal Cakes

"Mould the dough made of maize meal, cut into cakes larger than a saucer. Open a place in the side of the wood fire on the hearth, and put the cakes, each between two cabbage leaves." 1800.

This is probably Mark Twain's ash cake, which no tramp came for twice!

Maize meal will make a pleasant bread, but should be cooked in flat cakes, or long-shaped rolls like French bread, as the grain is such a poor conductor that the middle of the bread remains raw, while the crust is overcooked—hence the emphasis on the shape of all maize bread. Huck Finn says make it the shape of a "pone".

Maize v. Potatoes

In 1845 all the potato provinces of Europe rang with the intelligence that a blight had wasted the fields. In 1847 a tract was published giving "a case for the Times . . . showing the practicability and necessity of cultivating Maize".

Among other uses the tract points out that maize husks can be used to stuff mattresses, to make door mats, and can be worked into brown paper production. The pitch of the cob makes excellent fuel, and the stalks will light the fires and heat the bread oven all winter. The pigs fed on maize make good bacon and can be smoked by the burning stalks, etc. However, maize did not flourish in England.

(*See* Vegetables for Maize—green corn.)

Maize Pesto

A curious "famine" recipe. I found the same idea in Ireland during the famine of 1900. It is a sauce made of cheese and scraps of fat, poured over a cereal foundation and raw green herbs—in Ireland potatoes or bread.

Take basil, marjoram, parsley, and onion (or garlic), pepper, salt, and a bit of old dry cheese, and beat all well together in a mortar, mix with boiling water to a smooth paste, boil up, stir in bacon fat or dripping, pour it over the dishful of hot mush and greens, brown and serve quickly.

The raw greens and cooked starch are interesting as an instinctive attempt, by people who knew nothing of the value of vitamins, to balance an inadequate diet.

Furmente (made of wheat)

" Take wete and pyke hit fayre and clene, and do it in a morter shene. Bray hit a lytelle with water it spryng [sprinkle] Tyl hit hulle, without blesyng. Then wyndo hit wele, nede thou most, washe it fayre and put hit in pot, Boyle hit tylle hit brest [burst] then; Let hit down, as I thee kenne. Take new mylke, and play hit up. Till hit be thykkerede to sup. Lye hit up with yolkes of eyren, and kepe it wele, lest hit berne. Coloure hit with safron and salt it wele and servys hit forth, sir at the mele; with sugar candy thou may it dowce, If hit be served in grete lordys howse. Take black sugar for mener menne, Beware therewith for hit wylle brenne [burn]."

The new wheat makes this dish; it must be shelled, cooked slowly in milk, and flavoured and sweetened. It used to be possible to buy this creed wheat already dressed, but it is easy enough to make, depending simply on the long slow cooking to bring out the sweetness of the starch in the grain.

" A boll of furmenty and in the midst of it sticking a dozen of hornspoons in a bunch as the instruments meetest to eate furmenty porage withall.

A dozen, as a number of plenty, complete for full chere . . . and of horn, as a substance most estimable . . . being neither so churlish in weight as mettall nor so forward and brittle as stone [i.e. pottery] nor yet so soiling in use no rough to the lips as wood is, but lyght plyaunt and smooth, that with a little licking will always be kept as clean as a dy [die?]. Wear it not indeede that horne be so plentie hornware I beleeve would be more set by than it is."

Antient Mynstrals Sollem Song, 1575.

*Natural Forms
of Horn Spoons
in Use as Scoops*

DRINKS

GENERAL NOTES ON BREWING AND WINE MAKING

" Oh, Peggy, Peggy! when thou goest to brew,
Consider well what you're about to do;
Be very wise, very sedately think
That, what you're going now to make, IS DRINK.
Consider who must drink that drink, and then,
What it is to have the praise of honest men."

KING.

OF OLD, every household made its own beer to suit its own purpose. The light beer for the harvest workers was no more intoxicating than barley water. In the west and south its place was taken by cider, whose strength varied according to requirements. Brewing was not heavy work. In the author's home the brewing copper was in regular use within the last generation. Brewing was not considered any special accomplishment— it was taken for granted that "any housewife knew how to brew"; perhaps it was a little more difficult than the baking of bread, but then beer was not brewed so often.

Brewing was one of the jobs that "fitted in" with the ordinary affairs of the house (such as the collecting of feathers when plucking, and the occasional making up of the accumulation into another pillow or bed). Incidentally, it is this leisurely taken-in-the-stride-methodicalness that gives the appearance of slowness to country actions. The "I've had it in my mind to do it for some time" or "I'm waiting for a day to do so and so" is not dilatory. The countryman *is* waiting a convenient opportunity, *because it will save time* if he can fit in that particular job with something else.

Brewing, today, as a private enterprise, has been suppressed. You may not brew for sale without paying a heavy tax.

Similarly with wines. Tucked away in cottages are scores of skilled workers, who can produce delicious wine. Some of the English wines are old and golden. Some are delicate as spring cowslips. Some wines are little more than light syrups, faintly flavoured with flower perfume. Some wines are sparkling, some are smooth, and one is a rich liqueur, made of pure black-currant juice, slowly warmed in the sun. Only a few of the country wines are coarse and sour; and used for their curative properties.

536

When English workers *made* their drinks, they made strong beer, and good wine; now they *buy* weak beer and gas waters.

So, when you try these recipes, try to find some old hand to "come and put you in the way of it"—then you will make an old drink and a new friend simultaneously.

CELLAR NOTES

Racking (or clearing)

The mechanism of racking was realised long before the scientific reasons were understood. The downward current caused by cold, in standing water, can be seen by anyone watching a pond or canal before frost. The dirt in suspension, which makes such water muddy in ordinary weather, drops downwards during frost, and the pond stands clear as crystal, with the sediment, still and soft, at the bottom. Sometimes a dead leaf can be watched, sinking slowly downwards, though no current is visible. The reason is that cold water contracts and becomes heavier, so as the surface of water in frosty weather is chilled, it sinks down, and the warmer water from beneath rises and, in its turn, is chilled and falls, so that the movement downwards goes on. (The same thing happens when you throw a spoonful of cold water into the coffee-pot to settle the grounds.) The gradual chilling of the water proceeds from top to bottom till all the pond is the same temperature, and the further chilling causes ice to form on the surface, growing thicker and thicker downwards, till all is solid.

The wine or beer in the cellar does not freeze, but the brewer knows that when the quiet frost has stilled and cleared the standing water in his pond it will also have stilled and cleared the wine standing in his cellar, so it can be drawn off at that time perfectly bright and clear, leaving the sediment resting quiet at the bottom. That is "racking".

Fining

Fining is the same mechanism as "clearing", but done by introducing some liquid of a different gravity, or some substance that makes a change in the gravity of the liquid in the cask. Sometimes it is a colloidal solution, such as milk, or a substance which makes one, such as isinglass or glue. Albumen, such as egg-white or blood, are variously used. Without attempting scientific language, consider "racking" and "fining" as the action of sweeping the particles of sediment down through the liquid, till clear.

"Set Casks Atilt!"

Casks of beer should be "set" at least a week before use, longer if the weather is sultry.

Barrel stands are cheap to buy, or easy to make. There should be two to each barrel, and as soon as the barrel comes, set it upon one pair, and as the beer grows low, get the next barrel and stand it on the second pair. Thus, by the time one cask is finished, the next is ready for use. It is customary for the brewers' men to collect one empty cask as he leaves a full one, so this arrangement makes no difficulty.

Learn When to Tilt

Through tilting badly, good beer is wasted. When the barrel is first "set" it may tilt back slightly, as the pressure is lessened, and the run steadier; then gently pull forward the front block till the beer is level. If one person steadies the cask as the other slides the block forward, the movement barely stirs the liquid. To get the last beer drawn clear, move the back block slightly forward. Finally, use the last drips for Welsh Rabbit, and start the new barrel.

If you set your casks atilt gently, directly *after* drawing the beer, and keep the cellar cool, you will always draw off clear bright beer.

Bottled Beer

Bottled beer should be stored flat (the corks well covered), but the current supply should be set upright. In cold weather these upright bottles may stand in the coolest part of the room where they are to be drunk (unless it's a very hot room). In hot weather a few bottles may be put into the refrigerator for a short time, but beer, being malted and therefore a living yeast product, should never be frozen, as this "kills" it. It is better to have a wooden tub full of cold water, standing on a stone floor, and kept full of bottles of beer standing upright. If a cube of ice is thrown in every time a bottle is taken out, the beer will keep excellently cold, and all the bottles remain an even temperature, for nothing is so bad as a glass of warm beer after a cold one.

Consult your brewers' agent as to the best types of beer for your special requirements—it's dull and stupid to go on serving the same drink summer and winter. As accompaniment to lunch on a hot day you want something light and invigorating. On a cold evening when sleep may overtake unrebuked, then a stronger, heavier brew is more warming.

Stout and porter are popular with manual workers and for "elevenses". Oatmeal stout, being considered "very strengthening" has a medical reputation in the ladies' bar. Porter was also considered strengthening and good for invalids. It is said that porter took its name from the London porters and carriers, who drank it in vast quantities "to work on". Porter was usually made with imported Belgian hops. Beer, ale, cider and mead are suitable to our climate, and natural to our temperament, so see that our native drinks are properly served.

Tankards

> " Magelanus, performing the first Voyage round the world,
> falling in with this post (St. Julien) . . . there had been a munity
> against him, for which he Executed diuers, upon a Gibbet close
> by the sea . . . which gibbet, we found there sound and whole . . .
> though being there 50 years at the least! Of which wood our
> cooper made Tankers for such of the (Ships) Company as would
> drink in them. Whereof for my owne part I had no great likeing
> seeing there was no such necessity."
>
> *Journal of Voyage to Cape Verde*, SIXTEENTH CENTURY.

Tankards should be kept in the same place as the beer (beer from a cold
cellar will make pewter from the dining-room feel unpleasantly warm).
In summer, keep jugs and tankards also in the cellar and bring them up
together. If the change of temperature "clouds" the metal it is no fault.
A scrubbed wooden tray is best for tankards and jug. Pewter on wood has a
pleasant thump; never use a traycloth for drinks, though a plain linen
napkin should be on the tray, for wiping spilt foam.

Tankards should be washed in hot soapsuds, rinsed, and upended to
dry. They should be polished inside and out with plain whitening, and
polished off with a soft cloth. Silver should shine with a clear bright
polish.

Pewter is best cleaned with fine bathbrick (sift the bathbrick through
muslin) and much attention should be given to keep the inside brighter
than the outside. Of old, pewter was cleaned with fine sifted sand, wood
ash, and coarse rushes or "mare's-tails".

The idea that "antique pewter" should be blackish grey is quite wrong.[1]
It should glow with a soft, velvety radiance, not hard and clear like silver,
but bright as pearl.

On no account should metal polishes or chemical preparations be used
for tankards. The smell clings past all cleansing, and many people have
been put off using tankards through this common error.

Glasses

Glasses and mugs should be well washed in warm soapy water, rinsed
in hotter water, and then held under the cold tap several seconds and set
to drain dry. When dry, polish with chamois till crystal clear.

If glasses are laid on the table, it will be necessary to bring them into
the warm room before the cool beer, otherwise they may so cloud that
they damp the cloth—but if carried in on a wooden tray with the beer,
this clouding does but show good serving.

---

[1] Old manuscripts show that pewter was kept polished brightly, and wooden platter
and bowls were scoured and bleached cream-coloured.

ALE *v.* BEER

In history ale is much older than beer,

> " Turkeys, Heresies, Hops and Beer,
> All came to England in one Year."

> " Ale is made of malte and water and they the wiche do put
> any other tings to ale than is rehersed except yest, barme or
> godes good doth sophisticate they're ale. . . it is a naturall
> drynke, for a Dutche man, and now of late days it is moche used
> in England to the delyment of many Englysshe men."
>
> BOORDE, 1547.

The introduction of hops began beer, and though "home-brewed"
in country pubs is now the exception, there are still a few places that carry
on the tradition, and the universities nearly all brew their own ale. Local
"herb beers" are sometimes brewed by country people, but the notice,
"herb beer sold here", usually indicates a commercial preparation.

Spruce beer may have had its origin in "tar beer", a brew which used
the sticky ends of fir boughs and had a "turpentiny" aroma. A consign-
ment of "essence of spruce, and other extra stores adapted to cold climates
and a long voyage" was taken by Captain Parry on his voyage of discovery
for the North-West Passage in 1819—he also took essence of malt and hops.
As malting is needed for both ale and beer, it is considered first.

Malting

> " Rigo: I like your Beere you have excellently well, I pray you
> tell me in what sort you make it?
>
> Cono: I will not hide my cunning in this matter, and herein
> I will follow the custome and order of the English, who are the
> great masters in all Christendome in this art . . . and other
> Nations but their Imitators. They first turn their Barley into
> Malt in this manner.
>
> They take a good quantity of Barley and put it into a Cesterne
> or Vat and so steepe it in water the space of 3 nights, then drain
> it from the water and let it drop a day, then lay it on a faire
> floore in a great thick heap or centre, and let it so lie 3 nights
> more, in which space it will sprout at one end (for it must not
> sprout at both) then they spread it very thin all over the floore,
> and either with a shovel or the hand it must be turned and tossed
> twice or thrice a day, for the space of 14 days or more (for to
> make perfect Malte it must have full 3 weeks Vat and Floor).
> Then they drie it upon the Kilne with a gentle fire, of sweete
> straw, (for any other fuel yields too stronge smoake and gives

the Malt an ill taste); after the Malt is dried colled, rubbed cleane skreened or winnowed, then it is sent to the Mill and ground according to the proportion of the Brewing, which if it be ordinary household Beere, then they drawe of every quarter of Malt, 3 hoggsheads of Beere.

But if it be for extraordinary strong March beere, then to every hoggshead you should allow one quarter of Mault, a peck of Pease, half a pecke of Wheate and half a pecke of Oates."

MARKHAM.

Brewing

" After the Malt is ground they put it into a mashvat and the liquor in the [cauldron] being ready to boyle, put it to the malt and mash together. Let it stand an hower. Then drain the liquor from the Malt and put it in the [cauldron] againe, and ad to it for every quarte of Malt a $1\frac{1}{2}$ lbs. of hops and boyle over for the space of an hower. Then clense the liquor from the hops through a strait sive into the Cooler . . . then put in your barme and after they have wrought, then heate them together, then tunne your Beere into Hoggsheads, let it purdege[1] well, and after closse them up. This Beere may be drunke at a forghtnight's age and is of long lasting."

C. MARKHAM.

Water

The water should be soft water, but not dead. Springs and rivers make good beer water, and some living wells are also good. White water—that is, waterfall or tumbled river water with air in it, is best; and the worst is rain-water or the peaty, brackish water of standing pools or slow muddy rivers. "Under chalk" water makes good beer (Dorchester beer used to be made with this).

The temperature of the water for mashing is important. Old hands gave "Three parts boiling water to one part cold water" to get the correct heat (about 1800), but they usually "waited till the steam had lifted, so they could see their face in the water" and "that was right heat".

Hops

These were grown on hedges around farm fields; gathered in September or October, dried in the old bread ovens and packed into bags. The essential oil and the curious resinous content (lupulin) vary in quantity and quality in different types of hop, and these differ with the soils. Hops are usually strongest when fresh, but are kept longer for light brews, and will keep, in good store, for over a year.

Nowadays the hops are often dried by electricity, and the oast houses

[1] "Pured" (Chaucer), is probably the origin of the word "purdege". That is, let it "work" till it has purged and purified itself.

no longer burn wood. The hop industry is localised in the southern counties, and the hop fields are one of the most interesting rural industries. Acrobatic men on high stilts put up the training wires in winter, old local hands twine the young hops encouragingly up the lines (some of the prunings are eaten as a delicate dish in spring). In autumn the East End of London removes itself to camps in the fields, and gathers the crop for the big breweries. Breweries buy the prepared product, but country households usually gather their hops themselves from hedges where they have run wild.

Things Needed for Home Brewing

Anne Corbet's notes are excellent for beginners—she wrote for households who also baked their own bread. Brewing thus automatically provided yeast suitable for baking. It is impossible to disentangle the household operations of a self-supporting family community, as one piece of work must fit in with the next job. The brewhouse usually adjoined the bakehouse (the woodshed adjacent, with fuel for both). Brew-boilers are distinguished from clothes-boilers by being of tinned copper, and usually boarded in overhead. This enclosing was to keep in the steam (and, in some cases, the tell-tale smell of brewing), but yeast can be bought, and any large six-gallon saucepan will serve as "a boiler".

Anne also requires a mash tub of wood, shallow and strong enough to hold all the beer at once. There must also be an "under-buck" (curiously the word "buck" (used for washing), continues in the stand upon which the wash tub was raised). This "buck" is merely a plain wooden stand, to lift the mash tub a foot or so off the floor, so that a drain hole and vessel for catching may be set underneath the tub. A barrel, sawn in two "unequal halves" will provide one large mashing tub and one shallow under-buck. A stick or "spider" is needed to stir the malt with, and plenty of clean old cloths to cover the tub and keep the brew warm. A strainer and a cooler tub, and a "tun-dish" or funnel with which to fill the cask, are all easy to obtain.

"The malt should be ground up as fine as meal, and the hops should be new and fresh and light and dry. If finings, or clearings, are needed, isinglass is best," but if the cask stands still in a cold cellar, and is drawn off in frosty weather, the beer should be clear and bright enough.

RECIPES FOR SOME ENGLISH BEERS

A Simple Recipe for Beginners (after Anne Corbet)

1 peck of malt, 2 ounces of hops, 1 teacupful of brewer's yeast.

Boil 3 gallons of water and when "just off the boil" (*see* Water), pour it onto the malt, which has been placed in a big raised-up tub. (This tub should have a tap near the bottom, or a plug hole, covered with clean straw and stoppered with a fitted cork that can be pulled out, to drain off the water.) Stir the malt till it is all a wet "mash" and, covering the tub to keep in the heat, stand it in a warm place for three days. Then drain off this water into another tub (Anne calls this the under-buck). Cover the malt with another 3 gallons of water (again stirring well) and leave for a day, and draw off and mix with the first "run". Now boil these 6 gallons with the hops for half an hour (while you clear out the malting tub) and then strain all the liquid back into the tub and, as soon as the brew is just warm to your hand, crumble the yeast into it and "leave it alone to work". Some people advocate skimming the surface daily, others say this "disturbs" the yeast plant. If there is much working, to skim off the froth is good; if the working seems sluggish, a very small sprinkle of sugar or warming the brew may liven it up (this is where only experience can advise). At the end of two days, if the brew does not "go quiet", skim it closely, for, after three or four days, the working *should have almost ceased*, and the beer must be run off into a cask. Leave the bung out for a day (as the shaking up may have started the working again and you do not want a fountain of froth bursting the bung). Then, if there is just a comfortable "hum" going on within the cask, bung it up and let it stand (level) till after the next frost (up to 6 months). Beginners should not try bottling until they can judge the strength of the ferment they have made, as blown corks and broken glass can be dangerous.

Gale Beer

> " The fenny part of Axholm bereth much galle a low frutex swete in burning."
>
> LELAND, 1538.

> " Gale beer brewed from a plant growing on the moor above Arnforth in Yorkshire was sold by Mrs. Sedgeworth of the Black Horse."
>
> *Advertisement*, 1863.

Though we have evidence that gale was used for beer far back beyond Anglo-Saxon times, yet I can find few early recipes in script.

This recipe was from a Scarborough woman, whose "grandmother made it for religious people". It is probably the same recipe that was used in St. Hilda's Convent at Whitby and inspired Caedmon.

In wide circles around any monastery, or community centre, vestigial remains of earlier cultures persist, and the plants used by the communities grow wild. Now, sweet gale does "grow wild on mountains and fenny grounds"; but not all the plantations of it that I have traced around the ruined dumps of early dwellings were wild. I am certain many were planted by the hand of man, and a man who drank gale beer.

That the plant was so long known to the common people, all of whom were illiterate, is one reason for the lack of early recipes, and the fact that Leland finds it necessary to explain the scent of gale to southerners is slight contributory evidence that the plant was almost exclusively used by Saxons in the Fens and in the north; a Saxon people, whose usages were not incorporated into the Norman till long after the Conquest. Some gale grows around Snowdon, and the oldest folk there remember its use in their metheglins. I cannot be certain whether the earliest gale ferments were of honey, rye, or of barley; in this recipe we ferment with barm.

Gale Brew

Take a wooden tub with a spigot near the base, and pack it full of gale in full leaf. Measure how much water this will hold, to cover the branches, and put half that amount of water on to boil, with honey, in the proportion of ½ pint to 1 gallon of water. When boiling, pour it over the gale in the tub, pressing it down under some wooden slat, to get a strong infusion. Boil the remainder of the water, and pour this on in turn, and with the second water, test the heat, and when cool enough, add just enough barm to make it work. Remove the gale and let the beer work about a week (according to the quantity you are brewing), then remove the spigot and draw off the gale brew into a cask, bung it, and later draw it off in frosty weather and bottle, as you would any other home-brew.

(If you drink a pint of this, with oatcake, cheese, watercress and salt, or a grilled chop and brown bread, you will have duplicated just such a simple, satisfying meal as Caedmon may have enjoyed.)

The small brown "tassells" of the gale in earliest spring are pungent and were said to have been used for wax, or threaded as a form of taper. Their slightly "resinous" content may have been used as that of hops.

Nettle Beer

This is made by country people for "summer visitors".

Take 1 lb. of sugar, 1 oz. of ginger, 1 oz. of cream of tartar, 1 oz. of yeast, 1 lemon, and a good truss of freshly gathered nettles. Boil in ½ gallon of water till well flavoured, and pour off into ½ gallon of cold spring water, in a wooden tub. Add the yeast, and let it work 12 hours, or longer, according to the weather. Skin and use a small cask for keeping, or bottle for quick use.

Ginger Beer

Many of the small cottages who "accommodate" cyclists specialise in this popular drink, and make it excellently.

Take 5 quarts of boiling water, 1¼ lb. of sugar, 1 oz. of whole ginger, 2 lemons, ¼ oz. of cream of tartar, and a good spoonful of brewer's yeast.

Into a warm earthenware jar put the sliced lemon, sugar, bruised ginger, and cream of tartar. Pour on the boiling water. When cool enough, ferment with yeast for about 24 hours, keeping warm by the kitchen fire. Skim and bottle securely.

Hop Beer (note, not malted)

In some districts the hedges are covered with hops that have grown wild. They are often very fine and are gathered and used by farmers' wives to make a light summer beer.

On a farm there are usually boilers and tubs available for large quantities.

Take 10 oz. of hops, 16 gallons of water, 5 lb. of brown sugar and enough yeast to ferment. Boil the hops for an hour, then draw the fire and strain out onto the sugar in a wooden tub. Work with yeast, while warm, about two days, then cask it.

Varieties of this recipe, in similar quantities, make dandelion beer, sage beer, and other local mixtures.

Mangel Wurzel Beer

(We believe the older recipe used the even sweeter parsnip root—and no hops.)

Wash, clean, and slice about 60 lb. of root and boil to pulp, making the amount to 14 gallons with fresh spring water; while boiling add a double handful of hops. The whole should boil a clear hour.

Dip it out into a tub through a linen cloth (to clear it) and as soon as cool, stir in 4 to 6 oz. of yeast. Let it stand and work till the yeast has all worked up to the top.

Skim and pour the beer into a cask (avoid the sediment) and let it finish working for a few days, then bung it up. It is ready in about a week, but improves if bottled.

Spruce Beer[1]

The gummy tassels of the spruce are brought gradually to the boil to release the essential oil and flavour. As soon as the oily scum shows on the surface, pass a large plate across the surface drawing the scum aside and slip out the spruce, put in another bough, and continue doing this till you have a thick scum of spruce oil, and the water is well impregnated with the essence. Strain, and to 16 gallons of warm spruce liquor, add 16 lb. of treacle, stir till dissolved, and put in about ½ pint of fresh yeast. Let it work, covered, for three days, and then strain off into a cask. Do not

[1] The Scotch pine is the only native fir. This must be a fairly late beer.

bung up until fermentation has practically ceased. It can be drunk within a week or so, but it is better kept some months.

Spruce beer is made all over Europe. The German black beer is made from spruce, and the Russian Army used to have a special brew enlivened with horse-radish, ginger, mustard and all manner of spicery.

Spruce beer has noted antiscorbutic properties.

I give also this recipe, as it has the laconic New England touch:

> " One pint good spruce extract, 12 lb. treacle, 3 gallons of water. Boil all and let stand 1 hour. Add 3 or 4 gallons of water, 1 pint of yeast (the water should be hand warm). Pour into a 10-gallon cask. Fill her up,—let her work. Bung her up. Bottle her off."
>
> FROM A MS. ABOUT 1890.

Sugar Beer (for harvest)

Take 1 gallon of water, in which a truss of barley has been steeped. (Sometimes barley water, very thin, formed the basis.) 1 cup of honey, some lemon peel, and a piece of yeast spread on a slice of toast. The honey is stirred into the water, as it cools, and when all is lukewarm, the whole is poured into an earthenware panshon and left to work for two days.

It is then skimmed and poured into a light cask and can be used almost at once. It is usually made on the farm for the harvest workers.

VARIETY OF ALES

> " I generous wine am for the Court,
>   The Citie calls for Beere!
>   But Ale! Bonny Ale! Like a Lord of the Soyle!
>   In the countrey shall domineere! "
>
> HALLIWELL, 1630.

Too many small breweries have closed down. They depended for their excellence upon their local water supply and the skill of the local brewer. The brewery at Llangollen, spoken of by Borrow, has long been closed.

Welsh Ale

> " I suppose you get your ale from Llangollen? . . ." " No, nor anywhere else. . . . It was brewed in this house by your honour's humble servant. . . . There, your honour, did you ever see such ale? Observe its colour! Does it not look for all the world as pale and delicate as cowslip wine? . . . Taste it, your honour! . . ." The ale was indeed admirable, equal to the best that I had ever before drunk, rich and mellow, with scarcely any smack of the hop in it, and though so pale and delicate to the eye, nearly as strong as brandy."
>
> G. BORROW.

" ' This is very bad ale . . . very different from what I drunk in the summer when I was waited on by Tom Jenkins.'

' It is the same ale, sir, but the last in the cask; and we sharn't have any more for six months, when he will come again to brew for the summer; but we have very good porter, sir, and first-rate Allsopp.'

' Allsopp Ale,' I said, ' will do for July and August, but scarcely for the end of October. However . . . bring me a pint.' "

BORROW, AT BALA.

Kentish Cherry Ale (best in England)

I had this first on a cold spring day at a very small inn near Molash. The hop poles were white with driven snow, the cherry trees gaunt against a grey sky, and icy puddles crisped in the cart tracks. The inn-keepers were Cockneys, who, in youth, came down for the "hopping" and lived to attain their ideal of "a public-house in Kent".

The recipe was the finest old ale and unlimited freshly plucked cherries. The resultant brew took me to Canterbury walking (fairly straight) on air!

"Collect all the spare cherries (the throw-outs or pecked ones from the gatherings in the orchards), and collect also a good handful of the darker cherries as well as the Kentish white hearts. Fill a panshon, and mash cold, cover with boiling water and work with sugar and yeast in the usual way. If the stones of the cherries are beaten with a hatchet back, till cracked, it will give a finer almond tang to the ale. Barrel and, subsequently, bottle." It is said to improve up to nine years, but is excellent after three. The use of cherry in ale was much considered by the cider makers of the west, and boats were sent around to Bristol with trees of cherries to grow and mix with the cider apples.

Cock Ale and Cornish Ale

A generation ago this was common in Oxfordshire. It approximates to Cornish Cider, which has sheep's blood drained into it.

This is a recipe of 1780: "Take 10 gallons ale, a large cock (the older the better). Slay, caw and gut him, and stamp him in a stone mortar. Add spice and put all into a canvas bag. Lower him into the ale while still working. Finish working and bottle."

In all cases where blood is used, the primitive idea was that the strength and courage of the animal was thus absorbed. Therefore, in some cases the creature was thrown in, still alive and, where blood was added, it was fresh and hot from the slaughter. Cornish men swore by a sheep's blood for their brewing, very much as the early American planters swore that a black negro's blood was best for refining sugar. The grim stories of men's bodies being concealed in hogsheads of wine and ale are not beyond belief. Andrew Boorde wrote that "Cornish Ale is stark nought, looking whyte and thycke as pygges had wrastled in it." He may have seen some Cornish cream brew, or it may have had something to do with the Cornish clay water? They used to put cream in their cider to fine it.

HOT DRINKS MADE WITH ALE AND BEER

> " There was laughing and chattering, and ' pass the cup round '
> Bargains and toasts and rounds, and so till Evensong,
> And Glutton had gulped down, a gallon and a gill,
> He could neither step nor stand, nor could he stand still!
> Like a blind man's dog, from side to side he sways,
> First to one side; then to that; then sudden, backwardways!
> Like a man, who goes to and fro, pegged-down nightlines."
> *The Vision of Piers Plowman* (free rendering).

Ale Gruel (or Ale Berry)

This was a famous drink in the north country. Men drank it over the kitchen fire, while their stiff dry nightshirts hung over a chair to warm, and the woman ran the big brass bed-warmer up and down, and put a blanket in the bed. Then they kicked off their shoes, stripped by the hearth, and got straight into bed—"it didn't do to go out after the hot ale for it made you sweat and put you to sleep, and the oatmeal kept you going till morning while you'd be too tired to eat anything".

Boil a handful of crushed oats in 2 pints of water till thick, grating a lump of root ginger into it; strain it off, boiling hot, into an equal quantity of just boiling ale, adding a generous scrape of nutmeg, or cinnamon, and a spoonful of rough sugar. Drink it as hot as possible—*and go to bed at once.*

The recipe was given to me by a woman who kept a stone pub by a river bridge in Wharfedale; she said that "it was wonderful if you'd bin drowned".

Ale Flip—a "Bonalay"[1]

This was a stirrup cup, after leaving a dance. Before driving back home in an open gig, you drank it, pulled the horse blankets well round you, and "T'hoss knew the way well as you did, if you fell asleep".

Put the ale (about 4 pints) into a saucepan with a blade of mace, a couple of cloves, a lump of butter (the size of a big walnut), beat 2 egg-whites and yolks *separately*—the whites till they are foam, and the yolks with a drop of cool ale. The eggs are then put into a huge jug and the hot ale poured onto them, from a height, and then the ale is poured back and forth in the jug till cool enough to drink (then you drove off).

[1] " Bonalay ", for a farewell drink, may have been Norman, more likely a later acquisition from the French wars—as our " Sanfairyan" and many other words.

Beer Flip (for bell-ringers before a long peal)

Eight yolks of eggs, beaten with sugar and orange juice and spices, the whites beaten separately till firm and stiff. One quart of strong beer, made hot and poured upon the yolks, and then poured back again from a height, so that it froths high. The white of the eggs are added to the froth, and the whole served swiftly while hot.

Wassail Bowl

> " Sometimes lurk I in the gossip's bowl
> In very likeness of a roasted crab,
> And when she drinks, against her lips I bob,
> And down her withered dewlap pours the ale."
>
> SHAKESPEARE.

Wassail bowl varies with every household. The following is the recipe of 1722 of Sir Watkin Williams Wynne.

Take 1 lb. of brown sugar, 1 pint of hot beer, a grated nutmeg, and a large lump of preserved ginger root cut up. Add 4 glasses of sherry, and stir well. When cold, dilute with 5 pints of cold beer, spread suspicion of yeast on to hot slices of toasted brown bread, and let it stand covered for several hours. Bottle off and seal down, and in a few days it should be bursting the corks, when it should be poured out into the wassail bowl, and served with hot, roasted apples floated in it.

Note. A "wassail bowl" is *not* a "punch bowl".

GENERAL NOTES ON WINE

> " Wyne y made is by crafte of good spicery and herbes."
>
> BART. ANGLICUS.

> " Good wine needs no bush."
>
> SHAKESPEARE.

Everyone knows a bush was hung out to denote the wine-shop, but why a bush? The reason is this: Yeast was made by each household, as a preliminary part of the brewing. Now yeast is a live thing, and difficult to keep active for long periods of time, and many were the schemes used; but the best proved to be storage "in a little bush or besom of twigs", as this kept the particles well exposed to the air. So, when you had a plentiful supply of yeast, you made some "little bushes or besoms of birch twigs", and dipped and stirred them in the yeast, leaving them in it "till a great quantity had adhered thereto". These little bushes were then hung

up on hooks; and "take care of the dust getting into it, or too dry, or cold, and when your beer is fit to set to work, throw one of these bushes into it, and it will soon work as well as if you had fresh yeast. You must whip it about in the wort, and then let it lie therein." When the beer works well, pull out the bush, and dry it again, and it will do for the next brewing.

These little bushes were also used to revive old ale or wines that had gone flat or stale. But *"Good wine needs no bush."* The quotation, then, makes far better sense.

THE MAKING OF WINE IN ENGLAND

" The toasts taken out of ale and wine should always be given
to the hens—it will encourage them mightily."

EIGHTEENTH-CENTURY MS.

The "toasts" are the slices of dry bread on which the yeast is put to float.

You must never strain wine : it destroys the texture. That is why country people insist on lump spices, and break them up (never using powdered spice). Sometimes if the ingredients are thick and "cloudy", the ferment is made to work through the standing wine, to "work up" the material into a thick scum on top of the panshon that can be skimmed off, leaving the wine liquid clear; but sometimes the liquid is clear itself. In that case, the ferment is spread upon a little raft, usually of toasted bread, and set to float on the surface of the liquid.

Good wines, made with fruit juice, use very little, if any water. Flower wines, of necessity, do use water; and this water must be very soft and pure, to absorb the aroma.

Flower wines are usually made by a cold process, or by dropping flower heads into boiling water and instantly cooling. (Neglecting this gives only a "greenery stew"!) The "heads" and blossoms must also be well "pressed-out" to extract the small honey washed loose in the steeping.

The ginger and spice and lemon and orange rind, flavourings now quoted in so many modern recipes, are used more sparingly by the real country makers, who concentrate on bringing out the true flavour of the wine, and only use other scents (such as sweet briar, rosemary, etc.) to intensify the natural aroma.

Spices are a help in locating a good wine-making district, or if you roll up in a car asking for wine, it may be thought you are come to detect illicit brewing! And no one will know anything for miles around, but you can locate a good wine-making district by the counter display at the local chemist's. I remember finding such a chemist near Brecon. At the right time of the year, his polished counter was set out with dishes full of spices labelled "Spices for Wine", "Mixture for Vinegar", "Hot Pickling Spices", and there were long trays of cinnamon sticks, brown and crackly, curls of red mace, like the palms of little pixie hands, crumbling piles of crushed spice root, baskets of papery bay leaves, peppers (white and black), twisted scarlet capsicums, powdery cummin, knobbed bone-white ginger roots. There were round glass saucers full of crystal gums, golden arabic, shandrac; and yellow, dusty resin; there were lumps of amber, honey-coloured, and spun isinglass, white as wool.

Outside, the cold wet dusk and the grey rain of early autumn closed down, but inside the shop all was golden, warm, scented spicery. The chemist's coloured glass jars spilt rainbows down from the little window, as if the footless Bird of Paradise had come to nest.

The wine-makers of the district spoke favourably of that chemist. As the "wine expert" explained, "He is a very knowledgeable man, and takes great credit for getting us 'the best', for in wine-making, my dear, there are very few things you must have, but the fewer those things *are*; the better they need to be."

Wine-making apparatus is simple. Some large earthenware panshons to stand on the wash-house floor and hold the mixtures. An old-fashioned pestle and mortar (or the axe-head and a piece of clean linen cloth on the hearthstone), to break the spices. Old spirit casks are used. (These are increasingly troublesome to obtain. Hence more wines these days are bottled too soon.)

When pouring off from the cask into bottles, put the cloudy dregs of the wine into a jar, and let the corks for the bottles soak in it a few hours before wiping and inserting in the necks and driving home with a wooden mallet.

Corks should be new, and of the best quality; reject any with dark rough streaks going across them.

If there is difficulty inserting the corks, a slight nick cut at the lower rim, may "start them down", but it should not be more than an eighth of an inch thick.

Corks should be left some little time driven half in, to be sure the working has ceased, before being rammed home level with the top of the bottles. Leave another 24 hours to dry off and then seal. Sealing wax or pitch are the best seals and should cover the cork and overlap the bottle rim completely.

Racking off from the casks should be done in frosty weather (*see* notes on Racking, p. 537).

SOME ENGLISH WINES

Parsnip Wine (one of the oldest)

To 4 lb. of parsnips, allow 3 lb. of demerara sugar, 1 tablespoonful of fresh yeast spread on a slice of toasted bread, and 4 quarts of boiling water. Spice according to discretion, and stir with rosemary or other scented wood. Boil the cut parsnips gently in the water for 15 minutes, add spices and cook gently for 10 minutes longer. Strain, add sugar, and when the liquid has become blood warm, float on it the toast spread with the yeast. Let it ferment 36 hours (according to weather). Then turn into a cask, which it should fill. As soon as fermentation ceases, bung securely and leave for six months unmoved. Rack off into bottles, during a frost. Store twelve months before using—improves up to ten years.

Turnip Wine

Slice the roots and press in the cider-press. To every gallon of juice, 3 lb. of lump sugar, and ½ pint of brandy. Barrel, and bung lightly for a week or so, until it has done working. Then stop it close for three months, and in frosty weather draw off; bottle when fine.

Dandelion Wine

Take 3 quarts of dandelion heads gathered in full flower, and let dry a little, spread on a paper in the hot sun at noonday. Drop into boiling water slowly, and leave till cool, covered closely.

Strain the water off, pressing the heads well, and reboil the water with

3 lb. of sugar, and put in some ginger and lemon and orange rind (optional). As soon as cool, ferment with yeast floated on toast and, well worked, cask it.

Coltsfoot wine is made in the same way as dandelion.

Burnet Wine

Owing to the dry nature of the burnet heads, they may be boiled to infuse. No other flavouring is used, but raisins are added to give "body".

Blackberry Wine (*see* Blackberry)

Cowslip Wine

The cowslip "pips" for making this wine were sold by the pint in the old open market at Nottingham. Take 5 gallons of soft water, and 12 lb. of loaf sugar. Boil and skim, add 6 egg-whites. Let cool slightly, add ½ pint of yeast, and pour into a barrel containing 4 quarts of cowslip pips. Stir each day for three days with a myrtle broom, then bung tightly and rack off in October.

This recipe is a basis for other flower wines, such as hawthorn or scented peony. There was a scented peony wine made in Wiltshire that was the colour of rose quartz.

Birch Wine

This is made from the birch in March. It need not hurt the tree, and is pleasant and warming. When the sap rises, tap the tree on the warmest side, using a little spigot of elder, or other hollow twig; or, if the tree requires trimming, a pail may be hung from a small cut bough, but take care it is only a small bough, as the sap runs like a faucet if it's a warm spring.

For a gallon of sap allow 2 lb. of sugar; boil and turn into a panshon, and when cool, work it with a spoonful of yeast floated on toast. Let it work four or five days, according to whether the working is strong or not, and then strain off into a cask. A few almonds may be put in the cask. Let ferment for a few days and then bung the cask up for six months. It can be racked off into bottles during the first frost in September and will be passable by Christmas. It is pale silvery gold, with little flavour, but a curiously pungent aroma. I think it might mature well.

Birch Wine in Sussex

" Take the sap of Birch fresh drawn. Boil it as long as any scum arises; to every gallon of liquor put 2 pounds of good sugar; boil it for half an hour, and scum it very clean. When 'tis almost cold, set it with a little yeast spread on a toast, let it stand five or six days in an open vessel, stirring it often, then take such a cask as the liquor will be sure to fill and fire a large match dipped in brimstone, and put it into the cask and stop in the smoak till the match is extinguished always keeping it shook. Then shake out the ashes—and as quick as possible pour in a pint of sack or Rhenish, which taste you like best, for the liquor retains it.

Rinse the cask well with this and pour it out. Pour in your wine and stop it close for 6 months, then if tis perfectly fine—you may bottle it."

MS., ABOUT 1700.

Rowan

" Diodgriafel is made of the berries of Solus Aucuparta by pouring water over the mashed berries and setting the infusion to ferment. When kept some time this is by no means an unpleasant liquor. In Scotland a spirituous liquor is obtained by distillation."

EVANS, 1798.

Potato Wine

Spoken of as "White Root" (as the distil of potato spirit is strictly illegal). 2 lb. raw potatoes grated into pan, 2 lb. of raisins, 4 lb. of demerara sugar, 1 pint of wheat, 4 gallons of boiling water, 1 oz. of yeast.

Mix in a deep panshon and stir at intervals for three weeks—strain off into a small keg—rack and bottle. If kept well for some years, it much resembles brandy (if the sugar be genuine demerara). The wheat should be husked, but not otherwise dressed, and should be "Michaelmas wheat" (i.e., mature, but fresh).

This is a wine, not to be confused with the Irish potato spirit, "poteen".

Bread Wine

This has taken many forms, according to the yeast used in making the bread and the type of corn used for the flour. The early forms, using honey and rye bread (*see* Rye), must have approximated to mead. In the pre-Reformation period this wine had religious significance and degenerated to witchcraft.

This recipe is compiled from several old instructions.

A 2-lb. loaf of brown bread—pulled to pieces and lightly browned in the oven (this browning makes the golden hue of the wine), 1 lb. of sugar, and rather more than 6 pints of spring water. Dissolve the sugar in water, and pour over the dry bread in a wine-jar. Keep the jar in a warm place till the ferment is well worked. Drain off into a cask, bung lightly till the working seems complete—then bottle. The wine, which is very lively, should be drinkable in three or four months—but improves with time.

This recipe came from near Nottingham, where many French settlers had followed the lace trade. The bread was home made.

Sage Wine

This is not often made nowadays (*see* Sage Tea).

Elder-blossom Wine

Shred a quart of elder blossom off the stalks, with a fork, into a deep pan. Take 1 gallon of water and boil it with 3 lb. of sugar and the juice of a lemon till the sugar is dissolved, cool slightly, and cream off a dessert-spoonful of barm from the blossoms onto a slice of toast and set the bowl in a warm place to ferment for three days, or a little longer if the barm works slowly; strain off and add the beaten white of an egg and leave another three days; then cask it up with a handful of raisins in the cask. It should be ready in six months, but, bottled, will improve if left longer.

This is a smooth, sweet wine.

BEE WINE

So called, because it makes a faint humming noise. This wine used to stand in glass jars in kitchen windows. It is quite epidemic in England: suddenly someone starts the "bee" and others are fascinated, and begin "beeing", and so it spreads a fashion from village to village or street to street, though it seems to be chiefly a country conceit.

It's something alive to watch, and the small "bees" going up and down, up and down, steady as clockwork (working a little faster in the sun, working a little slower in the shade), are companionable to a cook. "You get really fond of your 'bee'."

Bee wine was the basis of a simple ginger beer, being flavoured with ginger root and given an aroma with garden herbs. The "bee" is a yeast mass (*Saccharomyces pyriformia*) mechanically entangled with the bacterium (*Bacterium vermiforme*). It makes a small spongy mass that goes up and down because at the bottom it produces carbon dioxide, which makes it rise to the surface where it discharges the gas, and sinks again.

To make it; put a "bee" of the yeast into a jar of water in the sun and "feed" it with small quantities of sugar or honey. When the water has become well clouded and yellow, drain it off, flavour, and bottle it. Fill the jar with fresh water and sugar and start again.

Ginger Bee

For ginger "bee" add a root of bruised ginger and the rind of a lemon to each bottle of the strained-off bee wine—cork till "up" (time depends upon strength of solution and temperature of store).

OTHER ENGLISH DRINKS

NIGHTCAPS

Bishop

> " Fine orange well roasted, with wine in a cup,
> They'll make a sweet bishop when gentlefolks sup."
>
> SWIFT.

Make several pricks in an orange, stick in cloves, and roast the orange
by a slow fire. Put small quantities of cinnamon, cloves, mace, and allspice, and a race of ginger root, in a saucepan, with ½ pint of water, and let
it boil till reduced by half. Heat a bottle of port wine, burning off some
of the spirit. Put the roasted orange and the hot spice into the hot wine,
and let it stand by the fire for 10 minutes. Rub a few lumps of sugar on
the rind of a lemon and put it, with the juice, into a bowl. Pour the wine
over, grate nutmeg on it, and serve hot.

Lawn Sleeves

Use sherry instead of port, and lemon instead of orange, and add three
glasses of hot calves-foot jelly.

Cardinal

Use claret.

Pope

Use champagne.

Brown Betty

> " Brown sugar, dissolved in 1 pint of hot water, a slice of lemon
> in it. Add cloves, cinnamon, brandy, and a quart of strong ale.
> Heat it up, and float a round of brown toast on top of it—and
> on the toast grate nutmeg and ginger root. Serve hot."
>
> *Oxford Nightcaps*, 1827.

Rumfustian

Yolks of 12 eggs, 1 quart of strong beer, 1 bottle of wine, 1 pint of gin,
and cinnamon, nutmeg, sugar and ginger to taste. Beat and warm—but
on no account boil, as that would curdle the egg-yolks—and the rumfustian should be opaque and rather thick.

Currant Rum

2 pints of black currants, 1 lb. of sugar dissolved in 1 pint of boiling
water. Boil all up, and strain off, pressing the fruit well. When nearly

cold, add an equal quantity of rum, and bottle it. ("Good to clear the Captn's throat" is the remark that accompanies this MS. note.)

Scottish Hot Pint

Grate $\frac{1}{2}$ nutmeg into 1 quart of mild ale and set it to heat. Mix sugar enough to sweeten the whole with 2 well-beaten eggs, and a little cold ale, whip well, and stir into the hot ale, very slowly, lest it curdle.

Add half a pint of whisky, and pour rapidly from one jug to another till the hot pint is smooth, and the patient ready for it.

It can be made in the time it takes to get a man's boots off on a cold night.

Bumpo

"He and his messmates . . . were making merry round a table well stored with Bumpo and wine."

SMOLLETT.

Bumpo is rum, sugar, water, and nutmeg, hot.

Negus

Extract the juice of 1 lemon and cut 2 others into thin slices. 4 glasses of melted calves-foot jelly sweetened, and spice to taste. Pour 1 quart of boiling water on to these ingredients in a deep jug, cover and stand for 20 minutes. Add 1 bottleful of white wine.

A very "genteel negus" was made by old-fashioned friends, near Banbury, with a bottle of silvery-yellow cowslip wine and calves-foot jelly. Sweetened with broken clear sugar candy, which tinkled and splintered as it melted in the thin glasses. It was served after a ladies' card-playing evening, before the short walk home through the summer twilight.

PUNCH

Each family—nay, each member of a family—had their own special make of punch and often their own special occasion for making it. Punch is served in those large deep china bowls, and ladled out with small silver-mounted scoops.

A Nineteenth-century Punch

The juice of 10 lemons, and the thin rind of 3—the juice of 4 Seville oranges and the rind of 2. Cut the rinds into very fine thin strips.

6 glasses of melted calves-foot jelly, 2 quarts of boiling water, all stirred up together in a hot jug. Allow to cool slightly, then put 1 pint of French brandy, 1 pint of white wine, with a glassful of crushed sugar, into the punch-bowl; lace the whole with some Jamaica rum or orange shrub. Pour over the cooled jugful and stir with a twig of sweet briar.

A Milk Punch

> " Beat 15 eggs very well, and strain to ¾-lb. of white sugar, and
> 1 pint of Canary. Set it over the coals and keep stirring till it
> is scalding hot. Meantime grate some nutmegs into a quart of
> milk and boil it and pour it into your eggs and wine (they being
> scalding hot). Hold your hand very high as you pour it [another
> recipe suggests you mount on the kitchen table and teem it down
> from a height!]. Then set it before the fire for half-an-hour
> and serve it up."
>
> GLASSE, 1742.

GENERAL EXPLANATION OF THE CAUDEL

That the mixture of eggs and cereals and malt, etc., is very ancient is
shown by this recipe.

> " Nym euren and sweng well togedre. Cheuf [warm] ale a do there
> to. A porcion of sugar or a perty of hony and a party of safron,
> boille it, and gift it forth."
>
> TWELFTH-CENTURY MS.

We, who do not normally go long periods without a meal, expect refresh-
ments when we travel, and do not take long journeys on horseback, or
cold stage coaches; we do not realise the need for the caudel type of hot
"soup wine" or "ale meal". After long hours of travel, hot wine, or spirits,
on an empty stomach, were not too good, and yet often you were too tired
to eat. Thus, the compromise of a caudel, which warmed you, fed you, and
"kept you going till you could obtain a solid meal". That is why this type
of "food drink" has survived in working classes and rural circles, where
the same physical need still continues. The cocktail stimulant of modern
communities has not the same stamina.

"Ale berry" is a type of caudel; hot gruel with whisky and lemon is
another type. Genuine caudels were made in so many ways it is difficult
to choose the most popular. This is one that might have comforted Mr.
Pickwick after his immersion.

Mr. Pickwick's Caudel

2 tablespoonfuls of finest oatmeal stirred into 1 pint of hot water. Boil
till thick, and immediately strain out into a hot mug. Add sugar, nutmeg,
lemon peel, ginger according to taste, and serve piping hot, laced with fine
brandy. (For the ladies, use sherry and perhaps a well-frothed egg.)

This Caudel Would Please Sam Weller

Boil 2 tablespoonfuls of oatmeal in 1 pint of hot water with the rind
of a lemon, a blade of mace, a scrap of cinnamon, and 1 tablespoonful of
brown sugar. Pour off into an equal quantity of hot mild ale, or fresh porter.

Spinster's Blush

This caudel might restore the virtuous female after the departure of Jingle. 1 tablespoonful of ground rice boiled in 1 pint of water, sugar to taste, grate of ginger, and a glass of port wine.

A caudel was taken *before* a meal, a posset was taken *instead* of a meal. A posset was usually served in a specially made china posset dish, with a cover to it, but a posset could vary from a simple treacle cold cure to an elaborate confection.

POSSETS

A Simple Posset

> " A sparing diet did her health assure
> Or sick, a posset was her cure."
>
> DRYDEN.

Take 1 pint of milk, heat in a pan, and when it froths up, add a gill of white wine. Strain out the curd, rub some lumps of sugar on a lemon, and add with a spoonful of ginger and a grate of nutmeg if liked.

Posset (East-Indian style)

> " From far Barbadoes on the Western main
> Fetch sugar, ounces four, fetch sac from Spain,
> One pint, and from the East Indian coast,
> Nutmeg; the glory of the Northern Toast,
> On flaming coals let them together heat,
> Till the all-conquering sac dissolve the sweet,
> On such another fire put eggs, just ten,
> (New-born, from tread of cock and rump of hen),
> Stir then with steady hand, and conscience pricking
> To see the untimely end of ten fine chicken,
> From shining shelf, take down the brazen skillet,
> A quart of milk from gentle cow will fill it
> When boiled and cold, put milk to sac and eggs,
> Unite them firmly, like the triple league,
> And on the fire let them together dwell."
>
> POPE (?)

YPOCRAS

This interesting mediaeval spiced wine is mentioned by an old steward of a castle who laments that lords and ladies do not drink and dine in Hall as their fathers did, but have hot wines and small meals carried up to their bedrooms.

This spiced wine took its name from Hippocrates' sleeve (so they say), as the bags hung up for the wine to drip through were shaped like long mediaeval sleeves.

When working out this recipe, I was fortunate in obtaining some of the plain grape juice of Constantia, very like the plain Norman wine, though probably more sweet and sunripe. The spices were worked out by a wine-merchant's chemist, with the experts from Spicers Hall, some of the most curious—e.g., "quires" (which proved to be quince seeds), and "graynes" and galingale, etc.—being unobtainable through the ordinary chemist. It is interesting that "graynes" (of paradise) are still used to revive a faded vintage, and several other spices were tactfully mentioned by the merchants who "made wines to match the labels, not the labels to the wines". Ypocras is very pleasant and very potent—especially "hote".

For the smaller quantities now convenable, we suggest that small bags to hold the spices should be immersed in the wine jar, rather than the more cumbrous sleeve method; move the bags gently about in the wine, and remove while testing (as the spice works very rapidly when the wine is warm). Do not strain, simply decant gently, direct from the wine jar. The spices (see Boorde's own instructions) may be dried in the bags and used many times.

> " Good son to make Ypocras, hit were get lernynge
> And for to take the spice thereto aftur the proportionyne
>
> Ginger, Synamoune, Grayes, Sugar, Turnesole,
> That is good colourynge
>
> For common peple Gynger Canelle long pepur
> Hony aftur claythynge
>
> Look ye have of pewtur basons oon two or thre
> For to kepe in youre powdure, also the licour therein to remove
>   when that nede be
>
> To iii basouns ye must have iii bagges, renners so clepe them
>   well
> And hange then on a perch[1] and looke that sure they be
>
> Se that youre gynger be welle y pared a hit to powder ye bete
> And that hit be hard with owt worme bytynge and good hete
>
> Looke that your sikkes of synamone be thyn bretille and fayre
>   in colewre
> And in youre mowthe fresche hoot and swete that is best and sure

---

[1] Wooden hook on wall—hence hawk perches.

Graynes of paradice, hoote and moyst they be
Sugre of ii cut, white, hoot and moyste in his propurte

Sugre Candy is best of alle as ye tell thee
And red wyne is hote and drye to taste fele and see,

Graynes, gynger, long pepur and sugre hoot and moyste in worckyng
Synamone Canelle red wyne hoot and dry in theire doynge.

Turnesole, is good and solsoun for red wyne colourynge
Alle these ingredyentes they are for Ypocras makynge.

Good son youre powdure so made vche by thourself in bleddur laid,
Hange sure youre perche and bagges that they from your not brayd

Furst put in a basoun a galoum ii or ii wyne so red
(Then put in your powdurs if ye wille be sped)
And aftyr wite the rennere so lett bym be fed
So wite the second bagge so wuld it be ledde
And loke thou take a piece in thyne hand evermore amonge
And assay it in they mouth if hit be any thynge strong.

Now is the yprocas made, for to please many a wight
(The draff of the spicery is good for sweres in kychyn dight)
I would then the put it in staunche and clene vesselle
And the mouthe fe-ff y stopped more wicely and welle
And serve hit forth with wafurs bofe in chambur and celle."

SYLLABUB (spelt also Sillabub, Sillebub etc.) (*see* Hatted Kit)

Sill was a part of the Champagne country from which the wine Sill or Sille took its name, Bub was the common Elizabethan slang for a bubbling drink, later, by association, a belly, and a syllabub was made by mixing the wine Sille with frothing cream—to make a Sille Bub.

Syllabub under the Cow (sometimes called "Hatted Kit")

For this, milk (which naturally forms a fine froth on being milked from the udder) is drawn down direct into the wine. That was a simple syllabub, but it could also be a rich cold sweet.

A Rich Syllabub

Seven ounces of sugar melted in the juice of two large lemons, add the rasped rinds, two glasses of sherry, and two smaller glasses of brandy. When the mixture is made, whip in a pint of cream, and continue to whip till a fine froth rises.

This should be piled into glasses to serve. The old recipe adds that you may use more or less wine, in proportion to the cream, but syllabubs " are neither good nor wholesome without a portion of brandy ".

A Curd Syllabub

The milk is poured upon the sugar, wine and brandy mixture, and left to form a curd. This curd is then placed in the glasses, the whey poured on to the top and whipped cream sweetened and flavoured with lemon *rind* (not the juice) is floated to top off the glass.

If port or red wine is used for the curd, nutmeg is used to flavour the topping of cream.

The trick of holding the wine over the finger bowl was known as toasting the "King-across-the-water", and was a Royalist sign, after the expulsion of James II.

GENERAL NOTES ON CIDER AND THE CIDER-PRESS

" Materials for thy Mill, a sturdy Post
Cylindric to support the grinders weight
Excessive, and a flexible sallow entrench'd.
Rounding capacious of the juicy hord.
Nor must thou not be mindful of thy Press!
Long ere the vintage, but with timely care,
Shave the goats shaggy beard, least thou
In vain should'st seek a strainer. . . .
Be cautious next a proper steed to find,
Whose prime is past, the vigorous horse disdains
Such servile labours, or, if forced, forgets
His past achievements and victorious palms.
Blind Baynard rather, worn with work and years
Shall roll the unwieldy stone, with sober pace.
He'll tread the circling path till dewy eve,
From early dayspring, pleased to find his age
Declining, not unuseful to his Lord."

EIGHTEENTH-CENTURY CIDERMAN.

One can tell this was "border" cider. The "entrenched trough; rounding capacious" was of rough stone, with a basketwork rim of sallie willows, to keep "the juicy hord" in the path of the heavy rotating grindstone, and the "goats shaggy beard" was to provide the thick hair mats, in which the apple pulp is wrapped, when put under the screw press (after Baynard has "milled"). For there are two main "schools" of cider—"border" and "down west". The "border" sub-divides into Monmouth, Gloucester, Hereford, Welsh and Shropshire types. The "down west" sub-divides into Devon, Dorset, Somerset and Cornish types, and all types have their differences.

Briefly, in "border" cider, the apples are rolled over by heavy rough stone wheels, which crush the pips, releasing their almond flavour, and the pulp is then packed into loose, thick mats of horsehair (now coir) and pressed, in iron and stone screw presses, on the whole rather more swiftly than in the larger wooden presses "down west".

"Down west", the apples are packed between straw layers like enormous many-tiered sandwiches (sometimes reinforced by hurdles), and the pressure is put on more gradually in wooden presses; the hollow staves acting as drainage channels.

The final "pummace" of both types is equally dry, but the "west-type" is now full of flattened straw and the "border" pummace solid apple.

The "down west" school maintains that there "belongs to be a power of minerals raised up from the soil into the straw" and the apple acid "searches this out" and so their cider is enriched by the goodness from the golden corn straw. The "border" contests that *if* that is so, the natural acid of the apple is "neutralised" and "deadened by the straw", their mats being the purer vessel. The "stone" crushing also, "by reason of the apples passing between the grains of the stones" (stone trough below and stone grinder rolling around above; stone rolling on stone) the apple skins are "harassed" and "indent", thereby releasing the aroma which is *in* the substance of the apple skins. (Devon skins remain flat, but smooth), and on the "border", we have the flavour of the pip kernels!

Feeling runs very high! One tries to be impartial, but Devon folk are very self-opinionated! Our Monmouth cider is vastly superior, and shall be described forthwith!

Cider Apples

Nowadays large firms take great credit for scientific research in cider apples, but this was done for centuries, by the country people.

The carriage of apple trees from one part of England to another is an endless tale of patience and loving enterprise by country people. There are wharf lists, cargo records, shipping logs, private letters from ship-owners to orchard planters, unlimited evidence that the work has been carried on for centuries.

Here are the names of some of the old apples;—Deux Anna[1], Jerseys, French Longtails, Culverings, Rusticoats, Holland Pippings, Cowley Crabs, Kentish Pippins, Burlington Crabs, Cackagee, Kendrik Wilding, Herefordshire Styne, the Foxwhelp, the Woodcock, the White Swan, the Warrenden[2] (can't you hear them trundling along?), the Redstreak,

[1] " Deux Ans ", two years, later corrupted to " Jews' hands ".
[2] Warrenden or Quarenden.

Rubystreak and Longstreak Redstreak (they sound like a cider-mill creaking!) and a dozen others.

Besides apples, various localities used other ingredients. In Kent, cherries were used. In the West, blackberries were added.

Blood, Smoke, and Milk in Cider

Some additions were made of albumen, to "clean" rather than to flavour. The Cornish miners would run a sheep's blood into the cask.

In Devon, milk and cream were added. All sorts of things, from isinglass to eggshells, were used. Probably Spanish influence taught the scenting of casks with the smoke of aromatic spices.

One method was to soak linen strips in oil and aromatic gums. (The gum from cherry trees or apple trees was sometimes used.) These were burnt in the cask and the cider was poured in while the cask was still full of smoke.

Certain precautions were common to all makes of cider. Metal must never touch the acid fruit. I have known a stack knife carelessly used to cut the pummace for a second pressing to ruin an entire vintage, and the whole district remembers the enormity of that crime.

The apples must be left "to sweat" or to rot, or used comparatively fresh, according to local judgement.

"Racking" is a very vital process. Cider must never be *strained*, so to get it clear it must stand unmoved (either of its own working or movement of the cask) until the dropping of the temperature clears it (*see* Racking, p. 537).

Working Cider

The country people become lyrical when describing the sounds of "working"—how you are to listen with your ear to the cask, and hear the cider "singing low and sweetly".

Commercial enterprise may make adequate standard cider, but it cannot make the interesting, friendly variations that happen each season with the small private press. How one tree has borne rather well; how the apples another year run small, so that there is a predominance of pips, and the cider that year has a noticeable almond aroma—how they left it "perhaps a little too long?", or how "perhaps this year is the best we've ever had. . . ." All the anxious anticipation and mature judgement when we all gather round to pass opinion on our efforts of the season.

Mill and Press

It is a small mill, belonging to a comparatively small farmhouse. The mill is an old stone trough, with wide splayed wooden rim. The heavy stone crusher rolls round, pivoted on a worn oak beam.

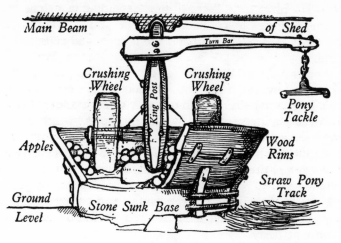

Section of a pony-turned cider mill. This has two balanced rolling stones.
Sometimes there is only one larger roller on the opposite side from the pony.

A Monmouth cider press: the apple pulp is wrapped in mats of black horse-
hair, with boards between each matful of pulp to keep the whole pile steady
and level under pressure.

The press is a plain stone "screw" press, standing in a stone trough.

In autumn the apples are gathered into a pile, and left to brown slightly. The old pony is then fetched up and the harness and collar lifted down from its pin.

The old pony picks up the sound as cleverly as he picks up the wind-fallen apples, and usually comes round (though the story that the intelligent animal utterly refused to grind one year when he thought the vintage wasn't worth it is not accredited). While the apples "weather", the cider shed is "got ready".

All the things that have accumulated for twelve months are cleared out, and the trough and press are washed, and the woodwork all well soaked with spring water.

The apples are shovelled in to the trough and stirred with a wooden shovel—the horse goes round, and the pummace is made, packed and pressed, without delay.

If it is a good year, it fills all the casks with first press, but sometimes the pummace is loosened, re-milled with more apples and a dash of spring water, and pressed again for the last casks; it all depends.

The cider mill and press are just a convenient size to be loaned to neighbours around, who bring their own creaking cartloads up the little lane, and do a couple of day's pressing for themselves; as each local orchard has its own variety of apple (*not* all special cider apples) there is always pleasant variety.

The Press and Mats

When the trough is full of crushed pulp this is collected into one of the pressing mats (previously soaked in clear water). These fold over the pulp into a well-made parcel (folds on top) and the mass "set" on the stone base of the press. The screw is "set on" and juice runs swiftly down into the under trough. As this fills, it is baled out into the tub (if for mixing) or direct to the cask. This is the point of production when some do "flavour" their cider, some smoke it, some spice the cask, some leave plain. Sweetbriar is sometimes laid in the press with the pummace, but a good cider relies on the selective blending of the apples and their correct "weathering" and pressing. Milling and pressing may begin as early as September and go on as late as December—it depends on the fruit.

Pummace

A few beekeepers "mill" once, very early, for their small bees dearly love the pummace.

Most womenfolk collect a jug of the plain run juice, when pressing, for special harvest cookery.

The pummace, when pressed dry, is mixed with meal and fed to the pig.

Cider Made in Small Quantities without Mill or Press

The pulp was sometimes crushed with mallets in stone or wooden troughs. An old shallow stone-ware sink (called a slopstone in the north) makes a good trough, raised on stones and with a wooden rim set on to it, the juice draining out through the sink hole into the "catch tub".

An old stone cheese press can often be found near a farm, and a strong linen sack will hold enough pummace for a small cask. Any enterprising countryman with an orchard of windfalls can make his own cider.

Perry

> "Of Peres, wyne is made, if they be grounde
> And through a rare saack with fors y wronge, . . .
> Of peares sour and wilde, it is no wronge
> Aysell (vinegar) to bringe . . . ."
>
> PALLADIUS ON HUSBANDRY (fourth century, probably translated
>   into English by a Colchester gardener and monk in the 1300s).

Made in England in the cider districts, but not given the care and research that attends cider making.

GENERAL NOTES ON MEAD

"Meade is made of honney and water boyled both together, if it be fyned and pure it preserveth helth."

Yeast was *not* used in the old meads. Mead was made from the washings of the honeycombs from which the honey had been extracted. Now the comb was hive-warm, and in contact with the wood or rye straw skeps, and it is more than likely that there was mycological infection from the rye straw. Also, some of the curious balm-like bee bread was always added "to help it ferment". That *Saccharonyces cerevisiae* accounted for the ferment is possible. The same wooden tub would be used to make the bread, brew the mead, or mash the apple pulp. Utensils were fewer. They were seldom boiled, never sterilised. Mediaeval stories of miracles and blessings, spells and curses, throw plentiful suspicion upon the utensils.

Many mediaeval record keepers of repute tell of hollow stones which turned water into wine of their own accord, and it's very likely these stone troughs had been used for previous ferments. A strongly impregnated wooden tub will continue to "work" for years, if it is kept damp and warm.

Certain monasteries guarded their special brews from year to year quite as jealously as modern brewers guard their special cultures of yeast (for innoculating their special worts). Practically every modern brewery now has its own culture which produces the individuality of its beer (and I believe there are certain old laws reminiscent of the Guilds, requiring brother brewers to give a sufficient start of a yeast plant if a culture is accidentally killed off).

The bee bread used in mead, being a plant pollen predigested and partly converted to diatose by the bees, is an excellent home for yeasts which would occur naturally (as they do in the skins of apples and pears used for cider and perry).

Till as late as the seventeenth century, it is pretty certain that there was a distinct mead ferment, just as now there is an ale yeast. In proof, some old Welsh skep clearings were put into the waiting honey mixture, and instantly started a strong ferment which made an exceptionally light frothed mead.

To Make Mead (eighteenth-century recipe)

This recipe makes a very light pleasant mead, with a fine white head.

The honey need not be the clear strained honey—in fact, the clearings of the hive, including bee bread and broken comb, work better; and "the gallon of hot water" may well be the water used to rinse out the honey separator. Any scraps or small impurities will work out in the scum of fermentation, and some rough pieces of bee bread have a special value in making the mead strong.

To 1 gallon of water take 1 pint of honey. Bôil it, and after boiling, immediately plunge in a handful of rosemary, sweet briar, or little lemon balm (a bay leaf, or some cloves and bruised mace, may be added if liked, but we do not care for mead in which the taste of the honey is burnt out with ginger and spices).

So consider the aroma of the special honey; and choose your "flower fragrance" to enhance this natural bouquet. When the honey-sweet water is flavoured and scented, and blood-warm, spread a piece of toasted bread with the finest yeast you can get, and float it on top. If it's your first try, it is helpful to sprinkle a little fine sugar around the floating yeast raft—then reassuringly soon you will see the yeast begin to work, making small soft bubbles, and a gentle purring sound. Keep the pan lightly covered in a reasonably warm room.

A creamy scum should have spread all over the top of the liquid in *about* a week, but much depends on the temperature of the room, and the shape of the tub, and strength of ferment and honey water. The yeast plant feeds on the sweetness in the liquid, taking it in, and giving it out, after a process rather like digestion. While there is plenty of sugar free in the warm liquid, the yeast will bubble and hiss and grow fast; when the liquid becomes cold, it will "work" slower. A deep crock makes it harder work; on a wide shallow crock the yeast cannot spread so quickly. Also you may not want the yeast to have worked through all the sweetness, but to have some left for the fermentation to continue after the liquid is in the barrel (or you may want it quite "worked out", so as to be able to bottle it sooner without fear of bursting).

Therefore watch and study your "working", and if it is singing to itself, let it alone. If it seems quite still, the ferment may have "died" or may have "ceased working" (because it has used up all the free sugar it worked upon). For the novice, it is reassuring to put a pinch of sugar on to one corner of the scum, and watch. If in a short time that one spot becomes active again, but as soon as that small pinch of extra sugar has been used up the activity ceases, then it is evident that the sugar content in the rest of the liquid has all been converted and "the yeast is not dead, but has ceased to work".

Now skim off the yeast (you can use it again if you want to), pour off into the cask (and a handful of raisins in the cask is a great improvement), let it be bunged up and rest for three months, and be drawn off in frosty weather, when it will be found very clear and bright, with a fine froth.

English Sack (a variant of mead)

To 1 quart of water put a sprig of rue and a handful of fennel roots. Boil, strain off, and to every gallon allow nearly 3 lb. of honey, boil again, till dissolved, and when cool, work it with yeast. "Turn it into such cask as is fit for it, keep it a year, and then bottle it and it is very good Sac."

SPIRITS

Wines and Spirits are linked, as are Meads and Metheglyns; euphonious but misleading, for, on the whole, the English drank "straight", they did not mix much. As with food, they worked to bring out the flavour rather than to blend.

Usquebaugh

> " For my mother was not only a Connacht woman, but an out and out Connamara quean, and had wrought with the lads who used to make the raal cratur on the islands between Ochlerard and Ballynahinch. . . . There's not such a place for Irish all in the world as Scotland Road [in Birmingham]."
>
> S. Borrow.

Drogheda Usquebaugh

Take 1 oz. of aniseed, ½ oz. of sweet fennel seeds, 1 oz. of green liquorice, 1 drachm of coriander seed, a drachm of cloves, 1 drachm of mace, 1 lb. of raisins, ½ lb. of figs, a slice of liquorice root; bruise all the ingredients and infuse in a gallon of best brandy for eight days. Strain and infuse ½ oz. of the best saffron for two days. Bottle.

Cherry Brandy

Pack an earthenware jar with dark Morello cherries, sprinkling crushed brown sugar candy. Fill up the cask with brandy, and tie down with bladder.

Keep several months before bottling. (*See also* Cherry Ale.)

Sloe Gin (*see* Sloes)

Sloes are best preserved in gin.

Sloe gin, blended with Penny Royal and Valerian, has for years been used by country wives in connubial emergencies.

Cold Tankard (Victorian)

All the rind of a lemon rubbed off on sugar, to taste, and ½ pint of brandy. Mix well, add 1 quart of cold spring water, 1 pint of white wine, and/or 1 bottle of cider.

Put a handful of borage and lemon balm into a flagon, pour the cold tankard into it, and embed on ice at least 1 hour.

Distilling

> " The knowledge of stilling is one pretty feat,
> The waters be wholsome, the charges not great.
> What timely thou gettest, while summer doth last,
> Think winter will help thee, to spend it as fast."
>
> TUSSER.

Distilled Scents and Essences

The "still room" was so usual a part of old housekeeping that the name continues in countryhouse use.

For country people with large gardens it is worth while to acquire a simple still: the management is no more complicated than many glass coffee machines. The different types of stills (obtainable through a chemist) have their own instructions.

It is usually better to distil each fragrance separately, and blend them afterwards. The oils of some herbs, such as rosemary, can be obtained by infusion and skimming, and pure melted lard, filled and refilled with flowers, will absorb their scent—distilling is beyond the scope of this book, but an interesting point for the plain cook; that basting fat used with aromatic herbs in cooking meat becomes very strongly aromatic, and thus a flavoured dripping should be kept separately and used to flavour other dishes.

Saffron Cordial (an example of domestic distilling)

" Fill a large still with marigold flowers, and strew on it an ounce of cafe-nutmegs, that is, the nutmegs that have the mace on them; beat them grossly, and take an ounce of the best English saffron; pull it and mix it with the flowers; then take three pints of muscafine, or tent, or Malaga sack, and with a sprig of rosemary dash it on the flowers; then distil it off till it begins to be sour; save a pint of the first running to mix with other waters on an extraordinary occasion, mix the rest together to drink by itself. This cordial is excellent in fainting, and for the smallpox or ague; take five or six spoonsful at a time."

MS. (about 1750?)

The Counsel of Chaucer

" A lecherous thing is wyne and dronkenesse
A dronke man, disfigured is thy face.
Sour is the breeth, foul art thou to embrace
And through thy dronke nose semeth the soun
As though tho seydest ay " Sampsoun Sampsoun "
And yet god wot Samsoun drank never no wyn,
Thou fallest as it were a stiked swyn
Thy tonge is lost and al thyn honest cure
For dronkenesse is verray sepulture
Of mannes wit, and his discretion
In whom that drinke hath dominacioun
He can no conseil kepe, it is no dred
Now kepe you fro the whyte and fro the rede."

GENERAL NOTES ON TEA

" All well-regulated families set apart an hour every morning for tea and bread and butter."

ADDISON, 1711.

Watch the care with which English people make tea—kettle rinsed, freshly drawn water, the pot warmed and polished.
Some teapots have special wool jackets, crocheted to fit neatly round their spouts, pulled up to their necks, and woolly mats to sit on.

Not only woman's tea is made with care; watch any workman, with his billycan of yellow, hot tea, and the sugar in a screw of newspaper. First thing he does on a job is to fix the bucket-of-coke fire and settle the blackened iron kettle to boil. Managing directors in "shops" and "offices" all allow for the "tea break".

In the engineering shops the apprentice boys come and fetch the men's cans, at "mashing time, regular to the tick". Married men bring real milk in glass bottles and bachelors use "condensed" out of a tin in their locker.

Boat-men on canals "boil" tea. "A well-boiled cup of tea" only means freshly boiling water, and well stood.

Discourteous indeed would be the English back-door that would refuse boiling water to a tramp's tea-can, "Save your screw [of tea]

The workman's tea-kettle—the most urgent part of any government contract

and have a filling out of our pot," is the courtesy of the road any time after four.

Tea came to England in about the seventeenth century. They say it was imported to Europe by the Dutch, at the end of the sixteenth century. It didn't sound any too good at first.

"The aforesaid warme water is made with the powder of a certain hearbe called chaa"—later "tay", later "tea".

One traveller from the East explained carefully that the water should remain on the tea leaves "for as long as it takes to say the Miserere Psalm slowly".

There was a tremendous lot of controversy about the new drink. The first tea-cups did not have handles. They were little round bowls, and you went to take tea with tremendous ceremony and palaver.

In 1660 Pepys sends "for a cup of tea (a China drink) of which I never have drunk before". (It's nice to think the date is in September, with the evenings closing in, when Pepys first fell for a nice hot cup of tea!)

By the 1700s tea was the English drink. It was ruinously expensive, anything between 16s.–50s. per lb., and the used tea-leaves would be dried, rolled, and re-sold again by the servants of the rich. This was illegal: "Geo. III. Act 17. Eney person . . . who shall dye or fabricate any sloe leaves, liquorice leaves, or the leaves of tea that has been used . . . " (a heavy fine if caught).

In the 1800s they tried to make wine of tea leaves (because about that date they made wine of everything), so tea was fermented, probably flavoured with briar, and casked and bottled.

At first there were two main types of tea, *Thea bohea* and *Thea viridis*—that is to say, black tea and green tea—and the names, Gunpowder, Pekoe, Formosa, etc., were mixed (in locality and variety), for some years. "Tea" as a drink was not new to England, we were well trained on our own earlier "infusion" herb drinks. So, instantly the foreign herb called "tea" arrives, all our old infusions become called "teas" also.

This is a very interesting point, as probably many of the earlier drinks called "tea" were not tea at all, but the old well-known plant infusions, which still continue in use in country places. In the sixteenth century the English medicinal teas crossed the Atlantic and now flourish in America (sage tea vying with sarsaparilla as universal and all-pervading).

In time all the old "cordials" and "waters" become called "teas"— even strengthening soup becomes "beef-tea". Sweet balm, camomile and hartshorn all made "tea". Cowslip tea is delicious, and lime-tree tea made of the blossoms of the lime trees is very fragrant and soporific).

Raspberry-leaf tea is known to village mothers for easy childbirth, and black-currant tea is sovereign cure for hoarseness of throat and cold in the chest.

Wild thyme, bugloss, willow and mint are other country teas; so is the stinking valerian, used to induce abortion.

The medicinal waters of Bath, so popular at the period of tea-and-coffee-houses, were referred to as "limestone tea"!

SOME ENGLISH TEAS

Catnip Tea

> " ' Is there anything I can do for you Aunt Fortune? '
> ' I don't care if you make me little catnip tea. The catnip is up in the store-room. Here's the key.'
> How to make catnip tea Ellen did not exactly know, but supposed it must follow the same procedure as black tea, so she put a pinch or two of catnip tea in the pot, poured over a little

water, and stood it to draw. Then she filled up her tea cup and carried it upstairs.

'My stars, Ellen! What do you call this?'

'Isn't it catnip?' said Ellen, in alarm.

'Catnip! It tastes of nothing but the tea kettle! It is as weak as dish water! Take it down and make some more. How much did you put in? You want a good double handful, stalks and all, to make it strong. I think if I could get into a sweat I should be better.'"

E. WETHERALL (Anglo-American).

And such was the potency of the catnip tea, that Aunt Fortune had her good sweat and slowly threw off her influenza.

Hyssop Tea

The flowers and leaves are used. Pour boiling water over them (a handful to 1 quart) infuse for 20 minutes. Sweetened with honey, it was considered good for chest coughs.

Raspberry-leaf Tea

The ordinary leaves of the raspberry canes from late spring to full summer should be gathered and used (fresh, if possible). Infuse in boiling water and drink freely with milk and sugar. It also makes a good drink with lemon and sugar. It is well-known as particularly good during the later months of pregnancy.

Black-currant Tea

The berries made into a thick syrup, sweetened with honey, are excellent for hoarseness of the throat or to loosen a cold on the chest. For the latter the tea is drunk hot at bedtime.

Black-currant Leaves

The leaves, gathered in early summer and dried and rubbed, made a good ordinary tea, and was used by old pensioners to supplement their allowance of "India blend".

Blackberry Leaves

Dry and roll the small "tips" of the runners.—When making "substitute teas" the blackberry is chosen to give a good colour.

BLENDING PLANTS FOR "TEA"

> " Tell, tell your griefs, attentive I will stay
>   Though time is precious, and I want some tea."

A. POPE, LINES TO MRS. LOVET.

It was during the acute rationing period that all these "teas" were used in England to adulterate the imported teas.

A serviceable English "tea" may be made with hawthorn for bulk, and sage, lemon balm, woodruff (the plant), and black-currant leaves for flavour. Do not omit at least three out of the four flavouring herbs, but let some flavour predominate. Thus, if currant and sage predominate, the tea will somewhat favour Ceylon; if the lemon balm predominates, it will be more a China cup; if the "woodruff", it will have the smoky aroma of Darjeeling.

Pick over the leaves, and spread to dry in the sun. As they dry, rub them with a rolling motion under the flat palm of your hand to give a tightly folded texture, then rub them through a coarse sieve.

It is advisable to make the base first, and then add the other prepared leaves separately—a measure at a time, till you have the blend you require. Realise that the flavour will mature further in the canister, the stronger flavouring leaves permeating the whole. Let this tea steep rather longer than ordinary Indian tea.

If China tea is wanted, lemon balm, lime-tree blossom, cowslip pips and a very few lavender leaves or sweet briar will give a delicate golden brew. The lavender leaves should be used very sparingly, but a few give a slight bite, whereas the sweet briar, lime blossom and cowslip blossom merely give fragrance.

The old-fashioned sweet briar makes a good pale tea, also dried jessamine flowers. A few "blackberry-tip leaves" can be added to any tea blend to give a stronger colour.

> " It is impossible to make a fire, boil water and make tea, drink it, wash up the things, sweep up the fireplace and put all to rights again in less space of time than 2 hours . . . besides the waste of a man's time hanging about waiting for the tea."

COBBETT.

CHOCOLATE

In the eighteenth century chocolate was "vastly modern". The early chocolate was prepared from the "nib" direct. The nibs were pounded and stewed for hours (like bones making stock). When cold the white fat (cocoa butter) was removed and the chocolate reboiled with milk and flavouring, and, just before serving, thickened with eggs.

Chocolate made thus is mentioned by all early American writers, and continued in England till fifty years ago, when the "prepared" cocoas and chocolates replaced it.

In its early forms, chocolate was considered as good for breeding women as coffee was for men. One health expert in the eighteenth century described how, by the use of chocolate, his wife was "brought to bed of twins, three times". After which two learned doctors bravely undertook personal experiment, and "lowered several pounds of chocolate into their stomachs", and sat all one afternoon awaiting events. (Dr. Wills.)

Cocoa was curiously popular with unexpected people; hunters and soldiers drank it, and Sherlock Holmes and Dr. Watson had it for early breakfast before an expedition.

SALOP [1]

> "Provision for three weeks, according to the daily proportion of 1 lb. biscuit, two thirds of a lb. of Donkins preserved meat, one ounce of salop powder, one ounce of sugar and half a pint of spirits for each man."
>
> *Parry's Voyages in Search of the North-West Passage,* 1819.

Salop is seldom made in England now, though I have found it in a few places.

It is the root of *Orchis mascula* (also called "dogstones"), washed, dried and ground to powder.

Glasse describes it as obtainable, compressed into a stone, subsequently ground and scraped to powder, and "sold at a shilling an ounce". "Use one large teaspoonful to one pint boiling water, and stir till a fine jelly."

It was a common, soft drink before the period of coffee-houses, and, being a cheaper product, continued in country use for centuries later. It is mentioned often in Victorian tracts, as drunk by porters, coalmen, and workers of all kinds, who bought it at the small "car-men's rests". In Cardiganshire I had it at an old seaman's cottage after a long, wet sea crossing; it was made very thick and hot and served with a spoon and sugar. In Scotland (Durness) I had it laced with spirit in a glass. In Ireland it was served in a teacup, thickened with cream and egg yolk.

"*Salop, How Tis Made*" (1742)

"Take one quart water and let it boil $\frac{1}{4}$-hour, then put in $\frac{1}{4}$-oz. of salop, fine powdered, and let it boil $\frac{1}{2}$-hour longer, stirring it all the time. Season with white wine and juice of lemon, and sweeten it to your taste, and drink it out of china cups, as chocolate. It is a great sweetener of the

[1] From the Dutch slemp, a drink made of thickened milk with clove and sugar, served hot to skaters.

blood . . . or if you please to leave out the wine and lemon, put in a pint of thick cream, a stick of cinnamon, and thicken it up with 2 or 3 eggs."

With the more general use of sago, a salop-like drink was made thus:

1 teaspoonful of sago, 1 pint of milk, boil, and cover closely, to thicken in a hot place by the fire. Strain and sweeten as a drink for invalids. This was sometimes called salop, but it wasn't.

COFFEE

Coffee is a modern example of how a change in diet permeates the country. The Blitz evacuated thousands of city workers used to "coffee elevenses" into the country, the soldiers serving overseas were given coffee, and tea rationing happened at the same time. Nowadays you can trace the coffee makers around American camps, newly placed industrial areas, and where displaced foreigners have come to live in England. In many English farm-houses, and hotels, these days you can get excellent coffee with cream—or *café au lait*—and gifts from colonial friends help this trend in spite of raised prices (curiously price has often little effect on food fashions).

Dandelion Coffee

The gypsies and some herbalists make a coffee from dandelion roots, dried and ground. This is supposed to be good for the liver. It makes a pleasant milk coffee, and many people like it who cannot take real coffee.

Dig the roots in early autumn and wash thoroughly; the easier way to wash is to put in a net under a waterfall, turning and shaking the net often. Dry the roots spread out in the sun till "bone dry", then roast the roots slightly, as giving a better colour and flavour. Grind them rather coarsely, and use as ordinary coffee.

Acorn Coffee

Roasted and ground, acorns make a rough coffee-like drink in emergency, but it is unpleasant and bitter.

Chicory we only use for salading.

> " Be content that the Creator
> Has blest the World with so much water."

THE INDUSTRIAL REVOLUTION

STARVATION AND PLENTY

A NOTE ON THE INDUSTRIAL REVOLUTION

IT IS difficult for the historian housekeeper to explain the divide between poverty and wealth, and good food and poor food; they are not the same division. In early English history the division between the few enormously wealthy and powerful, and the completely penniless multitude, is not a division of food. The overlord might feast, and the hireling fast, but both could do it on the same basic English materials. The game laws, penalties for sheep stealing, the hordes of helpless vagrants, obscure the main dietetic facts. Population was scanty, large tracts of the country free, and the land fertile. A countryman's family, even under almost slavish conditions, often had as good food as their own industry could provide *for themselves*. The wool on his back, the leather shoes on his feet, the pork in his larder, and corn in his bin, were a man's own growing. Beyond an iron pot and a few tools, there was little he could buy. He lived in good clean air, had clean water, and was able to make a fire and build a house (of materials no worse than many an Irish cabin of today). In some cases, where the wealthy lived in cadaverous stone castles cut off from the sun and air, and where they ate costly unsuitable food, the balance of rude health was with the peasant and his simple life. The misery and starvation in the early rural communities, are usually caused by epidemics, tempests, and war. The slave was bought and sold like cattle, but it behoved the owner to keep slaves in good condition to do their work. The bestial cruelty and misery, the dungeons and lash, existed, and the large feudal estate levied service, for the estate fields, but air surveys show historians more; the number and size of the "small holdings"—the little cultivated lands show like shadows below the turf—and those small lands all supported their own independent population.

With the Industrial Revolution the people are driven off the land; they are cut off from their natural food supply, and are compelled for the first time to *buy* food. The cruelty of the Industrial Revolution was that it made money a necessity of *life*; it is not the crowding into towns, to work in the factories, nor the land, neglected, ceasing to provide food, *it is a dislocation of the food supply*.

Townspeople today rarely realise the necessary continuity of country work. On the land one must wait three years before it is possible to live; it is corn bought two years previously that is today's bread, beef is two years, or more, agrowing; one ewe, even if she have twin lambs, must suckle and graze them into the second year before mutton is available; even the cheaply bought runkling pig must be well-fed for months before it is slaughtered, and without the year's work and growth in the field, there is nothing to feed the pig! This is elementary, yet so many people say unthinkingly "Why did they not return to the country?" The "country" is like a door that slams shut!

Only country people realise the impossibility of leaving the land, for even a few months, without losing all livelihood from it for at least a year. For the unfortunate victims of the industrial townships, there was no "return home". Once away from their basic proportion of arable land, they were dependent, for the first time in history.

WHAT THEY LEFT

Rural life on £12 a year

Housekeeping of a farm labourer in Scotland.
The following extract concerns one of the finest parts for mixed farming —the Carse of Gowrie, the fertile land on the sea coast of Fife.

Wages of a farm foreman in Fifeshire in 1870

Money £12.
65 stone of oatmeal (nearly 100 lb).
1 drill of potatoes (1,200 yards long in a field).
House and garden and the keep for his own cow. He also got an extra allowance of bread and beer during harvest. So much was *pay*.
Now—onto this he probably kept a pig on waste from house and garden —and some hens loose about the land. He would have only one fire (around which the family sat after the cooking was done) and this burnt peat, cut and carted by himself. The garden would provide rough kail, soft fruit (raspberries are a speciality of the district), onions and summer greens, and he'd keep bees.
Now, stock his wife's larder.
Oatmeal scones, biscuits, bread and porridge. Bacon, lard, pork, ham, eggs, boiling fowls, fruit, vegetables and potatoes, honey, milk, butter, cream, and cheese (*see* One-cow Cheese). Milk puddings, bone and vegetable broths, and probably mild beer or souse drinks. All these without spending a penny at a shop.
Add small quantities of tea, coffee, cocoa (nibs), lemon, ginger and

condiments (salt, sugar and spirits, etc.) and you give scope for cakes and cookies (Scotland is fine for cakes), and a full varied diet of the best type, even without the probable mutton, or a piece of beef that could be obtained by exchange for some other commodity. The £1-a-month wage had to cover clothes and coal (a little) and light (oil and candles) and soap, etc., *but the standard of nutrition was independent of cash.*

This was a well-to-do man. As a contrast, the hired labourer, a *brothy man*, was expected to use his wages to supplement his basic diet. He got a sleeping bunk, blankets and bedclothes, fuel, and the use of a furnished kitchen, but only one simple diet of oatmeal brose (i.e., oatmeal and water) and milk. The amount was ample and the diet, with the fresh milk and garden, healthy. Again the idea was to provide the necessities of life as part of the basic wage, but any variety had to be provided by the individual.

It is interesting to note that brothy men were expected to provide their own wooden bowls and horn spoons. The cooking pots would be of cast-iron, knives and forks of steel, and the coarse linen sheets and homespun blankets almost indestructible (no laundries!) so that the replacement wastage was reduced to a minimum. Variety in pay according to the district is interesting. In Berwickshire the carriage of coals is included, and a space of land for flax growing. In Northumberland rye and peas are given, with wheat and barley and oats and wool for spinning. Poultry are prohibited but pigs permitted.

Where a farm labourer does *not* live on the same farm but does skilled seasonal work the enormous rise in *cash* payments *shows the value of the basic living costs.* Thus a hedger may expect £40 or £50 a year but any "smallholding" he attempts must be at his own costs. (A *good* farm house could be built for £300 at this date.)

The problem of the tied cottage arose in 1861. "Stewards, plough-men, shepherds, cattlemen, ditchers, hedgers and field workers are hired by the year, and lodged where they have to walk long distances to work. The obvious remedy is to build cottages near the steading. One would suppose sense would fix the lodging of a man who has worked 10 hours a day upon the farm with his horses, where he might rest his weary body, and from which he might tend the animals under his care; rather than fatigue him by a long journey, and remove him entirely from the animals under his charge."

"The payment of weekly money wages entices the English farm servant into the village beer shop, the Scotch farm servant is paid greatly from the produce of his farm, lives on the spot, and spends his leisure hours with his family" (STEPHENS, *Book of the Farm*).

The country folk missed their old brick ovens, and in towns the
local baker always baked for "Sundays"

THE BAKE HOUSE, AND SUNDAY DINNER

Their weekly bread oven was missing when country people moved into towns,
so the baker had a regular custom to " take in baking " at a penny or so a dish.
Pies, cakes, puddings, joints of meat, were left with him and called for when
the big oven was next opened. The " range " of fireplaces did not include an
oven till well on in the nineteenth century. In many country places the local
baker still " obliges " customers with his oven on Sunday morning, and a
small bakery, exactly like that in the illustration, continued in Osnaburgh Square
(London, N.W.1) up to the end of the war.

WHAT THEY CAME TO

Town life on £150 a year

These notes (1832) were to instruct the thousands of small householders who came to live in London. They would probably be small farmers' sons who had married wives with social ambitions, or men who disliked hard labour and dreamt of easy money and "refined life" in some town employment. London streets were "paved with gold". Hundreds of new shops and new buildings, businesses, etc., opportunities in the offices of factories, or even on the new railways, would tempt men to "sell out" and come to Town.

> " To choose your house, notice the water is well laid on [the pump at the end of the street is only a century old]. Study the chimney; it must not smoke as the coal fuel [now general] is very dangerous smoke. See the cellars are dry [the river still floods many districts]. Ask about the King's taxes? the poor rates? and any liabilities to Parish assessments? See the closets [not water] are well arranged for; [night soil men were still paid to empty the earth closets] and test the kitchen stove [a new enclosed type].
>
> N.B. Make sure the Landlord does *all* repairs.

The introduction of lead plumbing pipes into old houses was agreed as "very labour saving" but unreliable

EXPENSES 1832

Servants get through friends; obtain a Decent Girl from *at least* twenty miles out of Town, give her £6 a year, and see she puts part of it into a Savings Bank.

For Household Expenses by the Month.

Of Groceries buy: sugar (brown and white), rice, coffee, tea (black and green), mustard, spice and vinegar, raisins, almonds and cummin, etc. Total cost per month £28 14 6.

Chandlers for tallow dips, candles and soap £5 14 0.

Coal, 4 chaldrons, bought at the coal wharf on the river by the Strand steps, £8 8 0.

Wood from an oilman anywhere £1 0 0.

Potatoes are cheapest by the sack from Covent Garden £1 15 0.

Flour also by the sack and store it carefully £2 5 0.

Bread 365 quarten loaves (1 a day) at 10½ £15 10 4.

Beer 2 pints a day £4 11 3.

Wine, for Sundays and Visitors £3 0 0.

Milk at the door £2 0 0.

Cleaning materials—chiefly blacklead [for the grates], whitening [for the steps and hearthstones], sandstone [for scouring], bath-brick [for knives], dusters and brooms and mops £1 0 0.

All these things buy and pay for each month.

Butter for table 2 lbs. at 1/1 lb. and ½ lb. salt butter for cooking	£6	6	0.
Cheese [not much thought of by ex-country folk]	1	0	0.
Hams	1	0	0.
Bacon [again not much liked?]		10	0.
Fish and poultry	4	0	0.
Butcher's meat [3 joints a week!]	20	0	0.
Greengrocery from Covent Garden	3	10	0."

It is curious to see about 10s. a week for meat in contrast with 1s. for fruit and vegetables; but the dress problems of these would-be Londoners are even more difficult. "£30 a year must cover it all. £15 for yourself, £10 for your husband and £5 for the children." *All* clothes must be *sold* at the end of each year!

Washing should be "put out" to a respectable woman. "You will gain nothing by doing it at home!—£12."

"This scale of expenses for your housekeeping is *liberal*! And admits of your occasionally having company to visit your house. For coach hire, summer excursions out of Town, theatre seats, etc., you must 'Make a purse' by saving a little out of the general expenses."

CHILDREN

"*Education* after 8 years old, is essential for children"; very cheap boarding schools are to be avoided. Therefore, "send the boys to a good day school and educate the girls yourself."

After education is complete get the boys into employment as soon as possible; "if you have four boys, two ought to go to sea"!

The girls may be even earlier employed at their needles; a young girl, scarcely 14 years old, makes a guinea a week by her industry working as dressmaker and sewing for other friends who are "respectable but poor". "Have no foolish pride to interfere with the lasting advantage for all concerned in letting your girl seek employment."

The Housewife in this account is told to rise at 7 a.m. or earlier. Let the children and servants dine at 1 o'clock economically; (she is presumably to have a cup of coffee only?) and Dine with your husband at 5 or when he returns from work. She must also put one day a week to mending and sewing (bed linen has to be made) and she must always keep her children exquisitely clean and given plenty of exercise.

SWEATED LABOUR

The preceding paragraph speaks of uneducated girls being "brought up to sew" only. That explains the grinding poverty and misery of hundreds of girls.

For every family which made good, hundreds failed, leaving girls untrained and unprovided for, a prey to the first employer who would exploit their necessity. They were the sweated labour of the period, the origin of the "Song of the Shirt". The new ready-made clothing factories paid the poor creatures about 1*d.* an hour, so that only by slaving could they earn the 1*s.* a day they existed upon. There was no time to stop and search for other work—and as slow starvation and weariness wore them down, they had no strength to rebel. They could not return to the country life their parents had left, and only the bravest few survived.

One of the new possible employments for "ladies" was "office work" and there is sheer pluck behind these housekeeping accounts.

EDUCATED LABOUR—1880

The housekeeping of three girls in London from a contemporary magazine.

"The kitchen had a nice gas-stove fitted up on the 'penny-in-the-slot' system and by this all the cooking was done. Gas for 5 hours could be had by putting in a penny; this formed their only gas bill, for they used a lamp in their sitting-room and candles in the bedrooms. The gas bill was under a shilling a week.

Two shelves went all round the walls, one above the other, with nails in the edge for hanging jugs, measures, the dredger and the grater. A very small kitchen table stood just by the window, with two drawers in it. In one of these the tea and glass cloths were kept, and in the other the knives and forks.

The iron and wooden spoons used in cooking were kept in a box on the shelves. By its side the paste-board and rolling pin might be seen, the

ROLLING PINS HAVE CHANGED SHAPE!

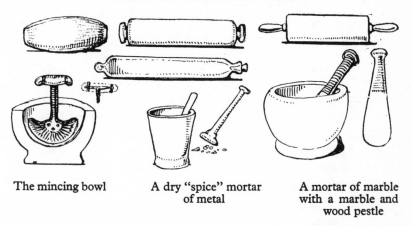

| The mincing bowl | A dry "spice" mortar of metal | A mortar of marble with a marble and wood pestle |

latter a good straight thick one that rolled very evenly. The dripping-tins, baking-tins, baking-sheet, and meat-rack were on the shelves as well, and also the small dinner service.

Under the shelves was a cupboard. On this was a row of coloured tins, containing tea, coffee, brown sugar, loaf sugar, rice, lentils, tapioca and sultanas, several jars of jam, a packet of cornflour, and a few other things. On the lower shelf were kept all cleaning materials: soap, soda, sand, emery, house flannel, and a spare scrubbing brush.

Fortunately there was a cupboard under the stairs in which the house-maid's box with its blacking-brushes and the zinc pail and pan used for scrubbing and washing could be kept. The six enamel saucepans of varying sizes stood on a tripod stand in one corner.

The fittings were all new and it was economically managed.

Sample of their dinners for a week:
Sunday. Stewed Steak. Mashed Potatoes. Mince Pies.
   (Supper: Poached eggs on toast. Cocoa.)
Monday. Tripe à la Normandie. Sago Pudding.

Tuesday. Sheep's Head. Vegetables and Dumplings. Treacle Tart.
Wednesday. High Tea: Fish Mould. Gingerbread.
Thursday. Brown Soup. Fish in Milk. Cottage Pudding.
Friday. Mutton Cutlets. Boiled Potatoes. Brussel Sprouts. Macaroni Cheese.
Saturday. Celery Soup. Minced Callops. Mashed Potatoes. Cup Puddings.

"Coals were only needed for the sitting-room fire as the *three hardy country girls* never indulged in such a luxury as a fire in their bedrooms and they found that half a ton of coals lasted them for six weeks."

These were adaptable, educated girls, and they have country friends who sometimes sent them presents of poultry or eggs.

Kitchen Ware	s.	d.
2 small enamel saucepans @ 8½d. & 6½d.	1	3
2 medium ditto @ 1s. 2d. & 1s. 4d.	2	6
2 enamel stewpans @ 1s. 9d. & 2s.	3	9
1 paste-board	1	9
1 rolling pin	1	0
1 dripping-tin		8
1 dripping-tin with meat-rack	1	0
1 baking-sheet		8
3 pint pie dishes @ 3¾d.		11¼
2 large basins @ 6½d.	1	1
3 pudding basins @ 2d., 4d. & 6d.	1	0
3 wooden spoons @ 1d.		3
3 iron spoons		3
Flour dredger		8½
Fine wire sieve	1	9½
Enamel omelette pan		6½
Small iron frying pan		10
Enamel pint & half-pint measures 4½d. & 6½d.		11
3 jugs; quart, one and a half pint, and pint	1	9
Weights and scales	14	6
Set of skewers		4½
Tin fish-kettle	8	6
	£2 6	0¼

Food for 3 for one week   s. d.

	s.	d.
1½ lb. chuck steak	1	3
2 lb. best end of neck of mutton	1	8
1¼ lb. tripe		9½
1 sheep's head		7
½ lb. suet		3
4 callops	1	0
¼ lb. mushrooms		3
Flavouring vegetables		4
1 lb. sprouts		2
8 lb. potatoes		6
Plaice		6
Fresh haddock		6
½ lb. macaroni		2
1 tin of cocoa		6
1 dozen best eggs	1	6
6 cooking eggs		6
1½ lb. fresh butter @ 1s. 4d.	2	0
Milk	1	7
2 lb. demarara sugar		3½
1 lb. loaf sugar		2
3½ lb. ham	2	4
½ lb. tea		10
8 loaves	2	6
	£1 0	2

Magazines of the period may be sentimental, but they shrewdly reflect contemporary life. They are full of stories of spinster daughters left to care for aged parents because there is no money after the father dies. The girls usually take some post where they can have their parents with them in return for their services, and schools "where a resident staff is employed" are frequently mentioned as a pleasant solution, if the girl has *been so fortunate as to be well educated.* Another interesting corollary of the Industrial Revolution from country to town are the many stories in which poverty-stricken ladies retire to the country, take one of *the numerous labourers' cottages now standing empty,* and live on £1 a week for two! They expend 1s. 6d. of that for "help with the rough work", but "decide to do their own cooking".

EMIGRATION

EMIGRATION—THE ONES WHO ESCAPED

The rations and clothing suitable for working girls in 1880 can be judged by the "equipment and feeding" of the girls sent out on a Government-approved scheme to New Zealand. There were a hundred to a shipload, varying from rebellious young governesses to adventurous daughters of farmers and derelict Irish housemaids. There were also a few "upper-class" daughters of landowners, who should have gone into service or factories, but had "that in their breeding which made them prefer the harder life but higher chances of a young community to the pampered menialism and limited range of the old civilisation". As the report is by an emigrant, it is probably fairly assessed.

She finds the worst part is the "crowding together all in one huge common room under deck" and "only being allowed up in the open air at certain times". "Before breakfast we take out our bedding boards, and scrub them with sand and holystone and sweep the floor. After breakfast we scrub all the forms, tables and painted walls with soap and water, and scrape the floor with a kind of hoe, before stoning it." Food issued includes beef, pork, preserved meats, suet, butter, biscuits, oatmeal, peas, rice, potatoes, carrots, onions, raisins, tea, coffee, sugar, treacle, mustard, salt, pepper, water, "mixed pickles, and lime juice[1] twice a week." She and her friend had taken with them a large biscuit tin containing 2 lb. of good tea, sugar, figs, meat extract, and a bottle of strong home-made calves'-foot jelly (for the seasick period). They also took fruit, and while it lasted, contrived to bake a pie in their galley.

Their clothes are interesting, being uniform issue. "6 shifts, 2 strong flannel petticoats, 6 pairs of stockings, 2 pairs of strong boots, and two gowns, of which one must be wool." They supplement this basis with "aspartagrass shoes" for deck wear (a "new" idea), some strong cotton gowns, nightwear, and took with them some "ready-cut-out" underwear to sew on board. They took one thick wadded hood each, and one "antiquated wide straw hat" for the tropics. In the hold were plain cool white dresses, neat ribbons, cotton gloves, washing frills (rough dried, not ironed), and straw bonnet material, packed flat (the straw-plait Buckingham rural industry much taught in orphanages), for sewing into shape, and the ribbons to trim it, and the lining ready folded, so that it can be "made up" on landing.

As the writer is one of a party of "lady emigrants" she also takes some "foreign writing paper, a strong inkstand, pencil, pens, and a few sheets of drawing paper for sketching upon". (All Victorian girls loved sketching!

[1] Compulsory against scurvy.

The emigrant was often the bravest and best type of countrywoman

It was as usual as it is to "take snapshots" now.) For £1 they hire "Ship's kits, 1 pillow, 1 bed, 1 rug, 2 sheets, 1 wash basin, 1 plate, knife, fork and spoon, 3 pounds of marine soap (for washing in salt water) all packed in a canvas bag".

On arrival in Brisbane ("which looks an incomplete place, splendid buildings side by side with rickety sheds") they find "necessities are cheap but luxuries very dear", and that "No one keeps a servant who can possibly do without one!" However, the women soon find work, they are made very welcome, well paid, and we leave them happy in this new world with every reasonable chance of early marriage ahead.

A LETTER SENT HOME FROM A HAPPY EMIGRANT

> "We have had green peas and cherries on Xmas Day! We have got fruit of all kinds just now. We burn nothing but wood here *so there are no grates to clean!* We make our own bread and candles and butter from our own cows and kill our own meat so there seems nothing to buy but tea and sugar. There are no beggars here in this country and no workhouses. Servants need never be out of a place, they are *wanted* here."

> LETTER FROM BRISBANE, 1837.

The desire to emigrate outran the opportunity. Professor Johnstone, the same year (1837), finds in one small village (Yetholme) over 30 able-bodied men all out of work and wishful to go overseas—but unable to get the money together to take their families. The sons can get away, and thoughtful women are doing their utmost to make it possible for the daughters to go also. But—womenfolk have not yet won the right to make their voice heard. It is coming, and rapidly; for these Victorian women, adventuring so gladly, are the true descendants of the Elizabethan adventurers—pilgrim children.

It was the children of these emigrant women who laid the foundations of the British colonies. As cooks they carried the traditions of England to the lands of their adoption. Many times in the far places of the earth it is the women cooks who have made adventure possible, by the simple skill learnt in an English kitchen.

Note. Lady Anne (one of the first to live in Government House in Cape Town), made a note to "bring a chart or plat from home to show the natives how to chop up the sheep into proper joints", and as Lady Anne's home was a good Scotch household, the Cape Town butchers still cut up their Cape mutton according to the Scotch method!

RICHES IN TOWN

Breakfast in the 18th century.

<pre>
                                  Tea
    Ham in jelly   Chickens
                          Spongecakes
              Potted shrimps   Potted salmon
              Preserves   Anchovy butter
                      Caramel custard
    Ginger cream   Jelly
              Butter   Butter
                          Fruit
    Chocolate   Sugar   Sugar   Cocoa
                Cream   Cream
                        Eperge on
                        stand glass
                Sugar   Sugar
                Cream   Cream
                          Fruit
                Butter   Butter
                      Caramel custard
    Wine Jelly   Coffee cream
        Tartlets   Preserves
                      Lemon cakes
    Lobster salad   Potted pigeons
        Raised pie   Tongue in jelly
                          Coffee
</pre>

Note that boiled eggs, hot rolls, muffins and toast were handed round also.

POVERTY IN TOWN

Grey Coat Hospital in Westminster in the 18th century

The Vestry of St. Margaret agrees to let the Trustees hire a large House rent free for 7 years for the reception of as many Parish children as the Trustees can undertake to maintain and employ.

They are all set to work upon spinning wool, housework, sewing and knitting, and the incomes of the charity with their earnings are appointed towards finding them in Diet and Lodging.

The Master of the House gets £40 a year and the Matron £20, the Singing Master £15 and 3 Nurses £15. The Laundry maid gets £10 and the Cook £10.

Their meals are as follows:

	Breakfast	Dinner	Supper (always the same)	
Sunday	Bread & Butter	Beef Broth & Peas	Bread & Cheese	
Monday	Bread & Butter	Bread & Butter	,,	,,
Tuesday	½ penny roll	Broth	,,	,,
Wednesday	Bread & Butter	Frumenty	,,	,,
Thursday	½ penny roll	Broth	,,	,,
Friday	Bread & Butter	Peas porridge	,,	,,
Saturday	½ penny roll	Milk porridge	,,	,,

Soyer's Poor Soup.

Put 1 oz of dripping into a saucepan holding 2 gallons of Water, with a quarter of a lb. of Leg of Beef without fat cut into square pieces of about half an inch, & 2 middling sized onions peeled & sliced. Set the saucepan over a fire, & stir the contents round for a few minutes until fried lightly brown. Add the peel of two turnips, green leaves or tops of celery, & of 2 leeks cut into small pieces. Then add half a pound of common flour, & lastly a pound of Pearl Barley, mixing all well together. Add two gallons of water, 3 oz salt & a quarter of oz of Brown sugar & allow all to simmer gently for 3 hours. — —

Soyer, who did so much to reform army cooking, was a practical man, who believed in basic simplicity. This soup, by modern standards, is thin, but it was infinitely better than the customary gruel.

Wood sawdust was made into bread in the hungry days of industrial starvation (1827 *Philosophical Transactions*). It required strong leaven and was "improved" by admixture of cereal flour.

THE COMING OF THE "PEA SOUPER", 1780–1880

This "century" divides the rural population from town dwellers. There had been fairs and markets, and London and other cities had definite street and trading centres, but the cities were so small and the country around so close that hens, pigs, cows, and farms, were still part of the town people's lives. Fuel was wood, and pumps and wells and gardens existed; many of the houses were still country-built with the farm buildings set around them. The Plague and the Great Fire had swept away much of this old-fashioned rural look from London streets.

In this century the population more than doubles, and Walpole's long uneasy peace gives hundreds of traders and shopkeepers, taverners and merchants, time to establish their businesses. Read the signs upon old firms when shopping and see in catalogues and advertisements the proud boast, "Established 1780" or thereabouts.

This is the period when they "started business"—probably by some small countryman selling his farm, investing in some overseas speculation, and setting up his shop sign in London.

Large manufacturers do not come into being before the nineteenth century, but the influx into the town has started.

Coal is being used, and is being tried out successfully for the smelting of iron (and a good job, too, for the woods of the Weald have gone, and timber grows scarce). Now with coal fuel—so fierce and strong—come the boilers and closed kitchens ranges and all the new metal contrivances. Enamelware is on the way—as yet called Japan ware, because it is but bright tin washed over with transparent brown varnish[1] to prevent rust. The Londoners' coal is brought from Newcastle and the north and sold on wharfs in London. Kitchen fires gulp and roar with the new fuel; the wide wood-burning hearths close inwards to a long shallow trench of heat, cooks burn the joints and chimneys are set on fire.

Not for generations will gentle elderly folk consent to sit by the horrible coals! The sitting-room fire must remain of wood for some time yet. Meanwhile here comes London's first pea souper!

> " *The Smoak of London.*
> That this glorious Antient City, which from Wood might be rendered Brick and from Brick Stone and marble . . . which commands the Proud Ocean to the Indies and reaches to the farthest Antipodies, should wrap Her stately Head in Clowds

[1] A form of lacquer imported from the East to Bristol.

of Smoake and Sulphur, so full of Stink and Darkness, I deplore
with Just Indignation . . . against . . . the Immoderate use of Sea
Cole . . . for when in all other places the aer is most Serene and
Pure it is here Eclipsed with such a cloud of Sulphur as the Sun
itself is hardly able to penetrate. . . . It is this horrid SMOAKE
which obscures our Churches, makes our Palaces look old, fowls
our clothes and corrupts the waters so that the very Rain pre-
cipitates this impure vapour which with its black and tennacious
quality spots and contaminates whatsoever is exposed to it. . . .
It scatters and strews about those black and smutty ATOMES
upon all things where it comes. . . . This Smoake poysioning the
aer with so dark and thick a Fog as I have been hardly able to
pass through it . . . there is under Heaven such coughing and
snuffing to be heard as in London churches and assemblies,
where the Barking and spitting is incessant and most impor-
tunate . . . from this intemperate use of Sea Cole in great Cities.
Sea cole . . . and Newcastle cole, . . . as expert Physicians affirm
causeth Consumption Phithisists and Indisposition of the Lungs."

EVELYN.

THE COMING OF QUEEN VICTORIA

In 1830 a "National Union of Working Classes" existed, and the banding
together of larger numbers of workers in town factories (rather than
scattered country workshops) made collective action possible. The French
Revolution was within memory, and there was now a constructive spirit
working within the discontent. When the Government ordered a general
fast to try to stop the spread of cholera, a procession of hungry people
marched, displaying a piece of beef and a slice of bread labelled "The
True Remedy Against Cholera."

The Iron Duke Wellington and William IV (from behind bullet-proof
shutters), still spoke of the "Constitution of England" as "perfect" but
Lords Grey, Palmerston and Russell and others fought to put through
the Reform Bill. While yet the Bill was fighting, Birmingham blacksmiths
worked overnight forging spiked iron caltraps, the same type of iron spikes
which had stopped a cavalry charge at Bannockburn! These caltraps
were the same pattern as the iron "cat" which they made for their wives
to hold the placid buttered toast before the fire; so one could make enough
of these "cats" to break the horse hoofs of an army, and yet only be
"stocking up" enough "useful kitchen stands" to last the winter! They are
nicknamed "cats" for no matter how thrown down, they alight on three
or four feet—with the other feet spiked up in the air.

The Reform Bill was passed, and Imperial Holy Russia spoke of the
"English Crown being thrown into the gutter"—but then Russia was
on the up-wane of Imperial Control. (By 1898 Fredric Maco, chef, in his

journal of cookery, writes that "even the cookery books are passed through the censors' hands; a short time ago, in one of them, the words 'to be boiled over a slow fire'—in Polish, over a 'free' fire—were suppressed because of the word 'free'.")

However, Russia was vast and impersonal. England was a smaller unit, and with the young child Queen, the Crown was transferred from the unsteady hands of the Georgian Lords to the hearts of the people. This was not sentiment. The young Queen might be helpless, but she was already a personality. Remember that the varied peoples who had become "*the* English people" had all, long ago, belonged to some chieftain of their own. Times had changed, but they still felt they had the right of direct ownership. Too long the statesmen had been "jack-in-office" over them. Now they claimed *their right* to *their Crown*. (The traditional "right", that had carried the voice of the lowest serf, past the upper servants, *direct to the head of the household*, where he sat at dinner in the great hall.) That right has again and again been claimed by the common folk of England. The "Crown" is theirs, *and therefore its ministers must be their choice*. By the half-century (1850) the new freedom was working like yeast all over the kingdom: slaves were being freed in the colonies; a new London University made learning free to all scholars (hitherto excluded from Cambridge and Oxford because they could not afford the fees); freedom for Dissenters, non-comformists, Jews, Roman Catholics, and all other small religious sects; poverty and misery were in the crowded towns; but there was new freedom and hope coming.

There had been attempts to supply free education made by many religious parties, but now the State took over the enormous task of general education, by insisting on at least two hours a week free teaching for every child. At first, this did little more than institute some slight "inspection", or "bringing to light" of the masses of children imured in factories, or hidden away in remote districts. The task was too large for free education to reach all districts; of the few children able to attend school, less than half could read, less than a quarter write, and only about two children in a hundred could do simple arithmetic, but it was the beginning of state education—and free. (In 1900 it was still common to find old people who could not read and write, and today a few can only "make their mark".) Till Victorian times cook-books were for the "housewife"; from 1850 onwards they are largely written for the instruction of the servant girl, for it is taken for granted that "any girl going as servant to a respectable household can read and write enough to inform her mind". These textbooks are often sanctimonious, but they give instructions on how to cook; how to bath (daily in a tub, with a jug of hot water and a cold sponge); how to revive a black silk dress with stewed ivy leaves; how to turn a poke bonnet; how to write a love letter; how to have a

baby; and how to do "simple interest for a banking account" (on wages
£8 per annum!). The hours of the servant are hard and long and the
skill and industry hopelessly underpaid, but their working conditions are
more comfortable; their Freedom begins. The drudge of Dickens' day
is gone, the overworked general going, already the charlady is on her way!

CHILD LABOUR

CHILDREN FILLING BOXES IN A FACTORY

HOUSEHOLD FURNISHING ABOUT 1800 (Studied from a Sale List)

Coach House. 2 light riding saddles for daily use; 1 quilted saddle for
long distance work; 1 pack saddle (luggage carrier). Coach (this had plate
glass windows); a jack for lifting coach to repair wheels; harness for coach
horses. A rick of hay (about 6 tons); a lead water trough; an old horse
chair or litter (for use of invalids or ladies breeding). Blankets; tubs;
stable gear; cornbins. Also a stone for grinding paint and tools for painting
and repairing the coach.

Item: a featherbed, bolster and blankets for the stableman sleeping
in the loft.

Cellar (not the wine cellar—the store). Hogsheads with stands; cyder
casks (one 40-gallon size); some "brewing tubs and gear" (everyone knows
how to brew, so they are not described).

Inner Cellar. Copper stewing pans and covers; kettles; a large round pot and cover (for bread yeast?); a "bel kittle" (bell-metal kettle for use with acids and vinegars where copper could not be used); a hog-scalding tub and small pickling tubs. An old-fashioned churn, a frying pan (burnt); a chocolate mill, etc.

Kitchen. 3 dozen pewter plates, 1 dozen of each size; 4 large pewter dishes and a fish dish; 7 other dishes of varied sizes; 4 tin saucepans and covers; 2 dish covers; cheese plates in pewter; 5 pewter water plates (these continued to be very much used—they were plates set over a dishful of boiling water to keep the contents hot).

2 coffee mills; 2 brass candlesticks; 6 flat-irons and chintz irons (rounded for polishing work); 2 box irons and an Italian iron for ribbons, etc.

Italian irons were heated by inserting a hot iron, and the work was drawn across them. Very good for lace and cravats (*see* p. 640).

Pantry. Candlesticks of brass (a lot, probably); meat screen for roasting (to go behind the spit); towel horse, hangers and spits; saucepans and covers; scales and beams (large scales that hang from the ceiling and could weigh a whole pig); large iron boiler with a top; spouted kettle; cheese press (iron stand and stone weight); copper coal scuttle and "grate furnace" (these are small braziers or side fires made for small cookery); one large iron cauldron, napkin press; copper bottle cistern and a lot of earthenware and stoneware; a Dutch tea kettle and lamp; a washing cistern.

Plate (the list, except for the narrow marrow spoons, is curiously modern and unchanged). 12 tablespoons; 12 soup spoons; 12 marrow spoons; 12 dessert spoons; 12 three-pronged forks; 12 dessert knives and forks with silver prongs; 12 knives with silver handles; 1 punch ladle; 1 pair of tongs; 6 silver teaspoons. 2 coffee pots; 1 teapot; 1 lemon strainer; 2 cream ewers; 2 sauce boats.

China (a curiously short list, which tells us its value!). 7 coffee cups; 24 fine blue and gold table plates; 9 fine old blue and white dishes (tall); 24 small plates; 10 baking dishes; 11 blue and white plates; a pair of china sauce boats; 12 soup plates; a tureen and cover; 6 coffee cups; 6 saucers; 4 small plates; 6 *coloured* tea cups and saucers; a teapot stand; a glass salver; 12 sillabub jelly glasses.

Note that china was carried on pack-horse from the new English factories at great expense, but all pottery and earthenware was *made in local potteries because of the weight in transport. This accounts for the variety in design in good English earthenware and cooking pots—they were made in each district to suit the cooking of that district.*

China is classified by the *maker* and the *period.* Common kitchen pottery by the *locality.*

HOUSEHOLD ACCOUNTS 1864

For two bachelors living "in quiet comfort".

THE VICTORIAN HOUSEHOLD 1800–1900

The Victorian breakfast was the hearty reward of early rising, and followed an hour's "office work" and family prayers. The time was usually eight o'clock. The maids rose at five-thirty (five o'clock for the kitchen maid). The daughters of the house were down by seven o'clock, and did an hour's music practice, study, or brisk exercise. (In the new Methodist households, an hour's devotional study was quite usual.) The master of the house used his early hours for letters, estate work, and business affairs; the matron used hers for household affairs, and while she had a very young family she was permitted to wear a morning wrapper and spend part of this time in the nursery. The household work is that of a country house today, but with no gas or electricity, and no labour-saving appliances. The housemaid first opened the wooden shutters and windows, cleared the grates, and lit fires. She swept and dusted the break-fast-room, hall and staircases, while the other maid carried up the huge polished brass cans of boiling bath water, set down the flat tin "splash baths" from their stands against the bedroom walls, and carried jugs of scalding shaving water to the gentlemen's dressing-rooms.

In the kitchen the cook now descended, and woe betide the kitchen wench who has not a scuttle full of soot to show for her cleaning of the kitchen flues! The kitchen maid must then "do" the back door and fetch the morning's milk, collect the eggs, and wait upon the cook while she "makes the breakfast". Soon muffins are hot, toast crisp, fish cooked, bacon cut ready for grilling, plates set to heat; and, the table laid, cook, housemaid, and all the servants hurriedly put on clean aprons, wash their hands, and join the gardener and his boy, to file solemnly into the break-fast-room for family prayers.

In our engraving, the master of the household has opened the glazed bookcases (date 1700? His father's inheritance?), withdrawn the great Family Bible, and all are listening respectfully while he "reads the chapter".

A simple prayer followed, and, the Book being replaced, cook leads the procession of servants back to the kitchen, and the bustle of serving the breakfast begins.

Breakfast was a "family" meal. The servants usually had theirs at the same time, so it was a point of "consideration" not to need "waiting on" during breakfast. The "huswife" herself made the tea, using the expensive teas kept in the beautifully made tea-caddy of the period (lined with lead foil, it had two lidded compartments for "green" or "black" teas, with a cut-glass sugar bowl between them).

The kettle boiling upon the hearth was of polished brass, with a china or glass handle, and a neat woolwork tea-kettle holder hung alongside the fireplace. Hot teacakes, breakfast rolls, or muffins, were on a trivet before the fire. The boiled eggs were kept hot in a china dish—the cover shaped like a hen (some of these dishes were beautifully modelled)—or on a silver egg-stand.

After breakfast the domesticated matron usually made a small rite of "washing-up the breakfast things herself", either in an adjoining pantry, or the maid carried in a wooden bowl of hot soapy water, placed it on a japanned tea-tray on the table, with a clean cloth, and the washing-up was done "with neatness and despatch". China was a treasured possession![1]

[1] In the late eighteenth and early nineteenth centuries the fine painted " china sets " made for larger opulent households often had " duplicate saucers " (i.e. there were twelve large breakfast cups and twelve small tea cups, but only twelve saucers common

The mistress herself put the china back "together with the breakfast cruet and sundry etceteras", into the special china cupboard in the breakfast room.

Many "corner cupboards" of this period, now used for "show" china, were originally made for daily use.

In theory this "washing-up" of the breakfast things left the maids time to go upstairs and "do" the bedrooms, which, by the time they had plumped up the feather beds, emptied gallons of bath water and slops, arranged clean towels and draped the bed hangings, kept them busy till ten o'clock.

Cook, too, scurried around, and by nine o'clock was waiting respectfully to receive her mistress in consultation over the day's meals.

Another item in the Victorian illustration is the lamp (a heavy brass pillar, with leaded base and ground glass shade over a clear glass chimney), which diffused a mellow light. Paraffin was the usual oil, and the wicks of cotton fibre were boiled monthly in vinegar.

There would be as many as twenty lamps in some houses. One large hanging lamp in the hall; one large hanging lamp in the kitchen, one smaller one over the sink and one in the pantry; one in the dining-room over the table; smaller lamps in the passages and on the staircase landings; one standard lamp on the sitting-room table with smaller reading lamps by the armchairs; a "desk lamp" in the master's room or library; a lamp in the nursery; a lamp in each bedroom; and in some households great ruby-globed floor lamps called "moderators" lit each evening to take the chill off bedrooms or landings. These lamps had to be collected each morning and filled and cleaned and trimmed. The work was usually done in a "lamp room" or in a back kitchen. At the same time, also, were cleaned the bedroom candlesticks, one for each person, often of polished brass, which were set out at the foot of the staircase each evening.

The servant who attended to the lamps usually made the floor polish, using the candle-ends, beeswax, and turpentine. Paraffin was also used for cleaning windows, mirrors, and painted woodwork (and illicitly for lighting fires and firing chimneys). Owing to the number of coal fires, lamps were seldom used for cooking upon before the twentieth century (though spirit stoves were used by travellers).

The flap table under the tea-caddy was an early form of sewing table. The top drawer pulled forward and held scissors, bodkins, stilettos, netting and tatting, knitting and crochet needles, etc. (All stockings were "hand knit", and so were purses and fine lace edgings, and heavy cotton

---

to both sizes). As cups break first, this fine economy enables the acute antique dealer to produce a " perfect set " of twelve cups and saucers, and twelve plates; but if some of the cups vary in size, then it is a " cut down ", old duplicated set and not a complete original.

bedspreads.) The lower part supported a deep square bag which contained the needlework and mending.

In the evening the shutters at the windows would be closed, the curtains drawn, the lamp lit, and the "work"-table wheeled out (this period invented castors). Sewing machines were not invented till the turn of the century and all household linen was made by hand. The frilled caps of the two servants are counterparts of the "kappies" worn by Cape Dutch and the fashion—like the hyacinth bulbs flowering in blue "bulb glasses" on the mantelpiece, which were a vogue of the period.

The great bookcase, probably made of mahogany, is a century old, and probably a family piece, as the outlines show the room to be that of an old house (probably built early in the 1700s) but the table and chairs and all the furnishings are modern 1890. Two centuries have removed the delicate engraving or the perishable chalk drawing to back bedrooms, an oval miniature portrait hangs on a side wall, but the "modern picture" hangs over the mantelpiece, and this original painting, in oils,[1] of a full noonday pastoral landscape with its solid naturalistic statement of sentiment is as typical of the Victorian taste as the reproduced Van Gogh's "Sunflowers", seen in scores, are typical of the taste of yesterday.

VICTORIAN HOLIDAYS IN "APARTMENTS".

English visitors in a Welsh market typify the discovery of "rural delight" and "delicious country fare". Young Queen Victoria's children gambol upon Scotch heather, and all Victorian families "spend a country visit". The new railway and Telford's high roads lead west. Travellers return from the European "grand tour" with tales of Swiss Alps and Italian lakes, so mountains now become "scenery" and Windermere, Barmoutn, Rhyll and Colwyn Bay afford "rural retreats". Prices in hotels were high, "up to 10s. a day" and "late dinner is always an expensive item", but guide books advise the "simpler life of smaller places". "Apartments are moderate in price: three good rooms can be had in the Welch valleys for 30s. a week. The best plan is for a family to 'take rooms' and board themselves." This means they can purchase what they wish and have it prepared to their liking. So after breakfast, before going into the sea water, Mother leaves the "apartment" and goes shopping. The market stalls held the baskets of fish, nicely dressed poultry, packets of sage and onions, parcels of leeks, bundles of root vegetables, cheese, barra cierch, barr brieth, crepog, pot plants and pork pies.

[1] It is an interesting point that the careful tone values of these Victorian oil colours helped in the appreciation of the photograph and set the fashion for the gloomy " sepia prints ", so general a generation later.

SEA BATHING

The eighteenth century took spa waters internally, the nineteenth sea water externally.

Brighton became fashionable, and "arrangements were made for ladies to enjoy the benefit of bathing in salt water, with the utmost privacy"— using wooden bathing vans, with an arrangement like a hen coop that let down before the door, so that you would enter the water unseen.

In the home cold baths were usual each morning for the young and every advice-book of the period insists on "the refreshment of cold water on rising". It became a fetish in some households. Children who were found to have "benefit from sea bathing" often had little bags of sea salt called "tideman's sea salt" dissolved in icy cold water and sponged down the spine.

By the half century sea bathing, though still "adventurous", was part of the holiday treatment. You went "in" before breakfast; or between 10 and 11 a.m.—afterwards drinking hot milk and taking a brisk walk. This account is from a novel of 1850 in which the hostess entertains a young guest:

"I go into the water every morning," the lady explained; "of course I mean the *salt* water . . . you must come, it will do you good! You want Bracing!"

Diana clothed herself in a loose gown of brown mohair and slipped out after her hostess. "How far do we go in?" "As far as I can." It was never to be forgotten! that first taste of salt water! when they were in the flood up to their necks. Her companion made her duck her head under! It filled her mouth and eyes at the first gasp! But what a new freshness seemed to come over her!

AT THE PICNIC 1880

" Fitted baskets are only suitable for a small party, of three or four persons, for whom one pie and one sweet would be sufficient. For a picnic party, it is better to divide the loads, and if enough guests attend, there should be plenty for all without anyone being unduly overloaded.

A few hints upon packing the hampers.

Put the tablecloth and knives and forks on the TOP of the first basket to be unpacked. Cabbage leaves pack well around cool dishes, and contrast well with the pure white of the table-napkins. Cold meat dishes should be carried in the tins, in which they are set. Butter should be moulded, into balls, and parsley taken to garnish it after being set out. A cold shoulder of lamb is an excellent joint for a picnic, accompanied by a bottle of mint sauce.

It is perhaps better to take the ham ready sliced.

Meat pies, and pigeon, and veal and ham pies are standard for a picnic.

In all pies, the gravy within should be strong enough to form a jelly when cold.

Lobster, the meat picked out and carried in the main shell, with mayonnaise and salad packed separately, (it is thought expensive perhaps?) but fish dishes, such as eel moulded in jelly, are cool.

Cold roast ducks are sure to be popular, and cold dressed green peas not to be despised with them. We have known people take cold new potatoes, but did not consider them a success.

THE VICTORIAN PICNIC (*with Conversation*).

A PLEASANT LUNCHEON.

A well made salad everyone will enjoy, and a cucumber is indispensable! The picnic would not be a picnic if it were absent.

Jellies and creams should be taken in their moulds and turned out on the spot. Compot of fruit, with a mould of well boiled rice is excellent.

Turnovers are to be preferred to ordinary jam tarts, because the open jam in the latter is so sticky.

A sufficient quantity of bread rolls, and do not forget sugar, salt, corkscrews, a lump of ice, oil and vinegar, and cold water. Wrap the ice in a blanket and put it under the seat of the waggon. Claret cup is sure to be wanted, to be mixed on the spot by one of the men of the party. I have noticed that when a man has made a claret cup which is appreciated he feels thoroughly satisfied and at peace with the world in general. It is such a small thing to produce such a result (but then he has perhaps given years of his life to acquiring the knowledge!). I have known two young men who performed prodigies of touring on bicycles and cold tea ... but their friends were either amused or pitied them ..."

The picnic was so well arranged that we also give the setting for the resultant Wedding breakfast!

"The long mahogany table was polished and covered with damask, down the centre a narrow strip of white satin bordered with maidenhair fern, laid flat, like fine green lace—and within this a border of white flowers laid flat. At each guests' place was a small white bouquet, the ladies all white, but the gentlemen's having a faint colour, such as a pink rosebud."

                                          GIRLS' OWN PAPER, 1880.

MAN ABOUT TOWN. (And the After Dinner Smoke)

" A man may find a bedroom in one of the streets off the Strand for 8/- a week. When he arrives he pays 1/- for a glass of brandy, pays 2/- for his bed, and gives the Chambermaid 6d to make it up. He breakfasts next morning on coffee and egg for 1/6d, gives the waiter 6d for serving him, and gets his boots cleaned, for 3d.

In Town, he should find unfurnished lodgings to the west of Tottenham Court Road. Begin west of Berners Street, and you should soon get 2 rooms for 5/- a week on the second floor. Have them cleaned and furnish them yourself. Beyond Westminster Bridge get your bedding and feather mattress. Buy also chairs and a plain table, pillows, washstand, etc., £4. A chest of drawers £1. Arrange for them to be sent to your lodging when you can be there to meet them. Blankets and 2 pairs of sheets and 4 towels and 2½ yards of Holland for blinds should cost about £2 from Simon Bros., in Holborn. The earthenware wash basin, etc., should cost 5/-.

Having got a bedroom to sleep in, furnish the sitting room at sales.

On £100 you could live for a year, but beware of visiting. For exercise, a walk before breakfast costs nothing and will give you an appetite.

At several places you may dine for 1/- and give the waiter 1d, taking Meat and Vegetables and ½ pint of stout; apple pie and cheese is 5d extra.

At Garrick's Head in Bow Street table d'hote is 2/- and served at 5 p.m.

At a Coffee House you may dine for 2/6d, and there is also a Cigar Divan in the Strand or in Regent Street where you may lounge in the evening and have admirable coffee, a cigar and newspaper to read in a splendid well warmed room for 1/-. Haircuts are 6d and razor's set cost 3d each."

"The Cigar Divan in Regent Street", an illustration of the actual divan mentioned in the text

TIMETABLE OF A MILL OWNER ABOUT 1890

5.30 a.m. He rose, went to the mill (about half a mile) to see the night watchman. Returned in time for family prayers at seven-thirty.

8 a.m. Breakfast; smoke; newspaper; in company with his sister.

9 a.m. The foreman came to the house. The sister always waited till he came because he had to report to her if anyone was ill and needing special diet, as they "sent up word" by the foreman at this time for "anything needed" (comprehensive phrase!). The sister then left the men to talk "shop" and "work", while she went to see the cook, to decide how many

"soups" or "emergency dinners" were needed, or if some mother "needed the nurse" or had "better be seen to".

II a.m.   A cup of tea and "snap" was brought in for the owner and his sister—signal for the foreman to leave. He had waited for her return, because now he had to be told "when to send up for the things" or to tell whoever it was, "the things would be sent."

By 12 noon   "At the mill" and "about the place" till five o'clock. He usually took a "wallet" with him, and "had a sup from so-and-so's can" is a frequent entry in his diary.

5 p.m.   He returned, washed and dressed, and enjoyed one of the sumptous "Yorkshire teas" that have game pies, apple pie, cheese, teacakes, and tea. In the evening, after tea, he retired to his workroom and carried on with some hobby or interest, or his sister recounted whom she had "seen", and what "ought to be done about" anyone who was "off" ill. Tea was brought in to the drawing-room fire at about eight-thirty, and the night watchman was supposed to call for last instructions about nine o'clock; but as often as not the old man would "go down himself" (in Sherlock Holmes cap and heavy old Inverness cape). It was his special custom to do this evening walk if he thought any of the hands "wanted a word with him privately", as they could "happen along and walk a piece with him".

10 p.m.   Bedtime.   MS. PRIVATE DIARY

It is the knowledge of the enormous housekeeping bills: the joint of meat and stewing beef, the sacks of flour and stones of sugar used up in that kindly kitchen by, apparently, two gentle old people that makes one understand the inside working of the mediaeval kitchens.

I am glad to draw this portrait of these mill owners, as so much of this period being cruel and callous, the kindly family concerns are overlooked.

PIES, PUDDINGS, PASTRIES, CAKES

" He could roste and sethe and broille and frye
  Maken mortreux and wel bake a pye."

CHAUCER.

" One solid dish his weekday need affords,
  An added pudding solemnized the Lords."

POPE.

PIES AND PUDDINGS

PIEDISHES

See that the piedish is deep: most enamel dishes are far too shallow. See that the rim is wide enough to support the crust edge, but not too wide. Time the paste and fruit to be cooked together. It is better to make a pastry that takes longer to cook, than keep it too long in the oven to "finish" the fruit. It is better to cook the fruit a little first if very hard. Mix the sugar with the fruit, don't put it directly under the pastry. Fill well with juice. Serve pies hot, and if not all eaten at once, it is sensible to cut the lid off and bake it crisp again, rather than leave it damp, on wet fruit, in a cold larder.

PIES OF ENGLAND

THE PIES of England hold history—the pastry cases were first called coffers, or boxes of pastry. Not only fruit was put in tarts. A very handsome "fissche tarrte" made by a mediaeval recipe was of fine pork-pie-type crust, raised a foot and a half high, and within, the base was jet black, being compounded of figs, raisins, prunes and ginger; the middle layer was white spotted black, being white fish with currants in it; the next layer black spotted white, being the same date and prune mixture with white almonds in it. The whole was most richly gilt with gold leaf and the fish's tail sticking out of the top. That was a mediaeval "fysshe tarte".

The seventeenth-century tart was sometimes in pottery, with an imitation pie-crust lid (now called pie-crust ware); this was mostly for double cooking and game pies, etc. Their real pastry tarts and pies were delicious, the pastry being flaky or puff, very light and fine, and the fillings considered with care. Modern pies and tarts are made under various names, the Turnover, the Pastie, the Crowthie, the Fruit-between-two-skins, the Checky Pig, the Puff, the Cornet, the Open Tart, the Gable Tart, the Lattice (and all varieties of the pie-plate tart), the Proper Pie, the

Plate Pie, the Raised Pie, the Mould Pie, the Shell Pie (Scotch and most early English in design), and the Cottage Pie.

PASTRY

Puff Paste

> " Of the best kind you shall take finest wheat flowre, after it hath been a little bak't in a pot in the oven, and blend it well with egges whites and yolkes all together and after the paste is well kneaded, roule out part as thin as you please and spread cold butter on the same. . . . There be some that to this paste add sugar, but it is certain to hinder the rising thereof."
>
> ABOUT 1600.

Pastry

> " Dear Nelly! learn with care the pastry art,
> And mind the easy precepts I impart:
> Draw out your dough elaborately thin,
> And cease not to fatigue your rolling pin:
> Of eggs and butter see you mix enough,
> For then the paste will swell into a puff,
> Which will in crumpling sounds your praise report,
> And eat, as housewives speak, exceeding short."
>
> KING.

"Open Apple Tart after The Pig" (1700)

Make a small quantity of fine short crust and add a generous dust of cinnamon and a spoonful of sugar. Roll out thinly and line a buttered pie-plate. Stew the windfall apples with 4 cloves, and brown sugar, till solid and clear as amber. Spread a very thin layer of the pork scratchings on the pastry, cover with the apple amber and put four pretty wide, straight bars of pastry, which nail down with the 4 cloves that were used in stewing the fruit. Cook in a fairly hot oven. This excellent plate pie was usually served with whipped cream spiced with rum.

Note. "Scratchings" are the small scraps of crisp fat, scratched up from the bottom of the pan after rendering down flead for lard. They make a waterproof base under the apple pulp.

Lemon Pies (ancestral)

The yellow rind of 1 large lemon pounded with 4 ounces of fine white sugar. Add the yolks of 3 eggs, and half the whites whisked to snow. Continue whisking while adding $\frac{1}{2}$ lb. of just-melted butter (or half butter and half clotted cream), the juice of the lemon being beaten in last, with a few spots of orange-flower brandy. Line patty-pans with very fine puff paste, fill with the lemon mixture, and bake.

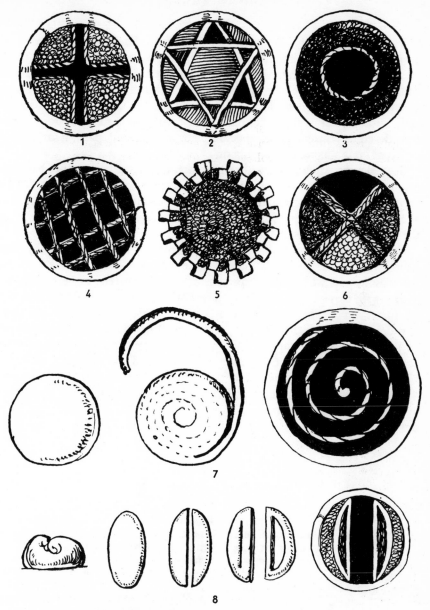

SOME ENGLISH JAM TART DESIGNS

1. Red Cross.
2. The Star.
3. The Well.
4. Lattice.
5. Gable.
6. A Cross Tart.
7. How to cut for a Whorl or Tail.
8. A very small scrap will make a "Slits".

Open Tarts

These became very decorative in the north. Each housewife vied in designing something handsome and fanciful! The old-fashioned thick glass dishes, with the raised glass handles, that held four different sorts of jams side by side (yellow apricot, black damson, red gooseberry, and green rhubarb), were no less fashionable than the tarts, prepared across and across, each section holding a different-coloured jam. Eight was considered a reasonably good show, but a diamond pattern of twelve different jams was really showing off!

Special tarts, such as the chitterling tart, treacle tart, etc., that had one colour only, were usually called "lattice", "trellis" or "gable" tarts. (The gable was where you made inch-wide cuts round the edge, folding the alternate ones inwards. This particular pattern was probably as old as the first embattled castle.)

Certain fillings had tradition; for example, an apple tart usually had plain strips of fairly wide lattice, as these were less likely to sink into the juicy pulp, and where the strips crossed, it was correct to nail them together with cloves. The drawings show better than I can describe how the designs evolve. The covering ring was cut first. The scraps are then kneaded up again and rolled out, which gives one little oblong of pastry, and you can see how cutting this into strips suggests the various lengths across the tart. How to use these strips has taxed the ingenuity of every cook who has ever made an open tart.

Note. The pastry must not be rolled out more often than absolutely necessary, and any restriction imposed by material is a challenge to a designer!

JAM TARTS (*see* p. 609).

1. The " Red Cross ". Red currant jelly, curd outside.
2. The " Star ". When made for the Church Social, was called " Epiphany ". You could use 12 different sorts of jam if you wanted to show off.
3. The " Well ". Very effective with greengage round blackcurrant, but it was a " good Pattern " if you wanted to use up a small scrape of jam in the middle, and it could be " done " in any colours.
4. The " Lattice ". Only one jam, and if over apple, the lattice was wide, and " nailed down " with cloves where it crossed.
5. The " Gable ". Customary with treacle.
6. The " Cross ". A Two-or-Four jam tart.
7. The " Whorl ". The number of turns depended on how much pastry you had left over and it tended to " sink " unless the jam was properly stiff.
8. The " Slits ". Showed you had measured very well, and had very little pastry left over for decoration.

Lemon Pies (modern)

Melt 1 large tablespoonful of butter in a thick pan, and into it rasp the fine yellow zest from 4 lemons (the butter should be just hot); now add fine flour gently, blending it with the butter, till it will take up no more, but becomes crumbly in the hot pan. Cook gently for several minutes like this. Now add, very gradually, a large cupful of boiling water, stirring all the time, and making a clear stiff thick gold sauce. Continue cooking, and add the strained juice of the lemons, and sugar to sweeten. When all is well cooked together, take the pan off the fire, and beat in the well-whipped yolks of 2 or 3 eggs. Line a deep pie-pan with fine short crust, fill with the lemon cream, and set in a hot oven, till the pastry is done. Meanwhile beat up the whites of the eggs to a stiff froth, add sugar, and a single spot of lemon juice, and pile it all over the top of the pie. Set it back in the oven for one moment to set. Dredge sugar over, decorate with candied peel, or marmalade and angelica, and serve hot or cold.

PASTRY CAKES

Banbury Cakes

These used to be carried around, all hot and crisp and fresh, in specially made chip baskets, wrapped in white cloths; they were very light and flaky, and "crunchy crusted", and the mixture inside was spicy fruit. There is a type of "solid filling" sometimes sold inside imitation Banbury cakes but the real thing was chopped peel and fruit and sugar and spice, and the whole cake was very brittle and always eaten fresh and hot. This is one of the oldest filling mixtures I can find, but several makers had their own variations:

Cream ½ lb. of butter with 1 tablespoon of honey, ½ lb. of candied lemon-peel, and ¼ lb. of candied orange-peel, 1 lb. of currants, 2½ oz. of all-spice, and ¼ oz. cinnamon; beat all well (if the weather is cold, warm the butter and honey). Keep this mixture in a closed jar. Make some finest flaky pastry, roll thin and cut into squares (about 4 or 6 inches), put a spoonful of the mixture on each, fold sides to middle, tucking in the ends,

The Banbury cake basket

reverse and roll again lightly to flatten; cut a slit (very small) on top just enough to encourage the pastry to rise evenly, brush over with white of egg and crushed sugar, bake lightly, and eat quickly.

Clifton Puffs

Clifton is the small hilly district aside from Bristol, and a direct route runs through Cheltenham to Banbury. These cakes somewhat resemble Banbury cakes, but the form is different. For the filling, mix $\frac{1}{4}$ lb. of apples chopped up finely, $\frac{1}{2}$ lb. of currants, $\frac{1}{4}$ lb. of stoned raisins, $\frac{1}{4}$ lb. of candied peel, $\frac{3}{4}$ lb. of sweet almonds chopped, $\frac{1}{2}$ nutmeg grated, and a glass of brandy. Put all into a closed jar in a warm place for an hour or so. For the pastry, use a very fine puff paste to which you add a little ground rice and ground almonds. (The best way to do this is to use them to dust the board on which the paste is rolled out several times.) Proportions given in the old recipe are 1 lb. of butter to 12 oz. of dry flour, 2 oz. of ground rice, 2 lb. of ground almonds, the juice of a lemon, and 1 tablespoonful of fine sugar.

Roll out the paste the final time as thin as possible, and cut into squares of about four inches; put the mixture into the middle of the squares, and fold each over cornerwise, making triangles; brush with egg, dust with crushed sugar, and bake quickly and lightly. Serve hot.

Eccles cakes were originally made with black currants and mint leaves; they are now made with dried currants.

Coventry Godcakes (these are the same type as Banbury Cakes, but more solid)

For the pastry, 1 lb. of flour, 1 lb. of fat, salt, and water to mix. Make a flaky pastry and roll out to an eighth of an inch thick—cut into triangles, put some mincemeat on one half, and fold over to form triangles; press the two edges together, and the folded edge to match; trim, and cut three slashes across the tops (as for Eccles or Banbury Cakes) glaze and frost with sugar and bake. As they are sold on New Year's Day and Easter, their triangular shape may have some reference to the Trinity, but the origin is obscure.

The Foot

" She's left his foots in t'oven and they're burnt to cinders."
Our Florrie, 1900.

A foot is popular as a snappin (i.e., an odd meal that miners take down the pit). It fits into the oval tin they carry. The oval section bottles and tins are a direct result of the miner's cramped job. The name "foot" belongs to the shape, and a miner's cook usually makes a pair of feet, thus:

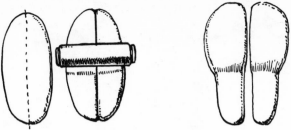

The "foot" (made in pairs)

Roll out some good short crust to a plain oval shape; then roll one end again, only, to the centre. This gives the "foot" shape, and if two are made at once, by cutting down the centre before the last roll, the likeness is more striking. It is a simple device for keeping the pie's bottom crust thick, and makes the top crust thin, and larger, to flap over the filling.

The filling is not always meat, but cheese, greens, egg, and, less often, fruit and sweet stuff.

Collier's Foot

Use bacon fat for the crust and spread a little extra over the heel side of the slice, after rolling out. Cover with thinly cut onion rings; cover these with wafer-thin slices of cheese and finally cover with a slice of bacon. Top each layer with seasoning, pepper on the cheese, salt on the onions, mustard on the bacon. Fold over and seal down. Bake well.

Often, to make the filling juicy, a spoonful of broth or beer is put over the onion rings, or an egg is beaten up with a little seasoned milk, and half poured over each foot. Sometimes a slice of apple is added for the same reason.

Scotch Black Bun

An interesting survival of the huff paste, and one of the few Scottish recipes in this English book. The recipes vary very much; this is an adaption from 1700, when yeast dough was used instead of bicarbonate of soda: 1 lb. currants, 1 lb. raisins, 4 oz. candied peel, 4 oz. almonds (mixed), 1 teaspoonful cinnamon, ½ teaspoonful ground cloves, 1 teaspoonful ground ginger, strong dust black pepper (these two were mediaevally supplementary), 2–4 oz. brown sugar. Mix to firm dough with buttermilk and brandy, beaten eggs and brandy, or brandy and water—adding ½ teaspoonful bicarbonate of soda in solution. The buttermilk would have a small butter content, otherwise note the absence of fat and cause for the huff to preserve the aroma of spice and brandy. The huff pastry was made with a little butter rubbed into plain flour, rolled out very thinly, and used to cover the entire bun closely. Baked for about 4 hours, according to size.

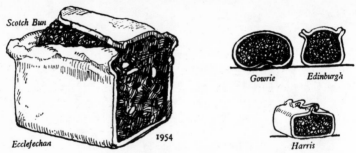

Scotch Bun

Gowrie   *Edinburgh*

Ecclefechan   1954   *Harris*

The black bun has burst through its huff on top, which is incorrect,
but shows the construction excellently.

Huff Paste (*see* Poultry & Ham Sections)

The name given to the close unleavened paste used to wrap round food
before baking. This paste served to keep in the juices and aroma, and
where the food was to be eaten cold was left on till just before the serving.
It originated in the clay covering (known to all campfire cooks) developed
by potters and clay workers. You find this type of cooking all round the
potteries and it followed around the hundreds of small potteries that used
to work about fifty miles distant from each other all over England (till
rubber tyres made mass transport possible—and the bracken used for
packing was left uncut). This huff paste, though not intended for eating,
often absorbed enough fat and flavour to become very tasty, and was
served cracked off in pieces for those who liked it (*see* Marrow-bones).
Later the name was given to the pastry that divided pies inside. This
paste, having been previously cooked over part of the pie was cut up and
incorporated in the finished article. For example, steak might first be stewed
under a boiled suet crust till enough rich gravy was ready, then the soft
cooked paste was sliced and slipped between the pigeons, oysters, or whatever was added later, and the whole finally covered by a thin, quickly
baked piecrust. The piecrust was on top and the huff crust (which needed
less fat) was within. This method of cooking caused the potters to make
those charming old "piecrust ware" dishes; the huff paste was still left
within, but the "top crust" was china. Sometimes these dishes have wide
rims, along which the cook runs a strip of paste to seal the cover tight while
cooking. It is worth doing this when preparing any very slow hot-pot
dish, as it keeps in the aroma and prevents gravy spilling over down the
sides of the pot, and so there is less fear of the contents drying up.

Hams were usually baked in a huff paste which was left on till cold,
then crushed to form the crumbled finish, and blistered before the fire.
Stuffed goose or capon is treated in the same manner. The paste was folded
to give double thickness over the breast bone (always liable to be over-
cooked in large birds).

MILK PUDDINGS

Hasties

Hasty pudding has been an English stand-by for centuries. It dates from the days when there was always a bin of bread-flour in the house, a cow in the byre, and butter in the crock. With a spice-box from the mantel-piece and a skillet stood over the fire, the pudding could be made in an otherwise empty kitchen. Well-made, the pudding tastes better than it sounds.

Hasty Pudding

> " I sing of food by British nurse designed
> To make the stripling brave and maiden kind
> Let Pudding's dish most wholesome be thy theme,
> And dip thy swelling plumes in fragrant cream.
>
> Sing then that Dish so fitting to improve
> A tender modesty and trembling love,
> Swimming in butter of a golden hue,
> Garnished with drops of rose's spicy dew.
>
> Sometimes the frugal matron seems in haste
> Nor cares to beat her Pudding into paste;
> Yet milk in proper skillet she will place,
> And gently spice it with a blade of mace.
>
> Then set some careful damsel to look to't,
> And still to stir away the bishop's foot;
> For if burnt milk should to the bottom stick,
> Like over-heated zeal it would make folks sick.
>
> Into the milk her flour she gently throws,
> As valets now would powder tender beaux;
> The liquid forms in Hasty Mass unite,
> Forms equally delicious as they're white.
>
> In shining dish the Hasty Mass is thrown
> And seems to want no graces but its own.
> Yet still the housewife brings in fresh supplies
> To gratify the taste and please the eyes;
>
> She on the surface lumps of butter lays,
> Which melting with the heat its beams displays,
> From whence it chases, wondrous to behold,
> A silver foil bedecked with streams of gold."
>
> KING.

A Hasty Pudding of 1742

" Break an egg into fine flour, and with your hand work up as much as you can into as stiff paste as possible [the size of the egg and dryness of the flour make it impossible to give quantities, but go on adding flour till the egg rubs into fine crumbs]. Add milk boiling, and put in a little salt, some rose water, or orange-flower water, a few drops put to your taste, some butter, and keep stirring all one way till it is thick as you would have it, pour it oute and when it is in the dishe stick it all over with littel bits of butter, and beaten cinnamon over."

A Modern Version (seems to have had no egg in it since 1800)

Melt a tablespoonful of butter in a thick saucepan, and beat in fine flour till the mass leaves the sides of the pan clean, and begins to crumble. Cook for about 3 minutes, then add milk slowly, beating till the whole is smooth and thick, add a few drops of rose water, or elder-flower wine, or some delicate aroma, and sugar and salt (a little only). Pour it boiling hot into a well-buttered dish. Instantly put extra knobs of butter on top, here and there, pattern-wise, then strew thickly with crushed sugar, and cover the top brownly with grated nutmeg or powdered cinnamon. Serve quickly while the butter melts into small golden wells of sticky sweetness and the spice runs over into a luscious brown sauce. Serve this pudding in a deep silver bowl; otherwise use brown earthenware.

Malvern Pudding (a fruit and hasty-pudding mixture)

Make a thick hasty-pudding mixture and when cooked, beat in an egg, sugar to taste, and a grate of nutmeg; fill a deep dish with alternate layers of this mixture and cooked sweetened apple pulp. A little lemon rind in the apple is an improvement.

Bake for 20 minutes and serve hot or cold.

BATTERS

A seventeenth-century cookery book gives the following recipe:

Batter Pudding

" Take a large pint of milk, four spoonfuls of flour, and boil till smooth [hasty pudding]. When 'tis almost cold, beat five eggs very well into it. Sweeten to taste and grate nutmeg. Butter your custard cups, put in your stuff, tie it over with a cloth, and let them boil something more than half an hour, turn out and pour on them melted butter."

A Victorian "Hasty-Batter", called Dowset

Take a pint of new milk, 3 laurel leaves, and a little of the yellow rind of a lemon; cook till the milk is well flavoured, and, with fine flour, make it into a pretty thick hasty pudding. Stir in ¾ lb. of butter, 2 oz. of sugar crushed, the yolks of 4 eggs, and their whites well beaten separately. Whip all lightly together and bake in a deep pastry-lined dish. It would have a light sack or madeira wine sauce with it.

A Modern Batter (popular winter dish)

This is a simple foundation batter mixture.

Beat the yolks of 4 eggs with ½ pint of milk then beat in ½ lb. of flour till whipped creamy; let it stand till wanted for use. Meanwhile whip the white of the eggs to a stiff froth, and finally fold them into the batter. Mix stiffly, and boil for a good hour in a buttered pudding mould. Turn it out onto a hot dish and serve it *instantly* (it becomes like leather cold). Cold butter and brown sugar are best served with this pudding, which should be well risen.

Strawberry cake and fruit batter

Kentish Fruit Batter

In Kent, the batter is cooked over ripe stoned cherries, and served from the pudding basin, strewn with sugar. Very good.

Note on Toad-in-the-Hole: The same batter, salted and seasoned, is poured over hot sausages (previously fried) and served as Toad-in-the-Hole.

Toad-in-the-hole

Tiverton Batter Pudding

Tiverton is a little town in Devon, having a typically rich batter pudding.

Take 4 eggs—yolks and whites beaten separately—mix with the yolks 3 dessertspoonfuls of flour, 1 dessertspoonful of sugar, and spice, ginger,

and candied lemon rind to taste. Pour nearly 1 pint of milk into the
mixture, fold in the whites of the eggs, beat lightly, and steam rapidly.
Serve butter and sugar therewith. Grease the basin very thoroughly and
serve as quickly as turned out, because steamed batter puddings sink very
quickly. They should be eaten at once while light and spongy.

Tewkesbury Saucer Batters (quick and easy snack meals)

Around Tewkesbury and the fruit-picking districts, they make delicious
"saucer batters" for teatime. The woman pickers bring a handful of any
soft fruit back from the fields, collect an egg, and the whole dish is ready
by the time the kettle boils. Put the fruit into the oven in a pot with sugar.
Beat the yolk of the egg into as much flour as it will take up; add a cupful
of milk (so that it makes a thick batter) beat the white, and fold it in; pour
the batter into two hot buttered saucers, and set in the oven. After 10
minutes, lift the hot batter out of one saucer, pile the hot fruit on to it,

Tewkesbury saucer batters

turn out the other batter inverted on top, strew sugar over all, and serve
instantly.

Sometimes a few green peas or a few tiny young beans were used. In
that case the batter was seasoned with pepper and salt and the dish
"waited" while they cooked the chop. These small "saucer" or sandwich-
type batters may have been Welsh in origin. They are found all along
the Welsh border, and the fillings are very varied.

Gotham Pudding

> " There were three wise men of Gotham
> Who went to sea in a bowl
> Had the bowl been stronger
> My tale had been longer."

Gotham is a little country town outside Nottingham, very quiet and
pretty. They have a lot of specialities, and this Gotham batter pudding
is from a book published about 1870.

Beat 1 breakfastcupful of milk and 3 well-beaten eggs into 2 tablespoonfuls or rather more of flour, and when quite smooth add a pinch of salt

and 4 oz. of candied peel sliced. Beat all thoroughly for 10 minutes; add 1 teaspoonful of "baking powder" at the last beating; then at once pour into a greased mould; cover and steam for 1½ hours. Stand a minute to shrink, turn out, and "serve with cowslip wine and sugar".

Tunbridge Fried Cherry Batter

Tunbridge Wells is in Kent and had a special type of batter fritter. Boil 1 pint of milk, and stir into it as much slaked flour as will make a thick batter. Beat it and pour it out, and when almost cold, beat in 3 eggs, sugar and flavouring. Let the batter now get quite cold, and then cut into slices; egg-and-breadcrumb these (keep back a little egg for this) and fry them in lard or butter. Serve on a pile of hot, baked, stoned cherries.

Nottingham Batter and Apple Pudding

Take large apples, peel and core and stuff the corehole with butter, sugar and nutmeg—stand side by side in a piedish and cover with a light well-beaten batter.

To make the batter, drop the yolks of 4 eggs into 6 tablespoonfuls of flour, add a pinch of salt, a little cold water, and stir round and round adding milk till the whole is the consistency of thick cream. Beat well and leave to stand a couple of hours—just before using, whip the egg whites stiff and fold them in.

Bake the pudding till the apples are soft and the batter well risen and crusty. Strew with crumbed sugar and serve hot.

Trayne Roste

This is from the Teuton side of the English (like the haver, or catbread, of the West Riding of Yorkshire). The modern German cake, called "Bough cake", is made by the same method, but has a larger hole down the middle where it slides off the thick spit: this version uses a fine "bird" spit, and has a core of dried fruit.

> " Take dates and figges and kutte hem and take grete reysoms and almondes and prick hem through with a nedel into a threde a mannys length and one of one frute and another of another frute and then bynde the threde with the frute arownde the spete.
>
> Take a quarte of wyne or ale and fyne floure and make batur thereof and cast thereto pouder ginger, sygur and saffron, poudre cloves, salt (and make the batur not fully rennyng, nother stonding, but in the mene) that it may cleve. Then roste the trayne and caste the batur on the trayne as he turneth so longe, till the frute be hidde in the batur. And as thou casteth the batur thereon hold a vessell undere nethe for spilling of the batur, and when it is y rosted hit wol seme a hasselet.

Then take a hit uppe from the spete al hole, and kut in fair
paces a span lengthe and serue a pece or two in a dissh al hote."

DYET, FIFTEENTH CENTURY.

This is easy to do before a roasting fire. It is practically basting with
batter, which cooks as it is slowly poured on to the fruit centre. It can also
be done upright, if you have an old-fashioned roasting-spit and cage.
The batter crisps and bubbles as it cooks, so that the whole is a very
delectable crunchy exterior around the completely submerged fruit; but
unless you have a spit of some sort and a roasting fire, it is hardly possible
to get the effect.

Muffin Pudding

Muffins were, in the north, made into a delectable boiled pudding.

Butter a mould; split the muffins and pack in lightly with small spoonfuls of honey and a grating of spice; fill the interstices with a light batter
made by using the *whites* of the eggs *only*, beaten to a snow and folded into
the flour and milk—more like an omelette than a batter.

Boil for 1 hour and turn out gently.

PANCAKES

Abroad pancakes are usually open and piled up together. In England
our pancakes are symbols of our insular detachment, for each is rolled up
by itself, aloof, with its own small slice of lemon.

Insular English pancakes

Snow Pancakes

Snow pancakes are made in winter. Use an ordinary pancake batter,
and, when just ready to fry, stir in a spoonful of fresh firm snow and fry
quickly so that the batter firms, before the snow entirely melts, leaving
holes in the pancake.

Welsh Pancakes (Crempog)

½ lb. of flour, a piece of butter the size of a walnut rubbed in, buttermilk
to mix to a smooth batter. Beat 1 egg and add it, and let it stand for an hour.
Before frying, add ½ teaspoonful of bicarbonate of soda. If the buttermilk is not sufficiently acid, a few drops of vinegar should be added to it.

Piled-up pancakes

Butter the pan and fry to a clear light brown. This recipe was given to me by a Welshman from Carnarvon, out of his mother's old manuscript book written in Welsh.

A Froise

This word is used in so many different ways in so many old cook-books that a definition is difficult.

The commonest form seems to indicate something fried in batter(?), but not always fried and not always in batter. Having puzzled much we believe it is onomatopoeic and based on the sudden *sound* of things dropped into deep boiling fat. Now under the roast, before the fire, stood the long iron dripping pan, full and smoking hot. What easier, while basting the roast, than to drop ladlefuls of the batter (so often cooked before the fire) into this trough? Or batter would drip off (*see* Bough cakes), and puff up and cook deliciously. Therefore I believe food cooked in deep fat was a "froise" as distinct from shallow dry frying. To follow this theory a "froisey" or "frausey" in the west country is a "small feast or jubilation" (such as the cooks would make around the fire after the joint had been served and they were left free of the "froice". Whether frowsey and drawsey (meaning grandeur and finery gone past its prime) are a degenerate form of the same word is *non proven*.

Fritters

Anything, such as a slice of fruit, or piece of meat, dipped into batter and cooked this way, we now call a "fritter".

WAFERS, WAFFLES AND GAUFFRES

" Wife, make us a feast, spare fleshe neither corne,
    make Wafers and cakes, for our shepe must be shorne.
    At sheep-shearing neighbours no other thing crave
    but good chere and welcome like neighbours to have."

                                                    TUSSER,

This MS. drawing made in the twelfth century shows
a wafer being taken from the hot wafer iron.
(*From the Bodleian Library, Oxford.*)

Wafers have been made in England since at least the twelfth century—
probably earlier. They needed a very fine texture flour. The pre-Reformation holy bread was a fine small specially stamped wafer, but the ordinary
everyday wafer was made over the open fire, as a pleasant "extra" (much
as we make hot buttered toast nowadays). The wafer irons were usually
round, sometimes square, about the size of a small plate, and with long
handles to hold the wafer far out over the red coals, there were delightful
incised designs on both sides, and the irons printed these on the batter. It
was these wafer irons that went to America with the Elizabethan settlers,
and now return to us as waffle irons!

An Early English Wafer

"Take fine wheaten flour, mix with cream yolks of eyroun [eggs] spice
it and beat it, then warming your irons on a fire, anoint well with butter,
lay on your batture, press it and bake it white or brown [lightly or rather
dark]."

After the war in Holland, we find the English recipe alongside a more
elaborate one called "The Right Dutch Wafer" (about 1780).

Take 4 eggs and beat very well, and take a spoonful of fine sugar, some
nutmegs, grated, some cream (about 1 pint) and 1 lb. of flour. Mix with
1 lb. of butter melted, 3 spoonfuls of rose water and 2 spoonfuls of yeast.
Mix and bake in your wafer tongs. For the sauce (for a sauce was poured
over the old wafer as over today's waffle) take cinnamon, sack, and melted
butter, and sweeten to your taste.

These wafers were "turned off" their irons with a tap and twist, but
the similar gauffres were more sticky, and pliant, and done on a flatter
iron, or one side only of the wafer iron, and peeled off.

Now these two varieties give the reason why the gauffre iron was
originally supplied with a small iron rod: if the paste gauffre was made,

it slipped out like a crisp pancake, with the pattern of the mould marked on it; if the flat toffee type was made, *it had to be rolled off the iron*, curling it off round the greased rod with a little stick.

Gauffres (goffer crois)

The true gauffre (American waffle) was made in England, went out of fashion, and came back with the Flemish weavers.

The flat sticky brown curls called brandy-snaps sold in a few places nowadays are descendants of the old English gauffres—and some Flemish gauffres of the same date have much the same ingredients, but add more eggs, and some yeast.

"Wafers piping hot out of the Gleed."
CHAUCER.

Brandy-snaps, or Gauffres (an old recipe)

¼ lb. of lard or butter, 1 lb. of sugar (brown), 1 lb. of flour, 1 table-spoonful of brandy and a dust of nutmeg.

Mix to a soft dropping batter with *well-beaten* eggs (and a spoonful of water) drop spoonfuls on to hot greased cake tins and let them *spread*—(the size of a walnut should spread out to saucer size). When quite flat—lift and curl round quickly—using *a stick*. They dry crisp quickly with a shiny bright toffee surface—they should be pale toffee-coloured and full of airholes—delicious filled with ginger-flavoured cream.

Note that the brandy, in this recipe, is the only relic left in the modern name of "brandy-snap", and that name is now passing back from the thin brittle gauffre, to a more wafer-textured biscuit, called "ginger nuts *or* brandy snaps".

PUDDINGS WITH A BREAD BASE

Summer Pudding (using bread)

Called "hydropathic pudding" because it was served in nursing homes where pastry was not permitted. It can be made with any light summer fruits, raspberries, currants or strawberries being especially good. It is so simple, it is worth making superlatively well.

Butter a smooth deep basin, and cut a round of bread to fit the bottom, then cut slices sloping, dovetailing them so that they fit the sides; press into place, boil the fruit with enough sugar, and, when absolutely boiling, lift the fruit into the basin, packing it in carefully. Fill up with the hot juice and put the bits left over from cutting the bread on top. Fit a saucer or plate on top of the basin so that it presses down the fruit. Put a weight on it, and leave till next day. Turn it out on to a glass dish. Decorate it with whole fruit and serve with cream.

Monmouth Pudding (this pudding is white and red)

Take the white crumb of a small loaf, break it into a hot basin, and pour on boiling milk till *just* soaked; cover, and let it stand for 10 minutes; flake up with a silver fork, adding 2 tablespoonfuls of rough white sugar, 2 tablespoonfuls of fine lard (or butter), and, lastly, the stiffly whipped whites of 2 eggs. Flavour delicately, pour into a buttered dish with a layer of red jam at the bottom; put other layers alternately on top and bake till set, in a *very* gentle oven.

A red and white section

Manchester Pudding (is yellow)

Boil (not just soak) about 3 tablespoonfuls of fine white breadcrumbs in 1 pint of milk with the yellow rind of a lemon, and sweeten to taste. Take it from the heat and beat in a lump of butter (the size of a small egg) and the yolks of two well-whisked eggs. Put a layer of apricot jam at the bottom on the dish; pour over the thickened custard; cover again with jam, and, lastly, spread the top smooth with the white of the eggs whipped, a tablespoonful of sugar, and a spot of vanilla. (This top should be spread smooth, like white icing.)

Bake in a *very* gentle oven till the eggs are "set", and the top crusted crisp and lightly browned. When this simple pudding is made for festive occasions, the jam is moistened with sherry or spiced rum, and it is served cold, the top decorated with cut crystallised fruits.

New College Pudding

"A new college pudding of marrow and plums
Is a dish of all others that suiteth her gums."

Ingoldsby Legends.

College puddings in mediaeval recipes seem to have been fried like rissoles.

Take 6 oz. of chopped suet, 6 oz. of currants, 6 oz. of sugar, 6 spoonfuls of flour, $\frac{1}{2}$ lb. of fine fresh breadcrumbs, the fine rind of a lemon, 3 eggs well beaten, and about 3 spoonfuls of brandy, enough to moisten. Form the mixture into little round puddings, large egg size, roll in flour, or thin batter, and drop into boiling fat like doughnuts. Serve them very quickly, drained and rolled in crushed sugar.

Aromatic Shropshire Pudding with Brandy Butter

This is brown and aromatic, and, served with this butter and sugar, makes a good pudding for a frosty day.

Take the crumb of a stale brown loaf, and half as much finely grated suet. To about $\frac{1}{2}$ lb. of each add 4 tablespoonfuls of brown sugar, 1 generous teaspoonful of grated nutmeg and a very generous teaspoonful of brandy. Mix all well together, and bind with 2 eggs well beaten up with a spoonful or two of water, not milk (mix it rather moist). Put into a buttered mould and steam for 3 hours. Turn out and serve with brandy butter.

Brandy Butter. Warm, but do not melt, 4 oz. of butter, and cream into it as much castor sugar as will turn it to crisp snow. At the last beat, sop a tablespoonful of brandy on the last spoonful of sugar (this is the easiest way of incorporating the brandy). Give a final beat and set to chill. The pudding should be brown, crumbly, and hot; the sauce white, smooth, and cold.

Ipswich Almond Pudding (an old recipe; now we should use ready-ground almonds)

"Steep somewhat above 3 oz. of the crumbs of white bread in 1$\frac{1}{2}$ pints of cream, then beat $\frac{1}{2}$ lb. of blanched almonds very fine (till they do not glister) with a small quantity of orange-flower water, beat up the yolks of 8 eggs and the whites of 4; mix all well together, put in $\frac{1}{4}$ lb. of white sugar; then set it into the oven, but stir in a little melted butter before you set it in; let it bake but half an hour."

ROLY-POLIES AND DUMPLINGS

Treacle Roly-poly

This is a solid English pudding. Make a good firm suet crust and roll it into a long, smooth strip. Cover it, to within two inches of the edge, with fine breadcrumbs; over these sprinkle lemon juice in summer, and powdered ginger in winter. Cover the crumbs with syrup, wet the edges of the paste, and roll it up, damping and pinching the edges together so that the juice cannot escape. Roll up in greased paper (not too tightly)

Jam roly-poly

and finally in a pudding cloth, pleating the cloth to allow for swelling. Plunge the pudding into boiling water, and boil steadily for 1 hour at least—more if very large.

Roll it out onto a hot dish and serve instantly.

Another Roly

Season the suet-crust with pudding spice, sweeten slightly and, instead of treacle or jam, fill with a layer of mixed dried fruits, currants, sultanas, raisins, and peel, scalded till swollen and juicy, and a spoonful of marmalade to bind. Lay on the crust, seal up, and cook as usual.

Use the water in which the fruit was soaked to make a clear thin brown spice sauce—a dash of brandy in this sauce is good.

Plough Pudding (a savoury roly)

This used to be made for stable lads' suppers.

Take a lightly made suet-crust, and roll out to three-quarters of an inch thick—cover closely with strips of bacon (cut across the rasher) try to arrange lean and fat strips alternately, cover these with finely chopped onion, a fine sprinkling of sage, "and pretty well" of white pepper and a single trail of honey or syrup (a great improvement to the gravy broth that should drip out when cutting the roll).

Baked fruit roll

Galley Dumplings

An excellent version of the dumpling type of pudding, but lighter and more quickly served. Mix a light boiled crust as for sea pie, form into a long roll, and wrap in a floured cloth to boil in rapidly

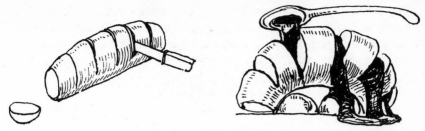

Galley dumplings are boiled as a long roll. The ends cut off and tucked under. The now bent roll is slit into dumplings and hot jam or treacle poured into the gashes.

boiling salted water. Lift, and roll out of the cloth in the usual way, but then cut off the two ends, and tuck them under the middle of the roll, so that it bends up. Cut the roll across, into thick slices, halfway through, put a lump of butter, a dust of nutmeg into each cut, and crust over with brown sugar. Serve hot, instantly. Hot treacle or jam may be inserted in the same way.

Tadcaster Pudding

Tadcaster is a small place, with individuality. It makes a pleasant ordinary baked suet pudding.

"Eight ounces suet, quarter of a pound of flour, salt, four ounces chopped fruit, currants, raisins, peel, etc., two teaspoonfuls of baking powder. Mix and stir together with a dessertspoonful of golden syrup in nearly one pint milk. Stir the liquid in carefully as the mixture should be stiff." Pour it into a shallow well-greased baking-dish and bake till well risen and firm—probably about 1 hour. Now comes the slight change: Turn out, upside down, and pour over it spiced hot treacle.

Spiced treacle. Melt 2 tablespoonfuls of treacle in 1 large breakfastcupful of hot cider, add a squeeze of lemon juice and a good scrape of spice. Serve extra sauce hot in a hot jug.

Lemon Pudding

"My dear, we always had roast chicken and lemon pudding for Easter Sunday."

The Aunt.

Make a good suet pudding with flour, chopped suet, sugar, and some fine white breadcrumbs, rub in the finely rasped yellow rind of two lemons, and instead of using milk to mix, use the lemon juice, and enough water to make a dry dough. Butter your pudding basin, and steam the pudding at least 1½ hours. Turn out and serve with hot orange sauce.

The hot sauce for lemon pudding. 1 tablespoonful of butter, melted and blended with 1 tablespoonful of flour, cooked, sweetened, and thinned down with orange juice. On no account use milk, or make a white solid sauce; the sauce should be thin, clear, and a bright orange tint.

USING EGGS

A Caramel Custard

Take an ordinary pint-size cake tin. Put a tablespoonful of sugar at the bottom and just wet it with hot water, and set it to melt over a low heat, then let it boil briskly away, till it is a mass of bubbling toffee, tilt the tin round and round, till all the bottom is covered with a layer of smooth golden brown toffee. Take it off the fire. Meanwhile flavour a pint of milk with almonds, and beat into it a large egg, or two small ones, sweeten to taste, and pour it on to the hard caramel in the tin; set the tin on a mat in the oven and bake at your lowest possible heat till the custard sets. The more slowly it cooks the richer the custard. Let it cool, slide a knife around the edge of the tin, and turn over on to a dish; the brown top will be glossy, and the juice that runs down forms the sauce.

Modern Boiled Custard

For a boiled custard today it is better to make a thick foundation (with cornflour, milk, and butter) that can be *well boiled*, then cool it slightly and beat in the eggs already beaten up in a little more milk, and keep *hot* only long enough to cook the egg.

Bakewell Pudding

This is named after a small town in Derbyshire; they are sometimes called Bakewell tarts. Line a deep earthenware piedish with short crust, cover the bottom with mixed preserved fruit and sugar and moisten with cider or wine. Melt $\frac{1}{4}$ lb. of butter with 1 oz. of ground almonds and 6 oz. of fine sugar, beat in the yolks of 3 eggs with a little milk and fold in the stiff whites—use this to fill the pastry-lined piedish over the fruit. The whole art is in getting this mixture the right soft consistency. More milk may be added to make the custard softer, or a *few* fine white breadcrumbs to make it set more steadily, but the result, when carefully baked, should be set, but must be quite soft and creamy.

Petyperneux (Pernollys; Little Lost Eggs)

The fourteenth-century version was "pety perdue oeufs"—"little lost eggs"(?). At least that is the Anglo-Norman-kitchen-English that seems to describe the recipe; which later is called Pernollys.

"Take flour, saffron, sugar, salt and make thereof paste—and make small coffyns [i.e., small pastry cases, like little pork pies]. Take the yellow yolks of the eggs from the whites, and let the yolks be whole, and not broken, and lay three or four in each coffin. Then take powdered ginger and sugar and currants and raisins, and cast them over the round yolks, and cover in the pies with their paste lids and bake them."

Cut open, this would give you a pie of three hard round yellow balls buried under a dark brown earth of fruit. Three golden balls?

I wonder if there was some subtle jest in the kitchen the day that new dish was set before some noble long ago?

OTHER PUDDINGS

Called after towns:

Canterbury pudding: plain sponge with hot wine sauce.

Cheltenham pudding: a baked suet with fruit—including candied ginger —and brandy sauce.

Chester pudding: a custard made of egg yolks, powdered sugar, chopped almonds, rind and juice of lemons, and butter melted, spread on a thin pastry case, and baked with the whites of the eggs frothed on top and lightly browned.

Chichester pudding is chiefly milk and egg yolks, thickened with white breadcrumbs, sweetened and flavoured, and made into a stiff custard, the stiff whites of the eggs folded in, and the whole baked lightly till set and browned; it cuts marbled yellow and white, *and Deptford pudding*, the same, only thoroughly mixed.

Exeter pudding: 7 eggs beaten with rum (to taste) and 6 oz. of sugar; fill this with light breadcrumbs (about 10 oz.), 7 oz. of very fine suet, and the rind of a lemon; beat well together.

Line a basin with buttered ratafias and raisins split and stuck to the buttered sides; fill with the mixture, adding layers of jam; bake till risen and firm, and serve with black-currant jelly melted with sherry.

Noodles (not Chinese, but English)

Here is a fourteenth-century recipe:

"Take whyte of eyroun and mylke and floure and a lytel berme, [barm] and bete to gedery [together] so that it be runney and not too styf. Caste sugre thereto and salt, then take a chafer ful of fresshe grece boyling, and put they hond in the bature and lat him renne down by they fyngerys, into the chafere, and whan it is ronne togedere, on the chafere and it is y now, nym a skymer, and take it up and let al the grece renne out, and put it on a fayre dysshe and cast thereon sugre and serue forth."

This is curiously like Chinese crispy noodles. The "chafere ful of fresshe grece" is of course deep drying; as this is difficult on the uncertain heat of an open fire, it has always been customary to have a side fire, a pan or stove into which the red-hot charcoal from the main fire could be placed, and upon which steady heat the cook could do any quick special jobs. The "skymer" which you take up (nym) and use would be exactly like the wire-basket spoons or skimmer used today, and the "fayre dyssche" would be a hot flat platter with (likely) a slice of dry bread at the bottom to ensure drainage. This is a satisfactory modern version which I have tried and found delicious:

Take the white of an egg beaten to a stiff froth, and about 2 tablespoon-fuls of flour beaten to a smooth paste with milk; add a pinch of salt (if for a sweet dish sweeten to taste) and stir the beaten egg lightly into the batter "so that it be runney, not stiff", and when the pan of deep fat boils, let the batter run into it in trickles. Keep the curls from clinging together, and give them a moment to firm—the crispies will float on top when it is done enough—lift out of the pan with a strainer, drain well, and serve loosely on a hot dish sprinkled with sugar (or if for a savoury, serve as required).

I have not yet the skill to make it trickle down all my fingers, and so make five crispies at a time.

PLUM PUDDINGS AND MINCEMEAT

As with Christmas puddings, every English family has its own mince-meat recipe so we only give one representative of many.

Mincemeat of Lemon

Take the rind off 12 lemons, squeeze out the juice and boil the white pith, in several changes of water, till quite soft. Pound it up to a pulp, and beat in raisins, currants, candied peel, chopped almonds, the lemon rinds and little fine suet, till it will hold no more, stir in brandy, lemon juice and sugar to your taste and cover well. This recipe (curiously) has no spice in it; at a guess it dates from 1650 onwards, when "marmalades" were made using the white pith of oranges and lemons.

Plum Pudding Cold Remains (if any; four local methods)

A rich mixture is most commonly sliced, set upon a hot plate in a hot oven till smoking hot, resuscitated with brandy, and served alight. Or dry fried, in a scrap of butter, and either dusted with crystal sugar, or given the rum butter of its origin (but in districts where they use rum butter the contingency of any pudding being left over is unlikely).

Lancashire sensibly uses the pudding, crumbled up with a little extra brandy, to fill a pastry case. This is then turned over, and rolled lightly, and slits cut on top (like an Eccles cake). It is then brushed over with egg and strewn with crystallised sugar (to make a glazed sparkling crust) and served as a crisp cake, piping hot, for tea.

In Devon an interesting way is to cut the pudding into blocks (and build these up in a deep piedish, criss-cross, so as to leave open spaces). An egg custard mixture is then poured in gently, and the whole baked gently till set.

The English Royal Family's Christmas Pudding

> 1¼ lb. suet.
> 1 lb. demerara sugar.
> 1 lb. raisins.
> 1 lb. sultanas.
> 4 oz. citron peel.
> 4 oz. candied peel.
> 1 teaspoonful mixed spice.
> ½ teaspoonful nutmeg.
> 1 lb. breadcrumbs.
> ½ lb. sifted flour.
> 1 lb. eggs (weighed in their shells).
> 1 wineglassful brandy.
> ½ pint milk.

Prepare all ingredients, well whip the eggs, add to milk, and thoroughly mix. Let stand for 12 hours in a cool place, add brandy and put into well-greased basins and boil 8 hours or longer. Sufficient for twenty to twenty-eight people.

Mince pies

SOME CAKES

Seed Cake

> " Wife, sometime this weeke if that all thing go cleare,
>   an ende of wheat sowing we make for this yeare,
>   Remember you therefore though I do it not
>   the Seede Cake, the Paties, and Furmenty pot."
>
>   TUSSER, 1477.

" Melt 2 lb. of butter, and then rub in 4 lb. of fine dried flour.
Mix in 8 eggs [whip the whites to snow] and pt. of ale yeast and
1 pt. of sack [any white wine]. Mix all together lightly and put
in 2 lb. of Carraway comfits. Put into buttered Hoops and bake
2 hours and a half. You may mix in ½ oz. of cloves and cinnamon if you like."

                                        CONDE, 1744.

Sponge Cake

5 eggs, the weight of 4 in sugar, and 3 in flour, is standard mixture for
sponge cake. Lemon juice, orange-flower water, rose water, etc., are added
at discretion. Separate the whites from the yolks of the eggs and beat the
yolks with the sugar till creamy and white, dredge in the flour very lightly,
and lastly the whisked whites. Butter a cake tin, and dredge thickly with
sugar and flour, pour (or rather lift in) the sponge mixture and bake at
once till just firm. Some cooks do the whipping over a bowl of hot water.
Sponge cake is turned into the more solidly textured Madeira cake by the
addition of fat and a higher percentage of flour in the mixture.

Hedgehog Pudding

> " Thus when the dame her Hedgehog Pudding breaks,
>   Her fork indents irreparable streaks,
>   The trembling lump with butter all around
>   Seems to perceive its fall and then be drowned;
>   And yet the tops appear, whilst almonds thick
>   With bright loaf sugar on the surface stick.
>
> . . . . ' Oh, delicious !'
>   But where must our confession first begin,
>   If Sack and Sugar once be thought a sin? "
>
>   KING.

Hedgehog was a sponge cake, the said cake being equal quantities of
sugar, flour and eggs (*see* Sponge Cake). This hedgehog cake was made
oval in form, and set in a dish, and soaked in sherry till it could soak up no
more—then split almonds were pushed into it, slanting backwards in rows
and the whole surrounded by rich custard.

Madeira Cake

5 fresh eggs, separated yolks and whites. Whip separately, and then blend together. Now, still beating, shake in 6 oz. of sugar, 6 oz. of flour, and 4–6 oz. of just-melted butter. Flavour lightly with almond, lemon peel, or orange-flower water, and small pieces of citron peel are sometimes added. Use 1 teaspoonful of baking powder and bake in a moderate oven. In both these cake mixtures, if the eggs be small, or the flour very dry, it may be necessary to add an extra eggcupful of cold water, but on no account use milk.

This was served, with Madeira wine, as a light refreshment in the nineteenth century as, today, we serve sherry and biscuits.

Strawberry Cake

This is a good way of finishing a small amount of raspberries or strawberries. Make the sponge cake as usual, and cool; cut it through half-way, and cut a circle out of the centre. Crush a basinful of strawberries with sugar and a few drops of lemon juice, and cover the bottom half of the cake good and thick with the crushed fruit. Put the top over it and now fill the centre hole with cream, putting a few whole berries on top. Serve at once.

If served as a sweet, the sponge cake is sometimes soaked in white wine.

Cornish Heavy Cake

1½ lb. of flour, dried well, ½ lb. of currants, cleaned and washed, a small spoonful of salt. Make into a paste with clotted cream; roll out till about an inch thick; bake flat, scoring the top for breaking apart when done.

Aberfrau Cake

Aber (mouth) of the Frau river.

Aberfrau is a small old seaside village in Anglesey. Between the salt spray and the sea wind huddles down a cluster of one-storey fisher-huts, and a graceful stone packhorse bridge, which springs wide over a tidal river full of geese and ducks. It is very isolated, so I was surprised to find a recipe for "Aberfrau cake" in Cassell's Dictionary of Cookery.

Aberfrau cakes are baked in scallop shells, or large cockle shells

The cakes are as simple as the village: ½ lb. of fresh butter beaten to a cream with ⅓ lb. of sugar and ½ lb. of fine flour. They were baked in the large flat scallop shells that abound on the estuary bar. The shells are the size and shape of small patty-pans. In the time when geese were so plentiful on the marsh, the cakes were, most probably, made with goose grease and sugar and flour.

Petticoat Tails

These simple biscuits are mentioned by Sir Walter Scott in his *Bride* and are still sold in Edinburgh. They date at least from the twelfth century. They were called "petty cotes tallis"; that is, little cases, or "cotes" (we have the word in sheep-cotes—small enclosures), made of pastry and cut into triangular pieces. Now "tallis", or "tallys", were cuts made on sticks to count or measure by (*see* Tally), so the word tally came to mean any sort of cut-out pattern (old mechanics still speak of a former plate as a tally plate).

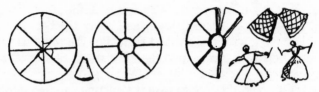

Centuries ago the brittle points broke from our triangular
slices—and centuries ago cooks invented this for us!

Every cook knows how the pointed ends of cut cakes and biscuits break off—so, after several centuries of broken tips, someone evolved the cure: they cut a circle out of the centre before baking. By then the filling had come out of the "cotes", and they were biscuits only—"pettycotes tallys". By this time ladies' "petty cotes" had become wide skirts, so that by the time Queen Elizabeth was wearing "petticotes" the little biscuits were exactly the pattern (or tally) for a full gored skirt, and by another century were called "petticote tallis" (or petticote tails?).

The recipe varies slightly, but this is a good modern one.

2 lb. flour, 1 lb. butter, ¼ lb. sugar, flavour to taste with almond, and after creaming all together—bind with an egg if required—roll out very thinly, and bake lightly.

N.B. Mark and remove the centre circle before slicing the main round.

Gingerbread, Gilt

The eldest gingerbread was not a cake, but a solid slab of honey, baked flour, ginger, etc. In the "tournament" period it was a popular gift (rather like expensive chocolates today). Appropriately, it seems to have been designed to copy cuir bouilli armour, being coloured a tawny brown with

Saunders, polished (with egg white?), and decorated with clusters of six small box leaves, set to form a fleur-de-lis, and gilt-headed cloves, driven in like nails. The resemblance to a piece of tooled and gilt-studded leather was very effective.

On a glossy dark slab of brown cake set a clove (clue), gilt for a nail, and box leaves, green or gilt

This dark heraldic decoration was as appropriate to the early mediaeval period as the frilly white sugar icing is appropriate to the early Victorian period.

The gilding of the moulded gingerbreads continued till the late nineteenth century, but some of the very elaborate wooden moulds were more likely made for marchpane (*see below*), that could be pressed in while warm, and could take the fine impress. Therefore, as a compromise for cooks who would like to put the gilt on the gingerbread, I give this ginger-and-honey bread, as the gold leaf may be "pressed on" while still hot and tacky, or (more easily) laid on with white of egg. Paint on the (unbeaten) white, let it almost dry, and then lay down the gold leaf (brush off surplus when dry). Gold leaf is quite harmless, and a little goes a very long way, as only touches of gold are needed.

Proportions: $3\frac{1}{2}$ lb. of fine flour, $1\frac{1}{2}$ lb. of honey, $\frac{1}{2}$ lb. of butter, $\frac{1}{2}$ nutmeg grated fine, 1 tablespoonful of ground ginger (1 teaspoonful of baking powder unless self-raising flour is used). Melt the honey with a little hot water and melt in the butter; blend into the dry ingredients, roll out the dough, or press into greased moulds and bake for about 20 minutes in a cool oven, "An if you will have hym gilt doe it now."

Dublin Rock (a cold sweet)

This sweet of the 1890s is rich, rather expensive, and very decorative. It probably graced the long polished dining-tables of the period. It is a form of St. Mark's Pain, the marchpane of the earlier time, or marzipan of later times.

Heat an earthenware bowl really *hot* and melt into it 4 oz. of sweet butter or *very* thick cream. Beat into this $\frac{1}{2}$ lb. of ground almonds, 2 oz. of finest white castor sugar and 1 dessertspoonful of brandy. A few drops of orange-flower water should be sprinkled in while you continue to beat till the bowl is cold and the mixture setting light and white and stiff. Leave it then till set stiff. Next day break it into rough lumps (it should be soft but *firm*), and pile them up on a platter like craggy rocks, putting shreds of green angelica and shreds of split almonds here and there in the crannies, like weeds (or shamrock?) growing on the "rock" (*see* p. 16).

Peggy's Leg

This is an Irish toffee, learnt in Liverpool, about 1928.

Take 1 lb. of brown sugar, 1 lb. of black treacle, and 1 lb. of brown treacle, ¾ lb. of lard, 1 teaspoonful of ground ginger, and 4 tablespoonfuls of vinegar. Melt all together, and stir them once. Then let boil till about to set. Divide into two parts: the one you pour out onto a greased slab, the other you leave in the pan, and add a small teaspoonful of baking soda till it rises white. Put this light upon the dark, and roll them together, and draw out into bars "the way you'll be having them all striped".

It was controversial taste whether you should add a spot of peppermint to the ginger or not. Peggy's Leg was hot stuff.

Mediaeval Chewing Gum (or chewing wax)

The comb honey must be used so that the wax pieces solidify. If you have to use the beeswax separately, it takes 1 cupful of beeswax to 1 table-spoonful of honey, with ginger, cinnamon, or spice to taste. For the authentic resinous taste obtained from the tips of fir trees, use a single spot of oil of terebinth. Melt wax, honey, and flavouring ingredients together, heating to boiling point, beat well till cool and pour it to set.

Another mediaeval version is like our modern treacle-fried bread. Make the mixture as before but pour it out hot on to slices of hot toast till they are thoroughly sodden. When cool, cut into squares and roll in cinnamon powder.

The same simple sweetmeat, with the substitution of lemon juice for the spice or terebinth, makes a good simple sweetmeat for a child's sore throat.

Cinnamon Sticks (1600)

Cinnamon was considered good for colds, or children in church. This sweetmeat was also a medical one. 1 oz. of powdered cinnamon; 1 lump of gum arabic. Melt the gum in hot rose water, and fill the liquid with sugar and cinnamon. Work it and beat it out flat on a slab and cut it into thin strips as it stiffens, and "roule" them a little into the "forme" of a cinnamon stick.

SUNDRY HOUSEHOLD MATTERS

LAUNDRY

Passing the Buck

> " Let her keep close her stubble and lopping of trees for fuel for
> the oven. Let her not suffer the stalks of Beanes Peasom Fetch,
> Thistles Danewort, the refuse of pressed things, and other un-
> profitable herbs to be lost, for in winter they being burnt to
> ashes will afford provision to lay Bucks withall."
>
> MARKHAM.

FALSTAFF WAS hidden in the buckbasket by the "merrie wives of
Windsor" and it was a big creaking willow basket full of washing.
Soap was made in each household from fat and wood ash, etc., but it was
also a matter of commerce from at least the thirteenth century, and
probably earlier. Like everything in mediaeval economy, soap followed
regular cause and effect in production. All large towns had drover roads
down which the beasts came to market; the slaughter houses and tan
yards were built below the town on the riverside (so that the refuse would
wash away down stream); and the soap boilers (who got their grease
from the scraped hides) had to boil their stinking soap lye downstream.
Bristol is a good example of this; the great drover road that brought the
hill cattle down across Clun and past Gloucester caused leather works
(still there), horn works (still there in Gloucester), and, finally, soap works,
as far down as Bristol. Bow Bridge Soap Works, Eastend, are another
example of the dirty work being done downstream from a city.

Toilet soap seems to have been "served" soft in bowls, and certain
roots and plants (ragged robin, for example) were used for cleaning also.

But apart from soap, which was used for washing, they also washed with
"soap substitutes", liquids that were poured over and through the linen.
This process was followed by rinsing and beating in running water, and
bleaching on grass—and this process was called "bucking". The arranging
of the linen in tubs for the cleansing fluid called "lye" to run through was
called "laying bucks". The diagram on p. 638 shows better than words
how it was done.

Old homespun linen was thick and heavy, and if packed solid, no liquid
would ever penetrate, so a tub with a false bottom and a spigot was filled
with the clothes, over clean sticks, placed across and across, as the weight

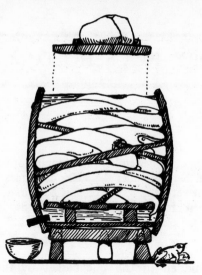

A buck tub (*section*). Linen packed in folds over sticks for bucking. The stone-weighted lid was put on to press out the lye when the spigot was withdrawn to let the lye water run out.

of the linen needed; as the laying went on, dirty places were specially damped with lye, and arranged downwards so as to catch the full force of the running water. The lye was then poured slowly in at the top and let run through; this was done over and over again, sometimes the spiggot plug was left in for soaking a while, before drawing off and using fresh lye. When the lye came through clean, the bucks were carried down to the running water and rinsed and spread out to dry. Most houses had a set of tenter hooks on to which new flannel or woollen goods were stretched out to dry and these were used for woollen washing.

On Tenter Hooks

Tenter poles were (and still are, near blanket mills) the size and shape of football posts, with iron hooks along top and sides and a log of heavy wood, also with hooks, that hung loose, fastened last into the bottom of the cloth, so that its weight hung onto it, and kept it stretched—it was "on tenter hooks" the whole drying time, so did not need pressing.

Meanwhile the linen was being dried and folded and pressed under weights. The old oak linen presses with their thick wooden screws are only used now for folding napkins and sheets, etc., after they have been ironed, but originally they took the things straight from the rollers (i.e., from the wide stone-weighted wooden rollers that ran over and over the folded linen as it lay on a long flat table in the wash-house).

Lye

The washing ley or lye was made of so many things that space forbids mention of more than a few.

Wood ashes, soaked and strained, gave a basis, hen dung, and also pigeon dung. The bleaching properties of urine were utilised, and lyes of bran water (still used today for chintz). Size, made by boiling down hoof-parings. Mixtures of soda were followed by acid washes.

Starch

The size mixtures were probably used to stiffen the mediaeval head-dress veils, but by Elizabeth's time starch was used, and was tinted yellow, till someone was beheaded in a wide yellow neckruff, which made it suddenly unpopular. Woollen stuff was trodden in streams by the feet, but linen was mostly hit with a rounded boll or stick-like beater; sun, wind, and water were the best bleachers.

Soap (as distinct from lyes)

A scented soap, 1615.

> " To make very good washing balls, take storax of both kinds, Benjamin Celanus, Aromatic, Aromaticus Labdanum, of each alike and braie them to powder with cloves and arras, then beat them with sufficient quantity of sope till it be stiffe. Then with your hand you shall work it like a paste and make round balls thereof."

The early pictures of bathing show soap being handed to the bather in large wooden bowls; this may have been "soft soap" made with woodash and soft fats. We know it was sometimes solid by 1400 (having seen pictures of it, in balls), and there is evidence of its being an urban commodity, bought and sold generally. But all isolated households boiled their own soap, from refuse fat, and the price dropped after the Reformation, when less tallow and wax was perquisite for church candles and scriptorums (*see* note on Mutton Fat). The first settlers in America always made their own soap, and as late as the 1890s my aunt (a traveller) spoke quite casually of their running out of all soap and using "a soap root found for us by the Zulus, though the Dutch used a sort of bush to lather with".

Other Washing Substances

Potato water for silks. The raw potato grated into cold water and the strained starchy water used to sponge the silk. This was sometimes boiled before use.

Ivy leaves, boiled and mashed till the water was dark, for black silk.

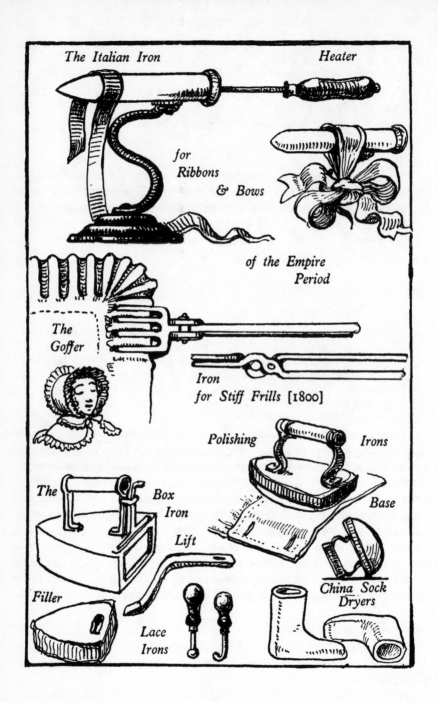

The Italian Iron   Heater

for
Ribbons
& Bows

of the Empire
Period

The
Goffer

Iron
for Stiff Frills [1800]

Polishing   Irons

The   Box
Iron

Base

Lift

China Sock
Dryers

Filler

Lace
Irons

Old tea leaves boiled with a few nettle tops, for "nankeen", or the "holland" linens.

Size, made by boiling down clean horse hoof parings, or glue, used for woollens. Bran, boiled, for chintz. (Both size and bran are used today by some experts.)

Hot vinegar and water was used for washing polished (waxed) furniture. Dry snow, and clean fresh grass clippings, were used for carpet cleaning.

WHITEWASH

Recipe Used for Whitewashing the White House at Washington

" The following is the recipe for making the celebrated stucco whitewash used in the White House at Washington, United States.

Take half a bushel of good unslaked lime, slake it with boiling water, cover it during the process to keep in the steam. Stir in a peck of salt dissolved in hot water, 3 lb. of ground rice, stirred in while the whole is boiling hot, $\frac{1}{2}$ lb. of Spanish whitening and 1 lb. of clean glue well soaked and melted down and liquid. Add 5 gallons of hot water to the mixture, stir, and let it stand covered several days. Reheat and put on hot.

One pint will cover one square yard and it will retain its brilliance for years."

A TRADE BOOK OF 1841.

Whitewash as Made for an Anglesey Cottage

Collect a bucketful of waste fat, butcher's trimmings, skin scrapings, or any household scraps that have gone bad, a proportion of tallow ends of "ship's grease" may be added. Chop all roughly with a peat spade (i.e., a narrow blade that will go into a pail). Put the fat at the bottom of an old cauldron, and strew over it twice as much dry unslaked lime broken into pieces. Pour over all the soapy water from the wash tub and cover with a board while it boils. The fervent heat of the slaking lime will entirely melt the fat and more water may be added as long as the heat continues. Next day the cauldron will be full of spongy whiteness; scoop out as much as you need to use into a bucket, wet down to a stiff creamy consistency, and paint in onto the house and walls with a stubby broom of Marrun grass.

If it brushes off, you have not used enough fat.

Modern usage substitutes powdered size for interior whitewashing but it is no use outside, as it melts when wet; fat stands the continuous rain and stays white.

PATENT

WASHING AND DRYING

MACHINES.

MACALPINE'S PATENT WASHING MACHINE.

This Machine is the most effective Washing Mach ne yet introduced; it is also in action the *safest*; as the finest Lace or Muslins may be washed in it without the least injury to the texture, and even the buttons on the shirts are not disturbed. It is at the same time equally effective in operating on stronger fabrics. As the articles being washed are operated upon whilst the liquid is in a boiling state, many impurities are removed that could not at ordinary temperatures be touched, and this also at a much greater speed than would otherwise be possible. The advantage of securing this effect for many of the articles required to be washed in Hospitals, Asylums, and Workhouses, will be at once understood. One great novelty of the machine consists in its application to the *wa shing boiling, and rinsing* the goods in the *same* vessel, so that they do not require removing until they are ready for the drying process. Large articles, such as Blankets and Counterpanes, can also be thoroughly washed, the weight of which renders them a very difficult operation in

A.—Beaters. B.—Revolving Steam Vessel. C.—Steam Pipe.

the ordinary methods. There is at the same time a great saving of Soap, (25 per cent. at least,) and one person will do the work of twelve, the work also being better done. The machines are made to work either by hand or by steam power. A machine can be seen at work daily, on the premises of the Patentee, Spring Vale Works, Hammersmith; also at the Bloomsbury Baths and Wash Houses; and at the Works of

MANLOVE, ALLIOTT & Co.,
SOLE MAKERS,
BLOOMSGROVE, NEAR NOTTINGHAM,
Of whom any further information may be obtained.

This machine reproduces the old "stamping mill" used by Cornish tin miners. It works on a camshaft which lifts the stamp hammers in rotation.

Patent Centrifugal Drying Machines.

These Machines form the most valuable and effective improvement in Drying Machinery yet introduced. As the water is thrown out by centrifugal force alone, all mischief to the goods that occurs in the ordinary operation of wringing is entirely obviated, and not the least disturbance of the texture of the materials being produced. The goods operated upon come out of the Machines very nearly dry, and a very great saving of time and fuel is thus obtained in the finishing process.

A very large number of these Machines are at work in different Asylums and Hospitals, Bath Wash Houses and Laundries, and in all cases with complete success.

SCOURING

Floors and table tops were scoured with chloride of lime water and silver sand, fuller's earth and soap being used for greasy places. Windows and glass were polished with a spot of paraffin. Sticky tins were cleaned by a solution of boiling water and soda and whitening; brass and copper, with boiling vinegar or crushed coarse rhubarb leaves. Cane and basketwork was first scrubbed with the "lye" from the wash tub, and then with strong salt water. Pewter was polished with fine bathbrick dust and oil. Mare's tails (the plant) was used for burnishing. In the coach-and-horse periods

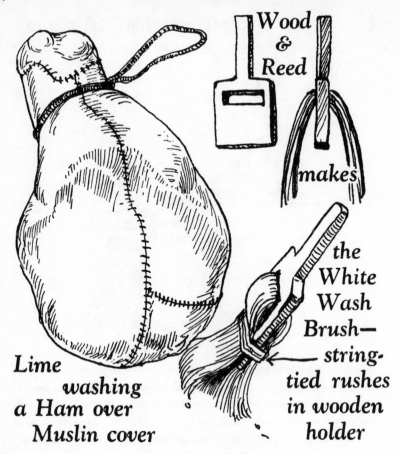

Wood & Reed makes the White Wash Brush— string-tied rushes in wooden holder

Lime washing a Ham over Muslin cover

Whitewash and Hams

saddle soap was a consideration, and most "houses" made their own, also bootblacking and black lead.

Kitchen-floor tiles were washed over with strong lyes on a small mop—then swilled with rain water—and finally dried off with red raddle. If of stone they were washed, swilled, and then sanded (which see).

Interestingly the huge slate slabs of floors, in the mountain district houses, were polished to black marble gloss with hot mutton fat. Where the cracks between the flags (and sometimes across them) dried white from their scouring with sand, the veined floor had the gleaming beauty of a black moth's wing.

Many of the sandstone-slab districts favoured yellow stoning, which was bright, and probably started the fashion for "yellow-painted floors" in New England.

INK

Till the eighteenth century most households made their own ink. Previously the inks used in the mediaeval scriptoriums were so individual that they proved one of the safest guides in locating the source of ancient manuscripts. The monasteries and convents guarded their ink recipes jealously. The recipes varied. One of the inks was obtained from the sooty bark of the blackthorn. Relays of the twigs were immersed in rain water till a thick black deposit was formed. This was dried off and the cake ground down with gum from cherry or pear trees. Other recipes used preparations of tannin from the oak and willow tanyards, oak galls, and minerals. The majority of these inks have lasted clear and strong through centuries. The small horns of the early English sheep, besides being used for bow notches, made a good natural ink-horn, and was inserted in a hole in a wooden desk, or fitted with a cap and carried through the scribe's belt. This, with a quill pen in it, has given the name to the fungus.

This is an eleventh-century ink recipe—12 lb. of oak galls pounded, 5 lb. of gum pounded, 5 lb. or less of green sulphate of iron, 12 gallons of rain water boiled each day till sufficiently done, letting it settle overnight.

The fraud of the fabulous Baron of Arizona who claimed the vast Peralta properties, hoodwinking the U.S. Government and enjoying a millionaire's life for years, was discovered by chemical analysis proving the original fifteenth-century MS. was written with iron ink, and the forgeries of 1880 were written with dogwood ink.

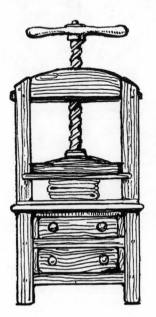

An oak linen press. Old thick linen sheets were more heavy and stiff than modern cotton; after mangling they were folded and "laid in the press" till quite smooth.

Later the word "press" came to be used for the cupboard in which linen was kept *after* it had been taken from "the press".

Upright Mangle
about 1880

There was much good design in the first upright mangle. This had fixed wooden rollers in a cast-iron frame, it was heavy but mobile, and was usually delivered from the makers by rail and pulled to the wash-house by a horse.

A roller

Section showing box with stones

This "box mangle" was in use in the laundry of a Convent near Euston Station till 1926. The oak rollers were worn smooth, and the stones were builders' rejects. The iron fitments consisted of a rack and pinion, which carried the "box" forward and backward over the rollers, and a chain, which took the weight when the rollers were removed.

CANDLES AND RUSHLIGHT

" I was bred and brought up mostly by rush light and do not find that I see less clearly than other people. My grandmother, who lived till 90 [that would make her early 1700s] never I believe burnt a candle in her life. . . . She used to get meadow rushes, such as they tie the hop shoots to the poles with, she cut them when they had attained full substance, but were still green; she cut off the top end to leave the prime part, which may be 1 ft. to 1½ ft. long. Then you peel off the green skin except for a fifth part a little strip all the way up, which is necessary to hold the pith together. The grease is melted and put into some iron pot as long as the rushes, and the rushes are soaked in it. Then take out and laid in a strip of bark [a natural rounded trough] fixed up against the wall by a couple of straps put round it— and there it hangs . . . for holding rushes. . . ."

COBBETT, 1822.

Rushlight holders were iron clips, mounted into wooden (or in some quarry districts slate or stone) bases, the rush being pulled up higher as it burnt down. Some small round tables will be found to be supported on four short pillars directly under the table top. These made a small square rack which held long bundles of the rushes, handy for use in the stand on the table above. Such rushlights often served to light several workers seated around the one table, and for fine lace work, or delicate sewing, a globe of water (like a water bottle or goldfish bowl) was used to throw a spot of light on the work, and the principle is used today in microscopes.

The peeled rush or pith was also made into elaborate favours and nose-gays and used to decorate the artificial wax-flower decorations of the eighteenth and nineteenth centuries. Up till 1900 I know of these favours being made at mill fairs in Lancashire, and lads made them for their girls, sitting out in the summer fields, at harvest time.

Among the play-time accomplishments of the late Victorian period, was "pith work" done with the ivory-white pith, bent, and secured on to thin boards with gum, in imitation of carved ivory pictures. Baskets made of the ivory-white pith, filled with small brightly coloured seaweeds, pressed and mounted, were popular efforts, brought back from summer holidays between the river and the sea.

So dipped down and faded out the pretty small flame of the rushlight that had lit kings to bed. And the little moorland ewes and their lambs nibble the juicy broom tassels that bend silver in the wind and stroke the music from the centuries.[1]

[1] *Bog Reeds—Arunde phragnites*—are used for thatch in central Wales. They are brought down from the mountains on sledges and used fresh. The bright, shining green

"Where candles are used see that the snuffers for the different candlesticks are completely emptied and wiped clean, and that there is a pair for each bedroom candlestick."

1850 (and later in many country districts).

Yellow candles are still used by miners, as melting at a higher temperature, and also being cheaper and less liable to blow out, or get damped out. The candles are set in the miner's tin bowler hat with a lump of clay. Quarry men also use them, since they are less liable to freeze and become brittle in cold.

LAMPS

Lamps must still be used in many districts, and in any country houses it is advisable to keep one lamp and a small airtight supply of oil in case of failure of other lighting system. Oil should be of the best quality, stored in an airtight tin out of doors, and a small funnel and some clean rags kept by the tin.

Lamps are safest with metal containers. See that you have a reserve lamp glass. Never let a cold wind blow on a hot lamp glass or it will crack it. Polish glasses with a spot of paraffin. See that wicks move easily, and rub the screws with beeswax for easy turning. Wicks act as filters in sucking up the oil, and when clogged and foul they may be cleaned by scraping and boiling in vinegar; but it is easier to buy a new wick. If the wick is slightly too large for the burner, thin it by pulling out some threads rather than by cutting. Wicks of circular lamps are most easily singed level with a red-hot poker.

There are elaborate oil cooking ranges, though in the country a good kitchen range which also heats the water is the best investment. But there are small duplex oilstoves (such as the Beatrix) capable of boiling a kettle and cooking a simple meal which will save the trouble of lighting a fire on a summer day.

A small oil heater is also useful in frosty weather, and very small lamps, placed safely under an inverted flowerpot, will often save a pipe freezing or warm an outside lavatory.

POT-POURRI

For scenting rooms it should be kept in a jar (some beautiful china jars, with openwork lids inside the close-covering top lids, were designed and made by various English chinaworks up to the eighteenth century). At the

---

tops to the round gold stacks catch the blue light from the sky and are often dotted black with roosting turkeys.

end of the nineteenth century, and in modern times, the old-fashioned open punch bowls were miscalled by dealers "pot-pourri bowls" but though they served the purpose, and standing open on the bureau or table scented the room slightly, the pot-pourri in them soon dried off and lost its fragrance. The genuine pot-pourri *jar* was kept close shut all day, and at evening was set before the fire, on the hearth, being turned till the jar was pleasantly warm, when the lid was taken off, and the imprisoned perfume suddenly permeated the room. The hot jar was then removed and replaced on its stand (that is why the best type of jar had stands, as part of the complete design) till cool, when it was closed again. Such a jar, well filled, would last in fragrance several years, though it was customary to refill each year about a month before Christmas.

The fragrance varied with each room: a warm damask rose predominated in the drawing-room; dried walnut leaves, bay leaves and tonquin beans make a very pleasant fender bowl for a library. For bedrooms, fresh verbena and lemon balm gave a cool fragrance; while for the linen press room lavender was used—plain—in bags.

So do not think one mixture should fill all jars.

For modern people unable to obtain the old-fashioned pot-pourri jars, a plain ginger jar, with a wooden lid fitted, and a simple wooden stand to match, is easy to make and will stand before a gas or electric fire to heat through quite suitably. There is real use in these scented jars, as they keep moth away, and the scents are never obtrusive.

Pot-pourri for a Parlour

This old recipe gives a very delicious flowery fragrance, but each garden has its own special type of flower, and their sweet ghosts best haunt the houses belonging to that garden. This mixture is one in which no single flower overpowers the whole and so becomes monotonous.

2 parts of damask roses—for fragrance and base.
1 part of Province or House roses—or any coloured rose petals—for colour and base.
1 part mock orange (syringa).
1 part clove pinks.
1 part rosemary leaves. Strip the stalks from tip downwards.
1 part myrtle.
1 part jessamine flowers.
1 part lemon thyme.
1 part lavender heads.
2 parts stock flowers or phlox.
$\frac{1}{4}$ part marigold flowers.
$\frac{1}{2}$ part mint leaves.

½ part bay leaves.
The rinds of two lemons cut off thinly.
1 whole nutmeg and a few cloves.
A sprinkling of orris root.
And 1 part of bay-salt, dried in the oven.

Dry all the flowers as you collect them, and store when dry in an airtight box. When ready to mix (in the autumn) rub over a deep pan with oil of cloves, and toss in all the ingredients, grating the nutmeg and crunching the salt, as you work it in.

POMANDERS

Tonquin beans, lavender bags, crushed spice, and aromatic gums make pomanders.

An orange stuck with cloves is a pleasant pomander, and easy to make.

Take a tangerine orange and stick it close with cloves, pressed stalk inwards like nails through the thin rind. Start at the top and work around in circles, setting each clove betwixt the row above, honeycombwise. Leave about the size of a clove between each clove. Set the orange to dry out on the warm hearth (or above the boiler in the airing cupboard) and keep squeezing it lightly and turning it as it dries; in a week or so it will have shrunk so that the clove-heads touch each other all over. Now go on drying it out, till it is quite hard and tight and firm. It will last fragrant for years.

If you stick the cloves too close, they will be pulled out of the rind, and crack away as they dry; if you do not stick them close enough, patches of dried peel will wrinkle between the rows and the orange will be ill-shaped. Stick evenly, and keep pressing the orange as it dries—that's all.

LAVENDER

There is much difference between the scent from the flowers, and the pungent, almost turpentiny scent from the spikes (the stems and leaves make spikenard or spike oil of lavender). The latter is better against flies, or moths, and should be rubbed over the insides of oak chests where blankets

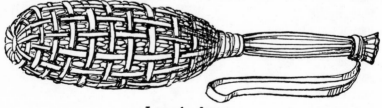

Lavender faggots

are stored. But beware of putting loose lavender *flowers* near anything of wool, as they cause tiny holes like moth bites. The flowers are best rubbed off and used in muslin bags in the linen-chests. The stems, bundled up, should be kept in a tin box near the medicine-chest, as a few burnt like a torch in a sick-room will clear the air more quickly than anything else, and, held before the opened window, their faint blue smoke will blow through the room, leaving a clean, refreshing scent.

A few old recipes mention lavender as a cookery herb. Its best eating service is to candy a few small grains to add zest to the Christmas box of candied fruits, and please the few who do not care for the ordinary type of sweet, but like the pungent "bite" of the lavender.

Lavender Faggots for Linen

Loose lavender should never be left in drawers or boxes, as I have already said. Keep lavender in muslin bags. To make the faggots that marked the dozens and half dozens when packing the dowry chest, the lavender must be freshly cut and still pliant. Gather about a dozen heads, and arrange as shown in diagram. Tie tightly with narrowest ribbon or a strip of binding; bend back the stalks, arranging them to cage in and cover the heads, and wind the ribbon in and out, pulling tighter as the bulge of the heads is covered in. Wind around and tie tightly, carry the ribbon down the stems, trim them all to one even "handle length" and fasten the ribbon off here. The "handles" are left sticking out to mark the "dozen".

A set of a dozen such lavender batons with loops to hang them together on a hook in the linen cupboard was a dainty small betrothal gift from girl friends.

Lavender Water, 1832

1 pt. of spirits of wine.
½ oz. of oil of lavender.
30 drops of oil of nutmegs.
30 drops of essence of Bergamot.
2 drachms of essence of amber grease. Mix and bottle.

HOW TO MAKE TEETHING CORALS

" ' Take his coral my dear,' she said, ' and rub it well with carrot juice. Rub it till the juice dries on it and then give it him to play with ' . . . ' Not got a coral? how can you expect that he should cut his teeth?' "

TROLLOPE, *Barchester Towers.*

Smooth branches of red coral were used as handles for silver rattles, or for children's teething necklaces.

The modern strings of lumpy beads sold for babies are direct descendants of the teething beads of our forebears.

Coral for babies' teeth

"To Make Children's Necklaces for the Teeth"

"Take roots of hen bane, of orpin and vervain [all rounded firm roots] and scrape them very clean with a sharp knife, cut them in long beads and string them green [i.e., while green and soft for the needle to pierce easily], first henbane, then orpin, then vervain, till it is the bigness of the child's neck. Then take as much red wine as you think the necklace will take up and put thereto a dram of red coral, and as much single peony root, finely powdered [Singles, old-fashioned bright scarlet]. Soak the beads in this for 28 hours, and rub the powder on the beads, and when red and dry, let the child wear them"—and probably the wine flavour was soothing, and the texture hard, and the chewing induced did help the teeth through.

OAT CHAFF FOR BABIES' BEDS

Oat chaff is an excellent filling for children's mattresses. It is very light and elastic, and yet gives a firm flat surface. Being of a wood basis, it is non-conductive, and being porous, is both warm in the winter and cool in summer. It is far more healthy than wool or hair fillings. If the mattress gets soiled the filling can be shaken out, the cover boiled, and refilled easily. I believe some enlightened trained midwives are taught the value of these chaff beds as part of their training; but it is really sad to see modern mothers wasting money on expensive made-up bedding that is not nearly so healthy.

The expensive "upholstered bedding" once it has been wetted, is never clean and fresh again, but a chaff bed can be changed completely in five minutes. As it "flattens smooth" in use, it cannot wear into a hollow, or ridge, and makes fine straight spines.

VINEGAR FOR TRAVEL

" Dry vinegar to carrie in your pocket! Take the bladder of green corn, either wheat or rye, and beat it in a mortar with the strongest vinegar you can get, till it is a paste. Roll it into balls, drie them in the sun, and when you need vinegar, cut a piece, and dissolve it in wine, or water to make vinegar."

1615.

Black Hair-dye in the Eighteenth Century

"Take gum dye and boil it with a handful of leaves of Beete and a handful of sage leaves, a dram of Myrtle and Bay leaves, and the outward peels of Walnuts. With this dye your hair—after you have wetted your hair well with a brush and comb—use a sponge to wash your face with white wine [to remove spot of the stain]. Let your hair dry of itself."
The Ladies Guide, 1700, says:

" Black hair is particularly useful in setting off the whiteness of neck and skin.
Cheeks should have a degree of Plumpness—
The Chin be white, soft, and agreeably rounded.
Neck, white, straight, soft and flexible, increasing gently towards the shoulders—the Bosom white and the Hands should unite insensibly with the arms, being long and delicate.
The sides long, hips wider than the shoulders, knees rounded, legs straight and feet white and little."

BEES, HIVES AND HONEY

" The hives thou set a little space asunder
Their enter, turn thou fair upon the South
No larger than a bee may tread thereunder
Wicketts two or three thou make there couthe
That, if a wicked worm one holes mouth
Beseige or stoppe, another open be,
And from the wicked worm,—thus save the bee.
To buy the bee, behold them rich and full
To prove them by their murmured magnitude
Or see the swarm; and carry them if thou will
By night, upon they back then safe enclose
But buy them not too far out of their air
For change of air may put them in despaire."

                                        TWELFTH CENTURY.

Bees and the history of English bee-keeping has been dealt with by experts, so this cook-book needs only enough outline to bring the honey into use. The first hives of which I can find pictures are almost trees in their simplicity. At a guess, some hollow tree full of bees had been plastered with clay and carried into the bee garden, laid upon stakes, and fitted with a movable plank front—but the MS. drawing is too rubbed to be certain. The interesting point is that the honey is being cut off by a curved knife, into a bowl, and the bees are flying round indignantly. Now when taking wild honey, the bees are killed, so these were tame bees. Palladius recommends wood or woven hives.

" It is not hot or cold, unkind,
Take felures eke, or supple twiges take
Ye may, but potters hives forsake . . ."

which covers lines made of split-wood cooper ware, and basket ware, and probably the straw and reed weavers (so long known as beehive work) the early drawings in the Junius MS. show hives like the modern skep, but more pointed, and probably plastered over with clay (as wattle and daub houses were made at that time). I think the top spike was probably the stick around which the basket was woven, retained as a useful structural asset.

There were regular bee garths in the grounds of all large establishments. They are to be traced in old monasteries, and castle gardens, and their placing was well studied. As honey was the principle sweetener till about the eighteenth century (and continued in country places and for many cookery jobs till the nineteenth), almost every small household kept their own bees—the extra amount used by larger houses for banquets and curing accounts for the rent being paid in honey in many old manor rolls. The old rhyme:

> " A swarm of bees in May is worth a load of hay
> A swarm of bees in June is worth a silver spoon
> A swarm of bees in July is not worth a fly . . ."

is curiously accurate, because the economic value of hay varies with the value of livestock after a hard winter, and the value of silver as cash value varies with the cost of the food the cash will buy.

Note. By chance the load of hay from our paddock, at controlled Government price during the war, was valued at £7, and a large silver serving spoon, priced by weight the same year, was valued at £5. Swarms of bees during the sugar shortage were fetching £5 to £10 apiece, average £7.

Till recently there was no artificially made comb. Honeycomb taken from the straw skep hives used to be sold in Abergelly market in great bowlfuls. I remember my father bringing in a brown earthenware bowl (probably Buckley ware) full of rough chunks of bright yellow comb, glistening and crumpling in deep golden-brown honey, dark as a wall-flower, and rich with perfume; the comb was set at all angles,—and had rounded pendulous shapings, large as apples, where the comb had hung down, heavy, within the rounded skep. Such would be the mediaeval honey, probably set to drip clear into jars and the wax used to harden the candle wax. The same wax, melted and rubbed on, glazed the wood-work, was used to stopper bottles, and had a hundred other uses. The honey was used in the kitchen where we would use sugar[1], and also for its preservative properties. It was soon known that it would seep through wet parchment, and this system of osmosis was used to make pickles strike through the skin of hams, as well as soften my lady's hands and form a base for her toilet creams, and for medical use.

Sugar-cured hams were originally honey-cured, and fruit was preserved in honey solutions. The rinsings of the combs were used to make mead. The original ferment of mead was almost certainly of fungoid origin from the rye straw of the skeps (*see* Mead). The bee bread was also used in making mead, but whether this was an intentional use to encourage the culture ferment, or a chance discovery, I don't know. I was told, as recently as 1943, that "we always put in a piece of bee bread, it makes the

---

[1] When "sugar" takes over from honey in old recipes liquid must be added to compensate.

Hiving under difficulties, 1895

mead nice and strong" but the modern "starting" with a scrap of yeast seems to have entirely displaced the old rye culture; as with the lack of rye straw, with the change to wooden painted hives and modern ways, the spore infection has ceased.

The large amount of honey and wax used in old households is astonishing. It must be remembered that there were more flowery meads surrounding cities, more wild lands around small towns, and bee-keeping was not a specialised hobby, nor honey a trade, but part of rural economy. Many old houses today have combs, centuries old, filling inaccessible old roof holds, and staining the old walls below; these would be the ancestral bees, whose swarms filled the hives in the bee garth below. Just as hirshels of sheep populated one mountain for centuries, till they became adapted to their special environment, so certain districts had certain types of bee, that suited the conditions of that locality. Thus the amount of honey and wax collected in any district was large in proportion to the needs of the district, and caused no special comment.

In one small ruined farmhouse in a quite isolated district, we found two yellowish grey mounds that looked like cement. They were abandoned beeswax—that had been melted down in buckets and turned out when set. By deduction, they must have been about fifty years old. One of the lumps, rendered down and cleaned, made a large washbasinful of good wax. If you think of the amount of comb needed to produce a bucketful of wax, you understand the amount of honey given in many old recipes. The searcloths mentioned in old MSS. were strips of linen dipped in melted wax. They had many medical uses, and were much used to bind up wounds, being put on soft and warm. With medicated additions they formed plasters for blistering.

Moulds and death-masks were made with wax, and it was used to waterproof leather and polish saddlery. As the wax must stand up to the heat of the full hive, its melting point is high, and so it is suitable for all polishes and dressings exposed to heat. We believe it was also the basis of a mediaeval sweetmeat, something like chewing gum, that may have been another American preservation of an old English recipe.

HIVES

This picture (in period within the memory of the oldest readers) still shows the straw skep used for hiving, the banging on the pans to make a noise, and the cussedness of the little people in choosing the wrong time and most inaccessible place; also the comparatively recent ownership of bees. This is obviously a small household—and the job is obviously taken as part of any small households troubles! In the earlier centuries every hut had its own hive.

SUGAR, 1846

"The proprietes have apparently forgotten the observation of Adam Smith in his work on The Wealth of Nations, that 'in every improved society the farmer is nothing but a farmer, and the manufacturer nothing but a manufacturer'. In the West Indies Colonies, especially Jamaica the farmer not only raises his own sugar cane, but grinds and boils them into sugar, and distils the molasses, with rum, and carries the produce to the wharf for shipment.

The Metcalfe Central Sugar Factory and Timber Co., is projected at Annatho Bay . . . it has secured suitable land etc. etc. . . ."

The idea was to buy the timber, as the new lands were cleared, to process the cane, and act as auxiliary to the railroads. The factory would collect on a series of tramways through the district—and it is suggested that the planters should make enough out of the sale of their processing plants to pay for the field trams across their estates to the factory line. The fires will be made of the waste wood, the refuse of the cane sold back for manure, etc. Opinions of the Crown Surveyors and others are given at length, and the opinion of the Vacuume processes that are in operation in Demerara.

> " Children should eat as much as like at a time. They will never take plain food more than is good for them; they may indeed be stuffed with cakes and sweet things till they be ill, but of meat plainly and well cooked and of bread, they will never swallow one ounce more than is necessary—Ripe fruit, or cooked fruit— BUT NO SWEETNING, will never hurt them, but once they get a taste of suggary stuff and when Ices creams tarts raisins almonds etc., and all the endless pamperin is come—the doctor must soon follow."
>
> COBBETT.

FAMILY COOKING FOR ANIMALS

> " The steward of the Hall shall keep one bone a day for each hound."   THIRTEENTH CENTURY.

I am not going to write a cookery book for households and leave out the family dog and the cook's cat; and the hens many people keep in these days.

Dogs

One good meal a day, free *long* grass, and clean water.

The family scraps alone are not adequate, neither, except for special, delicate breeds, are the expensive prepared foods necessary. A hard dog biscuit is the main standard; bitten crusts, remains of puddings, oddments

The hound's bone

of pastry, etc., should be baked hard in the oven, and given, dribbled with gravy, the bones from the stockpot, and dinner scraps, of course (except splintery rabbit or chicken bones which are dangerous). Most dogs will enjoy the spoonful of milk pudding left by baby, or cheese rinds, but milk and meat should *not* be given at the same meal. Potatoes and vegetable scraps are good, and offal from the butcher, properly prepared, excellent; but keep all dog food hard and dry, give a little raw meat, mix a little raw green stuff into the food.

See that there is clean cold water in plenty and daily fun and exercise. Sedate perambulations with the pram are not exercise. The dog must be free of leads and restrictions and made to exercise hard, till really tired. There must be a clean dry place to sleep, free from draughts, and *flat* to lie on. The old barrel kennel is not good for a large dog, and a hound must always have a flat shelf on which he can stretch out full length; the round dog-basket cramps hounds.

A rough towel for rubbing down a wet dog before he comes into the house, a brush and curry comb for all dogs, and special care for long-haired breeds.

Washing only when really needed; most dogs enjoy a swim, but hot soapy water may irritate the skin badly. Lop-eared dogs should have special attention to their ears, a little mild canker ointment gently soothed in during damp weather is better as preventative than cure.

Don't give mutton bones to a sheep dog, or splinter bones to any dog, nor sharp fish bones.

For invalid diet, consult the vet. A meat cube spiked onto a tooth will sometimes persuade a sad puppy recovering from distemper to suck it down, and afterwards drink milk and begin to feel hungry again.

An old coat or dress belonging to an absent owner, is comforting for a "left behind" dog to lie on while waiting. Of course, never leave a dog tied up unless absolutely necessary, and make adequate arrangements for his exercise, as well as his food, if you are away for some days.

If he travels by rail, he must by law carry a muzzle attached to his collar.

If you have not kept a dog before, get a handbook on the dog, and look up his special breed, and make proper arrangements for his housing and feeding before he comes to you. With care and correct catering, your dog need never have a day's illness in his happy life.

Love him well and keep him lean.

Cats

> " There is no way of scaring rats and mice from a steading so effectively as by cats. Let one or two cats be brought up in the steading . . . they will become vigilant guards against vermin. . . . Let each cat receive daily at its own particular place at a stated hour, say 11 o'clock a.m., a mess of sweet milk porridge, when it will attend to receive it as the hour arrives. Let each have a soft, warm, comfortable bed made for it in some good part of the steading. At night and early in the morning they will watch and hunt on their respective beats, and in the course of a short time with free access to every apartment the vermin will disappear. Cats . . . neglected of food . . . will not hunt . . . a regular fed cat makes the best hunter, because it hunts for sport, and not pressed by hunger will watch at the same spot for hours. Being strong from its daily wholesome food it feels courage to encountering any vermin and will kill numbers in the course of a day. A starved cat which hunts for food (not sport) eats the first prey it catches and gorging itself lies down to sleep. . . . People who will not take the trouble to feed a cat daily and regularly must be troubled with vermin."
>
> STEPHENS, *Book of the Farms.*

What Stephens says with authority of a *well-fed cat being a better hunter than a hungry one is proved,* but in districts where game keepers and traps are used, night hunting out of doors should be firmly discouraged; in fact it is better to give them their meal late and shut them in an outhouse for the night.

Cats should be given one good solid meal each day, as much as they can eat, of food they like. They should be free to find water to drink, and green grass to eat. You cannot keep a cat on milk only—you must give it solid meat, fish, or some of the dried cat foods now on the market. Nursing queens should be given water to drink and solid food, as soon as they want it. With cats, more than dogs, you can trust them to take exercise, and not overeat themselves—they are extremely clever.

HENS

" Ore all let cleanliness preside—no scraps
Bewstrew the pavement—and no half-picked bones.
To wash the court, well paved, nor spare thy pains,
For much to health will cleanliness avail."
SOMERVILLE.

Poultry will eat almost anything properly prepared, but scraps should not be thrown out in lumps to lie about and get foul and attract flies. An old mincing machine or small chaff-cutter nailed down in an outhouse is invaluable for running the food through. Otherwise put the scraps into a bucket, pour boiling water on them and mash with one of the excellent mash-cutting tools on the market. Dry off this mixture with whatever dry food you are using for the birds, and serve the whole in troughs. Dry grain should be raked into chaff or sand to be scratched for, and something enjoyable and tasty like a well caterpillared cabbage should be hung up for the exercise of jumping. Whole eggshells should never be fed to hens; if anything could put an idea into their heads that would!

When you enjoy oysters or shellfish, pound the shells with a hammer and let the hens enjoy them too, and, as the charming householders of early centuries have written, "When you take the yeast toasts from wine or brewing, be sure to give them to the hens—it encourages them mightily." These days so many people keep poultry that everybody has their own theories on feeding them. Let the cook save her scraps intelligently, and count her eggs victoriously!

THE CONSTRUCTION OF A PRIVY

In the housing shortage and present trek into the country, the above diagram may be useful.

In most cases a well-dug "privy" is far better than any other arrangement, but it must be well supplied with dry (baked to powder) earth or *fine* cinder dust, so that the plant roots can do their work quickly. Chemical disinfectants should never be used as they defeat the natural process by killing the roots that should do the work. A good washdown (with hose or water buckets) should be given frequently; and garden fertilizers (or the powders used to hasten decay in a compost heap) are useful. Keep the place covered, clean limewashed, and well ventilated.

The drain marked B on the diagram is for household slops or soapy water.

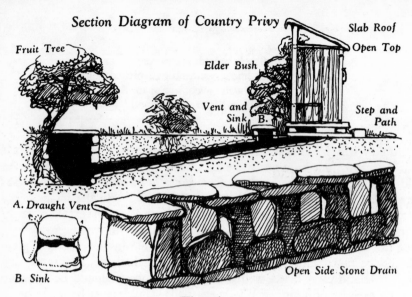

Section Diagram of Country Privy

Fruit Tree

Elder Bush

Slab Roof

Open Top

Vent and
Sink   B.

Step and
Path

A. Draught Vent

B. Sink

Open Side Stone Drain

The privy

Consult the local sanitary inspector before you start. If it's permitted to
construct a septic tank in your position, he will probably be very helpful in
obtaining an experienced workman for you.

A RAT REMOVER

" I Order all Rattons that be in this House,
All mannere of Rattons, and eke of Mouse,
By the grace of Mary cleane—
Go hence Rattons! and be no more seene—
And by Him, whom Mary bare aboute,
Let NO Ratton stay! within or withoute,
And by the Holy Ghost of grace,
That all Rattons! leave this place!
By the Father, and the Sone—
I bid all Rattons, to be Gone. . . ."

OLD CHARM.

BIBLIOGRAPHY

EARLY TO MEDIAEVAL PERIOD

Boke of St. Albans
Grosseteste (*Works*)
Walter of Henley
Bartholomaeus Anglicus
John Arderme
Visitations of Religious Houses
Chronicles of Grey Friars
Supplication for Beggars
Physicians of Myddvai
Book of Cookerie
Froissart (Lord Berners' Translation) also Jonville and others
Robert le Buenne
Joceland of Brakeland
Geraldus Cambrensis
Chronicles of Malmesbury (and other chronicles)
Palladius (*Works*)
Boorde (*Works*)
Langland (*Works*)
Chaucer (*Works*)
Gower (*Works*)
    Early English alliteration poems —(various). Reprints by Early English Text Soc.: Roxburgh Club: Camden Society: Soc. of Antiquaries and other Facsimiles.

MEDIAEVAL TO LATE-ELIZABETHAN PERIOD

Boke of Good Manners	1494
Letters from Ireland, Cuellar	1500
Description of English Fisheries	1500
Isle of England	1500
To Learne a Man to be Wyse in Building his House	1540

Boke of Introduction of Knowledge	1540
Diary of Jane Melville	1556
The Education of Children	1558
Book of Wines	1568
Holinshed Chronicles	1577
Garden of Health	1579
Tusser	1577
A Political Platt	1580
Stowe	1580
Mulcaster	1582
Anatomie of Abuses	1583
Itinerary Ireland	1599
Laws and Statutes for Relief of the Poor	1602
French Gardens for English Ladies and Gentlemen	1605
Gentleman's Exercise	1612
Hole (Maps)	1613
Skill of Oatmeal and other works, Markham	1615
County Household Guide	1615
Lawson Household Guide	1615
Charitable Physitian	1638
The Ladies Cabinet Opened and Enlarged	1639
Norfolk Gentleman	1640
Warme Beer	1641
Welsh Affairs	1648
Copyhold Tenants	1657
Perfect Husbandman	1658
Acelaria Eveleyn	1661
Hutchinson's *Industry*	1661
Norfolk Weavers	1663
The Complete Cook	1668
Culpeffer	1682
Making Mumm	1682
Note on Sugar Plantations	1682
Young Cooks Monitor	1683
Ladies Dictionary	1694

MEDIAEVAL TO LATE-ELIZABETHAN
PERIOD—*contd.*

Bread for the Poor	1698
Regulation Measures for Ireland	1695
Paxton (*Letters*)	
Society of Merchant Venturers of Bristol	
"Public Procession of Queen Elizabeth"	
Instruction of Henry Earl of Northumberland upon the Management of His Estates	
Guild of Merchant Tailors of Bath	
Sir Philip Sidney (*Letters*)	
Sir John Herrington	
Fitzherbert (*Works*)	
Proclamation Against Duels	
Markham (*Works*)	

FROM THE EIGHTEENTH CENTURY
ONWARDS

The Female Tatler	1709
Journeys and Customs of England, by a French nobleman	1710
Directors for Letters, Carriers, Waggons, and Roads	1710
Bee Master	1710
Work-house Accounts	1725
Defoe (*Works*)	1727
Pope (*Works*)	1732
Tull (*Works*)	1733
Slave Trade, Snelgrave	1734
Middleton	1734
Diet, by Arbuthnot, M.D.	1739
Mrs. Stephen's *Medicine for the Stone*	1739
Complete Housewife	1742
Yorkshireman	1743
The Female Spectator	1744
Ladies Magazine	1749
Prudent Housewife	1750

Glasse (*Works*)	1750
The Gentleman	1752
Complete Ciderman	1754
"Adulterated Bread"	1758
Curiosités de Londres et de l'Angleterre	1760
Wheel Carriages, by a nobleman	1763
Bath Guide	1766
Kitchen Garden Display'd	1767
Kitchen Garden, by Cook	1767
Raffold (*Works*)	1769
Designs for Farm Houses	1772
Letters from the Mountain, by a lady	1773
Catalogue of Household Furniture	1773
Kentishman	1776
Farmers Wife	1780
Gentle Shepherd, Ramsay	1780
Lady Accomplisht	1780
The Ladies Director	1785
Bread Pamphlets	1787
Complete Confectioner	1789
British Housewife	1790
Domestic Cookery	1790
"Petition of Englishman against confiscation of his property during his absence in Switzerland"	1794
Travels in England	1797
Young (*Works*)	
Somerville (*Works*)	

FROM THE BEGINNING OF THE
NINETEENTH CENTURY

Smollett (*Works*)	1800
"Information for Emigrants to Cape Colony"	1819
Treatise on Brewing	1821
Household Cookery	1824
New London Cookers	1827
Hone's *Table Book*	1831
Simple Housekeeping	1832
Stephen's *Book of the Farm*	1844
Young Women of the Factories	1845

Food for the Million or *Maize and Potatoes* 1847

Finchley Training Manuals 1849

Acton (*Works*) 1849

Commonsense for Housemaids, by a lady 1850

Emigrants' Handbook 1852

Bread, Anonymous 1855

Breakfasts 1860

Soyer's *Military Hospital Diet* and other works 1860

Burn's and Stephen's *Farm Buildings* 1861

Sea Products, Waste Products and Commercial Products, Simmonds 1862

Cook's Book for an American Family 1865

Good Cookery, Hall 1867

How to Economize Like a Lady 1874

The General Servant, by a lady 1875

British Immigrant 1875

Welsh Cook Book 1880

Comfort and Elegance on £150 a year in London 1880–1890?

Food Reform Magazine 1881

Housing of the Working Classes 1887

Coaching Guide, Hartleys 1889

Cobbett (*Works*)

Susan Warner (Elizabeth Wetherall) (*Works*)

INDEX

The butcher's block has
not changed for centuries